UNION, NATION, OR EMPIRE

AMERICAN POLITICAL THOUGHT

Wilson Carey McWilliams and Lance Banning
Founding Editors

UNION, NATION, OR EMPIRE

The American Debate over
International Relations,
1789–1941

David C. Hendrickson

University Press of Kansas

© 2009 by the University Press of Kansas

Published by the University Press of Kansas (Lawrence, Kansas 66045),
which was organized by the Kansas Board of Regents and is operated
and funded by Emporia State University, Fort Hays State University,
Kansas State University, Pittsburg State University, the University of
Kansas, and Wichita State University

Library of Congress Cataloging-in-Publication Data

Hendrickson, David C.
Union, nation, or empire : the American debate over international
relations, 1789–1941 / David C. Hendrickson.
    p.   cm. — (American political thought)
Includes bibliographical references and index.
ISBN 978-0-7006-1632-9 (cloth : alk. paper)
1. United States—Foreign relations. 2. United States—Foreign
relations—Philosophy. 3. International relations—Philosophy.
I. Title.
E183.7.H42 2009
327.73—dc22   2008047058

British Library Cataloguing-in-Publication Data is available.

Printed in the United States of America

10 9 8 7 6 5 4 3 2 1

The paper used in this publication is recycled and contains 30 percent
postconsumer waste. It is acid free and meets the minimum requirements of
the American National Standard for Permanence of Paper for Printed
Library Materials Z39.48-1992.

TO CLELIA, WESLEY, WHITNEY, AND MARINA

The Union of these States is the all-absorbing topic of the day; on it all men write, speak, think, and dilate, from the rising of the sun to the going down thereof.

DANIEL WEBSTER, JUNE 28, 1851

CONTENTS

PREFACE AND ACKNOWLEDGMENTS

The subject of this book is the way that American leaders have understood the world of international relations. It presents a history of international thought as seen through the prism of America's political experience from the founding until American entry into World War II. The domain of "international relations" as a field of study is potentially elastic because it can reach to all aspects of the relationship among distinct peoples. In entering this world, we confront a series of antinomies that have played a role in mapping what is a large and sprawling terrain: war versus peace, realism versus idealism, civilization versus barbarism, free trade versus protection, liberty versus despotism, freedom versus slavery, intervention versus nonintervention, nationalism versus internationalism, force versus law, empire versus equilibrium, union versus independence. Alongside these fearful antinomies stand a series of constructions—empire, nation, republic, state system, union, federative system, partnership, concert, alliance, society of states—around which certain questions cluster: what they are, how they adapt and change in response to circumstances, what values and interests they preserve or threaten. All these various conceptions are part of the discourse of international relations; they are essential concepts that enable us to construct "mental maps" of the intellectual world. They convey, in summary fashion, the basic subject matter of this book. We want to know how American leaders thought about and utilized these concepts with a view to understanding the basics of their international thought.

The American approach to international relations was distinguished by a multiplicity of questions that kept recurring, to which every generation proffered answers:

Do democracies live in peace with one another, or are they as addicted to war as monarchies?

Does the anarchical character of the international system conduce toward war?

Are the nations capable of forming federative systems to secure international cooperation, in advance of the hostility that has often prevailed, or are they doomed to self-help and conflict?

Would thickening ties of commercial interdependence make for peace
or embroil nations in dependencies that would end in embittered
conflict?

In a union of states, does expansion unleash centripetal or centrifugal
forces?

What role should the balance of power or resistance to aggression play
in relations among states?

When is war justified?

Should states adhere to a policy of nonintervention in the domestic
affairs of other states, or might they properly intervene in some
circumstances?

What is civilization, and how should "civilized powers" treat with
"barbarians"?

Are free institutions compatible with slavery?

Is empire compatible with free institutions?

These questions illustrate the range of empirical and normative questions
that were searchingly addressed in the past, all of which might comfortably be asked about the world of the early twenty-first century. In effect,
American history moves through a series of debates—many of them "great
debates"—in which these protean questions get canvassed in relationship to
the key events of the day.

At the core of this book is the attempt to exhibit what those debates were
about, that is, to set forth and illuminate the central claims of the various
advocates, the theories about the political world to which appeal was made,
and the prescriptions advanced for the conduct of American statecraft in
both its external and its internal dimensions. I am especially keen on understanding the way in which these various debates bore on matters of ideology,
identity, and institutions. Internationalism, nationalism, and imperialism
constitute herein the three ideologies of international relations that provide
distinctive frames of reference from which these theoretical questions are
addressed. These ideologies, in turn, have their analog in conceptions of
American identity and institutions that are focused on union, nation, or
empire.

Despite my interest in the various questions of international theory, my
method is historical. Only by setting these debates in the context of ongoing
events, I have believed, is it possible to make sense of them, and the book
is organized as a narrative keyed to the great events of American history.
I try to understand these events as much as possible through the voices of
the participants themselves. My emphasis, in keeping with the approach
of Thucydides, is on the dialectical confrontation of opposing arguments.

While I have my sympathies and antipathies with the various protagonists we shall meet along the way, I have tried to write with a modicum of detachment. It is the play of ideas that I find fascinating and that I want above all to recount.

Though not exactly a treatise in international relations, the book does seek to make a contribution to international studies and to what has been called the American science of international politics. The work demonstrates that international theory has a long history in the United States, a fact that is seldom registered in the field. I also try to show that theory had an influence upon history—that is, that the convictions and diagnoses that made up these complex debates often mattered greatly to the course of events. The work is informed, finally, by the idea that these dead American leaders have something to teach us. They make general and well-reasoned propositions that purport to be part of a science of politics and, as such, suggest truths as relevant in our age as in theirs. I think there is much wisdom in these now little-studied and mostly forgotten debates, so often consigned to irrelevance since 1945. They teach important civic lessons. They should not be lost from the consciousness of American leaders or citizens, as I fear in large measure they have been.[1]

The author of a book on the American debate over international relations might be expected to deal exclusively with the foreign policy of the United States, but it is my conviction that this domain is but half (though a very important half) of the proper subject matter. In fact, an equally rich vein of speculation into the manifold problems of international relations is America's experiment in federal union. *All* the antinomies and questions listed previously were raised in the debate over the Constitution in 1787 and 1788—that is, as part of an inquiry into what would now be thought of as America's "domestic" politics. The travails of the union, and of the states and sections that composed it, receive very little recognition in diplomatic histories of the United States, which alternately place the American nation-state or the vision of continental empire at the center of the narrative. In crucial respects, however, this customary placement is misleading, and a basic purpose of this history is to restore the federal union to its proper place in the understanding of American statecraft.[2]

From 1776 to 1787, the fear was often expressed that the states would be incapable of forming or maintaining a union and that they had to look forward to the conflicts and wars that were the common experience of neighboring peoples. In keeping with this perception that a raging state system might develop in North America, advocates for the Constitution put themselves in the "peace plan" tradition associated with the grand design of Henry IV, who had sketched "but the picture in miniature of the great portrait to be exhibited."³ This *novus ordo seclorum* was projected as the antitype of the old European system, hitherto ruled by a law in which peace was a duty but war a frequent occurrence. Despite the fond hopes vested in the federal union, its subsequent history was anything but placid. The whole dynamic of American politics from 1789 to 1861 lay in the occurrence, about every ten years, of a monumental sectional crisis that would be averted only through an unexpected turn of events or an inspired act of statesmanship. Because disunion was widely understood, sooner or later, to be a virtual synonym for war, the threat of force was not banished from the system.

To understand the course of politics and the tenor of thought under the federal union, we must put aside the myth that the "anguishing dilemmas of security that tormented European nations did not touch America for nearly 150 years."⁴ Far from being indifferent to the security problems that have drawn the anxious attention of internationalists in the twentieth century, Americans were obsessed by them from the American Revolution to the Civil War. They did not enjoy the alternative of withdrawing from "the state system" because they were squarely in the middle of one. This condition helps explain why their "domestic" discourse was filled throughout with language of a decidedly internationalist tenor, why there emerged doctrines of the balance of power, of intervention (and nonintervention), of the equality of states, of defense against aggression. That the greatest war in Western civilization from 1815 to 1914 was fought in North America gives some idea of the conflicts that lay embedded within the American union. Those conflicts created a much more serious security problem than is customarily appreciated and help explain the internationalist character of America's "domestic" political discourse.

This interpretation of the American founding as an experiment in international cooperation and one that, as a consequence, took up certain basic questions in the theory of international relations was advanced in my book *Peace Pact: The Lost World of the American Founding*, which the University Press of Kansas published in 2003. This work is a sequel to that earlier undertaking. Whereas *Peace Pact* looked back from 1787 and examined a range of historical precedents, dating from Greece and Rome, that helped explain the outlook of the framers of the constitution, this volume looks forward to the 150 years following 1787. That volume identified a vein of thought, which I labeled "the unionist paradigm," that was above all concerned with the predicaments of free states in union. At the core of the unionist paradigm was the belief that Americans had to create and perpetuate a form of political association by which republican governments committed to "life, liberty, and the pursuit of happiness" could be joined together in a workable federative system, so as to escape the anarchy of states, on the one hand, and the despotism of centralized empire, on the other. It looked toward the formation of a republican union of large extent, embracing a wide variety of peoples, interests, and ways of life, that would preserve peace within its zone and ensure protection from predators without. Though an attempt to escape from both the anarchy of states and the despotism of empire, it nevertheless sought to safeguard the two values with which each of these otherwise negative examples was closely identified: the liberty of states and the preservation of peace and order over a territory of imperial dimensions.

The founders sought institutions that would enable the union to acquire preponderance over the forces that threatened it while at the same time checking and controlling the power thus created. Guarding against undue concentrations of power either within itself or in the larger society of states, while providing sufficient power to secure its objects, was and remained its fundamental *problematique*. Achieving "a new order of the ages" meant establishing both internal and external relations on the basis of law and finding within the union a fair and workable division of burden-sharing and representation, but with the acknowledgment that the things they were to do in common were not to impair, but rather to preserve, their hard-won internal autonomy and independence. Provisioning and yet limiting arms, seeking to ensure the peaceful settlement of disputes, insisting on common action only in the limited spheres where such was indispensable, and then giving full power to obtain those ends, leaving all else to state responsibility and individual freedom and initiative—this cluster of ideas formed something like the first great consensus among Americans regarding a just and secure system of states.

Peace Pact explored this scheme of thought and sought to explain how and why it came about; this volume examines what became of it, especially as it was transformed under the impact of the great wars that followed: in 1812, 1846, 1861, 1898, 1914, and 1939. Though the old federal union crashed and burned in 1861, out of which fires emerged a far deeper sense of American nationalism, the categories of thought embodied in the unionist paradigm continued to receive expression, and I shall be seeking to show how the building blocks that lay behind the original paradigm were reassembled and reconstructed in the course of the twentieth century to inform the internationalist persuasion. As this book comes to a close, in 1941, the rival nightmares of international anarchy and imperial despotism prey upon the American consciousness even more deeply than in 1787, and out of that cauldron is forged a new reconciliation between independence and union, so long cast asunder since America's emergence as a world power in the twentieth century.

What I call "the unionist paradigm" is very close in substance to the "republican security theory" that Daniel Deudney explores in his pathbreaking work, *Bounding Power: Republican Security Theory from the Polis to the Global Village* (2007).[5] This scheme of thought is also deeply embedded in what J. G. A. Pocock calls "the Enlightened narrative," an account of European history preoccupied with two themes: "the emergence of a system of sovereign states—multiple monarchies, confederacies, and republics—in which the ruling authority was competent to maintain civil government and conduct an independent *Aussenpolitik*; and the emergence of a shared civilization of manners and commerce, through which, in addition to treaties and statecraft, the independent states could be thought to constitute a confederation or republic."[6] In the present work, over an extended period, we will be paddling along the American branch of this great river of speculation, whose springwaters lay in the Enlightenment. Nearly all works in the history of internationalism, which trace the rise and fall of the peace plans and the modalities of international cooperation from the seventeenth to the early twentieth century, focus exclusively on European developments.[7] The present work is informed by the assumption that American thought concerning international relations is just as important to the course of world history and just as rich in its capacity to inform speculation into the enduring problems of international cooperation as European thought over the same 150-year period.

This work is not a diplomatic history of the United States, but it is an attempt to reimagine and reframe the architecture of that history. Most students of American foreign policy carry around in their heads, and not improperly, an idea of American diplomacy divided into an Old Testament and a New Testament, and the question of their relationship must appear fundamental in understanding the broad sweep of our past. According to historian Walter McDougall, the Old Testament was based on a "promised land" devoted to the maintenance of liberty at home and committed to unilateralism, the Monroe Doctrine, and expansion. The New Testament that arose at the end of the nineteenth century, he argues, saw a "crusader state" developing new traditions of progressive imperialism, liberal internationalism, containment, and "global meliorism." My account of the Old Testament differs substantially from McDougall's, as it does from most interpretations of the nineteenth-century experience, in the centrality given to union. That different reading of the Old Testament, it is hoped, will enrich our understanding of the New Testament that emerges in the twentieth century.

Understanding that relationship is vital if we are to think clearly about the fundamental problem that hangs over this as other excursions into the past: Which "American traditions," as McDougall asks, ought we "to reaffirm and apply to diplomacy today," and which traditions should we "discard as irrelevant or even repugnant"? I feel a kinship with the other writers of my generation who have taken that problem seriously. Of these, McDougall, Robert Kagan, Walter Russell Mead, Michael Lind, and Anatol Lieven are the most prominent, but there are others. That each of us might, from the view of some other, be thought a wayward—nay, deranged—fellow traveler seems a firm deduction, since the pasts we imagine are often starkly different. The man from Mars could legitimately wonder whether it was the same country under the telescope. But we have each believed that there was wisdom in that distant heritage and set ourselves apart from the path of some historians, who from our perspective stumbled into a gold mine and made out with a lot of dirt. I have serious disagreements with Kagan, McDougall, and Mead, whereas my ideological perspective is largely in alignment with that of Lind and Lieven. Though I place much greater emphasis on the union in my historical reconstruction than either writer, each of us defends a position that I would describe as a blend or synthesis of constitutional realism and liberal internationalism, and each of us sees imperialism as a threat to international order and to the promise of American life.[8]

I wish to extend my thanks to the many people and organizations that have aided me in the completion of the work. I received a grant from the National Endowment for the Humanities in 1995–1996 that provided a solid foundation for *Peace Pact* and the present work. In 2004, President Richard Celeste made me the Robert J. Fox Distinguished Service Professor at Colorado College. The reduced teaching load and research support provided by the professorship has been of indispensable aid in the completion of the book, for which I am very grateful. I also owe a lasting debt to my colleagues and staff in the Political Science Department and to the prized students I have gotten to know over the past twenty-five years. I feel fortunate to have found a home at Colorado College and to be a part of its big extended family.

As with *Peace Pact*, the comments of Peter Onuf were very helpful to me in getting from rough draft to finished product, and once again I must express my profound thanks to him. Andrew Bacevich, Daniel Deudney, and Robert W. Tucker also provided shrewd comments and needed encouragement. Fred Woodward, my editor at the University Press of Kansas, has given good advice and borne with me patiently. It has been a pleasure working with him and his excellent staff. I have also learned a great deal from various Liberty Fund colloquia over the years, especially those organized by Karl Walling and the late Lance Banning, and I am grateful for the opportunity to have participated in such learned conclaves. My biggest debt is to my wife, Clelia, and our three children, Wesley, Whitney, and Marina, to whom the book is dedicated with deep love and affection.

David C. Hendrickson
Colorado Springs, Colorado
August 20, 2008
www.davidhendrickson.org

PART ONE
Introduction

I

The Problem and Its Modes

IF ONE CONSIDERS THE GRAND NARRATIVES of American foreign policy since World War II, it is fair to say that internationalism, nationalism, and imperialism are the outstanding explanatory concepts. One image visualizes the post–World War II multilateral system as a constitutional system or union with America as its leader. This interpretation emphasizes that the United States deliberately embedded itself in international institutions that would serve the common good and operate on the basis of consensus, alliances that were not narrowly instrumental but reflected common values and ideals. America was committed to building a peaceful world order based on law, and it was the acknowledged leader in a constellation of nations that came to be known at various times as the free world, the West, the international liberal community, the American system, the trilateral community, "the democratic zone of peace," and the "federation of free nations." Sir Alfred Zimmern gave an early anticipation of this community in 1951: "For as far ahead as political thought can see, the United States will occupy a preponderant position in the world, and the people of the United States, who might have set the crown of world empire on their brows, have decided to share their power in a constitutional partnership of free nations. Thus free nations everywhere are called, at a moment in world history corresponding to the moment of 1787 in your own constitutional annals, to a task of political construction."[1]

A second image visualizes the nation making instrumental alliances with others to preserve its security and to defeat evil and aggressive enemies. It emphasizes the intense nationalism and "exceptionalism" that animated the American people, the unilateralism to which its leaders sometimes resorted, and the insularity its people often felt. In this account, allies play at most a bit part—to be rallied when they are willing, ignored when they are not. Nationalist interpretations come in many different varieties—some conscious, some unconscious; some supportive of U.S. policy, some critical. It is, so to speak, the default position. The key preoccupation is with the nation's wants, needs, fears, interests, ideals, dreams, and delusions. Public displays of nationalism—crowds shouting "USA! USA! USA!"—bespeak not surface flotsam but the real animating impulse: a deep and overriding preoccupation, amounting in some accounts to a form of narcissism, with ourselves.[2]

A third image, which is compatible with the nationalist interpretation in some respects, sees the United States as an empire with dependents, protectorates, and satrapies, as having created a so-called Pax Americana that in fact was more than ordinarily bellicose. The imperial interpretation has two main variants. One emphasizes belief in the necessity of unlimited capitalist expansion as the wellspring of the imperial impulse and usually underlines the exploitative characteristics of global capitalism, with America at its head. The other sees an America that has been enthralled by the use of force and that has invariably insisted on exercising dominance within its sphere and in the larger international system. Both stress the importance of domestic factors and give "inside-out" explanations, making them compatible with a nationalist interpretation, but are distinctive in stressing that these domestically generated compulsions lead onward and outward to domination and imperialism.[3]

Union, nation, or empire? That protean question, far from being relegated to obscurity by the events of September 11, 2001, has instead in the years to follow pressed upon the country with dramatic force, implicating fundamental conceptions of the American purpose in the detritus of the Iraq war. Given all the revolutionary changes since 1945 in America's role in the world, it is of practical, historical, and philosophical interest that this triangular contest should go back to the beginning.

Internationalism, nationalism, and imperialism may be understood in two main ways, as signifying either *ideologies* or *social forces*. One might refer to a particular epoch as "the age of imperialism" or "the age of nationalism," as historians have often done, and mean by such an expression the dominant political force of the era. But probably the more familiar usage is as ideologies, where internationalism, nationalism, and imperialism signify doctrines, respectively, of cooperation, egotism, and domination (each in the context of relations across borders or among distinct peoples). Each purports to offer a way of understanding and of acting in the world that best secures the basic human goods of security, freedom, order, justice, and welfare, though the users and abusers of these doctrines understand differently the nature of these requirements and seek different routes to their fulfillment.[4]

Unlike "imperialism," "nationalism," and "internationalism," which are terms that did not come into widespread use until the late nineteenth and early twentieth centuries, "empire," "nation," and "union" have been fundamental categories of political discourse in the United States from the outset of the American experiment in 1776. These terms may also be understood in two distinct, but not incompatible, ways, as signifying either *institutions* or *identities*. In the first meaning, they denote a particular constellation of power and authority (for example, a hierarchical empire where power radiates from the "top down" or a republican union where it comes from the "bottom up.") In neither usage (that is, as identities or institutions) do they refer "to fixed and readily defined entities," in the words of the distinguished historical geographer D. W. Meinig. Rather, these symbols of the political community are "an essential, generalized shorthand for elusive formations that are continuously under construction and alteration."[5] As objects of devotion or detestation, as voices in mutual dialogue, these three images of the political community have figured largely in American history. Behind these terms lie differing complexes of value and purpose that capture vital aspects of the habitual inquiry into "who we are." Behind them, too, lie important theses and debates regarding American institutions and constitutional traditions. Behind them, finally, lie ideologies of cooperation, egotism, and domination, which compete for primacy in the struggle to determine the internal and external policy of the United States.

2

American Internationalism

AMERICAN INTERNATIONALISM, as it came of age in the first four decades of the twentieth century, was associated with a cluster of related ideas. It was committed to the peaceful settlement of disputes and held forth the ultimate ideal of a world at peace under the reign of law. It saw freer commerce as the indispensable means of maximizing wealth and making the nations useful to one another. It identified liberal democracy as the preferred method for organizing political life within nations and saw leadership in a partnership of democratic nations as the primary basis of America's world role. It emphasized both independence and union, recognizing that each of the peoples was entitled to rule itself according to its own forms and fastening on aggression as the key specter against which international society must unite. It envisaged forms of cooperative partnership as against the nightmares of international anarchy and imperial domination. It "rejected the idea of peace by universal empire or by the diplomatic juggle of balance of power," adopting instead "the ideal of the cooperative peace—the ideal which is the great contribution of the Americas to world thought."[1]

The quintessential expressions of the internationalist ethos in the twentieth century were Woodrow Wilson's embrace of the League of Nations and Franklin Roosevelt's championing of the United Nations, but it would be a mistake to identify internationalism solely with Wilson and Roosevelt or the international institutions they promoted. There were Republicans, such as William Howard Taft and Elihu Root, who also considered themselves internationalists. Internationalists divided on the portion of sovereignty or untrammeled discretion that would need to be ceded to any international body, they divided between "particularists" and "universalists" in their conception of the international community, and they divided over the degree to which the United States must pledge itself to the use of U.S. military force (as against economic sanctions and public opinion) in vindication of internationalist ideals. Despite these divergences, which made for a fairly big tent, internationalists held in common the vision of a peaceful world ordered by law and believed that America must play a vital role in bringing it about. Trying to put his finger on the phenomenon, George Kennan called it the "legalistic-moralistic approach to international relations" in his famous 1951 lectures on American diplomacy, and he noted that it had run "like a red skein through our foreign policy of the last fifty years." The tradition, Kennan observed, had in it "something of the old emphasis on arbitration treaties, something of the Hague Conferences and schemes for universal disarmament, something of the more ambitious American concepts of the role of international law, something of the League of Nations and the United Nations, something of the Kellogg Pact, something of the idea of a universal 'Article 51' pact, something of the belief in World Law and World Government." The essence of the idea, which Kennan shrewdly located in the historic experience of federal union, lay in the belief "that it should be possible to suppress the chaotic and dangerous aspirations of governments in the international field by the acceptance of some system of legal rules and restraints."[2]

As Kennan recognized, internationalism need not take a universal form, and to identify it simply with enthusiasts of the League of Nations or the United Nations is too restrictive an interpretation of the phenomenon. In the first part of the twentieth century, American internationalists imagined or projected various communities—the community of English-speaking peoples, a universal association for collective security, a Western Hemisphere community, an Atlantic Community, a Great Power Concert—and the study of internationalism must fully register that variety. But if our understanding of the internationalist idea must be broadened in some respects, it must be narrowed in another. Unless there is a conception of mutual exchange and reciprocal benefit within these various communities, sustained by pledges of good faith and commitment, internationalism can hardly be said to be present. The internationalist insists that there is a community beyond the nation, within which good faith, cooperation, and law are deemed essential.

Internationalism is distinct from cosmopolitanism on the one hand and nationalism and imperialism on the other. Whereas cosmopolitanism postulates a global society in which national identities and loyalties are abandoned, internationalism accepts that national loyalties are and will continue to be important. The internationalist does not seek a world from which nations are absent, but rather one in which they are enabled to flourish. Commitment to internationalism does not require states to cease pursuing their national interest, but only to pursue this interest in an enlightened way—that is, by taking account of the interests of others and requiring that the national interest be pursued within the limitations of justice and good faith. It is "the ideology of international bonding."[3]

Internationalism also stands in sharp opposition to the characteristic claims of nationalism and imperialism. The internationalist rejects a world in which egotistical nations pursue their interest without regard to a common international interest in the principles of a just and stable world order.

That is the way of anarchy, a condition that invariably gives succor to forces at odds with free government. Equally rejected, however, is the proposition that the world of anarchy can or should be mastered through imperial methods. From an internationalist perspective, any condition of unbound power, such as "empire" frequently connotes, is a remedy as fatal as the disease.

The most characteristic idea in the architecture of American diplomatic history is that internationalism did not make its appearance until the twentieth century. It is, so to speak, a Johnny-come-lately whose impact before 1900 was minimal. Whereas nationalism and imperialism are well-traveled historical routes, internationalism has been viewed as almost wholly a phenomenon of the twentieth century. Unilateralism, with which internationalism is often paired as an antonym, is normally seen as the defining characteristic of America's past. As the usual story goes, the United States rejected "its old tradition of unilateralism" and "laid the foundation for a new world of multilateralism" in the twentieth century. Once we were "isolationist," then we became "internationalist."[4]

These accounts are not wrong in stressing the revolutionary and epochal change represented by the abandonment in the 1940s of America's historic political detachment from overseas alliances, but they are wrong in dismissing the significance of internationalist currents in what may be termed the long nineteenth century (that is, from 1789 to 1914). In fact, all the big themes registered in twentieth-century internationalism—the league of free peoples, the peaceful settlement of disputes, the "commitment to the idea of commitment,"[5] the aspiration to bring the international anarchy under the "empire of law," the self-determination of nations, the preference for liberal democracy, the advantages of mutual exchange—are plainly registered in the eighteenth and nineteenth centuries. The normative order to which American internationalists appealed in the twentieth century had very deep roots in the American past. The years after 1945 brought a revolutionary change in American commitments and the determination to apply the full panoply of America's power to shape the international environment, but the *idea* of the order American internationalists wished to build was, in critical respects, previously formed.

The American statesman who contributed most to the development of American internationalism in the twentieth century, Woodrow Wilson, was himself emphatic on his debt to traditional American beliefs of a just world order. With every fiber of his being, he claimed in his great speaking tour on behalf of the League of Nations, he "shouted out" the traditions of the United States. Wilson once observed that because America was "compounded out of the peoples of the world her problem is largely a problem of union all the time, a problem of compounding out of many elements a single triumphal force."[6] That, in a nutshell, was his idea of the League of Nations. Historical judgments of Wilson emphasize the sheer novelty of his internationalism, but Wilson saw himself as a conservative who sought to apply old principles to new circumstances.[7]

One legacy of the eighteenth and nineteenth centuries was the traditional American commitment to international law. This "old internationalism" professed fidelity to the law of nations—the mother of multilateral norms—and was thoroughly committed to the "society of states" tradition. American diplomats attached vital significance to the law of nations in various spheres, especially the law of neutrality. They also sought to infuse into the law of nations "a spirit," in James Madison's words, "which may diminish the frequency or circumscribe the calamities of war." The "great increase which has taken place in the intercourse among civilized and commercial states," as Daniel Webster noted, had connected the United States "with other nations, and given us a high concern in the preservation of those salutary principles upon which that intercourse is founded. We have as clear an interest in international law, as individuals have in the laws of society." This posture is distinguishable, on the one hand, from an outlook, customarily identified with realpolitik, that sees the interstate world as an anarchy in which moral and legal restraints are irrelevant; and, on the other, from a cosmopolitan or revolutionary outlook that looks forward to the transcendence of the state system and its replacement by a new ordering of human relations. With but few exceptions this commitment to "the constitutional tradition in diplomacy" may be considered the characteristic worldview of American diplomatists in the eighteenth and nineteenth centuries, and the embrace of it by twentieth-century American internationalists requires no special explanation.[8]

A second feature of eighteenth- and nineteenth-century internationalism was the commitment to free trade. Throwing open the doors of commerce and breaking off its shackles was a deep impulse of the American Revolution. Among the bundle of arguments for free trade throughout the eighteenth and nineteenth centuries was the contribution it would make to repressing otherwise pronounced tendencies toward war and conflict. This vision of a liberal trading regime based on mutual interest and reciprocal benefit, and excluding all ideas of domination, was thought to offer a great contribution to international peace. America, as John Adams expressed that early faith, "will grow with astonishing Rapidity and England France and every other Nation in Europe will be the better for her prosperity. Peace which is her dear Delight will be her Wealth and Glory."[9]

These free trade visions, offering "a sort of Protestantism" in political economy, were sharply dented after the American Revolution by Europe's still deep attachment to the protective system, and there arose a school of American protectionists, whose early leaders were Alexander Hamilton and Henry Clay, that challenged the verities of the free trade gospel. In the confines of what might, from one perspective, appear the driest subject on the face of the earth—the discussion of the tariff—there arose a profound and fascinating argument concerning the relationship among free trade, protection, and peace, over which nationalists and internationalists waged ferocious battles.[10] Though the protectionists emerged as dominant during and after the Civil War, the American union was sufficiently big and diverse as to itself constitute an argument for free trade within the confines of an enlarged political community. "Inside of the union," noted William Graham Sumner in 1899, "we have established the grandest experiment in absolute free trade that has ever existed." The commitment to a vast free trade area behind high protective tariffs was the pattern that emerged after 1865, and it was, as Sumner observed, a very peculiar combination, "an interesting result of the presence in men's minds of two opposite philosophies, the adjustment of which has never yet been fought out."[11]

Though these ideas of the society of states and of free trade attest to the existence of strong internationalist currents in the eighteenth and nineteenth centuries, the phenomenon that most attracted to it the central perturbations of internationalist thought was the American federal union. We saw in the preface how the categories of thought radiating outward from the union had a decidedly internationalist tenor, in which the problem of cooperation among refractory states was of fundamental importance. Ideas commonly thought of as a special preserve of twentieth-century internationalism are given continual registration in this context. While the name—internationalism—did not yet exist, just about everything that came to be associated with the internationalist idea did exist. But instead of a "security community" or "international regime," the thing was called a "federative system."[12]

At the root of "the federal principle," writes one political scientist, was the notion of a covenant or *foedus* (its etymological root). This and "synonymous ideas of promise, commitment, undertaking, or obligating, vowing and plighting one's word" were joined together with two other things: "the idea of cooperation, reciprocity, mutuality," and "the need for some measure of predictability, expectation, constancy, and reliability in human relations."[13] These three concepts—commitment, reciprocity, predictability—are closely associated with contemporary ideas of international cooperation, and they were endlessly elaborated in debates over the nature and character of federal union from 1776 to 1861. A similar definition (serviceable, like the previous one, for "internationalism" as well) sees the federative principle as emphasizing "the political relation of adjustment among equals rather than the political relationships of inferiority and superiority, and methods of law rather than methods of force."[14] Both federalism and internationalism have a dualistic aspect in which particularity and commonality are, as it were, simultaneously reaffirmed. They propose union partly to aggregate power and partly to maintain distinctness. Each may be conceived as "an exercise in the difficult art of separation," as a "coming together to stay apart," as proposing devices "to cope with the problem of how distinct communities can live a common life together without ceasing to be distinct communities."[15]

The existence of this strong family resemblance between the old American federalism and the new Wilsonian internationalism is significant on a number of levels. It shows, at a minimum, that the historian of the American debate over international relations will not be wanting for abundant materials to prosecute his inquiry, even in a long epoch ostensibly given over to "isolationism." It suggests that one eminent authority was wrong in regarding nineteenth-century American thought on international relations as a "political desert whose intellectual barrenness and aridity was relieved only by some sparse and neglected oases of insight and wisdom."[16] But it also raises a question. What influence did this preceding experience of federal union have on those who defined a distinctively American version of internationalism in the first part of the twentieth century?

That is an important question for this book, and one of its main threads will be to trace the ways in which this inheritance came to matter in the course of the twentieth century. But it is also a complicated and somewhat mysterious question, and to those who saw the parallel in the early twentieth century it might suggest either a sense of providential mission or a warning of the sheer hazards of the undertaking. That the making of the American Constitution formed a template for the problems of world order was an oft-reiterated thought in the second decade of the twentieth century, as well known then as the "clash of civilizations" or the "end of history" theses are today. The inescapable reality, it seemed to internationalists, was that the threat of international anarchy or imperial domination, in a world now made suddenly compact by economic interdependence and revolutions in military technology and communications, required a union of some kind that would tame these malign forces of international anarchy and world empire. All internationalists saw that parallel and believed their world in need of union as an antidote to international anarchy and imperial despotism.

This sense of déjà vu all over again, that the breakdown of the European and world order had returned the United States to its founding predicament, was basic to the internationalist sensibility. As Horace Kallen, a member of Wilson's "Inquiry," put it in 1918, the independent states of America after 1776 "were in precisely the same position and confronted precisely the same problems, in principle, as the present states and governments of the world." James Brown Scott, the eminent authority on international law, gave voice to the same idea. Scott himself was no enthusiast of a federal state for the world, but he saw that the makers of the American Constitution had in fact mapped out the entire terrain regarding the possibilities and limits of international cooperation. Though acknowledging that the "Society of Nations may not be willing, and indeed even with good will may not be able, to go so far now or at any time as have the States forming the American Union," he insisted that "however many steps they may take or however few toward the closer Union, the experience of the framers of the Constitution who traversed the entire path should be as a lamp to their feet."[17]

As fraught with meaning as that parallel was, it was associated with one very troubling paradox. The more one traded on the analogy between the circumstances of 1787 and 1919, the more problematic the entire enterprise appeared. The problem, as Kallen observed, was in principle the same, but the solution—if there was a solution—would have to be different. However loose the old federal union was intended to be at the beginning, it had become much closer over time, and few wanted a degree of intimacy within "the civilized powers" or "the free world" that approached a common nationality. Certainly the American people did not want that. Off the table, therefore, was any international commitment that made a union as tight in its bonds as the Constitution of 1787—that is, which created state institutions and a community from which secession was, or might prove to be, impossible. Between the exigent need for a union among the peace-loving nations and the no less obvious foreclosure of a world state, American internationalism would have to carve out a new path. In responding to the potentialities and necessities of America's new world role in the twentieth century, the unionist paradigm was neither abandoned nor uncritically accepted, but rather modified and restated to fit the new circumstances of the case.[18]

3

Imperialism and Nationalism

To TRACE THE MOVEMENT OF A PARADIGM of thought across time does not necessarily establish its historical importance. The unionist and internationalist ideas we have briefly summarized are but one strand of American thought, and not necessarily the most powerful. Standing athwart any general acceptance of their significance are narratives in which nation or empire plays much the more prominent role. According to one influential school of thought, America's imperial urge is long-standing and utterly characteristic. It long predates the imperialist doings of the early twenty-first century or the moment of global ascendancy in 1945. It can in fact be traced to the beginnings of the nation's history. "The American nation was no sooner founded," writes Ronald Steel, "than its leaders embarked on an energetic program of expansion that—through diplomacy, conquest and theft from its original inhabitants—brought into the ever-expanding Union all the lands east of the Mississippi, then the vast territories of Louisiana, followed by Texas and a third of Mexico, the Pacific Northwest, Alaska, Caribbean and Pacific islands seized from Spain, and the once-independent kingdom of Hawaii." In this conception, American history moves in a sequence of dominations from continental empire to hemispheric empire to global empire. Historians Fred Anderson and Andrew Cayton sought to retell the American story in similar terms, emphasizing "the centrality of imperial ambitions to the development of the United States" and stressing especially the wars of 1812, 1846, and 1898. According to this view, only profound historical amnesia prevents Americans from appreciating how *traditional* and *characteristic* are America's imperial ambitions, which constitute for all intents and purposes the true American way of life.[1]

The imperial interpretation is in one respect incontrovertible. It is a fact that many peoples experienced their encounter with the American system as a form of domination, in which coercion rather than suasion was the overwhelming reality of the situation they confronted. Iroquois, Cherokees, Seminoles, Mexicans, Cubans, Filipinos, Nicaraguans, and Haitians are the predecessors of those peoples—Vietnamese and Iraqis, among others—that have latterly been on the receiving end of U.S. military power, in wars and occupations that can only be styled as imperial. It is no less true, however, that there are countervailing forces in American life that reject imperialism.

Indeed, the very historiography that most emphasizes and denounces imperialism—and there is a lot of it—is part of these anti-imperialist currents.
Taking the long view, it might be argued that the periods of sobriety and
reassessment that follow bouts of imperialism are also pretty typical, and
the country finds itself inoculated against further adventurism in its recoil
from the extravagant hypotheses and failed predictions of the imperialists.
Past performance, to be sure, is no guarantee of future results, but the larger
historical pattern is that American imperialism is both regularly recurring
and capable of generating antipodal tendencies that limit its reach.

There are far more denunciations than defenses of empire and imperialism
in the American tradition. "The American antipathy to imperialism," wrote
Walter Lippmann in 1944, "is not a humanitarian sentiment acquired in
some casual way. It is organic in the American character, and is transmitted
on American soil to all whose minds are molded by the American tradition."[2] American intervention in each world war of the twentieth century
was justified as an enterprise directed against imperialism, and indeed "anti-
imperialism" has often been a platform for the use of American military
power. It also figured strongly in the case for war in 1776, 1812, 1846,
1861, and 1898. This raises the possibility that "anti-imperialism" has itself been a disguise or mask for imperial impulses on the part of the United
States, that there is an "imperialism of anti-imperialism" in the American
tradition.[3]

In the 1960s, radical historians hit a sore point in charging this sin upon
the United States, which the keepers of established truths indignantly denied.
More recently, the indignant denials have been followed by seeming acceptance. What was once exculpated as a necessary evil by liberal historians has
been transformed, in neoconservative reconstructions, into a positive good.
"Once," as Jonathan Schell observed, "the left had stood alone in calling the
U.S. imperial and was reviled for defaming the nation. Now it turned out to
have been the herald of a new consensus. Yesterday's leftwing abuse became
today's mainstream praise." Niall Ferguson, in his book *Colossus* (2004),
advanced the view that the United States was now and had always been an
empire—though he added that it was an "empire in denial" whose aspirations were hypocritically (and unfortunately) denied by U.S. policymakers.
A similar stance was taken by historian John Lewis Gaddis. Though Gaddis
avoided the label of imperialism, he emphasized that preemption, unilateralism, and hegemony (the traits widely deemed imperial today) were defining
characteristics of nineteenth-century American foreign policy. There were
many other instances of the "Yes, we've always been an empire, and a good
thing, too" line in the early twenty-first century, but its enduring appeal is
doubtful. It is noteworthy that official interpretations vehemently rejected

that construction (in public at least) and insisted that "we have no empires to establish or utopias to promote."[4]

As important as the imperial interpretation of the American experience has become in recent years, fortified by an uneasy alliance of adherents across the ideological divide, its ascendancy is of fairly recent vintage. Such a view was not representative of twentieth-century interpreters of the American experiment. Overwhelmingly, they saw America in national terms. Michael Lind's formulation—"the United States has been, is, and should continue to be a liberal and democratic nation state"—well expresses the traditional view. Born in the Revolution, tested by fire in the Civil War, and coming of age as the "indispensable nation" in the twentieth century, the American nation is the lens through which the past is viewed, just as it is the vessel for the primary loyalty of Americans today. Few Americans, Lind comments, "are consistent liberals or conservatives; most are nationalists, by reflex if not reflection."[5]

An unusual feature of the historical development of American nationalism is its pluralism. In the 1950s, the distinguished historian Hans Kohn stressed this feature of American nationalism, something that in his view (he was a Jewish refugee from central Europe) blessedly distinguished it from most nationalisms of the European variety. Each of the distinctive historical expressions of American nationalism that Kohn explored underscored a plural identity: its roots in liberalism, "its relationship to the mother country; its federal structure; its multi-ethnic character, and finally, its position within the community of nations." America's liberal heritage featured the free individual entering into government to preserve liberty, reflecting an understanding of the relation of the individual to the state that was the inverse of European monarchy. *Matre pulchra filia pulchrior*—the fairer daughter of a fair mother—emphasized America as the offspring of Great Britain, itself a fountain of pluralism and constitutionalism. "A republic of many republics" told the story of American federalism, the great experiment in dividing authority between local and general governments. "A nation of many nations" concerned the reconciliation, on American soil, of the extremely heterogeneous collection of peoples, mostly European, who were folded into a single American nationality. "A nation among nations" emphasized that America brought to its conception of world order the new and exciting discovery it applied to the life of the individual—that free autonomous development, within the framework of law, would best achieve security and prosperity for nations as for individuals. In each of these instances, Kohn's account stressed the essential difference between American nationalism and that of continental Europe.[6]

In more recent studies, this pluralistic image of American nationalism has been steadily displaced by a view emphasizing the essential likeness of American nationalism to European variants. Especially among historians of foreign policy, the United States is seen as power-hungry and intent on relentlessly expanding its national domain, craftily outthinking and outannexing the apostles of European realpolitik. The pluralistic features of American nationalism, in this new and revised account, are not so much directly combated as ignored as being irrelevant to the matter at hand: explaining the rise of American power. The United States emerges, in this accounting, as the carrier of a *Herrenvolk* nationalism, defined by its racist exclusions and territorial aggrandizement.[7]

Kohn wanted to believe, with Horace Kallen, that "the most distinctive feature of American nationalism is its internationalism,"[8] but there is probably more evidence for the opposing view that the most distinctive feature of American nationalism is its rejection of internationalism. At a minimum, it would seem necessary to distinguish between "soft" and "hard" versions of American nationalism, with one trunk incorporating these pluralist and internationalist elements and the other defining itself as in combat, sometimes mortal, with threats to the nation from above or below, within or without. Many self-styled nationalists have regarded internationalism as a sort of large-scale identify theft, have asserted the prerogatives of national safety against individual rights and liberties, have insisted upon the supremacy of the national government as against the states, have called for high tariff barriers and special protection to American industry, have demanded the exclusion of immigrants as threatening to national identity, or have aggressively asserted the American national interest in conflicts with foreign states. Intense nationalism distinguishes the "persuasion"—nay, the spirit of brag and defiance—that Walter Russell Mead has dubbed "Jacksonian," ready to take up arms against insults to national honor, and chauvinistic in its cultural prepossessions. Theodore Roosevelt, who regarded the "professional internationalists" with derision, is probably the archetypal American nationalist. Every civilization worth calling itself such, Roosevelt believed, must be based on a spirit of "intense nationalism."[9]

As these remarks should make clear, the "imperial" interpretation of American history is not incompatible with a "nationalist" interpretation. Those who allege, and those who deny, that the United States was, became, or acquired an empire do not doubt that it was throughout a nation. With but few exceptions, they ignore the significance of the union. This larger compatibility of the "imperialist" and the "nationalist" schools is also shown in the interpretations of the wars that ostensibly define the American empire, because one would have to search high and low to find any that, in either their causes or their consequences, have not been closely tied by historical specialists to a burgeoning nationalism.

As a matter of philosophical congruence, the affinity between imperialism and nationalism seems intuitively plausible, for self-assertion, if carried to extremes, makes inevitably for domination if peoples are in proximity or otherwise in competition for scarce goods. It is difficult for calls to altruism or cooperation to stem the impulse to dominate, moreover, because "patriotism transmutes individual unselfishness into national egoism." That process was called by the commentator and theologian Reinhold Niebuhr "the ethical paradox of patriotism." "Loyalty to the nation is a high form of altruism," Niebuhr explained, "when compared with lesser loyalties and more parochial interests. It therefore becomes the vehicle of all the altruistic impulses and expresses itself, on occasion, with such fervor that the critical attitude of the individual toward the nation and its enterprises is almost completely destroyed."[10]

Nationalism may manifest itself as simply the pursuit of "the national interest." But students of nationalism also point to various cultural traits that in effect operate as a set of blinders upon the world and which belie the notion that the national interest rests on firm ground. The distinctive feature of these explanations is their emphasis on an "inside-out" analysis. To many critics, American conduct has grown out of a sort of deep narcissism in the national character, in which internal preoccupations and preformed worldviews push us out into the world and make us behave the way we do. Our sometime missionary zeal, our resentments against others, our religiosity produce a style of foreign policy that acts out a script driven by the sometimes delusional way Americans understand conflict rather than by the objective assessments of threats. The alteration from bouts of moral crusading to recrimination and apathy is rooted in an America driven by its own internal clock rather than by external compulsion.[11] The "Open Door" historians, descendants of Beard and Williams, also give an inside-out explanation, but with emphasis on economic rather than cultural compulsion. They see a highly consistent plan of action driven by elites that is not subject to the wobbles and reversals of public opinion, and they are best placed in the school emphasizing imperialism as an animating director of American conduct. They do share with other critics, however, the emphasis on the domestic roots of foreign policy.[12]

While it is easy to see various paths by which conduct rooted in nationalist impulses can give way to domination and to identify episodes in which nationalism and imperialism were joined at the hip, it would be misleading to conclude that they are always so intimately bound. What Anatol Lieven calls "civic nationalism"—the elements in the American creed that look to freedom, equality, and representative government—cannot be easily detached from what we understand American nationalism to be. In his eulogy of Henry Clay, Abraham Lincoln wrote that Clay "loved his country partly because it was his own country, but mostly because it was a free country; and he burned with a zeal for its advancement, prosperity and glory, because he saw in such, the advancement, prosperity and glory, of human liberty, human right and human nature."[13]

Once one reintroduces the creedal element, the intuitively obvious connection between nationalism and imperialism dissolves, and we are left with a posture intensely hostile to imperialism. The American nation, dedicated to the proposition that legitimate government rests on the consent of the governed, must by the same token reject the domination of one people over another. It must also reject, as deeply corrosive to free government, the institutional transformations at home required by the imperial project. Republicanism, in its classic American meaning, dictated opposition to both "having" and "being" an empire as that term was fleshed out in the practices and theories of rule of European monarchies. An empire, as John Adams put it, is "a despotism, and an emperor a despot, bound by no law or limitation but his own will: it is a stretch of tyranny beyond absolute monarchy." A monarch had to have his edicts "registered by parliaments," but even this formality, Adams thought, "is not necessary in an empire." Adams was capable of using the word "empire" in a far less sinister sense, as signifying simply dominion over a large territory, but the idea of empire always retained the despotic connotation as one of its potential meanings. The only empire Americans could have, under those circumstances, was an "empire of liberty"—a "steubendous *fabrick* of *Freedom* and *Empire*," as George Washington put it, erected "on the broad basis of Independency" and dedicated to "protecting the rights of humane nature and establishing an Asylum for the poor and oppressed of all nations and religions."[14]

There is a further sense in which nationalism may set itself apart from imperialism. Though nationalism is inseparable from the exaltation of the collective self and can easily produce the domination of others, many nationalists have been willing to respect the right of free autonomous development that they claim for themselves. In theory, the true nationalist must recognize this, even in the midst of the jostling for special advantage and the pursuit of the national interest. In theory, the wellspring of devotion to one's kith and kin, the little platoons of the great society to which men and women give their allegiance, must be recognized as belonging to all distinct peoples, and we can no more begrudge other nations their tender feelings for their own nationality than we can deny our own. If the rule of ethics is to do unto others as we would wish to be done unto us, the nationalist must concede to others the right he claims for himself—the joy, hardship, mutual history, and love associated with membership in a given *patria*. This form of nationalism makes its peace with internationalism—or tries to do so. A world society exists, but "no one is asked to transfer his allegiance from his own country to a new cosmopolitan fatherland. As he is a good patriot so he is a good neighbor, and by being a good neighbor he is loyal to the laws, the usages, and the requirements of the universal society."[15]

In practice, however, many nationalists are unwilling to concede that this simple rule of reciprocity applies to international relations. There are two characteristic forms of this rejection, both of which lead on to imperialism. One is the lure of *sacré égoïsme* and the belief that the national interest ought not to be controlled by any external constraint, a position basically equivalent to a kind of hard realism or realpolitik. The nation, according to a classic summary of this perspective, "is an organic being, engaged in a struggle for life, for strength, for the conquest of hampering limitations, for predominance. Its objectives are first to endure and then to expand. . . . Its chief and primary instrument is force. It is independent, self-centered, and concerned with other nations only externally, in the sense that they are regrettable, yet inescapable constraints on its pursuit of that interest. There is no community of nations, and there cannot be."[16]

The second departure is the adoption of a "nationalistic universalism" that seeks to replicate through coercion or intervention one's domestic model throughout the international system. Distinguishing between the nationalism of the nineteenth century and the "nationalistic universalism" of the twentieth century, Hans Morgenthau noted that the former sought "to free the nation from alien domination and give it a state of its own," whereas the latter entertained a "universal mission whose ultimate goal reaches to the confines of the political world." The one was limited and recognized that different nationalisms had similar and equally justifiable goals; the other claimed "for one nation and one state the right to impose its own valuations and standards of action upon all the other nations." It inspired its bearers "with a thirst and a strength for universal dominion of which the nationalism of the nineteenth century knew nothing."[17]

A key element in what Morgenthau called "nationalistic universalism" has been a pronounced feature of American foreign policy since the 1980s and was especially notable in the second inaugural address of George W. Bush, which called for the United States to devote itself to the "end of tyranny" and the achievement of democracy everywhere in the world. Advocates of this policy generally deny with indignation that it has anything to do with imperialism; on the contrary, it is justified as a policy of liberation. There is, however, a long and distinguished view in the American tradition which holds that such a policy has everything to do with imperialism. The reason is that it violates the law of nations and "the true principles of liberty," both of which privilege essential rights of national independence. Whether the newer view or the older view of this vital problem is most persuasive the reader may judge, but it is clear beyond peradventure that the new view justifying intervention for democracy is very different from the older view denying the legitimacy of this enterprise.

In the long nineteenth century, there was a consensus—reiterated in presidential messages and in other state papers—that intervention for such a purpose was illegitimate. Noninterference in the domestic concerns of other nations was continually avowed not only as a basic principle of American foreign policy but of the law of nations. "We recognize in all nations," observed President Polk, "the right which we enjoy ourselves, to change and reform their political institutions according to their own will and pleasure." That doctrine was dictated not only by "true policy" but also by "a sacred regard for the independence of nations." Whigs, who disagreed with Polk about many things, nevertheless agreed with him about this. Though united by commerce, as Webster put it, "The great communities of the world are regarded as wholly independent, each entitled to maintain its own system of law, and government, while all, in their mutual intercourse, are understood to submit to the established rules and principles governing such intercourse. And the perfecting of this system of communication among Nations, requires the strictest application of the doctrine of non-intervention of any with the domestic concerns of others."[18]

The nineteenth-century assessment of the relationship between liberty and nationality is key to understanding this question. American sensibilities privileged what would later be called "external self-determination" over "internal self-determination." The fundamental right was independence: every people had the right to devise its own institutions rather than to be ruled by foreigners. The very act of so devising—whether it took place through reform or revolution—was thought to conduce toward representative institutions, but if an independent people consented to a monarch or fell into a civil war from which a dictator saved them, that was their own business. In the conception of legitimacy then entertained, the men on the spot had the right, and outsiders none, to decide for themselves, even if this meant fighting it out among themselves. This was not an understanding that necessarily drew the United States into insularity, as it might be suspected of doing. At a minimum, it promoted commerce, and a case could be and was made in the nineteenth century for intervention on behalf of the nonintervention principle (an issue raised both by the threatened intervention of the Holy

Alliance in the Americas in the 1820s and by Russia's crushing of Hungarian independence in 1849).[19]

Nor should this view be equated with indifference to the cause of liberty. External self-determination (freedom from foreign rule) was a necessary condition of internal self-determination and was itself fundamental to the "liberty and independence" these nineteenth-century Americans prized. That commitment to "communal liberty" did not preclude support for "civil liberty." "What the laws of nations do not forbid," William Seward proclaimed in 1851, "any nation may do for the cause of civil liberty, in any other country." Seward's doctrine, expressive of the views of Lincoln and the Republican consensus, created a wide berth for the progress of free institutions but did not challenge the fundamentals of the society of states. These different understandings of the role of liberty and law, so central to America's conception of its purpose, and of vital importance today, make an issue between the present and the past on the question of American imperialism.[20]

The mutual relationship among union, nation, and empire forms the interpretive conundrum of the present work. It is a relationship of many dimensions. It reaches to the question of identity, with each of the terms suggesting an answer to the insistent question: Who are we? American institutional development—the relationship of states to nation, the role of the executive in relation to the legislative and judicial branches, the rise of a formidable central state apparatus and "military-industrial complex"—is also deeply implicated by these terms. At yet another level, these words may reflect deep-seated ideological antagonisms. They suggest rival ideologies of internationalism, nationalism, and imperialism, of cooperation, egotism, and domination, that meet one another in an elemental struggle throughout our history.

Which is primary, which secondary or tertiary? Which the main tradition, which the counterfeit one? Which blends most easily into the others? Which stand most at polar opposites? Alas, no straightforward answers can be given to these pertinent queries. In the immortal words of Oscar Hammerstein's king of Siam, "It is a puzzlement!"

While this work will offer distinctive interpretations of the development of American nationalism, internationalism, and imperialism, it differs from others perhaps most decisively in its commitment to hearing all three voices and the cacophonous dissents to which they gave rise. It rejects monodimensional accounts that assert the everlasting primacy of one of these factors, with the others registered sotto voce or not at all. A more accurate conception is that they are invariably to be found in conflict, collaboration, or coexistence with each other throughout American history. They are not, to be sure, of constant potency across the span of time. They undergo periods of great influence and subsequent contraction, in the fashion of the boom-and-bust cycles characteristic of stock markets and capitalist economies. But they are present, in various states of rise, eclipse, and renovation, throughout the years examined in this work. While this co-mingling makes the task of historical description and generalization more difficult, it also has seemed to me an exciting discovery in that it suggests that we might, through historical study, find debates of permanent importance illuminating the high purpose of these United States. These debates lay bare an intellectual landscape of great imaginative heights and take us to fundamental choices over how we should understand and act in the world.[21]

PART TWO
The Age of Revolution
and War

4

The Rival Systems of Hamilton and Jefferson

THE FEDERAL CONSTITUTION MADE AT PHILADELPHIA in the summer of 1787 deserves most of the accolades that have been bestowed upon it across the ages, but in the first decades of its existence it often seemed a frail and precarious thing. If it was, as the English statesmen William Gladstone later called it, "the most wonderful work ever struck off at a given time by the brain and purpose of man," it was also an instrument that allowed for profoundly different interpretations of its character. At its birth, it answered to each of the terms we have highlighted—union, nation, and empire—but it was, as James Madison insisted, "sui generis": "so unexampled in its origin, so complex in its structure, and so peculiar in some of its features, that in describing it the political vocabulary does not furnish terms sufficiently distinctive and appropriate, without a detailed resort to the facts of the case." Partly because of its silences and ambiguities, the government created under the auspices of the Constitution found itself in serious trouble after its establishment in 1789. Divisions over commercial policy toward Britain and France, recriminations over the locations of the capitol, and painful eruptions over Alexander Hamilton's fiscal system all split the First Congress along sectional lines. The Virginians were especially angered. Before 1789 was out, Madison declared in the House of Representatives that had "a prophet appeared in the Virginia ratifying convention and brought the declarations and proceedings of this day into their view, . . . Virginia might not have been a part of the Union at this moment." "The government which we both admired so much," wrote Henry Lee to Madison, would "prove ruinous in its operation to our native state." Lee pronounced himself ready to "submit to all the hazards of war and risk the loss of everything dear to me in life" rather than "to live under the rule of a fixed insolent northern majority."[1]

There were good reasons why New England and the southern states should each respectively be wary of too close a union with their erstwhile brethren. The United States, wrote one New Englander, had to "remain a collection of Republics, and not become an Empire . . . [because] if America becomes an Empire, the seat of government will be to the southward, and the Northern States will be insignificant provinces. Empire will suit the southern gentry;

they are habituated to despotism by being the sovereigns of slaves: and it is only accident and interest that had made the body of them the temporary sons of liberty." Democracy, added another New Englander, was "an indian word, signifying 'a great tobacco planter, who had herds of black slaves.'" Southerners, by contrast, had learned to fear domination by the "coalition of Monarchy men, Military Men, Aristocrats, and Drones" supposed to be ensconced in the northern states and who were stimulated by the prospect of "the Commercial plunder of the South."[2]

In 1790, the Virginians were most rattled by Hamilton's fiscal plans. The secretary of the Treasury proposed to fund fully the debt of the Congress, making no discrimination among the holders of the various notes it had issued, and to fully assume the debts of the states, thereby solving the hopelessly complicated problems with which the Congress of the Confederation had unsuccessfully wrestled. This audacious scheme was the very definition of killing several birds with one stone—it proposed at once to establish credit, undergird a stable currency, provide capital for development, and get southerners used to the idea of paying taxes. The financial stabilization that ensued, after the disorders of the confederation, seemed to admirers an amazing and extraordinary accomplishment, when "confusion heard his voice, and wild uproar/Stood ruled."[3]

To southerners, however, it appeared as a case of sectional aggrandizement. Thomas Jefferson would later recall that Hamilton had come to him in 1790 and had warned "in pathetic tones" of the danger to the union were the Treasury secretary's program not expeditiously approved by Congress. Two years later, Jefferson was warning Washington that the program to which Jefferson had reluctantly acceded (in exchange for getting the capitol in the District of Columbia) was threatening to break the union "into two or more parts." Jefferson could not imagine "a more incalculable evil. Yet when we review," he said,

> the mass which opposed the original coalescence [the ratification of the Constitution], when we consider that it lay chiefly in the Southern quarter, that the legislature have availed themselves of no occasion of allaying it, but on the contrary whenever Northern & Southern prejudices have come into conflict, the latter have been sacrificed & the former soothed; that the owners of the debt are in the Southern & the holders of it in the Northern division; that the Antifederal champions are now strengthened in argument by the fulfillment of their predictions; that this has been brought about by the Monarchical federalists themselves, who, having been for the new government merely as a stepping stone to monarchy, have themselves adopted the very constructions of the constitution, of which, when advocating its acceptance before the tri-

bunal of the people, they declared it insusceptible; that the republican federalists, who espoused the same government for its intrinsic merits, are disarmed of their weapons, that which they denied as prophecy being now become true history: who can be sure that these things may not proselyte the small number which was wanting to place the majority on the other side?

A good question that, to which the answer was that no one could be sure. To avoid the evil of a dissolution, Jefferson pleaded for Washington to stay as president: "North & South will hang together, if they have you to hang on." Washington was drawing away from Jefferson at this time, but he too saw grave peril in the drift of events. If partisan rancor continued, he wrote to Hamilton, he did not see "how the Reins of government are to be managed, or how the Union of the States can be much longer preserved."[4]

Developing alongside these disputes over union, which engaged the partisans in a deep sense of mutual betrayal, were the great controversies arising out of the French Revolution. In 1791, encouraged by French émigrés bitterly hostile to the Revolution, Prussia and Austria had, with the declaration of Pillnitz (August 27, 1791), made the cause of the French monarch their own. The French demand that Francis II of Austria withdraw his troops from the French frontier and expel the émigrés who had gathered in his dominions was refused; that in turn led to the French declaration of war. The subsequent invasion of France by the armies of Prussia and Austria was repulsed at Valmy (September 20, 1792); the French counterattack carried them into the Austrian Netherlands and the Holy Roman Empire. Late in 1792, the French Convention offered the support of France to any people wishing to recover its liberty; that declaration, together with the execution of Louis XVI, made wider war virtually inevitable. On February 1, 1793, France declared war on Great Britain and Holland, and on March 7 against Spain. With these acts, responsibility for which was bitterly disputed, a world war had begun. It raged on until 1815 with only one brief interval, the 1802 Peace of Amiens.

Even before the outbreak of war between Britain and France, which raised immediate and delicate issues for the resolution of the federal government, the ideological passions aroused by the French Revolution had reached the western shore of the Atlantic. At the beginning, American opinion had been generally sympathetic to the cause of revolution in France, but as the Revolution progressed toward war, regicide, and terror, there arose a strong revulsion against its course among the Federalists, which developed alongside, though in opposition to, the equally strong revulsion against the conduct of "the confederacy of kings" felt by the Republicans. That difference of opinion had set in early: Americans had read avidly the productions of Edmund

Burke and Thomas Paine, both of them famous names in North America; the rival views taken in America in 1791 of their respective pamphlets—with Burke bitterly and presciently hostile to the French Revolution, and Paine an avid fan—prefigured the ideological divisions of the two American parties in the coming decade, just as these pamphlets demonstrated the enormity of passion the French Revolution was capable of arousing everywhere in the Western world.

The bitter disputes over fiscal and foreign policy in the 1790s often put the union in peril; there were frequent reports, at home and abroad, of its imminent demise. In 1794, Rufus King of Massachusetts told John Taylor of Virginia, about to resign his seat in the Senate, that "it was utterly impossible for the union to continue." Noting that "the southern and eastern people thought very differently, and that the latter would not submit their politics to the former," King thought that "a dissolution of the union by mutual consent, was preferable to a certainty of the same thing, in a less desirable mode."[5] That Americans had not made, with their Constitution, an entire escape from the prospect of Machiavellian moments was strongly reinforced by the belief, held by both parties, that their opponents were strongly under the influence of foreign governments. "To be the pro-consul of a despotic Directory over the United States, degraded to the condition of a province, can alone be the criminal, the ignoble aim of so seditious, so prostitute a character," was Hamilton's malicious charge on Jefferson in 1798. Six years previously, Jefferson had written Washington that Hamilton's "history, from the moment at which history can stoop to notice him, is a tissue of machinations against the liberty of the country which has not only received and given him bread, but heaped it's honors on his head." That civil war would be the outcome of this fevered antagonism seemed to some observers highly probable; the escape from that dreaded condition, when it was made at the end of the decade, was very close indeed, with the patriotism of John Adams probably constituting the saving factor in the situation.[6]

The comprehensive systems of Hamilton and Jefferson seemed to oppose one another at every turn, posing a primordial choice between fundamentally different futures. Centralization versus decentralization, "implied powers" versus strict construction, judicial review versus the lack thereof—all these weighty constitutional questions stood alongside differing visions of future development, with Jefferson favoring western expansion and commercial reformation, and Hamilton cautious about western expansion and ambitious plans to reform Europe.[7] Whereas Hamilton most feared dissolution, and continued to see as a real historical possibility the emergence of the raging state system in North America, Jefferson most feared consolidation, and saw in Hamilton's program a set of aspirations equivalent to those that he and his fellow Virginians had once taken up arms to oppose. Virginians discerned "a striking resemblance" between Hamilton's financial system "and that which was introduced into England, at the revolution; a system which has perpetrated upon that nation an enormous debt, and has moreover insinuated into the hands of the executive, an unbounded influence, which pervading every branch of the government, bears down all opposition, and daily threatens the destruction of everything that appertains to English liberty. The same causes produce the same effects!" The memorialists apprehended that one of two evils would follow from the erection of such a powerful monied interest: either "the prostration of agriculture at the feet of commerce, or a change in the present form of foederal government, fatal to the existence of American liberty."[8]

Jefferson, who had become America's first secretary of state in 1790, strongly sympathized with the French Revolution. As minister to France from 1784 to 1789 under the confederation, Jefferson had witnessed the first scenes of the engulfing drama and had played a useful role in facilitating discussions among the parties. His counsel at the time was moderate; he hoped that France would settle on a constitutional monarchy. The course of the next few years turned him into a committed partisan and convinced him that the issue at stake in France was hardly different from the issue in America: in the one, revolutionaries were "exterminating the monster aristocracy, & pulling out the teeth & fangs of its associate monarchy";[9] in the other, "Anglomen" like Hamilton were attempting to foist upon the country a monarch and an aristocracy on the English model. Jefferson's enthusiasm for the French Revolution, as passionately felt as his hatred of Hamilton, carried him so far as to exculpate the acts of terror that chilled the bones of the rival Federalists. When the Jacobins employed "the arm of the people," Jefferson wrote in early 1793, they had killed "many guilty persons . . . without the forms of trial, and with them some innocent." The Virginian deplored those deaths but thought the actions justifiable: "The liberty of the whole earth was depending on the issue of the contest, and was ever such a prize won with so little innocent blood? My own affections have been deeply wounded by some of the martyrs to this cause, but rather than it should have failed, I would have seen half the earth desolated. Were there but an Adam & an Eve left in every country, & left free, it would be better than as it now is." Federalists would have paid dearly for the possession of this famous letter to William Short, not published until after Jefferson's death, for it would have provided wounding testimony of the misleading picture they drew of Jefferson throughout the decade: the committed revolutionary partisan and sansculotte, his teeth dripping with blood, awaiting his opportunity, in league with France, to bring the Terror to America.[10]

Jefferson's sympathies for the French alliance, however, antedated the Revolution and were a function of his strong anti-British sentiments. Throughout the 1780s and 1790s, Jefferson and Madison looked on the alliance with France as the sheet anchor of the public safety and continued to believe after the war broke out that French victories in Europe would check British ambitions in America. "One thing," Madison wrote in 1795, "is certain and conclusive": "Whilst the war against France remains unsuccessful the United States are in no danger from any of the Powers engaged in it." France was not only a barrier against Great Britain; it was also to be the means by which the commerce of the staple states was to be weaned from the British connection. When war broke out between France and Britain, the decision of Washington to follow Hamilton's lead and issue a proclamation of neutrality in April 1793 disgusted Madison, who found the proclamation abominable: "It wounds the national honor, by seeming to disregard the stipulated duties to France. It wounds the popular feelings by a seeming indifference to the cause of liberty. And it seems to violate the forms & spirit of the Constitution, by making the executive Magistrate the organ of the disposition, the duty, & the interest of the Nation in relation to War & peace, subjects appropriated to other departments of the Government." Jefferson had tried, but failed, to insinuate into the proclamation a reading of neutral rights that would, he thought, be more advantageous to France than American participation in the war. By breaking the British blockade of foodstuffs to France, it would defeat Britain's nefarious attempt to starve a nation out of its liberties. Madison and Jefferson were not oblivious to the importance of the balance of power; they believed, however, that the threat to it came principally from England and its associates. In their reasonings on the subject of British maritime dominion they gave expression to ideas long customary in France and America, seeing in those claims the basis of an insulting and atrocious tyranny. That attitude was reflected in their denunciation of the treaty with Great Britain that John Jay signed in December 1794, the proposed ratification of which further agitated the parties. Jefferson called it a "monument of folly and venality," an "infamous act, which is nothing more than a treaty of alliance between England and the Anglomen of this country against the legislature and people of the United States."[11]

In all these matters Jefferson and Madison were at odds with Hamilton. The secretary of the Treasury had already soured on the French Revolution when war broke out in 1793. The imperatives of his financial system had previously made him hostile to Republican plans of retaliatory commercial restrictions against British commerce; both before and after the outbreak of war, he saw infinite mischief in the Republican conception of "peaceable coercion," which he thought rested on a fatal misunderstanding of the limits of American power. Whereas Jefferson sought to maintain the French alliance as a counter to England and a source of pressure on Spain, Hamilton saw greater utility in an accommodation with Britain, and Jay's Treaty of 1794 and Pinckney's Treaty of 1795 with Spain represented the culmination of his diplomatic design. Those treaties made real the title to the western territories that had been dangled before America's eyes in 1783, but which was then rudely withdrawn by British intransigence and Spanish pertinacity. Hamilton and other Federalists, seeing a serious risk of potential disunion and war in the competition for the western territory, and understanding that an agreement with Britain over the western posts would frustrate any community of views between Britain and Spain, defended Jay's Treaty as essential to the preservation of peace. In the circumstances facing the United States, Hamilton argued, peace was an object "of such great and primary magnitude" that it was not to be given up "unless the relinquishment be clearly necessary to Preserve Our Honor in some Unequivocal Point, or to avoid the sacrifice of some Right or Interest of Material and Permanent Importance."[12]

At the outbreak of war, when French prospects looked poor, Hamilton's principal concern was that America would get dragged into the conflict through mistaken ideological sympathy for republican France. Much of his animus toward France arose from the contempt with which French diplomacy flouted the law of nations. France "gave a general and just cause of alarm to Nations" by its decrees of November 19 and December 15, 1792. In the former, the Convention, in the name of the French nation, declared "that it will accord fraternity and assistance to all peoples who shall wish to recover their liberty." In the latter, the Convention announced "that it will treat as enemies the people who, refusing liberty and equality, or renouncing them, may wish to preserve, recall, or treat with the prince and the privileged castes." Taken together, Hamilton argued, these decrees were "little short of a declaration of War against all Nations, having princes and privileged classes," equally repugnant "to the general rights of Nations, to the true principles of liberty, [and] to the freedom of opinion of mankind." Jefferson himself saw the vulnerability of France to that charge and confessed in 1793 that the French "have been guilty of great errors in their conduct towards other nations, not only in insulting uselessly all crowned heads, but endeavouring to force liberty on their neighbours in their own form." But his dominant portrait of the European war was one that saw a "confederacy of princes" warring "against human liberty." Responsibility for the war, he believed, lay with the despots of Europe, not the republicans of France, as did the first violation of the principle of nonintervention.[13]

Hamilton is the prototypical American realist and Jefferson the archetypal

American idealist. The contrast, though real, is easy to overstate because there is a considerable amount of idealism in Hamilton, the "Christian statesman," and much realism in Jefferson, the "practical idealist."[14] They disagreed sharply over the nature of "the dictates of national morality," while nevertheless recognizing the importance of the thing. In Jefferson's view, moral duty required gratitude toward France for its aid in securing American independence. To deny this sentiment as a proper motive of national conduct, Jefferson believed, was "to revive a principle which has been buried for centuries with its kindred principles of the lawfulness of assassination, poison, perjury, etc. All of these were legitimate principles in the dark ages which intervened between ancient and modern civilization, but exploded and held in just horror in the eighteenth century." Hamilton, by contrast, denied that gratitude could have any such claim. He did not "advocate a policy absolutely selfish or interested in nations," but rather insisted that "a policy regulated by their own interest, as far as justice and good faith permit, is, and ought to be their prevailing policy."[15]

A similar difference of outlook appears in their understanding of the law of nations, to which both men continually appealed in justification of their policy. The fundamentals of that law had been set forth by Montesquieu. It required the nations to "do to one another in times of peace the most good possible, and in times of war the least ill possible, without harming their true interests." It was basic to the law of nations that a state had a right to pursue its own interest, and an eminent task of political science was to find where that true interest lay. At the same time, the aims of statecraft had to be pursued within a recognized moral and legal framework. "Faith and justice between nations," as Hamilton summarized the teaching of the publicists and expressed his own deep conviction, "are virtues of a nature the most necessary and sacred." Jefferson agreed with that, but whereas Hamilton gave greater weight to considerations of customary usage and accepted practice—these were "of the highest authority"—Jefferson was led by his desire for a change in international law to greater reliance on "the natural or necessary law of nations," as discovered by the exercise of dispassionate reason. The Virginian believed that "with respect to America," Europeans "have been too long in the habit of confounding force with right."[16]

If anyone was guilty of confounding force with right, Hamilton believed, it was assuredly the French, and by 1798 he argued that France might well succeed in joining the empire of the land with the empire of the sea. The victories of French arms on the Continent and the possibility that Britain might go down under the onslaught of naval mutinies, national bankruptcy, Irish rebellion, and French invasion changed the face of world politics and had extraordinary repercussions in America. In response to the fear of a

French bid for universal empire, and capitalizing on the indignation that arose when Messrs. X, Y, and Z sought to bribe the American commissioners, the Federalists pushed through large increases in land and naval forces. In justifying these steps, Hamilton urged preparedness and collaboration with Britain to turn back this alarming threat to the balance of power and the liberties of the world. Britain, he thought, had "repeatedly upheld the balance of power [in Europe], in opposition to the grasping power of France. She has no doubt occasionally employed the pretence of danger as the instrument of her own ambition; but it is not the less true, that she has been more than once an effectual shield against real danger." That was the case in the War of the Spanish Succession, when Britain had ranged itself against the ambitions of Louis XIV; it was, Hamilton thought, certainly the case in the late 1790s. The recognition that American security would be gravely imperiled by the overthrow of the European system not only dictated cooperation with the English; it also underlined the necessity of permanent preparations for defense at home. "It can never be wise," Hamilton wrote at the end of 1798, "to vary our measures of security with the continually varying aspect of European affairs." In consideration of "the rapid vicissitudes, at all times, of political and military events" and "the extraordinary fluctuations which have been peculiarly characteristic of the still subsisting contest in Europe," the obvious policy was "to place our safety out of the reach of the casualties which may befal the contending parties and the powers more immediately within their vortex." Only by unremitting vigilance and exertion would America be able to secure its own destiny. "Standing, as it were, in the midst of falling empires, it should be our aim to assume a station and attitude which will preserve us from being overwhelmed in their ruins."[17]

The same specter—unlimited and arbitrary power, insatiable in its aims, destructive to liberty—haunted both sides in the great crisis of '98. For Hamiltonian Federalists, it came from abroad and dictated measures of preparedness and quasi alliance with Britain; for Jeffersonian Republicans, it arose at home and was to be found in the very measures advised by the Federalist Party. Republicans considered the Federalist (and British) claim that France posed a genuine threat of "universal empire" to be "a mere *bugbear*," designed to foist a standing army upon the people but otherwise to serve no legitimate purpose of national defense.[18] They vehemently condemned the Alien and Sedition Acts, repressive and unconstitutional legislation passed by Federalists (without Hamilton's concurrence) in 1798. Jefferson would later recall that the "usurpations and violations of the Constitution" by the Federalists "were so great, so decided, and so daring, that, after combating their aggressions inch by inch without being able in the least to check their career, the Republican leaders thought it would be best for them to give up their useless efforts there, go home, get into their respective legislatures, embody whatever of resistance they could be formed into, and, if ineffectual, to perish there as in the last ditch."[19]

The Republican resistance took the form of the Virginia and Kentucky resolutions of 1798 and 1799. The Virginia Resolutions, authored by Madison, were a sharp remonstrance that called for "interposition" but not "nullification" against the unconstitutional Alien and Sedition Acts. But the Kentucky legislature, in resolutions drawn secretly by Jefferson, went further, authorizing a direct nullification of the laws of the general government. Laws made outside the Constitution, the Kentucky Resolutions proclaimed, were "altogether void, and of no force." These were fighting words, and Jefferson knew it. As early as 1792, he had told Madison that the "only opposition worthy of our state, and the only kind which can be effectual," lay in the willingness to go to the wall on behalf of the constitutional rights of the states. Noting that "the power of erecting banks and corporations was not given to the general government," he deduced that whoever recognized such a "foreign legislature" would commit "an act of *treason* against the state." Anyone who participated in the day-to-day activities of such an illegal corporation, Jefferson then wrote, should "be adjudged guilty of high treason and suffer death accordingly, by the judgment of the state courts." Such was the hard-line view that informed the Kentucky Resolutions.[20]

Hamilton, who had come increasingly to believe that "the subdivision of the great states," and above all of Virginia, "is indispensable to the security of the General Government and with it of the Union," was alarmed at reports that Virginians were gathering arms to resist the execution of the laws, and he suggested that a "clever force" be collected from the armies then being raised, ostensibly to thwart the French menace, "to put Virginia to the test of resistance." For complicated reasons—the unexpected turn of the European war that diminished the French threat, the break in Federalist ranks brought into the open by John Adams's decision in early 1799 to send another peace mission to France, the Federalist overreaching on the sedition laws—the crisis broke in favor of the Republicans. Jefferson's election in 1800 put a temporary end to the possibility of a southern secession from the "monocrats" and "Anglomen" who had, to the Virginian's mortification, seized control of the general government. There is little doubt, however, that they had approached the brink and had just barely escaped, through a combination of luck and last-minute restraint, from falling into the abyss below. Far from being atypical, the experience of the 1790s was prototypical, constituting a dress rehearsal for the series of disunion crises through which the United States would pass over the next six decades.[21]

5

The Causes of War

A KEY ASPECT OF THE GREAT DIVIDE BETWEEN Federalists and Republicans arose over the causes of war. The question of whether democracy made for peace was frequently agitated during the debates over the making and ratification of the Constitution. Federalists had warned that in the absence of ratification the division of the continent was at hand; that as a consequence of this division regional confederacies would form that would entertain relations with one another indistinguishable from those prevailing in the European state system; and that this development—inevitably accompanied by perennial rivalries and by the standing armies and wars bred by these—would jeopardize the fragile growth of republican government on the American continent. "To be more safe," Publius warned in *Federalist* 7, the separate and rival confederacies of North America would "at length become willing to run the risk of being less free." In the absence of union, these confederacies would likely attach themselves to the interests of foreign powers, and the American continent would become, like the petty republics of Greece and Italy, the scene of foreign involvement and perpetual war. In those circumstances, "the face of America will be but a copy of that of the continent of Europe. It will present liberty everywhere crushed between standing armies and perpetual taxes."[1]

Anti-Federalists, by contrast, denied that the situation facing the American states was nearly as critical as the supporters of the new Constitution were maintaining. Centinel, a prominent Anti, dismissed projections of inevitable war as a "hobgoblin" that had "sprung from the deranged brain of Publius, a New-York writer."[2] "What will democratic states make war for, and how long since have they imbibed a hostile spirit?" asked William Grayson in the Virginia convention. The theory that democracies are inherently pacific was echoed by James Monroe, who believed that "all those terrors which splendid genius and brilliant imagination" had depicted were "imaginary—mere creatures of fancy." "The causes of half the wars that have thinned the ranks of mankind, and depopulated nations, are caprice, folly, and ambition: these belong to the higher orders of governments, where the passions of one, or of a few individuals, direct the fate of the rest of the community. But it is otherwise with democracies, where there is an equality among the citizens."[3]

Publius had been especially dismissive of the democratic peace theory. Republics, the *Federalist* had held, were no less addicted to war than monarchies; commerce had done nothing more than "change the objects of war." The author of the passages in the *Federalist* that denied both the pacific character of republics and the pacific consequences of commerce was Alexander Hamilton. Then, as later, Hamilton was frequently to be found ascribing the causes of war either to the infirmities of human nature or to the structural pressures of the state system; he did not believe, either as a matter of historical record or future conjecture, that republics had been or would be more pacific than other forms of government. It was not "funding systems," Hamilton argued, that produced "wars, expenses, and debts"; they were, rather, produced by "the ambition, avarice, revenge, and injustice of man." The seeds of war were "sown thickly in the human breast," and Hamilton considered it "astonishing, after the experience of its having deluged the world with calamities for so many ages, with how much precipitance and levity nations still rush to arms against each other."[4] Hamilton shared the general sense of the Enlightenment that war frequently failed to achieve its ostensible object and was continually involving its authors in unexpected calamities. Though Hamilton thirsted for military distinction—"all that is honor in the character of a soldier was at home in his heart"—the view that he was a military adventurer is unfair and misleading.[5] The Hamiltonian system, in both finance and diplomacy, was predicated on the achievement of peace.

The Republican credo was most famously laid out by Thomas Paine in *The Rights of Man*: "Why are not Republics plunged into war, but because the nature of their Government does not admit of an interest distinct to that of the Nation?" Dismissing the analysis of the Hamiltonians, Thomas Paine had insisted that war was "the common harvest of all those who participate in the division and expenditure of public money, in all countries. It is the art of *conquering at home*; the object of it is an increase in revenue; and as revenue cannot be increased without taxes, a pretense must be made for expenditures." Paine speculated that the "intrigue of Courts, by which the system of war is kept up," might "provoke a confederation of Nations to abolish it," and he believed that "a European Congress, to patronize the progress of free Government, and promote the civilization of Nations with each other, is an event nearer in probability, than once were the revolutions and alliance of France and America."[6]

Madison considered these issues in a remarkable essay published in 1792, where he took ground that differed substantially from that which Hamilton had urged in the *Federalist*. The propensity toward war, Madison argued, was strongly heightened by certain internal institutions—monarchy, aristocracy, "funding systems"—that created a profound disjunction between those who gained, and those who lost, from war. Dissecting what he termed "Rousseau's plan" for a "confederation of sovereigns, under a council of deputies, for the double purpose of arbitrating external controversies among nations, and of guaranteeing their respective governments against internal revolutions," he found it both undesirable and impossible—"preposterous" as well as "impotent." So long as war depended "on those whose ambition, whose revenge, whose avidity, or whose caprice may contradict the sentiment of the community, and yet be uncontrolled by it; whilst war is to be declared by those who are to spend the public money, not by those who are to pay it; by those who are to direct the public forces, not by those who are to support them; by those whose power is to be raised, not by those whose chains may be riveted, the disease must continue to be *hereditary* like the government of which it is the offspring." The regeneration of existing governments was the first, and indispensable, step toward a cure; the absurdity of Rousseau's plan for perpetual peace lay in the fact that it not only failed to allow for such regeneration but created a mechanism (the guarantee against internal revolutions) that might actively prevent it.[7]

In his comments on "Rousseau's plan," Madison was almost certainly basing his exposition on Rousseau's *Abstract* of the plan of St. Pierre, where Rousseau had refined the idea and concluded that "all the alleged evils of the federation, when duly weighed, come to nothing." If the plan lay unrealized, Rousseau wrote, "that is not because it is utopian; it is because men are crazy, and because to be sane in a world of madmen is in itself a kind of madness." Madison's unfamiliarity with Rousseau's far more critical *Judgement* (which was not published until 1782, though written contemporaneously with the *Abstract* in 1756) may be deduced from the fact that Rousseau, in the *Judgement*, gave voice to many of the objections against St. Pierre that Madison himself unfolded in "Universal Peace." The whole life of kings, Rousseau noted, was "devoted to two objects: to extend their rule beyond their frontiers and to make it more absolute within them." These twin objectives—war and conquest without, the encroachment of despotism within—gave mutual support to one another: "Aggressive princes wage war at least as much on their subjects as on their enemies." Madison said the same, and his clinching objection against "Rousseau's plan" was also stated by Rousseau in the *Judgement*: "It is impossible to guarantee the prince against the rebellion of his subjects without at the same time securing the subjects against the tyranny of the prince." There is little in the *Judgement* that Madison would have disagreed with, and much he would have relished, for Rousseau saw clearly the deformities of the military system, especially its seeming incapacity to achieve stability and its limitless ambitions: "I have beaten the Romans," said Hannibal. "Send me more troops. I have exacted an indemnity from Italy. Send me more money."[8]

Both Hamilton and Madison saw the causes of the great war that engulfed Europe through the lenses of their respective theories, with Madison viewing the war, with Jefferson, as a "confederacy of kings" that "warred on human liberty," and Hamilton taking a far more jaundiced view of the course of the French Revolution and France's responsibility for the war. For the Republicans, despotic governments were seen to cause war, and war was seen to reinforce despotic government. They were soul mates, near-identical twins who would protest vigorously any prolonged separation from one another.

Aspects of this republican credo would later draw a sharp objection from John Quincy Adams, then minister to Prussia. Writing from Berlin, and comparing the evils inseparable from the military government of Europe with the condition of human society in his own country, Adams could not forbear "an ejaculation of gratitude to Heaven." Adams went on to attribute the military system of Europe not, as Thomas Paine and the Republicans had done, to the bloated aristocracies and avaricious monarchies of Europe but to what he called "the European *condition of society*," by which he meant the fact that Europe was "divided into a number of wholly independent states." Given that division, it was "by their armies alone that they can defend themselves against the encroachments of the other." This opinion, Adams acknowledged, was not "conformable to that which faction so delights to prattle, and knowing ignorance to repeat," but it was nevertheless the truth. The "spirit of encroachment" stemming from this division was "so far from being extinguished by the flood of philosophy which poured upon that self-conceited dupe, the eighteenth century, that it never burnt with a more consuming blaze than at the birth of this her daughter." Expressing astonishment over the number of sovereign states that had been "swallowed up in the vortex of the last ten years," Adams thought it possible that this tendency "toward consolidation" was so strong that it might end with no more than "four or five sovereign states left of the hundreds" that once existed there. But there was no escape from the imperious demands of the system, which bore as much upon free countries that cherished their survival as it did on any others.

> An army, therefore, is as necessary to every European power which has any hope of long existence as air to the motions of the lungs, and France through the whole course of the revolution has been so convinced of this that she has not only kept on foot such armed myriads hitherto, but has settled for her peace establishment one of the largest armies in Europe. Now it is impossible that such armies should be levied, recruited, and

maintained, without principles and measures of continual compulsion upon the people. Hence France in her republican state has continued to practice them under the name of conscription, and requisition, and loan, more than the most despotic of enemies. Hence England, a country justly renowned for its liberty, has always been obliged to adopt the system as her insular situation modifies it with regard to her—by the impressment of seamen for her navy. And if she has hitherto avoided the other part of it, requisition or the compulsive raising of stores, provisions, labor, etc., it has only been by draining the pockets of posterity and loading their shoulders with debts which will end in bankruptcy.

The lesson this held for America was plain. On the basis of these considerations, "more than from any others," Adams looked to "the *Union* of our country as to the sheet anchor of our hopes, and to its dissolution as to the most dreadful of our dangers." With unity, "a large *permanent* army" would never be necessary, and the possibility of external invasion that would require a large temporary force would steadily diminish with the growth of population and strength. With disunity, however, the catalog of European horrors could not be avoided.

If we once divide, our exposure to foreign assault will at once be multiplied in proportion to the number of states into which we shall split, and aggravated in proportion to the weakness of every single part compared with the strength of the whole. The temptations of foreign powers to invade us will increase with the prospect of success which our division will present them, and fortresses and armies will be then the only security upon which the disunited states can rely for defence against enemies from abroad. This is not the worst. Each of the separate states will from the moment of disunion become with regard to the others a foreign power. Quarrels, of which the seeds are too thickly sown, will shoot up like weeds in a rank soil between them. Wars will soon ensue. These must end either in the conquest of one party by the other, or in frail, precarious, jealous compromises and momentary truces under the name of peace, leaving on both sides the burden of its army as the only guarantee for its security. Then must the surface of our country be bristled over with double and treble ranges of rock-hewn fortresses for barriers, and our cities turned into goals by a circumference of impenetrable walls. Then will the great problem of our statesmen, too, be what proportion of the people's sweat and blood can be squeezed from them to maintain an army without producing absolute death. I speak in the sincerity and conviction of my soul in declaring that I look upon standing armies, intolerable taxes, forced levies, contributions, conscriptions, and requisitions as the unavoidable and fatal chain of which disunion is but the first link.[9]

As this remarkable letter shows, it was virtually impossible to consider the causes that had prompted unending war in Europe apart from that which might prompt unending war in America. The gist of Adams's argument had been made by Publius and others at the time of the framing and ratification of the Constitution, and would be repeatedly affirmed in coming years; it lay at the heart of the unionist paradigm. These passages demonstrate not only that the analysis had a continuing relevance but that it touched the inner springs of thought, feeling, and devotion. The date of its composition—February 14, 1801—is significant. We can imagine his brother receiving this communication soon after the time that their father—having successfully packed the judiciary, and embittered over his defeat by Jefferson—took early morning flight to Quincy on the day his successor was inaugurated. If, as Jefferson later wrote, his election in 1800 represented "as real a revolution in the principles of our government as that of 1776 was in its form," the peaceful surrender of power to this putative revolutionary appears all the more significant. If it was, as historian Merrill Peterson would write, the most moving spectacle "a free people could ever witness," it was so because in the corner of every mind lay the dark specter that John Quincy Adams had unfolded.[10]

In the various analyses of the causes of war that occurred in this early period, we find each of the three "images" of war's causes that were highlighted by Kenneth Waltz in his classic work on the subject. Human nature (the first image) stands alongside the internal nature of the political regime (the second image) and the anarchical character of the state system (the third image) as the great lenses through which, across the ages, the causes of war have been diagnosed. Each of these images was invoked in the early American debate. In the debates provoked by the Constitution and the French Revolution, Federalists adhered to the first and third images, whereas Anti-Federalists and then Republicans put forward "second image" arguments relating to the democratic peace and the pacific effects of international trade.[11]

It is remarkable that so much of the rivalry both over the Constitution and over the foreign policy of the early republic can be seen in relation to these varying theories of war; at the same time, it would be misleading to array Americans into wholly separate schools of thought. The Anti-Federalists, proponents of the democratic peace, admitted that the Articles of Confederation needed improvement, and some among them were susceptible to the fear that, in the absence of union, war among the surviving fragments would be inevitable. As keen as Hamilton was on tracing the causes of war to the nature of man, he would not have disputed that republics and monarchies did act differently, that their internal composition mattered to the conduct of their foreign policy. His system, too, would promote commercial interdependence among the sections, and he saw that as a bond of union.[12]

Madison, who drew the distinction between monarchies and republics as pointedly as anyone and who cherished the pacific implications of republicanism, did not deny in "Universal Peace" that republics were subject to imperial temptations. In fact, Madison pointed to a key vulnerability by highlighting the disjunction between who paid and who profited from war. The republican principle, forcing a dependence of the rulers upon the ruled, would eliminate one cause of war, but the ability of republican regimes to borrow money to pay for war might reintroduce the fatal disjuncture between benefits and burdens, opening again the gates of "the temple of Janus." Madison's idea was not original with him but had been advanced by Adam Smith in the *Wealth of Nations*; it would be picked up also by Kant. But no one advanced the idea with more conviction and tenacity than the Virginian. "Each generation," Madison proclaimed, "should be made to bear the burden of its own wars, instead of carrying them on, at the expence of other generations." Then the people would proceed more cautiously. "Were a nation to impose such restraints upon itself, avarice would be sure to calculate the expenses of ambition; in the equipoise of these passions, reason would be free to decide for the public good."[13]

Nor did Madison's insistence in "Universal Peace" that the causes of war were closely linked to monarchy and aristocracy preclude recognition of the structural causes of war—that is, to the dynamic that John Quincy Adams spelled out in objection to the republican thesis. As Madison had written in *Federalist* 41, "If one nation maintains constantly a disciplined army, ready for the service of ambition or revenge, it obliges the most pacific nations who may be within the reach of its enterprises to take corresponding precautions." This security dilemma made a standing military force both necessary and dangerous: "On the smallest scale it has its inconveniences. On an extensive scale its consequences may be fatal. On any scale it is an object of laudable circumspection and precaution."[14]

A similar line of thought was pursued by John Marshall, a Federalist who was appointed in 1798 as one of the three American commissioners to France after the fallout from the Jay Treaty brought America and France to the edge of war. Noting that the powers of Europe had spent a third of the eighteenth century in war, Marshall observed to Talleyrand, the French foreign minister, that these nations had been induced to do so "by motives which they deem adequate and by interests exclusively their own. In all respects different is the situation of the United States. Possessed of an extensive unsettled territory, on which bountiful nature has bestowed with a lavish hand all the capacities for future legitimate greatness, they indulge no thirst for conquest, no ambition for the extension of their limits. Encircled by no dangerous powers, they neither fear nor are jealous of their neighbours, and are not, on that account, obliged to arm for their own safety." A different policy, Marshall noted, might compromise the peace of the country: "A long train of Armies, debts, and taxes, checking the growth, diminishing the happiness, and perhaps endangering the liberty of the United States, must have followed the adoption of such a System."[15]

If one were to characterize broadly the American outlook on such matters, it would run something like this. The modern commercial republic, unlike the ancient republics, is pacific in tendency, and America, especially, should reject the lure of conquest as highly unrepublican and dangerous to its free institutions. It was also recognized, however, that the American republics could not maintain their institutions intact unless they solved the structural pressures for war that exist in any system of independent states. Looking upon Europe, Americans generally saw a close match between internal institutions (aristocracy and monarchy) and the "military system." Whether the former had produced the latter or the latter had produced the former was a question that found advocates on either side. But though much might hang in theory on whether the chicken produced the egg or the egg produced the chicken, Americans were agreed that, in practice, their mission was to escape the birth cycle by which "war made the state, and the state made war."[16]

This objective, in turn, required both independence from the European system and the union of American republics. Democracy might be a necessary condition of peace, but it was not a sufficient one. The conviction that democracy was insufficient was not only the possession of those among the Federalists—such as Hamilton, Adams, and Ames—who viewed the wisdom of popular assemblies with suspicion. It was shared, in fact, by even the most ardent partisans of Jeffersonian republicanism. All agreed that the democratic peace had to be organized through union, on terms more or less intimate, and that unless you rightly distributed the powers of government to their appropriate levels and specified where you proposed to give primacy to the majoritarian principle—which in America's federal union meant putting the categories of state, section, and nation in some kind of settled relationship with one another—there could be little hope that the war system of Europe could really be transcended in North America.[17]

Despite this larger consensus, Federalists and Republicans also differed sharply over the role that commerce might play in either hastening or retarding the tendency toward war. The expectation of many Enlightenment thinkers that commerce would have pacific effects in the relations of states was sometimes voiced by Americans at this time, but in general the tenor of their thought saw no easy relationship between commerce and peace. Philosophically, both sides agreed that commerce had softened manners and was a key ingredient of improvement and progress, but in political and strategic terms the two parties fell out sharply. Hamilton's financial system, though dependent on the continuance of Anglo-American commerce, looked toward the development of an American system at home that would emphasize the strengthening of commercial ties within the union rather than the reformation of commercial practices without. He saw in the attempt to force free trade on the European powers via commercial interdictions and restrictions a likely road to war. The dominant idea of the Republicans, by contrast, was not so much that commerce led to peace but that the adroit use of trade boycotts and retaliating commercial restrictions would enable the United States to find a substitute for war—"another umpire than arms." Yet Republican thinking is not easy to briefly summarize; the views of Jefferson on the relationship among commerce, peace, and war in fact went through a wondrous cycle, comparable (and indeed contingently related) to the larger tension between "withdrawal and return" that marked his public life. Each decade from the 1780s onward saw a change of emphasis—sometimes subtle, sometimes dramatic, always different. Hezekiah Niles's pertinent query of 1832—"What *principle* in the political ethics of our country might not be *sanctioned* AND refuted by the writings of Mr. Jefferson?"—is perhaps most pertinent with regard to Jefferson's views of the relationship among commerce, war, and peace.[18]

In a famous letter of 1785, Jefferson had mused that, were he to indulge his "own theory," he would wish America "to practice neither commerce nor navigation, but to stand with respect to Europe precisely on the footing of China. We should thus avoid wars, and all our citizens would be husbandmen." Jefferson quickly added that it was "theory only, & a theory which the servants of America are not at liberty to follow. Our people have a decided taste for navigation & commerce. They take this from their mother country: & their servants are in duty bound to calculate all their measures on this datum: we wish to do it by throwing open all the doors of commerce & knocking off its shackles." Jefferson's rejection of the ideal of commercial isolation rested not merely on the "decided taste" of the people; it also owed to his own deep-seated vision of lateral expansion through space. If on one side lurked the danger of the foreign wars that an extensive commerce might bring on the United States, on the other lay the possibility that the American husbandman would be unable to find an outlet for his produce, eliciting sloth and anarchy in the western country. Both alternatives threatened a deeply held conviction, and hence were potential sources of corruption; yet one or the other appeared inescapable.[19]

Jefferson and Madison were, in the early 1790s, enthusiastically in favor of free trade, though they were never free traders of the sort that came to exist in the 1820s and 1830s in Britain, France, and America and who have, ever since that time, represented one pole of a continuing argument. The Virginians did not preach, in short, "the gospel according to the *Economist*"; they proposed instead a system of policy that required continuous retaliation to reach the goal of freer trade. Their position may best be described as one of "fair trade" or commercial reciprocity: they wanted equivalent reductions of duty or relaxation of regulations in reciprocal pacts and did not think the European powers—above all the British—would move one inch toward a relaxation of their closed systems unless they faced retaliating measures from America. Hamilton, by contrast, was highly skeptical of "fair trade." Though he favored protection as a shield against excessive dependence on Europe (and as much for reasons of security as of prosperity), he had an acute sense of the dangers of violent operations on commercial relationships with the idea of forcing them into a different pattern.[20]

The idea at the core of the Republican system was that the economic power of the United States was really quite prodigious. This was an authentic production of the colonial American mind that continued to be cherished by the Republicans. If, as Paine had said, America would have a market for its produce "so long as eating is the custom in Europe," it also had a potential source of power over European states. American power rested, in the Republican estimation, on its capacity, sustained by public virtue, to deny markets and supplies to the European powers and their possessions in the Western Hemisphere. Jefferson and Madison thus wanted "to conquer without war," in the phrase of a later French minister to the United States. They greeted the outbreak of war in 1793 with the idea that the occasion furnished the United States "a happy opportunity of setting another precious example to the world, by showing that nations may be brought to do justice by appeals to their interests as well as by appeals to arms." The objective of finding "another umpire than arms" was the leading idea behind the making of the Constitution. The Jeffersonians proposed that, through "peaceable coercion," the idea be extended to the relationship of America to Europe.[21]

Jefferson got the opportunity to implement these ideas in the final eighteen months of his presidency, with the ill-fated embargo of 1807–1809. This was an odd measure: it found the agricultural section of the country making immense sacrifices on behalf of commerce, which the commercial interest of the country (the eastern states) found unconstitutional, officious, tyrannical, and hostile to commerce. Even odder was the shift in purpose and meaning that the embargo underwent in the final eighteen months of his presidency, leaving historians (and contemporaries) rather perplexed over what precisely the sphinx in the stone house had in mind. In his brief message of late 1807 recommending the embargo to Congress, Jefferson spoke of no coercive purpose and placed exclusive emphasis on the precautionary motive that underlay it—the need, in view of "the great and increasing dangers with which our vessels, our seamen, and merchandise, are threatened on the high seas," "to keep in safety these essential resources." A coercive intent, however, was apparent in the embargo from the beginning, and in Jefferson's eighth annual message, the measure was justified as an honorable attempt to find a substitute for war in settling disputes between nations; a positive blessing by virtue of its reordering of the American economy; and, above all, a test of republican virtue. In its final months, the embargo that had been undertaken to free commerce and to overthrow the belligerent restrictions now became a device to insulate America by banning its commerce with the rest of the world. At the end, as one historian notes, Jefferson came full circle.[22]

The Republican dream of overthrowing European barriers against free trade—which Jefferson had embraced in the late 1780s and pursued throughout his public life—now yielded to Jefferson's still older conviction that commerce was an instrument of corruption by virtue of its tendency to involve the country in Europe's endless wars. His growing frustration over violations of the embargo became fixed on the low motives of commercial men, and he felt betrayed that his own administration had somehow been lured into defending them. He authorized acts and laws highly irregular and utterly inconsistent with previously articulated conceptions of power granted by the Constitution. "Between the embargo and the old Virginia theory of the Constitution," as Henry Adams wrote, "no relation could be imagined."[23]

It also occurred to Jefferson that the neutral rights on whose vindication his administration had staked its whole diplomacy were contrary to the interest of the United States to exercise. "As to the rights of the United States as a neutral power," he told one correspondent, "our opinions are very different, mine being that when two nations go to war, it does not abridge the rights of neutral nations but in the two articles of blockade and contraband of war. . . . With respect to the interests of the United States in this exuberant commerce which is now bringing war on us, we concur perfectly. It brings us into collision with other powers in every sea, and will force us into every war of the European powers. The converting this great agricultural country into a city of Amsterdam,—a mere headquarters for carrying on the commerce of all nations with one another, is too absurd." Absurd it may have been, but such was the object at which the administration had clearly aimed since 1806, when Madison set forth an extended justification of the rights of neutrals that, had it been accepted by the belligerents, would have inexorably led on to this result.[24]

Partly because of the searing experience of the embargo, it was the desire to withdraw from rather than reform the European system that expressed Jefferson's mature outlook in retirement. The idea of an American system that would spare the United States the necessity of extracting "its imports out of the external fires raging in the old world" then held great appeal, and he thought this even though he looked with suspicion on the proposals—a protective tariff, a national bank, and internal improvements—necessary to bring it to life. Jefferson's mature conviction paid ironic compliment to Hamilton. In the early 1790s, Hamilton had warned that it was neither possible nor wise to seek to overturn directly the system that regulated "the general policy of Nations." He had seen that the prevailing system of exclusion among the mercantilist nations of Europe made it dangerous to depend too heavily on their markets. His alternative was to encourage the development of "an extensive domestic market" capable of absorbing these surpluses, one of whose pillars would be domestic manufactures. He acknowledged that there existed a "want of reciprocity" in the treatment of American commerce by foreign nations. So long as the economy rested on agriculture, the United States would not be able to "exchange with Europe on equal terms," but this he regarded as a fact that American prohibitions and discriminations were powerless to alter. That it might be contrary to the interest of the European powers he readily conceded, but he thought it belonged to them to judge "whether, by aiming at too much they do not lose more than they gain. It is for the United States to consider by what means they can render themselves least dependent, on the combinations, right or wrong, of foreign policy." Hamilton's policy in this regard became part of the National Republican consensus after 1815, shared even by many southerners, and remained so until increases in the tariff rate in 1820, 1824, and 1828 convinced them that they had gotten the short end of the stick.[25]

6

Louisiana!

IF THE EMBARGO WAS THE GREATEST FAILURE of Jefferson's presidency, the Louisiana Purchase was undoubtedly its greatest success. Like the other great act of expansion in the 1840s, the "affair of Louisiana" was marked by surprising twists and turns. Napoleon had gained from Spain title to Louisiana in the secret Treaty of San Ildefonso in 1800, and the prospect that the France of Napoleon, rather than the weak Spaniards, would gain the outlet to the Mississippi was given a new and ominous significance once Britain and France made peace at Amiens in March 1802. "What a beautiful fix we are in now," mused Napoleon. "Peace has been declared!" Napoleon's scheme was to tie together in a single empire the sugar colonies in the Caribbean with Louisiana's great hinterland up the Mississippi, but France's inferiority in naval power made any such colonial project acutely vulnerable to British cancellation in war. It was European peace, then, rather than war, that presented a situation that both Republicans and Federalists regarded as perilous.[1]

The news that Spain had closed the deposit and thus shut up access to the river's outlet had caused an enormous furor in the West and had prompted Jefferson to dispatch James Monroe to Paris. He arrived there just after the offer by Napoleon to sell the entire province. In its negotiations with the French, the Jefferson administration had had its eyes on New Orleans and the Floridas and had secured congressional authorization in 1802 to seek to purchase these territories. Its negotiators returned with Louisiana, which included New Orleans but not the Floridas.

Napoleon's decision to sell demonstrated that Jefferson enjoyed, in addition to his other remarkable qualities, the ability to benefit from the Wheel of Fortune: Spain would never have transferred Louisiana to France had it known that France would surrender it to America; Napoleon might not have abandoned his scheme of maritime empire had he not suffered such disastrous reverses in Haiti; the purchase would have faced far more onerous financial terms, and perhaps have been impossible, had Jefferson's ideas on credit, or even his ideas on commercial retaliation, been followed in the 1790s; France might have quietly pursued the advantages of slow and steady commercial development had it not been led by a man of dangerous and all-consuming ambition. Federalists pointed to these factors, or most of them, with a view to tarnishing Jefferson's triumph, but these forebodings were submerged amid the tumultuous acclaim.

"Among the various acts of political wisdom, for which the present administration of the United States has been distinguished," wrote Allan Magruder in exultation at the purchase, "the late cession of Louisiana to this country, by the exercise of a magnanimous policy on the part of our government, may be classed as the most pre-eminent." According to David Ramsay, the acquisition of Louisiana stood alongside independence and the Constitution as "the greatest political blessing ever conferred on these states." Both Magruder and Ramsay traced out the pernicious consequences that would have ensued had the French plan for colonizing Louisiana been carried into effect. In the hands of Napoleon, wrote Ramsay, "New Orleans would have been the fulcrum of an immense lever, by which he would have elevated or depressed our western country in subserviency to his gigantic projects." With the "standard of discord" thus planted between the Atlantic and western states, "the union of our rising empire would soon have been severed." The history of Europe, "cut up into innumerable independent sovereignties" dependent for their survival on a balance of power that could only be maintained through frequent war, furnished "a summary of the evils" that America escaped with the Louisiana Purchase. America's "true policy" was "PEACE with all the world, and especially in our own country," and Louisiana brought that golden prospect much closer to fruition. Politically, it broke the connection between the Indian nations and the most powerful of European states, and it hastened the day when America might enjoy "a commerce of our own, as independent, as possible, of the ever changing politics of the old world." Not only would this commercial independence be "greatly promoted by the reciprocal wants and capacities of different portions of our now widely extended empire"; the bonanza had all been secured through peaceful methods. "We have secured our rights by pacific means," wrote the editors of the administration's most faithful newspaper, "truth and reason have been more powerful than the sword."[2]

When the time came to submit the treaty to the Senate, however, the candor promised in the administration's "new diplomacy" of peace and persuasion suffered a setback. Jefferson had come to power in 1801 fresh from having construed the Constitution narrowly for a decade. Upon the formation of the Washington administration, he had repaired repeatedly to the standard that no powers might be exercised that were not expressly given. Weighing the Louisiana Purchase, he had to acknowledge that the Constitution provided no authority for the general government to acquire new territory outside the previously acknowledged boundaries of the union. He restated his creed in a letter to John Breckinridge: "The Executive have done an act beyond the Constitution," and Congress ought not authorize it without making "appeal to *the nation* for an additional article to the Constitution, approving & confirming an act which the nation had not previously authorized." To another correspondent Jefferson explained, "When an instrument admits two constructions, the one safe, the other dangerous, the one precise, the other indefinite, I prefer that which is safe & precise. I had rather ask an enlargement of power from the nation, where it is found necessary, than to assume it by a construction which would make our powers boundless. Our peculiar security is in possession of a written Constitution. Let us not make it a blank paper by construction."[3]

Madison, Gallatin, and other friends denied that the acquisition of territory by treaty was an act "beyond the Constitution"; they rejected as unnecessary and potentially perilous Jefferson's terse constitutional amendment: "Louisiana, as ceded by France to the United States, is made a part of the United States." In justifying the measure, the Republicans were drawn to ideas that had previously formed part of the Federalist armory of constitutional ideas, appealing to the "necessary and proper clause," to "implied" powers, to the "inherent right to acquire territory" possessed by "the United States, as a nation." Such ideas were plausible interpretations of the federal Constitution, but they could not, without inordinate ingenuity, be found there if one adopted the rules of construction that Jefferson had affirmed repeatedly in the 1790s. But it was not only with the purchase that the Republicans went beyond their previous ideas on the subject of national powers. The legislation that Jefferson proposed for the government of the Louisiana territory, as John Quincy Adams noted, subjected the governor of that province to no constitutional restraint. The consent of the inhabitants, then about 50,000, was neither asked nor given.[4]

In the midst of the crisis brought on by the retrocession of Louisiana and the closing of the deposit, Federalists from the middle states, particularly Pennsylvania and New York, had bid boldly for western sentiment by calling for much sterner measures than Jefferson favored. Federalists professed little doubt that Bonaparte, in the construction of his empire of the Caribbean and the Gulf Coast, would aim to separate the western country from the United States and would have in his hands the means—the control of New Orleans and of the market in the West Indies for the produce of the western country—by which to make the attempt. Federalist warnings of disunion exasperated the Republicans. Senator George Clinton of New York had responded to such prophecies by noting that "there is no reflecting and well principled man in this country who can view the severance of the States without horror, and who does not consider it as a Pandora's box, which will overwhelm us with every calamity; and it has struck me with not a little astonishment that, on the agitation of almost every great political question, we should be menaced with this evil. Last session, when a bill repealing a Judiciary act was under consideration, we were told that the Eastern States would withdraw themselves from the Union if it should obtain; and we are now informed that, if we do not accede to the proposition before us, the Western States will hoist the standard of revolt and dismember the empire. Sir, these threats are calculated to produce the evil they predict, and they may possibly approximate the spirit they tend to warn us against."[5]

There was much merit in Clinton's objection, for once the Louisiana Purchase was announced, there were a significant number of Federalists who began thinking seriously of disunion for themselves. The entry of Louisiana into the union was itself cause for depression because it promised, over time, to derange the balance of power and forever condemn the New Englanders to the role of a despised minority. "Admit this western world into the Union," warned William Plumer of New Hampshire, "and you destroy, at once, the weight and importance of the eastern states, and compel them to establish a separate and independent empire." Bringing Louisiana into the union by treaty, the Federalists held, was clearly beyond the pale of the Constitution. Federalists did not deny that the treaty power conferred a right to acquire territory. They did deny, however, that such territories might be brought into the union. "We can hold territory," said Uriah Tracy of Connecticut, "but to admit the inhabitants into the Union, to make citizens of them, and States, by treaty, we cannot constitutionally do; and no subsequent act of legislation, or even ordinary amendment to our Constitution, can legalize such measures. If done at all, they must be done by universal consent of all the States or partners to our political association; and this universal consent I am positive can never be obtained to such a pernicious measure as the admission of Louisiana,—of a world, and such a world, into our Union. This would be absorbing the Northern States, and rendering them as insignificant in the Union as they ought to be, if by their own consent the measure should be adopted."[6]

Their incipient political insignificance prompted many New England Federalists to think seriously about the price of the union and the prospects they would have if separated from the southern states. The design to dissolve the union, as John Quincy Adams would note in a document prepared in 1808 but not published until the late 1820s, was formed in the winter of 1803–1804. Wrote Adams: "Its justifying causes to those who entertained it were: That the annexation of Louisiana to the Union transcended the constitutional powers of the government of the United States; that it formed, in fact, a new confederacy, to which the States, united by the former compact, were not bound to adhere; that it was oppressive to the interests and destructive to the influence of the Northern section of the confederacy, whose right and duty it therefore was to secede from the new body politic, and to constitute one of their own." When Adams published his charges in 1828, the aging leaders of New England Federalism vehemently denied his accusations, insisting that the project of a separate confederation "existed only in the distempered fancy of Mr. Adams." That was not true; though Adams exaggerated the scope of the conspiracy, the project had in fact existed and had acquired considerable support among Federalists in Congress, including Roger Griswold, Uriah Tracy, and James Hillhouse of Connecticut, and William Plumer and Samuel Hunt of New Hampshire. But it was Colonel Timothy Pickering of Massachusetts, a former intimate of Hamilton's and the rudely dismissed secretary of state under John Adams, who was the acknowledged leader of this enterprise. The letters he sent in 1804 to leading Federalists seeking to drum up support laid bare the grievances of New England. He complained of the unfair domination of the southern states owing to their slave representation, an advantage that, though evil, they would never voluntarily renounce. In the event of a separation of North from South, Pickering assumed that the western states would ultimately break off from the southern states and take Louisiana with them. He bid them all good riddance: "How many Indian wars, excited by the avidity of the Western and Southern States for Indian lands, shall we have to encounter, and who will pay the millions to support them? The Atlantic States."[7]

Pickering, though complaining bitterly of "the corrupt and corrupting influence and oppression of the *aristocratic Democrats* of the South," put a happy spin on the relations that would obtain between these now dissevered sections: "Our mutual wants," he averred, "would render a friendly and commercial intercourse inevitable." All the advantages, he maintained, "which have been for a few years depending on the general union would be continued to its respective portions, without the jealousies and enmities which now afflict both, and which peculiarly embitter the condition of that of the North. It is not unusual for two friends, when disagreeing about the mode of conducting a common concern, to separate, and manage each in his own way his separate interest, and thereby preserve a useful friendship, which without such separation would infallibly be destroyed." Pickering sometimes seemed unsure whether the purpose of a separate confederacy was to give up the idea of union with the South or simply to force a better bargain with it—an uncertainty over the purpose of disunionist schemes that would recur frequently in the future. The credible threat of a separation would be necessary, in either eventuality, if the northern states were to "regain their just weight in the political balance."[8]

Pickering was unsuccessful in uniting the Federalists around this plan—Hamilton, King, Cabot, and Ames were all opposed. Hamilton, indeed, had always set his face against the idea that disunion might be a remedy for anything, and in one of his last letters, written just before the fateful encounter with Burr, he adhered to that stand: the "dismemberment of our empire" would be "a clear sacrifice of great positive advantages, without any counterbalancing good; administering no relief to our real disease, which is democracy; the poison of which by a subdivision will only be the more concentrated in each part, and consequently the more virulent." Two years previously, Hamilton had called the Constitution a "frail and worthless fabric," but a departure from it nevertheless appeared to him as suicidal. He agreed with Rufus King "that one inevitable consequence of the annexation of Louisiana to the Union would be to diminish the relative weight and influence of the Northern section; that it would aggravate the evil of the slave representation, and endanger the Union itself, by the expansion of its bulk, and the enfeebling extension of its line of defence against foreign invasion. But the alternative was,—Louisiana and the mouths of the Mississippi in the possession of France, under Napoleon Bonaparte." Hamilton and King, however, hoped and believed that "the loss of sectional influence . . . would be more than compensated by the extension of national power and security. A fearful cause of war with France was removed. From a formidable and ambitious neighbor, she would be turned, by her altered and steadily operating interests, into a natural ally. Should even these anticipations fail, we considered a severance of the Union as a remedy more desperate than any possible disease."[9]

Despite the bitter complaints of New England Federalists, Jefferson swept the 1804 elections and marched boldly into the citadel of Federalism by winning every state except Delaware and Connecticut in that election. In his 1805 inaugural address, Jefferson acknowledged the Federalist refrain that the territorial extension of the union might endanger its existence. "I know," he said, "that the acquisition of Louisiana has been disapproved by some, from a candid apprehension that the enlargement of our territory would endanger its union. But who can limit the extent to which the federative principle may operate effectively? The larger our association, the less it will be shaken by local passions." Jefferson accepted that "neighborhood" seldom produced "affection among nations"—"The reverse is almost the universal truth"—and he could not exclude the possibility of separate confederacies in the Mississippi basin, divided from the Atlantic states along the spine of the Appalachian Mountains. Were a separation to occur, he did not think the Atlantic states had reason to dread it: "The future inhabitants of the Atlantic & Mississippi States will be our sons. We leave them in distinct but bordering establishments. We think we see their happiness in their union, &

we wish it," but if the westerners should see their interest to lie in a separation, he did not think it proper to meddle in this quarrel between "the elder and the younger son."[10]

If Jefferson could on some occasions profess diffidence as to the union's prospects, and even pronounce himself unwilling to use force to keep it together, his course of action in responding to the Burr Conspiracy suggested a different conclusion. Burr, who had fashioned a fantastic plan to conquer Louisiana and Mexico while separating the trans-Appalachian states from the union, was pursued relentlessly by Jefferson, who used every legal resource to secure Burr's capture and hanging for treason. When Burr escaped conviction in the federal district court of Richmond, in a trial presided over by Chief Justice Marshall, Jefferson hotly condemned the legal technicalities that had excluded the jury's consideration of the most telling evidence against the malefactor. Though heartened by the popular revulsion against the Burr Conspiracy, Jefferson considered Marshall's rulings as "equivalent to a proclamation of impunity to every traitorous combination which may be formed to destroy the Union."[11]

A threat to the union even more serious than the Burr Conspiracy arose with the reaction of New England to the embargo of 1807–1809. Much as Jefferson wished "to hug the Embargo, and die in its embrace," its progressively draconian character put New England on the edge of revolt. If "the monster" were not soon stifled, wrote one Federalist, "a Hercules will arise in the North who will put it to rest." Pronouncing the legislation enforcing the embargo to be "unjust, oppressive, tyrannical and unconstitutional," the Rhode Island General Assembly observed that "it would be a reflection on their discernment and sagacity, if they did not foresee that the dissolution of the Union may be more surely, and as speedily effected by the systematick oppression of the government, as by the inconsiderate disobedience of the people." As enforcement provisions were strengthened, particularly in the Fifth Embargo Act of early 1809, New England Republicans deserted the embargo en masse on the grounds that the choice had suddenly resolved itself into one between "repeal or civil war." The "sudden and uncontrollable revolution of opinion" that took place among the Republicans of New England and New York pointed toward active resistance and disunion in the North were the embargo not abandoned, and this was the central reason for the repeal of the legislation in March 1809.[12]

7

Balances of Power

THROUGHOUT THE WARS OF THE FRENCH REVOLUTION and Napoleon, both sides in the great debate recognized that the United States had an interest in the maintenance of a balance of power in Europe, yet believed also that it was vital to maintain American neutrality. Their understanding of what the balance was, how it operated, and where it might threaten American rights and interests, however, was vastly different, as were their respective conceptions of what precisely neutral rights and duties consisted of, and how they might be vindicated. As the Jefferson administration moved toward its showdown with Great Britain over neutral rights in 1806, John Randolph had questioned the wisdom of the United States throwing its weight "into the scale of France at this moment, from whatever motive—to aid the views of her gigantic ambition—to make her mistress of the sea and land—to jeopardize the liberties of mankind. Sir, you may help to crush Great Britain, you may assist in breaking down her naval dominion, but you cannot succeed to it. The iron sceptre of the ocean will pass into his hands who wears the iron crown of the land. You may then expect a new code of maritime law." Hamilton had pointed to the same danger in 1798. The necessity of "crushing the TYRANT of the SEA," he then wrote, "has been trumpeted as a motive to other powers to acquiesce in the execution of a plan, by which France endeavors to become the Tyrant both of SEA and LAND." Such was the ever-recurring lament of nearly all Federalists and many old Republicans. "Nothing," wrote Fisher Ames, "is wanting to the solid establishment of a new universal empire by France, that should spread as far, last as long, and press as heavily on the necks of the abject nations, as that of Rome, but the possession of the British navy. France, whenever she can get access to her enemy, is already irresistible."[1]

The importance of the balance of power as an objective of American diplomacy had not escaped the attention of Jefferson. Since the 1780s, the rivalries of the European powers were always of the first importance in the shaping of his diplomatic outlook. Though he normally saw France as the more useful counter to Britain, he prided himself on his skill in playing both sides of the street. Each of the two great European powers, he believed, were "necessary instrument[s] to hold in check the disposition of the other to tyrannize over other nations." Sometimes he sought advantage, at other times merely safety, in this competition among the great. It often occurred to him to play the jackal and to fatten on the spoils of European rivalry; from the 1780s on, his commercial and territorial objectives were always reflected through this prism. At the same time, he was fond of comparing the United States to a "common herd of cattle"—fat and innocent—looking upon a mighty "battle of lions and tigers."[2] Though he mainly saw France as a necessary check on the rapacity of Britain, he also recognized the danger to American security and to the law of nations were France to join the empire of the seas to her prodigious power on land. "Our wish," he said after Trafalgar and Austerlitz, "ought to be that he who has armies may not have the Dominion of the sea, and that he who has Dominion of the sea may be one who has no armies. In this way we may be quiet; at home at least."[3]

These ideas continued to find frequent expression in Jefferson's correspondence after his retirement from the presidency. Toward the end of the Napoleonic Wars, he readily acknowledged that "it cannot be to our interest that all Europe should be reduced to a single monarchy," and he hoped that "a salutary balance may be ever maintained among nations"; even at that late date, however, he hoped that Bonaparte would "be able to effect the complete exclusion of England from the whole continent of Europe." His hope and expectation that France would form a useful counterpoise to British ambition was joined to the conviction that French power was scarcely likely to grow so large and threatening as to pose a danger to the United States. A letter written in 1810 gave full vent to these views. "The fear that Bonaparte will come over to us and conquer us" he considered "too chimerical to be genuine." Too many obstacles—Spain and Portugal, England and Russia—loomed to block Napoleon's supposed design. And even were he to succeed, his attention would not at first turn to America:

Ancient Greece and Macedonia, the cradle of Alexander, his prototype, and Constantinople, the sea of empire for the world, would glitter more in his eye than our bleak mountains and rugged forests. Egypt, too, and the golden apples of Mauritania, have for more than half a century fixed the longing eyes of France; and with Syria, you know, he has an old affront to wipe out. Then come "Pontus and Galatia, Cappodocia, Asia and Bithynia," the fine countries on the Euphrates and Tigris, the Oxus and Indus, and all beyond the Hyphasis, which bounded the glories of his Macedonian rival; with the invitations of his new British subjects on the banks of the Ganges, whom, after receiving under his protection the mother country, he cannot refuse to visit. When all this is done and settled, and nothing of the old world remains unsubdued, he may turn to the new one. But will he attack us first, from whom he will get but hard knocks and no money? Or will he first lay hold of the gold and silver of Mexico and Peru, and the diamonds of Brazil? A *republican* Emperor, from his affection to republics, independent of motives of expediency, must grant to ours the Cyclop's boon of being the last devoured. While all this is doing, we are to suppose the chapter of accidents read out, and that nothing can happen to cut short or to disturb his enterprises.

The skepticism that Jefferson expressed here toward the maintenance of the balance is most characteristic of his diplomatic outlook, expressed in the policies of "watchful waiting" and "palliating and enduring" that usually distinguished his diplomacy.[4]

The "balance of power" was at issue not only with respect to the role of the United States in the great struggle between Great Britain and France; it also bore closely on the relationship among the American sections. The debates before the declaration of war in 1812 could not escape the obvious reality that any war against a European power would tilt American expansion in a way that had important implications for the sectional balance of power. In an 1811 speech urging war against Great Britain, Felix Grundy of Tennessee pointed to this factor, among others, in unfolding the glorious prospects that would ensue from a successful war. "We shall drive the British from our Continent," Grundy held; "they will no longer have an opportunity of intriguing with our Indian neighbors, and setting on the ruthless savage to tomahawk our women and children." Britain, he went on, would "lose her Canadian trade, and, by having no resting place in this country, her means of annoying us will be diminished." But what seemed to truly rouse his vision was bringing the Canadians into the American union "as adopted brethren." To do so, he maintained, "will have beneficial political effects; it will preserve the equilibrium of the Government. When Louisiana shall be fully peopled, the Northern States will lose their power; they will be at the discretion of others; they can be depressed at pleasure, and then this Union might be endangered—I therefore feel anxious not only to add the Floridas to the South, but the Canadas to the North of this empire."[5]

Grundy's vision brought forth immediate ridicule from John Randolph of Virginia. Randolph was never known to treat his opponents with anything other than sarcastic condescension—and more than once did a duel follow one of his speeches. He could, on this occasion, "but smile at the liberality of the gentleman, in giving Canada to New York, in order to strengthen the Northern balance of power, while at the same time he forewarned her that the Western scale must preponderate. Mr. R. said he could almost fancy that he saw the Capitol in motion towards the falls of Ohio—after a short sojourn taking its flight to the Mississippi, and finally alighting on Darien [Panama];

which, when the gentleman's dreams are realized, will be a most eligible seat of Government for the new Republic (or Empire) of the two Americas!" For Randolph, it was "agrarian cupidity, not maritime right," which urged the war. The "eternal monotonous tone—Canada! Canada! Canada!"—bespoke the desire to "acquire a prepondering northern influence."

Randolph set his argument opposing war in the context of the oft-reiterated doctrine "that Republics are destitute of ambition" and "addicted to peace." Such a "war of conquest," he held, would form "a new commentary" on that doctrine. Randolph knew how easy it was to make war—"nothing easier." "It was as easy to go to war as to get a wife; and many a poor blockhead had he seen strutting his hour, because he had, after vast exertion, married a shrew." But this war was mistaken even if one indulged proponents of annexation "their most romantic notions of success" and imagined "the American standard as hoisted on the walls of Quebec, and even at Nova Scotia and New Brunswick," for that outcome would be "a national curse." "You are laying the foundation for a secession from the Union—on the north, by the possession of Canada, and on the borders of the Ohio, for another division. The Ohio has been made the line between the slaveholding States and those which hold no slaves. He need not call the attention of the House to this distinction, nor to the jealousies and animosities growing out of the subject." At the core of Randolph's argument lay the conviction that expansion would destroy the union. "Are there no limits," he asked, "to the territory over which Republican government may be extended? Is it, like space, indefinite in its extent?"[6]

It is part of the strangeness of the preliminaries to the War of 1812 that the causes of the war cannot in the main be ascribed to the desire to acquire a "prepondering Northern influence." President Madison would insist "that conquest, with a view of extending our territory, was not the wish of his government." As one critic noted in January 1813, "The Idea of this Republic following the footsteps of foreign ambitious nations, was so repugnant to the genius of the American people, and the constitution under which we live, that few, if any, of the warmest advocates of the war dare avow it." The western counties, however, scorned such timidity and thought at a minimum that the war would offer an excellent opportunity to break the connection between Great Britain and the Indians of the Old Northwest, having ascribed their Indian wars not to their own mistreatment of the tribes but to British machinations. Somewhat incongruously, the Madison administration looked to a Canadian invasion primarily as a measure to reinforce the commercial pressure by which Britain might be brought to heel. During the embargo of 1807–1809, a large illicit trade had opened up between the northern states and Canada. It was the desire to shut this off that had led Jefferson to authorize the draconian bill enforcing the embargo. If Madison's strategy of starving the West Indies and throwing British workers into the streets were to be effective in 1812, the loophole would have to be closed again. What better way to do so than to simply seize Canada—for the purpose of winning the war, gaining a useful equivalent for peace negotiations, or deciding that, after all, the fruit was ripe and that Canada should be incorporated into the American union? For neither Madison nor the westerners who supported him was the motive for the invasion of Canada the desire to acquire a preponderating northern influence, but Randolph had reasonable grounds for fearing such a conquest would lead to that result and, that accomplished, to a disunion, as he predicted in his speeches in the winter of 1811–1812.[7]

The issue of how Canada, if conquered, might be incorporated in the union was not a new one in 1812. Jacob Crowninshield of Massachusetts, a firm ally of Madison on the commercial and maritime issues that were leading the United States and Britain into deepening conflict, had held in 1806 that Britain would concede these issues rather than go to war. "Our trade," he said, "is too valuable to her. She knows, too, that in such an event she will lose her Eastern provinces. The States of Vermont and Massachusetts will ask no other assistance than their own militia to take Canada and Nova Scotia. Some of her West India islands will likewise fall." Crowninshield's speech had provoked an immediate reply from Randolph. "I have no desire," he said, "to see the Senators and Representatives of the Canadian French, or of the tories and refugees of Nova Scotia, sitting on this floor or that of the other House—to see them becoming members of the Union, and participating equally in our political rights. And on what other principle would the gentleman from Massachusetts be for incorporating those provinces with us? Or on what other principle could it be done under the Constitution?"[8]

For proponents of the war, Randolph's sketch of the posterior consequences held no terrors. "What are we required to do by those who would engage our feelings and wishes" in Britain's behalf? asked Clay. "To bear the actual cuffs of her arrogance, that we may escape a chimerical French subjugation! We are invited, conjured to drink the potion of British poison actually presented to our lips, that we may avoid the imperial dose prepared by perturbed imaginations. We are called upon to submit to debasement, dishonor, and disgrace—to bow the neck to royal insolence, as a course of preparation for manly resistance to Gallic invasion! What nation, what individual was ever taught in the schools of ignominious submission, the patriotic lessons of freedom and independence?" Randolph's argument, said Calhoun, was "calculated to produce unqualified submission to every species of insult and injury." "Protection and patriotism," Calhoun averred, "are reciprocal. That is the road that all great nations have trod." Randolph's grim forecast of the costs of war, according to Calhoun, was merely a species of "calculating avarice" that was "only fit for shops and counting houses, and ought not to disgrace the seat of sovereignty by its squalid and vile appearance. Whenever it touches sovereign power the nation is ruined. It is too timid to have in itself the laws of self preservation. It is never safe but under the shield of honor." But Randolph stuck to his guns: "His imagination shrunk from the miseries" of a connection with Bonaparte, "the great deflowerer of the virginity of Republics." It was ignominious to "take Canada at the risk of the Constitution—to embark in a common cause with France and be dragged at the wheels of the car of some Burr or Bonaparte." "As Chatham and Burke, and the whole band of her patriots, prayed for [Britain's] defeat in 1776, so must some of the truest friends to their country deprecate the success of our arms against the only Power that holds in check the archenemy of mankind."[9]

Though Randolph gave the most powerful brief against the war, it was in New England where opposition was concentrated. When war came, New England barely qualified as a participant in the struggle. "The four eastern states," as Jefferson later remarked, were tied to the rest of the country "as dead to living bodies." The governors of its principal states positively obstructed the enforcement of the commercial restrictions that loomed large in Madison's strategy for the war. When solicited by the secretary of war to call their militias into national service, the request was refused by most states in New England on the ground that no actual invasion had taken place and that the president, while empowered to command the militia, could rely on no officers save those appointed by the state. The Connecticut General Assembly, while expressing a "deep interest" in the preservation of the Constitution and a willingness to yield a "prompt obedience" to all its legitimate requirements, nevertheless insisted that "the state of Connecticut is a FREE SOVEREIGN and INDEPENDENT state; that the United States are a *confederacy* of states; that we are a confederated and not a consolidated republic." The building could not stand, the assembly warned, "if the pillars upon which it rests, are impaired or destroyed. The same constitution, which delegates powers to the general government, inhibits the exercise of powers, not delegated, and reserves those powers to the states respectively."[10]

How far New England might travel in secessionist schemes was difficult to calculate, and indeed was one of the principal political mysteries of the time. Foreign diplomats had continued to predict it before the war. "If some material Change should not occur in the System of the Government," wrote Lord Liverpool of England in 1810, "the result will probably be, the separation of the Eastern from the Southern States. This Event, whenever it take place, (and it will take place at no very distant period) will have the effect at least of securing the British Possessions in North America, from any Danger arising from Foreign Aggressions." New England politicians, moreover, had continued to threaten that the dire eventuality was fast approaching the status of a historical inevitability. In 1811, objecting to the bill to enable the people of the territory of Orleans to form a constitution and to admit it into the union, Josiah Quincy had declared, "If this bill passes, it is my deliberate opinion that it is virtually a dissolution of this Union; that it will free the States from their moral obligation, and, as it will be the right of all, so it will be the duty of some, definitely to prepare for a separation, amicably if they can, violently if they must." The outbreak of war and the vexatious measures against the coasting trade disgusted New England further. From "the most perfect specimen of national happiness and the nearest approximation to the felicity of Paradise which since the fall of man this great globe ever exhibited," wrote petitioners in Massachusetts, there had been a profound degeneration into "a gigantic system of despotism" and the adoption of measures that had "a direct tendency to the Establishment of an Absolute tyranny over these States."[11]

By 1814, opinion as to the future duration of the union had sunk to a very low point. The European peace, which freed British forces from Continental entanglements, promised to make the military situation yet more untenable, and it seemed probable that Britain would regard its former colonies "not as a property to be recovered, and therefore spared, so far as is compatible with the end in view; but as an object of vengeance, and desolation."[12]

The New England convention that met at Hartford, Connecticut, in early 1815 was the most important political expression of the region's disaffection. The situation, in their view, was dire. Having entered the "national compact" to secure common interests, New Englanders had seen with mortification the formation of a "coalition, not less evident than if defined by the articles of a formal treaty, . . . between the national administration and that fearful tyrant in Europe, who was aspiring to the dominion of the world." It adopted in its report the same justification of interposition and nullification Madison and Jefferson had employed in the late 1790s. Unless the specific terms of the constitutional compact authorizing the national government to call out the militia were satisfied, the general government would have "no more power over the militia than over the armies of a foreign nation." Though the convention deemed it inconsistent with the "respect and forbearance due from a confederate state towards the general government, to fly to open resistance upon every infraction of the constitution," when the case entailed "deliberate, dangerous, and palpable infractions of the constitution," it was "not only the right but the duty of such a state to interpose its authority."[13]

The report proposed seven constitutional amendments, of which the most important were the abolition of the three-fifths clause and the requirement that the entry of new western states receive the concurrence of two-thirds of the Senate and the House, in effect according to New England a veto on the process. Had the injustice and inequality of the three-fifths clause been foreseen, the report alleged, "the privilege" accorded the southern states "would probably not have been demanded; certainly not conceded." The "harmony and mutual confidence" that an equal representation according to the number of free persons augured was far more "conducive to the happiness and prosperity of every confederated state, than a mere preponderance of power, the prolific source of jealousies and controversy, can be to any one of them." The amendment giving New England a veto over the admission of new states was equally mandatory. "At the adoption of the constitution, a certain balance of power among the original parties was considered to exist," together with "a strong affinity between their great and general interests." The admission of new western states, however, had already "materially affected" that balance and threatened over time to destroy it. "The southern states will first avail themselves of their new confederates to govern the east, and finally the western states, multiplied in number, and augmented in population, will control the interests of the whole."[14]

These two proposals had been made by Gouverneur Morris and Rufus King in the Philadelphia convention, and it seems exceedingly doubtful that from a yet weaker position New England would gain concessions that it had been unable to extract twenty-five years earlier. But the tone of the report was not such as to indicate an immediate threat to the union and was thought by some to be in arrears of New England opinion as a whole. While calling for a future convention "with such powers and instructions as the exigency of a crisis so momentous may require," the report nevertheless rejected disunion as a remedy reserved to the direst extremity. Pickering and his followers had wished to make the convention into a declaration of New England's independence and an announcement of its reunion, on the basis of equality, with the mother country. This expedient the convention firmly declined. "If the Union be destined to dissolution," the report held, "it should be the work of peaceable times, and deliberate consent. Some new form of confederacy should be substituted among those states which shall intend to maintain a federal relation to each other." If events were to show that New England's calamities were owing to "implacable combinations of individuals, or of states, to monopolize power and office, and to trample without remorse upon the rights and interests of commercial sections of the Union," then, and only then, might a separation of the states be justified. For such "an alliance by constraint, among nominal friends, but real enemies," would be "inflamed by mutual hatred and jealousy" and would invite, "by intestine divisions, contempt and aggression from abroad. But a severance of the Union by one or more states, against the will of the rest, and especially in time of war, can be justified only by absolute necessity." Until that time should arrive, disunion should be conclusively rejected.[15]

That the Hartford Convention both embraced nullification and rejected disunion has always made room for differing interpretations of its significance. Recent historians have emphasized its moderate character. In the years after 1815, however, the moderates at Hartford gained little credit for their moderation, and the frightful image of the convention was waved over the heads of New Englanders with almost as much frequency as the bloody shirt was waved against the South after the Civil War. For more than a generation, New England would be badgered by spokesmen from the South and West for its alleged infidelity during this time, the memory of which was not allowed to die: it formed a pointed and ever-recurring counterpoint, too delicious to be resisted, to its budding nationalism of the 1820s and beyond. In a speech of 1830 directed against Webster, and made for the purpose of ridiculing New England's loyalty and lampooning Webster's nationalism, Thomas Hart Benton recalled the time "when the five-striped banner was waving over the land of the North! when the Hartford Convention was in session! when the language in the capitol was, 'Peaceably if we can, forcibly, if we must!' when the cry, out of doors, was, 'The Potomac the boundary; the negro States by themselves! The Alleghenies the boundary; the Western savages by themselves! The Mississippi the boundary, let Missouri be governed by a prefect, or given up as a haunt for wild beasts!'"[16]

This was true history, in Jefferson's phrase; if the portrait erred it was in the imputation that New England really knew what its own mind was. It did not. Its fury was distempered; its grievances, sincerely felt, could find no plausible outlet. Pickering and Lowell, the great advocates of secession, spoke for New England when they detailed the oppressions under which the section labored, but not when they counseled disunion. Neither the generality of men nor their cautious leaders could quite bring themselves to that measure. The ally in such a venture could be none other than Great Britain. However much New Englanders sympathized with British claims and objectives in the European war, to take part with Britain in a war against the South and West constituted too radical a break from dear recollections and historic accomplishments. Thus paralyzed between two hates, it was almost as if an entire section began sleeping late in the morning, breaking off contact with her friends, and sinking deeper and deeper into a wallow of indecision. "Had she declared independence," as Henry Adams summarized the predicament of Massachusetts, "England might have protected and rewarded her. Had she imitated New York in declaring for the Union, probably the

Union would not have allowed her to suffer in the end. The attempt to resist both belligerents forfeited the forbearance of both."[17]

Viewing New England's predicament from the vantage point of Monticello, Jefferson stated the fact apparent to "every one": "that we can at any moment make peace with England at the expense of the navigation and fisheries of Massachusetts." In a letter written earlier in the year to John Adams, Jefferson had weighed the sectional equities thusly: "Massachusetts chose to sacrifice the liberties of our seafaring citizens, in which we were all interested, and with them her obligations to the co-States, rather than war with England. Will she now sacrifice the fisheries to the same partialities? This question is interesting to her alone; for to the Middle, the Southern and Western States, they are of no direct concern; of no more than the culture of tobacco, rice and cotton, to Massachusetts. I am really at a loss to conjecture what our refractory sister will say on this occasion. I know what, as a citizen of the Union, I would say to her. 'Take this question *ad referendum*. It concerns you alone. If you would rather give up the fisheries than war with England, we give them up. If you had rather fight for them, we will defend your interests to the last drop of our blood, choosing rather to set a good example than follow a bad one." It was, alas, in the nature of this weak sister's plight that she could face neither of the alternatives in Jefferson's referendum. She could not give up the fisheries. She would not join the war.[18]

It was something of a wonder in these circumstances that the peace negotiators at Ghent agreed to press New England's claims to the fisheries and to territory in Maine. Albert Gallatin, who sat at the vital center of that divided delegation, assigned the reasons: "If we should abandon any part of the territory [of New England] it would give a handle to the part there now pushing for a separation from the Union and a New England confederacy, to say that the interests of the North-East were sacrificed, and to pretend that by a separate confederacy they could obtain what is refused to us." Henry Clay objected strongly to this reasoning: "It was too much the practice of our government to sacrifice the interests of its best friends for those of its bitterest enemies—that there might be a party for separation at some future date on the Western states, too." But Gallatin's wiser counsels prevailed.[19]

Jefferson had concluded in 1814 that, were a secession to take place, it would not be successful. He thought the Essex Junto was playing a big bluff, and was in no mood to play along. The "defection" of Massachusetts was disagreeable, he told Short, but not dangerous: "If they become neutral, we are sufficient for one enemy without them, and in fact we get no aid from them now. If their administration determines to join the enemy, their force will be annihilated by equality of division among themselves. Their federalists will then call in the English army, the republicans ours, and it will only be a transfer of the scene of war from Canada to Massachusetts; and we can get ten men to go to Massachusetts for one who will go to Canada." Jefferson recurred to the theme in 1815. He was satisfied that the movers of the Hartford Convention could not raise "one single regiment (gambling merchants and silk-stocking clerks excepted) who would support them in any effort to separate from the Union. The cement of this Union is in the heart-blood of every American. I do not believe there is on earth a government established on so immovable a basis. Let them, in any State, even in Massachusetts itself, raise the standard of separation, and its citizens will rise in mass, and do justice on their own incendiaries." Just in case the citizens did not rise in mass, however, a body of federal troops marched in Connecticut shortly before the meeting of the Hartford Convention; the episode showed that even an outlook committed in theory to the right of peaceable secession might find ample cause for fighting a war against a seceding section.[20]

History works in the strangest of ways, but never more paradoxically than in the outcome of the War of 1812. The whole diplomacy preceding the war was a tissue of embarrassments. The Republicans, thinking that Bonaparte would get them the Floridas, had entered a silent entente with France and found themselves—to their own considerable mortification—standing athwart the great movement to throw off the despotism of Napoleon and to secure the liberties of Europe. Everywhere in Europe, and in many precincts of America, the government was deemed incapable of "any great or vigorous exertion"—with a constitution that was not made for war and a diplomacy that was not made for peace. Republican threats had not been taken seriously by either Britain or France; the military preparations for the war its diplomacy hastened were inadequate. During the war, the boasts made by Republicans before the war, the sum of which was that taking Canada would be a mere matter of marching, had been shown to be empty by the event. In the bleak winter of 1814–1815 the federal government had appeared at wit's end, its capitol in ashes and its financial affairs in utter disorder.

Yet from these unseemly ingredients a magnificent feast was made. The war settled nothing yet seemed to settle everything. At its conclusion, capped by the Treaty of Ghent and Andrew Jackson's victory at New Orleans, John Adams noted that Madison's administration had "proved great points long disputed in Europe and America":

1. He has proved, that an administration under our present Constitution can declare war.
2. That it can make peace.
3. That money or no money, government or no government, Great

Britain can never conquer this country or any considerable part
of it.
4. That our officers and men by land are equal to any from Spain and
Portugal.
5. That our trans-Alleghanian States, in patriotism, bravery, enterprise,
and perseverance, are at least equal to any in the Union.
6. That our navy is equal, *cæteris paribus*, to any that ever floated.

Jefferson noted a related set of proofs: "It proved the fidelity of the Orlea-
nese to the United States. It proved that New Orleans can be defended both
by land and water; that the western country will fly to its relief (of which
ourselves had doubted before); that our militia are heroes when they have
heroes to lead them."[21]

These letters cast an instructive light backward, showing the character of
the doubts that had existed for the first twenty-five years of life under the
Constitution: whether the government could make war or peace; whether
the inhabitants of Louisiana and the upper Mississippi Valley would prove
loyal or disloyal. But the general question surrounding these particulars had
always been whether the union would survive. That it had done so through
a severe trial gave wind to the idea that it might survive anything. Observers
discerned a newly recovered sense of nationality in the American people.
Before the war, wrote Gallatin, "we were becoming too selfish, too much
attached exclusively to the acquisition of wealth, above all, too much confined in our political feelings to local and State objects. The war has renewed
and reinstated the national feelings and character which the Revolution had
given, and which were daily lessened. The people have now more general
objects of attachment with which their pride and political opinions are connected. They are more American; they feel and act more as a nation; and I
hope that the permanency of the Union is thereby better secured."[22]

If Americans could take satisfaction that they had survived the war, and
could even revel in a sentiment of nationality, the experience of the preceding two decades had nevertheless confirmed for them the old proposition
that war with any European power would provide a spark that might well
produce the dissolution of the union. As Jefferson wrote Gallatin after the
war: "The war, had it proceeded, would have upset our government, and a
new one, whenever tried, will do it." The fear that war would equal disunion
had been of crucial significance for two decades in reinforcing Washington's counsel against permanent alliances and departures from neutrality.
In 1797, Jefferson observed that "if we engage in a war during our present
passions, and our present weakness in some quarters, our Union runs the
greatest risk of not coming out of that war in the shape in which it enters

it." Adams believed that devoutly in 1799; contrary to myth, Hamilton saw the danger too and was by no means the warmonger that Adams thought he was. The sentiment and policy of "isolationism" is often attributed to the belief in the moral superiority of America over Europe, and Jefferson in particular frequently gave vent to that sentiment. Of even deeper influence and significance in fostering the need for separation from Europe, however, was the fear that war with a European power would set in motion forces that would dissolve the union. Peace became, on this reckoning, the sovereign remedy for all such ailments.[23]

PART THREE
A Rage for
Federative Systems

8

The Confederation of Europe

WE HAVE BEEN CONSIDERING AMERICA'S federal union as a self-con-
scious escape from the European system, a *novus ordo seclorum* that was
to represent a vast improvement on the ancient practices of the Westphalian
system, but also as one that, from its first moments, was dogged by the
prospect of a sudden dissolution. At the end of the Napoleonic Wars, a
comparable attempt to escape the practices of the old system took place in
Europe itself. Called variously "the confederation of Europe," the "Concert
of Europe," "the Vienna system," and "the European Alliance," it entailed
the recognition by European statesmen that their previous discord and narrow self-seeking had brought upon them a series of disasters.

The Wars of the French Revolution and Napoleon had a profound impact
on the consciousness of European leaders. A keen sense of revulsion was felt
against the diseases of a system in which the leading states looked only to
their own interest and displayed, despite their protestations, a minimal sense
of Europe's interests as a whole. That experience produced the search for
new principles of European order. The political system that was established
on these ruins, Friedrich von Gentz wrote in 1818, was a "phenomenon un-
heard of in the history of the world. The principle of equilibrium, or, rather,
of counterweights formed by particular alliances—the principle which has
governed, and too often troubled and engulfed Europe for three centuries—
has been succeeded by a principle of general union, uniting all the states by a
federative bond under the direction of the five principal Powers. . . . Europe
at last forms a single great political family, reunited under an areopagus of
its own creation, in which the members guarantee to each other and to each
interested party the tranquil enjoyment of their respective rights."[1]

Contemporary and historical opinion of what was done at Vienna in 1815
and subsequently has varied greatly over the years. Was it progressive or
reactionary, a step forward or a step back? That there were restorative elements in the Congress of Vienna is clear, and in the subsequent century
the proceedings at Vienna were harshly criticized by liberals and nationalists for the indifference of the peacemakers to popular sentiment and for
its restorative—or reactionary—character. Gentz himself, "the Secretary of
Europe," treated it in both ways. In 1818, he proclaimed the utter novelty
of this federative system; but in his pamphlet, *Fragments upon the Balance*

69

of Power in Europe (1806), he had looked toward a restoration of the old Europe, and not toward a new arrangement. What needed to be restored in a Europe threatened by "universal monarchy" and "despotism," Gentz then thought, was "THE TRUE FEDERAL SYSTEM," "the old magnificent constitution of Europe," whose "characteristic object was the preservation and reciprocal guarantee of the rights of all its members." He contrasted it with "THE NEW FEDERAL SYSTEM" advocated by Bonaparte, an innovation in usage that Gentz put down to the "corrupted dialect" and "disgusting gibberish" of the press. The older system, Gentz then held, had "for centuries protected the liberty of Europe, with all its ornaments and excellencies, its constitutions and laws, its archives, its territorial limitations, and its adjudications of rights," but "the ignominious fall of the European commonwealth" before the onslaught of Napoleon had left everything in ruins.[2]

Gentz's distinction between "the true federal system" and "the new federal system" shows that, in Europe, what constituted a genuinely federal relationship was often a subject of dispute. The federal principle signified an ideal that men and nations with conflicting purposes wished to claim, just as it had done in the earlier competition between "Federalists" and "Anti-Federalists" in the debate over the ratification of the Constitution—with the latter charging, as Gentz had done, an outrageous linguistic appropriation on their adversaries. Among European publicists and statesmen, the use of the term "federal" conveyed, as yet, no intimation that a government with sovereign powers would be necessary to give effect to cooperative relations; nor had that been Montesquieu's conception of the federative tie among republics that, wishing to preserve the small scale and individuality necessary for their internal perfection, nevertheless had acute need of the power that could only come through an aggregation of their strength. Such an association, which he called a *république fédérative*, was "a kind of assemblage of societies, that constitute a new one, capable of increasing by means of farther associations, till they arrive to such a degree of power, as to be able to provide for the security of the whole body."[3]

A federal relationship—typically used synonymously with "confederal"—was distinguishable both from an empire, on the one hand, and from a civil association, on the other. It might range in size from a geographically limited area like Holland or Switzerland, to larger entities like the Germanic body, covering vast expanses of territory, all the way up to the society of states as such. Indeed, if we look at the use that early modern theorists and publicists made of the terms "federal," "federacy," and "federative system," we find that they were often employed to describe the nature of the society of states that had been constituted within Europe. The publicists spoke not only of "a kind of society and general republic" (Fenelon), "one great nation composed of several" (Montesquieu), "a sort of great republic divided into several states" (Voltaire); they also spoke of it as a "federative system." Lord Brougham, in his pamphlet "Balance of Power" (1803), wrote of a Europe that was "a united whole within itself, almost separated from the rest of the world;—a great federacy, acknowledging, indeed, no common chief; but united by certain common principles, and obeying one system of international law." In a treaty between Russia and Great Britain of April 11, 1805, the two kingdoms looked toward "the establishment in Europe of a federative system, to ensure the independence of the weaker states by erecting a formidable barrier against the ambition of the more powerful," and spoke of forming "an intimate union for the purpose of realizing their happy effects."[4]

The greatly agitated question, of tremendous political importance during the Wars of the French Revolution and Napoleon, was when and why this "federal constitution" had collapsed. In a work written in 1802, in response to the French publicist Hauterive, Gentz had considered the events in the eighteenth century that had "confounded, disordered, and overturned the public law of Europe," converting it "into a chaos of contradiction and an-archy" and at length putting "an end to its existence." But whereas Gentz attributed this collapse to the French Revolution, Hauterive had argued that the "federal constitution" of Europe, the term used by both authors to describe the political system established by the Treaty of Westphalia in 1648, had already collapsed by the late eighteenth century. The Frenchman ascribed the disorder to three great causes:

1. the entry into the European system of Russia, whose "plans of conquest and partition" had "made it doubtful whether the law of nations was not an empty name, invented as a cloak for power, and secretly despised by the powerful," and which had applied "the terms, sound policy, system of equilibrium, maintenance or restoration of the balance of power . . . to what, in fact, was only an abuse of power, or the exercise of arbitrary will."

2. the rise of Prussia, whose introduction of the "military system" had been "the cause of those unnatural efforts" to maintain the balance that had resulted in the "enervation of all the European states." "To main-tain great armies, and to fill their coffers, they oppressed their subjects so much by levies of men and money, excited such universal discontent, and strained all the springs of power so immoderately, as to occasion the general disorder which ensued, and 'of which the war against the revolution was only the last result.'"

3. the rise of England, whose commercial and colonial system had

"oppressed the industry of all other countries, . . . threatened their independence, . . . and encouraged their mutual dissensions."

As a consequence of these three great events, according to Hauterive, "there had long since ceased to exist any maxims of government, any federal union, any fixed political principles in Europe; that an imaginary principle of aggrandizement, in fact nothing more than a forcible, unnatural, and destructive exertion, had fascinated all governments." Were Hauterive's charges true, Gentz noted, "the French revolution will appear not only completely explained, but justified, and more than justified. It would, in that case, only be the natural end of a long series of evil, the breaking out, the decisive crisis of a disorder which had long preyed upon the constitution of society; a violent but salutary fever in a body long diseased."[5]

According to Gentz, however, Hauterive's account was not true. The partition of Poland was unjust and unprincipled, to be sure, but it was also uncharacteristic; so, too, it had been the failure of France to interpose in 1772 that explained why the partition took place. The "military system" Gentz attributed not to Prussia but to the France of Louis XIV: "The mighty armies, the brilliant administration, the splendid enterprises, the resources, and the system of finance of Louis XIV were models for all the states of Europe" and had already arrived at maturity by the time that Prussia was elevated in midcentury. The rise of the English colonial system, finally, had enabled that power "to save the independence and federal constitution of Europe from total ruin." Absurd was Hauterive's claim that, at the beginning of the eighteenth century, "France alone conducted herself in conformity to the true principles of the federal system, and the universal maxims of the political balance, while all other nations made no scruple of violating them." On the contrary, the salvation of the federal constitution of Europe and the preservation of the general balance "was the work and the merit of the coalition of which the Prince of Orange was the founder and director." Gentz's response to Hauterive, in sum, was also a defense of the old system. "Before the revolution there only needed a few wise reforms in the internal constitutions of states, and some happy combinations for ameliorating and confirming the federal system, to have raised Europe to a high degree of prosperity and happiness; whereas now all the means of attaining to this desired object must be sought for amidst a heap of ruins, and drawn forth, as it were, from chaos again."[6]

This dispute between Gentz and Hauterive prefigures much subsequent historiographical controversy. The magisterial accounts of Albert Sorel and Paul Schroeder—one at the close of the nineteenth century, the other at the close of the twentieth—bear a striking resemblance to Hauterive's diagnosis.

The "prejudice" that Sorel put aside in setting out on his great study of Europe and the French Revolution was "the representation of Europe under the ancien regime as a regularly constituted community of states, in which each directed its conduct by principles recognized by all, where respect for established law governed international relations and treaties, and good faith marked their implementation, where the sense of monarchical solidarity assured both the maintenance of public order and the permanence of engagements contracted by princes." That "Christian republic" had been, in Sorel's view, "nothing more than an august abstraction." The attempt made after the Napoleonic Wars to provide Europe "with the elements of an organization was a step forward, not a return to the past." Though in Sorel's judgment the step forward taken in 1815 covered no great distance, recent historians have concluded that the distance was very great indeed. Paul Schroeder, in his history of European diplomacy from 1763 to 1848, has made the contrast between the cynical and egotistical diplomacy of the ancien régime and the new diplomacy of the "Vienna system" the central theme of his work.[7]

Contemporary American opinion took a far harsher view of the Congress of Vienna than these judgments. For Jefferson, the proceedings appeared reactionary even by comparison with the practices of the eighteenth-century system. "There is no more moderation, forbearance, or even honesty in [the policy of the allies], than in that of Bonaparte. They have proved that their object, like his, is plunder. They, like him, are shuffling nations together, or into their own hands, as if all were right which they feel a power to do." Writing to John Adams a few months later, Jefferson gave vent to views that constitute an exact reversal of the now prevailing interpretation. "With some exceptions only," he told Adams,

> through the 17th. and 18th. centuries morality occupied an honorable chapter in the political code of nations. You must have observed while in Europe, as I thought I did, that those who administered the governments of the greater powers at least, had a respect to faith, and considered the dignity of their government as involved in its integrity. A wound indeed was inflicted on this character of honor in the 18th. century by the partition of Poland. But this was the atrocity of a barbarous government chiefly [Russia], in conjunction with a smaller one still scrambling to become great [Prussia], while one only of those already great, and having character to lose, descended to the baseness of an accomplice in the crime [Austria]. . . . How then has it happened that these nations, France especially and England, so great, so dignified, so distinguished by science and the arts, plunged at once into all the depths

of human enormity, threw off suddenly and openly all the restraints of morality, all sensation to character, and unblushingly avowed and acted on the principle that power was right?

Jefferson ascribed "this sudden apostasy from national rectitude" to the "treaty of Pilnitz" in 1791, but he acknowledged that France, "after crushing and punishing the conspiracy of Pilnitz, went herself deeper and deeper into the crimes she had been chastising. I say France, and not Bonaparte; for altho' he was the head and mouth, the nation furnished the hands which executed his enormities."[8]

Adams agreed with all of this and thought the partitions made at Vienna in 1815 had been "more daring" than the eighteenth-century partitions of Poland and "the intended Partitions of Pilnitz." He was reluctant to speculate on the subject—"A burned child dreads the Fire"—but attributed the cause of the conflagration to religious fanaticism: the fear of "The Priests of all Nations" that they were "Approaching such Flames as they had so often kindled about the Bodies of honest Men." As for why all Europe had "acted on the Principle 'that Power was Right,'" Adams speculated "that Power always sincerely, conscientiously, de tres bon Foi, believes itself Right. Power always thinks it has a great Soul, and vast Views, beyond the Comprehension of the Weak; and that it is doing God Service, when it is violating all his Laws."[9]

The same repugnance toward the Vienna system that immediately arose in America arose later in England, as is attested by the famous witticism that Castlereagh, listening to his European allies, was "like a great lover of music who is at Church; he wishes to applaud but he dare not." He dared not applaud because English opinion was distinctly out of sympathy with the legitimist principles on which the European alliance began to act. Canning's break from the European alliance in 1823 was far more in keeping with the English outlook than Castlereagh's earlier embrace of it had been, and Castlereagh himself had become disgusted at the lengths to which his confederates were taking the principle of legitimacy. His famous state paper of 1818 expressed that dissatisfaction and took a leaf (probably unwittingly) from the book of Rousseau and Madison: "The idea of an 'Alliance Solidaire,' by which each State shall be bound to support the State of Succession, Government, and Possession, within all other States from violence and attack upon Condition of receiving for itself a similar guarantee must be understood as morally implying the previous establishment of such a System of general Government as may secure and enforce upon all Kings and Nations an internal System of Peace and Justice; till the mode of constructing such a System shall be devised, the Consequence is inadmissible, as nothing would be more immoral or more prejudicial to the Character of Government generally, than the Idea that their force was collectively to be prostituted to the support of established Power without any Consideration of the Extent to which it was abused."[10]

Despite its repressive features, the Continental monarchs had put together a genuine "federative system." Historians frequently ignore or understate its repressive character and the networks of spies, ever on the outlook for seditious liberals, maintained by the Russian and Austrian governments. This not-to-be-forgotten feature apart, however, the system was in other respects an inspired example of cooperation among states. The peacemakers did consciously repudiate the idea that European order should rest on force rather than law, and they saw the Great Powers involved in a cooperative effort that was unprecedented, from which useful lessons may still be learned.[11]

North America, then, was not alone in having advanced toward the beau ideal of a federative system, and these respective constructions hovered over Christian civilization in the aftermath of the Napoleonic Wars. In Europe there stood a federative system joining in intimate union the crowned heads of Europe, the parties to which were pledged to uphold the peace treaties mutually agreed to in 1814 and 1815, and who were committed to the joint governance of their common affairs. In North America there stood a federal union, newly energized by late-arriving military valor, at the foundation of which was a constitution to which the parties were severally pledged. The European union held fast to prescription and settled authority and gloried in the past; the American union put government on a popular foundation and claimed to represent the future. The one sought to guarantee legitimate authority upon its throne and rested on the doctrine of indissoluble allegiance among subjects; the other held dear life, liberty, and the pursuit of happiness and believed legitimate government to rest on the consent of citizens. One considered it a solemn duty to repress seditious experiments in republicanism; the other guaranteed to the respective states a republican form of government. Neither Europeans nor Americans were disposed, in the years after the Napoleonic Wars, to note the similarities between their two federative systems—they were, as Monroe said in his famous message of 1823, "essentially different." And they did indeed differ with regard to both the institutions created to manage their respective associations and the principles of government that they represented. They were still, however, called by names that suggested much commonality: confederation, perpetual league, federacy, union.

Both had arisen out of what many observers took to be highly unpromising soil. The selfishness of monarchs in Europe and the inveterate localism of colonial and state assemblies in America had been the previous byword of seasoned observers. That these states should cooperate with their partners in the joint management of their respective worlds had always been deemed necessary by some but usually considered wholly improbable by those who had consulted their previous histories. Both were nevertheless now making a go of it, declaring their good faith and credibility against a background of mutual suspicion, the more cosmopolitan among them hoping that their partners would have the good sense to avoid the unnecessary quarrels, jealous rages, and stingy attitudes that had, in the past, nearly brought them to a common ruin. Central to both was the sense that they could secure their individual interests only through the pursuit of a general interest, securing their rights as states through the partial surrender of their freedom of action. Both renounced the balance of power insofar as that term signified "expediency and egotism in a collectivity of roughly equal and intensely acquisitive states which were bound and regulated by nothing but expediency and egotism," but both were nevertheless thoroughly informed by equilibrist notions and mechanisms of countervailing power.[12] A profound dread of war animated the architects and conservators of each system, though for somewhat different reasons. For the confederacy of kings, it was because war was a synonym for revolution and the destruction of social order; for Americans, because it would lead, through the introduction of the "military system" in the Americas, to the destruction of republican government. Both, in sum, saw their respective systems as an escape from the power politics that had at various periods characterized the European state system and believed devoutly that the rule of law needed to be substituted for "the empire of force."[13]

It was a characteristic mark of this interesting quarrel between Europe and America that each charged the other with the same defect and thought the miracle cure the opposing statesmen offered bespoke either present incomprehension or future comeuppance. Hegel had difficulty conceiving that America's federal union did or could exist. It seemed to have no state, or too many, which came to the same thing; and he was ready (like some theorists of the contemporary international system) to exclude the existence of this compound association because it did not fit anywhere within his philosophical system. Englishmen, too—albeit for more practical reasons—had a decided tendency to disparage the cohesion of the American union, and predictions of its probable future demise had filled up London's newspapers since the making of the Constitution.[14]

But Americans were ready with the same observation as to Europe. However much the European powers might now swear eternal fidelity to one another, or anticipate the day "when treaties shall be more than truces, when it will again be possible for them to be observed with that religious faith, that sacred inviolability, on which depend the reputation, the strength, and the preservation of empires," Americans were to be found disparaging the probable success of the enterprise, whose foundation they in any case found pernicious. In urging recognition to the Spanish American states in 1818, Henry Clay noted that the disunited condition of Europe sharply lessened the danger the United States might face from the consternation of the Holy Alliance. Clay "entertained no doubt that the principle of cohesion among the allies was gone. It was annihilated in the memorable battle of Waterloo. When the question was, whether one should engross all, a common danger united all." But "the consummation of the cause of the allies" meant "the destruction of the alliance. The principle was totally changed. It was no longer a common struggle against the colossal power of Bonaparte, but it became a common scramble for the spoils of his Empire." It was perhaps understandable, thought John Quincy Adams, that the allies might take "an eye for an eye," but in denying to France "all the principles of civil liberty and of national independence," they had "glut[ted] their vengeance for the wrongs which they have received." Can it be doubted, he wondered, "that they are laying up stores of wrath for the day of wrath in revenge for those which they are inflicting?" To Adams, the conclusion was unavoidable that "the foundation upon which the present peace of Europe is professedly laid is in its nature weak and treacherous."[15]

These two federative systems, then, were antipodes of one another, yet essentially alike. Observers on both sides of the Atlantic were grateful for the natural separation between them. Thank God, they both said, for the wide Atlantic. By 1817, John Quincy Adams was detecting a descent, in Europe, into "monkery and despotism," and he wished to have as little to do with the political system of Europe as possible. In response to a British effort to mediate the dispute between the United States and Spain over Florida, Adams declined the offer, appealing to "the policy, both of Europe and of the United States, to keep aloof from the general federative system, of each other."[16] That was Metternich's view as well. Despite his fulminations against sedition in the Americas, the social order in Europe was well enough preserved by geographic separation. Contrary to the fears entertained in the United States in 1823, which prompted the famous "doctrine" of President Monroe in December of that year, the Continental monarchs were little interested in counterrevolutionary interventions beyond Europe. Both the "Cominform of kings" and those republican firebrands in North America would largely agree in coming years to respect the protecting line of the two hemispheres.

9

New World and Old World

WHAT GAVE THE CONTRAST BETWEEN THE OLD and the new worlds great force in the years after 1815 was the development and progress of the Latin American revolutions. As early as 1808, Jefferson had written of an identity of interests between the United States and the independence movements in the South: "The object of both must be to exclude all European influence from this hemisphere." Later, he would insist that "the whole system of Europe towards America" was nothing "but an atrocious and insulting tyranny." "One hemisphere of the earth, separated from the other by wide seas on both sides, having a different system of interests flowing from different climates, different soils, different productions, different modes of existence, and its own local relations and duties, is made subservient to all the petty interests of the other, to their laws, their regulations, their passions and wars." Jefferson doubted that the independence movements would issue in free governments but still found the line of the two hemispheres desirable and meaningful. "In whatever governments they end they will be *American* governments, no longer to be involved in the never-ceasing broils of Europe. The European nations constitute a separate division of the globe; their localities make them part of a distinct system; they have a set of interests of their own in which it is our business never to engage ourselves. America has a hemisphere to itself. It must have a separate system of interests, which must not be subordinated to those of Europe. The insulated state in which nature has placed the American continent, should so far avail it that no spark of war kindled in the other quarters of the globe should be wafted across the wide oceans which separate us from them. And it will be so."[1]

Of the American statesmen of the time, none was a more inveterate defender of the Spanish American revolutions than Henry Clay, the "Hortensius of the West" whose orations on behalf of the liberty and independence of the new American states were read at the head of Simón Bolívar's armies. Clay had warned of the potential danger from the Holy Alliance as early as 1816, and in 1818 he presented resolutions in the House of Representatives authorizing expenditures for a minister to the United Provinces of the Rio de la Plata, an act tantamount to de facto recognition. Though holding that the forms of government the Spanish American states would establish was their business, and not that of the United States, he thought it likely, unlike

Jefferson, that the majority would establish free governments. The key belief that Jefferson and Clay shared was that, whatever forms the South Americans adopted, they would be independent and "animated by an American feeling, and guided by an American policy. They will obey the laws of the system of the New World, of which they will compose a part, in contradistinction to that of Europe." This system would lack "the influence of that vortex in Europe, the balance of power between its several parts, the preservation of which has so often drenched Europe in blood."[2]

Clay's resolutions were then defeated, but he returned to the charge in 1820. "It is in our power to create a system of which we shall be the centre, and in which all South America will act with us." The commercial advantages this "American system" promised, Clay held, would be substantial, but "infinitely more gratifying" was that "we should become the centre of a system which would constitute the rallying point of human freedom against all the despotism of the Old World." Justifying his course of action a year later, in a speech at Lexington, Clay excoriated the Holy Alliance for having "thrown off the mask of religion, and peace and hypocrisy," fully exposing "the naked atrocity of its designs" in its "recent lawless attack upon the independence of unoffending Naples." How far the alliance would push the "principle of *legitimacy*, a softer and covered name for despotism," could not be known, but he then raised the doubt he had earlier put to rest: the exemption of the United States from the designs of the Holy Alliance could not be taken for granted; the Continental powers might well act in concert against the Americas. Hence it seemed to him "desirable that a sort of counterpoise to the Holy Alliance should be formed in the two Americas, in favor of National Independence and Liberty, to operate by the force of example and by moral influence; that here a rallying point and an asylum should exist for freemen and for freedom."[3]

Clay's bold espousal of an American system met with often sharp criticism in the United States, but even its advocates disagreed over its precise contours. "What is the American system?" Representative David Trimble of Kentucky asked in 1822. "Why is it that it agitates two worlds? Why should kings shudder at it, while their subjects bid it welcome?" It had two aspects, Trimble argued, "two essential principles—one political, the other commercial. The first is known and distinguished by written constitutions, representative government, religious toleration, freedom of opinion, of speech, and of the press. The second, by sailors' rights, free trade, and freedom of the seas. Contrast it with the European system. The political character of that system is aristocracy, monarchy, imperial government, arbitrary power, passive obedience, and unconditional submission. Its commercial character is prohibition, restriction, interdiction, impressment, colonial monopoly, and maritime domination." The two systems, Trimble insisted, "are the antipodes of each other. They are sworn enemies, and cannot harmonize." Clay would have subscribed to much of Trimble's effusive assessment, but not to his encomiums on free trade, for in Clay's other "American system" a protective tariff directed against European manufactures was the paramount element in the whole scheme. Nevertheless, Clay did speak for free trade and reciprocity within the hemisphere, imagining a system in which the development of trade among the American republics would reinforce the separation from the Old World while providing an expanding market for North American manufactures.[4]

It must not be imagined, of course, that the enthusiastic embrace of the liberty and independence of South America passed without dissent. Clay had disclaimed any intention to interfere in the war between Spain and its rebellious colonies; he had insisted that recognition constituted no such interference. His opponents, however, continually objected that the United States were being asked to join in a "crusade"—a policy that, in their view, was "highly anti republican" and which had "wasted Europe from the middle ages to the present day." They denied the existence of a hemispheric community. "As to an American system," John Quincy Adams wrote, "we have it; we constitute the whole of it; there is no community of interests or of principles between North and South America." Like his father, Adams saw no prospect that the Latin Americans would "establish free or liberal institutions of government. They are not likely to promote the spirit either of freedom or order by their example. . . . Arbitrary power, military and ecclesiastical, was stamped upon their education, upon their habits, and upon all their institutions. Civil dissension was infused into all their seminal principles. War and mutual destruction was in every member of their organization, moral, political, and physical." Adams was insistent that the United States should take no part in the contest, and he saw little benefit in "any future connection with them, political or commercial." "The principle of neutrality to all foreign wars was . . . fundamental to the continuance of our liberties and of our Union."[5]

There were many Americans who agreed with Adams regarding South America but disagreed with him about the significance of the revolutions in Europe. "We have no concern with South America," wrote Edward Everett; "we have no sympathy, we can have no well founded political sympathy with them. We are sprung from different stocks, we speak different languages, we have been brought up in different social and moral schools, we have been governed by different codes of law, we profess radically different codes of religion." The case was far otherwise, Everett thought, with the revolution among the Greeks that had begun on the Morea in 1821, a rising universally approved in America, and which roused the enthusiasm and sympathy of a large array of important characters. The "appeal from the anxious conclave of self-devoted patriots, in the inaccessible cliffs of the Morea," Everett wrote, "must bring home to the mind of the least reflecting American, the great and glorious part, which this country is to act, in the political regeneration of the world." The sympathy elicited in America for the Greeks stemmed from many causes: partly from the avidity with which "the eyes of Greece were turned to this country as the great exemplar of states in the agonies of contest for independence," partly from revulsion against the outrages committed by the Turks, particularly the execution of the Greek patriarch of Constantinople and the fearful retaliations visited upon the whole population; partly from the conviction that this was a religious war, with Christians being put to death for the crime of professing their faith, making it a conflict, as Everett put it, of "the crescent against the cross." That the Greek Revolution broke out in the midst of contemporaneous movements toward constitutional government in Spain and Italy and had been sternly condemned by the powers reinforced its status as a great embodiment of the spirit of liberty.[6]

But what gave the Greek Revolution its quite extraordinary power over the American mind was the identity that existed between what was now happening in Greece and what had happened there in antiquity. No American could think of one without the other. Offering copies of American constitutions to a Greek patriot in Europe, Jefferson wrote that should the works prove useful, his correspondent was to consider it "a tribute rendered to the names of your Homer, your Demosthenes, and the splendid constellation of sages and heroes, whose blood is still flowing in your veins, and whose merits are still resting, as a heavy debt, on the shoulders of the living, and the future races of men." To the Greeks were owed "the fine models of science left by their ancestors, to whom we also are all indebted for the lights which originally led ourselves out of Gothic darkness." Unconsciously, whole libraries of learning kept getting mixed up in the American mind with the valiant Greeks, and Americans kept imagining that Demosthenes and Plato, Themistocles and Homer, were lurking in the shadows, ready to spring forward to revivify the glories of that ancient civilization.[7]

Experience, needless to say, did not keep up with these high expectations. Atrocities by the Greeks of a character no different from those that had been committed against them dimmed the luster of their cause. The countertheorem—of barbarous nations hacking their way to perdition in endless civil wars—was invoked by some even at the time. John Randolph could always be counted on to pour ridicule on the pretended similarities between the American experiment and revolutions elsewhere, whether in South America or Europe. But the prevailing popular feeling was one of ardent sympathy. Albert Gallatin, American minister in Paris, proposed aiding the Greeks with the American naval force in the Mediterranean—one frigate, one corvette, and one schooner. Calhoun was an enthusiast. Most American hearts were indeed beating in unison, as John Adams said his did, with the courageous Greeks—the descendants of virtuous and heroic forefathers.[8]

It was in response both to Clay's vision of a system pitting the liberty of the Americas against the despotism of Europe and to the contemporaneous call for American recognition and support for liberty and independence in Europe that John Quincy Adams composed his oft-quoted Fourth of July Address in 1821. On that occasion he told the citizens of Washington, "Wherever the standard of freedom and independence has been or shall be unfurled, there will be America's heart, her benedictions, and her prayers. But she goes not abroad in search of monsters to destroy. She is the well-wisher to the freedom and independence of all. She is the champion and vindicator only of her own." A contrary policy would involve the United States "in all the wars of interest and intrigue, of individual avarice, envy and ambition, which assume the colors and usurp the standards of freedom. The fundamental maxims of her policy would insensibly change from liberty to force. . . . She might become the dictatress of the world. She would no longer be the ruler of her own spirit."[9]

Adams meant this address, as he noted in a private letter shortly after its delivery, as a "reply to both Edinburgh and Lexington." Clay, or "Lexington," had proposed concord among the American republics to support liberty and independence in this hemisphere; a writer in the *Edinburgh Review* had proposed a combination between Great Britain and the United States to support liberty in Europe. "It is impossible," the *Review* held, "to look to the state of the Old World without seeing . . . that there is a greater and more momentous contest impending, than ever before agitated human society. In Germany—in Spain—in France—in Italy, the principles of Reform and Liberty are visibly arraying themselves for a final struggle with the principles of Established abuse,—Legitimacy, or Tyranny." In determining the issue of this contest, much would depend on the part taken by America. "It is as an associate or successor in the noble office of patronizing and protecting general liberty, that we now call upon America . . . to unite herself cordially with the liberal and enlightened part of the English nation, at a season when their joint efforts will in all probability be little enough to crown the good cause with success." Adams rejected in 1821, as he would reject in 1823, both Clay's vision of hemispheric collaboration to support liberty and independence in the New World and "Edinburgh's" vision of Anglo-American concord to support liberty and independence in the Old World.[10]

The same double rejection figured in the response made by the American government to George Canning's suggestion that the two governments of England and the United States issue a common statement in opposition to the Holy Alliance's efforts to help Spain recover its lost dominion in South America. Canning made his proposal to Richard Rush, American minister in London, but Rush, sensing the significance of a joint declaration, deferred the decision to his home government. President Monroe in turn sought the advice of Madison and Jefferson, both of whom counseled acceptance. Jefferson was alarmed by "the atrocious violations of the rights of nations, by the interference of any one in the internal affairs of another, so flagitiously begun by Bonaparte, and now continued by the equally lawless Alliance, calling itself Holy." He reaffirmed the line of the two hemispheres—that "America, North and South . . . should have a system of her own, separate and apart from that of Europe. While the last is laboring to become the domicil of despotism, our endeavor should surely be, to make our hemisphere that of freedom." He urged acceptance of the British offer and found himself in agreement with his old nemesis, George Canning, who had been British foreign minister during the tormenting years of the embargo, that a joint declaration would "prevent instead of provoking war."[11]

Canning's note of August 20, 1823, to Rush, indicated in outline what he had in mind. Conceiving "the recovery of the colonies by Spain to be hopeless," Canning wished to signal that the recognition of their independence would come when time and circumstance allowed. He also proposed to the United States one self-denying ordinance and one commitment: Britain, he told Rush, "aimed at the possession of no portion of the colonies for herself." Nor could Britain "see the transfer of any portion of them to any other Power, with indifference." Would the United States, Canning asked Rush, agree to make this self-denying ordinance and this commitment the basis of American policy? The United States had been committed to a form of the "no-transfer" principle since 1811, but what Canning proposed in 1823 was not quite what Madison had asserted in 1811. The United States was opposed to the transfer of sovereignty from the Spanish Empire to another European power; Britain now proposed to accept the self-denying for itself and invited the United States to do the same.[12]

The concrete issue that lay behind these high-toned declarations was the status of Cuba. Within the circle of Monroe's intimates who considered this issue in America, all had expressed the previous and common opinion that Cuba would one day fall into the lap of the American union. Its strategic importance, astride the outlet to the North Atlantic from the Gulf of Mexico, was obvious at a glance. In 1823, however, there were two obstacles to the consummation of this wish. One was that its acquisition, in Monroe's words, would likely cause a revival of the Missouri crisis and was certain to "shake our system, whatever might be the advantages" likely to attend its incorporation "if all the States would unite in it." The acquisition of Cuba through war or purchase, moreover, was certain to be opposed by Britain, France, and the newly emerging republics to the south.[13]

In 1823, Cuba existed in the same kind of diplomatic force field that protected the independence of the Low Countries during most periods of the historic European system. The value of its acquisition was not sufficiently great for any power for it to be worth the risk of war, yet ensuring that it did not fall into the hands of a hostile power might very well be worth that risk. Britain would probably fight to prevent its acquisition by the United States. The United States would probably fight to prevent its acquisition by Britain. In the careful equipoise of these probabilities, the status quo presented advantages for all the interested parties that outweighed the disadvantages that would be incurred by a rash claim upon the island for themselves. Adams and Monroe had for this reason rejected "a proposition from the strongest party in *Cuba . . . to join our union.*" Jefferson, who saw this diplomatic force field around Cuba, drew the following deduction. He had long thought that Cuba was "the most interesting addition which could ever be made to our system of States." The control of those strategic waters would "fill up the measure of our political well-being." Yet he thought that this could "never be obtained, even with her own consent, but by war." On the other hand, Cuba's independence, particularly its independence of Britain, could be obtained without a war. "I have no hesitation in abandoning my first wish to future chances, and accepting its independence, with peace and the friendship of England, rather than its association, at the expense of war and her enmity."[14]

Others, however, did hesitate; of those who did, the most important was John Quincy Adams. It was he, and not Jefferson, who was secretary of state, and on whose shoulders fell the primary responsibility of defining the position of the American government. Adams stood just a few years shy of opposing all expansion to the south and west (that is, to Cuba or to Texas) as an utterly wicked project of the Slave Power, and Cuba was thick with slaves in 1823. In that year, however, he remained an ardent expansionist. That the United States would expand from the arctic to the tropics was his settled conviction. Apples and pears, once ripe, would fall from their trees in Canada and the Caribbean in due course, where else but into the lap of the all-embracing union at the center of the continent? Until Europe, he wrote in 1819, "shall find it a settled geographical element that the United States and North America are identical, any effort on our part to reason the world out of a belief that we are ambitious will have no other effect than to convince them that we add to our ambition hypocrisy."[15]

To exclude as far as possible British claims in North America, and to extend as far as possible the claims of the United States, had been Adams's fixed line of conduct as secretary of state. He had, in the Transcontinental Treaty concluded with Spain in early 1819 (but not ratified until 1821), secured from Spain a claim to the Oregon country. (With this treaty, Spain ceded Florida to the United States, and the United States gave up Texas, to part of which there was a plausible claim under the terms of the Louisiana Purchase.) The prospect that Russia might make settlements in the Pacific Northwest (as far south as the fifty-first parallel) had elicited from Adams the substance of the declaration later to be included in Monroe's message of 1823: "that the American continents, by the free and independent condition which they have assumed and maintain, are henceforth not to be considered as subjects for future colonization by any European power." Directed against Great Britain and Russia, the "noncolonization principle" advanced in Monroe's message would be accepted formally by neither power. In conformity with his ideas on noncolonization, Adams also embraced the idea that no European power should gain any spoils from the collapse of the Spanish Empire in the Americas. The prospect that this might occur as a consequence of the intervention of the Holy Alliance in support of Spain had prompted Canning's note to Rush. But Adams smelled a rat: "The object of Canning," he observed in a cabinet meeting of November 7, 1823, "appears to have been to obtain some public pledge from the Government of the United States, ostensibly against the forcible interference of the Holy Alliance between Spain and South America; but really or especially against the acquisition to the United States themselves of any part of the Spanish-American possessions."[16]

John Quincy Adams, unlike Jefferson, did not want to make that pledge. He disclaimed the idea of taking Cuba or Texas by force but insisted that "the inhabitants of either or both may exercise their primitive rights, and solicit a union with us." This was one motive for a unilateral declaration from the American government. Another—shared by President Monroe—was the desire to avoid "the appearance of taking a position subordinate to that of Great Britain." These views prevailed. When President Monroe issued his warning to the Holy Alliance in late 1823—declaring "as dangerous to our peace and safety" any attempt on the part of the European alliance "to extend their system to any portion of this hemisphere"—he did not "come in as a cockboat" trailing meekly behind "the British man-of-war." Monroe had told Madison that he had no doubt "of the alleged project of the allied powers" or that, "if they succeeded with the colonies, they would, in the next instance, invade us." Adams, as historian James Lewis notes, viewed "any movement against Spanish America as unlikely and any attempt to restore Spanish rule as certain to fail." But in the chain of events unleashed by such an expedition, Adams feared the ultimate result would be the recolonization of the new states, "partitioned out among themselves." France would get Mexico and Buenos Aires; Russia would take the Pacific provinces, including California. "In this situation, Great Britain would claim Cuba 'for her share of the scramble.' This fear of a repartition of the New World drove the cabinet to make a stand in support of the new states and in 'opposition against the Holy Alliance.'"[17]

Neither John Quincy Adams, who discounted the likelihood of such an attempt, nor others like Calhoun, who thought it highly probable, failed to see the strategic significance of British naval power. With Britain's cooperation, wrote Madison, "we have nothing to fear from the rest of Europe, and with it the best assurance of success to our laudable views." To Rush, Madison noted, "With the British fleets and fiscal resources associated with our own, we should be safe against the rest of the World, and at liberty to pursue whatever course might be prescribed by a just estimate of our moral and political obligations." That "just estimate," for Madison, was "in the great struggle of the Epoch between liberty and despotism" to act so as "to sustain the former in this hemisphere at least."[18]

The presidential message appeared to do that, and Clay congratulated Adams on its tenor, commenting that the acknowledgment of South American independence had been too long delayed, and that "even a war for it against all Europe, including even England, would be advantageous to us." It was characteristic of the line that Adams followed in the crisis of 1823, with its insistence on the wisdom, for Europe and the United States, of keeping "aloof from the general federative system, of each other," that he took a dim view of such a prospect. Any such war, Adams commented, "might be inevitable, and, under certain circumstances, might be expedient," but because such a war would necessarily place the "high interests of different portions of the Union in conflict with each other," it could not fail to endanger the union itself. Preemption was the farthest thing from his mind; Adams wanted to preserve the peace. If the Holy Alliance was spoiling for a fight with the United States, he wrote, "it should be our policy to meet, and not to make it. . . . We should retreat to the wall before taking up arms, and be sure at every step to put them as much as possible in the wrong."[19]

Despite the unwillingness of the American government to join in a declaration with the British government, Canning's break from the European alliance in 1823 was nevertheless a highly significant development, as was the subsequent recognition by Britain (intimated in 1823) of the South American states as independent nations. That change in policy, Alexander Hill Everett wrote in 1827, "completely established the alienation of Great Britain from the continental alliance, gave that power a distinct and independent position in the world, and confirmed for ever, beyond the possibility of doubt, the emancipation of Spanish America." American diplomatic history had, up until the 1820s, mostly consisted of altercations with the British lion. Hamiltonian Federalists had moved closer to Britain in the late 1790s, but their repudiation in 1800 and even more dramatically in 1815 had made their policy seem a precedent to be avoided rather than imitated. Declamations against the atrocious tyranny that Britain practiced on the high seas had been, for a generation, the stuff of endless congressional orations. All of a sudden, the stars of the two countries seemed in alignment. Commercial and territorial issues continued to divide them, and the American refusal to join in a joint declaration with Britain in 1823 attested to that fact. The memory of their historic antagonism continued, too, to be cherished in many precincts of America and Britain. Still, as the maritime issues that had led to the War of 1812 receded in significance, there being no war to bring them to the surface, a reconciliation of views took place amid the realization that the two countries enjoyed, in certain points, a similarity of interests and an identity of sentiments.[20]

Alexander Hill Everett's book of 1827 is the most thoroughgoing statement of what he called "the new relation of political alliance and amity" that came to exist between Britain and America. Canning boasted of it at a public dinner in Liverpool in 1826, holding that "the mother and daughter . . . were now to stand together and make head against the rest of the Christian world." From "a state of continual and bitter collision," and without "a single moment of real cordiality," Everett concluded, the two countries had been brought "into a situation of virtual alliance and amity, so deeply and broadly founded in the interests of both, and in the established political system of Christendom, that it cannot well fail to supersede all the old motives of contention, and to endure as long, perhaps, as the national existence of either." The reconciliation had occurred "without any sacrifice of pride or principle on either side, without concession and indeed without concert." It had rather "taken place, as it were, against the will of the parties, whose sentiments are even now less friendly than their position, and who seem to glare on each other with eyes of hatred and suspicion, at the very moment when they are exchanging good offices of high importance, and taking the field, in fact, together against a common enemy."[21]

Everett's belief in the reality and permanence of an Anglo-American concert in large part reflected his analysis of the current state and likely future development of the European system. It was the present ascendancy and future expansion of Russia that he saw as the leading feature of that system. The "immense military empire" that had formed there, "resting its rear on the boundless regions of Asia, its right flank on the north pole, and its left on the deserts of Tartary and Turkey," would advance from its "inaccessible and impregnable position . . . to the conquest of the west." Even in the mid-1820s, he thought, Western Europe stood completely crushed "beneath the giant mass of this political Colossus," and he believed that the "natural termination" of this state of affairs would be "the union of the whole continent into one military monarchy." It was this fearful prospect that gave to Anglo-American collaboration and "virtual alliance" a solid foundation in interest and sentiment.[22]

Russia, Great Britain, and the United States, in Everett's estimation, were "now the three prominent and first rate powers of the civilized and christian world. All the rest stand at present, in an order secondary to one or the other of these." They were each "perfect models" of different systems. Russia was a despotic state par excellence; America represented the republican principle in all its purity. England stood, by contrast, in an intermediate position; it was a bundle of contradictions. It had "a king reigning by the grace of God, and parliament claiming and exercising the right of deposing him at pleasure; an established church, with universal liberty of conscience and worship;— equality of rights and hereditary privileges;—boundless prodigality in the public expenses, with a strict accountableness of all the agents." Possessing "a thousand other incongruities of the same description," it might have gone in either direction in the ten years after 1815. That Canning had displaced Castlereagh (whose penknife proved "more potent than his pen") was a momentous occurrence. Everett's witty jibe at Castlereagh's suicide in 1822 was unfair to the departed British foreign minister, for Castlereagh had joined the European alliance with the purpose of controlling his allies, and it is not obvious that his method was inferior to that of his successor. But whatever the cause of this change of policy, which led Canning to boast that he had called the New World into existence to redress the balance of the Old, it was, in Everett's estimation, highly significant and enduring.[23]

Everett's views reversed an important aspect of the traditional American view of the European system, for in the mutual scars and antagonisms of Anglo-American and Anglo-Russian relations there had lain the basis for a ready friendship. From the 1770s to the 1820s, the two great nations on the periphery of the European system had shared common complaints against Britain; Jefferson was more than once fired by the prospect that Alexander would come to his aid in his struggle with British maritime domination, and Adams and Clay continued to think of Russia as a useful check on Britain.

But it was Everett's glimpse of the coming alliance of England and America, cemented by their mutual fear of a Russian bid for universal empire, that saw deepest into the web of time. The pleasing forms of address made by Britain to Europe, and the mutual hatreds that continued to linger in Britain and America should not, Everett thought, obscure the solidity of this new alignment. In the relationship of Britain to Europe "a feeling of deeply seated animosity is veiled by a semblance of apparent good will," while in the relationship between Britain and America "the new sentiment of amity has hardly yet begun to beam out brightly, in the countenance of either party, through the sour and gloomy expression, which had been so long worn by both, that it had become habitual and in some degree natural." These outward expressions were insignificant: "the forms will accommodate themselves to the substance."[24]

It was Everett's firm belief that it had been the separate declarations of Canning and Monroe that had stayed the hand of the Holy Alliance. The belief, even if mistaken, is significant, because it attests to the idea that the Monroe Doctrine was felt to be something more than a vaporous utterance. It is also the case, however, that when Americans thought of the great contest between liberty and despotism then unfolding in the Western world, the battle of opinion was the foremost struggle they had in mind. Webster's oration on the Greek Revolution, in January 1824, reflected this newfound confidence in the opinion of the civilized world. "The time has been," Webster said, "when fleets, and armies, and subsidies, were the principal reliances even in the best cause. But, happily for mankind, a great change has taken place in this respect. Moral causes come into consideration . . . the public opinion of the civilized world is rapidly gaining an ascendancy over mere brutal force. . . . It may be silenced by military power, but it cannot be conquered. It is elastic, irrepressible, and invulnerable to the weapons of ordinary warfare."[25]

Webster's speech on this occasion was informed by the conviction "that a new era has arisen in the world, that new and dangerous combinations are taking place promulgating doctrines and fraught with consequences wholly subversive in their tendency of the public law of nations and of the general liberties of mankind." Webster had great fun with the declarations made at Vienna in 1815 pledging the contracting powers to observe the rules of justice and Christianity, holding up to the light this "solemn stipulation by treaty, to insure the performance of that which is no more than the ordinary duty of every government." Citing Pufendorf, Webster noted that "if one engage to serve another, he does not set it down expressly and particularly among the terms and conditions of the bargain, that he will not betray nor murder him, nor pillage nor burn his house."[26]

Webster's main targets, however, were the "two principles, which the Allied Powers would introduce as a part of the law of the civilized world": first, that "all popular or constitutional rights are held no otherwise than as grants from the crown"—the old doctrine, in other words, of the divine right of kings; and, second, the "still more objectionable principle" avowed by the allied powers of a "right of forcible interference in the affairs of other states." Webster acknowledged that the principle of nonintervention was not absolute: "A right to interfere in extreme cases, in the case of contiguous states, and where imminent danger is threatened to one by what is occurring in another, is not without precedent" in the "law of vicinage"; it might "perhaps be defended upon principles of necessity and self defence." The declaration of the Holy Alliance at Troppau in 1820—"that the powers have an undoubted right to take a hostile attitude in regard to those states in which the overthrow of the government may operate as an example"—went far beyond this narrowly drawn exception to the principle of nonintervention. It "established a sort of double, or treble, or quadruple allegiance. An offence against one king is to be an offence against all kings, and the power of all is to be put forth for the punishment of the offender." But this "asserted right of forcible intervention in the affairs of other nations" could not be admitted; it was "in open violation of the public law of the world." By proposing to divide society "horizontally," by insisting, in short, that there are "no longer to be nations," the Holy Alliance departed from the central principle that had lain at the heart of the law of nations. On the basis of the independence of nations there had been "reared the beautiful fabric of international law. On the principle of this independence, Europe has seen a family of nations flourishing within its limits, the small among the large, protected not always by power, but by a principle above power, by a sense of propriety and justice." There had been "occasional departures" from public law in the course of the eighteenth century, "as in the case of Poland," but on the whole the "harmony of the system" had been "wonderfully preserved." No longer. From a regard to its own interest, as well as from a regard for public law, the United States was duty bound to oppose these dreadful innovations.[27]

The opposition in Congress, led by John Randolph, found in Webster's speech "projects of ambition surpass[ing] those of Bonaparte himself," an invitation to a "crusade" in two hemispheres that would represent "a total and fundamental change of the policy pursued by this Government . . . from the foundation of the Republic to the present day." If such doctrines were to prevail, "every bulwark and barrier of the Constitution is broken down; it is become *tabula rasa*—*a carte blanche*, for every one to scribble on it what he pleases." But these charges were a highly exaggerated version of what

Webster had actually said. Webster was surely right in affirming that it was no offense against anyone to affirm a certain principle of public law; were this the case, the courts of Europe might as well put Vattel, and Pufendorf, and Burlamaqui to the torch, for these eminent expositors of the law of nature and of nations had affirmed the same doctrine as that maintained by Webster. Nor did Webster's sketch of the appropriate policy the United States should maintain in opposition to these doctrines resemble the caricature that Randolph drew of it. "What interest," Webster had asked, "do we have in opposing this system? The thunder, it may be said, rolls at a distance. The wide Atlantic is between us and danger; and, however others may suffer, *we* shall remain safe." His answer was twofold: the United States had an interest in the assertion of those principles on which their own governments were founded, and in addition "we have an interest in the preservation of that system of national law and national intercourse which has heretofore subsisted, so beneficially for all."[28]

In thus appealing to international law, Webster denied that the line of the two hemispheres was the relevant criterion: there was one public law for Europe and America, not two. "We shall not, I trust, act upon the notion of dividing the world with the Holy Alliance, and complain of nothing done by them in their hemisphere if they will not interfere with ours." In considering what the United States should do by way of action, however, he had denied the existence of the crusading impulse that Randolph would detect. "Are we to go to war? Are we to interfere in the Greek cause, or any other European cause? Are we to endanger our pacific relations? No, certainly not." Nor, he insisted, had any such commitment been implied in President Monroe's message of the preceding month, warning against the interposition of the Holy Alliance in the war between Spain and its colonies. The crucial distinction was between principle and policy: "The near approach or the remote distance of danger may affect policy, but it cannot change principle. The same reason which would authorize us to protest against unwarrantable combinations to interfere between Spain and her former colonies, would authorize us equally to protest if the same combination were directed against the smallest state in Europe, although our duty to ourselves, our policy, and wisdom, might indicate very different courses as fit to be pursued by us in the two cases."[29]

Despite Randolph's exaggerations, the Virginian had put his finger on one ambiguity in Webster's approach. Webster, Randolph noted, "would have us to believe his resolution is all but nothing; yet again it is to prove omnipotent, and fills the whole globe with its influence. Either it is nothing, or it is something." If the former, it was a vainglorious waste of time; if the latter, it was dangerous. Randolph's point against Webster applied also to the Monroe Doctrine of the preceding month, which seemed to be a commitment, but which was not really a commitment, to the independence of the South American republics. That it was not really a commitment was affirmed by Secretary of State Adams when he was queried on the point in 1824 by Mexico. Monroe's declaration, as Webster glossed the text in 1826, "did not commit us, at all events, to take up arms on any indication of hostile feeling by the powers of Europe towards South America. If, for example, all the states of Europe had refused to trade with South America until her states should return to their former allegiance, that would have furnished no cause of interference to us. Or if an armament had been furnished by the Allies to act against provinces the most remote from us, as Chili or Buenos Ayres, the distance of the scene of action diminishing our apprehension of danger, and diminishing also our means of effectual interposition, might still have left us to content ourselves with remonstrance. But a very different case would have arisen, if any army, equipped and maintained by these powers, had been landed on the shores of the Gulf of Mexico, and commenced the war in our own immediate neighborhood." Not only was there no actual commitment in the Monroe Doctrine; there was scarcely any power to enforce the commitment had one been made. Everyone understood that the first line of defense against the interposition of the Holy Alliance in South America was British naval power, not orations in Congress.[30]

Nevertheless, the larger claim that Webster had made—the importance and power of public opinion—is not so readily dismissed. Whether it was "elastic, irrepressible, and invulnerable to the weapons of ordinary warfare" might be doubted, but the appeals to public opinion, in both Europe and America, were surely significant. As early as 1816, Jefferson had pointed to the fact that the monarchs of Europe had sometimes felt compelled to cover their despotic power with the forms of constitutions, and that this would matter over time. He was right: it did matter. The very fulminations of absolutist governments against republicanism in the Americas betrayed, it was thought, real anxiety about the pretended durability of their own thrones. Everett judged from public pronouncements that "the cabinets of Europe are not yet satisfied, that the revolution, although it has taken refuge on the other side of the Atlantic, is a whit less dangerous to the old world, than if it had remained there." The mere idea of this, however, was itself a confession of the need for reform: "If such a person as Metternich, for example, a statesman of great experience and talent, really believes, as we have reason to think he does, that the internal peace of the empire of Austria is endangered by the existence of republican governments in the United States, and in South America, it must be because he knows that the government of that empire, (though it could not be probably changed all at once to one of a republican form) would admit of great improvement. Thus the very alarm that is now kept up, by the continental statesmen, respecting the existence of revolution and republicanism abroad, amounts to an indirect satire on their own policy, and a defence of the very proceedings and principles they mean to attack."[31]

IO

To the Panama Congress

AMERICANS HAD NO FIXED VIEW ON HOW this great battle of opinion would turn out. There stood, on the one hand, the immense military power of Russia looming over Western Europe, and the historic experience of endless European war, so fatal in its consequences to the prospects for republican government; on the other side of the equation, however, there stood a set of arguments for constitutional government that might yet prevail over fleets and armies. Jefferson resolved this question differently depending on which side of the big bed in Monticello he got out of in the morning, flitting back and forth from the opinion that Europe was hopeless to the idea that powers and principalities would fall before the republican principle.

A similar contest was seen to be raging in South America; there, too, much uncertainty was thought to attend the outcome. To the Protestants of North America, the priestly fanaticism that had historically exercised so dominant an influence over the "minds and bodies" of the South Americans was a very bad omen. "The people of South America," John Adams insisted in 1815, "are the most ignorant, the most bigoted, the most superstitious of all the Roman Catholics in Christendom. They believe salvation to be confined to themselves and the Spaniards in Europe. They can scarcely allow it to the Pope and his Italians, certainly not to the French; and as to England, English America, and all other Protestant nations, nothing could be expected or hoped for any of them, but a fearful looking for of eternal and unquenchable flames of fire and brimstone. No Catholics on earth were so abjectly devoted to their priests, as blindly superstitious as themselves, and these priests had the powers and apparatus of the Inquisition to seize every suspected person and suppress every rising motion. Was it probable, was it possible," Adams asked, that a plan of "free government, and a confederation of free governments, should be introduced and established among such a people, over that vast continent, or any part of it?"[1]

As this passage suggests, it was religion rather than race that evoked the most serious skepticism among North Americans over the prospects for republican government in South America. The Christian belief in the universal brotherhood of man, fortified by the spirit of the Enlightenment, had yet to give way to the race consciousness that characterized the middle and, even more, the late nineteenth century. Jefferson and Adams both thought religious

94

fanaticism of primary significance, though Jefferson, characteristically, occasionally gave vent to more optimistic projections. Others, like Henry Clay, placed little weight on such historical encumbrances and thought it probable that republican governments would be successfully established in South America; it was enough for him to read the fine state papers produced there and to deduce that they had caught the bug. Apart from religion, race, and "black legends" of wicked Spaniards, however, there was yet another factor thought to be of great importance in determining the fate of republican government in the nations to the south, one of which some leaders in South America were themselves acutely aware: What would be the relationship of the new governments to one another once independence was secured? Would they overcome their differences and form a republican union?

The federal problem presented itself in Latin America as a series of contrasting dreams, all of them mutually related to the others, none of them to be realized in the immediate future. The desirability of unity, as a means of both securing independence and avoiding, as in North America, a replication of the European experience, enjoyed wide appeal in theory. "If Spain," wrote a confidant of Simón Bolívar in 1814, "was able, from a distance of two thousand leagues, and with no large forces, to subject America, from New Mexico to the Straits of Magellan, to its harsh despotism, why cannot a lasting union be effected between New Granada and Venezuela? And further, why should not all South America be united under a single, central government?" The lessons of the European experience spoke as eloquently to many South Americans as to the peoples of the North: "The spectacle of Europe, bathed in blood, in an effort to restore an equilibrium that is continually being unbalanced, should be sufficient to bring about a change in our political life, if it is to be saved from those bloody perils. If our continent, like that of Europe, were to divide into nations, if the American government were to be guided by the principles which generally govern the European ministries, we also would experience upsets of continental equilibrium and would spill the blood which Europe sacrifices at the foot of her political idol."[2]

The ideal of unity, however, raised a whole series of questions: How many successor states would emerge from the ruins of the Spanish Empire? Would they follow the geographic lines of the four great viceroyalties that had existed under the Spanish dominion: New Spain, New Granada, Rio De La Plata, and Peru? Or would these great geographic constructions themselves splinter into pieces? Could the provinces of the Rio de la Plata—embracing what is now Argentina, Paraguay, and Uruguay—form a single state or federation? Would what is now Chile, Peru, and Bolivia, governed by Spain as the Vice-Royalty of Peru, join together or split apart? Would the federal ideas recognized in the Mexican Constitution of 1824 succeed in establishing that

equipoise between centralizing and decentralizing tendencies established, so
far successfully, by the U.S. Constitution? Would Venezuela and Colombia,
sundered by the experience of war, reunite under the leadership of Bolívar
and form the base of a state that might embrace Ecuador, Peru, and Bolivia,
a model and a leader for the larger project of Latin American union?

In answering these questions, amid the circumstances of sanguinary wars,
South Americans gave voice to a political rhetoric remarkably similar to that
which had unfolded in North America. There were manifold variations on
the federal idea in Latin America in this fermentative period, each mutually
related to the others, with no fixed conception of the boundaries of the states
that might come to exist, and within which, and among which, variations
of the federal idea were considered. The idiom in which South Americans
considered these issues was very similar to that which had unfolded in North
America, even in the midst of circumstances that were vastly different. Anarchy and despotism formed the rival specters, decentralization and centralization the rival solutions; the fear of foreign intervention lay in close
embrace with the danger of internal discord. That unity might give weight
and importance to Latin America was a fond hope; that discord would bring
wars and calamities rivaling, if not surpassing, those of Europe was the dark
specter that could not be banished.

Many believed that the federal union established in North America was a
model to be imitated. Venezuelans gave the sincerest form of flattery to the
federal republic of North America when they adopted a constitution similar
in crucial respects to that made at Philadelphia in 1787. But there were skep-
tics, Bolívar among them. Though an apostle of South American unity, he
distrusted North American federalism as a model for the southern republics.
It was a "marvel," he thought in 1819, that federal union in North America
"endures so successfully and has not been overthrown at the first sign of ad-
versity or danger . . . a marvel, I repeat, that so weak and complicated a government as the federal system has managed to govern them in the difficult
and trying circumstances of their past." Whatever its successes there, to apply it to Venezuela, as the makers of its "magnificent federative system" had
done, was to reason incorrectly about the making of constitutions. "Does
not [Montesquieu's] *L'Esprit des lois* state the laws should be suited to the
people for whom they are made . . . ?" It would, he thought, be a "major
coincidence" were the laws of one nation—so different in climate, size, land,
religion, and mode of living—found readily adaptable to those of another.
Like the North Americans, he sought a constitutional balance between "anarchy" and "despotism," but in drawing that line was far more Hamiltonian
than Jeffersonian in emphasis. He thought that the makers of Venezuela's
constitution had "responded more to the spirit of the provinces than to the

sound idea of creating an indivisible and centralized republic," yielding to "the ill-considered pleadings of those men from the provinces who were captivated by the apparent brilliance of the happiness of the North American people," a happiness he attributed as much to "the character and customs of their citizens" as to their form of government. These remarks were made in 1819; a decade later he would write that the federal form of government was nothing better than an "organized anarchy," one that "implicitly prescribes the obligation of dissolution and the eventual ruin of the state with all its members. I think it would be better for South America to adopt the Koran rather than the United States' form of government, although the latter is the best on earth." Like Hamilton, Bolívar deeply feared the centrifugal tendencies embedded in the circumstances he confronted—fears that, as experience would show, were quite well founded.[3]

The climax of Bolívar's plans for political union in South America came in 1826. This involved two rival visions: one for a confederation or "amphyctonic council" of the American states, meeting in Congress at Panama in 1826; another for a Confederation of the Andes, which he projected as a powerful centralized state that would embrace what is now Venezuela, Colombia, Ecuador, Peru, and Bolivia. The forlorn quest for the former, which Bolívar likened to "that mad Greek who from his rock tried to direct the course of ships sailing by," produced, by default, his vision for the latter. It, too, would fail. Bolívar's subsequent desire to use force to prevent the secession of Venezuela from Gran Colombia failed to command widespread assent, badly tarnished his fame abroad, and reduced him to isolation. He died amid the wreckage of his dreams, the fact of discord and the reality of civil war triumphing over his "sublime" hope that the "union of the five great states of America" would make of "this part of the world a nation of republics," a "colossus which, like Homer's Jupiter, will cause the earth to quake." His dark prophecies had all come true: "I see," he had written in 1825, "civil war and disorder breaking out in all directions and spreading from country to country. I see my native gods consumed by domestic fire." "There is no faith in America," he wrote in 1829, shortly before his death by tuberculosis. "Treaties are pieces of paper; constitutions, books; elections, combats; liberty, anarchy; and life, a torment."[4]

Bolívar opposed the participation of the United States in the Panama Congress. Great Britain, he thought, was of far greater utility to his cause, and he assumed that the participation of the North Americans might offend the British. But other counsels prevailed, and the United States received invitations from Colombia, Mexico, and the United Provinces of Central America. The two delegates sent by the United States never reached the congress: one died en route, and the other learned before his departure that the congress had adjourned to meet again at Tacubaya, Mexico (which rendezvous also failed). But there was much that came of the episode. The decision of President Adams to send delegates provoked a storm of controversy in Congress, and the voluminous debates that arose there over the mission provided a clear signal of the evolution of American thinking. The division in Congress was largely sectional: the South was hostile to the mission partly because it might give recognition to the Republic of Haiti, and partly because the South American republics were, as primary producers, their competitors in certain articles. The Northeast, seeing the possibility of advantageous commercial contacts and markets for its manufactures, was, by contrast, hospitable to the mission.[5]

The advocates of the Panama mission were more than a little astonished at the vehemence of the opposition it aroused. President Adams had specifically disclaimed the idea of entering into any kind of alliance with the South American republics: "All notion is rejected," wrote Secretary Clay in his letter of instruction, "of an Amphyctionic Council, invested with power finally, to decide controversies between the American States, or to regulate, in any respect, their conduct." Adams and Clay aimed, rather, for a concert of views, particularly on the three issues—maritime rights, commercial policy, and noncolonization—where the attitude of the American government was certain to be in opposition to that maintained by Great Britain. An important object of the mission was to counter the prospect of an invasion of Cuba and "Porto Rico" by "the united forces of Mexico." That invasion, Adams noted, was "avowedly among the objects to be matured by the belligerent States at Panama," but it raised questions of the deepest import. "The convulsions to which, from the peculiar composition of their population, they would be liable in the event of such an invasion, and the danger therefrom resulting of their falling ultimately into the hands of some European power other than Spain," made it imperative to devote "all our efforts . . . to preserve the existing state of things."[6]

These cautious declarations seemed not to matter in the ensuing political whirlwind in 1826. The congressional uproar left foreign observers mystified, unable "to reconcile the supposed anxiety of the United States to form a general Federation of America, with themselves at the head of it, with the backwardness and the opposition which has been manifested by both Houses of Congress" toward the Panama mission.[7] The knowledge that Panama would be the scene of a more ambitious attempt of a union of the Latin American republics, together with an incautious remark of Joel Poinsett, minister to Mexico, adverting to the willingness of the United States to place itself at the head of a hemispheric federation, provided ammunition to the opposition. There was something faintly ridiculous in all of this. In

1826, almost no North American thought to join the northern and southern hemispheres in a union like that made in the Articles of Confederation in 1777.[8] Poinsett's remark had been put forward to the Mexican government as a way of wringing concessions out of them. Supporters of the mission in Congress, and Secretary of State Clay, had repudiated it. Despite these careful discriminations and disavowals, the opposition charged that the mission and the ideas underlying it represented a perilous departure from the counsel of President Washington against entangling alliances.

The congress in Panama, charged Senator Robert Hayne of South Carolina, was to convene together the "confederated belligerent states, . . . for the great purpose of bringing the war, by their combined efforts, to a speedy and successful termination, and, at the same time, of establishing a plan of general cooperation, in all cases whatsoever." Joining in such a congress "unquestionably must be a total departure from our neutrality." As proof that Adams's administration contemplated this novel project, Hayne adverted to the letter that Poinsett had sent Clay on September 29, 1825, in which he had appealed to the "fraternal ties" that existed between the United States and the Republic of Mexico.

> To some objections urged against our claims on the ground that we had not yet taken part in the war, our Minister replied in the following words, viz.: . . . "that, against the power of Spain, they had given sufficient proof that they required no assistance, and the United States had *pledged themselves not to permit any other power to interfere* either with their independence or form of Government; and that, as in the event of such an attempt being made by the powers of Europe, we would be compelled to take the most active and efficient part, and to *bear the brunt of the contest*, it was not just that we should be placed on a less favorable footing than the other Republics of America, whose existence we were *ready to support at such hazards*." The Minister then goes on to state, that, after explaining what we had already done, he declared "what further we were ready to do, in order to defend their rights and liberties; but that this could only be expected from us, and could only be accomplished by a strict union of all the American Republics, on terms of perfect equality and reciprocity; and repeated, that, it was the obvious policy of Europe to divide us into small Confederacies, with separate and distinct interests, and as manifestly ours to form *A Single Great Confederacy*, which might oppose one united front to the attacks of our enemies."

Hayne went on to score the administration on the following grounds: that Monroe's message of 1823 did not imply a positive commitment to take up arms on behalf of South American independence; that, had it done so, the president acted without authority, since that prerogative belonged to the Congress; that a forcible interposition by the United States against the right of Britain or Russia to plant settlements in North America was either dishonorable or dangerous, but in any case unwise; and that the implied recognition of Haiti would constitute a flagitious case of interference in the domestic affairs of the South.[9]

Hayne's warnings about slavery had been thrown out with abandon during the Missouri crisis and were a foretaste of things to come. "The question of slavery," he said, "is one, in all its bearings, of extreme delicacy, and concerning which, I know of but a single wise and safe rule, either for the States in which it exists, or for the Union. It must be considered and treated entirely as a *Domestic Question*. With respect to foreign nations, the language of the United States ought to be, that it concerns the peace of our own political family, and therefore we cannot permit it to be touched; and in respect to the slaveholding States, the only safe and constitutional ground on which they can stand, is, that they will not permit it to be brought into question, either by their sister states, or by the Federal Government." Were the North to proceed on a different ground, it would blow up the American union. "To call into question our rights, is grossly to violate them—to attempt to instruct us on this subject, is to insult us—to dare to assail our institutions, is wantonly to invade our peace." On the day such intervention occurred, "we will consider ourselves as driven from the Union."[10]

The two different claims asserted here would be repeatedly affirmed over the coming decades. The right of the South to exercise an absolute veto over anything in foreign relations that touched on slavery—a doctrine spectacularly reaffirmed by Calhoun in 1844 when he was secretary of state—together with the assertion that any challenge to or even discussion of slavery would constitute an atrocious invasion of southern rights and instantly produce a dissolution of the union, were claims that thereafter enjoyed endless reiteration. What Everett had said about the sensitivities of the Holy Alliance respecting republicanism was true of the sensitivities of the South respecting slavery. The very alarm that southerners kept up regarding a supposed willingness of the federal government or their sister states to attack the institution was an acknowledgment that something was deeply wrong—it was "an indirect satire on their own policy, and a defence of the very proceedings and principles they mean to attack."[11]

There was one incongruity in the approach of Adams's administration that the opposition took particular pleasure in exploiting. That the president and his secretary of state were now joined together in promoting these wild schemes for cooperation in the Americas was decisive proof that a corrupt bargain had been made in the election of 1824, when Adams had asked Clay to be his secretary of state after Clay had swung the vote in the House of Representatives in Adams's favor. To suspicious minds, the denial by both Adams and Clay that there had been any prearrangement had appeared ludicrous from the first moment. Both were statesmen of great ability and were accustomed to peer far into the future: had they not, in 1824, foreseen the next two months? Before this pleasing bargain, if bargain it was, the issue on which Clay and Adams had most prominently locked horns was over the idea of forming a counterpoise to the Holy Alliance in the Americas. Yet here they were, operating in concert. This raised the possibility that one or the other was an apostate or an imposter, and John Randolph gave a delirious speech in 1826 that threw out random imputations on these and other scores—a speech which showed that long residence in Congress was not incompatible with progressive movement toward insanity. Generally, however, the opposition took the view that the administration was acting on Clay's ideas of 1821.

"The great object" that seemed "to lie so near to the hearts of some of our statesmen," Hayne said, lay in the construction of "what they are pleased to call 'An American System'—terms which, when applied to our domestic policy, mean *restriction* and *monopoly*, and when applied to our foreign policy, mean 'entangling alliances,' both of them the fruit of that prurient spirit which will not suffer the nation to advance gradually in the development of its great resources, and the fulfillment of its high destinies, but would accelerate its march by the most unnatural and destructive stimulants." To act on this basis, Hayne claimed, was to imitate the Holy Alliance, an utterly discreditable procedure. "This combination of nations at peace, to maintain certain principles and institutions, contains the most atrocious violation of the natural and social rights of man that the world has ever seen. It is wrong—most fatally wrong—and it makes no difference, in reason or justice, what the principles to be maintained are. It is of the essence of national independence, that every country should be left free to adopt and to change its principles and its policy according to its own views of its own interests; and from the very bottom of my soul I abhor the idea of combinations among sovereign States, for any purpose whatever." If it is realized that this was said by an advocate of the "State rights" school, who looked upon America's federal union as nothing other than a combination among sovereign states, it might be deduced that the orator had gotten a little ahead of himself. Other opponents of the Panama mission, like James Buchanan of Pennsylvania and Thomas Hart Benton of Missouri, did not advance as far as Hayne, a forefather of the fire-eaters, but they too were utterly opposed to any such concert with the South American republics and joining either in the deliberations of the Convention or in "the proposed Federative system." They expressed, on this score, the convictions of the Democracy that would soon come to power with the election of Andrew Jackson in 1828. "The maxims of prudence are the same among individuals and nations," held Senator Benton. "Neither can become too intimate with the other, without danger of breaking up all friendship between them. The sweetest wine makes the sourest vinegar; the best of friends become the worst of enemies! No feuds so bitter as those of families; no cause of quarrelling so common as intimacy overmuch! No peacemaker half so powerful as distance, independence, and complete separation of interests!"[12]

Webster's reply to opposition charges was masterly, certainly the equal of his oration on the Greek Revolution. Webster readily demonstrated that opponents of the mission were guilty of primitive misunderstandings in conflating a confederation and a diplomatic assembly. The whole argument of the opposition rested on one great proposition: "That because, at the same time and place, the agents of the South American governments may negotiate about their own relations with each other, in regard to their common war against Spain, therefore we cannot, at the same time and place, negotiate with them, or any of them, upon our own neutral and commercial relations. This proposition, Sir, cannot be maintained; and therefore all the inferences from it fail." But what gave the speech its memorable character was the contrast Webster drew between America and Europe. He quoted with approval the statement of "the intelligent and distinguished statesman who conducts the foreign relations of England [Mr. Canning], that when we now speak of Europe and the world, we mean Europe and America; and that the different systems of these two portions of the globe, and their several and various interests, must be thoroughly studied and nicely balanced by the statesmen of the times." They were part of the same civilization, alike in being "Christian states, civilized states, and commercial states," drawing on the same "fountains of intelligence."[13]

In matters of government and social institutions, however, they were essentially different. There had never, Webster thought, "been presented to the mind of man a more interesting subject of contemplation than the establishment of so many nations in America, partaking in the civilization and in the arts of the Old World, but having left behind them those cumbrous institutions which had their origin in a dark and military age." The new career that "America, the whole of America," had opening before her consisted in this happy combination between "whatever European experience has developed favorable to the freedom and the happiness of man, whatever European genius has invented for his improvement or gratification," and the "full power of erecting forms of government on free and simple principles, without overturning institutions suited to times long passed, but too strongly supported, either by interests or prejudices, to be shaken without convulsions." This combination constituted a splendid opportunity "to establish national intercourse upon . . . principles tending to peace and the mutual prosperity of nations." The whole significance of the Latin American revolutions, as of America's own federal union, might be seen in that "unprecedented" state of things. "If we look back on the history of Europe, we see for how great a portion of the last two centuries her states have been at war for interests connected mainly with her feudal monarchies. Wars for particular dynasties, wars to support or prevent particular successions, wars to enlarge or curtail the dominions of particular crowns, wars to support or to dissolve family alliances, wars to enforce or to resist religious intolerance,—what long and bloody chapters do not these fill in the history of European politics!" In the Western Hemisphere, by contrast, there lay "the noble hope of being able, by the mere influence of civil liberty and religious toleration, to dry up these outpouring fountains of blood, and to extinguish these consuming fires of war." [14]

I I

Into the Deep Freeze

IN THE COURSE OF THE LAST THREE CHAPTERS, we have been examining a variety of "federative systems" that arose in the decade after 1815 throughout the Western world. In Europe and the Americas, projections of such systems were all the rage: the European concert, the American federal union, plans of union within and among the successor states to the Spanish Empire, the emergence of a dividing line between the two hemispheres that put these federative systems in opposition—all this attested to a common movement of opinion within Western civilization. The decade from 1815 to 1825 announces themes that in both hemispheres would be of great importance in the future. Much of the American debate over foreign policy in the twentieth century is prefigured in this decade: whether the United States should be a crusader or exemplar for freedom, whether the world might change as a consequence of the mild influence of opinion or would obey, as ever, the dictates of force; whether nations could join together in cooperative ventures that fell short of the tight bonds of a federation, yet were in advance of the hostility that normally prevailed; whether circumstances now pointed to a "virtual alliance" between Great Britain and the United States, the fair mother and the fairer daughter reconciling in order to promote common purposes and to resist a Russian bid for universal empire; whether in the Western Hemisphere a natural affinity existed between the northern and southern parts, bound together by common political institutions, a common geographic position, and common ideals—all these questions were greatly agitated in the decade that opened with the ending of the Napoleonic Wars; all would be important in the twentieth century.

The irony is this: by 1830, nearly everything that had seemed significant in the decade from 1815 to 1825 had gone, or was going, into deep hibernation. Every federative system and "virtual alliance" that had earlier been projected looked very different by 1830. Despite the enthusiasm with which many North Americans had hailed the independence of the states of South America in the early 1820s, by 1830 there had emerged a profound disillusionment over their course. For the friends of Bolívar in America, like Henry Clay, the events of the late 1820s were mortifying. Clay himself had anointed Bolívar as "the Washington of South America" on January 1, 1825, but had finally become convinced that "he has conceived and actually commenced the execution of a vast project of ambition, which involved the overthrow of the liberties of South America. That project was no less than the ultimate establishment of an Empire which should stretch from the Isthmus of Darien to Cape Horn." That Bolívar was said to have taken Bonaparte for his model was barely comprehensible: "Was ever man guilty of greater folly? What glory awaited him, if he had been true to Liberty and to his Country!"[1]

A few years later, in 1830, Francis Baylies, American chargé d'affaires in Buenos Aires, ridiculed the idea that the United States had anything in common with the sister republics to the South. Describing the summary executions and deportations he had witnessed there, he concluded, "Such, Sir, is the happy condition of society in this Sister Republic of ours, whose free and liberal principles and hatred of despotism have so often been themes for the panegyrics of our mistaken, romantic, and imaginative politicians. I think one week's residence here would cure them of this hallucination."[2] North Americans had only to consult their own experience to see the basic cause of all of this. "What is now the condition of South America, in whose emancipation we felt so deep an interest, and where we hoped to find the cause of free Government strengthened against the alliances of its enemies?" asked Henry Storrs of New York in 1830. "Disunion has blasted our hopes. Slavish Congresses have there betrayed their country, and the power of that whole continent is swayed by bands of reckless despots." Tocqueville, who visited America shortly after Storrs made this declaration, commented in *Democracy in America*, "It is generally believed in America that the existence and the permanence of the republican form of government in the New World depend upon the existence and the duration of the Federal system; and it is not unusual to attribute a large share of the misfortunes which have befallen the new States of South America to the injudicious erection of great republics, instead of a divided and confederate sovereignty."[3]

The same disappearing act occurred in relation to the intimations of "virtual alliance" between Great Britain and the United States that Alexander Hill Everett had detected in the 1820s. This, too, went into the historical deep freeze. Though the idea of an Anglo-American concert in opposition to Russia regained some prominence after Russia's crushing of Hungarian independence in 1849, the general tenor of Anglo-American relations did not for a long time resume the cordiality glimpsed in the 1820s. In the two decades that followed the Monroe Doctrine, there was hardly any trouble at all between the United States and the Continental monarchies of Europe. The United States ran the greatest danger of war in those decades with Great Britain and France, the two European states with which there existed the greatest degree of concordance in political belief and institutions. With

France the Jackson administration drew close to war in the 1830s, and with Britain there was a war scare in 1837.

Thereafter, Anglo-American relations settled further back into their previous condition of mutual hostility and loathing. A war between the two powers often seemed likely in the 1840s, and there was significance in the fact that the successful negotiation and ratification of the Webster-Ashburton Treaty of 1842 needed the aid of secret service money. Had the issues settled by the treaty been still extant when the conflict over Oregon arose in the mid-1840s, and had the hawkish Palmerston remained in office, a war between the two powers would have edged from distinct possibility to probable outcome. With those "troublesome neighbors," as Lord Ashburton (Alexander Baring) observed, "nothing was more easy than to get into war." Ashburton thought that Britain would fare badly in such a contest—"our weavers and spinners will bring upon us the most humiliating disgrace after the first six months of any conflict"—and hence thought it best that when "the wild beast" approached "you walk if you can on the other side of the way." The American union, besides, "is always in danger and the danger will increase as ambition swells the Leviathan's back. Texas and Canada added, and a split will be inevitable."[4]

In Europe, too, the federative system that the peacemakers at Vienna had projected in 1815 looked very different in scope and purpose by 1830, when France took on a government and outlook more in keeping with Great Britain than its putative Continental allies. The concert among Russia, Austria-Hungary, and Prussia continued to flourish. The sense that these monarchs were arrayed together against their own societies provided a crucial basis of their solidarity. A concert confined to the three great Continental thrones, however, had a different meaning from that which had been projected at Vienna, for the earlier system had brought together the two great flanking powers—Britain and Russia—in apparent harmony and concordance, their antagonism mediated by the creative statesmanship of Metternich. This had made for a concert that squinted at universality, which the holy league uniting the Continental monarchs could scarcely pretend to do.

What lay at the core of the Vienna system was the deliberate abandonment by all the powers of the aim of mastery over Europe. "If," as F. H. Hinsley put it, "no Power now sought the mastery of Europe; if all accepted instead a common responsibility for maintaining the territorial *status quo* of the treaties of 1815 and for solving the international problems of Europe; if, when the *status quo* had to be changed or a problem had to be solved, they proceeded on the principles that treaties should not be set aside by unilateral action and that gains should not be made without common consent—and these were the essential restraints of the Concert of Europe—this was in the last resort because the aim of mastery was deliberately abandoned, these restraints deliberately accepted, within a framework of thought and experience which limited ambitions to the effort to make London or Vienna, St. Petersburg or Paris, the diplomatic centre of the Concert."[5] But if the deliberate abandonment of mastery was characteristic of the Vienna system from 1815 to 1848, and not even seriously challenged in the subsequent years of war and upheaval, the same abandonment is not so apparent in the case of the United States. During the same period, on the contrary, America's "Philadelphian system" would be torn apart by a struggle among the sections for mastery within the union. From the 1820s until 1861, the political trajectory of federal union in North America more closely resembles Europe's explosive and fearful epoch of 1871–1914 than the relatively tranquil era of 1815–1848. In both we discern the same restless and rapid change in the bases of power, the same breaches of faith, the same fears of domination, the same collapse in hegemonic war.[6]

PART FOUR
The Travails of the Union

12

Great and Fearfully Growing

IN THE PERIOD FROM THE CLOSE OF THE WAR OF 1812 to the Mexican War there occurred a dramatic change in conceptions of distance. The inauguration of the steamboat, the railroad, and the telegraph had an effect on imaginings of distance comparable to that which the radio, the airplane, and the ballistic missile had in the early to mid-twentieth century. Edmund Burke observed in 1775 that one of the difficulties of governing America was that "waves toss, and seas roll" between the order and the execution; this meant that imperial control over the colonies had to be exercised in a mild fashion, leaving much to colonial autonomy and self-government. The distances projected in the mind of Burke in 1775 were the same as those projected in the mind of Fisher Ames when, after the Louisiana Purchase added "an unmeasured world" beyond the Mississippi, he saw America rushing "like a comet into infinite space."[1] A lapse of three decades, from 1775 to 1805, made no difference: this was still an age of sail, still an epoch of wood-wheeled wagon and hoofed animal over primitive roads and bridgeless streams. These conceptions of distance were somewhat altered by the experience of the Napoleonic Wars: there was something in the scale of Bonaparte's ambition that suggested closeness and proximity even over vast distances. Still, the near-comic way in which the War of 1812 began—with the congressional declaration of war following by two days the relaxation of the British orders in council that provoked the declaration, the news of which had yet to reach America—suggests the eighteenth-century conception of distance; so, too, does the way the war ended. The most important battle of that war—Jackson's victory over the British at New Orleans in early 1815—occurred more than two weeks after the signing of the peace treaty.

By the 1820s, conceptions of distance were shortening. *Niles' Register* could speak of distance as being "annihilated by science and the spirit of adventure," but this, as yet, was prophecy and not fact. It was only with the commercial development of steam—allowing boats to chug upriver, and railroads to defy natural obstacles—that the compression of distance began impressing itself on the political imagination. These two developments, in turn, were capped by the introduction of the telegraph in the 1840s. That a surge of opinion on behalf of "Manifest Destiny" should arise concomitantly with these developments was not, it would seem, entirely accidental.

Distance was being radically and palpably shortened. "The day cannot be far distant," wrote the *Democratic Review* in 1845, "which shall witness the conveyance of the representatives from Oregon and California to Washington within less time than a few years ago was devoted to a similar journey by those from Ohio." The telegraph would enable Pacific coast newspapers "to set up in type the first half of the President's Inaugural, before the echoes of the latter shall have died away beneath the lofty porch of the Capitol, as spoken from his lips." Such developments, the *Review* argued, would facilitate intercourse among the sections of the union, binding them "more closely to the other, beyond the power of an increased population or sectional difficulties to disunite."[2]

Speculation about the effect that lateral expansion would have on the endurance of the union had been coeval with its birth, and was a subject of often intense inquiry. The question had been given much consideration in the eighteenth century, with the weight of enlightened opinion holding that sovereignty over imperial distances would either cause the development of opposing forces tending toward dissolution or conspire to produce tyrannical and arbitrary government. These two opinions, in turn, were closely related, for the likelihood that force rather than opinion would be the mainstay of government was all the greater because these centrifugal tendencies existed. So, too, the question had been central to the argument over the federal Constitution, with the Anti-Federalists clasping tightly Montesquieu's argument that republics were threatened by large size, that the greater they became, the more they risked internal deformation. The momentous technological revolution, collapsing distance, that occurred in these decades put this old problem in an entirely new light and contributed to much earnest speculation over the relationship between "widening" and "deepening."[3]

Contrary to the old opinion that republics had to exist on a small scale, the practicable sphere of a republic had been extended with the federal Constitution. While it was still in 1820 "the opinion of all, and the hope of many" Europeans that the great extent of America, "when it came to be thickly peopled," would lead to its separation, many Americans saw in increased size a potent contributor to political stability. James Monroe, in a message of May 7, 1822, expressed confidence that the "extension of our Union over a vast territory cannot operate unfavorably to the States individually. On the contrary, . . . the greater the expansion, . . . the greater advantage which the States individually will derive from it." In Monroe's view, expansion, "provided it be not beyond the just limit," would be advantageous to each level of government and would redound to the security of the whole American people. "Extent of territory, whether it be great or small, gives to a nation many of its characteristics. It marks the extent of its resources, of its population, of its physical force. It marks, in short, the difference between a great and a small power." Monroe did not say where the "just" or "practical" limit lay, but he did acknowledge it existed somewhere—that expansion might, if pressed too far, become a centrifugal rather than centripetal force. "It is only when the expansion shall be carried beyond the faculties of the General Government, so as to enfeeble its operations, to the injury of the whole, that any of the parts can be injured. The tendency, in that stage, will be to dismemberment, and not to consolidation. This danger should, therefore, be looked at with profound attention, as one of a very serious character."[4]

Another set of reasons for seeing the incorporation of additional states into the original union as a centripetal rather than centrifugal force was given by Francis Baylies on the occasion of a bill providing for the occupation of the Columbia River. Baylies, who spoke for the Massachusetts whaling interest, considered the objection that by adopting such a measure "the limits of our empire would be extended too far, and that the Union itself would be exposed to the danger of dismemberment." To the contrary, Baylies insisted: "The unity of this nation depends in some measure upon its extension. . . . If there were only two interests in the country—a Northern interest and a Southern interest—a slaveholding and a non-slaveholding interest—the hazard of separation would be greatly increased. But, by multiplying and extending the States of the Union, you will create so many different interests that they will neutralize each other. On some questions the interest of the Eastern and Southern States might be found to be the same; others the Eastern and Western; others the Middle States and the Southern, Eastern, and Western, and so on; and so conflicting interests which might arise from time to time (so great at times as to threaten dismemberment) be rendered less dangerous, and the angry passions of the few be controlled by the sober feelings of the majority." Baylies's theorem showed the continuing appeal of the hypothesis Madison had advanced in the Tenth *Federalist*. Though Madison had not in 1788 cast his argument for the extended republic in explicitly sectional terms, as Baylies did, Madison was thinking along the same lines in 1820. The tariff, he then observed, divided the nation "in so checkered a manner, that its issue cannot be very serious." The greater the variety of interests, the less likely it was that political alignments would pivot on a geographic line; such a state of parties, Madison had long believed, posed the gravest threat to the union.[5]

Despite the various paeans to expansion, there had always been plenty of observers who thought, with John Randolph and the New England schismatics, that expansion would give a boost to centrifugal forces. A balanced analysis, indeed, could hardly escape the conclusion that expansion seemed, somewhat mysteriously, to have both centripetal and centrifugal effects. John Calhoun had suggested as much in an 1817 speech on internal improvements. Exhorting his fellow congressmen to "conquer space," Calhoun was recorded as saying that "no country, enjoying freedom, ever occupied any thing like as great an extent of country as this Republic. One hundred years ago, the most profound philosophers did not believe it to be possible. . . . What was then considered as chimerical, said Mr. C., we now have the felicity to enjoy," yet he noted that large extent nevertheless "exposes us to the greatest of all calamities, next to the loss of liberty, and even to that in its consequence—disunion. We are great, and rapidly, he was about to say fearfully, growing. This, said he, is our pride and danger—our weakness and our strength."[6]

Given the importance of this factor in the political speculation of the age, it is surprising how little it figures in historical reconstructions. The dominant understanding more closely resembles the image of national expansion once famously evoked by Edmund Wilson: "In a recent *Walt Disney* film showing life at the bottom of the sea, a primitive organism called a sea slug is seen gobbling up smaller organisms through a large orifice at one end of its body; confronted with another sea slug of an only slightly lesser size, it ingurgitates that, too. Now, the wars fought by human beings are stimulated as a rule primarily by the same instincts as the voracity of the sea slug." Wilson was thinking of the Civil War, but his statement is probably not a bad summary of the outlook of the American historical profession today with respect to the process of white expansion. Contemporary historians, conscious of the humanity and just claims of the Indian peoples who were run over, expropriated, or ingurgitated in the process, have insisted that it was by no means an "empty continent," in the once common expression, over which the United States expanded in the first half of the nineteenth century.[7]

Other voices praise the successful realpolitik of American leaders and see nineteenth-century expansion not as "a matter of regret, but of pride." American expansion, on this view, "did not take place in a fit of absentmindedness but rather as a result of a sustained, relentlessly expansionist foreign policy that used all means necessary—diplomacy, money, and war—to achieve its goals." Whether viewed with guilt or pride, however, the dominant mental picture is the same: it is of a nation, awash with ideas of Manifest Destiny, advancing headlong to the Pacific. What is required, writes historian Walter McDougall, "is not a long explanation of U.S. expansion, but rather a short explanation of why U.S. expansion needs no explanation."[8]

This consensus view invites serious distortion in several particulars. It vastly understates, for one thing, the sheer contingency of the process. Though demographic growth and technological advance undoubtedly ensured that the west coast of North America would get settled—and sooner rather than later—there was great doubt that the republics to be established there could, because of the vast distances involved, be part of a common government. From our vantage point, Jefferson's sponsorship of Lewis and Clark's trek to the Pacific is the first step to a foreordained expansion, but Jefferson thought that the "free and independent Americans" who settled beyond the stony mountains would be "unconnected with us but by the ties of blood and interest." Jefferson is often quoted as predicting that North and South America would one day be populated from the "nest" on the Atlantic coast, but he also spoke in his first inaugural address, when American territory reached to the Mississippi, of "a rising nation" that possessed "a chosen country, with room enough for our descendants to the thousandth and thousandth generation." Thomas Hart Benton, who looked to Oregon as the gateway to Asia and thought a new republic would be formed there, also believed in 1825 that "the Western limit of this republic" should be drawn on the back ridge of the Rocky Mountains and that "the statue of the fabled god, Terminus, should be raised upon its highest peak, never to be thrown down." In 1830, Benton scoffed at the idea that goods from the western country would be sent by railroad across the Appalachians rather than down the Mississippi River, a conception of the material possibilities that also prohibited expansion to the Pacific Ocean and that made the East an appendage of the West and South. If it is remembered that what is now considered inevitable was once widely considered as undesirable or improbable, we shall have a better sense of the debates that unfolded over expansion in the era that followed the War of 1812. When territorial expansion came in leaps and bounds, as it did in the mid-1840s, it was because an unusual concatenation of factors overwhelmed the restraints, largely sectional and constitutional in character, that made for territorial stasis.[9]

A second objection to the grand narrative of "nationalistic expansionism" is that it obscures the dynamics of the process, which were strongly rooted in sectional impulses. Although expansion was always justified by virtue of the benefits it would bring the whole union and the entire nation, these justifications were invariably advanced amid the profound suspicion, repeatedly voiced on the floors of Congress by the opponents of such measures, that much narrower and selfish purposes underlay the projects they condemned. In the midst of the War of the Rebellion, Horace Greeley gave classic expression to this sectional emphasis when he argued, against those who wondered why the North would not let slavery alone, that

Slavery never left the North alone, nor thought of so doing. "Buy Louisiana for us!" said the slaveholders. "With pleasure." "Now Florida!"

"Certainly." Next: "Violate your treaties with the Creeks and Cherokees; expel those tribes from the lands they have held from time immemorial, so as to let us expand our plantations." "So said, so done."
"Now for Texas!" "You have it." "Next, a third more of Mexico!"
"Yours it is." "Now, break the Missouri Compact, and let Slavery wres-
tle with Free Labor for the vast region consecrated by that Compact to
Freedom!" "Very good, what next?" "Buy us Cuba, for One Hundred
and Fifty Millions." "We have tried; but Spain refuses to sell it." "Then
wrest it from her at all hazards!"

All this while, Greeley argued, slavery had used "the Union as her
catspaw," had dragged "the Republic into iniquitous wars and enormous
expenditures," and had grasped "empire after empire thereby." Greeley,
of course, exaggerated. New England's response to the expansion of the
Slave Power was far less gracious than he indicated, and western expansion
cannot be attributed exclusively to an "aggressive slaveocracy." Sectional
considerations, however, were present in every act of expansion realized or
contemplated, and the story cannot be understood without signal attention
to this factor. The struggle for empire over North America, an aim pursued against both aboriginal peoples and European powers, was also a dual
struggle for empire and a balance of power among the sections.[10]

A further reason for caution in identifying expansionism with nationalism
is that "the expansionists were not nationalists, and the nationalists were
not expansionists," in the inimitable expression of historian David M. Potter. Those advocating centralization, as George Bancroft put it, "must wish
& have ever wished to narrow our territory," whereas Democrats "with
States Rights, know no limit to the possible extent of the Federal Union."
John O'Sullivan, a northern Democrat and editor of the *Democratic Review*, considered the question in the same light. The advocate in the 1840s
of the right granted to the union by Providence to spread its ever-multiplying
millions over North America would also condemn the North's use of force
in 1861 and saw no inconsistency between these two views. The latter conflict he thought exemplified "the fable of the dispute between the head and
the tail of the snake for the right to lead." For many southerners, as Potter
noted, "there was but a short interval between their last efforts to bring new
potential states into the Union and their decisions to take their own states
out." By contrast, many nationalists—those who supported the concept of
extensive powers lodged in the general government, or who believed that
secession might be repressed through force—were very cautious or hostile
toward territorial expansion.[11]

This pattern was not simply an outgrowth of the bitter struggle preceding the Civil War but was in fact established in the first generation of the government. While there existed a consensus on the need to bring the territories beyond the mountains into the union, there was also an important division between Federalists and Republicans over how far such expansion might extend. The western country, as Hamilton expressed that consensus, "must have an outlet for its commodities. This is essential to its prosperity, and if not procured to it by the United States must be had [at] the expence of the Connection with them." Hence Hamilton would always insist that "the unity of our Empire, and the best interests of our nation, require that we shall annex to the United States all the territory east of the Mississippi, New Orleans included." But Hamilton warned of the tendency toward dismemberment reflected in the acquisition of territory beyond the Mississippi; in regard to western expansion, he was a "thus far and no further" man. It was Jefferson, the radical decentralist, who declined to set limits on "the extent to which the federative principle may operate effectively."[12]

Taking these factors together, it is evident that expansion was tied in a knot with secession from the Louisiana Purchase to the Civil War. The game was thus not one of addition alone but also potentially of subtraction, with each in play against the other. The "inevitability" of what happened, from our distant perspective, is just an optical illusion. What was inevitable is that the West Coast was going to get settled, but the political form this would take—whether independent republics, states of the union, or pockmarked battlegrounds of a sectional war—was unknown and unknowable. California and Oregon did not really figure in widespread consciousness until the early 1840s, when suddenly the whole circumference—Cuba, Canada, Oregon, California, Texas, Mexico—seemed up for grabs. In the 1820s and 1830s, if you had told an American that a country starting with the letter C was going to be rather promptly added to the union, Cuba or Canada (or both together), rather than California, would have garnered the overwhelming predictions. The thing that contemporaries thought was inevitable—Cuba and Canada falling like ripe pears into the union—did not happen. The thing they discounted as unlikely did.

13

The Title Page

AMERICAN NATIONALISM CRESTED IN EARLY 1819 with two extraordinary proclamations. In February, Secretary of State John Quincy Adams announced the Transcontinental Treaty that extended American claims to the Pacific Northwest. In March came Chief Justice Marshall's opinion in *McCulloch v. Maryland*, which "emphatically, and truly" declared the general government to be "a government of the people" and not a mere "league of states." Invoking the vast expanse of a republic that now extended "from the St. Croix to the Gulf of Mexico, from the Atlantic to the Pacific," Marshall held that the framers could not have intended any construction of the Constitution that rendered the defense of this realm hazardous. Marshall admitted, "as we all must admit," that the powers of the national government were limited and enumerated, but he nevertheless found that Congress enjoyed "the right to legislate on that vast mass of incidental powers which must be involved in the constitution, if that instrument be not a splendid bauble. . . . Let the end be legitimate, let it be within the scope of the constitution, and all means which are appropriate, which are plainly adapted to that end, which are not prohibited, but consist with the letter and spirit of the constitution, are constitutional."[1]

Marshall's opinion in *McCulloch*, though stirring in its nationalism, had ironic effects. Its very scope elicited a reaction, and it fell upon a country increasingly agitated by a range of other issues. Westerners were deeply displeased with Adams's treaty with the Spanish minister Luis de Onís, which secured American claims to the Oregon country and Florida (favored objects of the Northeast and South) but which gave up Texas. The panic of 1819 threw the West into depression and reawakened its sense of itself as an exploited colonial appendage of the East. When to these sources of agitation was added the bitter controversy aroused by Missouri's application to join the union as a slave state, all hell seemed to break loose at once. The Spanish treaty was one immediate casualty, for the Missouri question had "operated to indispose every part of the Union against the treaty; the North and East, because they do not wish even to have Florida as another slave State; and the South and West, because they wish to have all the territory to the Rio del Norte for more slave States." Fears for the Spanish treaty, however, paled before those for the union. "After the successful termination of the late war," as President Monroe expressed the prevailing mood in February 1820, "our system might be considered as having escaped all the perilous trials to which it was inevitably exposed, in its early steps." But the Missouri crisis was of a "more serious character . . . than any which preceded it." "It was a shocking thing to think of," Clay told Adams, "but he had not a doubt that within five years from this time, the Union would be divided into three distinct confederacies." To one correspondent, Clay lamented, "The words, civil war, and disunion, are uttered almost without emotion."[2]

The great question presented by admission of Missouri to the union, as Clay later observed, was "whether it was competent or was not competent for Congress to impose any restriction which should exist after she became a member of the Union?" Those in favor of Missouri's admission without restriction said that, "by the Constitution, no such restriction could be imposed" and "that, whenever she was once admitted into the Union, she had all the rights and privileges of any preexisting state of the Union." To restrictionists, Congress enjoyed a clear authority to make Missouri's admission contingent on the manumission of slaves, for to it was confided by the Constitution the authority to admit states and to make all needful regulations concerning the territories. To nonrestrictionists, however, the claim violated the equality of the states and, if accepted, would collapse the constitutional order.[3]

The Missouri crisis not only showed the ease with which contrary schools of construction could make the Constitution bend to exigent need. It also saw repeated predictions on the floor of Congress of civil war and horrible bloodshed, and it produced the awful sense among the most discerning of American observers that these prophecies, despite their wishes, really did foretell the future. The crisis was the "title page to a great tragic volume," wrote the younger Adams; the knell of the union, wrote Jefferson. It was likely to issue in "another Peloponnesian war to settle the ascendency between" rival confederacies. The triumphalist spirit evoked by the "Second War of American Independence," while reassuring in one respect, was disconcerting in another. Without an external enemy, could the union hold together? On that point, historical precedents were not favorable. "No confederation," as was observed during the Missouri crisis, "can long outlive the occasion which gave birth to it, unless it is the interest of all the parts to continue united. The Roman and Grecian confederacies, formed for external defence, were powerful for that purpose while the causes which produced them were in operation. But no sooner was the outward pressure withdrawn, by which, like a spell, their component parts had been bound together, than the discordancy of the political materials with which they were composed began to appear; and they became the unhappy victims of disunion and civil war!"[4]

Thomas Jefferson was deeply angered by the efforts of northern restrictionists in the Missouri crisis. The moral case, he believed, was all on the side of the South, since it was only through diffusion that peaceful emancipation might be effected: by spreading slaves "over a larger surface, their happiness would be increased, & the burthen of their future liberation lightened by bringing a greater number of shoulders under it." He agreed with Monroe's contention that the reviving federals wished to effect a division along the mountains that would drive the entire trans-Appalachian West from the union. Jefferson thought that the states of Ohio, Indiana, and Illinois could "scarcely separate from those who would hold the Mississippi from its mouth to its source," and believed that a new confederacy, if it resulted, would confirm the alliance between the South and the West. At the same time, he could feel the ground shifting under his feet. Instead of a solid and preponderating phalanx of the South and the whole western country against an isolated enclave in the eastern states, old Federalists like Rufus King made bold to create a new and "preponderant" division along the line of the Potomac and Ohio, "throwing 12 States to the North and East, & 10 to the South & West."[5]

To Jefferson, this was shocking, in the sense that it marked a change from his settled expectations, a kind of vast trembling of the political calculus. One half of his mind took as a matter of course that this was a pathetic revival of Federalism, and he hoped the people would see through their cynical party trick. But the other hemisphere of his brain saw the power of the new combination, saw the South slipping into dreaded minority status, there to furnish themes, like New England schismatics, "for the invective and irony of those who rule the nation." So long as Pennsylvania and Virginia held together, he wrote reassuringly to Gallatin, "the Atlantic states can never separate"; alas, Pennsylvania had "become more fanaticised than any other state." To a northern congressmen who had urged compromise, Jefferson evoked the union of the fathers and saw an unthinking conspiracy against it, wrong but inexorable. He regretted "that I am now to die in the belief, that the useless sacrifice of themselves by the generation of 1776 . . . is to be thrown away by the unwise and unworthy passions of their sons, and that my only consolation is to be, that I live not to weep over it." Jefferson broached the same theme to John Adams, alternately forecasting sectional war or servile rebellion as the two main possibilities unleashed by the restrictionists and hoping that both men would die before they saw the denouement. "Surely, they will parley awhile, and give us time to get out of the way."[6]

In contrast to Jefferson, Adams seemed to take the Missouri crisis more calmly, though he confessed to his old friend that for half a century he had seen slavery hanging over the country "like a black cloud." So terrified was he by the phenomenon, and by the prospect of violence that it disclosed, that "in former times" he had "constantly said . . . to the Southern Gentlemen, I cannot comprehend this object; I must leave it to you. I will vote for forcing no measure against your judgements." That line of policy had indeed occurred to Adams from the first moments of the American confederation, and it was on the broad principle of noninterference that the union had been reared. Whether it represented a wise counsel in the here and now, however, Adams left for God and posterity to decide: "I have none of the genius of Franklin, to invent a rod to draw from the cloud its Thunder and lightning." Adams the pessimist and Jefferson the optimist are well-established figures in historical consciousness, but here the roles are reversed. It was Jefferson in whom the Missouri crisis induced the most profound despondency. Everything else—"the banks, bankrupt law, manufactures, Spanish treaty"—seemed insignificant. Adams, by contrast, expressed the hope that the Missouri crisis would do no harm. It was "high treason," he declared, "to express a doubt of the perpetual duration of our vast American empire and our free institutions; and I say as devoutly as father Paul, Esto perpetua ['be thou everlasting']." Like Jefferson, however, he was "sometimes Cassandra enough to dream that another Hamilton, another Burr, might rend this mighty fabric in twain, or, perhaps, into a leash, and a few more choice spirits of the same stamp might produce as many nations in North America as there are in Europe."[7]

The specter of disunion had always provoked in the past the warning that foreign alliances and intervention would follow inexorably on a separation. An exchange between John Calhoun and John Quincy Adams, in the heat of the Missouri crisis, showed how intimate that connection continued to be (while also foretelling the deep logic of a future war). Calhoun warned Adams that if a dissolution of the union were forthcoming "the South would be from necessity compelled to form an alliance, offensive and defensive, with Great Britain." Adams in turn warned him that this not only would return the South "to the colonial state," which the Carolinian acknowledged, but also that the North would never accept a condition in which it would be "cut off from its natural outlet upon the ocean." Adams then suggested that the North, in those circumstances, would be forced "to move southward by land," to which Calhoun replied that the South "would find it necessary to make their communities all military."[8]

Adams did not press the matter further with Calhoun, but the Missouri crisis did set him and many others to thinking about the circumstances under which the dissolution of the union might be justified and how it might play out. Though he favored the Missouri Compromise, "believing it to be all that could be effected under the present Constitution, and from extreme unwillingness to put the Union at hazard," he wondered whether it would have been wiser "to have persisted in the restriction upon Missouri, till it should have terminated in a convention of the States to revise and amend the Constitution. This would have produced a new Union of thirteen or fourteen States unpolluted with slavery, with a great and glorious object to effect, namely, that of rallying to their standard the other States by the universal emancipation of their slaves." Adams, who saw slavery as "the great and foul stain upon the North American Union," believed that "if the Union must be dissolved, slavery is precisely the question upon which it ought to break." Many southerners were coming to that conclusion as well, though from entirely contrary premises. Adams reported that Senator James Barbour of Virginia "was going round to all the free-State members and pro-posing to them to call a convention of the States to dissolve the Union, and agree upon the terms of separation and the mode of disposing of the public debt of the lands, and make other necessary arrangements of disunion."[9]

The resolution of the crisis of 1819–1821 in the first and second Missouri compromises, by which Missouri was admitted as a slave state, was also a settlement of the status of slavery within the entire territory west of the Mississippi brought into the union by the Louisiana Purchase. Missouri apart, Congress forbade its existence above the line of 36°30′ and permit-ted it below that line. Missouri's pivotal location astride the two great wa-ter systems—the Missouri and the Mississippi—together with the fact that its territory lay largely above the line of the Ohio River, was such that its admission as a slave state in one sense constituted a highly significant vic-tory for the southern states. In another respect, however, the South signed a back-loaded mortgage in 1820–1821, with interest payments steadily rising, which promised both present gain and future distress. There was, in any event, less of a compromise between North and South than met the eye. Only the willingness of a narrow band of compromisers to vote contrary to sectional sentiment enabled Clay to put together his narrow margin of victory. As the "Great Pacificator" saw, the question could only be adjusted through delicate equivalents and compensations. Justifying the linkage of Maine's admission to that of Missouri, Clay remarked at the outset of the crisis that "this notion of an equivalent was not a new one; it was one upon which Commonwealths and States had acted from time immemorial."[10] Po-litical settlement occurring in the aftermath of threats of the use of force was also an expedient to which commonwealths and states had recurred from time immemorial. And so they did here.

Clay's prediction of a split into three separate confederacies attested to the sense, which if anything deepened in the 1820s, that the people of the Northeast, South, and West were quite sharply opposed in their political agendas and legislative programs. The West, as Ray Billington once summarized this trilateral alignment, wanted low-priced public lands, protective tariffs, and federally built internal improvements. The South wanted low tariffs, no nationally supported internal improvements, and high-priced public lands. The Northeast, finally, wished for high protective tariffs, high-priced public lands, and federally built internal improvements. Opinion in the West over the protective tariff was more evenly divided than Billington allowed—Clay of Kentucky was the author of a system that Benton of Missouri thought larcenous in its sectional injustice—but the larger constellation held good.[11] The South, as Billington noted, was placed in a relatively weak position, but it was also true "that no single section could hope to carry out its program without aid from one of the others. That might be achieved by happenstance; thus Northeast and West could unite behind a protective tariff bill beneficial to both. Or an alliance might be formed if one section consciously tried to win the support of another; conceivably the South might work for cheaper lands in return for western help in securing a lower tariff. Those bargains would necessarily involve agreements on secondary issues, for no one of the three antagonists would back down on its major demands; the Northeast and South would never compromise on the tariff, nor the West on land policy." These sectional alignments "were the basis for the legislative conflicts that kept the nation in a turmoil for the next generation." Statesmen from the three sections made sure that others understood that their interests were vitally concerned in these matters, and that disunion lay at the end of the road if their demands did not receive consideration. Webster had perfected this argument by warning in 1814 that "in the commerce of the country, the Constitution had its birth. In the extinction of that commerce, it will find its grave. I use not the tone of intimidation or menace, but I forewarn you of consequences." Clay said the same in 1826 when he warned that he "had no doubt" that "there would be a dissolution of the Union by the mountains" if Congress failed to use its powers for internal improvement. Southerners, who had dismissed this sort of talk as unctuous in preceding years, learned to employ the same menace as the waning of their power made them anxious to calculate "the price of the Union."[12]

14

Constitutional Disorder

THE FEROCIOUS POLITICAL ARGUMENTS OF THE 1820s and 1830s had many dimensions, of which the triangular controversy over political economy was but one. Constitutionally, there persisted and deepened the controversy between the nationalists and the state rights or compact school, which set forth utterly antipodal interpretations of the federal Constitution. Nationalists argued that the Constitution was a creature of the American people, and not of the states; that the resolution of conflicts over its character lay with the appropriate branches of the national government, not with the states; and that it established a union meant to be perpetual, from which no state or group of states enjoyed a legal or constitutional right of withdrawal. The "implied powers" that Alexander Hamilton insisted were invested in the general government by the Constitution, the judicial decisions of John Marshall, the legal commentaries of Joseph Story and Nathan Dane, and the orations of Daniel Webster and John Quincy Adams all buttressed these claims.

Compact theorists, by contrast, insisted that the Constitution was a creature of the people of the states, and not the instrument of a sovereign American people; and that the parties to the compact retained the right to determine when the general government had exceeded the powers granted to it under the Constitution. They rallied round "the principles of 1798" associated with the resolutions of the Virginia and Kentucky state assemblies. Some, like John C. Calhoun, insisted that each state enjoyed a right to nullify a federal law within its jurisdiction that, in its judgment, was unconstitutional; others who subscribed to the compact theory, like John Randolph, were content with affirming a constitutional right of secession. Both nullification and secession, though different things, found support in the writings of Thomas Jefferson, both in his authorship of the Kentucky Resolutions in the late 1790s and in letters written in retirement at Monticello.

One point of tension between these rival schools was whether the federal government was to be the judge of its own powers. Jefferson regarded that pretension as a "fatal heresy"; neither the state governments nor the federal "is authorized literally to decide which belongs to itself or its co-partner in Government; in differences of opinion, between their different sets of public servants, the appeal is to neither, but to their employers, peaceably assembled by their representatives in convention." Nationalists viewed Jefferson's doctrine as incompatible with the preservation of the union. The judges of the Supreme Court were "called to sit in judgment on the acts of independent States; they control the will of sovereigns," said Webster. "Sir, there exists not upon the earth, and there never did exist, a judicial tribunal clothed with powers so various, and so important. . . . I am persuaded that the Union could not exist without it." Webster believed that if Jackson's view of the limited power of the Supreme Court should receive general acceptance, "the constitution will have perished even earlier than the moment which its enemies originally allowed for the termination of its existence. It will have not survived to its fiftieth year."[1]

Nationalists also appealed to majority rule as "the first great principle of republican liberty," as Webster called it. "The great principle, which lies at the foundation of all free Government," Clay argued in 1832, "is, that the majority must govern; from which there is or can be no appeal but to the sword. That majority ought to govern wisely, equitably, moderately, and constitutionally, but govern it must, subject only to that terrible appeal. If ever one, or several States, being a minority, can, by menacing a dissolution of the Union, succeed in forming an abandonment of great measures deemed essential to the interests and prosperity of the whole, the Union, from that moment, is practically gone. It may linger on, in form and name, but its vital spirit has fled forever!" Clay had then urged that the union was more threatened by the abandonment of the American system than by its preservation; but a year later he not only consented to but urged the partial abandonment of that system in his promotion of the compromise tariff.[2]

The most elaborate and systematic statements of a theory of the American Constitution in opposition to the doctrine of majority rule were given by John C. Calhoun, who distinguished between the rule of the numerical and the concurrent majority. The theory that regarded the union "as a government of the mere numerical majority," Calhoun argued, rested "on a gross and groundless misconception." Such a government would be a despotism, as absolute as any of the monarchical governments of Europe, a result surely not intended by the framers of the Constitution. Instead, they took care to give "to each interest or portion of the community a negative on the others." Called by various names—"veto, interposition, nullification, check, or balance of power"—it was this negative power "of preventing or arresting the action of the government" that formed the Constitution. For Calhoun, then, it was "the negative power which makes the constitution—and the positive which makes the government. The one is the power of acting—and the other the power of preventing or arresting action. The two, combined, make constitutional governments."[3]

In one respect, at least, there was no disagreement between the two sides on whether the Constitution embodied the principle of a concurrent majority. "It is full of such checks and balances," as Webster remarked. "In its very organization, it adopts a broad and most effective principle in restraint of the power of mere majorities." But though Webster and Calhoun alike drew attention to features of the Constitution that pointed to forms of concurrent majority, Calhoun went much further, arguing that a state, if it judged an act of the general government to be unconstitutional, might "interpose" its authority and nullify within its borders the acts of the general government. This nullification was to stand unless three-fourths of the states signaled, through a constitutional amendment, their judgment of the constitutional controversy.[4]

The theory of nullification was undoubtedly ingenious, and Calhoun spun his web with characteristic boldness. Still, Calhoun's theory was seriously weakened by the proposition that a state might remain within the union and enjoy its benefits while thus arresting the operation of the union's laws. It was for this reason that Webster pronounced nullification a less "respectable" doctrine than secession. "Whatever other inconsistencies" the doctrine of secession might entail, Webster said, "one, at least, it would avoid. It would not belong to a government, while it rejected its authority. It would not repel the burden, and continue to enjoy the benefits. It would not aid in passing laws which others are to obey, and yet reject their authority as to itself. It would not undertake to reconcile obedience to public authority with an asserted right of command over that same authority. It would not be in the government, and above the government, at the same time."[5] Nullification thus violated the very principle of equity, or of a proportionate distribution of burdens and benefits, that it was ostensibly committed to preserving. It was criticized as such by many southerners, like John Randolph, who agreed with Calhoun that the protective tariff was unjust and unconstitutional, but who thought it nonsensical that a state might somehow be both within and without the union. That concession fortifies the view that nullification was, as its critics alleged, a doctrine of "organized civil War," "an impractical absurdity," "a sophistical construction," "a metaphysical subtlety, in pursuit of an impracticable theory." Andrew Jackson certainly thought so, holding in a special proclamation that nullification was "incompatible with the existence of the Union, contradicted expressly by the latter of the Constitution, unauthorized by its spirit, inconsistent with every principle on which it was founded, and destructive of the great object for which it was formed."[6]

Alongside the nationalist and compact schools lay a third view, distinct from both antipodal theories and in a precarious middle position between them. The adherents of such a view might accept that Calhoun's theory of nullification was a metaphysical absurdity while also believing that it would be utterly contrary to the spirit of the Constitution to preserve the union by force, a position taken by constitutional commentator William Rawle in the 1820s. They might reprobate secessionists as counseling a course of action that was patently unconstitutional and indeed disastrous while nevertheless regarding Hamilton's theory of implied powers as equally destructive of the constitutional order, a view taken by James Madison and Andrew Jackson. Much as these distinct views differed on the legitimacy of a forceful response to secession, it is apparent that these trimmers were attempting to reconcile the same incongruities. They all devoutly believed that to push the Constitution too far in the direction of centralization or decentralization would destroy it, and that its stability consisted in the maintenance of an elaborate equipoise between these opposing forces. Jackson did not have the disposition of a trimmer, but he gave an eloquent statement of the philosophy in his 1832 Bank Veto Message, six months before threatening Calhoun with the noose: the government, he insisted, could not be maintained nor the union preserved by invading the rights of the states: "In thus attempting to make our General Government strong, we make it weak. Its true strength consists in leaving individuals and States, as much as possible, to themselves; in making itself felt, not in its power, but in its beneficence, not in its control, but in its protection, not in binding the States more closely to the centre, but leaving each to move unobstructed, in its proper orbit."[7]

A great many people internalized the conflict and gave equal attention to both specters. A good example is William Pinkney's conduct in the crisis of 1819–1821. Pinkney was then the leading member of the American bar whose oral argument in *McCulloch v. Maryland* had been closely followed in Justice Marshall's opinion. Before the court, Pinkney had endorsed a "fair and liberal interpretation" of the powers of "the constitutional government of this republican empire" and contended that, "since the sovereign powers of the Union are supreme," the state governments must give way when conflicts arose.[8]

In his capacity as senator from Maryland, however, Pinkney strongly opposed the attempt by northern congressmen to impose conditions upon Missouri's admission. The assumption by Congress of this power, he held, would convert the union "into a unit." What is that union? he asked:

A confederation of States equal in sovereignty, capable of every thing which the Constitution does not forbid, or authorize Congress to forbid. It is an equal Union between parties equally sovereign. They were sovereign, independently of the Union. The object of the Union was common protection for the exercise of already existing sovereignty. The parties gave up a portion of that sovereignty to insure the remainder. As far as they gave it up by the common compact they have ceased to be sovereign. . . . The Union provides the means of defending the residue; and it is into that Union that a new State is to come. By acceding to it, the new State is placed on the same footing with the original States. It accedes for the same purpose, that is, protection for its unsurrendered sovereignty. If it comes in short of its beams—crippled and disparaged beyond the original States, it is not into the original union that it comes. For it is a different sort of Union. The first was Union *inter pares*: This is a Union between *disparates*, between giants and a dwarf, between power and feebleness, between full proportioned sovereignties and a miserable image of power. [The power claimed by Congress was one] of colossal size; if, indeed, it be not an abuse of language to call it by the gentle name of a power. Sir, it is a wilderness of powers, of which fancy, in her happiest mood, is unable to perceive the far distant and shadowy boundary. Armed with such a power, with religion in one hand and philanthropy in the other, . . . you may achieve more conquests over sovereignties, not your own, than falls to the common lot of even uncommon ambition. By the aid of such a power, skillfully employed, you may 'bridge your way' over the Hellespont that separates State legislation from that of Congress; and you may do so for pretty much the same purpose with which Xerxes once bridged his way across the Hellespont, that separates Asia from Europe. He did so, in the language of Milton, "the liberties of Greece to yoke." You may do so for the analogous purpose of subjugating and reducing the sovereignties of States, as your taste or convenience may suggest, and fashioning them to your imperial will."[9]

It was in one sense deeply incongruous that the winning side in *McCulloch* should give so eloquent a statement of the sensibility of the state rights school, but in another sense quite representative of the trimmers' philosophy: it was in the nature of the federal union that it must navigate the narrow passage between anarchy and empire. That position of the trimmers, in turn, was emblematic of the theme that the great historians of nineteenth-century America—George Bancroft, Francis Parkman, and Henry Adams—found so central. Each, notes scholar Richard Vitzthum, interpreted "American history as an intensely dramatic journey along a narrow path of moderation between abysses of excess yawning on either side. Though they establish many polarities in their works, the one they all see as fundamental consists of anarchy, or complete diffusion and decentralization, at one extreme and tyranny—complete subordination and centralization—at the other. Between anarchy and tyranny, they argue, America has charted and must continue to chart a wary middle course."[10]

The parameters of constitutional discourse shifted little from the 1790s to the 1830s, but in one respect it was deeply in flux. A vital discovery was that leaders who at one time could earnestly advance a theory of national supremacy or of state rights were to be found a decade later espousing the opposite principle. The experience of the first twenty-five years was particularly instructive in this regard, for it found even the highest of high Federalists moving toward nullification in the face of Jefferson's embargo and Mr. Madison's War, and quoting the Virginia and Kentucky Resolutions with approval, and the Jeffersonian Republicans governing on the basis of theories of sovereignty and implied powers at variance with their doctrines of the 1790s. The pattern continued under the second generation. Webster reversed his position on the protective tariff, opposing it as unconstitutional in 1816 and becoming its fervent advocate by the late 1820s. Calhoun embraced the protective tariff of 1816; intent later on showing the protective tariff unconstitutional, he denied having done so, in the 1830s insisting that his unvarying opinion had been that the Constitution authorized no such thing.[11]

The antipodal interpretations of the Constitution, together with the various reversals of position according to changing political interest, cast the Constitution into a dark twilight, its features difficult to make out. The cumulative effect of the argument, all sides to which affirmed the supremacy of constitutional values, was to subtly undermine the sense that the appeal to the Constitution could resolve anything, because the versions to which appeal was made were so utterly inconsistent with each other. That this had happened in the first quarter century of the government's existence was bad enough. That it happened again in the 1820s and 1830s was taken as a very bad omen, as indeed it was. Nothing, as Clay complained in 1833, seemed fixed. "After 44 years of existence under the present Constitution, what single principle is fixed? The Bank? No. I[n]ternal improvements! No. The tariff? No. Who is to interpret the Constitution? No. We are as much afloat at sea as the day when the Constitution went into operation." In 1834, John Quincy Adams confided to his diary that his "hopes of the long continuance of this Union" were "extinct." "The people must go the way of all the world, and split up into an uncertain number of rival communities, enemies in war, in peace friends."[12]

The constitutional crisis, then, was also a security crisis, a point that received repeated affirmation. "The great good of the Union," as the Unitarian minister William Ellery Channing observed, "we may express almost in a word. It preserves us from wasting and destroying one another. It preserves relations of peace among communities, which, if broken into separate nations, would be arrayed against another in perpetual, merciless, and ruinous war. It indeed contributes to our defence against foreign states, but still more it defends us from one another." The great compromises of 1820 and 1833 were justified in these terms, just as they were likened to the diplomatic settlements of European congresses, with Henry Clay calling the 1833 compromise "a treaty of peace and amity." The most distinguished early interpreters of the Constitution—John Marshall and Joseph Story, St. George Tucker and William Rawle—disagreed on much else, but all affirmed the view that the Constitution was "our last, and our only security."[13]

Saying, however, was easier than doing. With the individual states still commanding loyalty and reflecting "much nationality," the problem of ensuring effective coordination and cooperation among these refractory units, of keeping them in union, often seemed insuperable. "The States in our system," wrote Rufus Choate of Massachusetts, "may be compared to the primordial particles of matter, indivisible, indestructible, impenetrable, whose natural condition is to repel each other, or, at least, to exist, in their own independent identity,—while the Union is an artificial aggregation of such particles; a sort of *forced state*, as some have said, of life . . . a system of bodies advancing slowly through a *resisting medium*." Whereas the states were "natural" and were "a single and uncompounded substance," the union was "a totally different community—a community miscellaneous and widely scattered." It was "more delicate, more artificial, more recent, far more truly a mere production of the reason and the will—standing in far more need of an ever-surrounding care, to preserve and repair it, and urge it along its highway . . . a beautiful, yet fragile creation, which a breath can unmake, as a breath has made it." A writer in the *Democratic Review* agreed. Far from being "a union that nature dictated," America's "federal nationality" was the "result of consummate art to unite those whom God separated, making some of them powerful and others feeble, scattering them also apart with vast intervening distances; diversifying them with great differences of climate, natural productions, social habits, industrial pursuits and capabilities."[14]

A lot depended on finding a resolution to the disputes that put the Constitution into twilight and the union in jeopardy. Hugh Legaré, the talented South Carolinian who observed the nullification crisis from a distant perch as chargé d'affaires to Belgium, was delivered unto despair in contemplating the grim alternatives. He had resolutely opposed the high tariffs of the late 1820s and considered them unconstitutional centralism and sectional extortion, but he thought the course of nullification was perfectly mad. The future of the union, and its possible dissolution, oppressed him: "There is no subject that has a thousandth part of the interest this has for me,—I think of it continually, though . . . it ends in my not knowing what to think, except that dangers are around and above and below and within our poor little State." It was in the controversy over the tariff that Legaré first felt "the spirit of civil war burning within me," but that ominous heaving actually drew him back from the brink. He observed with alarm the growing anti-slavery sentiment in England and France, which found the South increasingly denounced for its barbaric institution, and warned friends in South Carolina that, if the union were dissolved, the South would "encounter assaults from across the Atlantic, to which the machinations of the Yankee zealots . . . are mere child's play." The only security, precarious though it was, lay in the union, for it was certain that "if the Union should go to pieces, it will be one hideous wreck,—of which, excepting New-England, no two parts will hold together. None of us will have any country . . . there will be no *flag* known to the nations, and none of the ennobling and sacred charities that bind, or rather bound us together but the other day." Instead, the inevitable result would be "piratical depredations . . . and ignoble border warfare, and the rudeness, coarseness and ferocity of a race of mounted barbarians."[15]

15

Decentralizing Tendencies

UNCERTAINTY OVER THE "TRUE THEORY" of the Constitution should not obscure the fact that in practice much in the way of effective power remained with the states. Even in those few and well-defined areas in which the claim of the federal government's authority was strongest—"war, peace, negotiation, and foreign commerce"—the system had considerable decentralization built into it. Furthering these tendencies was the Jacksonian persuasion, which stood foursquare against the institutions of Hamilton's Republic and gained notable victories against the national bank and the protective tariff in the 1830s.[1]

Under the Constitution, Congress gained the power of establishing and maintaining an army and a navy, but military power resided primarily in the militia of the states. The president enjoyed the power, under the Constitution, of calling the state militias into national service, and Congress the power of "organizing, arming and disciplining the militia, and for governing such part of them as may be employed in the service of the United States," but to the states were reserved "the appointment of officers, and the authority of training the militia according to the discipline prescribed by Congress." As the War of 1812 showed, this "recessed" system governing the distribution and balance of military power could operate so as to place the power to opt out of such requisitions effectively in the hands of the states. Hamilton, indeed, had intimated this peculiar distribution of military power in *Federalist* 28 when he asked: "When will the time arrive that the federal government can raise and maintain an army capable of erecting a despotism over the great body of the people of an immense empire, who are in a situation, through the medium of their State governments, to take measures for their own defense, with all the celerity, regularity, and system of independent nations?" The measures of military preparedness Virginia undertook in 1798, together with the defiance of New England in 1812, were two early instances of this phenomenon. Another was the query that Charles Pinckney addressed in 1820 to those who wished to impose the requirements of manumission on Missouri if it were to be admitted as a state. If Missouri refused the terms, Pinckney asked, how did the proponents of slavery restriction propose to use force? "By whom, or by what force can this be effected? Will the States in her neighborhood join in this crusade? Will they, who, to a man, think

Missouri is right, and you are wrong, arm in such a cause? Can you send a force from the eastward of the Delaware? The very distance forbids it; and distance is a powerful auxiliary to a country attacked."[2]

From the 1830s to the 1850s, much consideration was given to whether the federal government might repress the secession of a state through force; but up until the 1830s, when the debate really got going, the distribution of military power was such as to make this a very hazardous enterprise against any group of states. Tocqueville believed in the 1830s that "patriotism is still directed to the State and has not passed over to the union. . . . If the sovereignty of the Union were to engage in a struggle with that of the States at the present day, its defeat may be confidently predicted; and it is not probable that such a struggle would be seriously undertaken." When Jackson proposed his Force Bill in response to South Carolina's nullification of the tariff, it astonished observers, as much for the boldness of the threat of force as for the apparent reversal of Jackson's convictions (for the president had seemed to go from ultra–state rights to ultra-nationalist in less than two weeks). The Force Bill was represented by advocates as "a measure of peace," to which Calhoun replied: "Yes, such peace as the wolf gives to the lamb—the kite to the dove! Such peace as Russia gives to Poland, or death to its victims!"[3]

But the resolution of the crisis of 1833 with the compromise tariff was not generally thought to have established the principle that the federal government might coerce a refractory state. Whigs like Adams thought the Carolinians had prevailed. Generally speaking, there was probably more uncertainty about the outcome of such a struggle than Tocqueville's summary would suggest, with the key variable being whether a single state or an entire section would be the object of coercion. Standing alone, South Carolina's position was untenable, but as the leader of a united South it appeared unassailable. Undoubtedly, however, there were many observers who calculated the balance of power as Tocqueville did. Even in 1861, Europe and the southern confederacy scoffed at the union's threats of force, which recalled for them Britain's losing effort in 1776 to subdue its rebellious subjects. An inevitable deduction from this state of affairs is that there was no effective "monopoly on the use of legitimate violence" in the American system of states but rather, at the constitutional level, a duopoly whose boundaries were uncertain.[4]

The monetary system of the "U States" also resisted centralization. The circulating medium—actually media—was for long periods "practically and effectually under the control of the several State governments," as Daniel Webster complained in 1830. While the excesses of state banking systems were reined in to a considerable degree under the first and second Banks of the United States (1791–1811, 1817–1836), which performed a central banking function, the periods following the collapse of these institutions witnessed a high degree of monetary disorder—"anarchy," in the expression of economic historian Bray Hammond. However much Federalists and Whigs might plead for federal measures to sustain a sound and uniform currency, Jeffersonian Republicans denounced the first bank as unconstitutional in the 1790s, and Jacksonian Democrats killed off efforts to secure the renewal of the second bank's charter in the 1830s. "Experience has shown," wrote Amos Kendall, one of Andrew Jackson's intimate advisers, "how fallacious is the idea of regulating the currency by means of a National Bank. . . . Indeed, the scheme of sustaining a paper currency of uniform value throughout a country so commercial and extensive as the United States is an absurdity." The monetary system of the union from the 1830s to the 1850s more closely resembled Kendall's ideas than Hamilton's or Webster's, and there were hundreds of notes issued by different state banks that circulated widely and fluctuated wildly—a true mecca for the sharp-eyed speculator and a misfortune for the unwary. As Hamilton had foreseen, government debt played an important role in support of a national currency in the early period; but with the retirement of the national debt in the 1830s, that function was never passed successfully to state bond issues, on which there were a number of spectacular defaults in the 1840s.[5]

The tension between centralizing and decentralizing forces also played out in the arguments over trade and tariff. The federal Constitution established "what was in effect a customs union among member states," authorizing free trade among the thirteen states and a common external tariff, while prohibiting export duties. In the first two decades of the century, however, there was little in the way of economic integration among the sections. In urging his "American system," Henry Clay urged that it would be "favorable to the preservation and strength of our confederacy." "Now," he said in 1820, "our connection is merely political. For the sale of the surplus of the produce of our agricultural labor, all eyes are constantly turned upon the markets of Liverpool. There is scarcely any of that beneficial intercourse, the best basis of political connection, which consists in the exchange of the produce of our labor."[6]

Commercial interdependence among the sections grew dramatically after 1820, in large part due to the protective tariffs enacted under Clay's guidance in the fifteen years after the end of the Napoleonic Wars. Though there were protective elements in the tariff passed by the First Congress in 1789, these were more pronounced in the preamble than in its actual provisions; the broad program that Hamilton proposed for the support of American manufactures (which argued for a judicious mixture of bounties and external tariffs) was turned aside. The real birth of the protective system came in 1816, when protection was given to the manufactures that had sprung up in the course of the trade embargoes and nonintercourse laws adopted before and during the War of 1812. The tariff was increased in both 1820 and 1824, increases that culminated in the "tariff of abominations" of 1828. (Of this legislation, Webster famously said that its enemies spiced it with toxins in order to kill it, but its friends took it, "drugged as it was.")[7]

In one sense the antagonism between free trade and protection is misleading, for both sides entertained a keen suspicion of the restrictive systems on industry and commerce that still characterized the political economy of most European states. Perhaps the most important cause in promoting American prosperity, believed Albert Gallatin, was "the absence of those systems of internal restrictions and monopoly which continue to disfigure the state of society in other countries." What on first approach seems a dispute between free traders and mercantilists is better construed as a disagreement over the proper size of the free trade area or customs union at which America should aim. Thus James Buchanan, a Pennsylvania "protectionist," exclaimed in 1844, "Ours will be a glorious system of free trade, and the only one which the jealousy and the interest of foreign nations will ever permit us to enjoy." Buchanan recalled "the magnificent idea" and "grand design" of "Henry the Great, of France . . . of dividing Europe into fifteen confederated states, for the purpose of preserving peace and promoting free commerce among its different nations," and noted the beneficial results that had accrued to Germany since it "confederated in the Zoll Verein league, for the purpose of enjoying the benefits of free trade among themselves." Buchanan foresaw, "if we are wise," a "system of free trade at home on a more extensive scale than any which the world has ever witnessed." America's "system of confederated republics" he deemed "capable of almost indefinite extension with increasing strength," partly because of the advantages that membership within this free trade area provided. "If there were no other bond to preserve our Union, what State would forego the advantages of this vast free trade with all her sisters, and place herself in lonely isolation?"[8]

The aim of the protective system, according to one of its advocates, was "the broad and impregnable principle of national independence." It sought to give to the entire American people "employments of their own, resources of their own, strength of their own, and happiness of their own; which cannot be injuriously affected in war or peace, through stratagem or design by any other people." But Clay, the chief architect of the American system, went further, hoping not only to limit the dependence of the United States on commerce with Europe, which experience showed had led to war, but also to create a web of interdependent relations within the union whose severance would be unthinkable, thus reinforcing the political ties among the American states and sections.[9]

The ambition to conciliate the sections through commerce proved far from a straightforward process of ever-increasing harmony. The South considered the tariff an oppressive and unjust exaction, increasing the cost of its goods and decreasing the value of its exports (to the tune, it was alleged, of forty bales of cotton out of a hundred). "Through our political connection," said the South Carolina *Exposition and Protest*, "by a perversion of the powers of the Constitution, which was intended to protect the States of the Union in the enjoyment of their natural advantages," the North had stripped the South "of the blessings bestowed by nature, and converted them to their own advantage." Were free trade with the world restored, claimed the Carolinians, "we would become, what [the manufacturing states] now are by our means, the most flourishing people on the globe." The quarrel that the Carolinians had with the tariff was not theirs alone; in this matter, as Clay came to acknowledge, they spoke for the entire South. "Throughout the whole South," Clay had concluded by 1833, "there is a sympathy of feeling and interest" for the Carolinians. Other southern states might disagree with the strong remedy of nullification, but all agreed (great though Clay regarded their error) "in the substantial justice of the cause." Preponderant opinion in the South, that is to say, had come to the conclusion that the tariff had become "an instrument of rearing up the industry of one section of the country on the ruins of another" and had agreed "that its burdens are exclusively on one side and its benefits on the other."[10]

The argument over the tariff brought forth opposing visions of international relations—one nationalist, the other internationalist, and both in ostensible opposition to empire. Southern free traders embraced a liberal vision of international cooperation that pointed toward perpetual peace, rejecting the "barbarous and unenlightened" strictures of mercantilist statecraft. According to southern advocates of free trade, the protective system was a prolific breeder of war: "Three fourths at least of the wars in Europe for these one hundred and fifty years, have originated from the jealousies of trade, from the stupidity, and the selfishness of merchants and manufacturers." Free trade, by contrast, would "bind diverse interests into a solemn league of good-will." "National prejudices would be corrected," wrote the *Democratic Review*, and "the relations of distant people would be made so close and vital, that it would be next to impossible to foment a war." Free trade within the United States, insisted the *Review*, had had this effect. Despite profound sectional differences, Americans "feel themselves to be fellows; they know themselves to be one." If the same relations were "instituted among the nations of the earth," then the "same prosperity and peace" would follow. Such was the trajectory of the "modern movement," which pointed toward freedom, goodwill, and "universality."[11]

Thomas Cooper of South Carolina agreed with the *Democratic Review* that war "is seldom the interest of any nation, and is likely to be less so in future than formerly." It was absurd to look to "the past history of Europe, during its most barbarous and unsettled state," for the likely future trajectory of international politics. But he gave no encomiums to the American system. It was equally absurd that American congressmen "were debating and denying the plainest conclusions of political science, which every man in Europe pretending to a good education would blush to doubt." Cooper was heartened that in Britain a new generation of statesmen (Liverpool, Canning, and Huskisson) were fully persuaded that they must "disentangle the perplexed and vexatious system of monopolies, restrictions, and prohibitions in which the mercantile interest and the manufacturing interest have involved the commerce of that country," a system that in the past had "carried war and desolation into every quarter of the Globe and . . . made that island in particular the scourge of mankind." The "wicked and destructive tendency of the old maxims" had been overthrown, and now most Englishmen accepted "that men and nations gain in prosperity, in proportion as their neighbors gain also. That cutting the throats or devastating the property of those who would be our customers and consumers, are not the best means of enriching ourselves." Altogether, these developments provided a "glimpse of the dawn of a new day; and of peace on earth, and good will toward men."[12]

Advocates of the protective system, by contrast, rejected these rosy prophecies and insisted that the only prudent course was to assume that the future would resemble the past. "Should the international relations of the great powers of the Christian world be on no worse a footing for the next two centuries than they have been the two last," claimed one protectionist, the only rational deduction was "that on an average, every alternate year will be one of war." The great claim of the American system was that it would profoundly lessen the probability of the United States being drawn into some future European maelstrom. The system, Clay averred, "is favorable to the maintenance of peace. Foreign commerce is the great source of foreign wars. The eagerness with which we contend for every branch of it, the temptations which it offers, operating alike upon us and our foreign competitors, produce constant collisions." Advocates of the protective system urged that it would also raise up essential sources of supply and contribute to preparedness in case of war, but their larger claim was that protection meant peace: the interdependence fostered by free trade with Europe would in fact be a source of endless collision, contributing to neither security nor prosperity.[13]

The debate over free trade and protection raised vital issues of American identity. Declared one Carolinian in 1832: "I belong first to No. Carolina, and then to the Southern Country, and then to the U. States, and then to the Human Family." The tariff bore on all these attachments, but unequally. The southern free traders developed a cosmopolitan viewpoint and looked toward mutual dependence and prosperity among the nations. Advocates of the protective system, by contrast, rejected these misguided "doctrines of universal philanthropy." "The romance of the Free-Trade doctrine," wrote Calvin Colton, was "the assumption that all nations are one family, and that therefore a system of perfect Free trade would be best for their aggregate interests." This gravely mistook the real character of international relations. "The globe is divided into different communities," argued Clay, and it would ever be the case that each would seek "to appropriate to itself all the advantages it can, without reference to the prosperity of others." From the protectionist point of view, free trade was in fact an illusion. It would simply be the means by which Great Britain succeeded in driving out all competitors, making "the young and weak nations slaves to the old and strong."[14]

These perceptions on both sides threw union and independence out of kilter and exposed a severe fault line in the nation. For both northern protectionists and southern free traders, commitment to the union could be seen, if their adversaries prevailed, as fundamentally threatening to independence—for free traders, because protection entailed a colonial dependence on the North; for protectionists, because free trade entailed a colonial dependence on Great Britain. From the Carolinian point of view, the result beggared the imagination and put the American union in a new light as against the European society of states. Within the American union, noted George McDuffie in 1835, "The rights and liberties of the minority States are in much greater jeopardy from the majority States, acting through the federal government, under an assumed and practical omnipotence, than they possibly could be, if there existed no compact of Union, and each were separate and independent. . . . The smallest state on the continent of Europe, amidst the gigantic struggles of warring monarchies, holds its rights and liberties by much surer guaranties, under the laws of nations, than South Carolina now holds her rights and liberties, under the federal constitution, subject to a construction which absolutely inverts its operation, rendering it a chain to the oppressed, and a cobweb to the oppressor."[15]

The South received some satisfaction from the Compromise of 1833 and won a big victory in the 1846 downward revision of the tariff sponsored by Robert Walker, but the sense that the southerners were the victims of oppressive sectional legislation never really abated. Contrary to Clay's expectation that sectional harmony would ensue from commercial interdependence, the sections drew apart politically just as they grew closer together commercially. William Seward noted in 1853 that "the steam engine, the iron road, the electric telegraph, all of which are newer than the Union, and the metropolitan press, which is no less wonderful in its working than they, have already obliterated state boundaries and produced a physical and moral centralism more complete and perfect than monarchical ambition ever has forged or can forge." Tracing the growth of the "irrepressible conflict" between the slave and free states, he later observed, "Increase of population, which is filling the states out to their very borders, together with a new and extended network of railroads and other avenues, and an internal commerce which daily becomes more intimate, is rapidly bringing the states into a higher and more perfect social unity or consolidation. Thus, these antagonistic systems are continually coming into closer contact, and collision results."[16]

From the 1820s onward, it was a common observation that the development of the United States had far exceeded "in amount and rapidity the most sanguine expectations of the founders of the Republic"; but alongside this growth there was also a sense, as Joseph Story observed in 1833, that the centrifugal or "disturbing" forces "which, more than once in the convention, were on the point of breaking up the Union, have since immeasurably increased in concentration and vigor. . . . The North cannot but perceive that it has yielded to the South a superiority of representatives, already amounting to twenty-five, beyond its due proportion; and the South imagines that, with all this preponderance in representation, the other parts of the Union enjoy a more perfect protection of their interests than her own. The West feels her growing power and weight in the Union, and the Atlantic States begin to learn that the scepter must one day depart from them." The passage nicely expresses one of the great oddities of the federal union's political trajectory from 1787 onward: every decade saw an increase in both centripetal and centrifugal forces, a strange and symbiotic advance in national and sectional dynamism, each of which managed to grow in velocity and power until the crack-up in the 1860s.[17]

16

The Hope of the World

FOR ALL THE TRAVAILS OF THE UNION, it was nevertheless something in which Americans could take a great deal of pride. In the Western world had arisen a system that had successfully substituted law for force, in which great and little states were each accorded an equal station to pursue their distinctive and independent lives, and that had managed, "by the mere influence of civil liberty and religious toleration," to dry up many consuming fires of war. America, of course, was a byword for democracy, and the claim that government must rest on the consent of the governed posed a dramatic issue between American republicanism and European monarchy. But Americans understood that in the science of government their real claim to fame was not democracy but rather the successful creation and management of their federal union. "Of all the presumptions indulged by presumptuous man," as Webster observed in a commemorative address, "that is one of the rashest which looks for repeated and favorable opportunities for the deliberate establishment of a united government over distinct and widely extended communities. Such a thing has happened once in human affairs, and but once; the event stands out as a prominent exception to all ordinary history; and unless we suppose ourselves running into an age of miracles, we may not expect its repetition."[1] To the North American mind, the overriding fact was that the United States had succeeded in this unprecedented aim, and Europe and South America had no less clearly failed. Tocqueville, as we have seen, noted the widespread opinion in the United States that South America's bid for republican governments had collapsed because they had not taken the path of federal union. Europe often appeared a more hopeless case because the constituent elements of any such union—on the model perhaps of Henry IV's long-dead federative system—were too addicted to war and plunder to find any such prospect attractive.

America therefore stood alone: its "Federal orb, like the sun in the physical hemisphere, supports and maintains each revolving satellite," even those states "too weak to be secure and too small to be respectable," whereas Europe's balance of power locked states in bloody rivalries apt to break out at any time in a general conflagration. Despite the obstacles to improvement elsewhere, federal republican union provided a template for the amelioration of international relations and its movement in a progressive direction. One

Jeffersonian pamphleteer, Allan Bowie Magruder, concluded that "upon this liberal plan of government, the whole world might be regulated in peace and harmony." When Charles Sumner accepted nomination for the Senate in 1851, he responded thusly: "With me the Union is twice blessed: first, as powerful guardian of the repose and happiness of thirty-one States, clasped by the endearing name of country; and next, as model and beginning of that all-embracing Federation of States, by which unity, peace, and concord will finally be organized among the Nations." The sober Madison was not immune from exploring these dreamy possibilities. Reviewing his notes of the federal convention, Madison speculated in his retirement that "were it possible by human contrivance so to accelerate the intercourse between every part of the globe that all its inhabitants could be united under the superintending authority of an ecumenical Council, how great a portion of human evils would be avoided. Wars, famines, with pestilence as far as the fruit of either, could not exist; taxes to pay for wars, or to provide against them would be needless, and the expense and perplexities of local fetters on interchange beneficial to all would no longer oppress the social state."[2]

There was, to be sure, no prospect, in the then existing circumstances, that America might join a European congress. When William Ladd, the head of the American Peace Society, proposed in 1840 a Congress of Nations and wished to see American participation in it, the proposal made no headway in Washington. Ladd's *Essay on a Congress of Nations* looked to the formation of a body in which each civilized nation would have one vote, with decisions taken on the basis of unanimity and after ratification by the nations. The congress would be authorized to "enact a code of law; establish a court; promote trade, transportation, and communication, and seek uniformity in such standards as weights and measures. It could not intervene in the internal matters of states." There was no executive—enforcement was left to public opinion—but Ladd did propose a judicial body, with each country to name two judges, capable of hearing both justiciable and nonjusticiable matters. "The tribunal could hear cases referred to it by governments, settle boundary disputes, suggest laws for enactment, and render decisions by majority vote."[3]

When Ladd's plan was submitted to the Congress for action, the House Foreign Affairs Committee (chaired by Hugh Legaré) agreed "that the union of all nations, in a state of peace, under the restraints and protection of law, is the ideal perfection of civil society." It acknowledged, too, that America's federal union was a template for the reform of the European system: "That happy compromise by which the wisdom of our fathers—availing itself, it is true, of such circumstances as have never occurred elsewhere—has reconciled, on this continent, the sovereignty of the States with the rights of individuals, under a peaceful, judicial administration of the law, is still, and is likely long to continue, a *desideratum* [in Europe]." Peace was especially desirable because its prolongation would inevitably redound to the benefit of "limited or constitutional government." Whereas war had always been "the most fruitful source of arbitrary power," peace was "the hope of liberty." "A state of opinion that opposes large armies and military discipline . . . will inevitably lead . . . to the general establishment of representative institutions." The committee also praised the virtues of free trade, whose "great cardinal truth" was that "'self-love and social are the same.'" Nothing, it believed, "can be more shallow in science, as well as sordid and narrow in spirit, than a restrictive policy founded upon the idea that a nation can only enrich itself at the expense of its neighbors."

Despite these paeans to internationalism, the committee rejected the memorial. It was impractical—the requirement of unanimity would make any controversial project easily baffled. The plan exaggerated the impact of "mere positive legislation" as a factor in human affairs. The committee's objections were strongest, however, with respect to the proposed international board of arbitration. The "only republic in the world should be very careful not to commit its destinies, in any serious degree, to institutions which might and would be controlled by influences hostile to its principles." So long as any confederacy in Europe would be a confederacy of kings, it would be a body in which American participation was undesirable and unlikely. There was, withal, reason to hope: "The spirit of the age is gradually becoming more favorable to [representative] institutions, just in proportion as it is becoming less disposed to war."[4]

Hope indeed seemed to quicken its pace as Americans observed in 1848 "the efforts in progress to unite the States of Germany in a confederation similar in many respects to our own Federal Union." Commented President Polk: "If the great and enlightened German States, occupying, as they do, a central and commanding position in Europe, shall succeed in establishing such a confederated government," it would have momentous consequences. "Whilst it will consolidate and strengthen the power of Germany, it must essentially promote the cause of peace, commerce, civilization, and constitutional liberty throughout the world."[5]

Whether viewed as "our last and only security" or as a model world order, the union elicited intense devotion among Americans. To maintain the union in all its powers and limitations could appear as both manifest necessity and sacred cause, as the offspring of both inescapable reason of state and idealistic purpose. Without the union, as Americans were often reminded by their public figures, all would be lost; dismemberment "would leave the country,"

in Webster's words, not only bereft of its prosperity and happiness, but without limbs, or organs, or faculties, by which to exert itself hereafter."

Other misfortunes may be borne, or their effects overcome. If disastrous
war should sweep our commerce from the ocean, another generation
may renew it; if it exhaust our treasury, future industry may replenish
it; if it desolate and lay waste our fields, still, under a new cultivation,
they will grow green again, and ripen to future harvests. It were but a
trifle even if the walls of yonder Capitol were to crumble, if its lofty pillars should fall, and its gorgeous decorations be all covered by the dust
of the valley. All these might be rebuilt. But who shall reconstruct the
fabric of demolished government? Who shall rear again the well-pro-
portioned columns of constitutional liberty? Who shall frame together
the skilled architecture which unites national sovereignty with State
rights, individual security, and public prosperity? No, if these columns
fall, they will be raised not again. Like the Coliseum and the Parthe-
non, they will be destined to a mournful, a melancholy immortality.
Bitterer tears, however will flow over them, than were ever shed over
the monuments of Roman or Grecian art; for they will be the remnants
of a more glorious edifice than Greece or Rome ever saw, the edifice of
constitutional American liberty.[6]

PART FIVE
Empire and Its Discontents

17

Reds and Whites

WHEN THE CONSTITUTION WAS FORMED, one of the most important responsibilities lodged in the federal government was the making of treaties and regulation of relations with the Indian nations of eastern North America. The North American mind, swayed by the speculations of Enlightenment thinkers, had long looked with repugnance on the barbarous treatment meted out to aboriginals by Spanish conquerors. "What good could the Spanish not have done the Mexicans," Montesquieu had asked in *The Spirit of the Laws*. "They had a gentle religion to give them; they brought them a raging superstition. They could have set the slaves free, and they made freemen slaves. They could have made clear to them that human sacrifice was an abuse; instead they exterminated them. I would never finish if I wanted to tell all the good things they did not do, and all the evil ones they did." Vattel, too, had distinguished between North and South America in his treatment of the aboriginal question, condemning the Spanish and justifying the policy of the English colonies. In treating the "celebrated question which has arisen in connection with the discovery of the New World"—"whether a Nation may lawfully occupy any part of a vast territory in which are to be found only wandering tribes whose small numbers can not populate the whole country"—Vattel held that "these tribes can not take to themselves more land than they have need of or can inhabit and cultivate. Their uncertain occupancy of these vast regions can not be held as a real and lawful taking of possession; and when the Nations of Europe, which are too confined at home, come upon lands which the savages have no special need of and are making no present and continuous use of, they may lawfully take possession of them and establish colonies in them." It was no departure from "the intentions of nature" to "restrict the savages within narrower bounds," for "if each Nation had desired from the beginning to appropriate to itself an extent of territory great enough for it to live merely by hunting, fishing, and gathering wild fruits, the earth would not suffice for a tenth part of the people who now inhabit it." Vattel, fiercely anticlerical, was fortified in these views by his belief that the vast lands arrogated to unproductive monks by the Catholic Church had badly retarded human happiness in Europe. On these broadly utilitarian grounds he had justified European colonization and had praised "the moderation of the English Puritans" and of William Penn and the Quakers for their purchases of Indian land.[1]

In 1789, when the new government came into operation, the contrast between the colonizing policy of the Spanish and the English continued to be made, and among North American whites there was near-universal acceptance of the justification Vattel had offered for colonization. Strong doubts, nevertheless, had entered into the minds of many whites as they reflected on what was occurring before their eyes. In two previous wars, the Indian nations had suffered badly, ground between the millstone of the rivalry of the British and French colonists in the Great War for the Empire, and then between American and British forces in the American War of Independence. The pattern that would so often characterize the future—white encroachment, horrible atrocity committed by one or the other side, then retaliation—had already established itself. It was often impossible for outsiders to discover what had really happened; news of the battles always arrived in an atmosphere charged with rumor and fraught with horror. In the Declaration of Independence, Jefferson had charged against George III the crime of bringing "on the inhabitants of our frontiers the merciless Indian savages, whose known rule of warfare is an undistinguished destruction of all ages, sexes, & conditions of existence." Whites on the frontier saw their conflict with the Indians in those terms and ascribed it to an evil that must be extirpated, moral indignation supplying the fuel of counteratrocity and conquest.

More reflecting observers in the settled regions of the American states doubted that it was all so simple. It was obvious that white encroachment was responsible for much of the fighting; so, too, white expansion was often caught up with intestine conflicts among the Indians themselves. White land hunger and Indian disunity—a mirror for white Americans in which they often saw one possible future for themselves—operated together with the ready propensity on both sides to resort to violence to produce a cumulative picture that was profoundly disturbing. "It is a melancholy reflection," wrote Henry Knox, secretary of war in the Washington administration, "that our modes of population have been more destructive to the Indian natives than the conduct of the conquerors of Mexico and Peru. Evidence of this is the utter extirpation of nearly all the Indians in the most populous parts of the Union." Knox believed that unless the federal government adopted different and better policies, the next twenty-five years would bring a similar result for the tribes of the eastern Mississippi valley. In the 1790s, Knox saw the root cause of this in terms that, nearly a hundred years later, would be described by Carl Schurz. "Most of the Indian wars grew," Schurz held, "not from any desire of the Government to disturb the Indians in the territorial possessions guaranteed to them, but from the restless and unscrupulous greed of frontiersmen who pushed their settlements and ventures into the Indian country, provoked conflicts with the Indians and then called for the protection of the government against the resisting and retaliating Indians, thus involving it in the hostilities which they themselves had begun."[2]

For reasons we have already explored, however, the claims of the frontiersmen could not, in the last analysis, be denied. Both before and after the years in which Knox drafted his reports on Indian policy, the claim of the West was "protect us, or we will separate." Rumors of foreign alliance and of conspiracies of western separation were rife for three decades after the Treaty of Paris in 1783. The Spanish Conspiracy in Kentucky of 1787 to 1789, the Whiskey Rebellion of 1794, the Blount Conspiracy of 1797, the Louisiana crisis of 1802, and the Burr Conspiracy of 1806–1807—all attested to the anxiety with which people viewed the prospect of a durable union between the Atlantic and transmontane territories. That the western interest had to be protected and supported in order to secure its loyalty to the union seemed axiomatic. Unconditional support, however, promised to secure the union only at the cost of indicting the United States at the bar of posterity, because the cycle of mutual outrage and war would end in the destruction of the tribes. "A future historian," Knox warned, "may mark the causes of this destruction of the human race in sable colors."

In warning of this result, of course, Knox predicted the future; contemporary historians now so treat it. The image that formerly prevailed in national memory—of brave pioneers establishing self-governing democratic communities across the wilderness and prairie, repelling the attacks of barbarous Indians ever ready to employ inhumane means of warfare—has been displaced by its near opposite. The encounter is still defined by the opposition between "civilization" and "savagery," but the roles have been reversed. The treachery, inhumanity, and genocidal intention of the white man now has pride of place in the story and is set against a revised picture of the Indian nations who were displaced. The new understanding emphasizes their collective and democratic modes of decision making, their communitarian values, their development of agricultural systems more sedentary than previously thought, their more harmonious relationship with nature.[3]

Both accounts, traditional and revised, have been heavily influenced by the moral issues that inescapably are raised by the story. The unflattering portrait of Indians in earlier accounts eased the troubled white conscience and contributed its share to a narrative that made the violation of established right a historical necessity. The unflattering portrait of white men in more recent accounts, together with the more humane portrait of Indian communities, is rooted in the desire of historians to condemn an encounter marked by acts of injustice and inhumanity. That has drawn them irresistibly to the image of despotic empire. Of the new government inaugurated in 1789, D. W. Meinig writes that Indians "could only regard it as an ominous transformation of one empire into another, from one whose distant king had actually made some real effort to befriend and protect them to an empire run by the very people who had proved relentless in their destructive advance. . . . for Creeks and Cherokees, Chickasaws, Shawnees, Winnebagos, and many others, the new city of Washington was what St. Petersburg was for the Finns, Peking for the Miao, or Constantinople for the Serbs: the seat of a capricious, tyrannical power"; it could "punish, devastate, conquer, expel any people that stood in its way and challenged its authority."[4]

To arrive at a fair interpretation, in the midst of these clashing moral claims, is no easy task, but certain salient factors in the development of the story deserve consideration. Burke's plea of incapacity—"I know not the means of drawing up an indictment against a whole people"—may, in the first instance, be recalled. From the 1790s to the 1820s, the attitude and intention of the government in Washington was not the same as the attitude and intention of frontiersmen; the approach of New England came to differ vastly from that of the South; the various Indian nations displayed as much, if not more, diversity in their modes of existence as did Massachusetts and South Carolina. Just as it was unfair and misleading for frontiersmen to ascribe guilt, collective responsibility, and vicious traits to all Indians, based upon what some had done, we should be cautious in ascribing collective guilt to whites. The federal government was often a powerless spectator of events beyond its control, and even had greater power existed, there remained the dilemma, as Meinig notes, "that any attempt to bring the Western frontier under closer control would require such a severe braking of those forces actually driving it forward that it might create a friction so intense as to ignite and destroy the whole system." The forces driving it forward, as Meinig also shows, were overwhelmingly sectional in character; the armed populace involved in the thrust outward, whether to the Ohio Valley or the southern borderlands, did not need "the assistance and protection of the central government in their expansions into new lands."[5]

These facts imposed severe constraints on federal officials. They suggested that a separation of the western country from the United States would actually render the encounter more rather than less lethal for the Indians because it would unfold under the auspices of a raging state system in which American sections, European powers, and Indian nations struggled for primacy. At the same time, these facts, so centrally tied to the logic of the unionist paradigm, imposed severe constraints on the ability of the federal government to block depredations on the Indians. The constraints of policy were very narrow, but within those constraints it does not seem reasonable to doubt the sincerity of many of those within the federal government who struggled to find a humane outcome. At a minimum it would seem necessary to introduce into the account of these relations a greater sense of the sectional differentiation on the white side.[6]

The desire to arrest the cycle of mutual outrage, war, and extermination entered deeply into the Indian policy of the federal government after its establishment in 1789. The consensus held that a different policy must seek to make the expansion of white settlement compatible with the preservation of peace, with advance taking place through purchase and treaty, and with the ultimate aim of assimilating individual Indians into the larger white society. In order for this to succeed, it was necessary, in Washington's summary,

That [the Indians] should experience the benefits of an impartial dispensation of justice.

That the mode of alienating their lands, the main source of discontent and war, should be so defined and regulated as to obviate . . . controversy concerning the reality and extent of the alienations which are made.

That commerce with them should be promoted under regulations tending to secure an equitable deportment toward them, and that such rational experiments should be made for imparting to them the blessings of civilization as may from time to time suit their condition.

That the Executive of the United States should be enabled to employ the means to which the Indians have been long accustomed for uniting their immediate interests with the preservation of peace.

And that efficacious provision should be made for inflicting adequate penalties upon all those who, by violating their rights, shall infringe the treaties and endanger the peace of the Union.[7]

Though an early statement of government policy, Washington's guidelines were not only his own but those of successor administrations. The revision undertaken in 1802 by the Republican Congress largely followed these parameters. The control of Indian commerce was to be in the hands of federal agents, who were to license white traders, supervise government stores, and instruct Indians in agricultural arts. White settlement would advance as their lots were contracted. Government trading houses would display to the Indians the better lifestyle to be obtained through the abandonment of hunting and adoption of agriculture. The government would aid the Indians by teaching agricultural methods and provide them with needed capital through the purchase of lands made extraneous by the abandonment of hunting. Philanthropists and humanitarians like Jefferson believed that the greatest good for the Indians would be to encourage their assimilation into the white, agricultural society, and they were insistent on the importance of preserving peace with the tribes. As president, notes historian Peter Onuf, Jefferson "never tired of preaching to his Indian children the great advantages of a settled, agricultural regime that would enable them to have more children, thus countering the devastating and demoralizing effects of population loss on native societies." If the right policies were followed, the founding generation had believed, it might be possible to break "the fearful connexion" with "fraud and violence" theretofore endemic.[8]

This early policy was not without cynical elements. Jefferson, alarmed by the prospect of a French military colony in New Orleans and anxious to secure a stronger foothold in the Southwest, had noted in 1803 that the Indians might be forced to yield their lands as a means of paying their debts and had seen indebtedness as a most promising means of dispossession.[9] Then the Old Northwest was brought to war by settler mistreatment of the tribes and by the decision of Tecumseh, joined by his brother Tenskwatawa the Prophet, to gather the transmontane Indians into a grand confederation to resist further white encroachment. The war that ensued drove the Northwest Indians to defeat and exile. Unlike the maritime issues that had provoked the War of 1812, which saw neither America nor Britain retreating from its claims in the peace treaty, the war in the interior had proved decisive. Though in 1814 British negotiators were still holding out for a vast Indian protectorate covering most of the territory of the Virginia cession that made up the Old Northwest, they relented at Ghent. New dictated treaties followed, confirming the dispossession.[10]

In the Southwest, peace was maintained with the Cherokees, but there was vicious fighting with bands of Seminoles, "Red-Stick" Creeks, and runaway slaves during the War of 1812, which continued on after the war. In 1818, Andrew Jackson invaded Spanish Florida, seized the Spanish forts at Pensacola and St. Marks, and hung two British traders in the territory. Jackson's instructions had authorized him to take retaliatory action against piratical depredations but not to do what he did, and his actions provoked strong remonstrance in Congress. "*Veni, vidi, vici*," exclaimed Clay. "Wonderful energy! Admirable promptitude! Alas! That it had not been an energy and a promptitude within the pale of the Constitution, and according to the orders of the Chief Magistrate!" The justification offered by Jackson's defenders that the executions "were only a wrong mode of doing a right thing" was rejected by Clay: "A wrong mode of doing a right thing!" In no code of public law or system of ethics could one find "any sanction for a principle so monstrous." It was dangerous to create a precedent for the abuse of the war power, which had been "expressly and exclusively granted" to Congress under the Constitution to guard against precisely "that species of rashness which has been manifested in Florida." The members of the "immortal Convention" saw "that nations are often precipitated into ruinous war, from folly, from pride, from ambition, and from the desire of military fame." By committing the subject to the legislature, the hope was to spare the United States "from the mad wars that have afflicted, and desolated, and ruined other countries. . . . It was in the provinces were laid the abuses and the seeds of the ambitious projects which overturned the liberties of Rome. . . . The influence of a bad example would often be felt when its authors and all the circumstances connected with it were no longer remembered."[11]

Within the cabinet, Jackson's actions were condemned by Calhoun as raising the risk of war: "However improper the conduct of Spain has been, and however desirable to us to possess the Floridas, I am decidedly of the opinion that the peace of the country ought to be preserved. Should other powers be involved and the war general, the wisest man cannot see the result we must suffer. We want time. Let us grow." Incongruously, the lone defender of Jackson in the administration was John Quincy Adams. The seizure of the Spanish forts, as Adams justified the measure to the British government, arose "not by virtue of any orders received by [Jackson] from this Government to that effect, nor with any view of wresting the province from the possession of Spain, nor in any spirit of hostility to the Spanish Government; that it arose from incidents which occurred in the prosecution of the war against the Indians." Adams reviewed the murders committed by the "mingled horde of lawless Indians and Negroes" and argued that Jackson took the Spanish forts "as a necessary measure of self-defence; giving notice that they should be restored whenever Spain should place commanders and a force there able and willing to fulfill the engagements of Spain towards the United States. . . . By all the laws of neutrality and of war, as well as of prudence and of humanity, he was warranted in anticipating his enemy by the amicable, and, that being refused, by the forcible occupation of the fort. There will need no citations from printed treatises on international law to prove the correctness of this principle. It is engraved in adamant on the common sense of mankind. No writer upon the law of nations ever pretended to contradict it. None, of any reputation or authority, ever omitted to assert it."[12]

Years later, Adams recalled the infamous episode in an interview with Henry Wise, a representative from Virginia whom Adams corralled on the floor of the House. No sooner than graciously inviting Wise to take a seat beside him, Adams told the Virginian that he was a "bad man" and had "bad principles" because he justified human bondage, but that Wise was at least better than Andrew Jackson, who "has no principles at all." "When I was Secretary of State," Adams went on to say, "Andrew Jackson invaded Florida, and hung Arbuthnot and Ambrister. He was arraigned for that conduct before the Cabinet of Mr. Monroe. I alone defended his course, and put him on the high ground of international law, as expounded by Grotius, Puffendorf, and Vattel, and his conduct was justified by Mr. Monroe and by Congress." But though Jackson "was justified in doing right by the highest authorities on the law of nations," he preferred, Adams said, "to plead orders to do wrong." Jackson published a forged certificate, renounced by Monroe on his deathbed, supposedly authorizing the general to invade Florida. "He chose rather to rely on a forged order to do wrong than on the laws of nations to do right. He said, 'D—n Grotius! d—n Puffendorf! d—n Vattel!—this is a mere matter between Jim Monroe and myself!'" As Wise comments, "Jackson was the very man to d—n Grotius, Puffendorf, and Vattel; and Adams was the very man to condemn him for that above all other things as a great malefactor."[13]

Reviewing the history of Indian-white relations in 1820, William Pinkney asked: "What was the settlement of our ancestors in this country, but an invasion of the rights of the barbarians who inhabited it? That settlement, with slight exceptions, was effected by the slaughter of those who did no more than defend their native land against the intruders of Europe, or by unequal compacts and purchases, in which feebleness and ignorance had to deal with power and cunning." The Indians had been swept away "by the injustice of our fathers, and their domain usurped by force, or obtained by artifices yet more criminal." The determination that this should no longer be so ostensibly went to the essence of government policy under Washington, Knox, and Jefferson, but Pinkney saw little in the way of progress. With the Indians driven back "by the swelling tide of our population," he argued, the practice of making contracts and treaties with the "miserable remnant" that remained had only further sealed their ruin. The entire process, he observed, was both thoroughly shameful and utterly inexorable. "Will you recur to those scenes of various iniquity for any other purpose than to regret and lament them? Will you pry into them with a view to shake and impair your rights of property and dominion?"[14]

From before 1754 and up to the War of 1812, the encounter between red and white was often expressed in terms of the dialectic between unity and division. The whole subject was thoroughly infiltrated by the categories of the unionist paradigm. This was so, in the first instance, because federal norms and values were understood and celebrated on both sides of the encounter. The Iroquois League was the most famous of the Indian confederacies that recognized the federal principle, and it is fairly considered as the first great enterprise of federal union in North America. A recognition of the importance of union, and the danger of division; a pledge of perpetual peace within, and of concerted action toward enemies without; an understanding of how individuality might be preserved by common action; the vital significance attached to sworn oaths and plighted faith—all these hallmarks of the federal principle were reflected in the institutions and norms of that distinguished confederacy (also known as the Six Nations, the Long House, or the "Haudenosaunee political system"). This does not mean, as some enthusiasts have claimed, that the Iroquois League exercised a commanding influence at the Philadelphia convention; the recorded debates do not bear out that thesis. The experience of the Six Nations was but one example relevant to the building of the American union and not nearly as important as a host of precedents from Europe.[15]

In a basic respect, however, the question of relative influence is misplaced. The interesting thing is not whether Indians and whites directly influenced the other in the building of their institutions so much as that they hit upon the same ideas independently. There existed a close proximity of reasoning and experience resulting from the mutual recognition of federal norms. In his comments on the Confederacy of the Six Nations, for example, Calhoun found support for his theories of the concurrent majority. The individual veto accorded to each member of the confederate council (forty-two in all), with its unmistakable likeness to the Polish Diet, showed for Calhoun that an absolute negative, far from "making the Confederacy weak, or impracticable, had the opposite effect. It secured harmony in council and action, and with them a great increase of power"—as Calhoun expected a similar principle to do for the American Constitution.

Among the Indian nations of the interior, and reaching even to the solitudes of Canada and the vistas of Chapultepec, the ideas so central to the unionist paradigm—universal empire, international anarchy, unity and division, balance of power, liberty and independence, aggression and neutrality—had extraordinary relevance and resonance. The co-mingling of Indian and white perception and reasoning is especially marked by the attention given to union. Discerning observers on each side understood the importance of unity for themselves, while seeing in "the other" a spirit of union that might be emulated, a dangerous confederacy with formidable powers, or an experience of discord that taught the fatal lesson of disunion. Notes historian Joseph Ellis: "At the same time that state delegations were meeting at Philadelphia in the summer of 1787 to form 'a more perfect union,' all the Indian tribes south of the Great Lakes, to include the Iroquois,

Hurons, Mohawks, Wyandots, Oneidas, and Shawnees, had convened with the Creeks and Cherokees to create an Indian alliance, their Native American version of the Constitutional Convention." When Longfellow had Hiawatha say that "all your strength is in union, all your danger is in discord," he said what had been said a thousand times on both sides; and the wise men on both sides knew it.[16]

18

The Removal of the Cherokee

THROUGH ALL THE EARLY ADMINISTRATIONS, an invariable aim of federal policy was to confine the negotiation of treaties and cessions of land to itself. On the understanding that the whole relationship could only be managed by a general authority, the Constitution had lodged the power in the federal government. But though the union had exclusive control of Indian negotiations and treaties, it did not have an uncontested claim to western lands. The intractable issues that had arisen between landed and landless states in the confederation were resolved, in effect, by individual treaties between the federal government and states with extensive land claims. Following Virginia's precedent in the 1780s, which surrendered its title to the Old Northwest, the southern states also made compacts with the federal government in the first fifteen years after the Constitution came into operation. The 1802 agreement with Georgia, which lay at the center of the controversy in 1830, obligated the United States, "at their own expense," to "extinguish, for the use of Georgia, as early as the same can be peaceably obtained, on reasonable terms, the Indian title to lands within the State of Georgia."[1]

The federal government treated the Indian nations, in law, as "domestic dependent nations." They were dependent on the federal government because it asserted the exclusive right, as against both the states and foreign powers like Britain, to treat with the tribes; but they were nations because they were considered as "distinct, independent political communities, retaining their original natural rights, as the undisputed possessors of the soil from time immemorial." As Justice Marshall observed in *Worcester v. Georgia*, the "right of discovery" recognized in the law of nations "could not affect the rights of those already in possession." It applied only as against other European powers. "It gave the exclusive right to purchase, but did not found that right on a denial of the right of the possessor to sell."[2]

The political pattern that developed, from one vantage point, was "a suzerain-state system," in which one large power enters into a "protectorate" relationship with a string of lesser powers.[3] The difficulty is that there were two potential suzerains—the federal government and the states. The federal government had made two different sets of compacts—one set with the Indians, the other set with the states. The crisis of the late 1820s arose when these compacts came into collision. The refusal of the Creeks and

Cherokees to submit to any further alienations of their territory, together with the discovery of gold on their lands, led to a conflict between Georgia and the federal government in the Adams administration. Adams refused to coerce the tribes; Georgia insisted that "the lands in question belong to Georgia—she must and she will have them." Attributing bad faith to the general government, Georgia held that all the lands "which lie within the conventional limits of Georgia, belong to her absolutely; that the title is in her; that the Indians are tenants at her will; that she may, at any time she pleases, determine that tenancy by taking possession of the premises; and that Georgia has the right to extend her authority and laws over the whole territory." The whole grant of power to the federal government, the legislature insisted, had been made on the condition that the federal authority would in due time secure white title, and this it had failed to do. In view of her regard for the union, she would not "enforce her rights by violence, until all other means of redress fail." We will give you a bit of time, in other words; then, if not satisfied, we are going to use force.[4]

Georgia's threats played out alongside the movement toward nullification in South Carolina and the rising demand in the West for a virtual surrender of federal control over the public lands. They all raised constitutional issues that, while not identical, were certainly similar, and they were linked politically in the alliance of South and West, friendly to state rights, that brought Jackson to power in 1828. The surprise and astonishment over Jackson's Force Bill in early 1833 occurred against the background of Jackson's wholehearted support of Georgia in its claims against the Cherokee; for Georgia had made, and made repeatedly, the same threat of nullification that Jackson would brand as treasonous when made by South Carolina over the tariff.

Soon after the Twenty-first Congress had convened in December 1829, a report on a plan of Indian removal was presented by John Bell of Tennessee. This recognized the validity of Georgia's claim and proposed that the federal government undertake a plan of removal. The Adams administration had presented a plan of removal in 1826 but had insisted that nothing take place, in reference to the Indians, "without their own consent." Adams's secretary of war, James Barbour, was somewhat diffident about the reasons for this; it arose partly from "expediency"—above all the interest in peace—and partly from considerations of right or "authority." It was, withal, the settled policy of the government. The Bell report, in keeping with Jackson's outlook, now proposed that the Indians be removed without their consent, but for their own good. No individual Indian was to be removed involuntarily, but if they chose to stay they were to be "distinctly informed," as Jackson put it, that "they must be subject" to the laws of the states. The legislation was represented as a piece of humanitarian policy that would save the Indians. Supporters condemned the false humanitarianism of northern sympathizers whose advice, if followed, would doom the Indians to destruction.[5]

Because the preceding policy of the government has been subjected to a sharp eye by historians, the moral significance of this change of policy has often been blurred or eroded. The policy of Jackson and the Democrats no longer stands as a singularly bad act but is seen to be of a piece with the whole tenor and thrust of previous policy, only a shade blacker than "conquest by purchase." Among contemporaries, however, it was seen to have vast moral and political significance. Theodore Frelinghuysen (senator from New Jersey), Edward Everett (representative from Massachusetts), and Henry Storrs (representative from New York), together with others in the coalescing Whig opposition to Jacksonian democracy, launched blistering salvos against the change in policy. Jackson's intention to tear up the treaties, they charged, was unconstitutional. For the purpose of treaty making, Storrs insisted, "the Senate is the council of the States, and the treaties are the acts of the States." To violate these treaties on his own authority was a claim such as only a despot would make. The states-righters who supported Jackson in this instance were warned by Storrs that they were not to be freed from the evident implication. "If the friends of State rights propose to sanction the violation of these Indian treaties, they must bear him out to the full extent of this thoughtless usurpation." He chided the transparent cynicism of its supporters. Suppose, he asked, that the president had acted unilaterally to annul land cessions made by the Indians to some of the states. "Should we not have heard something—and that, too, quite earnestly, of plighted faith, of solemn treaties, and the constitutional securities of the states?" But it was the gross abrogation of the right of the Cherokee that filled him with the greatest indignation. "We cannot approach our Indian treaties on any side, without finding them secured by sanctions which cannot safely be despised." The committee report had not assigned "much weight to 'the stately forms which Indian treaties have assumed, nor to the terms often employed in them,' but considered them as 'mere names' and 'forms of intercourse.'" If this were so, Storrs held, "words no longer mean what words import, and things are not what they are." "It requires no skill in political science to interpret these treaties. The plainest man can read your solemn guarantees to these nations, and understand them for himself."[6]

In tracing the history of relations between whites and reds, Storrs noted that "we came to these people with peace offerings, and they gave us lands. As we increased in numbers we increased our demands, and began to press upon them. . . . They resisted at last, and flew to their arms. Fierce and bloody wars followed. We felt their power; and if they had been united, or had foreseen what we are now doing, we should not now be in these seats. We met them again in friendship, and established our treaties with them. We pledged our faith, and gave them our solemn guaranties that we would come no further." The "hospitality to our fathers" perpetuated "on the gorgeous panels which surround us," showing these distinguished ceremonies, were now to stare down in mockery on the proceedings in Congress. By throwing this away "by a dash of the pen," consequences threatening to constitutional liberty would inevitably ensue. "The passage of this bill will light up joy and hope in the palace of every despot. It will do more to destroy the confidence of the world in free government, than all their armies could accomplish." Storrs noted that republics, like monarchies, had been charged "with insolence and oppression in the day of their power. History has unfortunately given us much proof of its truth, and we are about to confirm it by our own example."[7]

It was the point of national morality to which Storrs continually recurred, the violation of which alarmed and disgusted him. It was customary, in this epoch, to appeal to the judgment of posterity, to "bid the distant generations hail!" But Storrs's appeal was frantic, even desperate. "We must stand at last at the bar of posterity," he warned,

> and answer there for ourselves and our country. If we look for party influence to sustain us now, it will fail us there. The little bickerings in which we now bustle and show off our importance, will have then ceased and been forgotten, or little understood. . . . Our country will be brought by the historian—*custodia fidelis rerum*—to that standard of universal morality which will guide the judgment and fix the sentence of posterity. . . . The character of this measure will then be known as it is. The full and clear light of truth will break in upon it, and it will stand out in history in bold relief. . . . Your history—your treaties and your statutes, will confront you. The human heart will be consulted—the moral sense of all mankind will speak out fearlessly, and you will stand condemned by the law of God as well as the sentence of your fellow-men. You may not live to hear it, but there will be no refuge for you in the grave. . . . Nor will this transaction be put down as a party measure. Our country, too, must bear the crime and the shame.

As Storrs observed, it was impossible to accept the Bell report without simultaneously charging bad faith and utter cynicism upon six presidential administrations. The only fair reading of the committee report was that the founders of the government had made all these treaties for the purpose of breaking them. "I would not darken the living light of that glory which these illustrations of the justice of our ancestors have spread over every page of their history, for all the Indian lands that avarice ever dreamt of, and all the empire which ambition ever coveted. . . . There is nothing to be won in this controversy that is worth a moment's thought, in comparison with the condemnation that lies beyond it."[8]

The proponents of forced removal were not without resources to combat these attacks. What, they asked, of the federal government's pledge, made in 1802, to alienate the lands over time? What, too, of the provision in the Constitution that forbade the creation of a new state from within the borders of an old state without the latter's consent? From the publications of New England, Lumpkin noted, "not only the stranger in a foreign land, but the honest laboring people of New England, who stay at home, and would mind their own business if let alone by these canting fanatics, verily believe that the Georgians are the worst of all savages. . . . Upon the other hand, they are taught to believe that the Cherokee Indians are the most prosperous, enlightened, and religious nation of people on earth—except, indeed, the nation of New England." The case was otherwise, Lumpkin insisted: the Cherokees were ruled by an "aristocracy" of about a hundred men, most of them with white blood, who used the federal dollars given in annuities from previous land sales to create a corrupt and dependent enclave within Georgia and other southern states.[9]

The debate over Indian removal pitted the North, especially New England, against the South, especially the Deep South; accusations of sectional jealousy, treachery, and unavowed but malicious motive flew thick and fast, just as they were doing in the concurrent debate over national supremacy, nullification, and the public domain among Webster, Hayne, and Benton in the Senate. That New England had done itself, or worse, what it was now condemning was frequently alleged, as was the fact that its real desire was to hamper the growth of the southern states. Martin Van Buren would later recall that the Whigs had made a "persevering" attempt to protect the Indians in their possession, but he would not credit their sincerity: "Few men would now venture to deny that it was a factious opposition waged to promote the interests of party at the expence of the highest interests of the Country, upon grounds which were not tenable and for avowed purposes which were not practicable,—or, if practicable, could only become so thro' the agency of the U.S. Army and the probable destruction of the Confederacy." The prospect of force, as Van Buren indicated, hung like a dark cloud over the debate. Taking note of the "strong and powerful feeling in favor of the Indians, which pervades an extensive portion of this country," Foster of Georgia professed that he had "no disposition to recriminate. Sir, I have a higher purpose in view—defence is my object. I take my stand on the borders of my State, for the purpose of repelling the attacks which have been made, and are still making, upon her rights and character; and if, in the prosecution of this duty, I should find it necessary to make an incursion into the territories of our assailants, I shall endeavor to do it in such a way as to be guilty of no departure from the established rules and principles of a strictly defensive war." Hayne and Webster spoke of similar excursions in their famous duel. That real menaces lay behind this sort of rhetoric could hardly be doubted.[10]

Jackson and the Democracy, the South and the West, in the end had their way, and Indian removal was authorized by Congress. What William Wirt, an advocate of the Cherokee, called "the omnipotent sophistry of interest and passion" prevailed. Commenting on what had been done, Tocqueville contrasted Spanish and Anglo-American modes of conquest. Like the Whigs, who also made the comparison in the 1830 debate, Tocqueville shared Montesquieu's judgment of the Spanish conquest: "The Spaniards pursued the Indians with bloodhounds, like wild beasts; they sacked the New World like a city taken by storm, with no discernment or compassion; but destruction must cease at last and frenzy has a limit: the remnant of the Indian population which had escaped the massacre mixed with its conquerors and adopted in the end their religion and their manners." The conduct of the Americans, by contrast, was characterized "by a singular attachment to the formalities of law. . . . The Spaniards were unable to exterminate the Indian race by those unparalleled atrocities which brand them with indelible shame, nor did they succeed even in wholly depriving it of its rights; but the Americans of the United States have accomplished this twofold purpose with singular felicity, tranquilly, legally, philanthropically, without shedding blood, and without violating a single great principle of morality in the eyes of the world. It is impossible to destroy men with more respect for the laws of humanity." Actually, a great moral principle had been violated in the Indian removal of the 1830s, and Tocqueville's summation is not a little peculiar in light of the objections raised in Congress. His larger judgment, however, was undoubtedly correct: the sincere humanitarian desire to maintain the tribes in the possessions guaranteed to them had been overwhelmed by tremendous resistance in the several states, forcing the abandonment of these efforts "in order not to endanger the safety of the American Union."[11]

That the union would be endangered were the federal government to deny the Southwest its claims was a frequently reiterated thesis. As it happened, however, the union was also endangered by the propitiation of Georgia, because this meant to defy other important pillars of the constitutional order. Such was the result when the authority of the Supreme Court, and the sanctity of compact, got bloodied in its confrontation with more powerful political forces. While the case of the Cherokee Nation against Georgia was pending before the Supreme Court, a Cherokee named George Tassels was convicted of murder and lay in a Georgia jail awaiting his sentence. A writ of error from the Supreme Court, signed by Chief Justice Marshall, was secured, and Georgia was ordered to appear before the federal tribunal and defend the judgment of its court. Georgia's response was contemptuous; the state legislature found Marshall's interference "a flagrant violation of her rights" and directed the governor to disregard it. He did. Tassels was hanged shortly thereafter.[12]

When the Court issued its opinion in the case brought by the Cherokee, which prayed that Georgia stop its acts contrary to treaty, Marshall denied standing to the tribe, holding that it was not a "foreign nation" as that term was understood in the Constitution when jurisdiction was granted to the Supreme Court. A year later, however, in *Worcester v. Georgia*, the Court ruled against Georgia in an opinion that constituted a sharp denial of the state's claims. Georgia refused to appear before the Court; to do so would "compromit her dignity as a sovereign State." Marshall found the acts of the Georgia legislature asserting jurisdiction over the Cherokee (and under the terms of which Worcester, a missionary, had been convicted) to be "repugnant to the constitution, laws and treaties of the United States." The treaties and laws of the United States fell within "the due exercise of the constitutional powers of the federal government." Those laws "throw a shield over the Cherokee Indians. They guaranteed to them their rights of occupancy, of self government, and the full enjoyment of those blessings which might be attained in their humble condition. But, by the enactments of the State of Georgia, this shield is broken in pieces—the infant institutions of the Cherokees are abolished, and their laws annulled." The peculiar relations that subsisted between the United States and the Indians, which were those of a stronger to a weaker power, did not enable the stronger to do anything it pleased. "A weaker power does not surrender its independence, its rights to self-government, by associating with a stronger, and taking its protection."[13]

In the course of his opinion, Marshall attested to the significance of the case. "If the judicial power," he said, "fall short of giving effect to the laws of the Union, the existence of the federal government is at an end." Were the acts of the national legislature not binding on the states, "the federal government would exist only in name. Instead of being the proudest monument of human wisdom and patriotism it would be the frail memorial of the ignorance and mental imbecility of its framers." Ten years previously, Marshall's tributes to and constructions of the Constitution had been made in a confident spirit. By this time, an element of despair had entered strongly into his personal correspondence and even, as here, into his formal opinions. The disposition of the case confirmed his worst fears. Whether Jackson actually said what he is reputed to have said—"John Marshall has made his decision. Now let him enforce it"—the fact was undeniable that the decision was irrelevant to the course of events over the next decade, when the remainder of the southern Indians were moved, in desperate circumstances, across the great river.

Though Marshall's opinion in *Worcester* would in the future constitute the broad foundation on which American Indian law was reared, it was, in 1832, worse than an irrelevance. The effect of the decision was to demonstrate that the role Marshall had claimed for the Supreme Court was faltering aspiration, not fact, and that it seemed destined to be swept aside in the new order betokened by "State rights Democracy," for which Marshall felt great repugnance. If, as Webster had said, the Supreme Court was "the great arbitrator between contending sovereignties"; if, as he often affirmed, "the Union could not exist without it," its inability to enforce any meaningful judgment on Georgia, together with the denial of its authority by President Jackson, seemed to push it on the road to irrelevance. "I yield slowly and reluctantly to the conviction," Marshall wrote to Story, "that our constitution cannot last. . . . The union has been prolonged thus far by miracles. I fear they cannot continue."[14]

19

Annexation of Texas and War
with Mexico

AS THE SOUTHEASTERN INDIANS MADE THEIR TREK along trails of tears, most of them to settle in Oklahoma, the Anglo-Americans who had come to the Mexican province of Texas were engaging in a struggle for their independence. In this controversy, characteristically, the idea of a federative system was central to the dispute. It was under the terms of the Mexican Constitution of 1824—a federal constitution allowing great autonomy to the provinces—that Texas had been settled in the 1820s. The revocation of that federal constitution by Santa Anna in 1835 was the avowed cause of the Texan War of Independence. Texans justified that war on the same grounds as the American colonists had justified their own war for independence: they were resisting tyrants who sought to erect a consolidated despotism over them. On March 2, 1836, their delegates assembled in general convention at Washington and in their declaration of independence held that "the federal republican constitution of their country, which they have sworn to support, has no longer a substantial existence, and the whole nature of their government has been forcibly changed, without their consent, from a restrictive federative republic, composed of sovereign States, to a consolidated, central, and military despotism." When Santa Anna annihilated "the constitutions of the sovereign States of the confederacy, and convert[ed] them into mere departments of the central government established at Mexico City," the Texans rebelled. Independence having been secured by the victory of Texan forces at San Jacinto, Texas was recognized as an independent state on the last day (March 3, 1837) of the outgoing Jackson administration, which had made reiterated attempts to purchase Texas from Mexico. Those negotiations had failed. Its independence now presented another route by which it might be brought into the American union.

When this issue presented itself in 1836 and 1837, it was apparent that much had changed from only a few years before. For one thing, the Lone Star Republic claimed all the territory on the left (or northern) bank of the Rio Grande del Norte, land that stretched across four Mexican departments. Though advocates of Texas annexation would speak in coming years of the "re-annexation" of Texas, there was no plausible way to deduce the vast empire claimed by Texas from the ambiguous terms of the Louisiana Purchase. And there were two further difficulties raised by the prospect of annexing Texas into the American union. One was that Mexico refused to recognize the independence of Texas; to incorporate Texas also meant incorporating the preexisting state of war with that disorganized government, which had repudiated the agreement extorted by the "Texian" authorities from Santa Anna after his capture in 1836. A second difficulty was that the territory claimed by Texas might embrace several more states, perhaps as many as five. Within the part settled by Anglo-Americans, slavery was already deeply entrenched, and the Texas constitution contained a provision stating that slavery could not be abolished without the consent of every individual slaveholder. From 1836 onward, therefore, Texas annexation was closely associated with two separate but related possibilities: war with Mexico and a sudden, dramatic shift in the sectional balance of power.[1]

After the entry of Maine and Missouri in the early 1820s, no states entered the Union until Arkansas (1836) and Michigan (1837), at the same time as the Texan War of Independence. In only fifteen years, however, the perception of relative power among the sections had changed profoundly. The equality between the free states and slave states that was maintained in the Senate was not maintained in the House of Representatives. Independent freeholders voted with their feet and moved their families north rather than south of the Ohio River. Population, industry, the spirit of improvement—the growth of all these had greater pace in the northern than in the southern states. While the South could expect that Florida, the only slave territory left, would sooner or later gain admission, there were in the late 1830s three northern territories (Wisconsin, Iowa, and Minnesota) that would also soon be clamoring for statehood.[2]

To many anxious southerners, Texas independence appeared providential. No better method than annexation proposed itself as a remedy for their incipient political insignificance. In resolutions presented to the Senate in December 1837, Calhoun had held that "the Union of these States rests on an equality of rights and advantages among its members; and that whatever destroys that equality, tends to destroy the Union itself." Already looking at Texas, Calhoun insisted that "to refuse to extend to the Southern and Western States any advantage which would tend to strengthen, or render them more secure, or increase their limits, or population by the annexation of new territory or States, on the assumption that the institution of slavery . . . is immoral, or sinful, or otherwise obnoxious, would be contrary to that equality of rights." Aiming, he insisted, at a broad settlement of the slavery question, Calhoun held in the subsequent debate that it "was the only question of sufficient magnitude and potency to divide the Union, and divide it it would, or drench the country in blood, if not arrested." The assaults made by abolitionists on slavery, he warned, threatened to "make two people of one, by destroying every sympathy between the two great sections, obliterating from their hearts the recollection of their common danger and glory, and implanting in their place a mutual hatred, more deadly than ever existed between two neighbouring people since the commencement of the human race."[3]

From the beginning, the question of Texas annexation was caught up in the deadly struggle that Calhoun prophesied. Seeing nothing but trouble, Van Buren had shelved the project when he became president in 1837. Nearly all Whigs were opposed to bringing Texas in, and the Whigs won the election of 1840. It looked then that the issue would sleep for a long time to come. A bizarre sequence of events at the beginning of the 1840s, inaugurating a period of increasing political turbulence and upheaval, would ultimately succeed in bringing Texas back to the center of the stage. The decade began with a tragedy or a farce, as the reader so wishes, when William Henry Harrison, the military hero chosen by the Whigs to carry their banner in preference to Clay, died of pneumonia a month after his inaugural. The old patriot had deemed it unvirtuous to dress warmly on the day of the unusually frigid ceremonies. His successor, John Tyler of Virginia, had been placed on the ticket at the insistence of the southern Whigs, and he was reported to have wept at Clay's loss of the nomination. Events rapidly showed, however, that he was the antipode of Whiggery. In outlook and sensibility, he was a Jacksonian Democrat. The whole cabinet resigned, save Webster, who thought it his duty to bring the negotiations with England, mainly over the Maine boundary, to a successful conclusion. Webster stayed on for a time after the Webster-Ashburton Treaty was ratified in 1842, to the disgust of many of his friends, but when Tyler showed increasing interest in reviving Texas annexation, Webster resigned. He was replaced as secretary of state by Abel Upshur, who thought like Tyler that Texas was ripe for resolution. Upshur negotiated, in secret, a treaty with the Texans in 1843 and 1844, but before he was quite done he got blown up, along with other members of the cabinet, in an explosion on the *Princeton*, an American warship. Tyler then gave the post to Calhoun, who had lost two close friends in the accident. So the victory of the Whigs in the presidential election of 1840 had produced Tyler and Calhoun at the head of the government, agitating for an annexation that was widely opposed within the party whose victory had put them there.

When Tyler and Calhoun announced the terms of the Texas treaty, their leading opponent in the Senate was Thomas Hart Benton. This, too, was a surprise. Benton was a man of the democracy and the West; easterners had long thought that he and land hunger were one. He had stood with Hayne and Calhoun in 1830 as a champion and representative of the new alliance between the West and South, the selfsame alliance that, a decade and a half later, produced Texas annexation. When Benton led the campaign in the Senate against annexation in 1844, and thus departed from the true Jackson faith, he broke many old friendships. His target in 1844 was John C. Calhoun, whom Benton pursued in philippics that later, affectionately, he called "Calhouniacs." Benton called Calhoun's letter to British minister Richard Pakenham (April 18, 1844), in which the secretary of state defended slavery and charged an abolitionist plot on Great Britain, "the most unfortunate in the history of human diplomacy." The British had disavowed four times the abolitionist plot that Calhoun alleged against that power. Benton showed why the alarms that had been raised against the prospect of Britain acting contrary to its public pledge were altogether implausible, and he proved that the territorial claims the Texans and the Tyler administration had made were far from representing the "true title." Noting the vast size of the territory claimed, Benton remarked:

All this—being parts of four Mexican departments—now under Mexican governors and governments—is permanently reannexed to this Union, if this treaty is ratified; and is actually reannexed from the moment of the signature of the treaty, according to the President's last message, to remain so until the acquisition is rejected by rejecting the treaty! The one half of the department of New Mexico, with its capital, becomes a territory of the United States; an angle of Chihuahua, at the Passo del Norte, famous for its wine, also becomes ours: a part of the department of Coahuila, not populated on the left bank, which we take, but commanded from the right bank by Mexican authorities: the same of Tamaulipas, the ancient Nuevo San Tander (New St. Andrews), and which covers both sides of the river from its mouth for some hundred miles up, and all the left bank of which is in the power and possession of Mexico. These, in addition to the old Texas; these parts of four States— these towns and villages—these people and territory—these flocks and herds—this *slice* of the republic of Mexico, two thousand miles long, and some hundred broad—all this our President has cut off from its mother empire, and presents to us, and declares it is ours till the Senate rejects it! He calls it Texas! and the cutting off he calls *re*-annexation! Humboldt calls it New Mexico, Chihuahua, Coahuila and Neuvo San Tander (now Tamaulipas); and the civilized world may qualify this re-annexation by the application of some odious and terrible epithet.[4]

Benton saw that Texas annexation could not possibly pass the Senate, with its high hurdle of a two-thirds majority, and had registered the warning of thirteen prominent northerners, who included John Quincy Adams, that "annexation, effected by any act or proceeding of the federal government, or any of its departments, WOULD BE IDENTICAL WITH DISSOLUTION." Recognizing these various obstacles to annexation, Benton deduced the spectacular charge that Calhoun had put it forward in the foreknowledge that it would fail and thus provide a basis for the formation of a southern confederacy. "Disunion," Benton alleged, "is at the bottom of this long concealed Texas machination. Intrigue and speculation cooperate; but disunion is at the bottom, and I denounce it to the American people. Under the pretext of getting Texas into the Union, the scheme is to get the South out of it. A separate confederacy, stretching from the Atlantic to the Californias (and hence the secret of the Rio Grande del Norte frontier), is the cherished vision of disappointed ambition; and for this consummation every circumstance has been carefully and artfully contrived." Though Benton may have badly misread Calhoun's real intentions at this time, he had certainly snuffed out the two ultimate possibilities between which Calhoun proposed to navigate. Were the North to block the annexation of Texas to the union, a southern confederacy embracing Texas was the ever-beckoning alternative, and it lurked in Calhoun's mind as both potent threat and serious possibility.[5]

Benton's assertion of a disunion plot depended on the assumption that Texas annexation would be blocked in the Senate. The treaty did indeed go down to defeat by a lopsided margin. But though dead in the Senate, it was very much alive politically, and it became the central issue in the 1844 elections. Van Buren nixed his chances for the Democratic nomination by coming out against it. Many of Van Buren's delegates, anxious for Texas, supported adoption of a rule requiring a two-thirds vote for nomination, a ploy that successfully killed Van Buren's chances. The nomination instead went to James Polk of Tennessee; the platform the Democrats adopted called for the "re-annexation" of Texas and the "re-occupation of Oregon." The Democrats had always been associated with territorial expansion; they now emerged as the party of Manifest Destiny, their orators claiming a right granted by Providence to spread over the continent. Their program promised expansion to both Northwest and Southwest, and thus stood in apparent conformity with the system of equivalents by which territories had been purchased, and states brought in to the union, in the past, and it was strongly justified as a national cause against the depredations of the European powers. That it might produce a simultaneous war with Mexico over Texas, and with Britain over Oregon, was considered highly improbable by its advocates in the election of 1844, who represented it as a measure of peace.

Polk narrowly won the 1844 election. Clay was an anathema to many abolitionists, who gave their votes to a third party; the loss of their support in the razor-thin election cost Clay his margin of victory. Since a Whig victory in 1840 had brought Tyler and Calhoun to power by 1844, it was only natural, and entirely in keeping with the strange whirl that American politics had now become, that the abolitionists should be responsible for the victory of Polk. Tyler, judging the results of the election as a referendum favorable to the immediate annexation of Texas, submitted the project to the old Congress in early 1845, a month before Polk's inauguration. The joint resolution passed in the House by a comfortable margin, and in the Senate by a vote of 27 to 25. Texas was admitted as a state on December 19, 1845, after complying with certain conditions stipulated in the joint resolution approved March 1, 1845.

By bringing in Texas through a majority vote in both houses instead of a two-thirds vote in the Senate, Tyler and the Congress stood in clear violation of the Constitution. The irregularities of the Louisiana Purchase were a trifle in comparison with this. In 1804 and 1819—indeed, even prospectively in the debate of 1844—it was a matter of course that a treaty of annexation had to find its way to the Senate and there bow before the constitutional requirement of a two-thirds majority. Secretary of State Calhoun, the strictest of strict constructionists, raised no objection to the objectionable procedure of flouting this rule. The stance was especially opportunistic and hypocritical for Calhoun, for the treaty clause according a veto to one-third (plus one) of senators present was the most striking illustration, in the American Constitution, of the idea of a concurrent majority. Holding the concurrent majority sacred in theory, he yet supported in practice ramming through Texas annexation via a razor-thin numerical majority, which majority might produce ten new senators in the bargain. Tyler paired his violation of the Constitution with a deception of a group of senators, led by Benton, who introduced language in the Senate resolution that looked toward instituting a negotiating mission on the model of 1798–1799 and 1814, led by a representative group of prominent Americans, who were to resolve the boundary dispute between Texas and Mexico, and thus avoid war. Tyler ignored the Senate resolution and brought Texas in on the basis of the more permissive House resolution. Polk had agreed to Benton's proposal during the negotiations over the resolution; he too broke his word when he came into office.[6]

Worse was to come. The Mexican government, itself in turmoil, refused to meet with Polk's emissary, John Slidell, in 1845; the failure of the Slidell mission led Polk to move American troops to the disputed area between the Rio Grande and the Nueces in early 1846. When Mexican troops fired on American soldiers in the disputed border area, Polk rushed to Congress asking that it recognize the existence of a state of war between the two countries. American blood has been shed on American soil! Congress complied by an overwhelming majority, with the war resolution passing in the House of Representatives 174 to 14 and in the Senate 40 to 2. Polk avowed no territorial objectives in his message—the war was portrayed as vindicating American rights and defending American territory—but he had set his sights on Upper California and New Mexico and was determined to secure them. Invoking the Monroe Doctrine, which had been directed against the threat posed by the Holy Alliance to the liberty and independence of the Spanish-American states, Polk refurbished it to argue against any European interposition in North America.

President Polk had no sooner gotten the war with Mexico that he had premeditated than he disclosed agreement with Britain on a resolution of the Oregon question. Britain, anxious to avoid war, agreed to the boundary along the forty-ninth parallel, the line that previous American administrations had angled for. For northern Democrats, this constituted a gross betrayal. Senator Edward Hannegan of Indiana had foreseen this result in December 1845 and insisted that a solemn compact had been made in the Baltimore convention of 1844. "Texas and Oregon," said Hannegan, "were born in the same instant, nursed and cradled in the same cradle—the Baltimore Convention—and they were at the same instant adopted by the democracy throughout the land. There was not a moment's hesitation, until Texas was admitted; but the moment she was admitted, the peculiar friends of Texas turned and were doing all they could to strangle Oregon!"[7]

In the space of two years, politics in the American system of states had resolved itself into a repetitive breaking of compacts. The pledged word among gentlemen, the law of nations, a solemn agreement among the sectional wings of the Democratic Party lay aside the wreckage of the Constitution that the annexation of Texas had wrought. The way the Mexican War ended just proceeded according to form and showed that the pattern had become deeply ingrained. The progress of American victories had led finally to the occupation of Mexico City by U.S. military forces; that remarkable advance led to an expansion of war aims. A surge of opinion in the northern newspapers pronounced itself in favor of the annexation and "regeneration" of all Mexico. "Like the Sabine virgins," wrote the *New York Herald*, "she will soon learn to love her ravisher." Lewis Cass, the Democratic presidential nominee in 1848, seemed a strong supporter of the idea (though what Cass really wanted was the land, not the people). Nor would Stephen Douglas or James Buchanan rule it out. By late 1847 Polk himself had determined on a line that ran from Tampico to near the entrance of the Gulf of California, far south of his previous desire. He recalled Nicholas P. Trist, the U.S. negotiator in the Mexican capital. But Trist, pleading with guile a change of circumstances, violated his instructions, negotiated a treaty in his capacity as a private person, and returned with a document almost precisely conforming to the instructions that Polk had abandoned. As Trist later explained his motives, his object throughout was "not to obtain all I could, but on the contrary to make the treaty as little exacting as possible from Mexico, as was compatible with its being accepted at home." Two considerations lay behind this conduct: "One was the iniquity of the war, as an abuse of power on our part; the other was that the more disadvantageous the treaty was made to Mexico, the stronger would be the ground of opposition to it in the Mexican Congress."[8]

Polk was furious with Trist's "arrogant, impudent, and very insulting" dispatch to him, but he feared that the rejection of the treaty might mean the loss of his principal territorial objects. The president reluctantly supported ratification, as did a significant number of Whigs, who feared that a rejection of the treaty would mean a continuation of the war. The sense of radical uncertainty was hardly surprising, given the record of the immediate past. Who knew what the next month might bring in the way of an astonishing development? It was heightened by the outbreak of revolution in Europe in early 1848, with the abdication of Louis Philippe and the publication of *The Communist Manifesto* occurring simultaneously on February 24 and seeming to portend "a general dissolution" of Europe's "ancient social systems."[9]

20

The Great Debate of 1848

ON FEBRUARY 23, 1848, IN THE MIDST of these wondrous events in America and Europe, John Quincy Adams died, having collapsed at his desk two days previously in the House of Representatives. A eulogy delivered a few months later by William Seward of New York described the debate in the capitol that had arisen before Adams's death but after American forces had "planted the banner of burning stars, and ever-multiplying stripes on the towers of the city of the Aztecs." A bewildering range of questions had been posed:

> Shall new loans and levies be granted to prosecute still further a war so glorious? or shall it be abandoned? Shall we be content with the humiliation of the foe? or shall we complete his subjugation? Would that severity be magnanimous, or even just? Nay, is the war itself just? Who provoked, and by what unpardonable offence, this disastrous strife between two eminent republics, so scandalous to democratic institutions? Where shall we trace anew the ever-advancing line in our empire? Shall it be drawn on the banks of the Rio Grande, or on the summit of the Sierra Madre? or shall Mexican independence be extinguished, and our eagle close his adventurous pinions only when he looks off upon the waves that separate us from the Indies? Does freedom own and accept our profuse oblations of blood, or does she reject the sacrifice? Will these conquests extend her domain, or will they be usurped by ever-grasping slavery? What effect will this new-born ambition have upon ourselves? Will it leave us the virtue to continue the career of social progress? How shall we govern the conquered people? Shall we incorporate their mingled races with ourselves, or shall we rule them with the despotism of pro-consular power? Can we preserve these remote and hostile possessions, in any way, without forfeiting our own blood-bought heritage of freedom?

Americans, as is apparent from Seward's passage, had stumbled on a whole series of Machiavellian moments, which implicated everything they were, thought they were, and hoped to be.

Seward went on to describe the impact of Adams's passing, in mournful words that suggested a close ideological relation to the questions he had raised. "All nations," he warned, "must perpetually renovate their virtues and their constitutions, or perish. Never was there more need to renovate ours than now, when we seem to be passing from the safe old policy of peace and moderation into a career of conquest and martial renown. Never was the duty of preserving free institutions, in all their purity, more obvious than it is now, when they have become beacons to mankind in what seems to be a general dissolution of their ancient social systems." Over his long career, Adams had accepted that duty, but the political winds had not gone his way in the years since he had left the presidency and taken up the lonely bastion of antislavery in the House of Representatives. Deeply embittered over the annexation of Texas and the forthcoming war with Mexico, Adams wrote in 1845, "The Constitution is a menstrous rag, and the Union is sinking into a military monarchy, to be rent asunder like the empire of Alexander or the kingdoms of Ephraim and Judah."[1]

A remarkable feature of the opposition to the Mexican War is that it joined a group of men who were all a step away from the grave. Clay, Webster, and Gallatin were each, as was said of Adams, "a living bond of connection between the present and past—the venerable representative[s] of the memories of another age."[2] Their common opposition to the belligerence and "palpable lies" that distinguished American policy; their appeal to the fact that American policy was thought utterly unjustifiable in the common opinion of Europe; their evocation of the true standard of policy and the true mission of the United States; their understanding that expansion and conquest threatened a dissolution of the union—all this signified a revolt of the older generation against the new. A sense of bereavement over the loss of what they and their country had stood for, and the understanding that the new spirit of the age was utterly incompatible with the preservation of the union as they had known it, hung over their speeches. The occasion often heightened the effect. Clay's speech against the Mexican War, on November 13, 1847, was on a day "dark and gloomy, unsettled and uncertain, like the condition of our country in regard to the unnatural war with Mexico." Like the season in which he spoke, Clay's "springtime has gone by, and I, too, am in the autumn of life, and feel the frost of age." Webster, in deep depression from the loss of his son Edward in the war, had a distorted and even grotesque countenance when he denounced the "Objects of the Mexican War" in his speech of March 17, 1848. Their own deaths and the death of the old union were unmistakably mingled in the debates over the Mexican War, just as they would later be mingled in their efforts on behalf of the Compromise of 1850.[3]

In the great debate over territorial expansion, the Whigs compiled a solid record in predicting the course of events. Clay's opposition to the annexation of Texas in 1844 had hung on the prediction that the annexation of Texas and war with Mexico were "identical." Events proved him right, though it was also true, as he noted in 1847, that "actual hostilities might probably have been averted by prudence, moderation, and wise statesmanship." Clay believed "that no motive for the acquisition of foreign territory" would be more fatal than obtaining it for "the influence which it would exert, in the balance of political power, between two great sections of the Union." Such a principle, put into practical operation, not only would threaten to dissolve the union but also would "proclaim to the world an insatiable and unquenchable thirst for foreign conquest or acquisition of territory. For if today Texas be acquired to strengthen one part of the confederacy, tomorrow Canada may be required to add strength to another. And, after that might have been obtained, still other and further acquisitions would become necessary to equalize and adjust the balance of political power. Finally, in the progress of this spirit of universal dominion, the part of the confederacy which is now weakest, would find itself still weaker from the impossibility of securing new theatres for those peculiar institutions which it is charged with being desirous to extend." Clay's final comment was a warning to the South that it was playing a dangerous game; subsequent events would demonstrate the veracity of the observation. The accession of power that the South received from the annexation of Texas—sufficiently important that the two senators from Texas cast the decisive votes in passing the dramatic change in the tariff in 1846—did not prove lasting once the war propelled by Texas annexation resulted in the acquisition of California and New Mexico. The alliance between the South and the West that made the war in the first place, in short, was broken by the results of it.[4]

Webster drew attention to the strange anomaly that hovered over the aggrandizing policy of the northern and southern wings of the Democratic Party. Both were willing "to carry on the war for territory, though it be not decided now whether the character of newly acquired territory shall be that of freedom or of slavery." The "Southern Democracy" was, "in general, in favor of new territory and new States, being Slave States," whereas the representatives of the "Northern Democracy . . . are for acquiring property; they are for more States; and, for the sake of this, they are willing to run the risk of these new States being slave States, and to meet all the convulsions which the discussion of that momentous question may hereafter produce." From the beginning, Clay and Webster saw that the conclusion of a peace by conquest would form the preliminaries of a great war among the sections.[5]

Though the debate over expansion passed through many phases from 1844 to 1848, the Whig critique was focused on certain key themes. Senator

Rufus Choate of Massachusetts noted in 1844 that the new union proposed with the annexation of Texas would not be "the Union which we have known; which we have loved, to which we have been accustomed," but rather "a new one, enlarged by the annexation of a territory out of which forty States of the size of Massachusetts might be constructed; a territory not appended equally to the East, the West, the Centre, and the South; not appended equally to the slave States and the free States; to the agricultural and planting; to the localities of free trade and the localities of protection; not so appended as to work an equal and impartial enlargement and assistance to each one of those various and heterogeneous elements of interest and sentiment and position out of whose struggle comes the peace, out of whose dissonance comes the harmony, of our system."[6]

Webster, too, expressed fear that "extension often produces weakness rather than strength; and that political attraction, like other attractions, is less and less powerful, as the parts become more and more distant." He commended to Americans "the admonition of the ancient prudence: 'You have a Sparta; embellish it!'" Though opposed to the annexation of Texas, the Whigs were not in principle opposed to further expansion if conducted in accordance with constitutional procedure and international law. Many of them looked longingly at the magnificent bay of San Francisco and saw it, as Polk did, as a stepping-stone to Asia. The Founders, said Garrett Davis, a Kentucky Whig, in January 1845, "glanced far into the vista of the future; . . . they saw the vast expanse of country which was not theirs, and which was stretching away from three fourths of their borders, teeming with swelling millions of people and swayed by alien governments. They looked into history, and they saw, as reflected from a mirror, wars, and conquests, and alliances, and treaties, and vicissitude, checkering the course of the mighty nations that are to enact their destiny on this continent. They saw that acquisition, for commerce, for defence, for security—that cession, for alliance, for pacification—and both, for general welfare, would be convenient and necessary." As Davis noted, however, the Founders lodged that capacity in the president and two-thirds of the Senate. It was vital to respect the constitutional requirement rather than flout it, as advocates of Texas annexation proposed to do after the election of 1844. "I prefer," said Davis, "this Union as it is to any breaking up and reconstruction of it. I would not put it in serious hazard for Texas, or Cuba, or Canada, or California, or all together. . . . I have a superstitious presentiment that if the golden chain which binds these States together be shivered, there will be no one to reconstruct it. What, then, will be the fate of this portion of the continent? Go read the history of Europe, the annals of her wars and her desolations—of her crimes, her oppressions and her sufferings."[7]

The Whigs also laid stress on the ravages brought by war. "War, pestilence, and famine," Clay held, "are the three greatest calamities which can befall our species; and war, as the most direful, justly stands in front." Unlike pestilence and famine, war was the work of our own hands; its effects, unlike these other scourges, are of much longer duration. "In the sacrifice of human life, and in the waste of human treasure, in its losses and its burdens, it affects both belligerent nations; and its sad effects of mangled bodies, of death and of desolation, endure long after its thunders are hushed in peace. War unhinges society, disturbs its peaceful and regular industry, and scatters poisonous seeds of disease and immorality, which continue to germinate and diffuse their baneful influences long after it has ceased. Dazzling by its glitter, pomp, and pageantry, it begets a spirit of wild adventure and romantic enterprise, and often disqualifies those who embark in it, after their return from the bloody fields of battle, from engaging in the industrious and peaceful vocations of life."[8]

The dissent aroused by the annexation of Texas and the Mexican War followed in part ideas that had been raised against the War of 1812. The potential that expansion held for introducing centrifugal forces that would break up the union was a leading feature of both critiques. The danger proved hypothetical in the first instance, when the conquest of Canada proved not to be a mere matter of marching, and very real in the second. But one vital difference lay in the use and abuse of the war power. There was no comparison between the way that President Madison and the Twelfth Congress had reached a declaration of war, and the way that Polk got his. For the first time, the commander in chief had shown it possible to exercise his control over the armed forces in a way that left Congress with little practical alternative but to acquiesce; the power of the purse was a poor instrument to rein in an executive who was in a position to move forces into a position provocative of war, and who could get war requisitions from a reluctant Congress by charging against a negative vote a betrayal of the valiant soldiers in the field. "What is the value of this constitutional provision" lodging the war power in Congress, asked Webster, "if the President of his own authority may make such military movements as must bring on war?"[9]

The martial enthusiasm of the time was paired with the conviction of the American people that successful military leaders were competent to any task of governance. The election of General Jackson in 1828 and of General Harrison in 1840, the war heroes of an earlier epoch, was followed by the election of General Zachary Taylor in 1848. Taylor's views were barely known in 1848; that, as a satirist noted, was one of the things that recommended him to the generality of the people. This outlook, together with Polk's vast expansion of executive powers, suggested a receptivity toward Bonapartism and Caesarism in the office of the president, alarming to many minds still steeped in British, French, and Roman precedents.[10]

The great spokesmen for Manifest Destiny were Robert Walker of Mississippi, Stephen Douglas of Illinois, James Buchanan of Pennsylvania, Lewis Cass of Michigan, and Levi Woodbury of New Hampshire. They were all ardent expansionists; all ardent states-righters; all boasters of the racial superiority of the American stock. Generally, they were both "Anglo-maniacs" and "Anglo-phobes"—"a combination not unusual in America," noted one British correspondent. Walker, an ultra expansionist famous for arguing that Texas annexation would siphon off blacks from, and weaken slavery in, the southern states, and then in Texas itself, emphasized the unity of the Anglo-Saxon people and promoted the idea that "the race" should act in concert against European and Latin despotism. Buchanan and Douglas, by contrast, rejected a narrow focus on the "pure Anglo-Saxon race" and held the American people as the best of a mixture of European bloods. Both views, however, professed intense hostility to the British government.[11]

Democrats denied that expansion would unleash centripetal forces and insisted instead that it would prove inconsistent with and antithetical to centralization. This was one of its charms for them, and their avowed nationalism was emphatically not of the central-state variety. But they saw themselves as part of a single American people and felt a providential mission in its behalf. They also displayed the tone of bellicosity that had entered American diplomacy in Andrew Jackson's day. Calhoun took note of this bellicosity by recalling Jackson's threat of a French war in the mid-1830s, averted through the mediation of Great Britain. The example had "contributed much," Calhoun feared, "to give the strong tendency, which we have since witnessed, to resort to menace and force in the settlement of our differences with other powers." Spokesmen for the Democratic Party relished that spirit of brag and defiance while generally asserting, before the war, that a firm stand would render all recourse to force unnecessary.[12]

Though Polk's paramount objective was California and the great ports that would rise up on that coast, it is also the case that preclusive motives—or preventing the acquisition of such territories by a European power—were also of considerable significance in prompting the move toward annexation and war. In the 1840s, no advocate for the annexation of Texas and, later, the war with Mexico failed to advance the hypothesis that Britain, certainly, and France, probably, were meditating designs on Oregon, California, Texas, and Mexico. Were the admission of Texas refused, John Tyler declared in 1844, that independent republic would inevitably "seek for the friendship of others. In contemplating such a contingency it can not be overlooked that the United States are already almost surrounded by the possessions of European powers. The Canadas, New Brunswick, and Nova Scotia, the islands in the American seas, with Texas trammeled by treaties of alliance or of a commercial character differing in policy from that of the United States, would complete the circle."[13]

Polk recurred to the same danger in his first annual message of December 1845, as Jackson had done in periodic effusions from the Hermitage. These statements produced alarm in European capitals. If the United States were encircled by hostile powers in 1844 or 1845, was not every power on the continent of Europe also encircled, only more so? In January 1846, French premier François Guizot noted that the United States was not the only nation in North America. There were "other independent nations," especially Mexico, whose rights were entitled to respect: "What was not good for Europe under the form of universal monarchy," Guizot held, "would not be good for America under the form of universal republicanism."[14]

While Democrats pressed the argument that independent republics in Oregon, California, and Texas would have hostile relations with each other and the American union were they to remain outside the fold, the Whigs maintained that such a system of independent republics would likely maintain relations of amity and concord. "In the future progress of events," wrote Henry Clay in 1844,

> it is probable that there will be a voluntary or forcible separation of the British North American possessions from the parent country. I am strongly inclined to think that it will be best for the happiness of all parties that, in that event, they should be erected into a separate and independent republic. With the Canadian republic on one side, that of Texas on the other, and the United States, the friend of both, between them, each could advance its own happiness by such constitutions, laws, and measures, as were best adapted to its peculiar condition. They would be natural allies, ready, by co-operation, to repel any European or foreign attack upon either. Each would afford a secure refuge to the persecuted and oppressed driven into exile by either of the others. They would emulate each other in improvements, in free institutions, and in the science of self-government.[15]

In speculating over the extent of future expansion, some Democrats set their sights well beyond North America. In principle, said Woodbury, the expansion of the union could be universal. Under "the American theory of self government, no reason existed why we should not be allowed to admit any State that would conjoin to our representative system, and whose union with us should, by the majority of both countries, or the proper authorities, be considered mutually advantageous, and that we might well wish to extend the blessings of our government as widely as practicable." On such a construction, Woodbury held, "States might be admitted, not only contiguous, but in the West Indies, South America, and even Europe." He cited with approval the conclusion of Mansfield's *Political Grammar*: "So far as convenient and beneficial, the whole world may thus become partners."[16]

It was not, however, the prospect of a universal partnership but the extent of American conquests that was the great issue in the debate that arose after the subjugation and occupation of Mexico City. Those who contended for "All Mexico" in the winter of 1847–1848, when the prospect seemed to seize the country, wished to regenerate the Mexicans and to lead them, via military occupation, to free institutions. John O'Sullivan, who anticipated those ever-multiplying millions streaming to the Pacific coast, was actually disgusted by Polk's turn toward militarism, but others in the northern Democratic penny press were enthused. The Illinois *State Register* demanded the "conquest, subjugation, and annihilation of Mexican sovereignty." Robert Stockton, the naval commodore who captured the Mexican capital of California in 1845, urged in late 1847 that the war be prosecuted "for the express purpose of redeeming Mexico from misrule and civil strife." Disdaining an indemnity—"no man here or elsewhere will consent to weigh blood against money"—Stockton evoked instead "a duty before God which we cannot—we must not evade. The priceless bond of civil and religious liberty has been confided to us as trustees," and even were the war to last for fifty years and cost "half of all that we possess, I would still insist that the inestimable blessings of civil and religious liberty should be guaranteed to Mexico." Senator Sidney Breese of Illinois, who urged "the *complete subjugation* of Mexico," did not believe it "contrary to the spirit and genius of our Government, nor against its settled policy, to conquer, in a defensive war, any country, and annex it, which might be thought, from its contiguity, to be necessary to our own safety." Though acknowledging that the Mexicans were not "at this time fitted for an equal union with us," he believed "the period of their pupilage will be of short duration."[17]

Whigs were appalled by the vast expansion of American war aims and were convinced the war had been waged on false pretenses. To push forward, wrote Daniel Dewey Bernard, the editor of the *American Whig Review*, would be "the hugest piece of folly and injustice in modern times." Bernard poured scorn on the idea "that it is the inevitable destiny of the Anglo-Saxon race to overrun and ruin its neighbors." It was "among the worst of those speculative delusions which have infested modern nations" and would inevitably bring disaster on the United States. To become "a rapacious, a warlike, a conquering nation" meant the "denial of the fundamental principle of the Republic" based on the freedom and equality of "not only men, but nations." In his grim augury of the future, he beheld "all seas covered by our fleets; our garrisons hold the most important stations of commerce; an immense standing army maintains our possessions; our traders have become the richest, our demagogues the most powerful, and our people the most corrupt and flexible in the world."[18]

The Whigs' opposition to the annexation of Mexico is often put down simply to a sense of racial superiority. That American rhetoric at this time was abounding in expressions of contempt and imputations of inferiority to the Mexicans is true enough. But for Clay and Webster, this was altogether peripheral to the question. In thinking it impossible "that two such immense countries, with territories of nearly equal extent, with populations so incongruous, so different in race, in language, in religion, and in laws, could be blended together in one harmonious mass, and happily governed by one common authority," Clay made appeal to the "warning voice of all history, which teaches the difficulty of combining and consolidating together, conquering and the conquered nations." The antagonism between Spaniard and Moor, Englishman and Irishmen, and French and British in Lower Canada—which "remains a foreign land in the midst of British provinces, foreign in feeling and attachment, and foreign in laws, language, and religion"—demonstrated that the same factors would operate were the United States to conquer Mexico. Religious differences would be a particularly "fruitful cause of dissatisfaction and discontent" were the two peoples forcibly united. "Why should we seek to interfere with them in their mode of worship of a common Saviour? We believe that they are wrong, especially in the exclusive character of their faith, and that we are right. They think that they are right and we wrong. What other rule can there be than to leave the followers of each religion to their own solemn convictions of conscientious duty toward God?" At only one point in his speech did Clay declare a sentiment ascribing inferiority to the Mexicans, and this of a political and not racial kind. "Unprepared, as I fear her population yet is, for the practical enjoyment of self government, and of habits, customs, language, laws, and religion, so totally different from our own, we should present the revolting spectacle of a confused, distracted, and motley government. We should have a Mexican party, a Pacific Ocean party, an Atlantic party, in addition to the other parties which exist, or with which we are threatened. . . . The Mexican representation, in Congress, would probably form a separate and impenetrable corps, always ready to throw itself into the scale of any other party, to advance and promote Mexican interests." Vast expansion, Clay believed, would produce parties on a geographic line; geographic parties would produce a dissolution of the union.[19]

Of the opponents to Mexican annexation, none made more explicit appeal to racial premises than Calhoun. "I protest against the incorporation of such a people," he declared. "Ours is the government of the white man." The "better class" of Mexicans, he allowed, "have Castilian blood in their veins, and are of the old gothic stock—quite equal to the Anglo-Saxons in many respects, and in some superior"; the rest were "impure races, not as good as the Cherokees or Choctaws." It was, however, the "Castilians" who ruled Mexico; Calhoun believed that they would never reconcile themselves to a degrading submission to an external power. "Of all the people upon earth, they are the most pertinacious; they hold out longer, and often when there would seem to be no prospect of ever making effectual resistance. It is admitted, I believe, on all hands, that they are now universally hostile to us, and the probability is, will continue so."[20]

Calhoun bottomed his case on an appeal to the Constitution: "It would be contrary to the genius and character of our Government, and subversive of our free popular institutions, to hold Mexico as a subject province." "You know the American constitution too well," he told his fellow senators,

> you have looked into history, and are too well acquainted with the fatal effects which large provincial possessions have ever had on the institutions of free states, to need any proof to satisfy you how hostile it would be to the institutions of this country, to hold Mexico as a subject province. There is not an example on record of any free state holding a province of the same extent and population, without disastrous consequences. The nations conquered and held as a province, have, in time, retaliated by destroying the liberty of their conquerors, through the corrupting effect of extended patronage and irresponsible power. The conquest of Mexico would add so vastly to the patronage of this Government, that it would absorb the whole powers of the States; the Union would become an imperial power, and the States reduced to mere subordinate corporations. But the evil would not end there; the process would go on, and the power transferred from the States to the Union, would be transferred from the Legislative Department to the Executive. All the immense patronage which holding it as a province would create,—the maintenance of a large army, to hold it in subjection, and the appointment of a multitude of civil officers necessary to govern it,—would be vested in him. The great influence which it would give the President, would be the means of controlling the Legislative Department, and subjecting it to his dictation.[21]

It was said of Calhoun, after his death, that "it was easy to fancy, when you heard him, that you were listening to an oration from the lips of a

Roman senator, who had formed his style in the severe schools of Greece." Never more so than on this occasion. "When the Roman power," Calhoun warned, "passed beyond the limits of Italy, crossed the Adriatic, the Mediterranean, and the Alps, liberty fell prostrate; the Roman people became a rabble; corruption penetrated every department of the Government; violence and anarchy ruled the day, and military despotism closed the scene."[22]

Webster especially feared the effect of large Mexican acquisitions on the constitutional balance of the union. Though Webster insisted in 1848 that the 1845 agreement with Texas providing for as many as five new states should be honored, he argued that the addition of the new Mexican territories would increase yet further the number of thinly peopled states. He warned that "if States formed out of territories thus thinly populated come into the Union, they necessarily and inevitably break up the relation existing between the two branches of the government, and destroy its balance. ... The Senate, augmented by these new Senators coming from States where there are few people, becomes an odious oligarchy. It holds power without any adequate constituency. Sir, it is but 'borough mongering' upon a large scale. ... We are now fixing on the Constitution of the United States, and its form of government, a monstrosity, a disfiguration, an enormity!"[23]

Of all the appeals made against the war, none was so eloquent as Albert Gallatin's. In 1844, at the age of eighty-four, Gallatin had warned that "the annexation of Texas under existing circumstances is a positive declaration of war against Mexico; . . . and in that assertion I will be sustained by every publicist and jurist in the Christian world. This war would be a war founded on injustice, and a war of conquest." When war took place, as Henry Adams would later observe, "Every moral conviction and every lifelong hope of Mr. Gallatin were outraged by this act of our government. The weight of national immorality rested incessantly on his mind." The crisis stirred in Gallatin, as frail as a wisp, a renowned statement of the mission of the United States in his pamphlet, *Peace with Mexico*, a hundred thousand copies of which were printed. That mission, Gallatin wrote, "was to improve the state of the world, to be the 'model republic,' to show that men are capable of governing themselves, and that this simple and natural form of government is that also which confers most happiness on all, is productive of the greatest development of the intellectual faculties, above all, that which is attended with the highest standard of private and political virtue and morality." The Founding Fathers, Gallatin believed, had not deviated from these principles. "The sound sense, wisdom, probity and respect for public faith" with which they had managed public concerns had "made our institutions an object of general admiration. Here, for the first time, was the experiment attempted with any prospect of success, and on a large scale, of a representative democratic republic. If it failed, the last hope of the friends of mankind was lost or indefinitely postponed; and the eyes of the world were turned toward you. Whenever real or pretended apprehensions of the imminent danger of trusting the people at large with power were expressed, the answer ever was, 'Look at America!'" Aiming to restrain the appeal to "cupidity" and to "the thirst of unjust aggrandizement by brutal force," he insisted, "Your mission was to be a model for all other governments and for all other less-favored nations, to adhere to the most elevated principles of political morality, to apply all your faculties to the gradual improvement of your own institutions and social state, and by your example to exert a moral influence most beneficial to mankind at large." Gallatin thought the "allegations of superiority of race and destiny" to be manifestly absurd. Such pretensions, he wrote, "neither require nor deserve any answer; they are but pretences under which to disguise ambition, cupidity, or silly vanity."[24]

21

Intervention for Nonintervention: The Kossuth Tour

THE DEMOCRATIC EXPANSIONISTS OF THE 1840S not only looked west; they also looked east. As Guizot had suggested, something very much like universal republicanism did inform a large current of expansionist opinion in the 1840s. The "general dissolution of ancient social systems" that occurred in 1848 suggested to many that the republican tide that had swept westward to the Pacific Ocean was poised to exert a profound influence on the course of events in Europe. The revolutions of 1848 and the brutal crushing of Hungarian independence by Russian armies in 1849 called forth a strong gust of sympathy for despoiled peoples from America, and when Louis Kossuth arrived on these shores in late 1851 at the invitation, and through the good offices, of the American government, he came with the slogan of "Intervention for Non-intervention." He did not come, as one hostile senator objected, "to seek an asylum here. No, sir; he comes here for the purpose of propagating a political principle; to assert the right of the people of every nation to regulate their own affairs, uncontrolled by the action of any foreign power; and to ask from this Government a pledge that it will aid him, not merely by moral, but by physical force, if it becomes necessary, in any future struggle in Hungary, to enforce and establish that principle." Kossuth's request, then, was that America say to every foreign power: "'You must abstain from all interposition. The people of Hungary have the right to establish the principles of their own government. They are engaged in a contest with the power of Austria. You must not interfere.' . . . We are to become the champions of this principle, and, in union with Great Britain, we are to say to the Emperor of Russia: 'Stand off! If you attempt to interpose in this contest between Hungary and Austria, we shall feel bound to render such interposition fruitless.'"[1]

The debate provoked by the Hungarian Revolution and the Kossuth tour was mostly a replay of the colloquy between Webster and Randolph that had occurred a generation earlier, though now the voices urging direct intervention, while still a distinct minority, were more numerous and powerful. In the midst of the "Magyar-mania," the *Washington Union*, the leading Democratic newspaper, urged the United States and Britain to stand "shoulder to shoulder to oppose the march of despotism, and to vindicate everywhere the rights of oppressed humanity," a declaration Webster regarded as a bold avowal "in favor of an utter reversal of our established policy." So powerful did he believe these sentiments to be that he feared they would sweep into national office a "warlike administration" with a new "zeal . . . for intervention in other states." Webster's position remained the same as it had been in 1824; he continued to occupy what Rufus Choate would later call the "high, plain, yet dizzy ground which separates influence from intervention." At the Kossuth Banquet in January 1852, he had affirmed again the power of public opinion. "We are too much inclined," he said, "to underrate the power of moral influence, and the influence of public opinion, and the influence of principles, to which great men, the lights of the world and of the age, have given their sanction. Who doubts that, in our own struggle for liberty and independence, the majestic eloquence of Chatham, the profound reasoning of Burke, the burning satire and irony of Colonel Barre, had influences upon our fortunes here in America?" But though Webster was willing to speak up for the principles for which America stood, he was firmly opposed to any departure from neutrality. He would treat Kossuth "with all personal and individual respect, but if he should speak to me of the policy of 'intervention,' I shall 'have ears more deaf than adders.'"[2]

The same stance was taken by Henry Clay, on his deathbed in a Washington hotel, who told Kossuth that nothing would be gained, and everything hazarded, by American intervention in a war for Hungary against Russia. After "abandoning our ancient policy of amity and non-intervention in the affairs of other nations," those nations would be justified "in abandoning the terms of forbearance and non-interference which they have hitherto preserved toward us." Far better it was "for ourselves, for Hungary, and for the cause of liberty, that, adhering to our wise, pacific system, and avoiding the distant wars of Europe, we should keep our lamp burning brightly on this western shore as a light to all nations, than to hazard its utter extinction amid the ruins of fallen or falling republics in Europe."[3]

Neither Webster nor Clay had really departed from their ground of the 1820s, but the fact that they found themselves on the other side of the debate in 1851 indicated that its parameters had shifted. There were now indeed strong intimations that a departure from the established policy of the government was no longer the augury of a distant future. Young America began thinking in earnest of "a future alliance of America with a federation of the free peoples of Europe."[4] Lewis Cass introduced a Senate resolution declaring that the United States "had not seen nor could they again see, without deep concern, the intervention of European powers to crush national independence." In America, Cass said, there were "twenty-five millions of people looking across the ocean at Europe, strong in power, acquainted with their rights, and determined to enforce them." Stephen Douglas held that "we should sympathize with every liberal movement—recognize the independence of all Republics—form commercial treaties, and open diplomatic relations with them—protest against all infractions of the laws of nations, and hold ourselves ready to do whatever our duty may require when a case shall arise." Douglas drew back from describing the precise character of those circumstances but made clear that he would abhor the prospect of acting in concert with England. "I wish no alliance with monarchs."[5]

Robert Stockton, now a Democratic senator from New Jersey, also declined any projected alliance with Great Britain and believed that the development of the United States, "far exceeding in amount and rapidity the most sanguine expectations of the founders of the Republic," would require "a modification of our national policy, in various respects different from that which prevailed in the infancy of the country." While it was reasonable to have nursed "the infant Hercules, until he should be able to encounter, upon more equal terms, the monsters he was destined to overthrow," the growth in national power would require a change, most particularly in "the amicable struggle now going on for British or American ascendancy on the ocean." Stockton desired "to see the trident of the seas wrenched from the tenacious grasp of that haughty and kingly empire—not for the purpose of ambitious extension—not to tyrannize or dictate, in the spirit of an intermeddling propagandism; but to hasten the time when the sword shall no longer be the arbiter of national disputes. Peace is the true policy of this Republic. Peace is the animating genius of our institutions."[6]

The advocates of intervention divided over whether the proper aim was to eliminate force as an arbiter of disputes, to propagandize democratic institutions, or to assert "the right of the people of every nation to regulate their own affairs, uncontrolled by the action of any foreign power." They differed, too, over whether England was a fit partner in these enterprises. But there was considerable strength for the sentiment that America must begin reconsidering its previous policy, particularly in the great West, the heartland of "Young America." In the East, too, there were voices that went beyond the expressions of sympathy and declarations of principle that had been given by Webster and Clay in 1824. Seward objected to a policy that would carry nonintervention so far as to treat coldly a refugee from oppression. To do so would "discourage the hopes and expectations of the friends of freedom throughout the world" and "encourage the advocates of oppression throughout Europe in their efforts to prevent the transition of the nations of Europe from under the system of force to the voluntary system of government which we have established and commended to their adoption."

What had happened in the aftermath of the revolutions of 1848, when seen together with the precedent established earlier by the Holy Alliance, could not but appear as profoundly alarming. Whenever the nations of Europe sought to throw off despotic systems of government, Seward observed, "we see it invariably happen that the existing despotisms of Europe combine to repress those struggles—combine to subdue the people. The consequence is, that despotism is a common cause, and it results also that the cause of constitutional liberty has also become one common cause."[7]

The Whigs like Seward who pressed "our mission of republicanism" were careful to keep their enthusiasm within the bounds of international law. "The comity of nations I respect," declared Charles Sumner. "To the behests of the law of nations I profoundly bow. As in our domestic affairs, all acts are brought to the Constitution, as to a touchstone; so, in our foreign affairs, all acts are brought to the touchstone of the law of nations—that supreme law—the world's collected will—which overarches the grand Commonwealth of Christian States. What that forbids I forbear to do. But no text of this voluminous code, no commentary, no gloss, can be found which forbids us to welcome any exile of freedom." Cass readily agreed that the law of nations was controlling—"Every country under heaven has an interest in its immunity and preservation."[8]

Most proponents of a forward policy were unwilling to go to war, though critics believed that war was intimated in circumstances "which gentlemen do not exactly define." "I take it for granted," Cass said, "that there is not a sane man who dreams even of intervening by force in this affair" (though he also said that intervention might be justified "at the proper time"). In the then existing circumstances, it was public opinion, rather than physical force, that he emphasized. "Moral force," he declared, is a "powerful lever in the affairs of the world, which sooner or later will do its work." Cass protested that critics confused "interference" with "non-intercourse." To break diplomatic relations with Austria gave that government no just cause of complaint. "If I choose to have no intercourse with a man, it is not interfering with him."[9]

Seward also acknowledged that "we shall best execute [our mission of republicanism] by maintaining peace at home and peace with all mankind." If he saw in a cordial reception of Kossuth "a step in advance towards the bloody field of contention in the affairs of Europe," he "would hesitate long before adopting it." Faced with these prevarications, many critics raised the same question—is it something, or nothing?—that Randolph had raised a generation before against Webster and Clay, with Clemens of Alabama warning, for example, that "to indulge in the use of threats towards Russia is either to cover ourselves with ridicule or involve the country in war."[10]

John Tyler, the retired president and no friend of the Whigs, also objected to threats of American intervention to establish the principle of nonintervention. Such a policy, he wrote, would be equivalent to intervention against Austria and "make us in truth the most forward in overthrowing our own doctrine." Though friendly to the idea that "the edict" of America might in the future "arrest the cohorts of tyranny in their march to trample out the flame of liberty," Tyler objected to inciting revolts "through paper bulletins and governmental declarations" and saw an unhappy end in this beginning. It would be better, he wrote mischievously, to "proclaim ourselves the knights arrant of liberty, and organize at once a crusade against all despotic governments. This would be to meet the question fairly—'to beard the Lion in his den.' Then our proclamation would go forth in a different form. We should announce to all Nations our determination to advance with the sword the doctrines of republicanism. The gonfalon of Mahometism would be our banner; *there is but one form of govt. upon earth which we will tolerate and that is a republic.*"[11]

Clay also found incongruous and disturbing the gap between the enormities complained of and the remedies proffered; he could discern no limit to a policy that assumed "the right of interference in the internal affairs of foreign nations." Where, he asked, "are we to stop? Why should we not interfere in behalf of suffering Ireland? Why not interfere in behalf of suffering humanity wherever we may find it?" The right system, Underwood said, was one that tried "to enlighten the substratum of society; to make all the nations of the world—the little boys and girls of the world—learn and understand their rights—civil, political, and religious. When you can indoctrinate mankind by teaching them what their rights are, and show them that the physical power belongs to the multitude, you have the foundation on which to erect a pyramid of Republican governments to enlighten the whole earth, just as ours is doing. But you may as well attempt to make a pyramid stand by inverting it, as to attempt by war and conquest to establish a government. It cannot be done." That, Underwood alleged, was nevertheless the method of Senator Cass: "He can swallow Mexico without being injured."[12]

Throughout the debate a close connection was drawn between the implications of nonintervention at home and abroad. Webster had taken up his pen against the Austrian minister in his "Hulsemann letter" more for domestic than foreign purposes. If he had gone beyond strict diplomatic proprieties in comparing the Austrian Empire to a "patch on the earth's surface" in comparison with the United States and if, as he acknowledged, the letter had been "boastful and rough," it was because he wanted "to write a paper which should touch the national pride, and make a man feel sheepish and look silly who should speak of disunion." The distinctly chilly reception that met Kossuth in the South—the "whole opposition" to Kossuth comes from there, wrote Horace Mann—was also due in part to the understanding that intervention, even for the avowed purpose of establishing the principle of nonintervention, was a doctrine that could readily be applied against southern institutions.[13]

Kossuth himself got badly tangled in the ongoing American debate: wishing to get "intervention for non-intervention" from America, he himself adopted in effect a policy of "non-intervention for intervention" while in America, professing neutrality in the dispute between North and South so as not to alienate any potential supporters of his cause, a posture that earned him a denunciation from the abolitionists as a rank betrayer of the cause of human freedom. Clay's warning that "foreign Powers . . . when they see us assuming to judge of their conduct, will undertake in their turn to judge of *our* conduct" was not mere rhetoric but must be set in the context of the ongoing dispute between North and South. Were the right of intervention made good, he intimated, foreign powers, and particularly Great Britain, could easily urge a right of intervention in North America in the event of a conflict between the sections.[14]

But it was not only Europeans who might be tempted to intervene in America's "domestic affairs" if America stepped forward in the "struggle between liberal and absolute principles, between Republicanism and Despotism." If Americans were to cast "the execrations of the world upon the Austrian and Russian despots," should they not also condemn with equal vehemence the wrong of domestic slavery in their own land? "I see no reason," noted Horace Mann, "why my sympathies as a man, or the obligations of my oath as an officer, should be inversely as the squares of the distances." The same idea was expressed in 1850 by John Parker Hale, a Free Soil Democrat from New Hampshire. Satirizing the idea that the American Senate should erect itself "into a high court of indignation . . . to try the nations of the earth for 'atrocious acts of despotism,'" Hale announced trial upon trial of the nations, the powerful along with the weak. But the trials, he insisted, could not stop there. After the Senate had passed judgment on all Christendom, it would then be necessary to "go from these high places down before the bar, and plead ourselves." For in "the capital of the Model Republic . . . within sight of the flag of freedom that floats over our heads . . . men are to be bought, and women are to be bought, and kept at twenty-five cents per day, until ready to be transported to some other market."[15]

The proper scope and limit of the nonintervention principle, which was fundamental to the debate over American foreign policy, was yet more important to the struggle between the sections. Inability to reach agreement on that question was a formidable impetus to the Civil War. The issue did not reach to the existence of slavery in the states where it existed. All but a tiny handful of abolitionists were willing, in theory, to give what was "written in the bond." But where antislavery opinion balked and drew an incontrovertible line was in the extension of slavery. Declared Sumner: "Vowing ourselves against Slavery, wherever it exists, whether enforced by Russian knout, Turkish bastinado, or lash of Carolina planter, we do not seek to interfere with it at Petersburg, Constantinople, or Charleston; nor does any such grave duty rest upon us. Political duties are properly limited by political responsibilities; and we are in no just sense responsible for the local law or usage by which human bondage in these places is upheld. But wherever we are responsible for the wrong, there our duty begins. . . . Slavery, where we are parties to it, wherever we are responsible for it, everywhere within our jurisdiction, must be opposed not only by all the influences of literature, morals, and religion, but directly by every instrument of Political Power."[16] The South was equally determined to reject the *odium theologicum* cast upon its institutions and to secure the right of extending slavery into the territories. Hence it was that the conquest of territory in 1848 wrote out the preliminaries of the great war to follow.

PART SIX
Into the Maelstrom

22

Invitation to a Beheading

THE UPHEAVALS INTRODUCED BY TERRITORIAL EXPANSION in the 1840s played a vital role in the controversies of the 1850s that ended in civil war. Congress was suddenly beset by "ultraisms"; there were, Henry Clay complained soon after the opening of the Thirty-first Congress in December 1849, "twenty-odd furnaces in full blast in generating heat, and passion, and intemperance, and diffusing them throughout the whole extent of this broad land." The introduction in 1846 of the Wilmot Proviso, which would bar slavery from any territories acquired from Mexico, reflected one pole of the debate. Southerners had reacted by denying that Congress had any power to restrict slavery in the territories (thus denying the constitutionality of both the Northwest Ordinance of 1787 and the Missouri Compromise of 1820). The territories, which were the common possession of all states in the union, ought to be open to slaveholders and nonslaveholders alike; any restriction on the emigration of slaveholders and their property the South regarded as "unconstitutional, unjust, inconsistent with their equality as members of the common Union, and calculated to destroy irretrievably the equilibrium between the two sections."[1]

Between these antipodal positions were two compromise formulas: one proposed to extend the Missouri Compromise line of 36°30′ to the Pacific; the other, known as "popular sovereignty," would have Congress adopt a "principle of non-interference" toward slavery in the territories, leaving the people of the territories free "to adjust it as they may think proper when they apply for admission as States into the Union." Such was the distribution of power in Washington, D.C., that none of these formulas could gain passage through both houses of Congress. A deadlocked Thirtieth Congress had adjourned in March 1849 having seen all four formulas defeated in either House or Senate, and leaving California and the other territories unorganized. Observers considered the union "more in danger" than ever before.[2]

The resolutions introduced by Henry Clay in late January 1850 indicated in broad outline the compromise that would ultimately be made by Congress in that year, though it was Stephen Douglas rather than an exasperated Clay who devised the legislative strategy by which compromise was secured. Under Clay's resolutions, California was to be admitted immediately as a state, "without the imposition by Congress of any restriction in respect to

the exclusion or introduction of slavery within those boundaries." The remainder of the lands (exclusive of California) embraced by the Mexican cession were to be organized in territorial governments on the same principle.
Clay's third and fourth resolutions restricted the western boundary of Texas
but compensated for the loss by having the United States assume the debt
of Texas. His fifth and sixth resolutions would abolish the slave trade, but
not slavery, in the District of Columbia. Finally, he would have Congress
formally declare that it had no power "to prohibit or obstruct the trade in
slaves between the slaveholding States," and that it would give "more effectual provision" to the requirement of the Constitution that mandated "the
restitution and delivery" of fugitive slaves. The plan of compromise, Clay
held, "contains about an equal amount of concession and forbearance on
both sides," though he thought that the free states of the North, being "numerically more powerful than the slave States," might in justice be required
to give "a more liberal and extensive concession." The South was required
to accept the admission of California as a free state, whereas the North, "for
the sake of peace, and in a spirit of mutual forbearance," would have to
surrender the Wilmot Proviso, which every legislature of the northern states
had instructed its representatives in the House and Senate to incorporate in
any legislation organizing the territories. Since it was the right of every state
to decide its own domestic arrangements, the South could not complain of
California's decision to bar slavery. Since "slavery does not exist by law, and
is not likely to be introduced" into any of the ceded territories, the North
should be content with a provision that would restrict slavery effectually but
without at the same time affording gratuitous insult to the South. Clay, with
Webster, "would not take pains uselessly to reaffirm an ordinance of nature,
nor to reenact the will of God."[3]

   With some elaboration as to detail, Clay's resolutions formed the substance of the Compromise of 1850. Defeated in the summer as part of an
omnibus bill, the elements of Clay's compromise plan were resurrected by
Stephen Douglas and won passage in separate legislation. As this switch in
legislative strategies showed, there was no genuine compromise in 1850.
Southern representatives voted against the admission of California by a
large majority, just as most northern representatives continued to support
the Wilmot Proviso and to vote against the strengthening of the fugitive
slave law. The package as a whole was carried by the small band of compromisers willing to cross sections either actively or through abstention. Despite
that fragile basis, the compromise measures were accepted by both Whigs
and Democrats in their 1852 platforms; "finality" became a slogan indicating that the legislation of 1850 was not to be disturbed, on penalties as dire

as those entailed by opening Pandora's box. Events showed, however, that it was impossible to keep the conflict down; the box would be reopened.[4]

In part this stemmed from the compromise itself, above all the strengthening of the fugitive slave act. The provisions of this act, which "contained a number of gratuitously obnoxious provisions," were such as to inflame northern opinion. It denied alleged fugitives the right to a jury trial, permitted cases to be tried before commissioners who were to obtain a ten-dollar fee if the fugitive were given up, but only five dollars if set free, and it required the complicity of northern citizens by empowering federal marshals to summon all citizens to aid in the act's enforcement. The essence of the dilemma, as one historian has succinctly observed, was that "no law for the recovery of fugitive slaves could be effective without being outrageous."[5]

The box was opened yet further with "the repeal of the Missouri Compromise" in 1854. On a bill for the organization of the Nebraska territories, Stephen Douglas had substituted the formula of 1850 for that of 1820. How far Douglas anticipated the storm of controversy this provoked is unclear, but the reaction was vehement. The "Appeal of the Independent Democrats" denounced the bill "as a gross violation of a sacred pledge; as a criminal betrayal of precious rights; as part and parcel of an atrocious plot to exclude from a vast unoccupied region immigrants from the Old World and free laborers from our own States, and convert it into a dreary region of despotism, inhabited by masters and slaves." This was not Douglas's announced intention; he claimed, as indeed had Webster and Clay, that popular sovereignty was as effectual a restriction on the expansion of slavery as the Missouri Compromise line had been. He argued in his defense that it was the very men condemning him now who had consistently opposed the line of the Missouri Compromise. "The first time that the principles of the Missouri compromise were ever abandoned . . . was by the defeat of that provision in the House of Representatives in 1848. By whom was that defeat effected? By northern votes with free soil proclivities. It was the defeat of that Missouri compromise that reopened the slavery agitation with all its fury. . . . Who was it that was faithless? I undertake to say it was the very men who now insist that the Missouri compromise was a solemn compact and should never be violated or departed from." Douglas's critics noted that the Missouri Compromise had covered the territory embraced by the Louisiana Purchase, not the Mexican cession, and argued that there was no warrant for Douglas's implicit assumption that the policy of the federal government must be uniform on the subject. In fact, it never had been. Those "northern votes with free soil proclivities," moreover, had generally opposed both the annexation of Texas and the war with Mexico. It was Douglas who had

strenuously supported territorial annexation in the blithe expectation that
the inevitable renewal of the question of slavery in the territories could be
met without serious difficulty. Thus did the Kansas-Nebraska Act reopen
the issues that the Compromise of 1850 had closed. It was the midwife of
the Republican Party; it gave renewed force to antislavery agitation in the
North and new impetus to attempts by northern legislatures to nullify the
fugitive slave law, while awakening the northern people "to the aggressive
character of slavery as a political power [and uniting] them in determined
hostility to its extension."[6]

The uproar over the Kansas-Nebraska bill in the winter and spring of 1854
occurred simultaneously with a crisis over Cuban annexation. The issues
were closely related; for the southerners, the motive for expansion in Kansas
or Cuba was the same: to restore a faltering balance of power in the councils
of the union. Franklin Pierce had pledged in his 1853 inaugural address that
his administration would "not be controlled by any timid forebodings of evil
from expansion," which southerners understood as an implied commitment
to obtain Cuba in the course of his administration. Many southern leaders
longed to bring into the union "a vast golden circle" of slave states in the
Caribbean and Central America so as to maintain their equality; northern
Democrats, in turn, saw the merit in reviving bisectional expansion in the
spirit of the Compromise of 1844 and were interested in Cuba "as a means
of diverting the southern consciousness from the West."[7]

But Cuba was lost. The administration, which sincerely wanted Cuba,
believed circumstances became propitious when Britain and France, which
had traditionally checked American ambitions for the island, went to war
against Russia in 1854, yet it could find no way around the multitude of obstacles that grew up before it. The filibustering expedition outfitted by John
Quitman of Mississippi bided its time until Pierce, stung by the furor over
Kansas-Nebraska, announced that his administration would move sharply
against any violation of the neutrality laws. "The Nebraska question,"
wrote Secretary of State Marcy, "has sadly shattered our party in all the free
states and deprived it of the strength which was needed & could have been
much more profitably used for the acquisition of Cuba." Thus weakened,
purchase seemed the only option now acceptable to northern public opinion, and indeed to Secretary Marcy himself, who wrote a friend that a war
of conquest "would degrade us in our own estimation and disgrace us in the
eyes of the world." Since the Spaniards preferred that Cuba should sink in
the ocean rather than be sold to the Yankees, desire faced a set of exasperat-
ing restraints out of which it was impossible to break.[8]

It was partly out of frustration that the administration solicited the advice of three American ministers resident in Europe—Buchanan in London,

Soule in Spain, and Mason in Paris—who met for consultations in Ostend, Belgium. Their communication back home—which when leaked to
the newspapers became famous as the Ostend Manifesto—announced that
"Cuba is as necessary to the North American republic as any of its present members, and that it belongs naturally to that great family of states of
which the Union is the Providential Nursery." If Spain refused to sell, and
if Cuba became "a second St. Domingo, with all its attendant horrors to
the white race," then the "great law of self-preservation"—indeed, "every
law human and Divine"—would justify the United States in wresting Cuba
from Spain, "if we possess the power." The ministers commented that, in
pursuit of this policy, "we can afford to disregard the censures of the world
to which we have been so often and so unjustly exposed," but that was not
an easy task given the ferocity of the denunciations that greeted it, both at
home and abroad. The Ostend Manifesto, by identifying expansion with
naked aggression and what Lincoln called the "plea of the highwayman,"
badly discredited the ideas of Manifest Destiny while weakening further
the relations between the northern and southern wings of the Democratic
Party. It, too, established "the aggressive character of slavery as a political power" and united the northern people "in determined hostility to its
extension."[9]

Three years after the dramatic confrontation over slavery expansion in
the territories and the tropics, the Missouri Compromise Act of 1820 was
declared unconstitutional by the Supreme Court in *Dred Scott v. Sandford*.
By adopting Calhoun's doctrine that the slave owner had a right to take his
property with him into territories governed by the United States, that the
Congress had gone beyond the Constitution in prohibiting slavery in federal
territories, and that to do so was to the slaveholder a violation of due process of law, the Court not only explicitly declared unconstitutional the Missouri legislation of 1820 but also cast grave doubt on the constitutionality of
the Compromise of 1850. Though Justice Catron of Tennessee had thought
that a decision denying that Congress had the power to govern the territories
"after a practice of 68 years" would subject the Supreme Court to ridicule,
Chief Justice Taney, a fierce southern sectionalist, had plunged ahead into
the political morass, in effect ruling out every political adjustment to this
much agitated question save the favored doctrine of the South. As historian
Kenneth Stampp has noted, the Court's opinion meant "that not only the
slavery provision of the Missouri Compromise but all other acts of Congress
excluding slavery from various territories had been equally unconstitutional.
A restriction thus imposed on congressional power to govern the territories,
unmentioned in the Constitution, unknown to its framers, undiscovered for
many years thereafter, but recently devised by John C. Calhoun and other

proslavery partisans, was now, according to the opinion of the Court, the law of the land."[10]

Dred Scott, though pretending to finality, settled nothing. Republicans were from the first moment determined to overthrow it. Northern legislatures nullified the operation of the fugitive slave law within their jurisdictions, as Georgians had nullified the decree of the Marshall Court in theirs. Kansas bled, as it became a battleground of proslavery and antislavery groups. In the firestorm provoked by Kansas-Nebraska, the Ostend Manifesto, and *Dred Scott*, the Compromise of 1850 was a distant memory. Americans were back in the condition from which Clay had more than once tried to rescue them—in which "nothing on earth is settled under this Constitution, but the principle that everything is unsettled." "Every day, still," said Rufus Choate in 1858, "we are in committee of the whole on the question of the Constitution or no Constitution."[11]

23

Causes of the War,
Causes of the Peace

THE MOST INVESTIGATED PROBLEM in American history is the coming of
the Civil War. Historians have differed over whether the conflict was inevitable (or "irrepressible"); whether slavery was "the sole cause"; whether the
war is best explained as a clash of distinct civilizations that, given their antithetical character, could no longer coexist within a common government, or
by pent-up economic grievances reflecting the irreconcilable differences between two distinct types of economic organization. Some have thought that
the central question must be why the South seceded, others why the North
fought to retain the South within the union through force. Blame has been
variously assigned for the catastrophe. In the years after its termination, responsibility for the conflict was placed on the minority of southern leaders
who had conspired, without ever enjoying the confidence of the people of
the South, to commit treason and rebellion. A later generation, impressed
by the futility of World War I, was disposed to grant that the Civil War, too,
was of that character, and saw its causes in the missteps of the fanatics and
agitators—whether of the abolitionist or "fire-eater" variety—who brought
about a needless war. Historians who lived through World War II, and who
believed that there were worse things than not fighting for principle, saw
the question yet differently. They rejected the "blundering generation" hypothesis and disputed the view that slavery might ever have been abolished
peacefully.[1]

Not surprisingly, the assumption of most writers is that the Civil War was
a shocking departure from the norm. While the insistent question, notes
geographer D. W. Meinig, has always been "Why did the war come?" an
equally pertinent question is "How could [the union] have held together
for so long under such dynamic circumstances?"[2] This way of posing the
question is strongly suggested by the unionist paradigm. Nothing was more
characteristic in discourse on the union than the idea that it was a "miracle,"
that it was attempting an experiment that had never been done before and
that, if done successfully, would constitute a precious example to mankind.
The "Union of so many States," noted James Madison in 1830, "is, in the
eyes of the world, a wonder; the harmonious establishment of a common
Government over them all, a miracle." But if, as Webster affirmed, "such a

thing has happened once, and but once," and if it stood "as an exception to all ordinary history," the logical implication is that the great war should not be considered as an accident or an anomaly but a reversion to the mean suggested by the historical experience of previous ages—a resumption of history, as it were, among a people (or peoples) who had entertained the enthralling but ultimately naive hope that they had found history's end.[3]

Rumors of war had in fact afflicted the federal union throughout its career, and many are the prophecies of the "great tragic volume" that lay waiting to be written in the future. If the state of war, as Hobbes once expressed it, consists not of battle only but of a tract of time, in which the will to contend by battle is sufficiently known, and if such a time may be compared to a long spell of inclement weather—always threatening precipitation, somehow never raining—the federal union often found itself under that dark cloud. Fisher Ames had observed in 1803 that he knew not "how many ages" it would take for the war to come. "I leave that problem to Thucydides the second to decide," he wrote mischievously, "in his new History of the American Peloponnesian War." Whether the war would be "between Virginia and New England, or between the Atlantic and Tra[ns]montane States," or whether it would be, as in France, the consequence of a turbulent democracy setting "the poor against the rich, and the vile against the worthy," Ames did not presume to say. "No muse has told me, and uninspired I cannot tell you." Lamenting in 1803 the vanishing significance of New England, he would doubtless have been surprised to learn that a fundamental cause of the American Civil War would be the growth in the power of the North and the fear this caused in the South.[4]

"The great and primary cause" of the "almost universal discontent" pervading the southern section of the union, as John Calhoun observed in 1850, was that "the equilibrium between the two sections, in the Government as it stood when the constitution was ratified and the Government put in action, has been destroyed." "Every census has added to the power of the nonslaveholding States," noted the Carolinian Robert Barnwell Rhett, "and diminished that of the South. We are growing weaker, and they stronger, every day." The South ascribed this growing disparity to sectional aggrandizement and to the unequal system of bounties, tariffs, and immigration that had augmented the industry of the North and depressed the agriculture of the South; the North traced the cause to factors of the South's own making, above all to slavery. Whatever the cause, however, there is no question but that the phenomenon of unequal growth played a critical role in stoking the fires that led to the Civil War. Though entering the government in 1789 in a minority position, the South had gained predominance in 1801 and held it until the Missouri crisis of 1820, after which there was a long recessional in its relative power. Sectional equilibrium proved impossible to maintain under expansion and growth.[5]

The significance of the crisis that followed the Mexican War, in southern eyes, was that it threatened to permanently derange the balance of power. "Now, for the first time," argued Jefferson Davis, "we are about permanently to destroy the balance of power between the sections of the Union, by securing a majority to one, in both Houses of Congress." The anxiety produced by the admission of California produced the search for ways in which the change in the balance might be reversed; there was, as Clay said, "a floating idea in the southern mind . . . of the necessity of an equilibrium of power between the two sections of the Union." Calhoun proposed a dual executive; Davis thought the best way to ensure this balance would be "that in one branch of Congress the North and in the other the South should have a majority of representation" (a possibility that Madison had broached but withdrawn in the 1787 convention). Neither alternative ruled out a third mode of adjustment, which was the annexation of new slave states from the Caribbean or Central America. Clay, in answering the proposals for constitutional revision in 1850, did not deny that a balance of power might be desirable, but he did insist that it was "utterly impracticable." The "rapid growth and unparalleled progress" of the North was such that the South could not "keep pace with it . . . unless the order of all republics shall be reversed, and the majority shall be governed by the minority." This was, in Clay's judgment, no reason for the South to despair. There were a great many other interests—navigation, the fisheries, manufacturing, commerce—that were in the minority; indeed, all economic interests save the "great and all-pervading interest of agriculture" were in the parlous condition in which slaveholders now found themselves. But it did not follow that slavery would be endangered by the South's minority status. It would still have available to it all the means of protection provided by the Constitution itself—the political concurrences of House, Senate, and president, the legal protections offered by the Supreme Court; it would enjoy, even as a last resort, the right "to make forcible resistance when oppression and tyranny become insupportable." These various protections gave the South "all reasonable security against any abuses which may be inflicted in the progress of events."[6]

Southern fears of a derangement of the balance of power were exacerbated by the swelling tides of immigration that occurred in the late 1840s and 1850s. Though numbers of immigrants had expanded each decade—151,000 in the 1820s, 599,000 in the 1830s, 1,713,000 in the 1840s, and 2,314,000 in the 1850s—it was only in the last two decades, when huge numbers came from Ireland, Scandinavia, and Germany, that the migrants, seven-eighths of whom settled in the North, had a vital impact on the balance of power among the sections. That great migration accentuated the hopelessness of the South's position within the union—one southern congressman estimated in 1856 that "by the next apportionment the North will gain upon the South twenty-four additional members from immigration alone"—and was a crucial factor in the assurance of northern victory during the war: A fifth of the Union army, approximately 500,000, was born abroad. Fears of the immigrant, ironically, were most prominent in the North and gave a meteoric rise to the Native American Party of the 1850s (rechristened as the American Party in 1855), but immigration remained essentially unrestricted. This ingathering of fugitives was of great significance in the decade before the Civil War, almost by itself suggesting that the war might have had a different outcome had it been fought in 1850.[7]

It was, however, not simply the loss of equilibrium, but how the South acted under the shadow of its minority status, that deserves emphasis in understanding the true cause of the war. Under the impetus of that declining position, southern representatives adopted an offensive strategy that awoke the northern people "to the aggressive character of slavery as a political power" and united them "in determined hostility to its extension." Texas annexation in 1845, the fugitive slave law of 1850, the Kansas-Nebraska Act of 1854, and the *Dred Scott* decision of 1857 were similar in three vital respects: each went beyond the law, each constituted a victory for the South, and each was a victory that cumulatively did grievous damage to the South's larger political position. Expansion into the tropics, though the conspiracy was defeated, had the same effect.

Every effort of the South to restore the faltering balance of power meant a corresponding defeat in northern public opinion, furnishing potent ammunition to the cause of antislavery. Much like Germany before World War I, every effort to escape encirclement simply made the ring tighter. Southerners, in their own minds, thought that they were simply building defenses around their beleaguered section and throwing up breastworks against the attacks of "fanatics" who wished to destroy the institution of slavery. But these defensive works, as if in perfect illustration of the "security dilemma," were seen by northern opinion, and not unreasonably, as highly aggressive. It was the consciousness of those aggressions that above all gave confidence and popularity to the Republican Party, and a realization, too, among southern leaders that all their victories had been for naught and had simply confirmed the ascendancy of their enemies that formed the immediate background of the secession crisis of 1860.

These considerations do not displace, but they substantially qualify, a Thucydidean explanation that would find the cause of the war in the growth of the power of the North and the fear this caused in the South. As important as these shifts in the balance of power were, they would not have enjoyed the significance they did in the absence of the slavery issue. Given the Negrophobia that existed in the North, and the conscious desire among whites to keep not only slavery but also blacks out of the territories, it is easy to minimize the significance of antislavery. "The army of liberation," as one historian laconically observed, at times "marched southward on its crusade under the banner of White Supremacy."[8] Despite these incongruous attitudes, the clash of moral principle was utterly real and of commanding importance. In the sectional conflict, the moral may have stood to the material, as in Napoleon's famous expression about war, as three to one.

The American people loved and cherished the union, and did so with deep conviction and sincerity. But the slavery issue shattered this pleasing consensus. The obloquy that attended the debate over slavery was a knife stuck into the body of the union, causing it to shriek and rear up. Each side, noted one historian in the 1950s, "charged the other with aggression. Each insisted that its opponent was carrying forward a program of encirclement aimed at the ultimate destruction of civilization. Vishinsky or Molotov or Dulles could not have conjured up a darker picture!"[9] This sense of the union as a compact with dark satanic forces, a partnership with one's worst nightmare, was felt, with more or less heat, on both sides of the Mason-Dixon Line. Such a state of affairs inevitably struck a formidable and cumulative blow at the foundation of the union. Calhoun was right, in his last speech, to argue that the "cords which bind these States together in one common Union, are far too numerous and powerful" for disunion to be "effected by a single blow. . . . Disunion must be the work of time. It is only through a long process, and successively, that the cords can be snapped, until the whole fabric falls asunder." Calhoun's account of how "the slavery question has snapped some of the most important, and has greatly weakened all the others," told of how the American churches had become divided on the question, how the two great political parties had dreaded its approach. With his insistence that the conflict must be resolved on southern terms and that compromise be rejected, he had also demonstrated, in his way, that it was inexorable.[10]

Both North and South had their explanations for the role that slavery came to play. One fascinating effect of the South's determination to see slavery as a positive good was its ready inclination to subject northern institutions to withering critique, and there is hardly a theme developed in the literature of Marxism and economic radicalism that was not urged against the North and its institutions by the proslavery intellectuals. But this exaggerated defensive reaction itself attested to the way in which the slavery issue poisoned the well of the union. To southerners, the widespread belief in the North that the "cornerstone" of southern institutions was immoral and unjust made it painful, and potentially hazardous, to remain in fellowship with their erstwhile brethren. The southern mind deduced that at some point slavery would be attacked directly, despite the protestations of Lincoln and the Republican Party, and it prompted the conclusion in 1860 that secession was better now than later. In their own minds, they were getting out while the getting was good.[11]

Most men and women in the free states, by contrast, attributed the prominence of the slavery issue to the aggressiveness with which southerners defended an institution that their forefathers had acknowledged was evil. Lincoln put great stress on this transformation, insisting that the change in the estimation of the institution—from necessary evil to positive good, and from one destined to pass away with time to one that grew in strength and sought to fortify itself—lay at the core of the sectional conflict. That change of opinion put an entirely different face on the "*declared* indifference" to the expansion of slavery in Douglas's proposals for popular sovereignty. Lincoln believed there was a "covert *real* zeal for the spread of slavery" reflected in Douglas's scheme, and he hated it. "I hate it because of the monstrous injustice of slavery itself. I hate it because it deprives our republican example of its just influence in the world—enables the enemies of free institutions, with plausibility, to taunt us as hypocrites—causes the real friends of freedom to doubt our sincerity, and especially because it forces so many really good men amongst ourselves into an open war with the very fundamental principles of civil liberty—criticizing the Declaration of Independence, and insisting that there is no right principle of action but *self-interest*."[12]

If the moral convulsions arising out of the slavery issue, together with the shift in the balance of power, form the two most important causes of the war, we are still obliged to ask: What caused the peace? In answering that question, one cannot simply appeal to the institutional characteristics of the federal system. There was a normative order attending federal union that lay at the base of these institutions, a triplet of mutually reinforcing norms of conduct consisting of good faith, equity, and compromise. It is to these moral qualities that we must look for the causes of the peace, because it was on those elements that the union had been reared and maintained. Emphasizing their impairment or loss is an equally illuminating way of understanding the dissolution of the union and the coming of the war.[13]

One of the best descriptions of the normative order was provided by Albert Gallatin, then a senior statesmen, in 1832. "The true problem to be solved in the United States," Gallatin wrote, "is not whether the people can govern themselves, of which not the slightest doubt can be entertained, but whether that government can be successfully applied to an extensive territory, embracing interests which must occasionally be in collision with each other; whether majorities formed by combinations of sectional interests will be so governed by a sense of justice and a spirit of conciliation as not to oppress those parts of the country, whose rights, though they may be a minority, ought, nevertheless, to be respected." A spirit of conciliation and a sense of justice were closely related norms. Though not identical, they were both responses to the heterogeneous character of the sections making up the union. Capping the normative order of federal union was *good faith*, a quality signifying the faithful performance of the obligations entailed by the constitutional compact. Gallatin, in a later address, summarized that value as follows: "The Constitution of the United States was from the beginning founded upon mutual concessions and compromise. When that Constitution was passed it appears that the southern states, alarmed by the difference of their social state and institutions from ours in the North, required some guarantees. They may have been granted with reluctance, but they are consecrated by the Constitution. The surrender of fugitive slaves and the non-equal principle of representation have been granted, and, however repugnant to our feelings or principles, we must carry out the provisions into effect faithfully and inviolate."[14]

Alongside the faithful performance of what was written in the bond was the imperative that the union accord to its members a fair distribution of burdens and benefits. An inequitable distribution of burdens and benefits threatened the union. As Hamilton had remarked, "There is, perhaps, nothing more likely to disturb the tranquility of nations than their being bound to mutual contributions for any common object that does not yield an equal and coincident benefit." And so the conservators of federal union pledged themselves to forgo the egotistical pursuit of special advantage. "I belong to no section or particular interest," the early Calhoun had claimed. "It has been my pride to be above all sectional or party feelings and to be devoted to the great interests of the country." "With me it is a fundamental axiom," said Daniel Webster in 1824, "that the great interests of the country are united and inseparable; that agriculture, commerce, and manufactures will prosper together or languish together; and that all legislation is dangerous which proposes to benefit one of these without looking to consequences which may fall on the others."[15]

Both good faith and equity were vital components of the normative order of federal union. Ironically, public figures would appeal to this normative order often for the purpose of demonstrating that some action embraced by an opponent represented a violation of it, so that we know its features from public debate as an ideal often crossed. A faithful adherence to the terms of the Constitution, though repeatedly invoked, had been often held up as a tarnished if not utterly forsaken ideal from the first years of the government until the great war of sections, so much so that American political history might almost be seen as a reiterated sequence of violations of the plain and emphatic edict of the Constitution. The same is true of the cherished ideal of a just distribution of benefits and burdens; there was not a year from 1789 to 1861 that did not ring out with charges that a system of iniquitous legislation, unfairly oppressive to one section of the union, had entrenched itself in the federal government.

Though each of the sections nursed certain deeply felt grievances, there was an understanding in all sections of the benefits brought by federal union. One bond of union, which James Buchanan regarded as "adamantine," was the powerful interest created by the mutual dependence of the states on each other. The locus classicus of this theme was Washington's Farewell Address, but it enjoyed continuous reiteration in the years to follow. Wrote Buchanan in 1850: "The numerous and powerful commonwealths which are spread over the valley of the Mississippi must seek the markets of the world for their productions, through the mouth of that father of rivers. A strong naval power is necessary to keep this channel always free in time of war; and an immense commercial marine is required to carry their productions to the markets of the world, and bring back their returns. The same remark applies with almost equal force to the cotton growing and planting States on the Gulf of Mexico and on the Atlantic. Who is to supply this naval power and this commercial marine? The hardy and enterprising sons of the North, whose home has always been on the mountain wave." This "mutual and profitable dependence upon each other" was for Buchanan "one of the strongest bonds of our Union."[16]

If some benefits were direct, others were indirect and "unseen." "The influence of the Government on us," as Alexander Stephens urged, "is like that of the atmosphere around us. Its benefits are so silent and unseen that they are seldom thought of or appreciated. . . . We seldom think of the single element of oxygen in the air we breathe, and yet this simple unseen and unfelt agent be withdrawn . . . and what instant and appalling changes would take place in all organic creation!" The influence of the government on the maintenance of peace among the sections was alone sufficient to give an entirely different reckoning to the supposed oppressions under which the South, or indeed any of the sections, was seen to labor. "What we would have lost in border wars without the Union, or what we have gained simply by the peace it has secured, is not within our power to estimate." In comparing the benefits of federal union to oxygen, Stephens did not mean to intimate that peace was the natural condition of the American republics. They owed their success to artifice, not nature. It was their institutions that had enabled the

American people, and most particularly the southern people, to prosper. Those institutions constituted "the basis, the matrix, from which spring all our characteristics of development and greatness." Look at Greece, said Stephens: "There is the same fertile soil, the same blue sky, the same inlets and harbors, the same Aegean, the same Olympus." Look at Rome, "once the mistress of the world." "There are the same seven hills now, the same soil, the same natural resources." In both Greece and Rome, however, "a ruin of human greatness meets the eye of the traveler." The cause, in both cases, was the same: it lay in the destruction of their institutions. Hence Stephens warned against the "fatal temptation" of disunion, of rashly trying the experiment "of pulling down and destroying, for, as in Greece and Italy, and the South American republics, and in every other place, whenever our liberty is once lost, it may never be restored to us again."[17]

The third great pillar of federal union, and truly its architectonic norm, was "reciprocal concession." An impartial consideration of the benefits and burdens of any system of policy might yield utterly irreconcilable opinions, as might the inquiry into the nature of the constitution to which good faith was pledged. Faced with such antinomies, all that remained, if the union were to be salvaged, was for the parties to approach one another in "a spirit of amity," and with "that mutual deference and concession which the peculiarity of the [American] political situation rendered indispensable." Such were the oft-quoted words of Washington in his letter transmitting the work of the federal convention. More, perhaps, than any of the framers had Madison inculcated the precept of reciprocal concession into the making of the Constitution, a standard that also shaped his insistence, in the First Congress, on a Bill of Rights. Among the second generation of American statesmen, none was more closely identified with the necessity of compromise than Henry Clay, "the Great Pacificator." Often would Clay appeal to "the great principle of compromise and concession which lies at the bottom of our institutions, which gave birth to the Constitution itself, and which has continued to regulate us in our onward march, and conducted the nation to glory and renown." The great compromises of 1820–1821, 1833, and 1850 were all justified in relation to "that spirit of harmony and conciliation"; all reflected Clay's anxiety "to find out some principle of mutual accommodation, to satisfy, as far as practicable, both parties." The compromising disposition entailed a genuine commitment to selflessness; for the union to be preserved, noted John Quincy Adams, every man must set himself and his opinions aside. Devotion to the union, as Lincoln described the tug of disinterestedness, "rightfully inclined men to yield somewhat, in points where nothing else could have so inclined them."[18]

For the advocates of compromise, the alternative to this process of reciprocal concession was well understood to be war, and the former took place under the shadow of the latter. "I tell gentlemen they must relieve the South or fight them," said John Quincy Adams in 1832. Noted Senator James Shields of Illinois in 1850: "Sir, where *compromise ends, force begins,* and when *force* begins, *war* begins, and the tocsin of civil war is the death knell of Republicanism." When Stephen Douglas reached the conclusion, in 1860, that a point had been reached when "a compromise on the basis of mutual concession, or disunion and war, are inevitable," he was not describing a new dilemma.[19]

Despite these many rumors of war, Americans of the antipodal parties went into the secession crisis of 1860 discounting the probability of war. Neither Republicans nor secessionists were willing to grant that adherence to their stands would lead inexorably to a great conflagration. The rank weed of secession, insisted the Republicans, would wilt before the refusal of the government to appease such noxious growths. The pretended use of force by the "black Republicans," thought the secessionists, would be stopped in its tracks once it confronted the steely backbone of southern resistance or the world awakened to its stark dependence on southern cotton. Perhaps it was a necessary condition of the war that this belief in its unlikelihood should be so marked a feature of the opposing camps' calculations in the winter of 1860. But there were also plenty of people at the time who distrusted these sunny forecasts and who saw the magnitude of the coming train wreck. They were among those, now a distinct minority, who trekked to the "Old Gentleman's Convention" of 1861, making one last fruitless stab at a settlement.[20]

Much as the disunion crisis of 1860 was unique in its outcome, in form it corresponded with unerring exactitude to past crises. The toasts at the Jefferson dinner of April 13, 1830, offer a classic symbolic moment of the fundamental quandary of federal union, in which rival constitutional claims, strongly foreshadowing the use of force, stand opposed to the appeal to reciprocal concession. Governor Troup of Georgia, a forefather of the fire-eaters, indulged with his toast in embittered sarcasm: "The Government of the United States: With more limited powers than the Republic of San Marino, it rules an Empire more extended than the Roman with the absoluteness of Tiberius, with less wisdom than Augustus and less justice than Trajan or the Antonines." There followed toasts by President Jackson: "Our Federal Union—it must be preserved"; by Vice President Calhoun: "The Union—next to our liberty the most dear; may we all remember it can only be preserved by respecting the rights of the States and distributing equally the benefit and burden of the Union"; and finally by Van Buren, who recorded the exchange in his autobiography: "Mutual forbearance and reciprocal concessions; thro' their agency the Union was established—the patriotic spirit from which they emanated will forever sustain it." The episode perfectly encapsulates the problematic nature of the federal union and sheds a bright light on both the causes of the long peace and the causes of the great war in 1861.[21]

24

D.I.V.O.R.C.E.

IT HAD LONG BEEN PART OF THE UNION'S LORE that it was like a marriage, and it was rich in the language of partnership, commitment, and infidelity. "We are in the Union," declared William Seward, "for richer or poorer, for better or worse, whether in a majority or in a minority, whether in power or powerless, without condition, reservation, qualification, or limitation, for ever and aye." That analogy to the married state not only indicated the conduct appropriate to its maintenance but also shone a light on the limiting condition, that is, the terms on which a separation might take place in the event the parties became estranged.[1]

If their relationship was to be preserved, they had to act in the spirit of Prior's ballad, describing a man's behavior to his wife:

Be to her faults a little blind;
Be to her virtues very kind.

Chatham quoted this couplet in his renowned speech of January 14, 1766, in the House of Lords, opposing a right of parliamentary taxation over the colonies; and it was an article of faith with him that parliamentary taxation was not compatible with this idea. Chatham's sentiments, of course, found great favor among the colonists themselves. When they became independent, and had formed a union of their own, Prior's ballad and Chatham's speech were recalled to describe the ethic the sectional partners should bear to one another.[2]

These metaphors did not mislead. The union *was* like a marriage, albeit a troubled and stormy one. The partners to this association spoke a language of commitment and betrayal; they thought often of what life would be like if they were to break asunder from their confederates; and their fellowship was often sustained by these fears of dissolution rather than by mutual good feeling. They each sustained a sense of rights and wrongs in their relations with one another, and they well understood that their partnership could not be sustained in the absence of a faithful performance of their obligations; but while agreeing in theory to that proposition, they often disagreed in fact over what constituted a faithless performance. They tended to quarrel perpetually over the burdens they were each respectively asked to shoulder, and resented with particular vehemence the imputation that they had not done, or were not now doing, their fair share. But there were the children to think of, and fond memories that bound them in a common sentiment, so even in the midst of their deepest acrimony they might be found searching for the basis on which they might reaffirm their vows.

This union was of the body as well as of the spirit. In affirming together the thing or things that they cherished, they did not believe that this spiritual affirmation was incompatible with the taking and giving of carnal pleasures. The acknowledgment of the practical and even selfish benefits they gained from their partnership—some of it quite excellent, much of it very mundane and ordinary—was compatible, in other words, with their spiritual commitment. Henry Clay once gave memorable testimony to the carnal character of the union (while incidentally causing his fellow senators to erupt in laughter) when he observed: "In private life, if a wife pouts, and frets, and scolds, what would be thought of the good sense or discretion of the husband, who should threaten her with separation, divorce, disunion? who should use these terrible words upon every petty disagreement in domestic life? No man, who has a heart or right feelings, would employ such idle menaces. He would approach the lady with kind and conciliatory language, and apply those natural and more agreeable remedies, which never fail to restore domestic harmony."[3]

The propensity to liken the union to a marriage bore directly on the problem of secession. Even the bitterest enemies of the South saw that the preservation of the union through force could only be a terrible last resort, and many denied that it could be any resort at all. "There are some rights, quite perfect, yet wholly incapable of being enforced," wrote the abolitionist Wendell Phillips on the eve of the war. "A husband or wife who can only keep the other partner within the bond by locking the doors and standing armed before them, had better submit to peaceable separation." "I love the Union as I love my wife," wrote John Quincy Adams in 1801, when he feared that the election of Jefferson and Burr might mean the union's breakup. "But if my wife would ask and insist upon a separation, she should have it, though it broke my heart."[4]

Adams took a very similar view forty years later in his speech on the jubilee of the Constitution:

> If the day should ever come, (may Heaven avert it,) when the affections of the people of these States shall be alienated from each other, when the fraternal spirit shall give way to cold indifference, or collisions of interest shall fester into hatred, the bands of political association will not long hold together parties no longer attracted by the magnetism of

conciliated interests and kindly sympathies; and far better will it be for
the people of the disunited states to part in friendship from each other,
than to be held together by constraint. Then will be the time for revert-
ing to the precedents which occurred at the formation and adoption
of the Constitution, to form again a more perfect union by dissolving
that which could no longer bind, and to leave the separated parts to be
reunited by the law of political gravitation to the centre.[5]

Seward and Jefferson are to be found speculating in the same vein. Though
Seward observed in 1844 that "disunion is no longer a real terror, but is
sinking into an antiquated superstition, haunting only minds which mor-
bidly court the enervating spell," he allowed that the dreaded divorce might
come. In that event, he prophesied, "long habits of discipline and mutual
affection may enable the American people to add another and final lesson
on the excellence of republics—that of dividing without violence, and reconstructing without the loss of liberty." Two or three years of a trial separation, Jefferson had predicted, "will bring them back, like quarreling lovers
to renewed embraces, and increased affections." Both men believed that just
about everything depended on keeping the marriage in good order. "Were
we to break to pieces," wrote Jefferson in 1820, "it would damp the hopes
and the efforts of the good, and give triumph to those of the bad through
the whole enslaved world. As members, therefore, of the universal society
of mankind, and standing in high and responsible relation with them, it is
our sacred duty to suppress passion among ourselves, and not to blast the
confidence we have inspired of proof that a government of reason is better
than one of force."[6]

If the comparison to the married state might be employed to show the
illegitimacy of force as a means of keeping the parties within the bond, it
was also true that an amicable divorce would be a contradiction in terms.
There were too many things once held in common whose division would
have to be agreed upon; if a willingness to bear, and forbear, could not be
found inside their partnership, it was most unlikely to exist once they stood
outside of it. Divorce, on that reckoning, would solve nothing. As Madison
observed in the course of the Missouri crisis, "The very discords to which
[the people] found themselves subject, even under the guardianship of a
united Government, premonish them of the tempestuous hostilities which
await a dissolution of it." It was precisely here, indeed, that the analogy
to marriage broke down, as Lincoln noted in his first inaugural address:
"Physically, we cannot separate. We cannot remove our respective sections
from each other, nor build an impassable wall between them. A husband
and wife may be divorced, and go out of the presence, and beyond the reach

of each other; but the different parts of our country cannot do this. They cannot but remain face to face; and intercourse, either amicable or hostile, must continue between them. Is it possible to make that intercourse more advantageous or satisfactory, *after* separation than *before*? Can aliens make treaties easier than friends can make laws?" [7]

Lincoln's rhetorical questions pointed to a consideration that had always been central to the unionist paradigm. By 1787, the American states were already so deeply enmeshed in one another's affairs that a decision by any group of states to go their own way would inevitably affect the rights and interests of others. Publius had shown in *The Federalist* that there were a great many different questions on which a war between the American states might take place. That problem never went away. Dismissing the prospect of "peaceable secession" in 1850, Webster observed that "we could not sit down here to-day, and draw a line of separation, that would satisfy any five men in the country." The same point was made during the crisis of 1860–1861. Were secession successful, wrote the *New York Times* in March 1861, "Questions of commerce, of the rights of navigation, of extradition . . . a thousand sources of hostility would be created by the very fact of separation. . . . It would be impossible . . . to avoid hostilities for any considerable length of time." [8]

Secessionists objected that this argument was nothing better than a self-fulfilling prophecy and took the same ground as that taken by the Anti-Federalists of 1788 and the New England schismatics of 1814. The dissolution of the union, said the secessionists, would remove the artificial conflicts that had been created by too close a connection, and the democratic character of the separated states, united by ties of commerce, would conduce toward peace. [9] This was, as we have seen, an old debate that had arisen in the argument over the Constitution, and its reiteration at this moment should occasion no surprise. Here as earlier, however, it does not appear clearly from the historical record which side had the better of the argument. The structural realist claim that war would inevitably ensue from the dissolution of the union did have the character of a self-fulfilling prophecy, as secessionists alleged, preventing a full trial of the experiment. By the same token, however, the outbreak and ferocity of the Civil War scarcely seem to vindicate the theory of the democratic peace. Today, political scientists propounding the law that democracies do not fight one another exclude the case from their purview, holding that the South, because of slavery, was both illiberal and undemocratic. At the time, however, the war was widely regarded as a scandal to democratic institutions. [10]

No period of the federal union had been without the specter of civil war, but the grim visage had been approached warily. Orators might insist that it was too terrible to contemplate, as they stood there contemplating it. With Webster, they might claim, "I have not allowed myself, Sir, to look beyond the Union, to see what might lie hidden in the dark recess behind. I have not coolly weighed the chances of preserving liberty when the bonds that unite us together shall be broken asunder. I have not accustomed myself to hang over the precipice of disunion, to see whether, with my short sight, I can fathom the depth of the abyss below." Webster's sight, instead, lay on the "high, exciting, gratifying prospects spread out before us" with the union; beyond that he would not seek "to penetrate the veil." "God grant that in my day, at least, that curtain may not rise! God grant that on my vision never may be opened what lies behind! When my eyes shall be turned to behold for the last time the sun in heaven, may I not see him shining on the broken and dishonored fragments of a once glorious Union; on States dissevered, discordant, belligerent; on a land rent with civil feuds, or drenched, it may be, in fraternal blood!"[11]

As Webster's remarks suggest, it was both impossible to look and impossible not to look at the dreaded specter of civil war. When he spoke of states "dissevered, discordant, [and] belligerent," he evoked a common image within the unionist paradigm. It was not unusual to warn, with Hamilton, of "an infinity of little, jealous, clashing, tumultuous commonwealths," with Jackson of "a multitude of petty States," or, with Lincoln, to see "the central idea of secession" as "the essence of anarchy." Secession, once begun, would on this view keep on going until the states were smashed into little fragments. The spirit that dictated the first step, after all, would still slumber in the breasts of the divorcees when they confronted the inevitable temptation to a second scission. If a minority refused to acquiesce in the decisions of a majority, but instead seceded, they would, Lincoln insisted, "make a precedent which, in turn, will divide and ruin them; for a minority of their own will secede from them, whenever a majority refuses to be controlled by such minority." Why, Lincoln asked, "may not any portion of a new confederacy, a year or two hence, arbitrarily secede again, precisely as portions of the present Union now claim to secede from it? All who cherish disunion sentiments," he warned, "are now being educated to the exact temper of doing this."[12]

Though the prediction of a division into a multitude of clashing sovereignties was common enough, it was also widely recognized that a division, were it to occur, would at first be into two or three confederacies. "The entire separation of the States into thirteen unconnected sovereignties," as Hamilton observed, "is a project too extravagant and too replete with danger to have many advocates. The ideas of men who speculate upon the dismemberment of the empire seem generally turned towards three confederacies." Hamilton himself thought the likely division would be in two, but his remarks capture the real alternative in 1787, just as they accurately characterize the real alternatives that existed over the next seventy years. The question was never, in the first instance, between union and "an infinity . . . of jealous commonwealths." It was between union and a system of regional confederacies, probably two or three in number. The sequence that Madison imagined in the 1830s in response to the nullification crisis is probably as representative as any: "a rupture of the Union; a Southern confederacy; mutual enmity with the Northern; the most dreadful animosities and border wars, springing from the case of slaves; rival alliances abroad; standing armies at home, to be supported by internal taxes; and federal Governments, with powers of a more consolidating and monarchical tendency than the greatest jealousy has charged on the existing system."[13]

The Civil War, when it came, pitted North against South. This was the division, as Madison put it in the convention, that was always arising "of itself," and that would lie embedded in the disunion crises of 1786, 1798, 1809, 1814, 1820, 1833, 1844, and 1850. It was the posture of the West that in 1860, as in many of the previous cases, was certain to prove crucial, for the West "held the balance" in the union. Conscious of its growth, the West had detected by the 1830s a vast scene of doddering decrepitude in the southern tidewater, a puzzled air of irrelevance in many precincts of New England; by the 1850s it considered itself the guarantor, savior, and director of the whole, charged with the task of arbitrating in equitable fashion the endemic quarrels between the parents. Thus Stephen Douglas objected in 1850 to all the "talk about the North and the South, as if those two sections were the only ones necessary to be taken into consideration, when gentlemen begin to mature their arrangements for a dissolution of the Union, and to mark the dividing lines upon the maps." The truth was that "there is a power in this nation greater than either the North or the South—a growing, increasing, swelling power, that will be able to speak the law to this nation." It was the "great West . . . one and indivisible," that was "the resting-place of the power that is not only to control, but to save, the Union." The idea that the control of the outlet to the Mississippi might pass into the hands of a foreign power, Douglas avowed, was unthinkable to western opinion: "We furnish the water that makes the Mississippi, and we intend to follow, navigate, and use it until it loses itself in the briny sea." As the holder of the political balance, the West, by the same token, was moderate in political doctrine as compared with the two older sections. "We indulge in no ultraisms—no sectional strifes—no crusades against the North or the South." Aiming to do justice to every section, the West wished instead to keep the Constitution "as it is," maintaining and preserving it "inviolate in its letter and spirit."[14]

As the stakes became ever higher toward the end, the disposition of the West remained highly uncertain. How it would turn depended on how the issue was framed. Clay's stance in 1850 is instructive in this regard. Though his real wish was to pass on to eternity before the blows were struck, he swore two things: one was to militarily support the union in case of secession; the other was to militarily support the South if the North attacked its domestic institutions. Webster's position was the same as Clay's, though his stance created far more peril in his region than Clay's did in his. "You in the South," Webster said at Capon Springs, Virginia, June 25, 1851, "have as much right to receive your fugitive slaves as the North has to any of its rights and privileges of navigation and commerce. . . . I am as ready to fight and to fall for the Constitutional rights of Virginia, as I am for those of Massachusetts." For his stand in support of the fugitive slave law, notes Potter, Webster was barred from Faneuil Hall and "was called a 'monster,' 'indescribably base and wicked,' the 'personification of all that is vile,' a 'fallen angel' who would receive the curses of posterity upon his grave, an 'infamous New Hampshire renegade.'"[15]

The defense of Webster came after his death from his friend Rufus Choate. Morality, Choate said, must "ponder thoughtfully on the complications, and impediments, and antagonisms which make the noblest politics but an aspiring, an approximation, a compromise, . . . a shadow of good to come, 'the buying of great blessings at great prices.'" Webster believed, according to Choate, that the obligation "of one State to allow itself to become an asylum for those flying from slavery into another State, was an obligation of benevolence, of humanity only, not of justice; that it must, therefore, on ethical principles, be exercised under all the limitations which regulate and condition the benevolence of States." Those limitations embraced "such things as the conflicts of the greater with the less; conflicts of the attainable with the visionary; conflicts of the real with the seeming." Choate asked whether Webster may not have in good conscience believed "that the evil which he found" in the fugitive slave provision of the Constitution "was the least of two; was unavoidable; was compensated; was justified" by a greater good: "unless everybody of consequence enough to be heard of in the age and generation of Washington,—unless that whole age and generation were in conspiracy to cheat themselves, and history, and posterity," was not "a certain policy of concession and forbearance of region to region . . . indispensable to rear that master work of man; and that same policy of concession and forbearance . . . as indispensable for its preservation?"[16]

Lincoln saw the need for concession and forbearance, much as he refused to compromise on the extension of slavery. His whole political career consisted of his trimming between the abolitionist impulse he sincerely felt, having always hated slavery, and his concomitant recognition that he must act to preserve the constitutional and political bases of union. His constitutional reliance on the union as it was also formed the base of the political alliance between North and West that was indispensable to victory in the Civil War. Nor was the West's role as holder of the balance lost on the most discerning southerners. Appealing for the avoidance of precipitate measures in 1860 in his speech before the Georgia legislature opposing secession, Alexander Stephens could speculate that if nothing rash were done it might be possible to secure support from "New York, Pennsylvania, Ohio, and the other Western States" and to go on with them "without New England, if she chose to stay out [of the Union]." "If the Middle States and Western States do not join us," Stephens argued, "we should at least have an undivided South." Secessionists, remembering Lincoln's prediction in 1858 that the union would be "all one thing, or all the other," that slavery would expand or wither and die, deeply distrusted his assurances in 1860 that slavery would be protected under Republican rule. Stephens answered: "Let us not anticipate a threatened evil. If [Lincoln] violates the Constitution, then will come our time to act. Do not let us break it because, forsooth, he may."[17]

Some observers in 1860 believed that if the North were to acquiesce in the separation of the South, the West would sooner or later cleave off from the East. Many Westerners feared they might become "slaves and serfs of New England" in a union shorn of the South. Southern secession, notes scholar Richard Bensel, "posed serious risks for the continued viability of the Republican coalition in the North and, if successful, could have begun a process of centrifugal disintegration of the entire Union." Bensel argues that "the choice for the North posed by southern secession was never between one nation and two but between one nation and many," and that an unwillingness or inability to suppress southern secession "would have fatally strengthened the centrifugal forces already operating within the federal union."[18] These considerations point to an ironic feature of Lincoln's warning in his first inaugural address: he had predicted to the South its impending disintegration if it acted on the logic of secession; a no less vital danger was that the northern alliance would be torn apart by that act.

The great moral principle on which Lincoln refused to compromise was the extension of slavery. From 1854 onward, Lincoln had insisted on the distinction "between the EXISTING institution, and the EXTENSION of it," and wanted to make that distinction "so broad, and so clear, that no honest man can misunderstand me, and no dishonest one, successfully misrepresent me." In effect, his was the standard of containment as against both "rollback" and "appeasement." Many believe that Lincoln's stance was the wrong one, and the abolitionists now receive a more favorable treatment from historians than they once did. It should be remembered, however, that slavery was abolished through the war for the union, and not otherwise. Had the abolitionists prevailed, at any time before the 1850s, in their battle for the conscience of New England, the result would almost certainly have been the secession of New England and the fortification of slavery in a grand confederation embracing the West, the South, and Texas.[19]

Garrison had pled for disunion soon after beginning publication of the *Liberator* on January 1, 1831. The Constitution he regarded as "the most bloody and Heaven-daring arrangement ever made by men for the continuance and protection of a system of the most atrocious villainy ever exhibited on earth." With him and other early abolitionists, as a contemporary put it, "slavery was not an evil merely, but a sin, and, as such, to be got rid of at any cost—even, were it necessary, at that of national dissolution. In strict consistency with this view they had, while the South was yet dominant, repudiated the constitution, branding it as 'a league with death and a covenant with hell,' and advocated separation, as, in the condition of affairs which then prevailed, the only practicable escape from the contaminating influence of the sin which they denounced." It is highly probable that a war undertaken not to preserve the union but to eliminate slavery would have been unsuccessful in gaining the support of the middle and western states and would have been in defiance of public opinion in these regions. It seems difficult to escape the paradox that the war that did end slavery could not have been successful had it been begun for that motive.[20]

It does not follow from these considerations that the Civil War was a "needless war," as was once a popular theme in American historiography (associated particularly with the "revisionist" historians J. G. Randall, Avery Craven, and George Fort Milton). There is, in particular, little reason to think that slavery was on the road to extinction. Since the 1830s, the South had been a closed society with respect to every question touching race. It was doing everything it could to fortify slavery, nothing to prepare the day for the emancipation that, revisionists claimed, was inevitable. Southern justice had long made penal all efforts to teach literacy to blacks, and continued to refuse its chattels any means of enlightenment and improvement. Jefferson had warned in 1797 that unless rapid steps were taken toward emancipation, "we shall be the murderers of our own children," but the South proved incapable of taking those steps and instead retreated to the absurd doctrine that made human bondage a great blessing. By refusing any reform, southern leaders made it far more likely that the necessary change would be effected by war or revolution.[21]

It was a familiar observation of the Enlightenment that the forms of a political association might be a kind of mask over its real nature and character.

In a celebrated aside in *The Spirit of the Laws*, Montesquieu had observed that the English nation might justly be "called a republic, disguised under the form of a monarchy." Edward Gibbon, in an ironic echo to Montesquieu, called the imperial system instituted by Augustus "an absolute monarchy disguised by the forms of a commonwealth."[22] The American union was distinguished by a like contrast: it was a raging state system disguised by the forms of a constitution, averted from periodic wrecks by skillful diplomacy. An international system in embryo, it was no more exempt from the specter of war than any other system of states. Seeing this predicament from the beginning of their association in 1776, Americans sought through constitutional innovation to keep war at a distance, and vital features of constitutional text and values were traceable to this commanding need. Alas, they were not altogether successful, and in the disunion crises of the 1790s and beyond the beast still sat there, with a grin on his face, thinking of his potential utility when matters came to blows. American statesmen had always managed to find escape from peril in the past. But then, in 1861, they did not. When the war finally came, it did so as 1914 did in the European system—as the long-prepared and seemingly inevitable cataclysm that nevertheless arrives as a profound shock.

25

The Tragedy of Civil War

THE FEDERAL UNION ENDED WITH THE RESORT TO ARMS IN 1861. Wherever responsibility is assigned for the origins of the war, an association dedicated to the peaceful settlement of disputes could not be the same once the appeal to arms was made. The normative elements of the original union—all the metaphors of friendship and marriage, of sisterly affection and loyalty—were inevitably transformed and rendered tragic or grotesque in the midst of the ensuing maelstrom. In 1850, Calhoun had warned that if force were used it might keep the states connected, "but the connection will partake much more of the character of subjugation, on the part of the weaker to the stronger, than the union of free, independent, and sovereign States, in one confederation, as they stood in the early stages of the Government, and which only is worthy of the sacred name of union." Calhoun's great opponent in the debate over the Compromise of 1850, Daniel Webster, deprecated and ridiculed the idea of "peaceable secession" and warned the South that the last logic of kings, *ultima ratio regum*, could not be avoided were disunion undertaken. At a deeper level, however, Webster and Calhoun were as one in considering the preservation of the union by force to be a violation of their most cherished aspirations.[1]

The American nation born in the fires of the Civil War summoned sentiments of patriotism and devotion equal to the union that preceded it, and the war brought a great good in abolishing slavery. Those beneficial consequences diminish but do not alter the tragic character of the war. It is not simply the immensity of the human loss—the children who were left fatherless, the wives and mothers who cried till they "felt no more"—that stamps a tragic character on the Civil War.[2] Nor does it lie simply in the way in which the war gave a new birth of freedom to African Americans, followed by a subsequent, and crushing, abortion of that hope in the course of Reconstruction. Also plumbing the depths of the tragic was the simple fact, for both North and South, that in seeking to protect that which they loved, they would destroy it.

That Lincoln loved the old union, and wished to keep it "as it was," is not in doubt. He was "for the old ship, and the chart of the old pilots." Though detesting slavery, he went far toward conciliating the South at the expense of the slave, and he did it all for the union. He confirmed in his first inaugural address the pledge of the Republican platform of 1860 that "the maintenance inviolate of the rights of the States, and especially the right of each State to order and control its own domestic institutions, is essential to that balance of power on which the perfection and endurance of our political fabric depend." He also offered to support a constitutional amendment "to the effect that the federal government, shall never interfere with the domestic institutions of the States, including that of persons held to service," giving what was already "implied constitutional law" a recognition that was "express, and irrevocable." He promised to find a way to secure the observance of the provision in the Constitution mandating the return of fugitive slaves, though the strengthened law enforcing that provision, passed in 1850, had angered and disgusted much northern opinion. During the preliminaries to the war, Lincoln always took his ground on the imperative need to preserve the old union. It was, however, in the nature of the case that, were the southern states to secede, and force employed to keep them in, the old union would cease to exist. To keep it, Lincoln would have to kill it.[3]

The tragic character of the war is especially pronounced if we view it from the vantage point of the South. Largely preservative were the aims of the southerners who—some with unbounded confidence, others with tearful reluctance—committed their "nation" to secession in 1860. After Robert E. Lee's death in 1870, his eulogist recalled the agonizing choice thrust upon Lee by the secession crisis, induced by the fact that this son of Virginia

loved the Union with a generous and passionate devotion. Had it been possible to close its yawning chasm by the sacrifice of his own life, no Roman Curtius would have leaped more freely into the gulf of death. But the Union around which were centered his affections and his obligations was not a consolidated Union, in which great communities, like his own mother Commonwealth, were sunk to the level of petty counties, but a Federal Union between sovereign and equal States. The Union which he had sworn to serve had been dissolved by the power which brought it into existence; and its dissevered and exasperated sections were now gathering up their every energy for a deadly struggle. Could any selfish or ignoble consideration have controlled Colonel Lee, he would have remained in the Federal army. He was opposed to the policy of secession. He had been through life a friend of emancipation. "If I owned four million slaves," he had declared, "I would give them all for the Union."[4]

Lee, certainly, was not representative of the South in his attitude toward emancipation, but a great many southerners, like him, had composed glowing tributes to the union in the generation before the war broke out. When Jefferson Davis foreswore "the government under whose aegis he was born, whose institutions he loved, whose battles he fought, and upon whose escutcheon he had shed a new and richer lustre," he was acting under preservative impulses similar to those that moved Lincoln; like his great adversary, however, the consequence of his acts was inescapably revolutionary and inevitably parricidal. For Davis, as for other southerners, this was so above all because a successful secession would have meant the creation in North America of that anarchy of militarized fragments that the founders had sought to banish. As the war progressed, the concentration of power in the government of the Confederacy—which alone might allow the South to glimpse the prospect of victory—meant also the destruction of the vision of "equal and sovereign" states that had informed the Confederate Constitution of 1861. That the exigencies of war, by its end, led southern statesmen to contemplate emancipation in exchange for service in the Confederate army only reinforces the larger point. From whatever angle the case is viewed, it is the essentially tragic character of the epic struggle that continually intrudes upon the story—of men being impelled, by sentiments of honor, duty, and filial devotion, to a kind of grand negation of their deepest values.[5]

So powerful, in "the Great Secession Winter of 1860," were the contending considerations on either side that for many a kind of paralysis set in. Such was the condition in which President James Buchanan found himself as he composed the lines of his last annual message in December 1860. Buchanan affirmed two great truths in this poignant message. One was his denial that secession was a constitutional remedy. Were secession deemed acceptable, the federal government would be "a mere voluntary association of States, to be dissolved at pleasure by any one of the contracting parties." Were that the case, "the Confederacy" would be "a rope of sand, to be penetrated and dissolved by the first adverse wave of public opinion in any of the States. In this manner our thirty-three States may resolve themselves into as many petty, jarring, and hostile republics, each one retiring from the Union without responsibility whenever any sudden excitement might impel them to such a course. By this process a Union might be entirely broken into fragments in a few weeks which cost our forefathers many years of toil, privation, and blood to establish." Buchanan, in short, affirmed the opinion of "General Jackson," using words almost identical to those the seventh president had employed in 1833 in contravening South Carolina's attempted nullification of federal authority within its jurisdiction.

But while Buchanan denied that secession was a constitutional remedy, he also denied, "after much serious reflection," that the Constitution had "delegated to Congress the power to coerce a State into submission which is attempting to withdraw or has actually withdrawn from the Confederacy." Not only was the authority to do this "not among the specific and enumerated powers granted to Congress," nor "'necessary and proper for carrying into execution' any one of these powers," but it was also "expressly refused by the Convention which framed the Constitution." The power "to make war against a State," in short, was "at variance with the whole spirit and intent of the Constitution." Buchanan had difficulty even imagining how such a union might be governed, even in the event of a successful war. "Suppose such a war should result in the conquest of a State; how are we to govern it afterward? Shall we hold it as a province and govern it by despotic power?" In distinct echo of the "friends of America" who had urged conciliation before the War of American Independence, Buchanan held not only that war would destroy the union, but that with war "would vanish all hope of its peaceable reconstruction," with the carnage "rendering future reconciliation between the States impossible." The union rested on public opinion, and not upon force: "If it can not live in the affections of the people, it must one day perish. Congress possesses many means of preserving it by conciliation, but the sword was not placed in their hand to preserve it by force."[6]

Buchanan's message drew harsh ridicule from Republicans. The president, Seward cagily observed, "has conclusively proved two things: 1st, That no state has the right to secede unless it wishes to; and 2d, That it is the President's duty to enforce the laws, unless somebody opposes him."[7] In a speech of January 13, 1861, Seward recalled again why it was that the union had been formed, and why its breakup into separate confederacies would mean "perpetual civil war." Under those circumstances, he prophesied, it would be "in the last degree important that the new confederacies . . . should be as nearly as possible equal in strength and power, that mutual fear and mutual respect might inspire them with caution against mutual offense." But such equality could not be long maintained: "One confederacy would rise in the scale of political importance; and the others would view it thenceforward with envy and apprehension. Jealousies would bring on frequent and retaliatory wars, and all these wars, from the peculiar circumstances of the confederacies, would have the nature and character of civil war." The confederacies would have no choice but to resort to the "hateful" system "of adjusting the balance of power which has obtained in Europe, in which the few strong nations dictate the very terms on which all the others shall be content to live." But that too would fail: "Foreign nations would intervene, now in favor of one and then in aid of another; and thus our country, after having expelled all European powers from the continent, would relapse into an aggravated form of its colonial experience, and, like Italy, Turkey, India, and China, become the theatre of transatlantic intervention and rapacity.

. . . Unstable and jealous confederacies, constantly apprehending assaults without and treason within, formidable only to each other and contemptible to all beside," would soon surrender, "on the plea of public safety," their "inestimable and unequaled liberty, and accept the hateful and intolerable espionage of military despotism."[8]

To men of Seward and Lincoln's persuasion, it was no use pronouncing a glowing tribute to federal union in theory, as Buchanan had done, if the consequence were to make it a eulogium in fact. Suddenly the realization dawned: not simply the political classes, but the generality of men and women, saw that the maintenance of Buchanan's attitude was an impossibility, and that to attempt to further cleave down the middle would land them in the vestibule of Dante's Inferno, scorned by themselves and by all others.[9] Despite the repeated insistence on both sides that they were acting faithfully to what had been constitutionally allotted to them, the war came in conscious recognition that the old union was lost either way. For several generations, the boast of American constitutionalism had been that it had shuttered the demon fires of war, had defied the law of history by which contiguous states fell into acrimony and remorseless conflict. No achievement of philanthropy, Rufus Choate ventured in 1850, "bears any proportion to the pure and permanent glory of that achievement whereby clusters of contiguous States, perfectly organized governments in themselves every one, full of energy, conscious of strength, full of valor, fond of war,—instead of growing first jealous, then hostile,—like the tribes of Greece after the Persian had retired,—like the cities of Italy at the dawn of the modern world,—are melted into one, so that for centuries of internal peace, the grand agencies of amelioration and advancement shall operate unimpeded."[10] To submit to the arbitrament of the sword, when the peaceful resolution of disputes by law had been the boast of America for generations; to take the "way of the world," when the whole logic of the American experiment had been to find a new way—this was the core of the tragic situation in which Americans now found themselves.

PART SEVEN
"At Last We Are a Nation"

26

The New Nation

IN 1866, AT THE ASSEMBLING OF THE SECOND SESSION of the Thirty-ninth Congress, the *Atlantic Monthly* posed two starkly different alternatives for the future. One was that "the tremendous war so heroically fought and so victoriously ended shall pass into history a miserable failure, barren of permanent results,—a scandalous and shocking waste of blood and treasure,—a strife for empire, as Earl Russell characterized it, of no value to liberty or civilization,—an attempt to re-establish a Union by force, which must be the merest mockery of a Union,—an effort to bring under Federal authority States into which no loyal man from the North may safely enter, and to bring men into the national councils who deliberate with daggers and vote with revolvers, and who do not even conceal their deadly hate of the country that conquered them." The second alternative was that "we shall, as the rightful reward of victory over treason, have a solid nation, entirely delivered from all contradictions and social antagonisms, based upon loyalty, liberty, and equality." This was a fair and eloquent way of posing the issue, though the outcome could not (as the writer, Frederick Douglass, unfortunately suggested) be "determined one way or the other by the present session of Congress." The issue remained to be fought over by the people of the era, and then by historians. It was in the nature of the case that, having "uprooted institutions that were centuries old, changed the politics of a people, transformed the social life of half the country, and wrought so profoundly upon the entire national character," the Civil War would have an influence that, as Mark Twain said, could not "be measured short of two or three generations."[1]

The cost was staggering. Altogether, 618,000 soldiers (of which 360,000 were Union and 258,000 Confederate) lost their lives in the war, more even than World War II's fearful toll of 405,000. The hegemonic war, notes political scientist Robert Gilpin, "is characterized less by its immediate causes or its explicit purposes than by its extent and the stakes involved. It affect[s] all the political units inside one system of relations between sovereign states"; the fundamental issue to be decided is "the leadership and structure of the international system." "Such wars are at once political, economic, and ideological struggles," characterized by unlimited means and profound transformations not only in the vanquished, who is remolded by the victor, but among the victors themselves.[2]

The Civil War readily fits these criteria. The outcome of the Civil War ensured that a federal state, "an indestructible union of indestructible states," would dominate North America instead of a multiunit system of regional confederacies that would "regulate their relations and maintain their identities by means of alliances and the balance of power." Fought by Lincoln to preserve the union, the war created the American nation, a "Yankee Leviathan" dramatically different from the federal union that existed before the war.[3]

Nowhere were the changes brought by the war more marked than in the understanding of the union; the result of the contest of arms was to resolve a set of fundamental ambiguities that had lain at the heart of federal union. "It was now established beyond peradventure," as Nicholas Murray Butler once summarized these changes,

> that the United States is a nation and not a confederation of nations or states; that sovereignty rests wholly and exclusively in the people of the United States, and that sovereignty means, as Lincoln defined it in his message to Congress on July 4, 1861, "a political community without a political superior"; that the sovereign people of the nation are the source of all authority, and that they bestow and distribute the powers of government upon and among the different organizations which they create or permit to be created, and that no individual or local government or section has any political rights as against the people of the entire nation; that the attempt to resist by violence the administration of the nation's laws or to take themselves out from under the supremacy of the national government is rebellion on the part of those who so act, and that therefore neither nullification by any state government nor secession on the part of any state is permissible under the political system of the United States; that the ultimate interpreter of the constitution is the national government set up thereby and not the several commonwealths or any of their representatives or agencies of government.[4]

None of these interpretations of the federal constitution had been established "beyond peradventure" before the great test of arms. Before they were so established, American nationality was like a grove of trees with shallow roots, a magnificent array whose ability to remain standing was doubted on every approach of a political storm. In a famous dictum, Supreme Court justice Sutherland declared in 1936 that "sovereignty is never held in suspense," whereas the reality under the preceding regime, as Clay dolefully reflected, was that nothing regarding sovereignty was settled except "the principle that everything is unsettled." Before the war, nullification and secession had strong if not wholly respectable support, sufficiently strong as to put every consensus in doubt. After the war, they were as dead as southern nationalism—"like the extinct monsters of a former geological period, to be seen only in the museum of history," as Charles Sumner put it in 1867.[5]

This represented a crucial change. The fiery death of nullification and secession profoundly altered the dynamics of American politics. Not only in the decade before the great war, but really since the Declaration of Independence, disunion had been a standing possibility, and scarcely a year passed without some observer pointing to the dread result as being immanent within the movement of events. No more: the South was now a devastated moonscape wrought by an enemy determined to "make war so terrible . . . that generations would pass away before [the people of the South] would again appeal to it," and whose strategy in the final two years of the war was to leave the southern people "nothing but their eyes to weep with over the war."[6] The grim specter that had risen up with regularity under the old federal union—the splintering of North America into a system of regional confederacies or an infinity of jealous commonwealths—was now entirely foreclosed. Sectionalism had previously signified the standing possibility of separate nations; all that now remained was "regionalism."

The surging sense of national identity drew wondrous comments from observers, convinced that a great gulf had opened up between the present and the past, and that they were living in a different country from that of their birth. The "territorial, political, and historical oneness of the nation," remarked a writer in the *Nation*, "is now ratified by the blood of thousands of her sons." It was not only the victory "but the long, hard struggle which preceded it" that "tended strongly to give new force to national ties. The preservation of the nation had been a supreme idea of a number of years. Every local interest and feeling had given way before it." The South did not share in this exaltation and had in 1865 a deeper sense of separate identity than it had ever entertained; among the victors, however, "publicists, intellectuals, and politicians indulged in a rhetoric of triumphant nationalism."[7]

Just as the Civil War evoked a profound affirmation of national identity, it also produced a massive shift in the character of American institutions. The federal government, having overcome the "shock of weakness" that afflicted it in the great secession winter of 1860–1861, vastly expanded its powers. Americans discovered "that there was in our . . . government a power of which we never dreamed." Before the war, recalled James Blaine, "every power was withheld from the National Government which could by any possibility be exercised by the State Government." Because of the war, which forced upon Congress the exercise of many useful powers, it was demonstrated "that every thing which may be done by either Nation or State may be better and more securely done by the Nation." The change of view was important, Blaine added, leading "to far-reaching consequences." Historians insist rightly on the revolutionary character of these changes. "The old decentralized federal republic," notes James McPherson, "became a new national polity that taxed the people directly, created an internal revenue bureau to collect these taxes, expanded the jurisdiction of federal courts, established a national currency and a national banking structure." The experience, writes another scholar, "both strengthened the American state in every dimension of institutional design and substantive policy and committed the entire apparatus to the promotion of northern industrial development and western settlement."[8]

Nothing the federal government had done previously compared in scale and scope to the powers it exercised in the course of the war. The suspension of civil liberties in the North during the war entailed an expansion in state power that was unprecedented. After the war had ended, the Supreme Court declared unconstitutional the suspension of habeas corpus. Justice David Davis, who had been appointed by Lincoln but now wrote in remonstrance against the virtually unlimited presidential powers that Lincoln had assumed during the war, proclaimed stirringly that "the Constitution of the United States is a law for rulers and people, equally in war and peace, and covers with the shield of its protection all classes of men, at all times, and under all circumstances." It was a grossly pernicious doctrine, Davis believed, that the provisions of this great charter could "be suspended during any of the great exigencies of government." Yet they *had* been suspended, and the decision of the court changed that fact not one iota. Nor was this willingness to sacrifice liberty on behalf of security confined to the North. Within a year of promulgating the Confederate constitution, its framers, recalled one southerner, "succeeded in consolidating all governmental power in the central agency at Richmond, and, upon the stale plea of *military necessity*, shamelessly trod under foot all the reserved rights of the states and people, and organized an irresponsible military despotism in the very bosom of the Ancient Dominion, as harsh and grinding in its character as has ever heretofore existed in any age of the world." The knowledge of the power that any American government might thenceforth assume in extremity could not be effaced from the memory and continued to cast a long shadow after the war.[9]

In monetary affairs, the Civil War witnessed the transfer of effective control over the currency into the hands of the national government, where it has remained ever since. To finance the war, the national government issued "greenback dollars" not redeemable in specie. The government borrowed lavishly, both from financiers and from the broader public, and gave bankers an incentive to lend money in exchange for a monopoly on the issuance of the national currency. The high inflation to which this experiment in fiat money creation led produced a sharp reaction in the postwar years, with the "sound money" advocates prevailing when the United States adhered to the gold standard in 1873. The long deflation from the 1870s to the 1890s brought cries that the western farmer was sacrificed on a cross of gold, but none of the subsequent controversies over bimetallism seriously threatened the national government's control of the currency and the banking system.[10]

In commerce, too, the Civil War brought the realization of Henry Clay's dream of an "American system" anchored to a high protective tariff. The departure from Congress of southern free traders made for a commercial revolution, facilitating the passage of sweeping protectionist barriers that remained largely intact until 1913, when Woodrow Wilson helped engineer a reduction of tariffs in the Underwood Act. The average rates on dutiable imports rose from 18.8 percent in 1861 to 47.6 percent in 1865, inaugurating what one specialist has called the "golden era of American protectionism." Fervently endorsed by Lincoln and his Republican acolytes, high tariffs remained central planks of the Republican platform until the Great Depression and were successfully established, with but few exceptions, as national policy. Despite challenges from Democrats, "in every year from 1862 to 1911, the average duty on all imports exceeded 20 percent ad valorem. In forty six of those fifty years the average rates on dutiable imports exceeded 40 percent ad valorem equivalent." Harrison and Blaine in the 1880s, McKinley and Roosevelt in the 1900s, and Harding, Coolidge, and Hoover in the 1920s were all enthusiasts of Clay's protective ideas. "Not until 1945," notes one political scientist, "did the United States fully endorse the principle of free trade at home and abroad."[11]

The Civil War, then, was "the Second American Revolution," as Charles and Mary Beard famously described it, out of whose ashes emerged a new nation, a second republic that dramatically differed from the first. The Civil War did not create a nation where before there was none, nor did it create nationalists where before there were none. Nationality existed in abundance in the early United States, but in addition to an American nation there were states that had "much nationality." There was also a "New England nation" and a southern protonation—that is, a "southern interest" with a sufficiently cohesive sense of identity to make itself a nation in short order. The Civil War causes a great eclipse in these competing affections, making the war a towering watershed. American nationality before the war, try as it might to escape the clutches of the union and soar above its messy compromises, could not do so. Fisher Ames had expressed this dependency in 1788 by noting that the union "is essential to our being as a nation." It was "the vital sap that nourishes the tree"; without it, "we girdle the tree, its leaves will wither, its branches drop off, and the mouldering trunk will be torn down by the tempest." The Civil War, in effect, inverted these relations, making the nation essential to our being as a union. When the war came at last that the fathers foretold, American nationality arrived not like vague portents in the spring but in the thunderous buckets and waves of prolonged summer storms.[12]

27

A New Birth of Freedom?

THOUGH THE WAR CREATED A NATION from which secession was now unthinkable, it was far less successful in securing a new birth of freedom for the liberated slave. Radical Republicans had sought that end in earnest and envisaged a revolutionary program of social and economic reconstruction based on the theory that the southern states were "conquered provinces" that had forfeited their constitutional protections. What followed, in the event, was a more limited program, enshrined in the Thirteenth, Fourteenth, and Fifteenth Amendments to the Constitution, which, respectively, abolished slavery, forbade the denial to any citizen of the equal protection of the laws or the forfeiture of life and liberty without due process, and forbade discriminatory attempts to abridge the right to vote. The postwar amendments established the principle, barely registered under the old federal union, "that civil rights are national in their origin and are placed under the protection and defense of the national government."[1]

What had been proclaimed in theory, however, faltered in practice. Groups in the southern states dedicated to white supremacy—the Ku Klux Klan and associated groups like the Knights of the White Camelia and the White Brotherhood—mounted a formidable violent resistance against northern control and the "carpetbagger" governments that followed the arrival of northern armies. "The wave of counterrevolutionary terror that swept over large parts of the South between 1868 and 1871," notes historian Eric Foner, "lacks a counterpart either in the American experience or in that of the other Western Hemisphere societies that abolished slavery in the 19th century." But the tactics employed—sowing fear and panic to deter previously oppressed groups from the assertion of their rights, terrorizing and killing collaborators and other representatives of the new order—are familiar enough from other conflicts and place the southern insurgency in a line that includes Algeria in the 1950s, Vietnam in the 1960s, and the Iraq war that began in 2003. The effect of these tactics on northern opinion was outrage over the heinous deeds, exasperation at their diabolical effectiveness, but ultimately submission to the incapacity of outside force to settle the problem. The southern planter class, though dispossessed of its slaves, retained control of its great landed estates, and its economic and political weight, symbolized by the rise of "redeemer" governments across the South, ultimately reasserted itself against what was felt by the vast majority of white southerners to be an alien and repulsive imposition. The end of slavery represented a net gain for blacks, who could now marry, own property, and enjoy more of the proceeds of their labor, but real emancipation was denied. Former slaves became sharecroppers. Voting rights were emasculated by poll taxes and literacy tests. Violence directed against the freedman was endemic, with no lawful recourse allowed against the perpetrators. Thus was the revolution left "unfulfilled," the new birth of freedom aborted.[2]

This grim result was bound up with the causes of the war. Lincoln's famous letter to Horace Greeley in 1862 attested to the tension between the two great objectives—the salvation of the union and the freeing of the slave—that came to define the northern war effort: "I would save the Union. I would save it the shortest way under the Constitution. The sooner the national authority can be restored; the nearer the Union will be 'the Union as it was.' If there be those who would not save the Union, unless they could at the same time *save* slavery, I do not agree with them. If there be those who would not save the Union unless they could at the same time *destroy* slavery, I do not agree with them. My paramount object in this struggle *is* to save the Union, and is *not* either to save or to destroy slavery." This had been Lincoln's consistent standard before and during the secession crisis, but not long after writing this famous letter to Greeley the moment came when Lincoln decided "that slavery must die that the nation might live." "Fondly do we hope, fervently do we pray," he said in his second inaugural address, "that this mighty scourge of war may speedily pass away. Yet, if God wills that it continue until all the wealth piled by the bondsman's two hundred and fifty years of unrequited toil shall be sunk, and until every drop of blood drawn with the lash shall be paid by another drawn with the sword, as was said three thousand years ago, so still it must be said 'the judgments of the Lord are true and righteous altogether.'"[3]

Frederick Douglass, the former slave whose talents and accomplishments were a living refutation of the slaveholding philosophy, knew Lincoln's history intimately. In his beautiful 1876 oration in honor of the dead president, one of the great speeches of our history, Douglass honored Lincoln as having been at the head of the great movement ensuring that "slavery should be utterly and forever abolished in the United States." Though

the Union was more to him than our freedom or our future, under his wise and beneficent rule we saw ourselves gradually lifted from the depths of slavery to the heights of liberty and manhood; under his wise and beneficent rule, and by measures approved and vigorously pressed by him, we saw that the handwriting of ages, in the form of prejudice and proscription, was rapidly fading away from the face of our whole country; under his rule, and in due time, about as soon after all as the country could tolerate the strange spectacle, we saw our brave sons and brothers laying off the rags of bondage, and being clothed all over in the blue uniforms of the soldiers of the United States; under his rule we saw two hundred thousand of our dark and dusky people responding to the call of Abraham Lincoln, and with muskets on their shoulders, and eagles on their buttons, timing their high footsteps to liberty and union under the national flag; under his rule we saw the independence of Hayti, the special object of slaveholding aversion and horror, fully recognized, and her minister, a colored gentleman, duly received here in the city of Washington; under his rule we saw the internal slave-trade, which so long disgraced the nation, abolished, and slavery abolished in the District of Columbia; under his rule we saw for the first time the law enforced against the foreign slave-trade, and the first slave-trader hanged like any other pirate or murderer; under his rule, assisted by the greatest captain of our age, and his inspiration, we saw the Confederate States, based upon the idea that our race must be slaves, and slaves forever, battered to pieces and scattered to the four winds; under his rule, and in the fullness of time, we saw Abraham Lincoln, after giving the slaveholders three months' grace in which to save their hateful system, penning the immortal paper, which, though special in its language, was general in its principles and effect, making slavery forever impossible in the United States. Though we waited long, we saw all this and more.[4]

Douglass insisted that the faith of African Americans in Lincoln "never failed," though he acknowledged that it "was often taxed and strained to the uttermost": when Lincoln

tarried long in the mountain; when he strangely told us that we were the cause of the war; when he still more strangely told us that we were to leave the land in which we were born; when he refused to employ our arms in defense of the Union; when, after accepting our services as colored soldiers, he refused to retaliate our murder and torture as colored prisoners; when he told us he would save the Union if he could with slavery; when he revoked the Proclamation of Emancipation of General Fremont; when he refused to remove the popular commander of the Army of the Potomac, in the days of its inaction and defeat, who was more zealous in his efforts to protect slavery than to suppress rebellion; when we saw all this, and more, we were at times grieved, stunned, and greatly bewildered; but our hearts believed while they ached and bled."

Douglass accepted that had Lincoln "put the abolition of slavery before the salvation of the Union, he would have inevitably driven from him a powerful class of the American people and rendered resistance to rebellion impossible," but Douglass could not accept that the same stern logic dictated retreat after the war from the program of the radical Republicans. In the 1880s and 1890s, Douglass turned increasingly bitter toward the Republicans—the Democrats he had written off long before—because they hypocritically treated the freedman as "a deserted, a defrauded, a swindled outcast; in law, free; in fact, a slave; in law, a citizen; in fact, an alien; in law, a voter; in fact, a disfranchised man."[5]

The conflict between "reunionists" and "radical reconstructionists" existed even before the war had ended. The basic issue was whether the southern states should be admitted as promptly as possible, accepting within limits the restoration of white control, or whether the South should be thoroughly revolutionized, its social order entirely overturned. Which choice would be made could not fail to be seen in relation to the immense sacrifices of the war; so, too, its resolution bore closely on political advantage among the sections, for if in the final settlement blacks were denied effective political representation and the three-fifths clause were eliminated, the South might win in peace the unfair privilege it had lost in war. To the radical reconstructionists, such as Charles Sumner, the United States could not, consistent with the sacrifices of the war and with its newly awakened identity as a nation, surrender the aim of granting full political and economic equality to the blacks. In Sumner's view, the United States was not "an empire cemented by conquest, like that of later Rome." Nor was it "a confederation in any just sense." The Republic was instead "One Nation . . . redeemed and regenerated, one and indivisible," in which local jealousies and geographic distinction would be "lost in the attractions of a common country." The centralization required by Reconstruction was "the highest civilization, for it approaches the nearest to the Heavenly example. Call it imperialism, if you please; it is simply the imperialism of the Declaration of Independence, with all its promises fulfilled.[6]

Ultimately, however, the nation took the other road and gave decided preference to reunion over social revolution. To the consternation of Sumner and other radical Republicans, Seward had adopted this view at an early date, and in all probability it was Lincoln's view as well.[7] Seward was in

accord with Charles Francis Adams in 1867 on the need "for an early restoration of constitutional peace, law, order, and progress among ourselves"
and feared that "centralization, consolidation and imperialism" would result if the radical reconstructionists prevailed. The work of reunion could
not "wait without danger of disorganization, anarchy, imbecility, and ultimate disunion."[8] Henry Foote reaffirmed that to push centralization too far
would destroy the American system. The coequality of the states, he argued,
was the foundation of the republic: "Extinguish this coequality in any way,
and, instead of a republic, we will necessarily bring into existence an imperial despotism, by whatever name called. Subject to enslavement the numerous distinct communities formerly enjoying liberty, and vest the power of
controlling all the domestic concerns of each of them in a central government, . . . and it will not be possible to prevent the rapid concentration of
all civil power in the legislative and executive department of the system first,
and very soon thereafter the consolidation of all power in the hands of a
single individual, which individual will, of course, be the executive officer
who wields the war power."[9] There were manifold factors of expense, fa-
tigue, and unrealized hope that, in addition to a still pervasive racism, made
the North turn away from the program of radical Reconstruction, but not
inconsiderable was the belief that prolonged commitment to such an enterprise would disorder American institutions, making them imperial rather
than republican in character.[10]

The Compromise of 1877 signaled the formal end of Reconstruction. After the contested election of 1876 induced a frenzy threatening to political
stability, the bargain that emerged in the late winter gave to the Republican
Rutherford B. Hayes the victory in the presidential canvass and to the South
the assurance that federal troops would be withdrawn to their barracks.
E. L. Godkin, editor of the *Nation*, founded by antislavery forces in 1865,
pronounced the unforgettable epitaph: "The negro will disappear from the
field of national politics. Henceforth, the nation as nation, will have nothing more to do with him." Ten years previously, men of similar persuasion
to Godkin had held that the "right of the negro is the true solution of our
national troubles. The stern logic of events, . . . disdaining all concern for
the color or features of men, has determined the interests of the country as
identical with and inseparable from those of the negro." That insight would
blossom again in the distant future, but it was in 1877 a distant memory.[11]

The "romance of reunion" that followed the compromise was a further
blow to the promise of individual freedom and equality for African Americans, but from it flowed a fervent patriotism in both North and South. The
Lost Cause was not forgotten and continued to be honored by southerners,

but a "New South" arose that accepted its defeat and conceded that it was for the best that the Confederacy had failed in its quest to preserve slavery and destroy the union. The Atlanta editor Henry Grady, whose overtures to the North in 1886 "turned a pleasant social occasion into a national event," saw it as a great good "that the American Union was saved from the wreck of war." Grady honored the heroism of the soldiers of the Lost Cause— "The South has nothing to take back; nothing for which she has excuses to make"—but emphasized that the South had "accepted as final the arbitrament of the sword to which we had appealed" and bore eloquent witness to "the imperishable brotherhood of the American people." It was a blessing, *"especially to us of the South,"* wrote one former Confederate officer, "that the war ended in the removal of the incubus of slavery and the consolidation of the entire nation under one flag and one government." Had the union been broken, the surviving fragments would have felt toward each other like the alien nations of Europe. "The result would have been vain attempts to maintain a durable balance of power, continual wars, conscription, standing armies, fortifications and custom-houses on every frontier, and burdens far more grievous than those under which all Europe is now groaning." So, too, it would have meant endless European intervention among the now weakened fragments of the former union. That reiteration of the old unionist paradigm attests to a basic continuity in how Americans valued the union, but it had a fundamentally different meaning from antebellum days. It no longer represented a distinct historical possibility. "The day of the sectionalist is over," proclaimed Henry Watterson of Kentucky in a Memorial Day address in 1877. "The day of the nationalist has come."[12]

It has recently been argued that the Civil War provided to Americans "the example of an aggressive war of conquest to implant American principles in a civilization that had manifestly rejected them," whence they discovered a "new lesson, that war could serve what they regarded as just and moral ends."[13] In light of the ultimate denouement of war and reconstruction, however, these judgments can scarcely be sustained. The acceptance by the South that the national government acted legitimately in saving the union, and the acceptance by the North that the South would regain control over its domestic institutions, suggest instead that the preservation of the union was indeed, as Lincoln had long insisted, the overriding war aim of the government. As such it was far from an aggressive war of conquest, that term being appropriately reserved for instances when states invade and occupy the territory of others without good claim of self-defense. Nor did the result of the war successfully implant American principles in a civilization that had manifestly rejected them. America's first experiment in nation-building ended in disillusion, recrimination, and renewed appreciation of the limits of military power and its potential threat to republican principles. Finally, it was not a "new lesson" that war could serve just and moral ends; no previous war in American history had been justified as serving unjust and immoral ends. The lesson learned, in any case, was not that aggressive wars of conquest were now somehow justified—quite the contrary.

28

"Free Security" and "Imperial Understretch"

ONE OF THE MOST REMARKABLE FEATURES of U.S. diplomacy in the nineteenth century is how little it changes at a formal level across the years. Taking virtually any point in the first hundred years of its constitutional existence, presidents and secretaries of state insist on a fundamental continuity with the policy of the fathers. In his first inaugural address in 1885, Grover Cleveland pledged "the scrupulous avoidance of any departure from that foreign policy commended by the history, the traditions, and the prosperity of our Republic. It is the policy of independence, favored by our position and defended by our known love of justice and by our power. It is the policy of peace suitable to our interests. It is the policy of neutrality, rejecting any share in foreign broils and ambitions upon other continents and repelling their intrusion here. It is the policy of Monroe and of Washington and Jefferson—'Peace, commerce, and honest friendship with all nations; entangling alliance with none.'" Adherence to the strict commands of neutrality and nonintervention, wrote Secretary of State Martin Van Buren in 1829, were "cardinal traits" of American foreign policy. "The obligatory character of this policy is regarded by its constituents with a degree of reverence and submission but little, if anything, short of that which is entertained for the Constitution itself." The bitter party battles over foreign policy that are equally a mark of the first hundred years—politics never then stopping at the water's edge—show that the application of these verities in particular circumstances was frequently controversial; nevertheless, the dominant tendency in all parties was to justify policy in relation to the original understanding.[1]

At a formal level, these traditional doctrines were barely disturbed by the Civil War. On the surface nothing had changed. Given the new constellation of power created by the war, however, everything had changed. Though presidents continued to reiterate the basic premises of the American system, the new constellation of power meant that the doctrines themselves had also in some measure been transformed.

The biggest change wrought by war and reconstruction is that it created a condition of near-absolute security. It would be a misnomer to call it "free security," for it had been purchased by enormous bloodletting and expense, for which the debt was still being paid. This condition was, nevertheless, a real achievement of the war. We have argued that to predate this sense of absolute security to the first republic is a mistake, because from 1776 to 1860 Americans had lived under the shadow of the destruction of the union, representing for those generations a kind of Armageddon. The war having come, and having vindicated the fears of the pessimists that it would all blow up, the conclusion of the war nevertheless put an end to the prospect of disunion and to the insecurity and war tremblings that prospect had bred. The true American security threat had always stemmed, in the first instance, from the danger of disunion; such threats as had existed from the European powers had always appeared most dangerous if they occurred in conjunction with a disunion crisis, raising the prospect that a foreign power might league itself with a disaffected American section. That prospect was now entirely in the past.[2]

The war also established, as a sort of inevitable deduction from the establishment of national unity, the hegemony of the United States in North America. Both the Canadian confederation and the eviction of Maximilian and France from Mexico followed swiftly upon the northern victory. The Mexicans would probably have accomplished that feat unaided—France, given its looming rivalry with Prussia, had no margin to spare in prosecuting new-world misadventures. Nevertheless, the United States concentrated large forces on the Mexican border after the southern defeat in 1865 and, sympathizing and cooperating with the forces of Benito Juarez (in character so similar to Lincoln), made clear that American forbearance would soon be at an end. The prodigious display of American military might, too, was the basic factor in producing the British North America Act of 1867 establishing confederation. The remarkable demobilization following the war, which reduced the size of the American army below that of Portugal, a minor European power, and left the navy to rust, did not seriously affect the new power realities. "The military power of the United States, as shown by the recent civil war," noted James Blaine in 1881, "is without limit, and in any conflict on the American continent altogether irresistible." That was the new fact.[3]

Having achieved such a commanding position in North America, it was predictable that the American colossus would embark on an energetic program of territorial expansion. Those unsympathetic to the northern cause had warned of this result during the war, and it was in many respects an inexorable deduction of the web of assumptions underlying the balance of power. For many leaders, certainly, the will was there. There were plenty of voices in national administrations and in public counsels who approved further expansion. In Andrew Johnson's annual message in 1868, the president declared: "Comprehensive national policy would seem to sanction the acquisition and incorporation into our Federal Union of the several adjacent continental and insular communities." Secretary of State William Seward, who placed those words in Johnson's address, had few peers in prophesying a vast enlargement of the union. He was, believed a contemporary, Gideon Welles, "almost crazy on the subject of territorial acquisition." House Foreign Affairs Committee chairman Nathaniel P. Banks, who defined the coming American role in world affairs as "the grand disturber of the right divine of kings, the model of struggling nations, the best hope of the independence of states and of national liberty," busied plans for the incorporation of Canada, Cuba, and Santo Domingo. Johnson's successor, Ulysses S. Grant, also made acquisition of Santo Domingo a priority of his presidency. Yet no bout of territorial expansion followed. Apart from the purchase of Alaska in 1867 and the claim to the uninhabited Midway Islands in 1868, the United States acquired no further territory for another generation, until the war of 1898 and its aftermath. Fareed Zakaria has called it "imperial understretch"—a nice expression because it highlights the contrast with the "normal" conduct of Great Powers. America, it would appear, wanted to expand, and enjoyed a mobilizable capacity that dwarfed that of any other power or combination of powers in the Americas. Yet it did not expand. Why not?[4]

Zakaria gives a straightforward explanation for the paradox. The United States went from "weak state" in 1865 to "strong state" by the turn of the century. The United States, on this view, did not expand because it lacked the state capacity to do so. But that is not a convincing explanation. The anterior question is: Why didn't the United States raise up the capacity, which it might so easily have done? America, moreover, did not have a "weak state" in 1865 but one that was stronger than it had ever been. If we are to understand the forces limiting American territorial expansion from the late 1860s to the 1890s, we need to take foremost account not of state capacity but of the web of identities, institutions, and ideologies that successfully blocked such enterprises as existed.

The lesson the Republican victors drew from the preceding two decades was a powerful restraint upon territorial aggression. "The Southern rebellion," Ulysses S. Grant concluded in his memoirs, "was largely the outgrowth of the Mexican war. Nations, like individuals, are punished for their transgressions. We got our punishment in the most sanguinary and expensive war of modern times."[5] Grant's view was the conventional wisdom among the Republicans who had opposed the Mexican War and won the Civil War. In the 1850s, they had seen an aggressive slavocracy and the Democratic Party continue on from Mexico with "Greytown, Ostend, Kansas, and all," each an obnoxious emblem of aggression. "The Democratic policy in dealing with our Republican brethren in South America and in Mexico," said Henry

Winter Davis in 1864, "has been that of the wolf to the lamb. Their growl was to frighten foreign wolves from the prey they marked for their own; they hectored, bullied, and plundered them, without even stretching out the hand of republican sympathy to appease their dissensions or consolidate their power. . . . Our policy is very different from the Democratic policy. We wish to cultivate friendship with our republican brethren of Mexico and South America, to aid in consolidating republican principles, to retain popular government in all this continent from the fangs of monarchical or aristocratic power, and to lead the sisterhood of American republics in the paths of peace, prosperity, and power."[6]

Equal in importance to the condemnation of aggression was the commitment to consensual union, which, as the following passage from Orestes Brownson shows, were really two peas in a pod. Brownson, an avid expansionist who prophesied the incorporation of Mexico and Canada, was equally insistent on the method by which this was to occur: "The Union will fight to maintain the integrity of her domain and the supremacy of her laws within it, but she can never, consistently with her principles or her interests, enter upon a career of war and conquest. Her system is violated, endangered, not extended, by subjugating her neighbors, for subjugation and liberty go not together. Annexation, when it takes place, must be on terms of perfect equality, and by the free act of the state annexed. The Union can admit of no inequality of rights and franchises between the States of which it is composed. The Canadian Provinces and the Mexican and Central American States, when annexed, must be as free as the original States of the Union, sharing alike in the power and the protection of the Republic." Brownson, though an idiosyncratic thinker in some respects, stated here the consensus of the Republican Party. "Empire obtained by force," wrote Charles Sumner, "is un-republican, and offensive to the first principle of our Union, according to which all just government stands only on the consent of the governed. Our country needs no such ally as war. Its destiny is mightier than war. Through peace it will have everything."[7]

The outcome of the Civil War also changed fundamentally many of the calculations that had driven expansion in the antebellum era. Given the evenness of the sectional competition, territorial expansion had been almost wholly subordinated to calculations of sectional advantage and disadvantage—a factor of great importance throughout the first republic but utterly dominant in the 1850s. "Under the former Union," noted the Confederate commissioners in appealing for British aid and recognition in 1861, "the slaveholding states had an interest in the acquisition of territory suitable to their institutions, in order to establish a balance of power within the Government for their own protection. This reason no longer exists, as the

Confederate States have sought that protection by a separation from the Union in which their rights were endangered."[8] To these changed calculations of political advantage were now added the reassertion of the constitutional restraint dictating the approval of two-thirds of senators for the acquisition of territory. Though Grant wished to annex Santo Domingo through a joint resolution of Congress, on the model of Texas in 1845, his path was blocked by Sumner, chairman since 1861 of the Senate Committee on Foreign Relations, who with many others viewed this mode of annexation as grossly unconstitutional.[9]

The most eligible candidate for incorporation into the union was Canada. Its ultimate annexation had long been prophesied. Seward noted in 1853 that "Canada, although a province of Great Britain, is already half annexed to the United States. She will ultimately become a member of this confederacy if we will consent, an ally if we will not allow her to come nearer. At least she can never be an adversary." Seward thought that the acquisition of Alaska in 1867 would give an inexorable impetus to the annexation of the Canadian northwest, but the voices in favor (on either side of the border) were never sufficiently numerous to make a voluntary agreement possible. And an involuntary one was foreclosed by the condemnation of conquest. After 1865, to be sure, everyone understood that Canada had become a hostage to British good behavior, and Grant and Sumner threatened the invasion and annexation of Canada in response to perceived British refractoriness over the Alabama claims. But Canada was protected so long as the British did not push things with the United States, and already the British were practiced at the art of dodging confrontations with the American government, one they would continue to deploy in futurity. With lust for Canada restricted to a perfectly civil marriage, and abjuring military conquest, expansion to the north was effectively blocked.[10]

Expansion to the tropics faced further obstacles. The frustrations of Reconstruction, in which the North confronted the race problem and then in effect gave up, argued against the voluntary incorporation of more people of color within the union. The Cubans, said *Harper's Weekly*, were "a people wholly alien from us in principles, language, and traditions, a third of whom are barbarously ignorant." Race played a vital role in sparking President Grant's interest in the annexation of Santo Domingo, ultimately defeated in the Senate. He wanted a refuge for freed slaves that would allow them self-government but that would also relieve the race problem in the southern states. Though the condescending and racist attitudes directed toward blacks and browns were vital factors for many in opposing expansion, a belief that all peoples were nevertheless entitled to self-government also played a role: "To the African belongs the equatorial belt," commented Sumner, "and he should enjoy it undisturbed." "Despite rhetoric of expansion," notes one historian, "powerful forces worked against an activist foreign policy. A widespread popular hostility to military adventurism, the pressure of internal demands on capital and organizing energy; ideological objections to empire building; strong and persistent American traditions of individualism, localism, and xenophobia; anti Grant genteel reformers: all tended to mute and restrict the outward thrust of American diplomacy."[11]

Formal adherence to the doctrine of nonintervention did not prevent presidents, secretaries of state, and houses of Congress from vigorously protesting the abuse of human rights abroad. The shocking treatment of Jews in the Austrian and Russian empires was especially singled out for condemnation. Secretary of State Hamilton Fish told the American minister in Vienna in 1872 that, though the American government "has no disposition or intention to give offense by impertinently interfering in the internal affairs of Roumania," it "heartily sympathizes with the popular instinct" against the outrages committed there.

Among the large number of Israelites in this country there are probably few whose sympathies have not been intensely excited by . . . the grievous persecutions of their co-religionists in Roumania. This feeling has naturally been augmented by the contrast presented by the position of members of that persuasion here, who are equals with all others before the law, which sternly forbids any oppression on account of religion. Indeed, it may be said that the people of this country universally abhor persecution anywhere for that cause, and deprecate the trials of which . . . the Israelites of Roumania have been victims." Twenty years later, Secretary of States James Blaine protested the cruel edicts against the Jews in Russia. While chiefly stressing that the interests of foreign governments, including that of the United States, would be strongly affected if they were forced to confront "the difficult problem of affording an immediate asylum to a million or more of exiles," Blaine also noted that the "prejudice of race and creed" had "in our day given way to the claims of our common humanity. . . . Much has been done [in Russia] which a humane and just person must condemn." In 1824 and 1851, protests in cases of comparable oppression had elicited the warning that the United States was embarking on a "crusade," but few such warnings appeared against these verbal remonstrances. The prospect of military intervention or even of economic sanctions to change the conduct of foreign governments in cases of internal oppression was understood to be nil, and faith was in any case often expressed that public opinion had great resources of its own. Rapid increases in the means of communication, noted Fish, "have brought into almost daily intercourse communities which hitherto have been aliens and strangers to each other, so that now no great social and moral wrong can be inflicted on any people without being felt throughout the civilized globe."[12]

The revolutionary changes in North America brought about by the Civil War received an echo in the Wars of German Unification that culminated in Prussia's defeat of France and the establishment of the Second German Empire. Like America, Germany had for a century been poised between decentralizing and centralizing impulses. Over this preceding century, writes a distinguished historian, "we can find in the German experience an especially intense conflict between variety and communality, between the obdurate facts of multiplicity and a stubborn struggle to attain or impose unity." The same struggle had been fundamental in American history over the same period, and the great conflict between these opposing principles, as Lord Acton wrote, conferred on the epoch "between the convention of 1787 and the election of Mr. Davis in 1861 an almost epic unity." Suddenly in both countries that great conflict was resolved by war, with the spoils of victory going to the forces of unification. Complementing the new nation in North America and the new empire in central Europe was the new Japan that arose with the Meiji Restoration of the late 1860s, after which Japan broke decisively from its preceding isolation and sought rational instruction in modernization from the Western powers. These developments, akin to earthquakes, constituted a giant shift in the tectonic plates, laying the foundation for a new geography of world power.[13]

29

A World of Its Own

HAVING BECOME A NATION-STATE, a veritable Yankee Leviathan, in the course of the war, the federal government shrank in the postwar decades. Its tax revenues were less than 5 percent of gross domestic product—mostly allocated to the veterans, widows, and bondholders of the Great War. By comparison with the great bureaucracies built up in the twentieth century, its administrative size was minuscule. Though small in number of employees, however, the government was powerful in its ability to shape the national economy. A fundamentally new economic order arose after the war, built on a protected continental market and laissez-faire doctrines that privileged capital over labor. Economists disagree on whether the Civil War advanced or retarded industrialization, but it undoubtedly concentrated capital and laid the foundations for many of the great industrial combinations that dominated the Gilded Age. The army, after returning to its barracks in the South, was employed to break strikes in the same year. The postwar amendments designed to free the Negro ultimately served mainly to free business enterprises from state control, and over time facilitated the erection of "Mr. Herbert Spencer's *Social Statics*" into the organic law of the republic.[1]

The American system of political economy set the United States apart from the world in one vital particular. Capital and labor poured onto American shores until 1914, but foreign goods were sharply restricted by high tariffs. The protective system was justified as giving the laboring man a higher wage than he would receive under a system of free trade, and there is little question that American labor had it better than the workers of other countries. Whereas protectionism had sometimes been justified as a necessary adjunct of national power in a competitive and ruthless international system, the American protectionists of the 1870s and 1880s stressed its pacific implications. The protectionists were no opponents of commercial civilization—they believed that commerce reflected a deeper law of service because it required men, as a condition of existence, to be of use to one another—but they felt America to be militarily, politically, and commercially impregnable. They relished the achievement of the world that Hamilton and Clay had espied, of one great system of trade centered on the home market, for in that golden circle lay a state of security and well-being that could not be "injuriously affected in war or peace, through stratagem or design by any other people."[2]

Free traders continued to question the protective system. It was obnoxious in the way that it introduced peculation into the government, with each tariff bill a riot of special privileges, and it bore unequally on the mass of American citizens, unfairly rewarding some and penalizing others. The grievance was felt strongly by the southern states. "It is no secret," as J. William Fulbright later summarized the southern sentiment, "that the South was considered like a conquered territory after 1865. Since that time, the tariff policy and the freight rate structure were designed by the North to . . . keep [the South] in the status of a raw material producing colony."[3]

But the protective system stood against its assailants, and the record of growth produced under its auspices could hardly be considered a failure. The economic expansion that took place from 1865 to 1900 was prodigious, awe-inspiring. America was becoming the storehouse of the world, vaulting forward to preeminent status in the production of its farms, industries, mines, and forests. By that latter year, John Hay noted, the position of commercial preeminence resulting from the superior quality and greater cheapness of American products "may result in shifting the center, not only of industrial, but of commercial activity and the money power of the world to our marts." Whether this success could be maintained was often subject to doubt. The desire to sell to foreign markets, after all, could not be satisfied in the long run without a corresponding willingness to buy foreign goods. If crisis should produce a vast reduction in external demand for American products, the collateral effects on the American economy would prove severe. Toward the end of the nineteenth century, Americans grew increasingly anxious over the sustainability of this system but still marveled at the stupendous growth it had achieved.[4]

Faced with such extraordinary growth, free traders found themselves in the awkward position that Adam Smith had faced in 1776, when he condemned the "mercantile system" for undermining what was, on the evidence of the customs statistics, an impressive accomplishment. The discovery of the Americas, Smith concluded, had raised "the mercantile system to a degree of splendour and glory which it could never otherwise have attained." Carl Schurz made the same point against the protective system. "The boast that the great advances of this country in wealth and prosperity were owing to the Republican policy of high protection is simply a slander on the American people. Our natural resources are so immense and the energy and ingenuity of American labor so exceptionally productive, that owing to the combination of these two tremendous factors the American people were bound to prosper and to grow rapidly in wealth under—or in spite of—any economic policy." Schurz found it "wildly preposterous" that America, with such abundant resources, "should need the highest protective tariff ever enacted in any civilized country to make our industries go and to save our people from ruin and starvation."[5]

Whether registered in class or sectional terms, the post-Appomattox republic saw a pointed increase in the stratification of wealth and power in American society. The great fortunes built on the northern war effort, the deluge of migrants from Europe (far larger, as a percentage of host population, than any other migration to the United States before or since), and the movement of population from rural idyll to urban agglomeration, in pace with industrialization, made for an America far different from what had existed at the time of the founding, when, it was commonly observed, property was "pretty equally divided." After the Civil War, frontier settlement was aided by the 1862 Homestead Act and continued to serve the purpose that Jefferson and Madison had given to such expansion—countering an otherwise inexorable tendency toward inequality—but the closing of the frontier in the 1890s brought that relief to the social question to an end. This growing stratification got itself but imperfectly registered in the political arena; there were many Americans, like Dwight Eisenhower, who "found out in later years that we were very poor, but . . . didn't know it then." The class divide, mitigated by the opportunity American society offered, nevertheless existed and had an important sectional dimension, but the sectional factor was fundamentally different in meaning from what it had been previously. The great war had made separation unthinkable, and the dark visions of the propertied classes, especially in the 1890s, now centered on populist revolt and proletarian revolution rather than disunion.[6]

Making one out of many has always been an American theme, but the dimensions of this problem changed with the Civil War. Before the war, the problem centered on creating a durable union out of disparate states and sections. The "new man" of whom Crèvecoeur wrote—melding together English, Scottish, Dutch, Swedish, German, French—was a leitmotif of the middle states, but the great problem of union centered around uniting the New England states and the slaveholding South, and especially Massachusetts and Virginia, in both of which the white population was predominantly English but whose original settlers had been drawn from opposing sides in the English civil wars of the seventeenth century. Ironically, the introduction of so many "foreigners" in the 1840s and 1850s had, in its consequences, immensely strengthened the national principle, but anxiety over the incorporation of a new heterogeneous wave rose strongly again toward the end of the nineteenth century. Weighing on many minds was the apparently insoluble problem of creating a distinct American nationality out of a wide mix of European nationalities, especially the great influx from southern and eastern Europe that occurred in the 1880–1914 period. "The writers of the Declaration of Independence and of the Constitution," as Horace Kallen put it, "were not confronted by the practical fact of ethnic dissimilarity among the whites of the country. Their descendents are confronted with it."[7]

This unprecedented amalgamation, which made America seem the "great assimilating nation of the modern world," as Rome had been in ancient times, was a source of pride to pluralists but a cause of alarm for many nationalists, who feared either the "degradation of the gene pool" or the loss of cultural identity. "We are submerged," wrote a professor at Harvard, "we are submerged beneath a conquest so complete that the very name of us means something not ourselves. . . . I feel as I should think an Indian might feel, in the face of ourselves that were." Pluralists like Randolph Bourne objected to putting the United States into "the tight and jealous nationalism of European pattern" and called instead for an international nationalism, "a cosmopolitan federation of national colonies, of foreign cultures, from which the sting of devastating competition has been removed." "The United States," wrote Kallen, "are in the process of becoming a federal state not merely as a union of geographical and administrative unities, but also as a cooperation of cultural diversities, as a federation or commonwealth of national cultures"—each of which contributed a theme and melody so that "the harmony and dissonances and discords of them all may make the symphony of civilization."[8]

There were parts of the country—New York City especially—where Kallen's depiction rang true, but beyond the Hudson the American people retained a keen sense of racial identity and were prey to anxieties that assimilation would be impossible for swarthy peoples "alien in thought and habit and allegiance." The Chinese were excluded from further immigration in 1882, and discrimination and xenophobia directed at Japanese immigrants were rampant on the American West Coast, constituting a potentially grave obstacle to a peaceful U.S.-Japanese relationship. The exclusion of Asians and the subjugation and segregation of African Americans were as much features of the new nation as the beautiful music that Kallen sought to orchestrate, though it seems excessive to say that the latter process rested on or required the former. The United States remained open to immigration until the outbreak of war in 1914, but there was a cultural emphasis on "Americanization" or "assimilation" that became ever more pronounced with each successive immigrant wave, with dominant emphasis placed on the melting of European ethnicities in a common cultural pot.[9]

The same homogenizing and nationalizing imperative reached to other areas of American life. Public figures came increasingly to insist that both plutocrats and proletarians would have to surrender narrow class interests to the larger demands of nationality. In Indian policy the promise of a "measured separatism," "islands of tribalism largely free from interference by non-Indians or future state governments," was displaced after 1865 by the virtual obliteration of the autonomy once enjoyed by the tribes. "Hereafter," Congress decreed in 1871, "no Indian nation or tribe within the territory of the United States shall be acknowledged or recognized as an independent nation, tribe, or power with whom the United States may contract by treaty." The separate loyalties of southerners, immigrants, and Native Americans were all condemned under the new dispensation. To the former, the architects of the system "waved the bloody shirt." To the hyphenate, the immigrant whose loyalties were divided between old country and new, they said: "Americanize!" The Indian, finally, was commanded to abandon his tribal loyalty and to merge, as an individual, into the great American mass.[10]

The Civil War had made America more democratic in signal respects, but it was also more oligarchic in its extreme disparities of wealth. It had become more homogeneous under the hammer of the war, and also more insular in having established its own American system seemingly beyond all possibility of challenge from the European powers. Emblematic of the degree of separation was Frederick Jackson Turner's famous 1893 essay on the significance of the frontier, which stressed that the basic features of American life were homegrown and owed little to European precedents. America had made a civilization of its own.[11]

30

The Unionist Paradigm Revisited

DESPITE THE DEATH OF "THE UNION AS IT WAS," interpretations of the significance of the war demonstrated the continued salience of the unionist paradigm. In his widely audited lectures on Manifest Destiny in 1885, John Fiske argued that the Civil War attested to "the pacific implications of federalism." Though noting that the United States had a greater cohesive force than any "ordinary federation or league," Fiske insisted that "the primary aspect of the federal Constitution was undoubtedly that of a permanent league, in which each state, while retaining its domestic sovereignty intact, renounced forever its right to make war upon its neighbours and relegated its international interests to the care of a central council in which all the states were alike represented and a central tribunal endowed with purely judicial functions of interpretation." This experiment represented "the first attempt in the history of the world, to apply on a grand scale to the relations between states the same legal methods of procedure which, as long applied in all civilized countries to the relations between individuals, have rendered private warfare obsolete." Emancipation was, on this reckoning, a "priceless gain," but the deeper question, "far more subtly interwoven with the innermost fibres of our national well-being, far heavier laden too with weighty consequences for the future weal of all mankind, was the question whether this great pacific principle of union joined with independence should be overthrown by the first deep-seated social difficulty it had to encounter, or should stand as an example of priceless value to other ages and to other lands." Fiske had no doubt that the war had been fought "in the direct interest of peace." It was far better to demonstrate "once for all, at whatever cost," the principle of pacific settlement among independent communities "than to be burdened hereafter, like the states of Europe, with frontier fortresses and standing armies and all the barbaric apparatus of mutual suspicion!"[1]

As important as the principle for which the war was fought were the consequences to which it led, for these

> falsified all the predictions that were drawn from the contemplation of societies less advanced politically. It was thought that the maintenance of a great army would beget a military temper in the Americans

and lead to manifestations of Bonapartism,—domestic usurpation and foreign aggression; yet the moment the work was done the great army vanished, and a force of twenty-five thousand men was found sufficient for the military needs of the whole country. It was thought that eleven states which had struggled so hard to escape from the federal tie could not be re-admitted to voluntary co-operation in the general government, but must henceforth be held as conquered territory,—a most dangerous experiment for any free people to try. Yet within a dozen years we find the old federal relations resumed in all their completeness, and the disunion party powerless and discredited in the very states where once it had wrought such mischief.

In Fiske's view, the American experience taught a keen lesson to Europe. The unifying theme in his lectures was that "the history of human progress politically will continue in the future to be what it has been in the past,— the history of the successive union of groups of men into larger and more complex aggregates." Europe could only stay on the forward march by learning "the lesson of federalism." Fiske drew a sharp distinction between warfare among Christian states, which he thought an absurdity, and that between civilized and "barbarous" nations. War "is with barbarous races both a necessity and a favourite occupation. As long as civilization comes into contact with barbarism, it remains a too frequent necessity." Fiske sympathized keenly with Russia's war against Turkey, concluded in 1878, that liberated Bulgaria from Turkish oppression, a war that set free "a kindred race endowed with capacity for progress" and that humbled "the worthless barbarian who during four centuries has wrought such incalculable damage to the European world." But European wars, such as a struggle between Germany and France for the Rhine frontier, deserved sharp condemnation. "Such questions will have to be settled by discussion in some sort of federal council or parliament, if Europe would keep pace with America in the advance towards universal law and order."

"All will admit," Fiske insisted, "that such a state of things is a great desideratum." The question concerned its practicality. Conceding that Europe had "an immense complication of prejudices, intensified by linguistic and ethnological differences," he nevertheless expected that the "pacific pressure exerted upon Europe by America" by virtue of its commerce was becoming irresistible.

The disparity between the United States, with a standing army of only twenty-five thousand men withdrawn from industrial pursuits, and the states of Europe, with their standing armies amounting to four millions of men, is something that cannot possibly be kept up. The economic competition will become so keen that European armies will have to be disbanded, the swords will have to be turned into ploughshares, and thus the victory of the industrial over the military type of civilization will at last become complete. But to disband the great armies of Europe will necessarily involve the forcing of the great states of Europe into some sort of federal relation, in which Congresses—already held on rare occasions—will become more frequent, in which the principles of international law will acquire a more definite sanction, and in which the combined physical power of all the states will constitute (as it now does in America) a permanent threat against any state that dares to wish for selfish reasons to break the peace.[2]

Fiske's lecture contained the essentials of the Wilsonian program that would emerge some thirty years later in the aftermath of the European firestorm. Independent states surrendering some portion of their sovereignty to a common authority, for the purpose of reserving the remainder; the resultant security allowing them to disarm to minimum levels, which in turn would be a boon to the commerce that it was the interest of all to cultivate; the state of profound peace discouraging the stale pleas of military necessity that had always formed a formidable bulwark to despotic government; law acquiring a more definite sanction, behind which stood a combined power directed against any state that dared for selfish reasons to start a war. In terms of the basic concepts, the agenda of internationalism was drawn word for word from the script of federalism. It was the same script, now to be thought out in relation to human communities arrayed "into larger and more complex aggregates."

Though Fiske's larger theme was not original—the contrast between Europe's military system and America's federative system was routine before the Civil War, as was the conception of federal union as a model world order—he advanced the argument by seeking to demonstrate that the war did not falsify the "lesson of federalism" but rather reinforced it. That was, to be sure, an optimistic reading of the titanic struggle in North America. With equal, perhaps greater, plausibility it might be maintained that the war and the preceding experience of federal union showed that there was no real middle ground between centralization and decentralization. A federal union might disintegrate or it might advance toward ever tighter centralization, but it could not exist indefinitely in a balanced state. It would either dissolve or its unity would be established by war, become all one thing or all the other.[3] Even if Fiske's reckoning of the Civil War is accepted and we understand it as a war whose fundamental object was peace, the irrefragable fact was that the war had occurred. Federal union had not eliminated war, and it was unlikely that the "Parliament of man, the federation of the world," which Fiske saw as the end of history, would do so either.

These bleak speculations apart, however, Fiske had put his finger on a vital problem, and he was right to believe that his contemporaries would share his conviction "that such a state of things is a great desideratum." Fiske delivered his lectures all across the country and spoke, by the invitation of President Hayes, at a White House gathering that included Chief Justice Waite, Senators Hoar and Dawes of Massachusetts, General Sherman, and George Bancroft.[4] Sensitive to the charge of utopianism, he joked that his own speculations reached to the millennium but fell short of the day of judgment. There was in any case no expectation by Fiske or anybody else that America would lead in the reconstruction of European order. America was the model for Europe, but Europe's task was not America's responsibility. America was utterly without interest in going to war over issues arising from Europe's contentious system of the balance of power. She felt herself impregnable. "Social convulsions from within," noted Lord Bryce, "warlike assaults from without, seem now as unlikely to try the fabric of the American Constitution, as an earthquake to rend the walls of the Capitol. . . . For the present at least—it may not always be so—she sails upon a summer sea."[5]

Of more immediate relevance to policy was the basic identification that Fiske posited with the civilized nations, seen here to have a unity of interest in combating barbarous nations. All across the world—in Central Asia by Russia, in Indochina and Africa by France, in South Asia and Africa by Britain—the European powers were engaged in wars with peoples regarded as "barbarians," and unmistakable is Fiske's sympathy with Europe's aims. It was the readiness to draw the sword in settlement of disputes that, in Fiske's view, constituted the chief mark of barbarism. On its political side, civilization "means primarily the gradual substitution of a state of peace for a state of war." "As the industrial phase of civilization slowly supplants the military phase," men become "less *brutal* and more *humane*."[6]

Much as peaceableness is a reasonable criterion of what constitutes civilized conduct, events would show that the comparison was often unfavorable to the "civilized powers," who frequently resorted to treachery, deceit, and appalling wastage of human life in their conduct toward "the barbarians." In 1885, the year that Fiske's lectures were published, the United States recognized the "Congo Free State" organized by Leopold II of Belgium, who accumulated the worst record in a general pattern of conduct that made a cruel mockery of the high and mighty professions of the European powers. Imperialism, nevertheless, professed itself to be the work of civilization, and the United States saw itself as fully a part—in the vanguard even—of the

framework of law and understandings identified with civilization and progress. A decade later, Massachusetts senator Henry Cabot Lodge proclaimed
that the "great nations are rapidly absorbing for their future expansion and
their present defense all the waste areas of the earth. It is a moment which
makes for civilization and the advancement of the race." Would the United
States fall out of the line of march?[7]

PART EIGHT
A Commission from God

3 1

The New Nationalism and the
Spanish War

IN 1881, JAMES G. BLAINE, secretary of state under James Garfield, issued invitations to the governments of the Americas for an international conference on "the means of preventing war among the nations of America." The purpose of the Peace Congress, as Blaine later explained, was to provide the South American states "external pressure to keep them from war" when at peace, and "external pressure to bring them to peace" when at war. The conference, however, was never held. Garfield's assassination brought a new president, Chester A. Arthur, and a new secretary of state, Frederick T. Frelinghuysen, who withdrew the invitations and repudiated the policy, writing, "Were the United States to assume an attitude of dictation toward the South American republics, even for the purpose of preventing war, the greatest of evils, or to preserve the autonomy of nations, it must be prepared by army and navy to enforce its mandate, and to this end tax our people for the exclusive benefit of foreign nations."[1]

By the late 1880s, however, the idea of a Pan-American conference was again popular. Prompted both by considerations of commercial advantage and by the desire for a new peace system in the Americas, Congress authorized a new Pan-American conference in 1888, a measure that became law despite Cleveland's opposition. After Cleveland's defeat in the presidential election, Blaine returned as Harrison's secretary of state in 1889 and, in a fitting twist of fate, presided over the first congress of American states attended by representatives of the United States. With reference to the major work of the conference, which was largely concerned with questions of trade and finance, Blaine noted, "Peace is essential to commerce, is the very life of honest trade, and yet there is no part of the world where a resort to arms is so prompt as in the South Spanish Republics." Harrison thought that the "crowning benefit" of the conference would be found "in the better securities which may be devised for the maintenance of peace among all American nations and the settlement of all contentions by methods that a Christian civilization can approve."[2]

The conference had mixed results. Though it did adopt an arbitration convention and standardized measurements for a new gold coin, the project for a continental customs union failed by a large vote, the Argentine delegate denouncing it not, he said, because he lacked love for America but because he felt no suspicion or ingratitude toward Europe: "I cannot forget that in Europe are Spain, our mother; Italy, our friend; and France, our elder sister." Despite interest in external remedies to counter the prompt resort to force in South America, there seemed little prospect of North American military involvement in hemispheric affairs. As Harrison himself had observed during the presidential canvass of 1888: "We Americans have no commission from God to police the world."[3]

The next ten years, however, would show that a commission from God to police part of the world would emphatically be claimed by the United States. A more assertive and belligerent posture developed in the 1890s, and even those nominally against the tide seemed nevertheless to become caught up in it. President Benjamin Harrison (1889–1893) and President Grover Cleveland (1893–1897) were both among the anti-imperialists of 1898–1900, but Harrison threatened war in 1891–1892 over a sailors' brawl in Chile, advancing far with preparations to sink the Chilean navy. Cleveland, who on returning to office in 1893 indignantly withdrew the treaty on the annexation of Hawaii from the Senate on the grounds that it was "a perversion of our nation's mission," nevertheless oratorically blasted himself to a victory over Great Britain in the 1895 Venezuelan crisis, as did his secretary of state, Richard Olney. The secretary's warning to Britain—"Today the United States is practically sovereign on this continent, and its fiat is law upon the subjects to which it confines its interposition"—laid down the law as it had never been laid down before. Olney later regretted the fulsomeness of his language, but his aggressive posture arose in part from the fear that a scramble for Latin America might develop alongside the concurrent scrambles for Africa and Asia, imperiling hemispheric security. Detailing the stakes of the Venezuelan crisis, Henry Cabot Lodge wrote that "if Britain can extend her territory in South America without remonstrance from us, every other European power can do the same, and in a short time you will see South America parceled out as Africa has been." Though the Monroe Doctrine had been announced in 1823 with considerably less in the way of blaring trumpets, it was true, as Cleveland observed, that the danger of a partition of South America was the precise thing "which President Monroe declared to be 'dangerous to our peace and safety.'"[4]

Alongside this newly assertive policy in the Western Hemisphere there developed a belief in the necessity of a "large policy" of colonies and commerce that would allow the United States to imitate the secret of British wealth and power. Earnestly supported by Theodore Roosevelt and Henry Cabot

Lodge, the discovery had been heralded by Captain Alfred Thayer Mahan in his book *The Influence of Sea Power upon History* (1890). This tome, detailing the rise of British sea power from 1660 to the War of American Independence, was much pondered by Roosevelt and Lodge. Mahan's work held the key to the puzzle of how America should manifest its new consciousness of power, and he, with TR and Lodge, looked in earnest toward the acquisition of Caribbean strongholds and Pacific bases in the 1890s.[5]

Underlying these shifts of policy was a perceptible change in the valuation of war, a disenchantment with the type of character molded by "industrial civilization" and a belief that, as Roosevelt put it, "Unless we keep the barbarian virtues, gaining the civilized ones will be of little avail." There seemed to have come over America, complained one anti-imperialist, "a sort of satiety of civilization, a hankering for a return to robust barbarism with its reign of force and disregard of moral ties. Churches, most of them, are carried away by the prevailing impulse, and lend the sanction of the Gospel to the love of war." The new dispensation held that "war is not only an occasional necessity, but a good thing in itself, and a moral tonic 'saving nations from the eating canker of those vices which too often grow up in a long continuance of peace.'" An eloquent statement of this philosophy had been given by Helmut von Moltke, head of the German General Staff: "Permanent peace is a dream, and not even a beautiful dream, and war is a law of God's order in the world, by which the noblest virtues of man, courage and self-denial, loyalty and self-sacrifice, even to the point of death, are developed. Without war the world would deteriorate into materialism."[6]

A strong affinity undoubtedly existed between Roosevelt's outlook and "the religion of the militarists in Germany." "Years ago," H. L. Mencken recalled after Roosevelt's death, "I devised and printed a give-away of the Rooseveltian philosophy in parallel columns—in one column, extracts from 'The Strenuous Life'; in the other, extracts from Nietzsche. The borrowings were numerous and unescapable. Theodore had swallowed Friedrich as a peasant swallows Peruna—bottle, cork, label and testimonials." His thirst whetted, TR went from Nietzsche to the kaiser. "Wilhelm was his model in *Weltpolitik*, and in sociology, exegetics, administration, law, sport and connubial polity no less. Both roared for doughty armies, eternally prepared—for the theory that the way to prevent war is to make all conceivable enemies think twice, thrice, ten times. Both dreamed of gigantic navies, with battleships as long as Brooklyn Bridge. Both preached incessantly the duty of the citizen to the state, with the soft pedal upon the duty of the state to the citizen. Both praised the habitually gravid wife. Both delighted in the armed pursuit of the lower fauna. Both heavily patronized the fine arts. Both were intimates of

God, and announced His desires with authority. Both believed that all men who stood opposed to them were prompted by the devil and would suffer for it in hell."[7]

Believing that "the country needs a war," Roosevelt was keen for war against just about anybody in the 1890s—Germany, Spain, and even England fell within his sights. It was this inordinate bellicosity that earned for Roosevelt and Henry Cabot Lodge the sobriquet of "degenerate sons of Harvard" from the president of the university, Charles W. Eliot. President Eliot's essay "Five American Contributions to Civilization" (1896) highlighted the commitment to the peaceful settlement of disputes as the first and leading American contribution but registered the new mood in the amount of time he spent refuting the "war has its virtues" doctrine.[8]

Even in the absence of these significant new developments, the United States may have ultimately intervened in the brutal war that Spain was fighting against revolutionaries in Cuba, which had begun again in 1895. The United States had faced essentially the same circumstances in the previous Cuban insurrection lasting from 1868 to 1876. Though tempted, it had avoided intervention. The different reaction in the 1890s bespoke the existence of a different country, with new wants, needs, and aspirations. McKinley's war message justified intervention "in the cause of humanity and to put an end to the barbarities, bloodshed, starvation, and horrible miseries now existing there." The action followed "many historical precedents where neighboring states have interfered to check the hopeless sacrifices of life by internecine conflicts beyond their borders." Though McKinley also insisted that serious American national interests were impaired by the continued fighting—including threats to American citizens and property—the humanitarian appeal was primary. In his annual message of December 1897 he had ruled out "forcible annexation," insisting that such an objective, "by our code of morality, would be criminal aggression." The prohibition, introduced as the Teller Amendment, was incorporated in the war resolution denying any intention "to exercise sovereignty, jurisdiction, or control over said island except for pacification thereof," and promising, "when that is accomplished, to leave the government and control of the island to its people."[9]

Had the United States acted precipitately? That was the opinion of legal experts, according to a 1908 study of the war: "In the opinion of nearly all writers on international law the particular form of intervention in 1898 was unfortunate, irregular, precipitate and unjust to Spain." The destruction of the battleship *Maine*, which played so large a role in inflaming American opinion, was not a sufficient ground, for Spain properly offered arbitration and had no motive for the attack. Of greater importance, the full Spanish concessions on the eve of war made the "technical basis" of the war in international law "very weak indeed." "Except for an uncontrollable desire for war on the part of the United States, diplomacy might, within all human probability, have accomplished the emancipation of Cuba."[10]

The aftermath proved more benign than it might have done, largely because of the soothing effect of the Teller Amendment on Cubans otherwise disposed to rebel against the new American overlordship. Though the U.S. treatment of the revolutionary armies was received with indignation—they, like their Spanish oppressors, were asked to surrender and turn in their arms—there was little armed resistance to the American occupation. In 1901, the United States imposed a protectorate on Cuba that gave its forces the right to come back into Cuba if it failed to meet its "international obligations." Leonard Wood, the governor-general of Cuba who wanted to annex the island, bowed to Elihu Root's preference for a protectorate but believed that there was "little or no independence left Cuba under the Platt amendment." Cubans were deeply ambivalent about the U.S. role in liberating their country from Spain—happy to be relieved from oppression, but anxious that they might have their liberators, at last, for their masters. The result was a strangely bifurcated outcome. Cubans saw their country slip into the control of a financial, commercial, and political oligarchy tied directly to American capital and underwritten by U.S. military forces. Americans, by contrast, congratulated themselves on their liberation of Cuba and thought they had done a grand thing. Both by "the pacification of Cuba and by the attempt to introduce a little order into the affairs of the turbulent Central American republics," argued Herbert Croly, the United States had made an effective beginning in the "great work" of building an "American international system." "Whatever may be the fate of Cuba in the future," wrote Harvard professor Archibald Cary Coolidge in 1908, "the treatment she has received at the hands of the United States in the decade since she was made free will remain something to be proud of." But even such enthusiasts of the American record saw, with William Howard Taft, that America's conduct, though "unselfish and self-sacrificing," was "treated among the South American people as an indication of our desire to enlarge our territorial control." The Monroe Doctrine, he sighed, which had "for near a century helped along the cause of peace," had been badly "misconstrued by the peoples who have so much profited by our enforcing it."[11]

32

Imperialism and the Conquest of the Philippines

THE WAR PROVED MOST CONTROVERSIAL not in its origins in Cuba but in its consequences in the Far East. The orders that sent Commodore Dewey to Manila Bay gave to the United States nominal possession of the Philippines; the great debate that subsequently arose over imperialism was centered on what the fate of the territory would be. For the broader public, the acquisition of a colonial empire across the Pacific was strikingly novel: they had gone to war against Cuba, as McKinley said, without "any original thought of complete or even partial acquisition" of the Philippine archipelago. Even for the imperialists, who had been thinking of naval bases and coaling stations, this was a new question. Mahan acknowledged that he had trouble wrapping his mind around the proper disposition of the new inheritance. At the same time, the imperialists did know in a general way what they wanted from the war—a much improved strategic position in the Pacific as well as in the Caribbean. They had not given serious thought to what they were going to do with Spain's decrepit empire, but to be in a position where they might dictate the terms was very much a war aim of the American government. Immediately upon the declaration of war, McKinley sent an army of 11,000 troops to the Philippines, indicating an intention from the outset to take military possession from Spain. Though the acquisition had elements of the unexpected, the president's explanation that "the march of events rules and overrules human action" was an attempt to blot out his own agency in bringing it forward. It was also quite convenient for one who had declared the year previously that military conquest and forcible annexation were un-American principles of which no decent man would think.[1]

McKinley was initially cool to taking the whole of the archipelago but nevertheless found great danger in all the alternatives—granting independence, establishing a protectorate, or selling or trading the islands to another of the Great Powers. After discovering that imperialism was popular in the country, his administration sought and attained the transfer from Spain of sovereignty over the Philippines in the Treaty of Paris. William Jennings Bryan, the Democratic challenger who intended to make opposition to imperialism a rallying cry in the 1900 presidential campaign, inexplicably directed wavering Democratic senators to vote in favor. Two days before Senate ratification of the treaty (February 6, 1899), savage fighting broke out between the Americans and the forces of Emilio Aguinaldo. One anti-imperialist, William Graham Sumner, had argued that the chief thing the United States would inherit from Spain would be the task of suppressing rebellions. So it proved to be.[2]

Albert Beveridge, the junior senator from Indiana now just bursting onto the stage as a spokesman for the Republicans, gave the most fulsome endorsement of imperialism. In his reckoning it was a grand thing to do, both for the regeneration of the world and for the nation's strategic and commercial interests. "Hawaii is ours; Porto Rico is to be ours; at the prayer of her people Cuba finally will be ours; in the islands of the East, even to the gates of Asia, coaling stations are to be ours at the very least; the flag of a liberal government is to float over the Philippines, and may it be the banner that Taylor unfurled in Texas and Fremont carried to the coast." Beveridge was as keen as anyone on the strategic bases and expanded commerce the acquisition would bring, but his larger appeal was to the world-transforming mission of the United States: "God," he intoned, "has not been preparing the English-speaking and Teutonic peoples for a thousand years for nothing but vain and idle self-contemplation and self-admiration. No. He has made us master organizers of the world to establish system where chaos reigned. He has given us the spirit of progress to overwhelm the forces of reaction throughout the earth. He has made us adept in government that we may administer government among savage and senile peoples. Were it not for such a force as this the world would relapse into barbarism and night. And of all our race He has marked the American people as His chosen nation to finally lead in the redemption of the world." Here, notes one student of American millenarianism, are "all the classic elements associated with the idea of 'the redeemer nation'" in capsule form: "Chosen race, chosen nation, millennial-utopian destiny for mankind; a continuing war between good (progress) and evil (reaction) in which the United States is to play a starring role as world redeemer." As a later observer dourly commented, the imperialists of 1900 spoke of expansion "in terms of an Inevitable Destiny which would carry American ideals and institutions to new lands and strange peoples and compel the Nation to assume the White Man's Burden as part of a great Plan which human volition could not alter."[3]

The imperialist case was troubled by serious tensions, if not outright contradictions. The imperialists were puzzled whether to justify the measure as primarily serving ourselves or serving others. They claimed that it did both, but the more one emphasized the strategic and commercial benefits to be gained by imperialism, the more its philanthropic motives were called into question—making the white man's burden "a sacred trust rich in dividends for the trustee."[4] The more its philanthropic motives were stressed, on the other hand, the more vulnerable the policy became to setbacks. "What's in it for us?" was a question the American people were bound to ask, and sooner rather than later. Lodge, sensing this, declared, "Whatever duty to others might seem to demand, I should pause long before supporting any policy if there were the slightest suspicion that it was not for the benefit of the people of the United States."[5] The question—for them or for us?—acquired particular urgency once the costs, contrary to expectations, began to mount. It was one thing to parade the idea of a "benevolent assimilation" happily accepted by the ignorant natives, quite another to "civilize 'em with a Krag," as the American soldiery in the Philippines had begun to do in earnest.

The imperialists were also of two minds with respect to the extension of American principles and ideals into the Philippines. On the one hand, the enterprise was justified as uplifting the Filipinos, but they were, at the same time, held to be incorrigible in their present barbarous state. Self-government was out of the question. "It is not true," Beveridge argued against the anti-imperialists, "that every race without instruction and guidance is naturally self-governing. If so, the Indians were capable of self-government." Roosevelt agreed: on Indian reservations, he wrote, "the army officers and civilian agents still exercise authority without asking the 'consent of the governed.' We must proceed in the Philippines with the same wise caution."[6]

The "national-imperialists" were keen to emphasize that their policy was novel and revolutionary; they had spoken repeatedly in the 1890s of the need to break from "the policy of isolation" and to become a world power. "I am an imperialist," as Mahan spoke the creed, "simply because I am not an isolationist." At the same time, they insisted that the acquisition of the Philippines was simply the latest stage in an ongoing story of American expansion—"a history of statesmen who flung the boundaries of the Republic out into unexplored lands and savage wilderness; a history of soldiers who carried the flag across blazing deserts and through the ranks of hostile mountains, even to the gates of sunset; a history of a multiplying people who overran a continent in half a century." "In the year 1898," began Roosevelt's gilt-edged presidential edition of *The Winning of the West*, "the United States finished the work begun over a century before by the backwoodsman." Roosevelt's generation was "but carrying to completion the work of our fathers and of our fathers' fathers." Both sides in the debate over empire believed that interpretations of the past were of crucial significance in conferring legitimacy in the present. If the anti-imperialists are right, Lodge declared, "then our whole past record of expansion is a crime."[7]

Though many advocates of the large policy had not been bashful in identifying it with an imperialist policy—Jefferson, said Beveridge, was "the first Imperialist of the Republic"—Roosevelt took strong exception to the use of the terms "imperialism" and "militarism." "The simple truth," he wrote when accepting nomination as vice president, "is that there is nothing even remotely resembling 'imperialism' or 'militarism' involved in the present development of that policy of expansion which has been part of the history of America from the day when she became a nation. These words mean absolutely nothing as applied to our present policy in the Philippines; for this policy is only imperialistic in the sense that Jefferson's policy in Louisiana was imperialistic."[8]

Given Roosevelt's belief that the civilized powers were all engaged in the same mission of repressing barbarism, the evident implication of his position was that European imperialism didn't exist either—a point that would be difficult to make out. The issue, moreover, of whether the United States was practicing imperialism is really to be separated from the purity of its motives, and on the former score there was no doubt that it intended to do the deed: it sought to rule another people by force, brandishing the sword while promising peace and civilization. There was also, as the anti-imperialists pointed out, a big difference between what Jefferson had done in Louisiana and what McKinley was doing in the Philippines. After the Louisiana Purchase, there was little doubt that "the *Gallo-Hispano-Indian omnium gatherum* of savages and adventurers"[9] would in due time be admitted to statehood, a promise incorporated in the treaty of cession with France; there was, by contrast, no possibility that the Filipinos would over time enjoy the same privilege. Even Roosevelt's characterization of U.S. policy toward the Indians rode roughshod over the facts: while approving of efforts to implant instructional missions among the tribes, Washington and Jefferson had acknowledged that the various Indian nations were self-governing communities entitled to rule themselves according to their accustomed forms, as well as to treat with others in a diplomatic mode. When shoved aside by Jackson in the 1830s, they were given the choice between assimilation and removal. That may have been a hard and bitter choice for the Cherokees, but it *was* a choice—one that was denied the Filipinos. It was only after Indian strength was entirely broken and the various nations were scattered into numerically small settlements that "the army officers and civilian agents" exercised authority over them. This experience was scarcely a cogent precedent for exercising rule over a vast archipelago containing some 8 to 10 million souls.

Roosevelt's larger appeal in "Expansion and Peace" was to military force as the only way to keep peace in a world still greatly populated by barbarians. The "indiscriminate advocacy of peace at any price" was cowardly and wrong. Invoking the Civil War, he maintained that the United States had "escaped generations of anarchy and bloodshed, because our fathers who upheld Lincoln and followed Grant were men in every sense of the term," allowing them to "do deeds from which men of over-soft natures would have shrunk appalled." He identified wholly, as Fiske had done, with the European powers who battled barbarians in Siberia, Hindustan, and Africa. "Every expansion of civilization makes for peace. In other words, every expansion of a great civilized power means a victory for law, order, and righteousness. This has been the case in every instance of expansion during the present century, whether the expanding power were France or England, Russia or America." Though Roosevelt claimed that there was "every reason, not merely to hope, but to believe" that wars between civilized communities would grow "rarer and rarer," the case was otherwise on the frontier between civilization and barbarism. Were the United States "to leave the Philippines and put the Aguinaldan oligarchy in control of those islands, . . . we should merely turn them over to rapine and bloodshed until some stronger, manlier power stepped in to do the task we had shown ourselves fearful of performing." Roosevelt pledged to keep the islands and "establish therein a stable and orderly government, so that one more fair spot of the world's surface shall have been snatched from the forces of darkness. Fundamentally the cause of expansion is the cause of peace."[10]

Events would show, however, that American expansion in the Philippines was the cause of a terribly destructive war. By insisting on full submission and dominion, the United States provoked revolt. The case is especially regrettable because it is evident in retrospect that the United States could have secured its vaunted strategic objectives without insisting upon sovereignty. Had the United States instead recognized the Aguinaldo government and offered to support its independence against external enemies—had it offered protectorate status to the Philippines—there is every reason for thinking that war could have been avoided and a reasonably stable government established. This course entailed collaboration with the wealthy and middle classes via a "policy of attraction," which the United States adopted, to evident success, in later years. Aguinaldo was not a social revolutionary but a representative of the very same forces with whom Washington subsequently collaborated. All it needed to do, but which it was initially incapable of doing because of its pigheaded militarism and hallucinations about barbarians, was to enter upon that collaboration immediately.[11]

The unnecessary war that resulted from such imperious conduct led to the loss of 4,000 to 5,000 American lives, 16,000 Filipino combatants, and approximately 150,000 to 200,000 dead civilians, who were ravaged by disease and starvation in the war zones. In short order the American people would discover that the army in the Philippines was engaged in the same practices that, when committed by the Spanish in Cuba, had aroused perfervid denunciation. Summarizing the evidence, one anti-imperialist noted in 1902 that "it seems to be well attested that Filipinos have been tortured to make them give up their hidden arms, while the language of some of the soldiers engaged in the work of subjugation has been reckless and ruthless in the extreme. On the other hand, the Filipinos are accused of burying American prisoners alive. Is this the promised reign of 'law, liberty and justice'? Will the character of the conquerors remain untainted by this competition in cruelty with a half-civilized race?"[12]

The best of the initial pamphlets appearing in opposition to imperialism was William Graham Sumner's *Conquest of the United States by Spain*. Sumner wrote before the outbreak of the Philippine rebellion, but he predicted it when the imperialists were oozing forth assurances about the acceptability of the American rule among the natives. Though the United States had bested Spain in the military conflict, Sumner declared, Spain had conquered the United States "on the field of ideas and policies." "Spain was the first, for a long time the greatest, of the modern imperialistic states," wrote Sumner. "The United States, by its historical origin, its traditions, and its principles, is the chief representative of the revolt and reaction against that kind of a state." Sumner showed that, with expansion and imperialism, "we are throwing away some of the most important elements of the American symbol and are adopting some of the most important elements of the Spanish symbol." This profound shift in identity and institutions made the anti-imperialists feel that they had lost their country. Its essential meaning had been inverted, its creed abandoned. To George Hoar, imperialism was "a greater danger than we have encountered since the Pilgrims landed at Plymouth—the danger that we are to be transformed from a republic, founded on the Declaration of Independence, guided by the counsels of Washington, into a vulgar, commonplace empire, founded upon physical force."[13]

Both imperialists and anti-imperialists were deeply devoted to the nation. Roosevelt believed that no excess was possible in national devotion. It was the only foundation on which "a vigorous civilization" could be built: "every civilization worth calling such must be based on a spirit of intense nationalism." The anti-imperialists were no less in love with America, but they saw grave danger to its "national character" in imperialism, for reasons assigned by Goldwin Smith: "The adoption of Imperialism by Americans can hardly fail to carry with it a fundamental change in the moral foundations of their own Commonwealth. Other polities, such as that of England, may be based on constitutional tradition. That of the United States is based on established and almost consecrated principles. . . . When the people of the United States, after recognizing the Filipinos as their allies, bought them with their land of Spain, as they would buy the contents of a cattle-ranch or a sheep-fold, and proceeded to shoot them down for refusing to be delivered to the purchaser, they surely broke away from the principles on which their own polity is built, and compromised the national character formed on respect for those principles."[14]

The leaders of the anti-imperialists were generally old men. As with Adams, Gallatin, Webster, and Clay when confronting the Mexican War, they were one step away from the grave. But they sang out with eloquence and clarity the elements of the old American creed that forbade the United States from doing what it purposed in the Philippines. It seemed to them morally objectionable and utterly inconsistent with the Declaration of Independence for Americans to rule over others without their consent. "No economic or diplomatic reasoning," notes a distinguished student of their thought, "could justify slaughtering Filipinos who wanted their independence. No standard of justice or morality would sustain the transformation of a war that had begun as a crusade to liberate Cuba from Spanish tyranny into a campaign of imperialist conquest."[15]

Most opponents shared the condescending sentiments toward the Filipinos—Sumner spoke derisively of "tutoring the Talags"—and were opposed to the admission of the Filipinos or the Cubans into the union as coequal states. Still, many anti-imperialists saw through this pervasive racism, and it was their appreciation that general principles of liberty forbade imperialism that enabled them to do so. The "doctrine that all men are equal," noted Sumner, "was set up as a bar to just this notion that we are so much better than others that it is liberty for them to be governed by us." "Who shall say," asked Goldwin Smith, "that the uncivilized or half-civilized races now being crushed by predatory powers in different parts of the world, may not have in them the germs of something which, spontaneously developed, would be as noble and worth as much to humanity as any of the powers themselves?" Senator Hoar of Massachusetts especially emphasized Filipino capacity for self-rule. The Filipinos were a people "that has a written constitution, a settled territory, an independence it has achieved, an organized army, a congress, courts, schools, universities, churches, the Christian religion, a village life in orderly, civilized, self-governed municipalities; a pure family life, newspapers, books, statesmen who can debate questions of international law, like Mabini, and organize governments, like Aguinaldo; poets like José Rizal; aye, and patriots who can die for liberty, like José Rizal."[16]

Just as the imperialists were unhappy with "imperialism" as a depiction of their policy, anti-imperialists were uneasy with "isolationism" as a depiction of theirs. Dismissing the isolationist epithet, Goldwin Smith noted that before 1898 the "American Commonwealth had the largest population of freemen in the world, and one which was rapidly growing. Its heritage reached from Arctic regions to regions almost tropical, with a range of production embracing nearly everything needed or desired by man. The world was full of its inventions and its manufactures. It was the tutelary power of this continent. It was in the van of political progress. Its influence was felt more or less in the politics of all nations. If such a state was isolation, it was an isolation the influence of which was as wide as humanity." The isolationists would subscribe to the isolationist label only after disposing of the malicious associations that their adversaries kept imputing to it. No, it was not hermitlike; no, it did not detract one iota from the benign influence that America should exert upon the world; no, it was not cowardly and pacifistic, but rather cautious, in keeping with the traditional precepts of the American system, about expanding justifications for the use of force. If it was isolation to incorporate into policy such sensible cautions, then they were isolationists. "When the others are all over ears in trouble," Sumner asked, "who would not be isolated in freedom from care? When the others are crushed under the burden of militarism, who would not be isolated in peace and industry?"[17]

Oddly, it was the trade protectionists of the Republican Party who were now clamoring after imperialism and the supposed extension of markets it would afford. The free traders, as Sumner summarized the argument of the preceding generation, had warned the protectionists "that they were constructing a Chinese wall." The protectionists answered "that they wished we were separated from other nations by a gulf of fire." Now, Sumner commented, it is the protectionists "who are crying out that they are shut in by a Chinese wall. When we have shut all the world out, we find that we have shut ourselves in." Here lay one more element showing the incoherence of the program: "At great expense and loss we have carried out the policy of the home market, and now we are called upon at great expense and loss to go out and conquer territory in order to widen the market." Renew the recently failed negotiations with Canada for a reciprocity treaty, Sumner advised. It did not cost a thing, and it would expand trade more effectually than any of the Spanish acquisitions.[18]

The anti-imperialists had a similarly nuanced approach to internationalism. If cooperation with the European powers meant participation in their ignominious rites, they were against it. At the same time, the ideological content of anti-imperialism did set forth a philosophy of international relations that was coherent and traditional. It affirmed the equality of all peoples and the wrongness of ruling over men without their consent. It found in militarism the chief threat to civilization. It privileged the peaceful resolution of disputes through law and arbitration. At the level of principle, everything the anti-imperialists said about the lineaments of a just and secure system of states had been said a thousand times before. It would be said again by internationalists in the coming generation.

Though it is easy to see a thematic affinity between anti-imperialism and internationalism, the imperialists could also lay a claim to internationalism. This interpretation of turn-of-the-century American imperialism is highlighted by scholar Frank Ninkovich. In Ninkovich's retelling, the "familiar old building blocks—the rise to world power, the pursuit of economic interests, racism, and social Darwinism—fail individually to hold up under the stress of examination, thus making for an explanatory structure that is quite rickety and unstable." The chief weakness of that narrative, in Ninkovich's view, is "the hard-edged emphasis on international struggle and self-interest." Instead, attention needs to be focused on "civilization, identity, the civilizing mission and great power cooperation." "Because the spread of civilization was a process that could not be described solely in nationalist terms, its rhetoric implied that imperialism was a common undertaking of the developed nations, a form of internationalism that was helping to build a common, better world. . . . Far from being interested in the Philippines, as such, Americans had fallen in love with the *idea* of empire as part of a broader historical outlook that caused people to thrill to McKinley's summons to 'duty.' More than any other argument it was the call of duty and civilization, the internationalist rhetoric of empire, that appears to have had the greatest impact" in prompting American support for the annexation of the Philippines.[19]

Ninkovich's perspective is especially welcome because it gives analytical primacy, as we have done, to the mutual relations among nationalism, imperialism, and internationalism. His argument, however, may represent an overreaction to the traditional accounts emphasizing nationalist preoccupations and struggles. It was the coincidence of desire and duty, of needing somehow to see policy in relation to both hard-won strategic gains and transcendent contributions to civilization, that was intrinsic to the imperialist sensibility of 1898–1900. That the economic gains attributable to imperialism would be nugatory is true, as was pointed out at the time by anti-imperialists like Sumner. More seriously, the strategic advantages of possessing the Philippines proved wholly illusory. Roosevelt, who with Mahan and Lodge had been very keen on the fulfillment of the "large policy," saw by 1907 that the United States had taken a bridge too far. The Philippines could not be defended against Japan, the most likely enemy, without large expenditures that were unacceptable to public opinion and which, even if made, would impinge greatly on Japanese vital interests. The discovery over time that there was no gold at the end of the rainbow, however, *was* a discovery. In the salad days, it was thought that whoever held the Philippines—"more resourceful and greater in area, population and opportunities than Cuba, and so situated as to command the commerce and trade of the Far East and the routes thereof"—would acquire "a vantage ground of inestimable strategical and commercial value." The archipelago provided a position "more valuable than the prizes for which the great nations of Europe have been scheming." It occupied "a favored location, not with reference to one part of any particular country of the Orient, but to all parts." Its possession "by a progressive commercial power, if the Nicaragua Canal project should be completed, would change the course of ocean navigation as it concerns a large percentage of the water-borne traffic of the world."[20]

Unless one has a Ph.D. in the mysteries of the human heart, it is not easy to award primacy to either of these factors. Historian David Healy's balancing of the relative importance of nationalism and internationalism in imperialism is judicious: "Had the American public seen no national advantage in imperialism, they would never have embarked upon it merely to do good; yet, had they seen no good in it, it is extremely doubtful that enough of them could have been persuaded to support it only for the sake of expediency."[21] This intermingling of selfish and idealistic motives might plausibly be adduced to show the ease with which humanitarian impulses are prostituted to the naturally stronger motives of mere profit, of reasons of state, but Ninkovich is right that American interventionism cannot be explained by sole reliance on the selfish motive. Both selfish and idealistic motives, in the event, were strongly appealed to and, for the imperialists, sincerely believed. That generalization is also true of anti-imperialists. In each case, opposing sides in the great debate joined differing readings of the national interest alongside a superheated appeal to the "symbolic spigots of a vast reservoir of popular idealism."[22]

Who won, who lost, the great debate over imperialism? It actually came to something of a draw. The fact that the imperialists had been betrayed in their prophecies hurt their cause, and there was no sentiment for a similar venture in the country. The people saw that the annexation of the Philippines had been a mistake but knew they could not go back and start over again. They wanted to withdraw but saw no clear way to do so. Those were points for the anti-imperialists. On the other hand, the opposition had not succeeded in forcing a withdrawal from the Philippines. The Supreme Court had affirmed the constitutionality of imperialism, holding in the *Insular Cases* that the inhabitants of the "unincorporated territories" had no constitutional rights that the court was bound to respect. Though the court conceded that these inhabitants could not be deprived of rights derived from natural law, these rights evidently did not include the right of self-government. Approving the power of the United States to rule "unincorporated" territories indefinitely, one justice remarked: "A false step at this time . . . might be fatal to the development of what Chief Justice Marshall called the American Empire."[23]

33

Informal Empire and the Protection of Nationals

THE BIGGEST APPARENT DEFEAT FOR THE ANTI-IMPERIALISTS was that their nemesis, Theodore Roosevelt, assumed the presidency in 1901 after the assassination of McKinley. Roosevelt's fulminations had driven the anti-imperialists to distraction. William James, a former teacher of Roosevelt at Harvard, was horrified with Roosevelt's conduct, which seemed explicable only by the idea that Roosevelt, though middle aged, was "still mentally in the *Sturm und Drang* period of early adolescence." He "treats human affairs, when he makes speeches about them, from the sole point of view of the organic excitement and difficulty they may bring, gushes over war as the ideal condition of human society, for the manly strenuousness which it involves, and treats peace as a condition of blubberlike and swollen ignobility, fit only for huckstering weaklings, dwelling in the gray twilight and heedless of the higher life."[1]

Though this depiction was unfortunately all too true of Roosevelt in the 1890s, it turned out not to be a good prophecy of Roosevelt's presidency. The possession of power moderated TR's outlook. Though he intervened further in Caribbean affairs, severing Panama from Colombia in order to build his treasured hemispheric canal and sending forces back into Cuba in 1906, he successfully warded off further European intervention in the Western Hemisphere and cleverly sent the dispute between three European powers and Venezuela to arbitration at the Hague. Convinced that the United States increasingly held the balance of power in the whole world, he practiced a prudent balance-of-power politics. Believing that order was best preserved by the recognition of spheres of influence among the Great Powers, he acquiesced in the Japanese incorporation of Korea. He gave cautious approval to the arbitration treaties of John Hay and Elihu Root, and he sought to cool and moderate the virulent anti-Japanese sentiment on the West Coast. His greatest triumph, for which he was awarded a Nobel Peace Prize, was his successful mediation of the Russo-Japanese War. That war constituted a grim foretaste of industrialized warfare and, together with the European crisis of 1905–1906, checked Roosevelt's previous confidence that the civilized powers were most unlikely to get into war among themselves.

Roosevelt retained his previous convictions about force, he never ceased to rail against the "peace at any price men," and he sought and achieved large increases in naval construction. But whether because of keen political circumspection or a genuine change in sentiment, he was no longer in public the fire-breathing celebrant of the "barbarian virtues" that he had been in the previous decade.[2]

The Spanish-American War reflected and further entrenched a new understanding of the Monroe Doctrine. Its original purport assumed the centrality of the norm prohibiting intervention in the internal affairs of hemispheric states, which neither the European powers nor the United States had a right to contravene. The United States, the thinking went, had an interest in the successful assertion of the rights of hemispheric nations to their own governments, under the control of the respective nations rather than by any European power. *Norteamericanos* were delighted when constitutional imitation proved the sincerest form of flattery, but when, in subsequent years, the continent seemed to be "swayed by bands of reckless despots," there was much lamentation over the fact but no accompanying assumption that the United States enjoyed a right of intervention to change this situation. What form these governments would take was their business, not ours or that of the European powers.[3]

In the early twentieth century, the pledge to respect sovereignty and the rights of national independence remained a formal stipulation of U.S. policy, but the prohibition against intervention began to be repeatedly breached along the shores of the American Mediterranean; the Monroe Doctrine, in turn, had come to mean something very different from the original. It now often conveyed unbridled unilateralism and meant, at a minimum, control over the foreign policies of these small states and stout resistance to European influence in the hemisphere, even at the expense of the principle of nonintervention. From the standpoint of Central American and Caribbean peoples themselves, this "informal empire" was but a hairsbreadth away from the real thing; for Roosevelt, however, it represented a contribution to civilization and a token of America's pledge to responsible partnership. Roosevelt saw his actions in Panama as a great boon to mankind, in which he exercised a sort of "international eminent domain" in securing the rights to build the canal. His other interventions in the Caribbean were conceived as attempts to ward off the circumstances that would invite European intervention. This put the United States in the odd position of intervening to ward off the dread evil of intervention, of practicing imperialism in order to suffocate in the Americas "the diplomacy of imperialism"—that is, the Great Power competition for the "waste spaces."[4]

The U.S. presumption to exercise effective control was perhaps most notably on display in Roosevelt's diplomacy over the hemispheric canal. Agreement had been reached with Colombia to secure the canal peacefully, but when the Colombian senate rejected the terms and held out for more, Roosevelt exploded in indignation against "the Bogota lot of jackrabbits"— "greedy little antropoids," John Hay called them—and engineered his Panamanian coup d'état, immediately recognizing the new Panamanian republic and preventing the sending of Colombian troops to the isthmus. Roosevelt insisted these acts were "justified by the interests of collective civilization" in the creation of an interoceanic canal, and he claimed possession of a "mandate from civilization," but all this was very irregular. Carl Schurz noted that Roosevelt had violated the law directing him, in case negotiations with Colombia failed, to negotiate with Nicaragua. He also "trampled under foot the principle for the maintenance of which" the American Civil War had been fought, namely, that "under a constitution like ours—and the existing constitution of Colombia is in this respect very much like ours, perhaps even a little stronger—a State has no right to secede from the Union." In addition to improperly recognizing the right of secession, Roosevelt "interfered with a mailed hand" in preventing the Colombian federal government from enforcing "its lawful authority in the rebellious community." In doing all this, Schurz noted, Roosevelt "flagrantly violated" the U.S.-Colombia treaty of 1846 under which Colombia guaranteed free transit across the isthmus to citizens of the United States, in return for which the United States guaranteed "the rights of sovereignty and property which New Granada now has and possesses over the said territory." What made these glaring violations of propriety especially disconcerting and badly undercut Roosevelt's appeal to an international mandate is the likelihood that "a little further haggling" and the introduction of separate negotiations with Nicaragua would in all likelihood have brought the Colombians to heel. "We might thus have had our canal without contemning our own law; without treading under foot principles we had maintained and fought for at a tremendous cost; without setting precedents which we pray may not come back to plague us; without the scandal of breaking a treaty."[5]

U.S. interventions in subsequent years—the imposition on Santo Domingo of a customs receivership in 1905, the reintroduction of American troops in Cuba in 1906, the overthrow in 1909 of José Santos Zelaya in Nicaragua— had motives that were usually mixed and difficult to order in relative importance, even in retrospect. When Smedley Butler, the cantankerous and disgruntled marine, recalled in the 1930s that he had been a "racketeer for capitalism" and a "high-class muscle man for Big Business," he did not tell the whole truth, though he did tell part of it. Protecting the American investments put at hazard by civil strife was often the leading motive for interventions, though the danger that European powers might intervene if the United States did not assert control was also a vital conditioning factor. In the aftermath of intervention, the U.S. government and public opinion saw elections as an essential means of establishing a legitimate government, but it was disorder rather than authoritarianism that prompted intervention, and even when successful, the new regimes were "aristocratic republics." "The primary U.S. goals," writes one scholar, "were strategic protection and economic expansion, for which engineering democracy was normally a tool or a subordinate objective." The larger thrust of American policy was arguably counterrevolutionary and sought to exclude the masses from democratic participation via a sharply limited franchise. The merest whiff of socialism set off alarm bells in Washington. This counterrevolutionary disposition made the little southern republics in name free, but in fact at the discretion of the president of the United States.[6]

The protection of nationals was especially important as providing a blank check to intervene for any motive policymakers wished. "Kill an Englishman at home," wrote the American ambassador in London, Walter Hines Page, "and there is no undue excitement. But kill one abroad and gunboats and armies and reparations are at once thought about."[7] American public opinion responded readily to the same plea. One American sojourner in Mexico, charged with coordinating all Protestant missionary activity in Latin America, assured donors of the safety of the Mexican missions, since "Uncle Sam has his troops" ready "for a hurry call" if necessary. "All parties concerned know this, and it gives us an added feeling of safety." The threat of intervention thus often arose from "incidents" in which the lives of American citizens were put in jeopardy. This roused in the government the need to act; the potential for disorder to bring European intervention if a government allowed the mistreatment of foreign nationals or was incapable of paying its debts formed an often vital corollary of the same idea.[8]

A striking example of the lengths to which the protection of nationals might be taken was the role played by the deaths of two American citizens in the overthrow in 1909 of Zelaya, who fled Nicaragua after Secretary of State Knox issued a blistering remonstrance against his conduct. The two U.S. citizens had joined the insurgency against Zelaya and, caught laying explosives to blow up a train, were executed. Senator Isidor Rayner, Democrat from Maryland, held that the Taft administration would be "a cowardly government if it does not make an example of Zelaya before the eyes of the civilized world. . . . If two American citizens—I care not who they were or what they were, citizens in high standing as they have been reputed to be or soldiers of fortune—have been murdered by Zelaya, then he must be made to pay the penalty of his crime. No other punishment will meet with the favor or the temper of the American people." Though taking a deep interest in Zelaya's alleged sexual depravities, Rayner said he was "opposed to participating in these Central American revolutions," did not care whether one party or the other was in possession of the treasury, and had insisted frequently "that we must keep aloof from these controversies." But America, he held, should not desist until Zelaya was in the dock. It would be extravagant to assume that the death of the two Americans was the cause of the 1909 Nicaraguan intervention, but it was certainly fuel to which could be easily attached any other motive.[9]

In theory, at least, the United States remained opposed to indiscriminate intervention. Roosevelt's 1904 "corollary" to the Monroe Doctrine threatened interference "only in a last resort," and then only if "our southern neighbors" proved unable or unwilling "to do justice at home and abroad," thus violating U.S. rights or inviting "foreign aggression to the detriment of the entire body of American nations." In cases of "chronic wrongdoing, or an impotence which results in a general loosening of the ties of civilized society," intervention would be justified both "in our own interest as well as in the interest of humanity at large," with the form of the action dependent "upon the degree of the atrocity and upon our power to remedy it."[10] This did not imply annexation—Roosevelt wrote in 1904 that he had as much inclination to annex the Dominican Republic "as a gorged boa constrictor might have to swallow a porcupine wrong end to"—but it did imply a continued readiness to intervene. Schurz, when he read of the doctrine, was appalled: "The task thus mapped out for us by Mr. Roosevelt is so unreasonable in itself, so adventurous, fraught with such arbitrary assumptions of power, with so many complications and with responsibilities so incalculable, that the statesmanship which proposes it may well be thought capable of any eccentricity ever so extravagant." Roosevelt joined a "naturally good heart" with a "lawless mind."[11]

Elihu Root, who became secretary of state after John Hay's death in 1905, had, by contrast, a mind deeply enthralled to the law. His ground for intervention within the ambit of the Monroe Doctrine was careful. "We deem the independence and equal rights of the smallest and weakest member of the family of nations entitled to as much respect as those of the greatest empire," he told the 1906 Pan-American Conference at Rio de Janeiro. "We neither claim nor desire any rights or privileges or powers that we do not freely concede to every American Republic." For Root, the Roosevelt Corollary was "a disclaimer of all that we ought not to arrogate to ourselves in [Richard Olney's] broad and somewhat rhetorical statement" of 1895. "It is a declaration that we arrogate to ourselves, not sovereignty over the American continent, but only the right to protect, that what we will not permit the great

Power of Europe to do on this continent we will not permit any American republic to make it necessary for the great Powers of Europe to do." Whenever, in short, the Europeans might make a valid claim of intervention, "we are bound to say that whenever the wrong cannot be otherwise redressed we ourselves will see that it is redressed." The legitimate claim of intervention, for Europeans or for Americans, did not reach to the internal forms of government adopted by these states but instead was tied to the performance, or lack thereof, of the duties of sovereignty—"that the citizens of other powers are protected within the territory; that the rules of international law are observed; that national obligations are faithfully kept."[12]

An outlook combining respect for sovereignty with punctilious regard for the rights of nationals also governed relations with China—though American policy in the Far East was devoted to keeping together the concert of European nations rather than, as in the Americas, preoccupied with keeping the Europeans out.[13] In 1900, when the Philippine War was raging, the United States sent 2,500 (later 5,000) troops to China as part of the multinational force raised up to repress the Boxer Rebellion, a xenophobic outburst in China against the annexations and humiliations of the 1890s. The U.S. willingness to participate in the European concert in Asia reflects a marked contrast with the detachment from the European concert in Europe but is readily explicable given the historic U.S.-China relationship. In 1844, the American envoy Caleb Cushing got the Chinese to accept a treaty that gave to the United States the same commercial rights as those accorded the most favored nation. Britain's success in the Opium War had reversed the relations of superiority and inferiority that had previously prevailed in the relations between China and the West. The "kowtow" that the Chinese emperor had imposed on Westerners, to the indignation of Americans like John Quincy Adams, was in effect imposed on China as a consequence of the Opium War, and American merchants were happy to pick up the scraps. This "hitchhiking imperialism" allowed the United States to tag along with the other powers, and especially the dominant power, Great Britain, in securing commercial benefits to itself and in extending the influence of Protestant missionaries.[14]

In the estimation of the Chinese government, the United States was often regarded as the best among a bad lot of barbarians. The high point of cordiality had been the appointment in 1867 of the former American minister, Anson Burlingame, as China's ambassador to all the treaty powers, a compliment paid "by the oldest empire in the world" to "the youngest nation on the globe." Burlingame, appointed by Lincoln as America's minister to China in 1861, had indicated his desire to resign his position, and on learning of this intention the Chinese government made him this remarkable offer. "It is a compliment which is without precedent probably," noted the *Boston Journal*, "for a foreign Government to select as its ambassador a representative of another country."[15] Compared with the other powers, the United States tended to be most solicitous of preserving Chinese sovereignty, in part due to its belief that nonintervention was the wisest course, but also increasingly due to the fear that the alternative was the breakup of the Chinese Empire and its partitioning by the European powers, a grim prospect that grew in probability in the 1890s. John Hay's Open Door notes in 1899 and 1900 reaffirmed the importance of both preserving China's administrative integrity and avoiding the parceling out of its territory into commercial spheres of influence, but the status quo these notes were designed to protect was visibly crumbling. It was challenged not only by the prospect that the European powers and Japan might partition China as the former had carved up Africa, but also by the universal Chinese belief that territorial dismemberment and the privileges accorded to foreign nationals, especially the greatly abused system of extraterritoriality, were outrages against the dignity of the Celestial Empire.

The dispatch of troops to China to protect endangered nationals and other Westerners from raging Chinese mobs (and also, though this was not admitted by the Western governments, from official Chinese forces) did not provoke anywhere near the controversy in the United States as the war in the Philippines. McKinley's decision to send troops was taken on his own authority and attested to the now expanded powers of the American presidency. The assertion of presidential power at the turn of the century demonstrated to an English observer that the presidency had become "neither more nor less than elective monarchy, limited as to duration, and regulated as to finance, but otherwise nearly unfettered. . . . The formless people when excited always hunger for a leader, and they get one."[16]

Comparatively speaking, U.S. forces behaved creditably in China and refused to join in the reckless punitive expedition proposed by Alfred von Waldersee, the German field marshal who became the Allied commander, but the western campaign as a whole was marked by much indiscriminate slaughter, with one official estimating that the western forces killed fifty ordinary Chinese for every Boxer after the fall of Peking. Tientsen and Peking were stripped bare by looters, who included the gleeful Western occupiers at the head of the pack.[17] "The Imperialist of to-day," noted Goldwin Smith, "when he attacks the weak, burns their homes, takes possession of their land, and if they 'rebel,' sends 'punitive expeditions against them,' laps himself in the delusion that he is the elect instrument of destiny, or if he is pious, of God. What is his 'destiny' or his 'God' but the shadow of his own rapacity projected on the clouds? What had destiny or God or anything but human greed to do with the atrocities perpetrated in China?" In the anti-imperialist reckoning, the influence of the American republic "must be greater if she stands aloof from European powers to whose aggressive attitude this uprising of Chinese nationality with its murderous consequences is due."[18]

Official U.S. policy justified the sending of troops as indispensably necessary to the protection of American nationals and tried with limited success to get European concurrence in the principles of the Open Door notes, but was otherwise impressed with the "inherent weakness" of the American position in China: "We do not want to rob China ourselves," wrote John Hay in 1900, "and our public opinion will not permit us to intervene, with an army, to prevent others from robbing her. Besides, we have no army. The talk of the papers about 'our preeminent moral position giving us the authority to dictate to the world' is mere flap-doodle."[19]

Writing at the same time from "the Wall Street point of view," Henry Clews noted that "China's reactionary defiance of the civilized world" had had important consequences: "The idea of a great union of civilized nations for mutual defense is rapidly developing in the minds of thoughtful people." Clews praised various contributors to this idea—Charles Beresford, George Clarke, Arthur Silva White, and Andrew Carnegie—but especially singled out Mahan for commendation. Mahan's "great apprehension of the future seems to be a possible inundation by countless hosts of outside barbarians, while he does not forget the inside ones in the shape of anarchists and socialists. He believes in the firm maintenance of the military system for accomplishing the highest objects of civilization." How, the author asked, did this accord "with the peace theory and the holding forth of the olive branch to the nations?" It was perfectly consistent, he answered: "Savages and barbarians bent on plunder do not understand anything about the significance of the olive branch until they are first made to feel the power behind it. Then they become docile." In order to accomplish the "great purpose" of making the barbarians "feel disposed to reason, so far as they are capable of reasoning," a "pacific alliance among all civilized nations, irrespective of language, will be an indispensable preliminary."[20]

34

Seward and the New Imperialism

ARE THE EVENTS OF 1898–1900 and the attendant striking displays of imperialism best seen as a "great aberration" or a "great culmination"? In the 1930s, diplomatic historian Samuel Flagg Bemis took the former view—an especially inviting judgment to make at that time, when public opinion was as anti-imperialist as it had ever been. While Bemis's view was not shared even at the time by maverick historians,[1] it was especially criticized by historians under the impact of the war in Vietnam and the rise of a "revisionist" school. The revisionists saw imperialism as much more emblematic of America's past. They argued, in particular, that the so-called new imperialism was really the great culmination of the vision of hemispheric and Pacific empire that had been unfolded by William Seward, who was for them "the central figure of nineteenth century American imperialism." Seward's commercial empire, writes one close student of his thought and diplomacy, Ernest Paolino, was simply the "large policy" of 1898, the vision of Roosevelt and Lodge that, as historian Julius Pratt described it, "aimed at no less than making the United States the indisputable dominant power in the western hemisphere, possessed of a great navy, owning and controlling an Isthmian canal, holding naval bases in the Caribbean and the Pacific, and contesting on at least even terms with the greatest powers, the naval and commercial supremacy of the Pacific Ocean and the Far East." On Paolino's view, "efforts to distinguish between expansionism as Seward is thought to have practiced it and the imperialism of the 1890's only serve to obscure rather than to illuminate the continuity of foreign policy from the 1860's to the 1890's." It was Seward's "new empire" that arose from the Civil War, writes another historian, that formed "the crucial incubation period of the America overseas empire" at the end of the nineteenth century.[2]

   The most striking continuity with the past is the reemergence in the "large policy" of the 1890s of the "Caribbean-Panama–Pacific Ocean relationship" that had been sketched out in the 1840s and 1850s by men such as William Gilpin, Asa Whitney, and Matthew Fontaine Maury. Since the emergence of a continental republic, the problem of linking the two coasts had excited attention on a transoceanic canal, with either Panama or Nicaragua as the most eligible sites. This in turn was seen to require strategic island fortresses and a navy that would guard the approaches and enjoy rapid communications between the coasts. The Philippines had never figured in this vision, but Cuba, Panama, Nicaragua, and Hawaii had definitely done so. These ideas, when they were first articulated in the 1840s and 1850s, looked both to national unification and to a revolution in the flows of trade, catapulting America to the summit of world commerce. Seward had shared in this vision and pursued policies looking toward expansion in every direction, though apart from Alaska without success. His treaty with Denmark for the acquisition of the Virgin Islands, enthusiastically supported by the 14,000 inhabitants, failed in the Senate, as did the 1867 Hawaiian reciprocity treaty. The consortium to build an isthmian canal was dissolving as he left office.[3]

Despite these continuities, the new imperialism represented a gross departure from Seward's vision. It would be extravagant to call the new imperialism an aberrant episode in American history. It was not the last time, or the first, that large swaths of the American people became bewitched with an imperialist ethos. In its implementation, the large policy of 1898 was, nevertheless, a severe distortion rather than culmination of the vision of empire held by Seward. The New Yorker may have been an imperialist—he spoke of empire often enough—but he was also a nationalist and a unionist; all these themes, somewhat miraculously, achieve an imaginative and brilliant expression in his thought. Those commitments conditioned one another and must be understood in relation to one another.

Seward was especially keen on the opening of Asia, for he foresaw that the lands washed by the Pacific Ocean would "become the chief theater of events in the world's great hereafter." America's great role in the future was to facilitate that transformation and to create a web of commerce binding Asia, America, and Europe. In his emphasis on commerce as the agent of renewal, however, Seward was much more a prophet of the 1990s than the 1890s; he gave sustained attention to the processes now known by the name of "globalization." The great destiny of the United States, which required a "Darien ship canal" and transcontinental railroads, was to "furnish a political alembic which, receiving the exhausted civilization of Asia and the ripening civilization of western Europe, and commingling them together . . . would disclose the secret of the ultimate regeneration and reunion of human society throughout the world."[4]

Seward's prophecies about the future course of American empire must be understood in light of his belief that commerce, rather than conquest, was to be the midwife of this "ultimate regeneration and reunion." Probably his most famous vision of the future came in 1853, when he exclaimed "that the borders of the federal republic . . . shall be extended so that it shall greet the sun when he touches the tropics, and when he sends his glancing rays toward the polar circle, and shall include even distant islands in either ocean; that our population, now counted by tens of millions, shall ultimately be reckoned by hundreds of millions; that our wealth shall increase a thousand fold, and our commercial connections shall be multiplied, and our political influence be enhanced in proportion with this wide development, and that mankind shall come to recognise in us a successor of the few great states which have alternately borne commanding sway in the world." If America could pre-serve its virtue, nothing was for Seward "more certain than the attainment of this future." It seemed "to be only a natural consequence of what has already been secured." A year later, in 1854, he bound union, nation, and empire together in the prophetic utterance in which he seemed to specialize. Intent on showing (quite mistakenly) that the union could not be broken and that neither North nor South would choose secession, Seward held that "political ties bind the Union together—a common necessity, and not merely a common necessity, but the common interests of empire—of such an em-pire as the world has never before seen. The control of the national power is the control of the great western continent; and the control of this con-tinent is to be in a very few years the controlling influence in the world."[5]

It is, however, emphatically clear that Seward did not imagine the unfold-ing of this "surpassingly comprehensive and magnificent" vision through military conquest, in either North America or elsewhere. He thought it in-evitable that Mexico and Canada would one day join the union but was equally insistent that the process not be rushed or the product of coercion. Of Mexico, he said in 1853: "Those states cannot govern themselves now; can they govern themselves better after they are annexed to the United States? No. Will you govern them? Pray, tell me how. By admitting them as equals, or by proconsular power?" Just as important as the forces leading to North American union, in Seward's view, was the manner in which it took place, which was of crucial significance in determining whether good or ill consequences would follow. None but ill consequences would follow unless annexation was by the free choice of both annexer and annexee. This vital condition, in turn, was a check upon a rushed or premature union that, unless handled carefully, could conceivably yield standing armies of occupa-tion or "the same disastrous drama of anarchy, civil war, desolation, and ruin at home" that afflicted Mexico.[6]

Seward's commitment to peace was profound. "The first want of every nation is peace, the last is peace. It wants peace always. So our forefathers understood the philosophy of government; for they established a system which dispensed with even the forces necessary for perfect defence, rather than cumber it with such as might tempt it to unnecessary collision with other states." Seward opposed the Mexican War. "I want no war," he said in 1846. "I want no enlargement of territory, sooner than it would come if we were contented with a 'masterly inactivity.' I abhor war, as I detest slavery. I would not give one human life for all the continent that remains to be *annexed*." Twenty years later, at the conclusion of the Civil War, he reiterated his long-standing advice: "I counsel no plans or schemes of military conquest. Not even the ancient plea of a necessity for the exhibition of our capacity for war remains. Wisdom, justice and moderation in the conduct of our foreign relations make it easy to acquire by peaceful negotiation, all the more than could be attainable by an unlawful aggression."[7]

In retrospect, it is evident that Seward underestimated the strong forces of resistance to forming a common political community that existed on both sides of the border. Racialism directed against the peoples of the South was too strong in the United States for these communities to enter on the basis of equality, and neither Mexicans nor Canadians showed much appetite for absorption into the American colossus. If it is remembered, however, that the idea of federal union proposed a limited national government, one that left the participating communities with profound discretion over their domestic affairs, the idea that these admittedly differently communities might come together and yet remain apart had a generous and enlightened aspect to it. It underscores the internationalist character of Seward's outlook and his resistance to conceptions identified more closely with either nationalism or imperialism, as does his belief that "exclusion of foreigners and hostility to foreign states always were elements of barbarism. The intermingling of races always was, and always will be, the chief element of civilization." Seward's vision of national greatness and of commercial empire—"which alone," he said, is "true empire"—relied on the powers of attraction, which "increases as commerce widens the circle of national influence." This vision, which Paolino calls Seward's "Law of Imperial Gravity," was not terribly different from Kant's notion of the expanding community of republics that was to form around "some great state." Seward's insistence that annexation could take place only through mutual consent makes his outlook as distant from imperialism as Kant's was from Napoleon Bonaparte's.[8]

Though Seward was not himself without the racial feeling of the time that exalted the Anglo-Saxon and looked downward at less enlightened peoples, he had much less of it than others. He was happy to welcome unlimited immigration from China and secured the Burlingame Treaty of 1868 that opened the gates of America's West Coast to Chinese laborers. The more intently racialist country of the 1880s and 1890s reversed this policy and excluded Chinese and Japanese immigration. Seward accepted the merit of the policy, "which acknowledges broadly the right of any people to work out its destiny freely and independently." His nephew George Seward, who was consul at Shanghai, identified that doctrine with "the advanced liberalism of the age." It was easy to stigmatize, the younger Seward allowed, but "the fact remains that one of the doctrines of the political faith of the age is that all intervention is harmful and should be avoided."[9]

Throughout his career, Seward insisted on the equality of all peoples as the essential framework for understanding the conduct of international relations. The philosophy of the American Constitution and the "supreme law" of the creation, he averred, "is necessarily based on the equality of nations of races and of men. . . . One nation, race, or individual, may not oppress or injure another, because the safety and welfare of each is essential to the common safety and welfare of all. If all are not equal and free, then who is entitled to be free, and what evidence of his superiority can he bring from nature or revelation?" Peace, in Seward's view, was dependent on mankind learning "the simple truth, that however birth or language or climate may have made them differ—however mountains, deserts, rivers, and seas, may divide states—the nations of the earth are nevertheless one family, and all mankind are brethren, practically equal in endowments, equal in national and political rights, and equal in the favor of the common Creator."[10] That was the language of the anti-imperialists of 1898–1900, the very text of George Hoar, who held that "the God who made of one blood all the nations of the world had made all the nations of the world capable of being influenced by the same sentiments and the same motives," of which none was more powerful than the proposition that "government derives its just powers from the consent of the governed." To back into the denial of this by invoking the eternal clash between the civilized and the barbarians followed the same route as the slaveholders had done as they had whittled away at Jefferson's doctrine in the Declaration of Independence.

Seward knew that litany well, and had followed out with Lincoln the implications of elevating the white race above all others in their possession of the right to freedom and self-government. Seward would have had difficulty recognizing the America that George Hoar confronted in 1902, when, after the defeat of Aguinaldo's forces, he summarized the grim record of the previous three years: "We changed the Monroe doctrine from a doctrine of eternal righteousness and justice, resting on the consent of the governed, to a doctrine of brutal selfishness looking only to our own advantage. We crushed the only republic in Asia. We made war on the only Christian people in the East. We converted a war of glory to a war of shame. We vulgarized the American flag. We introduced perfidy into the practice of war. We inflicted torture on unarmed men to extort confession. We put children to death. We established reconcentrado camps. We devastated provinces. We baffled the aspirations of a people for liberty."[11]

PART NINE
The New Internationalism Comes
and Goes

35

Before the Deluge

THE IDEA THAT THE AGE OF ISOLATION WAS OVER, and that the United States would have to take up an important role in world politics, was almost a commonplace at the dawn of the twentieth century. "The period of exclusiveness is past," declared President McKinley, in his last speech before being assassinated. Equally famous were Roosevelt's words: "We have no choice, we people of the United States, as to whether or not we shall play a great part in the world. That has been determined for us by fate, by the march of events. We have to play that part. All that we can decide is whether we shall play it well or ill." Roosevelt had no doubt that America's "proper place is with the great expanding peoples, with the peoples that dare to be great, that accept with confidence a place of leadership in the world."[1] What that calling would mean, however, was necessarily shrouded in mystery—an idea magically evoked in 1902 by Secretary of State John Hay, to whom it fell to memorialize the fallen president:

> Every young and growing people has to meet, at moments, the problems of its destiny. Whether the question comes, as in Thebes, from a sphinx, symbol of the hostile forces of omnipotent nature, who punishes with instant death our failure to understand her meaning; or whether it comes, as in Jerusalem, from the Lord of Hosts, who commands the building of His temple, it comes always with the warning that the past is past, and experience vain. "Your fathers, where are they? and the prophets, do they live forever?" The fathers are dead; the prophets are silent; the questions are new, and have no answer but in time.
>
> When the horny outside case which protects the infancy of a chrysalis nation suddenly bursts, and, in a single abrupt shock, it finds itself floating on wings which had not existed before, whose strength it has never tested, among dangers it can not foresee and is without experience to measure, every motion is a problem, and every hesitation may be an error. The past gives no clue to the future. The fathers, where are they? and the prophets, do they live forever? We are ourselves the fathers! We are ourselves the prophets! The questions that are put to us we must answer without delay, without help—for the sphinx allows no one to pass.[2]

The event that burst the horny outside case was the Spanish war, and imperialism was the answer given to the sphinx. By the time of Hay's address, however, the creature that emerged from the chrysalis did not seem nearly as lovely as initial appearances indicated. In the disappointments of the Philippines and the rousing popular opposition to England's fight against the Boers in South Africa, imperialism was discredited. Though William Howard Taft proved a capable and dedicated governor-general of the Philippines, an enlightened monarch to his "little brown brothers," by 1902 the American people not only had acquired "a distinct disinclination for further expansion but were inclined to regard the annexations we had already made as embarrassing liabilities."[3]

In the backwash from imperialism arose an enthusiastic public campaign for internationalism, which promoted a different conception of America's world role. Internationalists sought a new system of world politics that would realize the ancient dream of a peaceful world under the restraints of law. Internationalists were conscious that the world was turning into one social system, a web of interconnections in communications, trade, and technology that had never previously existed, which made the need for a new peace system all the more apparent. Public opinion seemed suddenly seized with the issue. "Great conferences were held annually; local societies sprang up all over the country; college presidents, clergymen, professors, teachers, club women, and community leaders by the hundreds" were drawn into the movement. "A rub-a-dub agitation once carried on in holes-in-walls became a national sensation which the most scornful politicians, even Theodore Roosevelt, could scarcely ignore."[4]

Running throughout the internationalist literature was the belief that the U.S. Constitution pointed the way toward the federation of the world. In the estimation of the internationalists, Hay was wrong: the fathers were not dead; the prophets were not silent. Benjamin Trueblood, the head of the American Peace Society, gave a full-throated rendition of the theme when he proclaimed, "The United States of America are the prefiguration and the first historical exemplification of what is sometime, in some form, to be the United States of the world, the result of which shall be universal and perpetual peace." Hamilton Holt, the editor of the *Independent*, was the most avid publicist of the idea. Though Holt began agitating for the federation of the world in 1904, his most eloquent statement came in 1914. The outbreak of war demonstrated the need, he believed, for "a great Confederation or League of Peace." He acknowledged that the "Federation of the World must still be a dream for many years to come" and would have to develop slowly, "step by step." But the "immediate establishment of a League of Peace" would constitute a "first step toward world federation" and did not, Holt thought, present "insuperable difficulties." It was the manifest destiny of the United States to lead in the establishment of such a League. . . . The United States is the world in miniature. The United States is the greatest league of peace known to history. The United States is a demonstration to the world that all the races and peoples of the earth can live in peace under one form of government, and its chief value to civilization is a demonstration of what this form of government is.

Prior to the formation "of a more perfect union" our original thirteen states were united in a confederacy strikingly similar to that now proposed on an international scale. They were obliged by the articles of this confederacy to respect each other's territory and sovereignty, to arbitrate all questions among themselves, to assist each other against any foreign foe, not to engage in war unless called upon by the confederation to do so or actually invaded by a foreign foe, and not to maintain armed forces in excess of the strength fixed for each state by all the states in congress assembled.[5]

Because of America's peculiar experience, wrote the internationalist William Hull, a professor at Swarthmore, "the great peaceful republic of the western hemisphere" was well fitted to take the lead in forming "a fraternal union between all the members of the family of nations." Such a union—"in which law and justice shall take the place of force and warfare, in which the smallest and the largest nation shall be on the same terms of equality before the law of nations, as are mighty Texas and 'Little Rhody' in the presence of the American Constitution"—would make "doubly dear to us the dear old flag." "The inclusion of forty-six commonwealths, some of which are like mighty empires in themselves, within a single political union; the enrollment within a single citizenship of men of every kindred, tongue and people; the peaceful residence, side by side, of men from every land and clime; and the maintenance of genuine local self-government"—such accomplishments of the American system gave the present generation "great hope and a great incentive" to realize this precious international ideal.[6]

One did not have to believe in the idea of a world state to find the parallel between American union and international union highly instructive. In fact, it entered broadly into all versions of internationalism; and it could easily strike the imagination of either a conservative Republican like William Howard Taft or a progressive socialist (as he then was) like Walter Lippmann. Throughout the Lake Mohonk conferences, which featured annual cogitations on internationalism, the "thought of the United States Supreme Court as the prototype of the federation of the world" was "dominant and pervasive." It received the apparent benediction of Theodore Roosevelt in his speech accepting the Nobel Peace Prize. Roosevelt noted "that the

Constitution of the United States, notably in the establishment of the Supreme
Court and in the methods adopted for securing peace and good relations
among and between the different States, offers certain valuable analogies
to what should be striven for in order to secure, through the Hague courts
and conferences, a species of world federation for international peace and
justice." Roosevelt acknowledged that there were "fundamental differences
between what the United States Constitution does and what we should even
attempt at this time to secure at The Hague," but still insisted on the utility
of the comparison: "The methods adopted in the American Constitution to
prevent hostilities between the States, and to secure the supremacy of the
Federal Court in certain classes of cases, are well worth the study of those
who seek at The Hague to obtain the same results on a world scale."[7]

President Taft was an especially keen supporter of arbitration and came
to believe that the wars of 1812, 1846, and 1898 had been unnecessary. "In
very few cases, if any, can the historian say that the good of war was worth
the awful sacrifice." His secretary of state, Philander C. Knox, concurred
with this idea and observed in a prewar commencement address that "we
have reached a point when it is evident that the future holds in store a time
when war shall cease: when the nations of the world shall realize a federation as real and vital as that now subsisting between the component parts
of a single state."[8]

Statements such as Knox's prophesying that war "shall cease" were much
ridiculed after war broke out in 1914. "Though a pacific nation," noted
one observer, America experienced in its first reaction to the war "a sudden revulsion against pacifism and Hague tribunals, as though it were the
pacifists who had brought on the war."[9] But though many American internationalists before the war were certainly guilty of an overly rosy portrait
of the then existing international system, making them wholly unprepared
for the cataclysm, some among them had well seen the dangers facing the
European system.[10] After all, the tremendous emphasis placed in the peace
movement on the need to arrest the armaments race reflected a sometimes
apocalyptic appreciation of the potential dangers. The most egregiously mis-
represented internationalist was the Anglo-American writer Norman Angell,
whose book *The Great Illusion* (1910) was widely attacked in subsequent
years as having argued that a great cataclysm was impossible. But Angell
argued nothing of the kind: his argument was "*not* that war is impossible,
but that it is futile." Angell described on ongoing struggle for military and
commercial predominance undertaken in the mistaken belief that wealth
could be procured by conquest, giving expression to a traditional liberal
objection to the war system voiced by such eighteenth-century luminaries
as Adam Smith and Josiah Tucker. But Angell also forecast "the likelihood

of an Anglo-German explosion" and thought "the pacifist effort then current was evidently making no headway at all against the tendencies towards rivalry and conflict." Such tendencies were "'so profoundly mischievous' and so 'desperately dangerous,' as to threaten civilization itself." On the essential points, the war confirmed his ominous prognostication.[11]

Even the figure, Benjamin Trueblood, against whom a verdict of idealistic utopianism might summarily be reached, pulled no wool over his eyes when surveying the tendencies of the then-existing international system. Trueblood's analysis ended with a prophecy of the triumph of Christian brotherhood, but he also saw the acute danger that the European system might descend into paroxysms of violence in the interim. Just when Roosevelt was insisting that wars among civilized nations were becoming "rarer and rarer," Trueblood noted that the "utterly inhuman system of militarism" had continued to grow "until it stands to-day, in appalling magnitude, fortified to heaven in the very heart of civilization. . . . There is no tyranny of our time like that which it exercises; no blinding of conscience and paralysis of will greater than that which it produces. Year after year the armies grow and the fleets expand. Year after year the war debts rise and the screw of taxation is turned down mercilessly another thread. Science is incessantly tortured in the hope of wringing from her some new death-dealing instrument, which will give one nation advantage over others." The technological dangers facing mankind were novel, but there was nothing new, in Trueblood's opinion, with this behavior. "The one feature of history, standing out above all others, has been the hating, quarreling and mutual destruction practiced by men of all ages and of all climes. This kind of history is still making itself." It had to end, Trueblood believed, and it would end with the ultimate acceptance throughout the world of the fellowship of Christ. He was just as certain, however, that it had not ended as yet. The reign of the war system continued. "The cup of its iniquity is not yet full, it seems."[12]

The prewar internationalist movement was extremely heterogeneous. One set of divisions concerned the degree of authority that needed to be vested in a world body. A handful—"the federalists"—took the view that this would require an apparatus of state control like that which existed in the American Constitution, with executive, legislative, and judicial branches. At the other end of the spectrum were pacifists who were opposed to sanctions of any kind save the moral and beneficent influence of public opinion.

The politically dominant approach—the legalists—fell in the middle of these two poles. In American time, their proposals were a long way from 1787 and fell well short even of the Articles of Confederation, but the legalists were nevertheless inching toward some kind of confederal arrangement. They were enthusiastic about creating a world court that would be empowered to hear justifiable disputes among the nations and looked to the Hague Conferences, at the first of which in 1899 a Permanent Court of Arbitration had been created, to take the next step along that road. They celebrated America's long record in utilizing arbitration as a method of diplomacy and pointed proudly to the Jay Treaty, the Rush-Bagot agreement demilitarizing the Great Lakes, and the Alabama Claims as part of that successful record. But Americans were not all of one mind over what sort of disputes were fit subjects of an arbitral panel. Roosevelt and Lodge opposed Taft's arbitration treaties of 1911 for their failure to carve out a sufficiently broad scope for national decision in matters concerning honor or vital interest—anything, in fact, that might actually prompt a war—and only emasculated versions of the arbitration treaties survived encounter with the U.S. Senate. Taft, furious with Roosevelt, refused to sign them. ("The truth is," Taft wrote, Roosevelt "believes in war and wishes to be a Napoleon and to die on the battlefield. He has the spirit of the old Berserkers.") Disappointment over arbitration, however, did not seem cause for great pessimism. "Leg over leg the dog went to Dover," emphasized Elihu Root. It was in keeping with the gradualist and meliorist character of the American philosophy that progress would take time. The important thing was to start walking along the road.[13]

Internationalists also divided on the question of who might be a fit partner of the United States in an enterprise intended to foster peace. Conservative internationalists looked toward a much closer relationship—perhaps even a grand reunion—with Great Britain, whereas progressive internationalists looked askance at the British Empire and, more generally, at the imperialist practices of the European powers. This had been an important division in 1900 in the debate over imperialism, and it would be a vital division in 1920 in the debate over internationalism and collective security. From the 1890s onward, the possibility of some kind of reunion between Great Britain and the United States excited intellectuals on both sides of the Atlantic. In 1905, anticipating the strategic basis of the two world wars, Henry Adams warned that "if Germany breaks down England or France, she becomes the centre of a military world, and we are lost." The only remedy was "to support France against Germany, and fortify an Atlantic system beyond attack." To his bewilderment, Adams wrote in the summer of 1917, the great object of his life had been accomplished "in the building up of the great community of Atlantic Powers." The English journalist-reformer W. T. Stead called for such a federation of the English-speaking peoples in 1902; indeed, most of Britain's "imperial federalists," driven by the haunting fear that Britain would be outclassed by the Continental-sized states, would have been delighted to accommodate a willing United States into a yet larger imperial federation.[14]

Andrew Carnegie, whose philanthropy watered many branches of the peace movement in the prewar years, had prophesied the rapid emergence of an Anglo-American reunion in the 1890s. Though he was disappointed in that expectation, the special relationship between the United States and Great Britain nevertheless became a factor in diplomacy. The Venezuelan crisis of 1895, which aught for the fine arts of British appeasement could have resulted in a war, was sobering to all concerned, and in its aftermath grew the conviction that war between the two great English-speaking countries was absurd and unthinkable. "There is a patriotism of race as well as of country," remarked Olney. It forbade such internecine conflict. The more that internationalism emphasized cooperation with England, to be sure, the more it could appear as simply a variant of nationalism. The completion of the project, if it were completed, would simply represent one more nationalism and could not offer itself as a solution to the nationality problem. The legalists, nevertheless, believed that the pattern of British-American relations served as an illuminating template for the extension of the practice of arbitration to the larger world of international relations.[15]

There was, however, a powerful strand of American opinion that looked with hostility to Great Britain. British professions of altruism and civilization received thunderous guffaws from Irish Americans and German Americans. Among many progressive internationalists, too, the world community they were beginning to visualize did not have cooperation between the United States and Great Britain at its centerpiece. It was a distinctive feature of progressive internationalism to argue that global interdependence was creating new "publics" who were mutually implicated in the consequences of interdependence, requiring new forms of international governance well beyond and in potential conflict with bilateral alliance. Finally, there was a powerful tendency among progressive internationalists to conceive of a new world order in terms of the impartial application of universal rules, and that more principled conception of internationalism was in tension with those forms that looked to buttress relationships with particular states.[16]

36

"Great Utterance" and Madisonian Moment

THOUGH IT WOULD BE POSSIBLE TO IDENTIFY ANTECEDENTS to all the forms of internationalism that prevailed after the onset of the Great War, the breaking of the dam in August 1914 "changed everything." It inundated pleasing expectations of inevitable progress and showed the vital necessity of devising a new system for the preservation of peace. At the outset, the near-universal reaction of Americans was that the country needed to stay out of the conflict. They luxuriated behind the walls of their federal union, reflected on the superiority of American to European institutions, marveled at the sheer stupidity of Europe's self-destruction. The war showed everything that was wrong with Europe, and everything that was right with the United States. Americans, as Walter Weyl commented, did not at the outbreak of war "put ourselves in the place of the fighting nations and acknowledge that in their circumstances we too might have been struggling in the dust. Rather, we boasted of our restraining democracy, and of our perfect co-operative union, which protected us from European anarchy."[1] At the same time, the outbreak of war confirmed the argument of those who had insisted that the old system was utterly dysfunctional in its purported aims of providing security and welfare to each of the striving nations. Once the accumulating armaments and poisoned relations of the European powers had yielded the vast cataclysm, and anarchy was no longer simply a theoretical expression but a living reality, the search was on for a new method of organizing international relations: "Here was an argument more persuasive than a thousand sermons, a demonstration that the deaf could hear and the blind could read."[2]

The most notable group after 1914 that organized itself in the United States on behalf of the league idea was the League to Enforce Peace, founded in 1915. Following up on the proposals for courts, the codification of international law, and arbitration prevalent in the prewar period, it advanced the cause one notch by allowing for forcible sanctions against a nation that refused to submit itself to arbitration. Under its proposals, the nations would submit their justifiable disputes to a council of conciliation for investigation and report, leaving to public opinion the enforcement of the decision of the court and the report of the council. This was a remarkably limited program; it did not threaten force against the state that, having shown up for its court date, nevertheless went ahead and launched a war. The result, according to one observer, was "a league to make war in order to secure a certain delay before war is made." Basically, the idea was to demand that the potential combatants meet in arbitration while reserving to public opinion and moral influences the enforcement of decisions.[3]

A more vigorous conception came, as usual, from Theodore Roosevelt, who in his first major statement on the war argued that "surely the time ought to be ripe for the nations to consider a great world agreement among all the civilized military powers *to back righteousness by force*." Roosevelt had suggested a similar idea in his 1910 Nobel address, noting then that the "power to command peace throughout the world could best be assured by some combination between those great nations which sincerely desire peace and have no thought themselves of committing aggressions." Nor had Henry Cabot Lodge rejected the league idea. In his Union College address in June 1915, Lodge had spoken of a "union of civilized nations in order to put a controlling force behind the maintenance of peace and international order." A year later, Lodge held, "I do not believe that when Washington warned us against entangling alliances he meant for one moment that we should not join the other civilized nations of the world if a method could be found to diminish war and encourage peace."[4]

Lodge made this latter declaration in a speech to the League to Enforce Peace on May 27, 1916. He shared the platform that day with former president William Howard Taft and sitting president Woodrow Wilson, who chose the occasion to issue his famous call for American participation in a new league of nations. The stage was not fully set, the destiny fully disclosed, in Wilson's "great utterance," but Wilson himself believed that the speech was the most important he had ever been called upon to make. Hamilton Holt told Wilson in its aftermath that it "cannot fail to rank in political importance with the Declaration of Independence and the Monroe Doctrine." "We believe these fundamental things," Wilson declared: "First, that every people has a right to choose the sovereignty under which they shall live. . . . Second, that the small states of the world have a right to enjoy the same respect for their sovereignty and for their territorial integrity that great and powerful nations expect and insist upon. And third, that the world has a right to be free from every disturbance of its peace that has its origin in aggression and disregard of the rights of peoples and nations." The United States, Wilson proclaimed, "was willing to become a partner in any feasible association of nations formed in order to realize these objects and make them secure against violation."[5]

It was the woe unleashed by the Great War of 1914 that made it necessary to invent a new peace system, but Wilson maintained his characteristic detachment from the then-raging hurricane: "With its causes and its objects we are not concerned. The obscure fountains from which its stupendous flood has burst forth we are not interested to search for or explore." Though Wilson portrayed Americans as "in no sense or degree parties to the present quarrel," he thought them fully aware that they must become full partners to the world in the war's aftermath. That required a "new and more wholesome diplomacy" in which right took precedence over "the individual interests of particular nations." Henceforth, "alliance must not be set up against alliance," but "there must be a common agreement for a common object," the heart of which was "the inviolable rights of peoples and of mankind." To secure these objects the United States must be prepared to join "an universal association of the nations to maintain inviolate the security of the highway of the seas for the common and unhindered use of all the nations of the world, and to prevent any war begun either contrary to treaty covenants or without warning and full submission of the causes to the opinion of the world,—a virtual guarantee of territorial integrity and political independence." Summarizing the message, the *New Republic* noted that the United States had said to the nations: "You may count on us to employ our power to curb any nation which attempts to destroy the peace you organize."[6]

This embrace of international union, though doubtless of great historical significance, was still limited and conditional: Wilson's desire to stay out of the war was genuine, and he assumed, as did most advocates of the League to Enforce Peace, that America would join such an association only after the conclusion of the European war. All attempts by Viscount Grey, the British foreign secretary, to pin Wilson down to a definitive guarantee to threaten war on behalf of a moderate settlement were unsuccessful. The United States, Wilson replied, would "probably" do so.[7] Republican leaders, moreover, continued to speak in tones of the most unvarnished nationalism, denouncing the "professional internationalists" in vitriolic terms. After the 1916 election, the *New Republic* found it absurd that Roosevelt and Lodge should join hands with William Borah and Albert Cummins in defense of American nationalism. "From every platform and editorial desk [the Republican Party] has been telling the country that it was the party of national responsibility and international purpose. The Democrats were negative, irresponsible, without policy, and blind to the facts of the modern world. Yet to-day it is a Democratic President who grasps the truth that isolation is over and strives to guide our entrance into world politics towards stability and safety. It is the Republican party which proposes to crouch at its own fireside, build a high tariff wall, arm against the whole world, cultivate no friendships, take no steps to forestall another great war, and then let things rip. The party which was inspired by the idea of American union is becoming a party of secession and states' rights as against world union."[8]

That precocious interpretation was right on the mark. Despite the seeming consensus among Roosevelt, Lodge, and Wilson on American participation in a league of nations, nationalism and internationalism were gearing up to fight the battle that had previously unfolded over the federal union. The two great political parties had switched roles: the Democrats, having previously been "the party of secession and states' rights," were now the party of international union, whereas the Republicans were executing the reverse maneuver. One side in this great conflict would speak of commitments that had to be made and rights that could only be vindicated in common; the other side of preserving "rights which ought not to be infringed" and refusing "obligations which might not be kept."[9] For the internationalists, the impossibility of isolation in an interdependent world meant that the nation was thrown back into the predicament facing the founders: it confronted an anarchy that would produce despotism unless arrested by a union. Nationalists did not entirely reject that analysis, but they were adamantly opposed to the commitments that Wilson would come to regard as indispensable. "Wilson has hoisted the motley flag of internationalism," wrote Beveridge. "That makes the issue, does it not?"[10]

The polar tendencies might be, and were, seen as a conflict between "idealism" and "realism"—"the eternal dispute between those who imagine the world to suit their policy, and those who arrange their policy to suit the realities of the world"—but the internationalists insisted that they represented a higher realism much more in tune with world realities than the hidebound proponents of national exertion.[11] Rather than a contest between realism and idealism, the dispute is better seen as the old wine of "union and independence" in the new bottles of internationalism and nationalism. Just as union had been necessary to secure the independence of the American states, so now the league of free peoples or partnership of democratic nations was necessary to secure the nation.

Both nationalism and internationalism had proponents who looked with utter scorn and contempt upon the other. There were many internationalists who shared the view of H. G. Wells (himself a cosmopolitan and a supranationalist) regarding the deficiencies of nationalism. Wells loathed it for its parochialism, egocentricity, and intolerance, because it "trumpets and waves its flags, obtrudes its tawdry loyalties, exaggerates the splendors of the past, and fights to sustain the ancient hallucinations."[12] There were, by the same token, great numbers of nationalists who viewed the internationalist project as a sort of large-scale and brazen identity theft. Both main tendencies or ideologies, however, were sufficiently important and powerful that the task of practical political intelligence became not elevating one to the utter exclusion of the other but showing how in a new relationship they could be made compatible and thus provide for freedom, security, justice, and welfare.

In keeping with this unwanted but intimate relationship, each of the forces would sometimes bow to the principle of the other: nationalists would say kind words about a strictly interpreted internationalism, and internationalists would pledge that the entire enterprise was necessary if the national interest were not to be compromised. Nor were these unreasonable postures. To push either variable too far might collapse the whole structure upon itself. Too tight a union would threaten independence; too much independence in the parts would destroy the union. That was at the core of the "Madisonian moment" in 1787; it had now recurred. What Lord Bryce had called the dilemma of federation—how "to keep the centrifugal and centripetal forces in equilibrium so that neither the planet States shall fly off into space nor the sun of the Central government draw them into its consuming fires"— was now the exquisite predicament into which America and the world were thrust by the Great War. There was one dramatic change in the terms of the paradigm: nationalism now signified the "lower" loyalty whereas previously it had signaled the "higher" one. In crucial respects, however, it was the same argument, now to be deployed to navigate a world arrayed "into larger and more complex aggregates."[13]

37

Safe for Democracy

DESPITE AN EARNEST DESIRE TO STAY OUT of the European war, the existence of the raging inferno on the old continent quickly drew the United States into a posture where the choice for war or peace rested with decisions made in Europe. This sequence followed the logic that had led to war in 1812, with the belligerents sorely tempted to violate the laws of neutrality if it afforded them a significant advantage, and the United States left with strong complaints against both sides. With important commercial interests at stake—both in exports of cotton from the southern states and in loans extended to Britain and France—Wilson's administration acquiesced in England's violations of neutral rights but took a stiff line toward Germany's. In 1915, Wilson exacted a pledge from Germany that it would rein in the submarine. Once German leaders, rolling the dice, decided to risk American belligerency by declaring unrestricted submarine warfare, Wilson was trapped by the logic of his previous positions and had no alternative but to ask Congress for a declaration of war.[1]

The war address was another thrilling performance by Wilson; it moved even Lodge to tears. Wilson himself had sobbed uncontrollably after the full weight of the inevitability of war had sunk in. He unburdened himself to the newspaperman Frank Cobb on the eve of the war address: "Once lead this people into war . . . and they'll soon forget there ever was such a thing as tolerance. To fight you must be brutal and ruthless, and the spirit of ruthless brutality will enter into the very fibre of our national life."[2] Wilson adverted to these fears in his war address. He was fully aware of "the solemn and even tragical character of the step" he advised and called it a "fearful thing" to lead America "into the most terrible and disastrous of all wars, civilization itself seeming to be in the balance." But Germany had "swept every restriction aside" in its war on the seas; its "submarine warfare against commerce is a warfare against mankind." Neutrality was no longer possible in those circumstances. "Neutrality is no longer feasible or desirable where the peace of the world is involved and the freedom of its peoples, and the menace to that peace and freedom lies in the existence of autocratic governments backed by organized force which is controlled wholly by their will, not by the will of their people." Wilson pledged "the utmost practicable cooperation in counsel and action with the governments now at war with Germany" and urged extension to them "of the most liberal financial credits, in order that our resources may so far as possible be added to theirs."[3]

Though now in the war, the objects of America had not changed: before and after entry, "our object . . . is to vindicate the principles of peace and justice in the life of the world as against selfish and autocratic power and to set up among the really free and self-governed peoples of the world such a concert of purpose and of action as will henceforth insure the observance of those principles." In thus promising to fight "for the ultimate peace of the world and for the liberation of its peoples, the German peoples included," Wilson declared: "The world must be made safe for democracy. Its peace must be planted upon the tested foundations of political liberty." Just as democracy would bring peace in the future, it was autocracy that had led to the war. It was not upon "the impulse of the German people that their government acted in entering this war. It was not with their previous knowledge or approval. It was a war determined upon as wars used to be determined upon in the old, unhappy days when peoples were nowhere consulted by their rulers and wars were provoked and waged in the interest of dynasties or of little groups of ambitious men who were accustomed to use their fellow-men as pawns and tools. Self-governed nations do not fill their neighbor states with spies or set the course of intrigue to bring about some critical posture of affairs which will give them an opportunity to strike and make conquest." Such "cunningly contrived plans of deception or aggression" were only possible "within the privacy of courts or behind the carefully guarded confidences of a narrow and privileged class."[4]

Despite Wilson's insistence that his thought had remained the same before and after the decision for war, he had changed in two outstanding respects. Both in his understanding of neutrality and in his larger identification of the causes of the war with German autocracy, the positions he took in April 1917 were very different from preceding views, and both transitions bear closely on the nature of the internationalism that Wilson now put forth as the salvation of the world.

Wilson's war address in 1917 actually marks the peculiar moment when the older and newer conceptions of neutrality stood side by side, eyeing each other warily but without full comprehension of their mutual incompatibility. The immediate justification and cause of America's entry was to vindicate its own grievously wounded rights as a neutral, but the war aims it announced included a league of nations that could function successfully only if neutrality were consigned to the past as a barbarous relic. "A league to enforce peace," as Roosevelt put it, "is merely another name for a league to abolish neutrality in every possible war."[5] So successful were the attacks on neutrality in the twentieth century that it is difficult to recapture the ways in which neutrality in the nineteenth century was considered an honored feature of the society of states—a vital point in understanding the evolution of internationalism.

Neutrality cannot be understood simply as the desire to "stay out of other people's quarrels," though it was that in part. It is also a legal institution recognizing certain rights and duties among belligerents and neutrals by which the society of states traditionally regulated its conflicts. The traditional doctrine, to which Americans made an important contribution, accepted that wars would occur but attempted to confine their consequences, so far as was possible, to the belligerents themselves. The rational arrangement, as Jefferson expressed it, was that "the wrong which two nations endeavor to inflict on each other, must not infringe on the rights or conveniences of those remaining at peace." It would be monstrous, he said, to prefer the alternative conception—"that the rights of nations remaining quietly in the exercise of moral and social duties, are to give way to the convenience of those who prefer plundering and murdering each other." Wilson's program of collective security stood foursquare against the older conception, but both were conceptions of the society of states. They both sought to keep the dreaded specter of all-out, universal war as a passing nightmare and not as a living reality; the means they proposed, nevertheless, were 180 degrees opposite. The older conception was that those making war were not, at the same time, to make a pest of themselves. Neutrality allowed states, by opting out, to continue their normal errands and preserve an ocean of peace amid islands of war. The new conception was that war was everybody's business; all states had to be prepared to "get in" if the peace were to be maintained.[6]

A change of emphasis also came in Wilson's evaluation of the relationship between democracy and peace. Before American entry, he had sometimes mused "that no people ever went to war with another people. Governments have gone to war with one another. Peoples . . . have not." At the same time, he did not identify the struggle taking place between the Central powers and the Allies as fundamentally involving the principles of democracy. During the period of American neutrality from 1914 to 1917, he tended rather to stress the structural causes of the European predicament, and indeed to look upon the competing pretensions of the Central powers and the allied coalition in terms suggestive of a kind of moral equivalence. "In the last resort," he had held, "the deeper responsibility for the war is borne by the whole European system, its combination of alliances and understandings, a complicated web of intrigue and espionage which inevitably caught the whole family of peoples in its meshes."[7]

Wilson was equally clear in his conviction that neither German militarism nor British navalism, if victorious in the war, would hold out the promise of an enduring peace. It was Wilson's secretary of state, Robert Lansing, who pressed upon the president the view that the war was a giant struggle between autocracy and democracy; but Wilson remained, for the moment at least, unconvinced: The "amazing thing to me," Lansing wrote in a confidential memorandum prepared in September 1916, "is that the President does not see this. In fact he does not seem to grasp the full significance of this war or the principles at issue. I have talked it over with him, but the violation of American rights by both sides seems to interest him more than the vital interests as I see them. That German imperialistic ambitions threaten free institutions everywhere apparently has not sunk very deeply into his mind. For six months I have talked about the struggle between Autocracy and Democracy, but do not see that I have made any great impression. However I shall keep on talking."[8]

Since the outbreak of war in 1914, Britain and France had been declaiming against German aggression and had defined their war effort in terms of opposition to German militarism. To them, Wilson had appeared in 1916, when he pledged to join a league after the war, like a fireman who promised unstinting cooperation in dousing the flames of a house to be built in the future, but who offered little to no assistance in preventing the then-existing structure from burning to the ground. To the Allied powers, there was no possibility of peace until Prussian militarism, "this system which places Force above Right and denies all international morality, has been defeated."[9] To the disgust of British opinion, Wilson had resisted this analysis for two and a half years; now suddenly he had not only caught up with the British conception but seemed to have lapped it. The new catechism was that the causes of war stemmed from the internal character of governments; that autocracies were warlike and incapable of keeping faith; that democracies were pacific and, by virtue of their dependence on public opinion, bound to keep their word.

As different as these explanations for the causes of war are—one stressing the internal character of states, the other the structural predicament of the anarchical European system—they were actually joined in Wilson's conception of a partnership of democratic nations and in his idea of a world made safe for democracy. Wilson accepted the peaceableness of peoples but did not embrace any theory of the automatic cooperation of democracies; their native hatred of war did not produce peace by itself but required them to be tied in solemn vows and organized in union. Wilson's conception of a world made safe for democracy, moreover, was not aggressive. It was Wilson's critics who charged upon him the absurd ambition of making all the world's governments democratic, but Wilson and his defenders repudiated the implication. "I am not fighting for democracy except for the peoples that want democracy," Wilson remarked in 1918. "If they don't want it, that is none of my business."[10]

A world made safe for democracy was a peaceful world in which liberal democracy could show its superiority to other forms of government and economy. Such a world, if it were to organize itself successfully against the possibility of an utter breakdown of international law and order, had to be one in which the democracies cooperated with one another in the achievement of goals they had in common, above all the preservation of their political independence and the assurance of civilized intercourse. This was an essentially conservative conception that registered appropriate horror at the novel destructiveness of war and sought through new institutions the realization of the very values of independence and amity that underlay the old law of nations. It did not authorize beginning a war for the purpose of changing the political institutions of another people; on the contrary, it forbade it. Its dominating impulse was to restrict, rather than expand, the various justifications that might be entertained (of which overthrowing despots and establishing democracy by force is but one) for resolving national differences through war.

Though Wilson is remembered today as a militant crusader for democracy, his Caribbean and Latin American policy conforms meagerly to the stereotype. In his interventions in Haiti and the Dominican Republic in 1915 and 1916, strategic considerations were probably decisive. The assassination of the Haitian president by a mob, itself the culmination of years of disorder, provoked Wilson to "take the bull by the horns" and intervene. The occupying U.S. military demanded a protectorate and control of the customs, but when the Haitian legislature refused these changes, notes one historian, the United States "adjourned the legislature and kept it adjourned for the next thirteen years." The occupation regime also "revived forced labor, enacted press censorship, removed restrictions on land ownership by foreigners, and introduced overt racial segregation." As Theodore Roosevelt noted in 1918, it was difficult to judge whether the administration's actions in the island were right or wrong because Wilson, with his "usual horror of publicity" and his "inveterate predilection for secret and furtive diplomacy," had kept most of the facts hidden. But one fact, Roosevelt noted, was apparent: "We have with armed force invaded, made war upon, and conquered the two small republics, have upset their governments, have denied them the right of self-determination, and have made democracy within their limits not merely unsafe but non-existent."[11]

It was in Mexico especially that Wilson took up the cause of "good government" for Latin America. At the outset of his first administration, Wilson had no thought of military intervention in Latin America: he wanted, like the professor that he was, to "teach" the South American republics to elect good men. But he was drawn, against his inclinations, into Mexico's internal politics by his refusal to recognize General Victoriano Huerta, who came to power in early 1913 and shortly thereafter murdered his predecessor, Francisco Madero. Wilson styled his effort to overthrow Huerta as a defense of constitutional government, "to secure peace and order in Central America by seeing to it that the processes of self-government there are not interrupted or set aside." The United States, he pledged, would "discredit and defeat such usurpations" as Huerta's "whenever they occur." Wilson intended to isolate Huerta completely and to force him out, and he warned the powers that if these measures were insufficient, "it will become the duty of the United States to use less peaceful means to put him out."[12]

Wilson's policy, as State Department counselor John Bassett Moore complained at the time, was a departure from the previous de facto recognition policy followed by the United States (which accorded recognition to those who gained "possession of the nation's goods"). But Wilson's refusal to recognize Huerta had special justification because of the unconscionable role that Taft's ambassador, Henry Lane Wilson, had played in Huerta's elevation and Madero's murder. President Wilson, who was horrified at the "government of butchers" and who reprobated the acts of Taft's ambassador and the rest of the European diplomatic corps in Mexico City, believed that Huerta had been brought to power in an externally driven coup and that his only hope of survival was support from Britain and Germany. In Wilson's mind, his confrontation with Huerta began not only as a defense of constitutional government but also as a case of counterintervention to even the scales against the unjust intervention of other powers. As such, the case fell within the Monroe Doctrine, which Wilson proved just as ready to enforce as his predecessors.

The odd feature of Wilson's Mexican policy lay in his simultaneous commitment to Mexican self-determination and his no less determined effort to intervene in Mexico's affairs. Even after he had succeeded in ousting Huerta, in which the U.S. occupation and blockade of Vera Cruz played an important role, he demanded from Venustiano Carranza, the "first chief" who succeeded Huerta, good treatment of foreign nationals, domestic opponents, and church officers as the price of recognition. He reminded Carranza that, with Europe at war, the absence of U.S. recognition (and the consequent denial of credit) meant the speedy breakdown of any Mexican government. Just eight days later, however, Wilson sharply rebuked his secretary of war, Lindley M. Garrison, for suggesting a military intervention in

Mexico's interior: "We shall have no right at any time to intervene in Mexico to determine the way in which the Mexicans are to settle their own affairs." Though many things might happen of which the United States might disapprove, there were in Wilson's view "no conceivable circumstances which would make it right for us to direct by force or by threat of force the internal processes of what is a profound revolution, a revolution as profound as that which occurred in France."[13]

Who, then, was the real Wilson? The zealous proponent of intervention for constitutional government? The zealous opponent of intervention in the name of self-determination? Or the stern taskmaster and segregationist who imposed a news blackout on Hispaniola and erected an arbitrary despotism right next door? The latter Wilson is, one supposes, best forgotten. The one remembered today is the one who, in 1913 and 1914, pledged to refuse recognition to governments that set aside constitutional processes in Central America and who affirmed that cooperation was possible only "when supported at every turn by the orderly processes of just government based upon law, not upon arbitrary and irregular force." That, too, was a real Wilson, for he never departed from his belief "that just government rests always upon the consent of the governed." But the Wilson that came to dominate was the one who, chastened by his Mexican holiday, concluded that the Mexicans would have to fight it out among themselves and that the American role would be limited to marginal pressures from the sidelines.[14]

"If the Mexicans want to raise hell," he remarked in 1915, "let them raise hell. We have got nothing to do with it. It is their government, it is their hell." He was willing to chase Pancho Villa deep into Mexico in 1916, after the revolutionary leader turned bandit shot up Columbus, New Mexico, but he stoutly opposed military intervention to protect American property rights or to avenge harm to the some 50,000 American nationals in Mexico, which many Republicans were urging. Wilson, as Walter Lippmann observed, "understood that the problem of order in Mexico was deeper than the question of armed protection of American property and lives, that permanent stability and progress could never be attained by intervention, and that Mexico would never be a good neighbor until the Mexicans had achieved a measure of self-government. Conquest would merely mean decades of insurrection against the American conqueror, and a perversion not only of Mexico's life but our own. There was no peace to be had by intervention or by the establishment of Huerta."[15]

Entry into the European war did not change these convictions, and Wilson resisted the strong pressures to intervene in Mexico (emanating from his own State Department) that arose after the conclusion of the armistice in

Europe. He applied the same ideas to the Russian Revolution: "My policy regarding Russia is very similar to my Mexican policy. I believe in letting them work out their own salvation, even though they wallow in anarchy for a while." American diplomats and military officers resident in Russia were not so punctilious as Wilson, and a number intervened happily and readily against the Bolsheviks, but Wilson's idea of what he was doing is important and reveals a vital component of his international thought.[16]

38

The Liberal Peace Program Goes to Paris

AMERICA'S ENTRY INTO THE WAR OVERCAME the anomalous situation in which Wilson had seemed to promise to back the peace the European powers organized. It was a moral and political impossibility that Americans should ratify any settlement apart from the merits as they saw them. As Wilson observed in his "peace without victory" address of January 22, 1917, "So far as our participation in guarantees of future peace is concerned, it makes a great deal of difference in what way and upon what terms [the war] is ended." With entry into the war the United States would now be in a position to greatly influence the terms. Wilson believed that American influence would be at its pinnacle during the peace negotiations. Though this was not his motive for entering the war, he was optimistic that the allied states would all be in his power. Wilson unfolded his vision of the liberal peace program both before and after American entry, in his January 1917 address to the Senate and then more fully in his "Fourteen Points" speech of January 1918. "Open covenants openly arrived at," though first among the Fourteen Points, was last in terms of significance, for Wilson made clear soon enough that this meant only no more secret treaties and did not forbid secrecy in negotiation. There was also less than met the eye to Wilson's invocation of the "freedom of the seas," his second point, for that principle was qualified to the point of nonexistence by his simultaneous insistence on the idea that resistance to aggression must displace neutrality as the architectonic concept of the society of states. The critical elements of the liberal peace program lay instead with the following goals:

- A peace without victory and among equals that would not be forced upon the loser. A harsh peace would leave "a sting, a resentment, a bitter memory upon which terms of peace would rest, not permanently, but only as upon quicksand." A peace settlement should not injure or block Germany from exercising "her legitimate influence or power"— but Germany must accept "a place of equality . . . instead of a place of mastery." The war was directed against the "German Imperialists," not the German people.

- "Justice to all peoples and nationalities, and their right to live on equal terms of liberty and safety with one another, whether they be strong or weak"—what subsequently became known as the right of national self-determination. That meant a territorial settlement ensuring an independent Polish state with guaranteed borders and access to the sea, the evacuation and restoration of Belgium, a settlement of the colonial question that made the interest of the populations concerned of "equal weight with the equitable claims of the government whose title is to be determined," and the adjustment of Italy's borders and recognition in the peoples of Russia, Austro-Hungary, and the Balkan States of a right to autonomous development along historically established lines of allegiance and nationality. Every people, Wilson declared, "should be left free to determine its own polity, its own way of development, unhindered, unthreatened, unafraid, the little along with the great and powerful." "No peace can last, or ought to last, which does not recognize and accept the principle that governments derive all their just powers from the consent of the governed, and that no right anywhere exists to hand peoples about from sovereignty to sovereignty as if they were property."

- The removal of economic barriers and the establishment of equality of trade for those nations associating themselves with the maintenance of the peace, allowing to each nation "free access to the open paths of the world's commerce."

- The reduction of armaments to the "lowest point consistent with domestic safety."

- The establishment of a general association of nations in which the members would make mutual guarantee of the political independence and territorial integrity of the league members. Political independence was to be "absolute in domestic matters, limited in external affairs only by the rights of other nations." Such an association was to represent a preponderating force in international politics, "much greater than the force of any nation now engaged or any alliance hitherto formed or projected." Anchored to the power of public opinion and draconian economic sanctions, but in the last resort resting upon the threat of war, such a league would offer a force that "no probable combination of nations could face or withstand." Joining other civilized nations in guarantees of peace entailed "no breach in either our traditions or our policy as a nation, but a fulfillment rather of all that we have professed or striven for." In July 1917, Lippmann summarized the national purpose as Wilson had summoned it: "We can win nothing from this war unless it culminates in a union of liberal peoples pledged to cooperate in the settlement of all outstanding questions, sworn to turn against the aggressor, determined to erect a larger and more modern system of international law upon a federation of the world." At this moment, Lippmann wrote, "that is what we are fighting for."[1]

It was on the basis of the liberal peace program that Wilson justified the war, and it was on the wings of that program that Wilson met the cheering crowds of Europe after the conclusion of the armistice. Wilson's European tour, after the war had ended but before the peace conference had begun, represented the pinnacle of his fame and influence, justifying the characterization of Winston Churchill that one man seemed to hold in his hands the destiny of the world. One must emphasize the dazzling heights that Wilson achieved in order to appreciate the sheer magnitude of the descent that took place over the next year and a half, for in that span of time every aspect of the liberal peace program fell to ruin. Critical aspects of it had been either ignored or honored in the breach in the Treaty of Versailles and the four associated treaties that made up the 1919 Peace of Paris:

- Germany received the treaty as a diktat and not as an equal partner, and at the urging of Western publics was subjected to bills for reparations that "made the pips squeak." German war guilt extended beyond the Imperialists whom Wilson had denounced; the German democracy must also do its penance.
- The innumerable territorial conflicts that broke out after the end of the armistice—Poland's military clashed with Ukraine, Germany, Lithuania, Czechoslovakia, and Russia between 1918 and 1921[2]—showed that "justice to all peoples and nationalities" was an extremely problematic goal. There was scarcely a border in Europe accepted as just by those on opposing sides, and much suffering by many nationalities who felt themselves badly cheated by the peace. The right "to hand peoples about from sovereignty to sovereignty as if they were property," it appeared to many, had been freely exercised by the victorious allies in Paris.
- Forced transfers of wealth as a consequence of reparations and economic controls imposed by the new states made European economic life less free than it had ever been. Germans shivered and starved under the allied boycott; Austria, "with its one great city supported by a thin strip of Alpine country," was "a nation economically deprived of arms and legs." Hungary was looted by Romanians and revolutionized by Bolsheviks.[3]
- Disarmament faltered. Though Germany saw its army reduced to

100,000 troops and was denied a navy and an air force by the Treaty of Versailles, the victorious Allies showed no inclination to moderate their own expenditures on armaments. The French boasted that they would retain eternal military superiority over their fallen rivals. Wilson, who had previously been a bashful advocate of preparedness, endorsed a navy intended to challenge British primacy and to counter Japanese aspirations in the Far East.

- A League of Nations was formed and made part of the Versailles treaty, but the U.S. Senate would approve the treaty only if Wilson accepted manifold reservations to the league. With Wilson's refusal to compromise, the treaty went down to defeat. Relations among the Western democracies turned to bitterness after the "great betrayal"; the partnership of democratic nations dissolved. "The Friendless Nations," the title of a *Nation* editorial from early 1921, summarized the almost atomized condition into which the frenzied nationalisms had worked themselves only two years after Wilson's triumphal European tour in the winter of 1918–1919.[4]

Thus it came to be that every leading aspect of the liberal peace program confronted something like its negation in the aftermath of the war. In the eyes of one disillusioned chronicler, the peacemakers had "gathered up all the widely scattered explosives of imperialism, nationalism, and internationalism, and, having added to their destructiveness, passed them on to the peoples of the world as represented by the League of Nations. . . . Prussianism, instead of being destroyed, has been openly adopted by its ostensible enemies."[5] When the ideals of Wilson's peace program were not realized, wrote another, "the world fell into the worst disillusionment the world as a whole had ever had, a universal disease, a sickness of spirit from which almost the whole human race suffered for years."[6] Far from producing a benign international environment, the "war to end war" produced a Europe seething with conflict in every quarter and an estranged and embittered America. Of all the great disillusions in American history, the crushed hopes of a liberal peace may take first prize in depth and suddenness. How did things go so utterly and completely wrong?

One factor was that the spirit of the Fourteen Points had nearly evaporated by the time of the armistice. Wilson's January 1918 program had been intended to collapse support for Germany's imperial policies among its Social Democratic opposition; even at the time, however, it was a "summons to the dead."[7] The decision by Germany, followed by its ally Austria-Hungary, to reject Wilson's peace terms and to aim for a knock-out blow in the west comparable to what it had achieved in the east with Brest-Litovsk, advanced the war to a new stage. The Allies now aimed for the breakup of Austria-Hungary and called for the liberation of its subject peoples, reducing to irrelevance Wilson's previous vision of a federalized Austria-Hungary. Wilson's opponents at home, especially Roosevelt and Lodge, shared in the Allied objectives and demanded Germany's unconditional surrender and the breakup of the Hapsburg empire. The United States, in their view, should "emphatically repudiate the so-called Fourteen Points and the various similar utterances of the President." In public opinion, Norman Angell recalled, the internationalist America of 1916 and early 1917, with its calls for peace without victory, had become in 1918 "more fiercely insistent upon absolute victory and unconditional surrender than any other of the belligerents. . . . The complete reversal of the 'peace without victory' attitude was demanded—cultivated, deliberately produced—as a necessary part of war morale." Those "emotions of coercion and domination," however, could not be "intensively cultivated and then turned off as by a tap. They made America fiercely nationalist, with necessarily a temperamental distaste for the internationalism of Mr Wilson."[8]

Wilson's own relationship to this great movement remains something of a puzzle. On his way to the peace conference, he told the journalists on the *George Washington* that "a statement that I once made that this should be a 'peace without victory' holds more strongly today than ever." He had "greatly deprecated" the desire of Lloyd George to fight the war "to a knockout of Germany." Attempting "to punish the German people would keep them solidly behind the Kaiser, and in sympathy with the military party," whereas the right policy was "to separate them from such influence and control and have them believe that we were ready to make a reasonable and just peace, as he was." Wilson wrote to House in late October that "our whole weight should be thrown for an armistice which will prevent a renewal of hostilities by Germany but that will be as moderate and reasonable as possible within those limits, because it is certain that too much success or security on the part of the Allies will make a genuine peace settlement exceedingly difficult if not impossible." In late 1918, Wilson was most conscious of all the Western statesman of the need to preserve some form of equipoise in the struggle on the central front if the peace were not to be lopsided; it is one of the ironies of history that Wilson, the professed opponent of the balance of power, should have then been seized above all others by the characteristic reasoning of the equilibrist.[9]

The end game, however, did not work out as Wilson planned and set the stage for subsequent recrimination. The Germans signed the armistice on the basis of the Fourteen Points and a lenient peace, whereas the Allies fully intended a peace dictated by the requirements of victory. They kept up an economic blockade against Germany that forced Germans into privations greater than the war years, with infants starving in great numbers. In the armistice negotiations, Wilson's key stipulation was that the declaration of peace had to be made by a new government shorn of the kaiser, which Germany dutifully produced, but this seeming advance in democracy was purchased at a heavy price. It was the new German democrats of Weimar rather than the old German militarists of Berlin who were saddled with responsibility for the armistice and the treaty.[10]

Despite Wilson's reputation for leniency toward Germany, he accepted as just various aspects of the settlement that the Germans themselves received with indignation. He believed that a delay in German membership in the league was reasonable—the German people, he insisted, must do penance—and he accepted and approved the Allied reservation to the armistice, accepted by Germany, that reparations would be paid. The Fourteen Points themselves bore adversely on Germany; they had called for an independent Poland with access to the sea, and this meant the partial dismemberment of the Reich. Even before Wilson was subjected to pressure from France and other associates for a Carthaginian peace, he himself had accepted and thought just the imposition of punishment on Germany. Toward the end of the conference, it was Lloyd George rather than Wilson who fought for German interests; Wilson was at that time more insistent on lecturing the Germans about the justice of the condign punishment they would receive.[11]

A second factor in explaining the outcome is that Wilson's power to shape the conference to his ends was much weaker than he had anticipated. His party lost the 1918 elections, which Wilson had styled as a referendum on his policies. His expectation that the Allies would be "financially in our hands" was dashed; that America was now a creditor to England and France gave it little to no influence in their relations. France and Britain tied reparations to America's willingness to cancel or mitigate the Allied war debts, and Congress made clear the United States would not forgive anything. The secretary of the Treasury wrote to Wilson in Paris expressing grave concern about the "possibility that the debts may be forgiven or exchanged for debts not as good" and noting that "Congress believes these loans are good and should be collected."[12]

Wilson had also expected that America's pledge to guarantee the settlement would be a source of leverage, but this crucial relationship proved to be difficult to exploit to his advantage. The basic dilemma was that Wilson could put pressure on the Allies only by threatening to abandon the settlement, but this threat undermined the solidity and automatic character of the American guarantee, depriving the intended beneficiaries of that felt security that they needed if they were to be merciful to their enemies. There was, unfortunately, no clear way out of this vicious circle. France wanted a separate security treaty with Britain and America guaranteeing France's security and capped by an international general staff that would provide credibility to the deterrent. Wilson was opposed to that type of military commitment and agreed to the French security treaty with reluctance. Any separate treaty, he well knew, created a different class of guarantee for the borders of France and all the rest. If the guarantee was strong here, was it not weak elsewhere? This Wilson and other advocates of collective security were loath to admit, and thus the pledge to come to the assistance of France was made "subject to the approval of the Executive Council of the League of Nations."[13]

A third factor in explaining the outcome was that Wilson placed the highest priority on the establishment of the League of Nations, which made him vulnerable to Allied threats to thumb their noses at a league. The main drama of the Paris negotiations centered on the tension created by Wilson's opposition to certain Allied war aims and his need to secure Allied consent for the league. In the summation of Henry White, the professional diplomat who served as the sole Republican on the American delegation in Paris, the importance vested by Wilson in the league—"in which he has been more deeply interested than anything else from the beginning"—was "played to the hilt by the French and Japanese in extracting concessions from him; to a certain extent by the British too, and the Treaty as it stands is the result. The Italians overshot the mark."[14] That dynamic long formed the basis of criticism, articulated by Walter Lippmann, that Wilson fundamentally miscalculated by basing his negotiations "on the idea that he must purchase assent to the League by accepting the program of Imperialism. His real politics should have been to purchase the renunciation of the Imperial program with the American guarantee."[15] While this criticism rightly highlights the view, urged also by the Republicans, that securing a reasonable treaty was more important than the creation of the league, it severely overstates the likelihood that Wilson could have accomplished this feat. The two aforementioned factors obstructed any such clever footwork. Ironically, Wilson's bargaining position was dealt a further blow by his need, forced upon him by the Republican Senate, to reopen the question of the covenant after his return to Paris, which cast him in the role of a supplicant. Given Wilson's devotion to the league, the Allies saw immediately that the satisfaction of American demands to alter the covenant—making way for the Monroe Doctrine, the right of withdrawal, and national prerogatives in trade and immigration—gave them an edge in the negotiation.

A fourth reason for the disparity between the vision of the liberal peace program and the actual outcome was the implicit underestimation of the sheer wastage the war had wrought, making reconstruction a hugely complicated and drawn-out affair. "When you have torn down," observed Lippmann, "you have torn down. We started to destroy a supremely evil thing and it is destroyed. The result of destroying it is destruction, and what is left are fragments, and possibilities, the stirrings of new life long suppressed, old hopes released, old wrongs being avenged, and endless agitation. It is chaos by every standard of our thinking, wild and dangerous, perhaps infectious, and thoroughly uncomfortable." Movement toward economic restoration, however, was very slow. In the peace conference, thought of reconstructing the delicate economic mechanism of Europe was entirely subordinated to the achievement of national and strategic aims. "It is an extraordinary fact," wrote Keynes, "that the fundamental economic problem of a Europe starving and disintegrating before their eyes, was the one question in which it was impossible to arouse the interest of the Four."[16]

On the shoal of these contradictions was broken up the bright vessel of liberal internationalism: previous comrades in this enterprise now divided into warring camps. Wilson would not admit that his vision of the liberal peace had been lost "in the morass of Paris." He defended the treaty as a just punishment of Germany perfectly consistent with the Fourteen Points and argued that whatever deficiencies existed would later be remedied by the league. Did he believe this? Keynes thought so, holding it probable that Wilson was "genuinely convinced that the Treaty contains practically nothing inconsistent with his former professions." On this view, Wilson freely embraced the "web of sophistry and Jesuitical exegesis" that clothed "with insincerity the language and substance of the whole Treaty." To admit the existence of the stark disparities between the liberal peace promised and the punitive peace imposed, an outstanding feature of the German reply to the treaty, would destroy Wilson's self-respect and "disrupt the inner equipoise of his soul."[17]

Keynes's charge was partly true, for Wilson was incapable of seeing his actions as actuated by injustice, but the president also saw keenly that to admit the deficiencies of the treaty would weaken his case for the league. Wilson himself often vented in the aftermath of the Paris negotiations that the Allies were hopeless: "When I think of the greed and utter selfishness of it all," he told Lansing, "I am almost inclined to refuse to permit this country to be a member of the League of Nations when it is composed of such intriguers and robbers. I am disposed to throw up the whole business and get out." Somewhat to his astonishment, Lansing noted that this was "the *third* time that the President has said to me that the present conduct of the nations makes him consider withdrawing from the League, though he never before spoke so emphatically. The other occasions were when the Greeks were demanding all of eastern Thrace and when France was insisting on her claim to Syria."

Wilson, believing rightly that it would injure his case for the league, kept these feelings mostly hidden in public but was often driven to distraction by the conduct of the Allies. "Foreign affairs," he sagely observed, "certainly cause a man to be profane."[18]

Wilson has also been severely criticized for setting loose the demon of rabid nationalisms that seemed to multiply in postwar Europe. Whereas the liberal critique of Wilson at Paris emphasized the disparity between vision and accomplishment (while holding that the vision itself was sound), the realist critique came to be associated with the dangers of "self-determination" as an ordering principle of international relations. Ironically, critics noted, self-determination called forth the very spirit—of nationalism—that clawed and spat at the international cooperation Wilson hoped to inculcate. "The spirit of nationalism," as Senator Charles Thomas of Colorado commented during the debate over the covenant, "was never more assertive than it is now. President Wilson's announcement of the right of self-determination was like deep calling unto deep. The response greeting it was universal." On the eve of the Paris conference, Lansing recorded in his diary the dangers that would be unleashed by this glittering generality: "Fixity of national boundaries and of national allegiance, and political stability would disappear if this principle was uniformly applied." It was, Lansing thought, a phrase "loaded with dynamite. It will raise hopes which can never be realized. It will, I fear, cost thousands of lives. In the end it is bound to be discredited, to be called the dream of an idealist who failed to realize the danger until too late to check those who attempt to put the principle in force."[19]

Lansing's fears were doubtless well justified, but it should be appreciated that it was the hard realists and intense nationalists like Clemenceau, Roosevelt, and Lodge who pushed the liberation of the subject peoples of Austria-Hungary as a war measure in the course of 1918; Wilson caught up with them ultimately in the summer in his "force to the utmost" phase, but the emphasis of his policy in early and late 1918 aimed at hiving off the German social democracy and the Dual Monarchy from the German Imperialists in pursuit of a negotiated settlement. The nationalists or hard realists considered that a high-sounding idea that cloaked "ignoble action" and wanted to beat the Central powers to their knees. The nationalists prevailed, such that by the time of the peace conference these new nations existed, and it was absurd to think that a settlement should not recognize the fact. Wilson's overarching phrases could indeed constitute a threat to international order if understood as a call to revolution in every multiethnic state, but Wilson did not so understand the matter. In fact, he saw as clearly as Lansing did the dangers of pushing the self-determination principle too far.[20]

Philosophically, Wilson's policy adhered to the traditional American view, articulated by Hamilton and Jefferson and subscribed to by various worthies thereafter, that every people had a right of revolution that could not be denied; outsiders were obliged to recognize that new status when it was achieved but should neither foment revolution nor come to the aid of despotic governments against internal enemies. To do either would be illegitimate intervention and equivalent to aggression. Self-government, an oft-used Wilsonian phrase, meant above all freedom from external rule, and Wilson thought the world was moving along its proper axis if *the nations* worked out their destiny themselves, after which they would be in a position to cooperate with others and to become yet more free. To his way of thinking, this was their elementary right.[21]

Wilson was thus faithful to the traditional nineteenth-century understanding of the relationship among nationality, democracy, and self-government. He shared the nineteenth-century equation—which the interwar experience would show as a rare combination—between liberalism and nationalism. Harold Nicolson, a member of the British delegation, later recalled the mood of progressive opinion: "It was the thought of the new Serbia, the new Greece, the new Bohemia, the new Poland which made our hearts sing hymns at heaven's gate." The experience of postwar Europe was badly disillusioning on this score, and Wilson, with other liberals, was undoubtedly guilty of unfounded optimism in believing that the new states would all choose constitutional governments and that their rival claims could be adjusted without much rancor.[22]

Much of this conflict, however, was simply inevitable, and responsibility for the state of affairs, if such would be assigned to the United States, would fall as much on Rooseveltian nationalists as on Wilsonian internationalists. Given that the new states were facts of nature by the time of the peace conference, all that remained was to argue over the contested frontiers, attempt to deal fairly with forlorn minorities sacrificed to the needs of strategic compactness or economic viability, and seek to preserve, so far as was possible, free intercourse among the newly independent states. Wilson fought bravely for these objectives at Paris and won some important victories, but these were marginal additions to the treaty that did not change its punitive character. Nearly all of Wilson's friends saw these deficiencies starkly upon the publication of the treaty terms, even those who stayed in Wilson's camp, but Wilson was resolved to defend the treaty as something substantially his and in keeping with the great promises of his public life. On this false note he returned from Paris to present the Versailles treaty and the covenant of the League of Nations to the Senate.

39

The Great Debate of 1919

It was Wilson's intention to tie the treaty to the league and force the Senate to accept the package or do the unthinkable and reject the American role in the league. When the treaty comes back, Wilson declared on returning to the United States in the middle of the peace conference, "gentlemen on this side will find the Covenant not only in it, but so many threads of the treaty tied to the Covenant that you cannot dissect the Covenant from the treaty without destroying the whole vital structure." Wilson the political scientist had long taken the view—expressed, for instance, in his *Constitutional Government* in 1907—that the president's authority in foreign affairs was near absolute because, despite his nominal dependence on the Senate, he could make it an offer it could not refuse. Holding all the threads of a negotiation in his own hands, the president could present the Senate with a fait accompli that, if rejected, would badly compromise the honor and good faith of the nation. Believing that his own thoughts perfectly mirrored those of the vast majority of his countrymen, and thinking that he held the moral and constitutional advantage, Wilson was resolved to fight for the league to the last ditch and thought that the Senate would have no alternative but to comply with his terms. "The stage is set, the destiny disclosed," Wilson told the Senate on presenting the treaty in July 1919. "We cannot turn back. We can only go forward, with lifted eyes and freshened spirit, to follow the vision. It was of this that we dreamed at our birth."[1]

The covenant that formed the object of this debate, in its great vows of mutual protection, closely resembled the classic form of confederation. The League of Nations, however, was the first such entity that embraced the world. Most of its members were drawn from the states of Europe and the Americas, but Japan, Australia, China, Siam, South Africa, and Liberia were among the original members. At its core were a set of procedures intended to safeguard the peace. The parties pledged, in Article 16, to submit their justiciable disputes to a panel of arbitration; failure to do so would yield automatic financial sanctions against the offender. They also pledged, in Article 10, to guarantee the territorial integrity and political independence of the league members, with discretion allotted to the Council of Nine to fashion an appropriate response. The Council of Nine was to be composed of five permanent members—Great Britain, France, Italy, Japan, and the United

States—and, in a bow to the smaller states, four members elected to three-year terms by the assembly. The council was the decision-making body, and nothing of substance could be authorized in the council save through the unanimous consent of all nine members. While pledging to act faithfully to their promise of mutual support, the big powers thus reserved their discretion in any particular instance and had the ability not only to withdraw from any proposed action but potentially to deny international legitimacy to projects they disapproved.[2]

Until the presentation of the covenant, which in its first draft was published in early 1919, speculation about a future league was exceptionally vague: "In some manner the states of the world were to come together in a more or less binding pledge to substitute law for force in their interaction. . . . But beyond that nothing was clear." H. G. Wells arrayed the League of Nations proposals "into a series between two extreme positions": one was the League to Enforce Peace program, a rehabilitation of the Hague Tribunal, which Wells called the "Weak League of Nations" and its proponents "the weak leaguers." The other was a world federal state with substantial concessions of sovereignty by the participating units, which Wells favored.[3]

The league that Wilson presented fell in between these two proposals. Though radically short of a world state, it represented also a sharp change of emphasis from the League to Enforce Peace conception. That older conception, as Elihu Root noted, had based hopes for world peace on "the reestablishment and strengthening of a system of arbitration or judicial decision upon questions of legal right." Wilson instead had proposed a political rather than a judicial body—a council rather than a court—as the key element in his scheme. To Root and other conservative internationalists, that held peril as "a government of men, and not of laws, following the dictates of expediency, and not of right." It also represented, in Root's view, a radical change from the traditional American conception: "For more than half a century the American government has been urging upon all the world the settlement of all such questions by arbitration. Presidents Grant, Arthur, Harrison, Cleveland, McKinley, Roosevelt, and Taft strongly approved the establishment of a system of arbitration in their messages to Congress." Now the American people were to be asked to approve a commitment to ensuring the political independence and territorial integrity of all league members.[4]

In the subsequent debate over the league in the United States, liberals were most critical of the treaty's concrete provisions, whereas conservatives, who had generally favored a punitive peace, placed emphasis on the dangers of the league. In a larger sense, however, opponents among the three emergent strands of critical opinion were united in condemning the iniquity of the thing. Liberal and progressive internationalists bemoaned the loss of

Wilson's program and excoriated the grossly punitive and irrational scheme of reparations; conservative internationalists saw the instability of the borders being created and believed a universal guarantee of them to be absurd; the irreconcilables clung to the exceptional qualities of the United States and damned the partnership with allied nations as a league with death and a covenant with hell.

The loss of liberal support hurt Wilson badly, robbing his position of the moral high ground that he had always claimed. And the critique was ferocious. The league, wrote J. A. Hobson in the *Nation*, was a sham, "a New Holy Alliance." Thorstein Veblen called it "an instrument of realpolitik, created in the image of nineteenth century imperialism." Commitment to the league, insisted another critic, meant sustaining "territorial and economic arrangements which are wrong in principle and impossible in practice." For the *New Republic*, which emblazoned "THIS IS NOT PEACE" on its cover, the treaty was an "inhuman monster" on behalf of which liberalism was committing suicide. The treaty was "vicious enough to incriminate the League," but the league, as Wilson hoped, was "not powerful enough to redeem the treaty." The band of liberals at the *New Republic*, having been among the most stalwart proponents of a league, now insisted on withdrawing "from all commitments under the Covenant which in any way impair [America's] freedom of action."[5]

The position adopted by the liberals was actually quite close to that adopted by many irreconcilables and "bitter enders," a new marrying of sentiment that exerted strong influence into the interwar period.[6] "You have here a League of Nations," complained Senator Borah, "composed of the great and dominant powers of the earth, some of whom are now engaged in oppressing and decimating weak nations and innocent peoples, and with those people you ask me to form a permanent combination and bring this Republic down to that level of debauchery and shame." The liberals basically agreed with that analysis. Lippmann regarded the league as "fundamentally diseased" and gave Borah confidential information culled from his days of government service with which to oppose Wilson. The liberals were in theory still committed to international cooperation, but they agreed entirely that this entangling alliance was hitched to an utterly illegitimate object.[7]

The irreconcilables or bitter enders stood their ground on the supremacy of the national interest and the traditional policy refusing entangling alliances with Europe. A supporter of the league, according to Borah, "no longer wants an American republic, no longer believes in nationalism and no longer desires to see the American flag a little higher in the heavens than that of any other nation." With the league the United States would forfeit and surrender, "once and for all, the great policy of no entangling alliances upon which the strength of the Republic has been founded for one hundred and fifty years."[8]

It was neither the disillusioned liberals nor the bitter enders, however, who held in their hands the fate of the treaty. That distinction belonged to the broad numbers of "reservationists" who thought the United States should join the league but only after appending reservations. Henry Cabot Lodge, the Republican chairman of the Senate Foreign Relations Committee, was the leader of the reservationists in the Senate. There has always been a controversy among historians as to whether Lodge was really a reservationist or an irreconcilable—a conservative internationalist or a die-hard nationalist—an uncertainty that arose partly from Lodge's need to bring together a heterogeneous coalition. That required eliciting the cooperation of moderate internationalists such as Root and Taft while not alienating the fourteen irreconcilables of the "Battalion of Death." Lodge's strategy for defeating Wilson's league lay in appending reservations to it that would eviscerate its basic character as Wilson presented it, while still allowing him to claim support for the league idea, which polls showed in the first half of 1919 to be still commanding majority support in public opinion.

Roosevelt and Lodge had long differed from Wilson in their approach to the peace. In one of his last editorials before his death in January 1919, Roosevelt had championed the idea of a victors' alliance, which Wilson deplored. The best hope for such a league, in Roosevelt's conception, entailed "a pledge by the present allies to make their alliance perpetual, and all to go to war again whenever one of them is attacked." In Roosevelt's view, moreover, it was essential that those entrusted with maintaining the peace not succumb to the delusion that they could do so by disarming themselves, and equally essential that the league be limited "at the outset to the Allies, to the peoples with whom we have been operating and with whom we are certain we can co-operate in the future." Such a league would exclude not only Austria and Turkey but also Russia and Germany: "Bolshevism is just as much an international menace as Kaiserism." Roosevelt urged that the American envoys to the peace conference not sit "as umpires between the Allies and the conquered Central Powers," as Wilson proposed to do, "but as loyal brothers of the Allies, as loyal members of the league of free peoples, which has brought about peace by overthrowing Turkey, Bulgaria, and Austria, and beating Germany to her knees."[9]

Republicans also opposed Wilson's fixation on tying the creation of the League of Nations to the treaty of peace with Germany. That was, in their view, a serious mistake. Ending the war and agreeing to terms with Germany ought to be done rapidly. Given the multitude of questions that a League of Nations would present, Lodge warned in December 1918, tying the treaty to the league "might endanger the treaty and force amendments. It would certainly lead to very long delays." "The words 'the league of nations,'" Lodge conceded, "are captivating and attractive. Everybody would like to bring about a world condition in which wars would be impossible. But we ought to be extremely careful that in our efforts to reach the millennium of universal and eternal peace we do not create a system which will breed dissensions and wars. . . . Intelligent discussion becomes difficult when the advocates of the league of nations drape themselves in trailing clouds of glory and omit to tell us the conditions to which they propose to bind the nations." The Republicans considered Wilson's secretive conduct and apparent determination to ram the league down the Senate's throat to be "offensively arrogant" and an unconscionable usurpation of the Senate's constitutional powers, about which Wilson was duly warned in the "round-robin" of thirty-nine Republican senators (enough to defeat the league) in March 1919. Despite these misgivings over the league, Lodge had long counseled that Allied unity should remain a paramount concern in the postwar period. "To encourage or even to permit any serious differences to arise between the United States and Great Britain, or with France, or Italy, or Belgium," he declared in the Senate in late 1918, "would be a world calamity of the worst kind."[10]

In the first half of 1919, forty-six hostile amendments were proposed to the covenant, which Lodge reduced to fourteen harshly worded reservations by the summer. These included some far-reaching provisions: the United States would be the sole judge of whether it had fulfilled its international obligations in case it decided to withdraw from the league. It would respect no vote in which the white dominions of the British Empire participated. It would exempt itself from obligation to respect the economic sanctions that might be required by league membership (either of the "automatic" kind specified in Article 16 or of the discretionary kind that might be imposed by the council under Article 10). It would not submit to arbitration any matter relating to the Monroe Doctrine, which was "wholly outside the jurisdiction" of the league. It withheld consent to the provisions according Japan a "mandate" in China's Shantung Province. It claimed a right to disregard unilaterally any plan for the limitation of armaments if the United States were threatened with invasion.[11]

Though each of these matters figured in the debate over the league, it was the second reservation, directed against Article 10, that struck the crucial blow: "The United States assumes no obligation to preserve the territorial integrity or political independence of any other country or to interfere in controversies between nations," unless Congress in any particular instance should so provide. The guarantee in Article 10, as Root noted, entailed a solemn commitment whose terms the American people did not really

understand and which they had no intention of fulfilling. In a world rife
with conflict, where change was the order of the day, Root questioned committing the prestige of the United States to the preservation, virtually everywhere, of the territorial status quo. "If perpetual, it would be an attempt to
preserve for all time unchanged the distribution of power and territory made
in accordance with the views and exigencies of the Allies in this present
juncture of affairs. . . . It would not only be futile; it would be mischievous.
Change and growth are the law of life, and no generation can impose its will
in regard to the growth of nations and the distribution of power, upon succeeding generations." In his first intervention in the debate, Root suggested
that Article 10 be limited to five years' duration; subsequently he urged its
entire abrogation. A perpetual guarantee, he believed, was madness: "The
vast territories of the Hohenzollerns, the Hapsburgs and the Romanoffs
have lost the rulers who formerly kept the population in order, are filled with
turbulent masses without stable government, unaccustomed to self-control
and fighting among themselves like children of the dragon's teeth."[12]

Root's thinking not only lamented the dangers of universality but also
highlighted the inadequacies of the particular commitment to France and
Britain, which he wanted to see strengthened. "If it is necessary for the security of western Europe that we should agree to go to the support, say, of
France if attacked, let us agree to do that particular thing plainly. . . . I am
in favor of that. But let us not wrap up such a purpose in a vague universal obligation, under the impression that it really does not mean anything
likely to happen."[13] Underlying this difference over Article 10 were differing conceptions of the relationship of war to international order. One side
insisted that wars had to be repressed everywhere because a single conflict
could grow like a prairie fire and ultimately involve the entire world in
its consequences, as the Great War had done. Wilson, who took this view,
was the first great exponent of what would later become known as "the
domino theory," which envisioned even a remote war as the first domino
to fall in a tumbling cascade. In this conception, "any quarrel, however
small, however limited the questions it involves, may again, if carried to the
point of war, kindle a flame throughout the world." The other side argued
that some conflicts were of merely local significance. A war between Chile
and Peru might be unfortunate for the combatants, but its significance for
international order was minimal as compared with the titanic stakes of the
war against Germany. To guarantee everything was to fail to make essential
distinctions between the greater and the lesser, the here and there, vital interest and quixotic endeavor.[14]

For Wilson, acceptance of the Lodge Reservations was unthinkable: "The
heart of the covenant" was the commitment contained in Article 10. Other

provisions might be compromised; this could not be. He equated acceptance of the reservations with the "nullification" of the treaty, and every American knew the analogy he had in mind in using that choice expression. There had always been a strand of internationalist opinion which held that no league at all would be better than a league of no consequential power and authority, and Wilson's resolution was to take his stand on that ground. Convinced that the rejection of the league would mean the return of the old system and the relapse into anarchy, Wilson pleaded that the failure to join the league as agreed in Paris, as the long-term consequences unfolded, would mean inevitably the near approach of despotism at home. He returned to the theme again and again in the great western speaking tour that he mounted in 1919 on behalf of Senate ratification of the covenant. The alternative to the league, and to the general disarmament it would make possible, was a set of institutions in the United States that would prove fatal to liberty: vastly enlarged executive powers, "a great standing army," "secret agencies planted everywhere," "universal conscription," "taxes such as we have never seen," restrictions on the free expression of opinion, a "military class" that would dominate civilian decision making, all of it "absolutely antidemocratic in its influence" and representing an "absolute reversal of all the ideals of American history."[15]

In justifying the league, Wilson did not directly invoke the precedent of the American union, as many others were doing at the time. He was, of course, well aware of the analogy: as early as August 6, 1914, the ex-president of Harvard, Charles Eliot, had suggested to Wilson a defensive league that would lead to "the future establishment and maintenance of federal relations and peace among the nations of Europe." Wilson had considered Eliot's suggestion "a momentous proposal."[16] For reasons somewhat obscure, however, Wilson's appeals to the union were furtive and indirect; instead, he characterized the league as "an extension of the Monroe Doctrine to the world." He would go to Paris, he had told William Rappard in late 1918, to do "what he had tried to do without success some years ago with South and Central America: to extend Monroe Doctrine so as to make it a principle of mutual protection. '*Not a big brother affair, but a real partnership.*'"[17] In the Pan-American Pact that Wilson presented to Latin American governments in January 1915, the parties were to "join one another in a common and mutual guarantee of territorial integrity and of political independence under republican forms of government." Though attracting the interest of the smaller Latin American states, the larger states of the southern cone—Argentina, Brazil, and Chile—were each uninterested, and the project had failed.[18] Thereafter, however, Wilson spoke of the Monroe Doctrine as if it had been spiritually transformed from a unilateral declaration into a multilateral treaty. This kind of talk drove Henry Cabot Lodge to despair: the Monroe Doctrine, Lodge insisted, was unilateralist in execution and geographically limited in scope; to multilateralize it and universalize it, as Wilson proposed to do, robbed it of its raison d'être. Though Lodge is perhaps not the best guide to the historic meaning of the Monroe Doctrine, it *was* strange that Wilson should claim the doctrine as the precedent for the league. What he meant was that the Monroe Doctrine had been based on the same principle as the league—the preservation of political independence as against external aggression. The comparison, however, also suggested that the territorial guarantee embodied in the league would be in the nature of a protectorate, whereas his true conception was much more on the order of "all for one and one for all." The better comparison, as he surely knew, was with the old federal union, and especially to the predicament of the American states to which union had been the response.

Certainly all the core elements of the old paradigm are present in Wilson's thought. The anarchy of states as fatal to liberty and productive of despotism; the armed camp as the unavoidable consequence for republican states caught in the maws of this unreformed system; the remedy seen in terms of a partnership or concert or union among democratic states that will achieve a preponderance of power while limiting armaments; the provision of equal rights to all states, great and small—all this showed that Wilson had drunk deeply of the unionist paradigm. There is no objection to characterizing this as the projection of "American domestic values" on the international system, as many historians have done, or as a fulfillment of American ideals, as Wilson did, so long as it is borne in mind that the "domestic values" and national ideals in question were derivative of the thought and experience concerning federal union, which was at its inception also an experiment in international cooperation. The unionist paradigm marked out both the great objects to be achieved and the great dangers to be avoided.

It did not mark out, however, the same institutional path to getting there. The League of Nations had none of the powers that were conferred on the general government in 1787, but most of the expectations it engendered. The objectives of 1787 were to be achieved with an instrument more resembling the league of states created by the Articles of Confederation, which meant that the league had many of the features (only more so) that the framers of the Constitution had denounced as grave defects in the right construction of federal government. Its requirement of unanimous endorsement by the league council raised a hurdle far higher than the voting provisions of the Continental Congress, more nearly resembling the *liberum veto* (conferring a veto on every noble) of the eighteenth-century Polish constitution, which provision had been the subject of great sport by discerning adepts in the science of politics. It was more dependent on the voluntary contribution of the state members than even the Continental Congress, which had the authority to issue currency in the name of the United States (even if it did not have the power to maintain its value).

This feature of the league covenant pointed to a highly paradoxical feature of the movement toward international organization. The more one looked to America's federal union as a model for world union, as large numbers of individuals did, and the more one traded on the analogy between the international anarchy the framers sought to master, and that which the world would have to master in 1919, the more problematic the enterprise appeared. Enthusiasts for world union had to admit it, and indeed did admit it: the league was a first step; insofar as it was reenacting anything, it was reenacting the Articles of Confederation, not the Constitution of 1787. But if the analogy was sound, the league would fail. If the principles by which unions might be made more or less perfect had been well understood by the framers, this new union would not work.

Advocates of the 1787 Constitution gave a thorough explication of why a system of voluntary contributions would fail in theory, while noting the many instances in which such collaborations had dissolved in practice. The American confederation, Hamilton noted, had been formed under the expectation "that a sense of common interest would preside over the conduct of the respective members, and would beget a full compliance with all the constitutional requisitions of the Union." But expectations were gravely disappointed: the delinquencies of the states multiplied, inducing paralysis. Hamilton deduced the law "that in every political association which is formed upon the principle of uniting in a common interest a number of lesser sovereignties, there will be found a kind of eccentric tendency in the subordinate or inferior orbs . . . to fly off from the common center." Any student of *The Federalist* could easily see that there was no reason why the league should not suffer from the same eccentric tendency. Advocates of the covenant might plead that there was no alternative, and that the sacrifice of sovereignty entailed by a charter for the world modeled on the U.S. Constitution was impossible. All this was quite true but was an evasion of the main point. There the framers stood, holding forth a way of thinking, a model . . . and a reproach.[19]

The existence of these objections may explain why Wilson, who was thinking like a unionist, saw hazard in appealing to the precedent of the federal union, so long "cherished by Americans as affording the hope that it might become a model for the rest of the world."[20] This disjunction between ends and means, between what Wilson hoped for the league and what the league was destined to be by virtue of its very nature and organization, is key to understanding the whole episode. Walter Lippmann—whose attitude toward Wilson at various points was that of sublime enthusiast, bitter critic, and grudging admirer—gave the most intriguing explication in his book *U.S. War Aims* (1944). At the core of Wilson's vision, Lippmann argued, was a series of prohibitions whose general purport was to "forbid national states to do the things which they have always done to defend their interests and to preserve their integrity." Disarmament to a point consistent with national safety meant that nations could not defend their surrounding regions, while the prohibition against special covenants within the League of Nations (like the security treaty with France) meant that nations belonging to a common strategic area were prevented "from organizing a combined defense and from concerting their foreign policy." Why did Wilson and his disciples believe that such negative principles would promote a universal society? The reason, Lippmann speculated, was their assumption "that they were laying the foundations of a world state under a world government." The Wilsonian principles, though irrational for the world as it is, "are quite rational if we imagine that the nations are about to do what the thirteen American states did when they formed the Federal Union." Lippmann was not quite right, because Wilson expected the league to work without a state, but he was essentially right, because Wilson did believe that the league would have the same effect on international society as the federal Constitution had on the union, making way for the "negative principles" and a virtuous circle of reassurance. Unfortunately, the profound institutional contrast between what was done in 1787 and 1919, quite apart from other formidable obstacles, ensured that this could not be the case.[21]

The *vis inertiae* built into the league, subjecting it to the same stresses as previous confederations, would have existed even had it been limited to Europe and the Americas. But the league, though far from including all peoples, squinted at universality and wished to embrace the whole of international society, now extending beyond Europe and the Americas to include important non-European powers. The classic confederation, notes one scholar, "is based on a decision by a particular group of states to act henceforth in common vis-à-vis the outside world. To act as one externally, to have common friends and enemies, means necessarily that the particular group of states concerned must be pledged to perpetual peace within. Inner unity is hence correlated indissolubly with the will to individuality or particularity externally. Interstate relations are transcended in one area in order that they may be the more effectively prosecuted elsewhere." Though it is an exaggeration to argue that this correlation was entirely missing in the league—the peace-loving nations were to join together against an aggressor, who could be a league member—the far greater extent of the projected society made inner unity more problematic than in any previous confederation.[22] In this particular, too, the League of Nations was very different from the American Constitution, whose framers had made axiomatic the relationship between inner unity and the will to individuality externally.

The weak structure of the league's constitution, together with the enormous lateral reach of its boundaries and membership, predestined it to be little more than an influential debating society at some moments, and this whether America entered with or without reservations. The constitution of the league required automatic sanctions if a state refused to submit to arbitration, but it did not have a government to make those sanctions automatic, and it was inherently left to the parties to decide their obligations in those circumstances. The league's constitution was permissive in the sense that it could form the nucleus of a concert of free peoples in taking legitimate action to preserve international society. Absent such a concert, the league as such could not add much independent influence over the course of world affairs.

While the weakness of the league was looked upon with trepidation by the world federalists like Wells, who saw these centrifugal tendencies clearly, the dominant image of the league conveyed in the American debate of 1919–1920 was its great and overpowering strength. This "New Holy Alliance," said the liberal critics, sought the same universal dominion for itself that it had struck down in Germany. Irreconcilables conjured pictures of American citizens ordered to battle by foreign governments, "many of which are laggards in the march of civilization and exponents of autocracy and tyranny." To critics of the treaty, the irreconcilable and the reservationists alike, it did not matter that the covenant expressly stipulated that action by the council required unanimous consent; this association, weak by all the standards of confederal theory, was yet an all-powerful thing that bid fair to dominate the world. These exaggerated portrayals gave the debate over the covenant a surreal character, since so many took as their starting point what was plainly not so.[23]

Yet the debate over Article 10 was serious and raised the most profound issues; it could not be readily compromised, if at all. Wilson had a transactional conception of the covenant very similar to that which the theorists of the social contract like Hobbes had imagined, but the debate over the league disclosed a large gap between the ends that he foresaw and the means that he and his party proposed. According to Senator Hitchcock, who led the pro-league forces in the Senate, the league would "not require armies or navies. . . . The power of public opinion in the United States and the power of public opinion through the civilized world will be the supreme power, the moral power, which will naturally bring compliance with any agreement duly made." According to the Democratic whip, America would vanquish "force by scorning its use." If that were so, then the league was "a covenant without the sword," in Hobbes's famous expression. If the league had a sword, however, then there seemed an unending series of conflicts into which the United States might be drawn. The opponents of the league saw the contradiction clearly and mercilessly exposed it in debate. Once again, "Something or nothing?" proved the fertile question.[24]

But for Wilson, holding to his transactional conception of the covenant, the critical thing about the Lodge Reservations is that they took back the promise; that is why he saw no essential difference among critics of the league. "Practically every so-called reservation," he wrote in March 1920 in his final rejection of compromise, "was in effect a rather sweeping nullification of the terms of the treaty itself. I hear of reservationists and mild reservationists, but I cannot understand the difference between a nullifier and a mild nullifier."[25] Wilson's final rejection stunned supporters, many of whom thought him stark raving mad, and historians friendly to Wilson have usually stressed his illness as providing the key to his behavior. But the rejection had a certain hard logic to it. The organization of the league was confessedly weak. Without the promise it was nothing.[26]

The most basic argument of the nationalists was that the country had grown to power and prosperity under Washington's admonition to steer clear of European alliances. The policy of independence and of the Monroe Doctrine, the ramparts of a distinct American system in the Western world, had brought the nation to a prosperity and security unmatched elsewhere. It was right and proper to make the well-being of this, our country, the anchor of American policy. Yet nationalists, while elevating the nation, also denigrated the foreigner, and indeed poured rhetorical volley after volley at what Roosevelt had called the "sorry crew" of "professional internationalists" who appeal to "weaklings, illusionists, materialists, lukewarm Americans, and faddists of all types that vitiate sound nationalism." Beveridge, who was once a leading voice of the imperialists, now called for a "pure and exclusive nationalism versus mongrel and promiscuous internationalism." Roosevelt agreed: he confided to Beveridge that his sops to the internationalists were merely "platonic" expressions designed to rope in Taft and his followers "and also to prevent any accusation that we are ourselves merely Prussian militarists." Lodge accused Wilson of substituting "an international state for pure Americanism" and for wanting to "move away from George Washington to . . . the sinister figure of Trotsky, the champion of internationalism." The "cheap, hastily constructed, foreign-made lamp of internationalism," concurred the critics, ought not to be given up for the "Aladdin's lamp" of nationalism.[27]

But the internationalists could persuasively reply that independence was just one part of the inheritance of the fathers and that union had always stood in close proximity with it in their scheme of things. Communication among the nations of the world was far more rapid than that which existed at the time of the making of the Constitution; the world had shrunk, and revolutions in communications and technology ensured that it would keep on shrinking. The prodigious expansion in the explosiveness and range of modern weaponry made for a world of nations more dangerously proximate than even the newly independent American states. Wilson evoked these dangers in his western tour, of weapons grown ever more powerful and destructive, and insisted that they must be mastered. That was also the central theme of the case for a League of Nations written by H. G. Wells and endorsed by great authorities in England. The marriage of science and militarism threatened to "so enlarge and intensify the scope and evil of war and of international hostility as to give what was formerly a generous aspiration more and more the aspect of an imperative necessity."[28] The terrifying new forces made it imperative that independence be substantially controlled by the exigent requirements of union. At the time of making America's own Constitution, wrote the *New Republic*, it was evident "that political independence, won by a group of nominally sovereign states, could not endure unless these states converted independence into interdependence and organized a federated nation." The essential meaning of American membership in a league of nations was consent "to a political reunion with Europe." America's independence as a nation had "come to depend on the acknowledgment and organization of the necessary interdependence of all free nations."[29]

This vision had been powerfully held among the internationalists, but it did not survive encounter with the peace. Two months after this passage appeared, the injustice of the peace put this new relationship between independence and union in grave question and led to the *New Republic*'s break from the treaty and the covenant. Disillusionment with the peace in turn fed disillusionment with the war, raising troubling questions in the liberal mind—shared strongly also by "peace progressives" like Borah—about the wrenching effect on America's free institutions if it were exposed again to the virus of large-scale war. Unlimited presidential power, popular frenzy against the Hun and his hyphenate collaborators, the censorship of news, the seizure of progressive publications, the jailing of dissenters—indubitably, the face of free institutions was contorted into an ugly shape in the pressure cooker of war. Like the Athenian plague chronicled by Thucydides, the propensity to sacrifice liberty on behalf of security struck young and old, strong and weak, aristocrat and democrat: the normally cautious and prudent Root declared to a New York rally in the heat of the war that there were men walking the streets of the city that night who ought to be taken out and shot the next morning for treason. The persecution of war critics was especially absurd: men went to jail, as Charles Beard noted, for retaining "Wilson's pacifist views after he abandoned them." Their crime, said another critic, was simply "loyalty to conviction." Wilson would not pardon Eugene Debs, the Socialist jailed for opposing the war, because in his own frigid mind he needed to keep faith with the boys he had sent to France, with the evident implication that the prize those boys had won was incompatible with respect for free expression at home. That Wilson had failed to achieve the liberal peace was understandable given the forces arrayed against him. But it was "forever incredible," as Lippmann wrote, "that an administration announcing the most spacious ideals in our history should have done more to endanger fundamental American liberties than any group of men for a hundred years."[30]

The historian Arthur Link has characterized the great debate of 1919–1920 as a contest between competing internationalisms, taking issue with the conventional depiction of a fight between "internationalists and nationalists" or "interventionists and isolationists." Supporting Link's view is the fact that many Republican leaders—Roosevelt, Lodge, Root—did stand for a conception in which the "league of free peoples" figured strongly. Their idea of an international community America might join was tied to the community of Atlantic powers and was at once narrower and stronger than Wilson's conception. Lodge warmed to the French idea of creating an international general staff—basically an Anglo-French-American triumvirate—that would enjoy powers akin to those later invested in the Supreme Allied Command under NATO. Wilson, by contrast, did not disavow the use of military force in his defense of the league—it lay there "in the background"—but he did assert that force would not be necessary "98 percent" of the time. The heavy lifting, in the president's conception, would be done by the combined force of public opinion and economic sanctions. Lodge considered this a thoroughly faulty conception because it sought to secure the pledge of the nation to overseas commitments by minimizing the real burdens that role would entail.[31]

The weakness of the Republican position was not their exposure of the fallacies of Wilson's league but their conception of the treaty. They were all in favor of smashing the Germans and inflicting on them defeat and humiliation without end. Events would show, however, that a draconian peace could not be sustained in the court of Anglo-American public opinion; even Lodge became disgusted with French conduct toward Germany in the early 1920s. But the most serious liability of the repressive solution was the likelihood that it would breed frightening new political movements out of the desperation such punishment would induce. The liberals believed that nothing good could come out of the infliction of such miseries. They could call to proof the ability of the Bolsheviks to seize power in Russia—a success not conceivable in the absence of the utter disorganization the war had spawned—and they feared that some rough and pitiless beast might also arise in Central Europe if the Germans were presented "a cup that is too full of misery." Let the world beware of doing that, warned the distinguished German statesman and industrialist Walther Rathenau, an assimilated Jew who briefly served as foreign minister under the Weimar Republic before he was assassinated by right-wing thugs in 1922. It is fully apparent in retrospect—it ought to have been apparent at the time—that the liberal internationalist analysis of this danger was right: the severities and hypocrisies of the peace, the stupid and insensate cruelties of the 1919–1923 period, deeply compromised the Weimar democrats and inculcated in Germany the moral and psychological basis for the rise of the Nazis.[32]

Was a different approach possible, one that combined the Wilsonian promise of a generous peace with NATO-like guarantees to forestall a revival of German aggression? Perhaps the peace might have had a chance if an attempt had been made early on to fix a grand bargain in which the reintegration of Germany into Europe's economic life, accompanied by sharply reduced reparations and war debts, was paired with restrictions on its military power and sustained by an American pledge to come to the aid of western Europe if attacked. Some internationalists had seen this logic early on, and at some moments it seemed to be Wilson's own conception: if America, by bringing its power to bear, could give France a sense of security, then France might be willing to deal less punitively with Germany, fostering German reintegration and the recovery of Europe.[33]

Much as this seems the course of constructive statesmanship, the obstacles facing it were severe. Neither side in the great debate favored this solution: it violated Lodge's desire for a punitive peace, and it crossed Wilson's insistence on universal guarantees and his wish to keep military power in the background. Both men, too, had to contend with the strong popular prejudice against anything that smacked of a traditional alliance. Instead of stating the obvious—that both Wilson's league and Lodge's victors' alliance were serious entanglements that required the abandonment of traditional policy—both men insisted that the departures they had in mind were not entangling alliances at all. If either scheme were to have a chance of working, however, they had to be just that.

Other political realities threw up further obstacles to such a grand bargain. It was soon evident that keeping American forces in Europe after the war was impossible: the "boys" were unanimous in wanting to come home, and the public agreed. Reparations also posed an apparently insoluble problem: France and Britain were unwilling to consider lessening German reparations unless America mitigated or canceled the war debts Britain and France owed to the United States, and Congress was strongly opposed to doing that. Nor were the French really interested in a grand bargain: they wanted the American guarantee, but in exchange they did not want to give leniency toward Germany. To do so, from their perspective, meant leaving Germany, with its greater population and industrial resources, in a dominant power position on the Continent, thus rendering all the sacrifices of the war pointless. Germany, in effect, would win in the peace what it had lost in the war. The comparatively greater sacrifices made by France and Britain in the war gave them a decided advantage in a showdown with the United States. Should the American president prove obstinate, the allies thought, "then the sacrifices of France and Great Britain were such that they were entitled to have a final say, and would say it."[34]

Beyond all these formidable obstacles was the fact that a tripartite pact among Britain, France, and the United States left unresolved the question of Germany's frontiers to the east. The league, as Henry Taft described it, "is designed primarily to give protection to the seven new republics and the four autonomous nations in the Near East, created as a result of the war." In reality, there was no magical political formula that could overcome the profoundly different perspectives among France, Britain, and America over the Eastern Question, and little likelihood in summoning the American people to any such commitment. And yet it was in the East, as Wilson predicted in his western tour, that the challenge to the postwar settlement was most likely to come.[35]

Perhaps the most interesting feature of the debate over the league is how the liberal internationalism of Wilson and the conservative internationalism of Lodge served to cancel one another out, leaving the nationalist Borah as the last man standing at the end of the contest. Both Wilson and Lodge could block the other's conception of the league of free peoples, and into the void created by this stalemate stepped the logical alternative: a return to normalcy and reaffirmation of the wisdom of the fathers in advising detachment from European quarrels. The Republican internationalists were a bit astounded at the force of the reaction that they themselves helped to precipitate: the sober reservations they wanted to incorporate into the league got overwhelmed by the wave of popular enthusiasm for nationalism and "one hundred percent Americanism"—and the great tide washed out not only Wilson's internationalism but also their own.

Wilson, then, was not alone in being guilty of "supreme infanticide"— Lodge killed his own baby just as surely as Wilson did his.[36] Lodge and other Republican internationalists had called forth nationalism in opposition to "Wilsonism" and expected the public would share their affinity to working with Britain and France in stabilizing the postwar world, but the public responded most enthusiastically to abuse directed at these selfsame allies. Opinion toward Britain, remembering the indignities of the neutrality period, soured further in 1919 because of British repression in Ireland and the callous shooting of demonstrators in India at Armistar, whereas the French were scorned because of their undisguised imperial ambition as they picked over the carcass of the Ottoman Empire. Twisting the lion's tail had again become popular sport and received the assiduous support of Irish, German, and Italian Americans, whose anti-British bias the Republicans shamelessly cultivated. Borah received his loudest and longest applause one evening when he declared, on the campaign trail for Warren Gamaliel Harding in 1920, that "I don't think any man ought to be elected President of the United States who thinks six times as much of Great Britain as he does of the United States."[37]

When the draft covenant became known in early 1919, Senator Gilbert Hitchcock declared that "internationalism has come" and that the United States "must choose what form the internationalism is to take."[38] In signal respects, however, it is evident that the new internationalism came and went. The election of 1920 was its obituary. Republican internationalists did not want the election of 1920 to be a referendum on the league and "isolation," and they pointed to various enigmatic utterances of Harding to show that he really did favor joining the league once the election was won and the necessary reservations were registered. But Harding made his position utterly clear in the final month of the campaign. "I do not want to clarify these obligations," he said. "I want to turn my back on them." The only league he favored—and he did favor a league "with all my heart"—was one that existed in his mind's eye. It was not the league that would soon be taking up residence in Geneva.[39] The public evidently liked what it heard from Gamaliel. The Republicans raked in 404 electoral votes, and their twenty-six-point margin in the popular vote was the largest between major party candidates in the twentieth century.[40]

Whatever else it was, the election was a repudiation of Wilson, who had fallen into a disgrace and isolation so deep and mortifying as to tax the resources of a tragedian to describe. In the bleak winter of 1919–1920, enfeebled by his stroke, Wilson found himself in complete estrangement from the American people. His only consolation, not inconsiderable, was that he gave his life fighting for his cause, but he had badly alienated the country and at the end sat almost friendless, bound to his wheelchair, in his shriveled body and straitened soul. The great cause on behalf of which he had enlisted America, which had seemed the most important thing in the history of the world two years previously, evoked palpable groans by late 1920. "I don't want to hear about it," "Please, can we change the subject," rang out across the broad expanse of continental America, from sea to shining sea. Disgusted by the potential human and financial cost of international commitments, and fearing that "another war means another Palmer," the vox populi heard by H. L. Mencken in the fall of 1920 went as follows: "Let the heart of the world bust if it will! Let Turk eat Armenian, and Armenian eat Turk! Let the Poles steal what they can grab, and keep what they can hold! Let the Russians try genuine democracy if they want to! Let the French lift everything that is not nailed down and the English take what is left! Let Europe, Asia, and Africa be damned!"[41]

PART TEN
The Crisis of the Old Order

40

Nationalism, Internationalism, and Imperialism in the 1920s

THE FAR-REACHING DEBATE OVER WAR and peace in 1917–1920 disclosed the principal alternatives that would confront American foreign policy in the twentieth century. Reformulating the choice between independence and union in the circumstances of a newly interdependent world, the great debate had cast forth a choice between nationalism and internationalism that would remain of fundamental significance. But the enduring significance of the new internationalism, it is important to appreciate, is more apparent in retrospect than it was at the time. Until the very end of the interwar period, "Wilsonism" seemed to be crushed, and across wide precincts of the country internationalism approached the status of a dirty word. The diminishing band of internationalists continued to weigh in on the importance of American cooperation and believed it in the interest of the United States "to let into our souls a certain percentage of regard for our position as world citizens." But the internationalists felt themselves besieged by the contrary force of public opinion: "The problem is how to get that percentage of world citizenship into the soul of the hundred per cent American citizen."[1]

The 1920s were very different from the 1930s in basic tenor. After the destabilization and turmoil of the years immediately following the war, culminating in the French occupation of the Ruhr in 1923, a measure of international stability returned. In the Pacific, the United States presided over a conference at Washington in 1921–1922 that produced two accords—a treaty of naval limitation that fixed the ratio of capital ships among the United States, Britain, and Japan at 5:5:3, and a Nine Power agreement pledging the parties to respect Chinese sovereignty and the Open Door. In Europe, the United States approved the provision of short-term loans to Germany by U.S. banks, which restored a measure of financial stability and prepared the way for the Locarno agreements among Britain, Germany, France, and Italy guaranteeing the Franco-German border. Following quickly upon Locarno was the Kellogg-Briand "peace pact" of 1928, the "international kiss" whereby the preponderant voice of international society agreed to renounce war as a legitimate means for the resolution of international differences. Sixty-two nations ultimately pledged their faith to this idea, but the treaty proved not to be a harbinger to an era of good feelings. The guarded optimism that prevailed at the end of the 1920s would not last. The American stock market crash of 1929 and the subsequent worldwide descent into economic nationalism and depression made the fortunes of the world turn much darker. The "low, dishonest decade" that followed, loosing anarchy and despotism upon the world, produced a crisis within Western civilization of greater magnitude than any it had previously experienced.

The outstanding paradox in the American position during the interwar period is the simultaneous existence of great power and psychological withdrawal. Never before had the United States so towered over the remainder of the international system; never before had its desire to escape the broils and caprices of the European state system been stronger. The emergence of the United States as the world's greatest power was due primarily to the decisive weakening that all the other Great Powers (with the exception of Japan) had undergone as a result of the war, with the victors suffering almost as much as the vanquished. By virtue of the Allies' liquidation of assets to pay for the war, the center of world financial power had shifted from London to New York, and the United States, owed enormous debts by the Allies, was well on the way to becoming "the most notorious absentee landlord in history."[2] This financial entanglement would prove to be of great significance in making the United States an intimate party to Europe's disintegration in the 1930s.

Though the outlook of the Republican presidents and their secretaries of state—Charles Evan Hughes, Frank Kellogg, and Henry Stimson—was nearly always described as isolationist in the post–World War II period, more recent historians have emphasized the "internationalist" character of the Republicans' mind-set. In fact, both characterizations are true, but the terms are being used to describe different things. The refusal of the United States to commit itself to using force outside the Western Hemisphere existed throughout; so, too, did the commitment to high tariffs, reaffirmed in the Fordney-McCumber Act of 1922. As if to punctuate America's determination to have a separate destiny, immigration was sharply restricted in 1921 and 1924. After the "closing of the gates," the great tidal wave of people that had come from Europe in the two decades before the war slowed to a trickle. These were all reflections of both isolationism and nationalism, and they were no less pronounced in the 1920s than in the 1930s.

Despite these characteristics, Republican leaders did subscribe to beliefs that are certainly part of the internationalist tradition. They thought that the American way would best prosper in peace. They sincerely favored methods of arbitration and the peaceful settlement of disputes. They hoped to limit armaments. They wanted to see peaceful economic development via loans to undeveloped regions and now thought of the Open Door, which had had its birth in response to foreign penetration in China, as a set of principles to be applied worldwide.[3] In speech after speech, notes one historian, the Republican presidents and secretaries of state "dedicated American foreign policy to the construction of a peaceful and stable world order."[4] They gloried in the triumph of commerce and civilization and accepted that worldwide interdependence was a basic fact of modern life. The nationalist and isolationist axioms the Republicans shared set sharp limits on the use of force to achieve these lofty aspirations; their "internationalism" was in this sense profoundly conditioned by their "isolationism," making them "semi-internationalists."[5] What might appear as internationalist to these satisfied citizens of the world, in other words, might seem hidebound and isolationist to others. Thus, while Secretary Kellogg was congratulating himself for proposing, and the world for signing, the multilateral pact to renounce war as a legitimate instrument of policy, the English were still wondering why "every time Europe looks across the Atlantic to see the American eagle it observes only the rear end of an ostrich."[6]

The relationship of these Republican administrations to imperialism is also somewhat ambiguous because "imperialism" was a concept used to identify differing phenomena. One usage focused on the competitive dynamics of the European empires—"the diplomacy of imperialism"—such as was manifested after World War I in the scramble between Britain and France for the spoils of the Ottoman Empire; the other usage referred to the relations of a metropole with a dependent "colonial" population. The former had always been deemed objectionable by American opinion (for the same reason that this opinion had objected to "the balance of power"), but one result of the Great War was to call into grave question the legitimacy of colonial rule. That in turn put a spotlight on America's practices within its own sphere of influence in the Caribbean basin. As we saw earlier, Roosevelt had denounced Wilson's policies in Hispaniola, and the new Republican administrations were keen to contract the commitment, but the complications of withdrawal proved interminable. Marines would leave the Dominican Republic in 1924, but they would not evacuate Haiti until 1934. For that and for the "slavish" imitation of "the policies upon which the British Empire was built," Republican administrations received the repeated denunciation of imperialism from Robert La Follette and other peace progressives in the 1920s. "We are today creating in Central and South America our Irelands, our Egypts and our Indias. Helpless peoples are being crushed into submission in order to compel them to pay tribute to our international bankers and industrial exploiters."[7]

The argument over American imperialism was renewed by Coolidge's decision, in late 1926, to send forces to Nicaragua. The 100-man legation guard that had been stationed in Nicaragua since 1912 was withdrawn in 1925, but what went back in was a much larger force intended to prevent the liberal forces from claiming the presidency against Adolfo Diaz. This followed an old pattern whose characteristics were summed up by John Dewey in 1927: "The natural movement of business enterprise, combined with Anglo-American legalistic notions of contracts and their sanctity, and the international custom which obtains as to the duty of a nation to protect the property of its nationals, suffices to bring about imperialistic undertakings."[8]

The Coolidge administration, which sent the troops on its own authority and without consultation of Congress, laid out a series of justifications for the step. First up was the "Evarts Doctrine," named for Secretary of State William M. Evarts, who had held in 1878 that "it was the first duty of a Government to protect life and property; that this duty was incumbent on a Government whose nationals were menaced by the neglect of a Government in whose territory they resided; that the United States Government was not solicitous about the methods to accomplish this protection of its imperiled nationals in a foreign land and that 'protection in fact to American lives and property is the sole point upon which the United States is tenacious.'" The administration also claimed that it was acting in accord with the 1923 treaty, signed in Washington, in which the states of Central America pledged not to "recognize any other Government which may come into power in any of the five republics through a coup d'etat or a revolution." This explanation was insufficient for Senator Borah, who noted that the party against which the United States acted, led by Juan Sacasa, had won a "perfectly legal election" in 1924. Faced with the opposition of Borah, the powerful chairman of the Senate Foreign Relations Committee, the administration then claimed to be acting against Bolshevism and charged that Mexico, under the influence of Bolshevik doctrines, had allowed arms shipments to Sacasa. As with many such interventions before and since, none of these justifications was without severe problems standing alone, but together they made a happy threesome and were sufficient to overawe the domestic opposition that arose. As Coolidge emphasized in a statement to Nicaragua, the United States had no desire "to influence or dictate in any way the internal affairs of your country." Everyone—the United States, the government and people of Nicaragua, even presumably Adam Smith's Impartial Spectator—appreciated that America had "no selfish ends or imperialistic designs to serve."[9]

From abroad, condemnation of the Nicaraguan intervention came swiftly. In London, the *Times* found the intervention "in logical accord with the recent evolution of the Monroe Doctrine, which, from the negative proposition that no European country should interfere on the American continent, has developed into a positive theory that the United States itself is free to intervene there at any time in defense of its interests." The intervention, wrote the *Daily News*, not only "excited the contemptuous comment of European newspapers as providing a glaring example of the hypocrisy of American moral philosophy in international relations" but had also "deeply angered the peoples of Latin America, who see their liberties menaced by their great and powerful neighbour." The real heat of these denunciations stemmed from the widespread expectation that Mexico was next. A French paper commented that the policy of Washington in Mexico "consists of making order impossible in that country and then accusing it of living in anarchy." Some day, the paper predicted, "this will finish in intervention."[10]

That further intervention was likely seemed the only possible anticipation. In 1927, one observer counted thirty-one separate military interventions in the Caribbean since 1898: "In Cuba, four; in Panama, five; in the Dominican Republic, five; in Nicaragua, six (the last still in progress); Haiti, one, still in progress; Mexico, two; Honduras, six; Costa Rica, one; Colombia, one." Despite this record, as Walter Lippmann noted, Americans did not think of themselves as imperialists and felt that there ought to be some other name than empire "for the civilizing work which we do so reluctantly in these backward countries." "We have learned to think of empires as troublesome and as immoral, and to admit that we have an empire still seems to most Americans like admitting that they have gone out into a wicked world and there lost their political chastity." But the failure to acknowledge the fact of empire, in Lippmann's view, had pernicious consequences, since it meant that the management of these protectorates was turned over to interested businessmen or inexperienced diplomats. Few others seemed to care. When crises occurred in the Caribbean, "the only voices heard are those of the oil men, the fruit men, mining men, bankers on one side, and the outraged voices of the Gladstone liberals on the other. The debate is conducted by the hard-boiled and the soft-hearted." Lippmann, taking cognizance of this record, recommended that the United States institute something like the British colonial office for the management of its protectorates; instead, a surprising thing happened: the United States turned away from the prospect of further intervention.[11]

The anticipation that the Nicaraguan intervention was but the prelude to a much larger and more difficult intervention in Mexico proved mistaken. Coolidge's ambassador to Mexico, Dwight Morrow, negotiated a settlement with Mexico that finally brought agreement on a range of issues and that conceded Mexican claims of a right to national possession of their subsoil. Far from being the wave of the future, the Nicaraguan intervention constituted something of a swan song for Caribbean interventions, at least for another generation. Herbert Hoover, Coolidge's successor, was against further intervention and put the United States on the road to formal acceptance of the policy of the "good neighbor."[12]

The complex of attitudes distinguishing Republican diplomacy in the 1920s—an anti-imperialism that carved a broad exception for U.S. intervention in the hemisphere, an "internationalism" that expressed traditional hopes for peace and amity yet was nationalistic in trade, immigration, and security—had one outstanding characteristic: it was not fearful. With the end of the war, the old sense of American impregnability returned. The country clung, almost feverishly, to what Calvin Coolidge called the "tremendous good fortune" that surrounded its international position. "We have no traditional enemies. We are not embarrassed over any disputed territory. We have no possessions that are coveted by others; they have none that are coveted by us. Our borders are unfortified. We fear no one; no one fears us."[13] Coolidge's optimistic rendering of the American position was repeated by Hoover in an Armistice Day address of 1930, when he observed that "the outlook for peace is happier than for half a century." This attitude only made sense on the assumption, which Hoover devoutly believed, that nothing might happen in Europe or Asia that could affect the fundamentals of American security. Lewis Einstein quoted Hoover's comment with some wonderment and noted the developments decidedly adverse to world peace that had already occurred by the time of Hoover's bland assurance: "Six and a half million Hitlerites in Germany had just voted for a programme bred by misery and which, if carried out, can only end in war; and four million German Communists had voted for upheaval. Mussolini had repeated his speech of last spring: 'Words are beautiful, rifles and cannon are still better,' and openly professed his belief in war within the next few years. Soviet Russia remained an outlaw State, planning to bring about World Revolution. Austria was overawed by armed bands and Hungary continued truculent and revengeful. Spain was in the throes of a dangerous crisis; France, Poland and the Little Entente were arming, not without cause, suspicious of their neighbors. Outside Europe, South America had been swept by a wave of revolution, India stirred by dangerous unrest, and in China civil war continued!"[14]

41

The Great Depression and
Economic Nationalism

THE REVOLUTIONARY TURMOIL OF 1930 only worsened in the coming years, as political stability was shattered by economic depression. The sharp fall in equity values on Wall Street in 1929 helped set it all in motion. The collapse of liquidity, of readily available credit, ensured that the least creditworthy could no longer secure loans. Germany had, ever since the Dawes Plan of 1924, relied on short-term credits from American banks to fund reparations. Without those credits, it could not pay reparations; without reparations, the Allies could not pay their war debts to the United States. Defaults followed. This seizing up of the international payments system was complemented and exacerbated by the Smoot-Hawley Tariff of 1930, which raised rates to the highest level ever. These mutually reinforcing shocks to credit and trade were the veritable one-two blows that put the world economy flat on its back. With surplus capacity everywhere, states were extremely reluctant to allow in imports that would increase domestic unemployment. Prices collapsed; a debt contracted in 1928 was two or three times as onerous by 1932, and for a large number of individuals and firms that meant default and bankruptcy. Everywhere the people followed "a flaming nationalism," as the *New York Times* summarized the situation on New Year's Day, 1933: "Swept by centrifugal force, each nation draws in upon itself to weather the storm, to conserve its own resources." The "inflammation of aggressive nationalism" had produced "tariffs and reprisal tariffs, embargoes, currency restrictions, campaigns to 'Buy home-made goods,'" all of which were justified "on the ground that a nation can do anything, no matter how drastic or in what manner it affects its neighbors, in order to survive."[1]

The rickety international payments structure that collapsed in the early 1930s had been set in place by the Great War and its aftermath. The public took Coolidge's reputed view—"They hired the money, didn't they"—and opposed cancellation of the debts owed by Britain and France. They also thought it perfectly natural that America should return to the tradition of the protective tariff, enshrined almost as part of the foundational law of the American system since 1862. But these two stances, standing together, were nothing better than a logical contradiction, for without access to the

American market the debtors could not earn the remittances to pay their debts. Economists, whose profession was largely committed to economic internationalism, screamed from the rooftops that these policies went to the nether regions of economic insanity, to which the consensus replied: "The Allies contracted the debts and should pay them. We have a right to protect our workingmen." The great majority of congressmen, the *Times* of London noted at the end of 1931, "are still without any real understanding of the condition to which the world has been reduced by the incubus of the war debts and by the ham-stringing of international trade through prohibitive tariffs, and fail still more completely to realize that their own troubles are merely the reflections of that condition."[2]

The domino theory is best known as a proposition in geostrategic thinking, wherein military aggression is depicted as the first in a cascade of tumbling dominoes, but the theory also took strong hold of economic reasoning during the Depression and remains of cardinal importance today. The events of the early 1930s were the textbook example of the dangers that protectionism and nationalism posed to economic prosperity. The economic dominoes, too, preceded and helped produce the military dominoes that subsequently fell. The experience was of tremendous significance not only for the devastation it wrought in the lives of millions and for its ominous consequences in the political realm but also because it would haunt future generations of policymakers. The crisis showed that economic nationalism had a self-reinforcing character; once the descent was on, there was no way to escape the whirlwind. Among the dominos was the growth everywhere of state control over the means of production, entailing various forms of national socialism. Another was that trade and commerce, the sweet solvents of international discord, became simply the pursuit of war by other means. "Nazi economics" took this furthest and achieved, in the new environment, the swiftest recovery, but all nations, even those professing internationalism, were thrown back on their own devices. Franklin D. Roosevelt came to office with the theory that "'no substantial progress toward recovery from the depression, either here or abroad,' could be achieved without abandonment of the Republican doctrines of high tariffs and economic isolation." In the course of the year, especially after the failure of the London Economic Conference, he had accepted that "in the current phase of the depression it was necessary for each nation to give priority to its own problems."[3]

Intense nationalism, then, was both the cause and the consequence of the economic collapse. The very factors that had brought about the catastrophe were immeasurably strengthened by it. The experience left every nation convinced that there was little hope of salvation through international action; if they were to be saved, it was by pulling themselves up by their own bootstraps. There were several variations on this theme in the world, of which the American New Deal, with its eclectic mix of whatever might work, was but one. Republicans, who remained wedded to the tradition of high tariffs, believed with Hoover that the United States would be able "to make a large measure of independent recovery because we are so remarkably self-contained," and they continued to believe it even when the promise was belied by the deepening of the Depression.[4]

The idea of an economically isolated America also had appeal on the political left. Charles Beard, in *The Idea of the National Interest*, gave the fullest explication of an autarkic America that would carve out its own civilization apart from the war and strife of Europe and Asia. Beard, like the conservative isolationists, feared above all that the United States would be drawn into a future European war and believed, with them, that economic internationalism would give a formidable boost to political involvement. "The supreme interest of the United States," he wrote, "is the creation and maintenance of a high standard of life for all its people and ways of life . . . within the frame of national security." If trade endangered that security, it ought to be given up as a game not worth the candle. To achieve security "there must be the utmost emancipation from dependence upon the course of international exchange. . . . Let us limit our trade in order to increase our security . . . the less trade, the less navy we require . . . the less risks we take."[5]

Beard had always been a great unmasker of received truths since he came to national attention with his *Economic Interpretation of the Constitution* in 1913, and he scored the internationalists for promoting, under the guise of the common welfare, sordidly narrow economic interests. Behind the claptrap about mutually beneficial exchange was the farmer seeking his market and the banker making good on his loan; the "superstructure" of justification to which internationalists appealed was of no influence save as it lulled the minds of utopians or diverted attention from reality. Foreign policy, he believed, "could easily be made the instrument to stifle domestic wrongs under a blanket of militarist chauvinism, perhaps disguised by the high-sounding title of world peace." Beard, though righteously opposed to internationalism, nevertheless distinguished his own nationalism from the "predatory nationalism which devours in the name of its own myths and racial bigotries." His nationalism, according to a sympathetic critic, "would file the claws of such predatory forces and achieve 'positive control over the domestic forces responsible for outward thrusts of power.'" In order to do this, however, America must give up the fatuous search for export surpluses achieved via the Open Door and substitute instead "an intensive cultivation of its own garden."[6]

Beard's belief in an autarkic American system was not shared by most economists and was condemned vociferously by internationalists. They insisted that American economic well-being was not separable from the condition of the world economy, giving America a vital stake in its functioning, and they especially rejected Beard's contention that protection meant peace and free trade meant war. "The calamitous situation of the world today," wrote four internationalists in reply to Beard, "only too eloquently proclaims the fact that the desertion of foreign trade in the quest for self-sufficiency invites war and imperialism." "As the old mercantilism was warp and woof with the old colonialism," the free traders believed, "so the new mercantilism is hand in glove with the new imperialism."[7]

This was an old argument in American history, a resumption in new circumstances of the bitter polemics surrounding the protective system that had raged throughout the nineteenth century. Both sides had ample precedent on which they could rely, with protectionists glorying in the tradition of Clay, Lincoln, and McKinley, and internationalists pointing to George Washington's hope that "the benefits of a liberal and free commerce will pretty generally succeed to the devastation of war." But internationalists had one more thing going for them: they had the better argument. We of this generation have the perspective to see, having witnessed something like a controlled experiment, that a world of economic exchange was a formidable creator of wealth, whereas the route of autarky, in either its right-wing or left-wing versions, was a no less efficient destroyer thereof. Had the world followed that route in the twentieth century, instead of reversing course in midstream, it would have meant impoverishment for untold millions.

42

Isolation and Neutrality

WHAT GAVE PROFOUND POPULAR APPEAL to isolationism in the 1930s was the fear of involvement in another European war. Americans, as Henry Luce recalled the interwar opinion, "didn't much want to be in any kind of war but, if there was one kind of war we most of all didn't want to be in, it was a European war." This attachment to nonintervention, strictly speaking, was not pacifism. Americans generally, and isolationists especially, were not interested in turning the other cheek or loving their neighbor as themselves; they rejected that as a basis for foreign policy and were in principle prepared to fight for the maintenance of national independence and the Monroe Doctrine. Nor may 1930s isolationism be understood as simply the possession of a party or an outlook; closer to the truth is that "never again" was the possession of all parties and all outlooks. "We are not isolationists," Franklin Roosevelt declared in his 1936 election campaign, "except in so far as we seek to isolate ourselves completely from war." That was the great end in view to which nationalists and internationalists alike pledged fidelity and which expressed the rock-hard consensus of American public opinion throughout the 1930s.[1]

The sources of this profound desire were multifaceted, but its overpowering weight with intellectuals and the people was an interpretation of the Great War and of America's role in it. Everything, it seemed, was reflected in "the afterglow of the last conflagration."[2] In the role America had played since 1917, noted one commentator in 1932, the "American people think they have been misused; many, nay, the majority think they have been 'the goat,' that they have made themselves ridiculous before the world by always helping to the wrong end." Nothing hence evoked more hostility in America than the plea to assist Europe for humanitarian reasons: "This kind of argument has fallen into disrepute since 1917 with every American." To the isolationist disposition, it was evident that the parties to the European quarrel were actuated by the same selfish motives. In Europe and Asia, wrote Beard, "greed, lust, ambition . . . do not seem to be confined to Italy, Germany and Japan; nor does good seem to be monopolized by Great Britain, France and Russia." "The alleged moral certainty" posed by the confrontation between dictators and democrats, complained Harley Grattan, "is as fervent as that which misled us twenty-odd years ago."[3]

These realists, in keeping with the argument that E. H. Carr would advance in *The Twenty Years' Crisis*, believed that the "have-nots" had legitimate grievances that deserved recognition. They accepted that the Japanese had a good point when, in their exit from the League of Nations, their delegate declared that the Western powers had won their colonial dominion through high-stakes poker and now wanted to settle down to a game of contract bridge. Given the greed and hypocrisy of the Western imperialists, observed Borchard, it was a wonder that they had the temerity to "lecture others, like Italy, on the observance of law and morality." These slighting references to the Western powers were intended to show that America, even if it wished to cooperate, had no fit partners for the enterprise.[4]

Supporting these sentiments was the revisionist historiography that had arisen quickly after the end of the Great War. It first called into question Germany's exclusive guilt for the war, pointing especially to the Russian general mobilization as a critical precipitating factor. Not far behind was the proposition that America had gone to war in 1917 due to the importuning of munitions makers and Wall Street bankers, anxious that an Allied defeat would cashier their investments. The machinations of the special interests were the focus of the Nye committee in 1935, and the ensuing national sensation led to the enactment of neutrality legislation that attempted to ensure that, were another European war to break out, the United States would not be sucked in. In a series of acts between 1935 and 1937, Congress required the president to ban the shipment of arms and ammunition to all belligerents, while also forbidding loans and American travel on the ships of nations at war. Whereas Wilson had stretched neutral rights to a very implausible degree, especially in his insistence of the right of Americans to travel on armed belligerent merchantmen, the neutrality legislation of the 1930s renounced the neutral's traditional rights in a way that went far beyond the dictates of international law. The rights in defense of which Wilson went to war were to be abandoned at the outset, and the whole sequence of events that produced intervention in 1917 was to be cut up at the roots and made impossible.[5]

The most comprehensive and able defense of neutrality as an objective for the United States came from Edwin Borchard of Yale University. America had difficulty seeing the virtues of neutrality, in Borchard's view, because the conduct of the Wilson administration had so badly distorted its meaning. Despite professing neutrality, Wilson had been far from neutral. He had acquiesced in the British blockade against Germany and had put forth the extravagant claim that Americans had an incontestable right to innocent travel on belligerent merchantmen. While maintaining the Allies' right to arm belligerent merchantmen, Wilson denied the right of German submarines to attack them without warning, erecting an illogical double standard. This posture pushed the administration onto a "limb from which it was later unwilling to retreat." Like his mentor, John Bassett Moore, Borchard did not accept the "devil theory" emphasizing greedy private interests as the cause of American intervention in 1917. Instead, he insisted that Wilson's conflicting emotions—"the desire to play the part of mediator, the spasmodic desire to keep out of the war, and the desire to see the Allies win"—had placed him in so untenable a position that anything was possible. "Unprotected from his own ultimata, which never should have been issued had peace been his policy," Wilson "had made himself the victim of an incident."[6]

Borchard and his friends also cast a penetrating light on the theory of collective security. They did not believe that "paper schemes" would work; they showed that it would be impossible to achieve agreement on economic or military sanctions among so many disparate countries. They drew attention to how difficult it was, in particular instances, to decide the rights and wrongs of foreign quarrels, a sentiment that Americans had felt acutely in contemplating the ruin of postwar Europe. Economic sanctions, promoted by the advocates of collective security, were unlikely to be anything other than a road to war, placing the United States in a situation where, if sanctions failed, the result would be total war or abject surrender. Ultimately, they believed, the very attempt to abolish war would promote its universalization. Instead of containing conflicts, as the nineteenth-century law of neutrality had done, collective security would broaden them. Wilson was the source of all these errors, in Borchard's view, "the Crusader bearing fire and brimstone in one hand and sweet-scented lavender in the other." With Wilson, "world war for peace, democracy and a new order . . . began its preposterous career."[7]

The noninterventionist movement reached its highest influence in 1937. In that year, 70 percent of the American public believed that U.S. participation in the Great War had been a mistake. They reacted coldly to Roosevelt's proposal, made in response to the Japanese offensive against China, that the peace-loving nations attempt to "quarantine" the aggressors. They feared with the isolationists that such a proposal could easily be made the preliminary to a war. They supported the amendment to the Constitution offered by Louis Ludlow of Indiana, which would require a popular referendum to enter another war. The desire to avoid repetition of "the mistake of 1917," George Gallup commented, had been "the great master-principle of the postwar period in the United States, explaining our attitude on neutrality, our unwillingness to lend money again to defaulting nations and our sympathy for the principle of a war referendum."[8]

The same sympathy for nonintervention was reflected in the Latin American

policy of the United States. The American government under Hoover and
Roosevelt had abandoned the policy introduced by Wilson and followed by
Harding and Coolidge of refusing recognition to governments brought to
power by extraconstitutional means.[9] Though Sumner Welles had in 1933,
as FDR's ambassador to Cuba, refused recognition to a provisional Cuban
regime on the grounds that it was "not approved by the great majority of
the Cuban people" and had demonstrated disastrous incompetence "in every branch of public administration," he justified the policy on the ground
that, with the Platt Amendment still in effect, any such recognition would
inevitably be seen as constituting U.S. approval of the regime. In the new era
that dawned under the Good Neighbor Policy, in which the Platt Amendment was abrogated and the right of intervention renounced, the Roosevelt
administration instead embraced the "Estrada Doctrine," propounded by
the Mexican minister for foreign affairs in 1934, that would accord recognition automatically to any government as it comes into power.[10]

Welles, who as undersecretary played a vital role in the formulation of
American policy, opposed the view, proposed by some liberals, that the
American government had been "gravely derelict" because it had not "pursued in the Western Hemisphere . . . a policy of 'revolutionary democracy.'"
Though Welles wished to encourage representative governments in Latin
America and believed that peace would favor their consolidation, he equated
nonrecognition with indiscriminate intervention and rejected the idea that
the United States "should have assisted in the overthrow of the established
governments of the other American Republics in every case where they did
not meet the requirements" of liberal opinion in the United States. Any
such policy, as he later recalled, "would signalize the termination" of the
inter-American system. The result was that by 1940 "the last vestiges" of
U.S. intervention in Latin America had been "liquidated." Every marine had
been withdrawn, and the treaties (like that with Cuba) providing a right of
U.S. intervention, which hung like "a perpetual sword of Damocles over the
heads" of Latin peoples, had been abrogated.[11]

43

The Final Reckoning

ONE BEDROCK ASSUMPTION OF VIRTUALLY ALL PARTIES to the American debate throughout the 1930s was the conviction that the next European war, if it came, would likely be a stalemate. To a world grown accustomed to depictions of the Germans' miserable plight, it seemed highly improbable that Germany—still in a weakened condition and dependent on imports for critical items—should be the victor in a European war. This assumption deeply conditioned views of American security. The military analyst of the *New York Times*, Hanson Baldwin, wrote in the summer of 1939 that "no military tidal wave could prevail against our continental and hemispherical impregnability." The only danger to American security lay in going "far beyond our borders, into distant seas," which would entail a loss "in treasure, human life and national destiny which no man living can foresee. By frittering away our great strength in foreign theaters, we may well destroy that impregnability which today means certain security for the American castle."[1]

By the spring of 1939, however, public opinion had undergone a substantial change. It had not been swayed by Japanese aggression against China, or by Italian aggression against Ethiopia, or yet by the moral passions unleashed by the Spanish Civil War. What broke the spell was Hitler's repudiation of the Munich accords signed only months previously. As the war clouds gathered, noted George Gallup, American opinion crystallized around the following propositions: Help England and France. Make the United States as impregnable as possible. Stay out of the war. There were no discernible differences between Democrats and Republicans on these attitudes, Gallup reported, "or even between the Atlantic seaboard and the Middle West." Well before the shocking events of late August and early September 1939—when in the space of a few weeks Hitler and Stalin signed a nonaggression pact that divided eastern Europe between them, Germany invaded Poland, and England and France declared war—62 percent of the public felt "that the totalitarian powers would represent an immediate menace to America in case they won." Would they win? That was still deemed unlikely. "The chances of England and France being defeated are slim indeed," averred Senator Henry Cabot Lodge Jr. in October 1939, and "even if Germany were victorious and desired to conquer the United States, she never could do so." In early spring 1940, one poll showed 90 percent of Americans were confident of an Anglo-French victory over Germany.[2]

Hitler's invasion of Norway and Denmark in April 1940, followed by the rapid occupation of Holland and Belgium and the smashing defeat of France, caused a revolution in opinion: overnight, noted one newspaperman, American thought went "from belief in security to dread of tomorrow." The eighteen-month period between the fall of France and American entry into the war formed the high point of the debate over intervention. Up until that point, nearly all entertained the expectation that America would stay out, but now there began an agonized argument that recalled the frenzy of the pre–Civil War period. The late Arthur M. Schlesinger Jr. called it "the most savage national debate in my lifetime—more savage than the debate over communism in the late 1940s, more savage than the debate over McCarthyism in the early 1950s, more savage than the debate over Vietnam in the 1960s. The debate between interventionists and isolationists in 1940–41 had an inner fury that tore apart families, friends, churches, universities, and political parties." In that respect, indeed, the bitter estrangement of 1940–1941 was very similar to what had unfolded before the Civil War. In each case, the frenzy was proportional to the stakes, with all participants aware that the very purpose and meaning of the nation—its institutions, its identity, its deepest beliefs—hung on the outcome.[3]

Discarding all pretense of neutrality, yet still seeking to keep out of the war, the Roosevelt administration justified America's new status of "non-belligerency" by appealing to the Kellogg-Briand Pact renouncing war, of which Germany was a signator. The president reformulated American aims in his June 10, 1940, address at the University of Virginia. His premise was "that military and naval victory for the gods of force and hate would endanger the institutions of democracy in the Western World—and that equally, therefore, the whole of our sympathies lie with those nations that are giving their life blood in combat against those forces." The idea, which some still held, that America could "safely permit the United States to become a lone island in a world dominated by the philosophy of force" was a "now somewhat obvious delusion." It would condemn Americans to "the nightmare of a people lodged in prison, hand-cuffed, hungry and fed through the bars from day to day by the contemptuous, unpitying masters of other continents." From that specter arose Roosevelt's determination to speed up America's rearmament and to "extend to the opponents of force the material resources of this nation," becoming thereby "the arsenal of democracy." Roosevelt was at pains to justify this stance as the best means of keeping America out of the war, and the Republicans in 1940 chose a presidential candidate, Wendell Willkie, who supported that policy. So the question of whether all-out aid short of war was the best means of keeping out of the war was not an issue in the 1940 presidential election, but it was neverthe-less the great issue before the country.[4]

The noninterventionists had now reached the moment of truth. They faced a president who seemed clearly to be leading the country to war, saying one thing and doing the opposite, and they believed the stakes to be tremendous. Empire abroad and dictatorship at home would be the inexorable outcome of participation. "The inevitable result of what this war party is urging," Robert Taft warned, "is an American Empire doing what the British have done for the past two hundred years. But our people don't want to be em-perors even if they could be." Taft believed that the varied peoples of Europe would have to work out their own salvation. America could not do it for them, and it was unlikely that they would "welcome an Anglo-American be-nevolent despotism any more eagerly than a German despotism." The con-flicts of Europe were so unending, and the 80 million Germans so numerous, that the United States would have "to maintain a police force perpetually in Germany and throughout Europe" to protect the small democracies. There were, Taft believed, intrinsic limits to the wisdom and power of the United States to solve Europe's historic problems: "There have been wars in Europe for a thousand years. There will probably be wars for years to come. Europe, its varied peoples and its small democracies must work out their own salva-tion. No outsider can permanently aid them."[5]

The deepest fear of the noninterventionists was that total war would entail a fundamental alteration of the American system. The constitutional alloca-tions of power would be irredeemably changed by participation in an all-out war. "I never was more convinced of anything in my life," wrote Senator Borah, "than that, if we become directly involved in these controversies, we will at no distant date find ourselves under the control of a wholly different form of government than what the Constitution now provides." Oswald Garrison Villard, who resigned from the *Nation* in 1940 over the support its editorial board, led by Freda Kirschner, gave to intervention, wrote that the editors would "some day awake to a realization that the course they are now proposing will inevitably end all social and political progress, lower still further the standard of living, enslave labor, and, if persisted in, impose a dictatorship and turn us into a totalitarian state." Far from safeguarding democracy, argued Senator Taft, "war is likely to destroy democracy right here in the United States." Enormous war debts "would probably break down the whole free enterprise system on which the American type of free-dom has depended." The powers the president would gain, even if some lapsed with the end of the emergency, would outlive the war: "If the war lasts for five years," Taft warned, "I doubt whether we ever return to our constitutional system."[6]

This belief that entry into the war would mean "regime change" at home was key to both right-wing and left-wing versions of isolationism. If for conservative isolationists entry into the war would bring the end of Lincoln's republic, for liberal isolationists it would bring the return of the America of 1917–1918, with its frenzied domestic suppressions and reversals of reform. But all variants of noninterventionists looked with trepidation on the two closely related consequences—arbitrary power at home and empire abroad—that they saw as the inexorable consequence of intervention. Undoubtedly, this conception was imbued with national feeling; it exalted the well-being of the nation above any other value. The noninterventionists rejected "isolationism" but fully accepted "nationalism" as a depiction of their policy: "The party of non-intervention represented by the America First Committee," wrote Beard in an open letter to the group, "includes no 'Appeasers,' no 'ostrich isolationists,' no foreigners of any nationality in letter or spirit, and no pacifists."[7] What was exalted, however, was not what is normally conveyed by "nationalism" as a motive force of state action; it was elegiac, nostalgic, intent above all on preserving the constitutional liberties and characteristic ways of life of a distinctive American civilization. Savaged by critics as abettors of "tyranny, sadism, and human defilement," the noninterventionists strapped themselves to the mast of the old republic and appealed to the vision of an America strong in its unassailable fortress, protected by the oceans from a world gone mad.[8]

Just as self-described nationalists rejected the "isolationist" label, many self-described internationalists rejected the "interventionist" label. Nor was this for the most part deceptive advertising, for the internationalist consensus as a set of fundamental beliefs and aspirations congealed in 1940 and 1941 even as most internationalists still wanted to keep out of the war. In urging all-out aid to the democracies, internationalists accepted that such a policy brought with it a greatly heightened risk of war, but the movement as a whole was greatly torn between the desire to see Hitler defeated and the desire to stay out. William A. White, the principal founder of the Committee to Defend America by Aiding the Allies, emphasized in December 1940 that "his only motive was 'to keep this country out of war' and that his organization opposed sending American convoys to Great Britain" and repealing neutrality provisions barring aid. White soon resigned because of the controversy stirred by his statement, but the dispute, as the *New York Times* editorialized, was just a reflection of the divided internationalist mind.[9]

Scholars have disagreed on what was most important to those who saw a vital stake in the outcome of the European war, even as they clung to the hope of avoiding all-out involvement. Three schools of opinion have emerged on the question, paralleling our tripartite explanatory apparatus. One, realist and nationalist in orientation, sees the new consensus as focused intently on national security to the exclusion of moral and material factors. A second, revisionist, stresses imperial aspirations and ascribes vital importance to the Open Door and the perceived need for international solutions to domestic economic crisis. A third, internationalist, sees an outlook that defined itself in opposition to totalitarianism and that projected a free world whose basis would be either a new union among the constitutional democracies or a new compact among the peace-loving nations.[10]

This scholarly controversy, though important, should not obscure the critical point that all three factors were of fundamental importance in the development of American foreign policy. Like Father, Son, and Holy Ghost, they formed a seemingly indissoluble trinity. Many of those who pointed to the danger to America's physical security if English seapower should fall before German might—Walter Lippmann and Edward Mead Earle avidly purveyed that theme—were equally convinced of the existence of a moral and civilizational unity that had been startled into existence by German nihilism. They appealed to the threat the Nazis posed to America's physical security, to the inestimable importance of maintaining the seas as highways of commerce and exchange, and to the existence of an "Atlantic Community" that embraced nations in Europe, the Americas, and the Pacific in common bonds of interest, sentiment, and civilization. In the internationalist view, both independence and union were threatened by the Nazi scourge—independence because totalitarian control of Eurasia threatened American national security and well-being, and union because the same specter threatened an open trading system and basic civilizational values treasured in the West. These imperatives of independence and union, so long cast asunder since America had entered the twentieth century, were now fused by Hitler into one indissoluble whole.[11]

The deep substratum of internationalist belief is best seen as a negation of Hitlerism. Everything he represented, the internationalists opposed. Hitler's open glorification of force and "the persecution and destruction of hundreds of thousands of human beings because they were Polish or Jewish or Christian," the flouting of constitutional and peaceful procedure in every interaction, foreign or domestic, the rejection down to the last jot and tittle of the civilized intercourse of Western nations embodied in the society of states—this irruption from Germany's gutter was a malignancy unlike any other that Europe had suffered in a long history of wars, crimes, and devastations. No one had really been prepared for this. The "ice cold evil" that

Hitler represented, as Lippmann noted, had been discounted as a possible reality by the modern skeptical temper, one among the many forgotten but essential truths that were lost when, "thinking we were enlightened and advanced, we were merely shallow and blind."[12]

Thus disillusioned with their own disillusion, the internationalists were not bashful in affirming the sacred value of their liberal heritage. "The creeds of Communism and Fascism," wrote Earle, the dean of American strategists, "are a negation of every accepted tenet—liberal and conservative—of organized society. Exploiting worldwide insecurity and fear, the Fascist states have played havoc with individual liberties, have exalted themselves to deity and have made faithlessness, braggadocio, blackmail and falsehood the new bases of international relations. War is exalted as the normal state of affairs, peace decried as the abnormal. Trade is a weapon of conquest and plunder, economics the science of military power rather than the search for a higher standard of human welfare."[13]

The Nazi conquest of continental Europe also induced a revolution of opinion regarding America's stake in the community of democracies. The security and well-being of this community were now seen as being indissolubly linked with America's own. Internationalists of all stripes believed devoutly in the World War I era that such a union would have to be built in the twentieth century, and they had thrilled to Wilson's vision of a partnership of democratic nations. But no such union had been built. The interwar period had largely featured poisoned relations among the Western democracies, which proved generally incapable of sustained cooperation in that era. But the Nazis, in their very rejection of liberalism, instilled a new faith in the liberal creed: opposition to totalitarianism and belief in the natural alliance of the free democracies fused in the mind as one fundamental and solemn conviction. This psychological shift came suddenly in 1940 and was of tremendous import in the development of American internationalism. In its approach to the League of Nations, Gerald W. Johnson recalled in mid-1941, the nation had cherished the traditional idea "that its own unaided strength was and would ever remain sufficient for its needs." "Blandly and blindly," Johnson wrote, the critics who opposed in 1919 what they took to be a unilateral American guarantee "assumed that Europe would always need American strength, but that the time would never come when America would need European strength. A majority of the people shared this belief and clung to it until the very hour when a tremendous combination of tyrannies seemed on the point of wiping out the last strongholds of free government in Europe, thrusting us suddenly into a form of isolation that we had never contemplated and most emphatically did not want." The plain lesson was that "our own safety is indissolubly linked with the safety of all free peoples, and that ours cannot be assured without assuring that of others."[14]

It followed from the nature of Hitler's threat that neutrality in such a war was impossible. From the first the Nazis had rejected the whole apparatus of law as of no value. Borchard, for all his sophistication, failed to see that neutrality was but one of the institutions of the society of states and had to be sacrificed as of lesser weight when the whole was in peril. It was made for an age of limited war, not one of brazen continental-sized conquest, fitted for monarchies and republics that recognized, even if they did not always obey, the "dictates of civilization." Hitler's rejection of the whole structure of international law, his contempt for the society of states, made this a war not over any principle within the law of nations but over whether there should be such a law at all—"an irreconcilable conflict," wrote Ellsworth Barnard, "as to what shall be the ultimate principle governing the relations among states."[15]

In a vital supporting role to these considerations was the belief, shared by all internationalists, that the world had to move beyond the system of closed trading blocs that defined the 1930s and find its way to a progressive lowering of tariff barriers. Cordell Hull, secretary of state from 1933 to 1944, was the great champion of this view in the American government. Holding that protection meant war and free trade meant peace, he made the relaxation of trade barriers his cause célèbre. Though his negotiations for bilateral reductions of tariffs were about the only way to make a start on this in the 1930s, these treaties had had little effect in prompting recovery. But the internationalists had big plans. Their premise was that national protection in trade, which had defined the American approach to political economy since the Civil War, was now utterly obsolescent. Future secretary of state Dean Acheson argued in 1938 that the remedies for the recovery of the world economic mechanism from paralysis were as plain as day: the rapid removal of tariffs, "a broader market for goods made under decent standards," "a stable international monetary system," new ways to make capital available for industrial production, and the elimination of "exclusive or preferential trade arrangements."[16]

Internationalists pointed to the new pattern of inter-American relations inaugurated by FDR as illustrating the contrast between the American and Nazi conceptions. The group of twenty-one nations that constituted the inter-American system, wrote A. A. Berle Jr., a confidant of Roosevelt, had "rejected the idea of peace by universal empire or by the diplomatic juggle of balance of power. It has adopted, instead, the ideal of the cooperative peace—the ideal which is the great contribution of the Americas to world thought."[17] In 1940, Roosevelt emphasized the Western Hemisphere community as representing a model world order. "We of this hemisphere have no need to seek a new international order; we have already found it. This was not won by hysterical outcries or violent movements of troops. We did not stamp out nations, capture governments or uproot innocent people from the homes they had built. We did not invent absurd doctrines of race supremacy or claim dictatorships through universal revolution." Latin Americans had seldom been in a mind to accept the glittering generalities of *norteamericanos* at face value, and Roosevelt over the preceding years had had to work through a thick fog of suspicion and mistrust. But to all appearances an American president had found an approach that was genuinely popular in the nations to the south. It was uncanny, said a Chilean diplomat, difficult to explain, a source of some amazement even to themselves: Roosevelt was popular, indeed greatly esteemed, in Latin America. By paying close attention, he had articulated the principles by which Latin America might gladly join in communion with the colossus to the north.[18]

The Western Hemisphere community that Roosevelt idealized could not accurately be described as a "democratic peace." Its foundation was not a common commitment to democracy but a common commitment to certain basic principles of international law. Though Latin America retained enough of the old Spanish liberalism to be recognizably of the West, its democratic institutions had faltered. At the end of 1938, according to historian J. Fred Rippy, twelve Latin American states were ruled by dictators, perhaps more if one looked to the "deep structures" of these regimes or dismissed various rigged elections for the frauds they evidently were. These juntas ruled "seventy-five million people in Latin America" and dominated "a land area almost twice the size of the United States." Those undemocratic tendencies, though discouraging, were not for Roosevelt an insuperable obstacle: "Peace reigns among us today because we have agreed, as neighbors should, to mind our own business. We have renounced, each and all of us, any right to interfere in each other's domestic affairs, recognizing that free and independent nations must shape their own destinies and find their own ways of life."[19]

The commitment to nonintervention lay alongside the aspiration to promote "the four essential human freedoms," as Roosevelt called them. "Everywhere in the world" would America seek "freedom of speech and expression," "freedom of every person to worship God in his own way," and "freedom from want." The fourth essential freedom was freedom from fear, which meant "a world-wide reduction of armaments to such a point and in such a thorough fashion that no nation will be in a position to commit an act of physical aggression against any neighbor." In the Atlantic Charter, signed with Winston Churchill on a ship off Newfoundland on August 14,

1941, these pledges were reiterated amid the plea "that all of the nations of the world, for realistic as well as spiritual reasons must come to the abandonment of the use of force." Pending "the establishment of a wider and permanent system of general security" that would permit a lessening of expenditure on armaments, the disarmament of the aggressor nations would be essential.[20]

Both sides in the great debate between nationalists and internationalists claimed the mantle of historic tradition, with one side emphasizing independence, the other the need to bring independence and union into a new relationship. The best statement of the noninterventionists was Beard's *A Foreign Policy for America* (1940), where he gave an eloquent rendition of the foreign policy of independence. In his writings on American history and foreign policy, Beard had been a relentless detector of hidden motives, sniffing about the pious declarations of policymakers like an indefatigable hound dog, and usually finding plenty of interested parties whose wealth stood to be affected by the decision of the government. In this book his tone was different, and he recapitulated the encrusted dogmas with respect and even veneration. Beard called the nineteenth-century approach "continentalism," though he acknowledged that no simple phrase could capture it. The strong sympathy Americans expressed for despoiled liberty abroad, as with Greece in 1821 and Hungary in 1849, did not dislodge the nonintervention principle from its central place in the American system. American leaders, expressing a broad public consensus, "were non-interventionists in respect of European wars which were not projected into the western hemisphere. They were also non-interventionists in respect of the purely domestic conflicts arising in other countries everywhere, including this hemisphere." American statesmen believed that the United States should concentrate on building a civilization in North America that would be "essentially extra-European," as John Quincy Adams put it, and that would keep the lamp of the republic "burning brightly on this western shore," in Clay's words, rather than hazard "its utter extinction amid the ruins of fallen and falling republics in Europe." Sympathizing with liberal movements abroad, American officials yet "made no invidious discriminations on account of forms, ideologies, morals or religions," carrying on business "with despotic Tsars, Mohammedan Sultans, and oriental tyrants, as well as with parliamentary Britain and republican France." The great state papers setting forth these principles, as Beard fondly observed, were "marked by gravity of style, simplicity, and clarity of statement" and employed "the language of restraint, dignity, and courtesy." From the vantage point of 1940, Beard acknowledged that both imperialism and internationalism had challenged this consensus over the previous fifty years and had been sufficiently appealing as to occasionally sweep the American people off their feet. As he read the record, however, the people over time regained their balance and saw that the promise offered by these heresies was essentially false.[21]

Despite Beard's exclusive claim to the mantle of historic tradition, the internationalists also had good authority on their side. The founders had put at the core of their philosophy of international relations the conviction that federal republican government could survive only by avoiding the twin demons of international anarchy and universal empire, yet there was no escaping the fact that anarchy and despotism were worse than they had ever been in Western civilization. Anarchy was worse because of the terrifying implications of new weapons technologies. Despotism was worse because the catastrophe of the world war had spawned regimes far more complete in their regimentation and more directly opposite to free government than anything that civilized old Europe had produced under the rule of monarchs and aristocrats. The idea that a union was required to arrest the malign forces of anarchy and despotism was no late arrival to American history but rather the oldest idea in the American approach to international relations; on it the republic had been built. Seward had indeed advised, as Beard noted, fidelity to the principle of nonintervention—"straight and peculiar as it may seem to others"—but he had also said that when despotism makes a common cause, "it results also that the cause of constitutional liberty has also become one common cause."[22]

The worst kind of despotism, according to the Founders, the one most menacing to civilization, liberty, and progress, was that which hitched its star to the dream of universal empire. Hamilton had denounced France in the 1790s for its embrace of this "hideous project," and the internationalists had oodles in Hamilton's oeuvres to make use of: Hamilton was deeply committed to the society of states tradition and emphatically saw the British navy as a shield against Continental conquerors. It is as certain as anything can be that he would have favored intervention in the crisis of 1940–1941. With Jefferson the case is more doubtful. Of the two great Founders, indeed, Jefferson was really the man for the crisis, because no one had so deeply feared the emergence of an American power state, with its centralized institutions, massive debts, and standing armies, but no one had more lyrically expressed the enduring liberalism of American life, to which Nazism stood in such deadly counterpoise. The debate of 1940–1941, then, brought forth a Jeffersonian moment of exquisite torment, and the nationalists and internationalists could each speak cogently to one half of his divided mind.

There would come a time, Jefferson had prophesied, when America might "shake a rod over the heads of all" the European powers, which would "make the stoutest of them tremble." Though Jefferson added the hope that "our wisdom will grow with our power," teaching us "that the less we use our power, the greater it will be," surely no better cause than the salvation of the Enlightenment may be imagined for some serious rod shaking. So, too, Jefferson had written in the early 1800s that American security dictated the wish "that he who has armies may not have the Dominion of the sea, and that he who has Dominion of the sea may be one who has no armies." He accepted in 1814 and 1815 that it could not be for the interest of the United States that Europe should be reduced to a single monarchy, and prayed that the "establishment of another Roman empire, spreading vassalage and depravity over the face of the globe," was not "within the purposes of Heaven." He was ready to join with Britain in 1823 to make this hemisphere one of freedom against the depredations of Continental monarchies.[23]

These considerations generally supported the internationalist case, but there were undoubtedly contrary indications in the oracular sayings of the sage of Monticello. Throughout the Napoleonic Wars, Jefferson had shared the belief—so characteristic a feature of 1930s isolationism—that there was an essential moral equivalence between the European parties. Britain was a pirate roaming over the ocean, France a robber despoiling the land, but both followed iniquitous policies fatal to the society of states. He had blasted away at the hypocrisy of Britain—"the friend and protector of Copenhagen!"—as readily as Beard and Borchard did later. So, too, Jefferson had often expressed skepticism that Bonaparte would succeed in the mad enterprise to dominate the earth, if indeed that was his aim, believing that the "chapter of accidents" would likely prove fatal to his plans.[24]

But if those convictions might have steered Jefferson away from intervention, the most agonizing question was what intervention would do to the character of America's domestic institutions. War undoubtedly would mean the multiplication to the nth degree of every Hamiltonian tendency toward centralization that he had looked upon as the knell of the republic. More than once for Jefferson did that specter lead him to favor creating an ocean of fire between the Old World and the New World. But the internationalists were not backward in invoking the same specter the isolationists had done. In their view, the failure to intervene, if it led to the victory of the totalitarian powers, would make inevitable in America a garrison state, armed to the teeth and necessarily subject to internal regimentation. Only if the Nazis were defeated, they argued, could a permanent garrison state be avoided. If this were an accurate forecast, even the faithful Jeffersonian would have no alternative but to take the plunge.[25]

An equally vital precedent about which everyone was conscious was afforded by Wilson and the Great War. Wilson was often criticized in later years, especially by the post–World War II generation, for not explaining to

the people the paramount strategic dangers posed by a threat to "the balance of power," preferring to dwell on the higher plane of moral principle
in justification of his every step. That was certainly the Wilson the American
public remembered, the one who had asked them to be Santa Claus for the
world and had considered it demeaning to tell them what they would gain
from the bargain. But their memory was somewhat faulty on that score, for
Wilson had in fact informed them of this danger. In his speeches of 1918,
and again in his great western tour of 1919, he articulated repeatedly the
great stakes involved in turning back the German bid for mastery over the
Continent. He had shuddered at that outcome in 1914, thinking that a German victory would "change the course of our civilization and make the
United States a military nation." He was even more preoccupied with that
danger from 1917 to 1920.[26]

Wilson objected strongly to the idea, which he associated with the "balance of power," that order could be had if each nation pursued its own
advantage without any consideration of the common interest, on the analogy of the free Smithian individual who, by pursuing his own economic
advantage, creates by an invisible hand the greater wealth of the society.
The catastrophe of the Great War, as Wilson rightly concluded, had shown
this concept to be an absurd basis on which to found a stable system of interstate relations. Nevertheless, Wilson was as committed as anyone to the
belief that for the security of each and all the universal dominion by any one
power over the state system had to be prevented, by force if necessary—and
this, after all, was the key historic meaning of the balance of power as an
objective of the European society of states. Wilson called this danger to mind
in 1918 as eloquently as Churchill would do in 1940. The German purpose,
he said in 1918, "is undoubtedly to make all the Slavic peoples, all the free
and ambitious nations of the Baltic peninsula, all the lands that Turkey has
dominated and misruled, subject to their will and ambition and build upon
that dominion an empire of force upon which they fancy that they can then
erect an empire of gain and commercial supremacy, an empire as hostile to
the Americas as to the Europe which it will overawe, an empire which will
ultimately master Persia, India, and the peoples of the Far East."[27]

That was also the specter that Wilson invoked in his 1919 western tour
when he warned that the rivalries of the world had not cooled but had been
rendered "hotter than ever." His warning against what would later be called
"the garrison state" presumed the threat of Continental domination that
Germany represented in 1917–1918 and that it had, against all expectations, achieved again in 1940–1941. From whatever conjunction of motives,
the logic of war had pushed Germany by 1917 toward the utter domination
of the European peoples. Unrestricted submarine warfare was the decisive

move in the victory of the most extreme forces in Germany, reflecting a thralldom to force that, in the war's final year, anticipated the state socialism, brutality, and regimentation of the Nazi period.

Given these similarities between 1917–1918 and 1940–1941, it is not surprising that after the fall of France the "ghost of Woodrow Wilson" had begun to stir again in the disturbed imaginings of the American people. Wilson had been the subject of countless books, wrote Gerald W. Johnson, but these authors had only succeeded in embalming him. It was Hitler who brought him to life. "Once more the gaunt old Presbyterian looms in the imaginations of Americans and his words and his ideas take on vitality and force again." It was generally conceded that Wilson had wrong-footed many things. He had an irritating personality. In his great moral appeals, he had left the impression that international cooperation was selfless service rather than enlightened self-interest. The denunciations of him, the jokes about him, the sad pathetic ending of him, could fill (had filled) many volumes. Withal, the great commanding ideals and conceptions of role that Wilson evoked now stirred the nation. The people were beginning to think he might have been right after all, and there suddenly loomed the possibility that, like a "drowsing Barbarossa," Wilson might "start from his sleep and rush to the field to lead his countrymen again." For Johnson and many others, that was a very happy thought: "Certainly Hitler could face no more appalling apparition than the ghost of Woodrow Wilson with America united behind him as it was united in 1917. For with the protagonists of hatred and intrigue and violence he can always find a way to live very comfortably, if he must; but a nation determined to secure 'not a balance of power, but a community of power; not organized rivalries, but an organized common peace' is his implacable, mortal enemy."[28]

The form that might be taken by this "organized common power" could be but barely glimpsed in 1940 and 1941, but the internationalists all knew and preached the catechism—at once liberal, republican, and unionist—whereby anarchy would give rise to despotism unless arrested by a union. In the concluding passage of a little pamphlet of 1940, Walter Lippmann predicted that the "anarchy will continue, it will expand and become ever more destructive, unless there is forged in the fires of the war itself—under the pressure of necessity and in the mood of heroic devotion—the hard core of an enduring union."[29]

What kind of union exactly? That, of course, was the rub. The alternatives were not unlimited. As in 1919, the key alternatives revolved around two separate questions: How deep? How wide? Would the new union, in other words, be a mere confederation or would it enjoy a statelike apparatus? Would the new union put the Atlantic Community at its core, or would it aspire toward universality? In that earnest time, which featured an "uproar of revolutionary spirits" crusading "anew for the ideals of 1917," nothing was off the table. At a 1940 seminar on American isolation sponsored by the American Historical Association, the "most applauded speaker expressed the opinion that the only road to a peaceful world lay in the creation of a super-state enforcing a universal order." The Council on Foreign Relations study group chaired by James Shotwell spoke in its concluding passage of the need to move from "league to federation." A protestant group chaired by John Foster Dulles, future secretary of state, proposed the creation of a federal government for the world consisting of a parliament, an international court, and suitable executive agencies. It would possess "adequate international police forces" and have the authority to impose "worldwide economic sanctions."[30]

The public seemed receptive to such speculations, but the sheer number and variety of conceptions were also doubtless confusing. Henry Luce spoke of an "American Century" that entailed remaking the world in America's image—a conception that most internationalists did not like because it had overtones of imperialism. Henry Wallace invoked a "Pax Democratica" that would undergird the "Free World" and chose "the century of the common man" as a better objective than Luce's American Century. Clarence Streit, the former *New York Times* reporter at Geneva, published a book, *Union Now*, that called for a federation of the North Atlantic that would be modeled on the Constitution of 1787. Streit's commanding idea was the need to overcome the gap that existed between the disorganization of the democracies and their great potential power against the totalitarians if they could somehow mobilize that preponderance in union. *Union Now*, a surprise commercial success, proposed a federation of fifteen nations that would embrace the United States, Great Britain, the self-governing British dominions, and the nations of Western Europe, including Belgium, France, Holland, Scandinavia, and Switzerland.[31]

Even in 1940 and 1941, the key tension within internationalism that would emerge during and after the war was already apparent. It lay between the particularists and the universalists. One side, wrote Ross Hoffmann, "is conservative and conceives the war as a conflict brought on by the attack of revolutionary and barbaric forces upon the concrete order of political society, states and constitutional structures, civil institutions, law, freedom, social order, and civilized international institutions running back through Christendom to Rome, Athens, and Jerusalem. The other is a revolutionary conception in which the war appears not only as an effort to beat back 'reaction' but also as an effort to arrive upon new horizons and to create a new age of universal peace, justice, and prosperity. The first emphasizes tradition and might be called Churchillian; the second emphasizes progress and is rather Rooseveltian."[32]

Perhaps the key difference between the universalists and the particularists lay in their contrary diagnoses of the causes of conflict. The Roosevelt administration, especially its key State Department officials, Sumner Welles and Cordell Hull, saw war anywhere as "an infectious disease against which there was no immunity in isolation, and which therefore must be totally eliminated." The only way to do that was by a collective security system "with teeth" that would immunize the world against aggression. The particularists, by contrast, saw a concrete historical community that included "the British nations, the American nations, and . . . the Latin nations on both sides of the Atlantic, and across the Pacific," whose interests were "so enmeshed by geography, by strategic necessity, and by historic formation that their paramount interests are, when tested in the fires of total war, inseparable." In this view, eloquently summarized by Walter Lippmann in his two little books of the war years, the Atlantic nations needed "a common foreign policy in their relations with the non-Atlantic World." Such a system of "organic consultation"—more than a formal treaty of alliance but less than a political federation—reflected a community with the deepest values in common but one that could not be held together through compulsion. It was to be not "one military empire ruled from one capital" but rather "a concert of free nations held together by a realization of their common interests and acting together by consent." Internationalists, then, were divided on the world they wanted to build, with one side insisting upon the construction of a universal society that would effectively forbid aggression everywhere and the other on the deepening of ties within the West. But both repudiated isolationism and imperialism, and both saw the need to subordinate the nation to a larger sense of international community.[33]

The great debate over intervention was resolved abruptly by the Japanese attack on Pearl Harbor on December 7, 1941, followed—in an unexpected act of benevolence and good faith toward his Japanese ally—by Hitler's declaration of war against the United States on December 11. Suddenly the great debate was all over. Isolationists had the slender consolation that it turned out as they had predicted, that the "short of war" strategy, far from being the best means of keeping out of the war, basically guaranteed that the United States was going to go all the way in. Historians still argue whether Roosevelt consciously chose the "back door to war," but there is no doubt that the precipitating cause of the Pacific War was the economic and military shock given to Japan by the U.S. sanctions imposed in the summer of 1941. Not wanting to be further complicit in Japanese aggression in China and Southeast Asia, the United States deprived Japan of the oil without which its

fleet could not function. Combined with the U.S. demand that Japan evacuate every foot of territory it had taken in China since 1931, Japan was forced
into a corner. Facing an effective choice between attack and surrender, it
attacked. The isolationists had warned that war lay at the end of the road,
but on December 8, 1941, they received no points for their perspicacity. It
no longer mattered. Americans united behind the president in prosecution
of the war. Isolationists fled to a dark and guilty corner of the American
imagination, there to await the merciless drubbing they would receive from
a new generation.

While it lasted, the great debate had touched the deepest chords of the
national faith, its bitterness a function of the tragic confrontation of irreconcilable goods. It was entirely in keeping with the nature of the question that
the frenzied arguments reminded observers of the days before the Civil War,
for the stakes in the two conflicts were very similar. We remember the Civil
War and World War II as fights for individual liberty, but in their origin and
purpose they much more reflected irreconcilable conflicts "as to what shall
be the ultimate principle governing the relations among states." The union
could tolerate a partnership with slaveholders, and the international order
could, as it had always done, accommodate monarchs and dictatorships,
but what neither could tolerate was the determined assault on its foundations, a challenge that threatened to cut it up by the roots. Unionists and
internationalists alike saw, in 1861 and 1941, that the failure to use force in
response would not leave in its wake the old union or the old international
order, which in each case had broken down utterly. Instead, the alternative
to war was an endless cycle of anarchy and despotism engorging upon the
entrails of the human race, the worst nightmare of the American imagination come to life.

In retrospect, it cannot be doubted that American intervention in this
second titanic war was necessary and justified, and we cannot really imagine
the world that might have transpired in its absence. Wrote one Russian in
November 1941, shortly before American entry: "To imagine for a moment
the possibility of Hitler's victory meant to forego all reason; if it were to
happen then there could be no truth, logic, nor light in the development
of human society, only chaos, darkness and lunacy; and it would be better
not to live."[34] Intervention, nevertheless, posed a tragic choice, placing two
fundamental but irreconcilable values in mortal antagonism. The noninterventionists were undoubtedly wrong about the necessity of American intervention, but they anticipated, sometimes with remarkable prophetic power,
the complications that would ensue once the United States undertook a permanent commitment to world order. Their predictions of dictatorship and
totalitarianism for the United States happily proved unfounded, but they

were not mistaken in believing that the old republic would vanish with the war and in its place would be a new American state with vastly magnified executive powers, standing military establishments, and centralized institutions. As devotees of constitutional liberty, it was not ignoble for them to fear these things: the danger that by fighting totalitarianism the United States would insensibly come to resemble the thing it fought haunted even the internationalist outlook and made the choice faced by the United States in 1941 one that was indubitably tragic.[35]

But there was promise as well as peril in the assumption by the United States of a globe-girdling role. The world of 1941 desperately needed a fresh reordering, a new constitution whereby the peoples of the world might develop freely in peace, and no one was then better equipped to offer this than the Americans. To no state fell more naturally the leadership role in a constitutional partnership of free nations, one whose purpose would necessarily be to establish the bases of a cooperative peace and to ward off insidious tendencies toward anarchy and despotism. There was much in the American constitutional tradition of intense relevance in the construction of a new world order, much in the old unionist paradigm that spoke directly to the new realities of global interdependence. If, as was said in 1841, "the union of all nations, in a state of peace, under the restraints and protection of law, is the ideal perfection of civil society," surely the American mission in 1941 was to hurry that ideal forward. The American political tradition, far from representing an obstacle to clear thinking about international relations, conferred decided advantages in that task. The United States, far from being the least prepared to preside over the creation of a peaceful world order, was the best prepared. [36]

SHORT TITLES AND
SELECTED BIBLIOGRAPHY

The notes are intended to provide a record of the scholarship that was most important to me in the composition of the book. I have used short titles for both primary and secondary sources; the works listed below consist mainly of books cited in more than one chapter. For easily accessible state papers, such as presidential addresses, congressional debates, and *The Federalist*, I use a more economical mode than customary. The annual messages of the presidents, together with much further valuable material, are available at www.avalon.org, a Web site maintained by the Yale Law School. I have also made extensive use of the electronic collections of the Making of America project undertaken by Cornell University and the University of Michigan. Many nineteenth-century titles (including the papers of Jefferson, Clay, Seward, and Webster) have different publication dates with the same editors, which I signify, if different from the standard citation, with the year of publication—for example, *Seward Works* (1853).

A new and exciting way of conducting research has been opened up by Google Books, which in recent years made great advances in digitizing the Stanford and Harvard collections, among others. One can type in a fifteen-word string at books. google.com and usually find the original document in which the phrase appears. Some eighteenth- and nineteenth-century titles are still behind a wall, but for the most part they're free as a bird. To one who has spent a good part of his existence chasing footnotes, while pained by a lack of ready access to rare titles, this seems like the arrival of the promised land and fair compensation for *all* the other ills that technology has brought upon us. It was very helpful in the final preparation of the manuscript.

SHORT TITLES OF PRIMARY SOURCES

Adams Papers	*The Papers of John Adams.* Edited by Robert J. Taylor et al. 14 vols. to date. Cambridge, MA, 1977–.
Adams Works	*The Works of John Adams.* Edited by Charles Francis Adams. 10 vols. Boston, 1850–1856.
Ames, *State Documents*	*State Documents on Federal Relations: The States and the United States.* Edited by Herman V. Ames. New York, 1970 [1906].
Ames Works	*Works of Fisher Ames, as Published by Seth Ames.* Edited by W. B. Allen. 2 vols. Indianapolis, 1983 [1854].
Annals of America	*The Annals of America.* Published by Encyclopaedia Britannica. 21 vols. Chicago, 1968.
ASP: Indian Affairs	*American State Papers: Indian Affairs.* Edited by

Walter Lowrie et al. Washington, DC, 1832–1834.

Bartlett, *Record* — *The Record of American Diplomacy*. Edited by Ruhl J. Bartlett. New York, 1964.

Benton, *Debates* — *Abridgment of the Debates of Congress, from 1789 to 1856*. Edited by Thomas Hart Benton. 16 vols. New York, 1857–1861.

Bryce, *American Commonwealth* — James Bryce, *The American Commonwealth*. New York, 1919 [1888].

Buchanan Works — *The Works of James Buchanan*. Edited by John Bassett Moore. 12 vols. Philadelphia, 1908–1911.

Calhoun, *Union and Liberty* — *Union and Liberty: The Political Philosophy of John C. Calhoun*. Edited by Ross M. Lence. Indianapolis, IN, 1992.

Calhoun Works — *The Works of John C. Calhoun*. Edited by Richard K. Crallé. 6 vols. New York, 1888.

Cappon, *Adams-Jefferson* — *The Adams-Jefferson Letters: The Complete Correspondence between Thomas Jefferson and Abigail and John Adams*. Edited by Lester J. Cappon. 2 vols. Chapel Hill, 1959.

Choate Works — *The Works of Rufus Choate, with a Memoir of His Life*. Edited by Samuel Gilman Brown. 2 vols. Boston, 1862.

Clay Papers — *The Papers of Henry Clay*. Edited by James F. Hopkins et al. 11 vols. Lexington, KY, 1959–1991.

Clay Works — *The Works of Henry Clay*. Edited by Calvin Colton et al. 10 vols. New York, 1904.

Commager, *Civil War Archive* — *The Civil War Archive: The History of the Civil War in Documents*. Edited by Henry Steele Commager and Erik Bruun. New York, 2000.

Elliot, *Debates* — Elliot, Jonathan, ed. *The Debates in the Several State Conventions on the Adoption of the Federal Constitution as Recommended by the General Convention at Philadelphia in 1787. . . .* 5 vols. Philadelphia, 1859.

Farrand, *Records* — Farrand, Max, ed. *The Records of the Federal Convention of 1787*. Rev. ed. 4 vols. New Haven, CT, 1937.

Federalist — Alexander Hamilton, James Madison, and John Jay. *The Federalist*. Edited by Jacob E. Cooke. Middletown, CT, 1961.

Franklin Writings — *The Writings of Benjamin Franklin*. Edited by Albert Henry Smyth. 10 vols. New York, 1905–1907.

Gallatin, *Selected Writings*   *Selected Writings of Albert Gallatin.* Edited by
E. James Ferguson. New York, 1967.

Gallatin Writings   *The Writings of Albert Gallatin.* Edited by Henry
Adams. 3 vols. Philadelphia, 1879.

Graebner, *Ideas*   *Ideas and Diplomacy: Readings in the Intellectual
Tradition of American Foreign Policy.* Edited by
Norman A. Graebner. New York, 1964.

Hamilton Papers   *The Papers of Alexander Hamilton.* Edited
by Harold C. Syrett et al. 26 vols. New York,
1961–1979.

Hamilton Works   *The Works of Alexander Hamilton.* Edited by
Henry Cabot Lodge. 12 vols. New York, 1904.

Hofstadter, *Great Issues*   *Great Issues in American History.* Vol. 2, *From the
Revolution to the Civil War, 1765–1865.* New York,
1958. Edited by Richard Hofstadter.

Jefferson Papers   *The Papers of Thomas Jefferson.* Edited by
Julian P. Boyd et al. 34 vols. to date. Princeton, NJ,
1950–.

Jefferson Works   *The Works of Thomas Jefferson.* Edited by
Paul. L. Ford. 12 vols. New York, 1904. All
references to *Jefferson Works* are to Ford's multiple
editions, one of which (New York, 1892–1899) has
the title *Writings.*

Jefferson Writings   *The Writings of Thomas Jefferson.* Edited by
Andrew A. Lipscomb and Albert Ellery Bergh. 20
vols. Washington, DC, 1905.

JQA Memoirs   *Memoirs of John Quincy Adams, Comprising
Portions of His Diary from 1795 to 1848.* Edited by
Charles Francis Adams. Philadelphia, 1874–1877.

JQA Writings   *The Writings of John Quincy Adams.* Edited by
Worthington C. Ford. 7 vols. New York, 1913.

LC   Library of Congress. I use this designation for the
multiple editions of congressional debates (e.g.,
Annals of Congress, Register of Debates), available
at http://memory.loc.gov/ammem/amlaw/lwac.html.

Lincoln Speeches   *Abraham Lincoln: Speeches and Writings, 1832–
1865.* Edited by Don E. Fehrenbacher. New York,
1989.

Lincoln Works   *The Collected Works of Abraham Lincoln.* Edited
by Roy P. Basler. 10 vols. New Brunswick, NJ,
1953.

Madison Letters   *Letters and Other Writings of James Madison.*
Published by order of Congress. 4 vols.
Philadelphia, 1865.

Madison Papers

The Papers of James Madison. Edited by William T. Hutchinson et al. Chicago, 1962–1977 (vols. 1–10); Charlottesville, VA, 1977– (vols. 11–).

Montesquieu, *Spirit of the Laws*

Montesquieu, Charles de Secondat, baron de. *The Spirit of the Laws.* Edited and translated by Anne M. Cohler et al. Cambridge, 1989.

Moore, *Digest*

A Digest of International Law . . . Edited by John Bassett Moore. 8 vols. Washington, DC, 1906.

MP

A Compilation of Messages and Papers of the Presidents, 1789–1897. Edited by James D. Richardson. 10 vols. Washington, DC, 1896–1899.

Paine *Writings*

Thomas Paine: Collected Writings. Edited by Eric Foner. New York, 1995.

Peterson, *Writings*

Thomas Jefferson: Writings. Edited by Merrill D. Peterson. New York, 1984.

Phelps, *League of Nations*

Selected Articles on a League of Nations. Edited by Edith M. Phelps. New York, 1919.

Roosevelt *Works*

Works of Theodore Roosevelt, Memorial Edition. Edited by Hermann Hagedorn. 24 vols. New York, 1923–1926.

Schurz *Papers*

Speeches, Correspondence, and Political Papers of Carl Schurz. Edited by Frederic Bancroft. 6 vols. New York, 1913.

Seward *Works*

The Works of William H. Seward. Edited by George E. Baker. 5 vols. New York, 1884.

Smith, *Commonwealth or Empire*

Smith, Goldwin. *Commonwealth or Empire: A Bystander's View of the Question.* New York, 1902.

Smith, *Republic of Letters*

The Republic of Letters: Correspondence between Thomas Jefferson and James Madison, 1776–1826. Edited by James Morton Smith. 3 vols. New York, 1995.

Smith, *Wealth of Nations*

Smith, Adam. *An Inquiry into the Nature and Causes of the Wealth of Nations.* Edited by Edwin Cannan. New York, 1937 [1776].

Stephens, *Constitutional View*

Stephens, Alexander H. *A Constitutional View of the Late War between the States.* 2 vols. Philadelphia, 1868–1870.

Storing, *Anti-Federalist*

The Complete Anti-Federalist. Edited by Herbert J. Storing and Murray Dry. 7 vols. Chicago, 1981.

Story, *Commentaries*

Story, Joseph. *Commentaries on the Constitution of the United States.* 3 vols. Boston, 1833.

Sumner, *Conquest of U.S.*

Sumner, William Graham. *The Conquest of the United States by Spain.* Boston, 1899.

Sumner Works	*The Works of Charles Sumner.* 15 vols. Boston, 1870–1883.
Tocqueville, *Democracy in America*	Tocqueville, Alexis de. *Democracy in America.* Edited by Phillips Bradley. 2 vols. New York, 1945.
Trueblood, *Federation of the World*	Trueblood, Benjamin. *The Federation of the World.* Boston, 1899.
Van Buren Autobiography	*The Autobiography of Martin Van Buren.* Edited by John C. Fitzpatrick. Annual Report of the American Historical Association for the Year 1918. Vol. 2. Washington, DC, 1920.
Washington Writings	*George Washington: Writings.* Edited by John Rhodehamel. New York, 1997.
Webster Papers: Diplomatic	*The Papers of Daniel Webster: Diplomatic Papers.* Edited by Kenneth E. Shewmaker et al. 2 vols. Hanover, NH, 1983–1987.
Webster Papers: Speeches	*The Papers of Daniel Webster: Formal Speeches and Writings.* Edited by Charles M. Wiltse et al. 2 vols. Hanover, NH, 1986–1988.
Webster Works	*The Works of Daniel Webster.* Edited by Edward Everett. 6 vols. Boston, 1851.
Webster Writings	*The Writings and Speeches of Daniel Webster.* Edited by Edward Everett. 18 vols. Boston, 1903.
Wilson Papers	*The Papers of Woodrow Wilson.* Edited by Arthur S. Link. 69 vols. Princeton, NJ, 1966–1994.
Wilson Speeches	*President Wilson's Foreign Policy: Messages, Addresses, Papers.* Edited by James Brown Scott. New York, 1918.

SECONDARY SOURCES

Adams, Henry. *History of the United States of America during the Administrations of Jefferson and Madison.* New York, 1889–1891, 9 vols.

———. *The Life of Albert Gallatin.* Philadelphia, 1880.

Adler, Selig. *The Isolationist Impulse: Its Twentieth-Century Reaction.* New York, 1957.

Anderson, Fred, and Andrew Cayton. *The Dominion of War: Empire and Liberty in North America, 1500–2000.* New York, 2005.

Bacevich, Andrew J. *American Empire: The Realities and Consequences of U.S. Diplomacy.* Cambridge, MA, 2002.

Banner, James M. *To the Hartford Convention: The Federalists and the Origins of Party Politics in Massachusetts, 1789–1815.* New York, 1970.

Banning, Lance. *The Sacred Fire of Liberty: James Madison and the Founding of the Federal Republic.* Ithaca, NY, 1995.

Bartlett, Ruhl J. *The League to Enforce Peace.* Chapel Hill, NC, 1944.

Beard, Charles. *A Foreign Policy for America.* New York, 1940.

Beisner, Robert L. *Twelve against Empire: The Anti-Imperialists 1898–1900*. New York, 1968.

Bender, Thomas. *A Nation among Nations: America's Place in World History*. New York, 2006.

Bensel, Richard. *Yankee Leviathan: The Origins of Central State Authority in America, 1859–1877*. Cambridge, UK, 1990.

Borchard, Edwin, and William Potter Lage. *Neutrality for the United States*. 2nd ed. New Haven, CT, 1940.

Boritt, Gabor S. *Lincoln, the War President*. New York, 1992.

Brands, H. W. *What America Owes the World: The Struggle for the Soul of Foreign Policy*. Cambridge, UK, 1998.

Carter, Paul A. *Revolt against Destiny: An Intellectual History of the United States*. New York, 1989.

Davis, S. Rufus, *The Federal Principle: A Journey through Time in Quest of a Meaning*. Berkeley, CA, 1978.

Deudney, Daniel. *Bounding Power: Republican Security Theory from the Polis to the Global Village*. Princeton, NJ, 2007.

———. "The Philadelphian System: Sovereignty, Arms Control, and Balance of Power in the American States-Union, *circa* 1787–1861." *International Organization* 49 (1995): 191–228.

Eckes, Alfred E., Jr. *Opening America's Market: U.S. Foreign Trade Policy since 1776*. Chapel Hill, NC, 1995.

Edling, Max M. *A Revolution in Favor of Government: Origins of the U.S. Constitution and the Making of the American State*. New York, 2003.

Ellis, Joseph J. *American Creation: Triumphs and Tragedies at the Founding of the Republic*. New York, 2007.

———. *Founding Brothers: The Revolutionary Generation*. New York, 2000.

Ellis, Richard E. *The Union at Risk: Jacksonian Democracy, States' Rights and the Nullification Crisis*. New York, 1987.

Fischer, David Hackett. *Albion's Seed: Four British Folkways in America*. New York, 1989.

Forsyth, Murray. *Unions of States: The Theory and Practice of Confederation*. New York, 1981.

Graebner, Norman A., ed. *Traditions and Values: American Diplomacy, 1790–1865*. Lanham, MD, 1985.

———. *Traditions and Values: American Diplomacy, 1865–1945*. Lanham, MD, 1985.

Hendrickson, David C. *Peace Pact: The Lost World of the American Founding*. Lawrence, KS, 2003.

Higham, John. *Strangers in the Land: Patterns of American Nativism, 1860–1925*. New Brunswick, NJ, 2002.

Hogan, Michael J., ed. *Paths to Power: The Historiography of American Foreign Relations to 1941*. Cambridge, UK, 2000.

Horsman, Reginald. *Race and Manifest Destiny: The Origins of American Racial*

Anglo-Saxonism. Cambridge, MA, 1981.

Howe, Daniel Walker. *What Hath God Wrought: The Transformation of America, 1815–1848*. New York, 2007.

Huntington, Samuel P. *Who Are We? The Challenges to America's Identity*. New York, 2004.

Jackson, Robert. *The Global Covenant: Human Conduct in a World of States*. New York, 2000.

Johannsen, Robert W. *Stephen A. Douglas*. New York, 1973.

Johnson, Robert David. *The Peace Progressives and American Foreign Relations*. Cambridge, MA, 1995.

Jonas, Manfred. *Isolationism in America, 1935–1941*. Ithaca, NY, 1966.

Judis, John B. *The Folly of Empire: What George W. Bush Could Learn from Theodore Roosevelt and Woodrow Wilson*. New York, 2004.

Kagan, Robert. *Dangerous Nation*. New York, 2006.

Kauffman, Bill. *Ain't My America: The Long, Noble History of Antiwar Conservatism and Middle-American Anti-Imperialism*. New York, 2008.

———. *America First! Its History, Culture, and Politics*. Amherst, NY, 1995.

Keller, Morton. *Affairs of State: Public Life in Late Nineteenth Century America*. Cambridge, MA, 1977.

Kennan, George F. *American Diplomacy, 1900–1950*. Chicago, 1985 [1951].

Kersh, Rogan. *Dreams of a More Perfect Union*. Ithaca, NY, 2001.

Kinzer, Stephen. *Overthrow: America's Century of Regime Change from Hawaii to Iraq*. New York, 2006.

Knock, Thomas. *To End All Wars: Woodrow Wilson and the Quest for a New World Order*. New York, 1992.

Knupfer, Peter B. *The Union as It Is: Constitutional Unionism and Sectional Compromise, 1787–1861*. Chapel Hill, NC, 1991.

Kohn, Hans, *American Nationalism: An Interpretive Essay*. New York, 1957.

Konig, David Thomas, ed., *Devising Liberty: Preserving and Creating Freedom in the New American Republic*. Stanford, CA, 1995.

Kuehl, Warren F. *Hamilton Holt: Journalist, Internationalist, Educator*. Gainesville, FL, 1960.

———. *Seeking World Order: The United States and International Organization to 1920*. Nashville, TN, 1969.

Kuehl, Warren F., and Lynne K. Dunne. *Keeping the Covenant: American Internationalists and the League of Nations*. Kent, OH, 1997.

Kupchan, Charles. *The End of the American Era: U.S. Foreign Policy and the Geopolitics of the Twenty-first Century*. New York, 2002.

LaFeber, Walter. *The American Search for Opportunity, 1865–1913*. Vol. 2 of *The Cambridge History of American Foreign Relations*. New York, 1993.

———. *The New Empire: An Interpretation of American Expansion, 1860–1898*. Ithaca, NY, 1998 [1963].

Lerner, Ralph. *The Thinking Revolutionary: Principle and Practice in the New Republic*. Ithaca, NY, 1987.

Lewis, James E., Jr. *The American Union and the Problem of Neighborhood: The United States and the Collapse of the Spanish Empire, 1783–1829.* Chapel Hill, NC, 1998.

Lieven, Anatol. *America Right or Wrong: An Anatomy of American Nationalism.* New York, 2004.

Lind, Michael. *The American Way of Strategy.* New York, 2006.

———. *The Next American Nation: The New Nationalism and the Fourth American Revolution.* New York, 1995.

———. *What Lincoln Believed : The Values And Convictions Of America's Greatest President.* New York, 2005.

Link, Arthur S. *Woodrow Wilson: Revolution, War, and Peace.* Arlington Heights, IL, 1979.

Lippmann, Walter. *U.S. War Aims.* Boston, 1944.

Malone, Dumas. *Jefferson and His Time.* 6 vols. Boston, 1948–1981.

Mayers, David. *Dissenting Voices in America's Rise to Power.* Cambridge, UK, 2007.

———. *Wars and Peace: The Future Americans Envisioned.* New York, 1999.

McCardell, John. *The Idea of a Southern Nation: Southern Nationalists and Southern Nationalism, 1830–1860.* New York, 1979.

McCoy, Drew R. *The Elusive Republic: Political Economy in Jeffersonian America.* New York, 1980.

———. *The Last of the Fathers: James Madison and the Republican Legacy.* Cambridge, UK, 1989.

McDougall, Walter A. *Promised Land, Crusader State: The American Encounter with the World since 1776.* Boston, 1997.

McPherson, James M. *Abraham Lincoln and the Second American Revolution.* New York, 1991.

———. *Battle Cry of Freedom: The Civil War Era.* New York, 1988.

Mead, Walter Russell. *Special Providence: American Foreign Policy and How It Changed the World.* New York, 2001.

Meinig, D. W. *The Shaping of America: A Geographical Perspective on 500 Years of History.* 4 vols. New Haven, CT, 1988–2004.

Merk, Frederick, with Lois Bannister Merk. *Manifest Destiny and Mission in American History: A Reinterpretation.* New York, 1963.

Morison, Samuel Eliot. *The Oxford History of the American People.* 3 vols. New York, 1972.

Morrison, Michael A. *Slavery and the American West.* Chapel Hill, NC, 1997.

Nagel, Paul C. *One Nation Indivisible: The Union in American Thought, 1776–1861.* New York, 1964.

Nevins, Allan. *Ordeal of the Union.* 8 vols. New York, 1971.

Ninkovich, Frank. *Modernity and Power: A History of the Domino Theory in the Twentieth Century.* Chicago, 1994.

———. *The United States and Imperialism.* Malden, MA, 2001.

———. *The Wilsonian Century: U.S. Foreign Policy since 1900.* Chicago, 2001.

Nordholt, Jan Willem Schulte. *Woodrow Wilson: A Life for World Peace*. Berkeley, CA, 1991.

Onuf, Nicholas, and Peter Onuf. *Nations, Markets, and War: Modern History and the American Civil War*. Charlottesville, VA, 2006.

Onuf, Peter S. *Jefferson's Empire: The Language of American Nationhood*. Charlottesville, VA, 2000.

Onuf, Peter S., and Nicholas Onuf. *Federal Union, Modern World: The Law of Nations in an Age of Revolutions, 1776–1814*. Madison, WI, 1993.

Osgood, Robert E. *Ideals and Self-Interest in America's Foreign Relations: The Great Transformation of the Twentieth Century*. Chicago, 1953.

Pagden, Anthony. *Lords of All the World: Ideologies of Empire in Spain, Britain, and France, c. 1500–c. 1800*. New Haven, CT, 1995.

Paolino, Ernest N. *The Foundations of the American Empire: William Henry Seward and U.S. Foreign Policy*. Ithaca, NY, 1973.

Paterson, Thomas G., and Dennis Merrill, eds. *Major Problems in American Foreign Policy*. 2 vols. 4th ed. Lexington, MA, 1995.

Patterson, David S. *Toward a Warless World: The Travail of the American Peace Movement, 1887–1914*. Bloomington, IN, 1976.

Peterson, Merrill D. *The Great Triumvirate: Webster, Clay, and Calhoun*. New York, 1987.

———. *Lincoln in American Memory*. New York, 1994.

———. *Thomas Jefferson and the New Nation*. New York, 1970.

Pocock, J.G.A. *Barbarism and Religion*. 4 vols. to date. New York, 2001–.

Porter, Bruce D. *War and the Rise of the State: The Military Foundations of Modern Politics*. New York, 1994.

Potter, David M. *The Impending Crisis, 1848–1861*. New York, 1976.

Prestowitz, Clyde. *Rogue Nation: American Unilateralism and the Failure of Good Intentions*. New York, 2003.

Randall, James G. *Constitutional Problems under Lincoln*. Urbana, IL, 1951.

Richards, Leonard L. *The Slave Power: The Free North and Southern Domination, 1780–1860*. Baton Rouge, LA, 2000.

Ruggie, John Gerard. *Winning the Peace: America and World Order in the New Era*. New York, 1996.

Schlesinger, Arthur M., Jr. *The Cycles of American History*. Boston, 1986.

Schulzinger, Robert D., ed. *A Companion to American Foreign Relations*. Malden, MA, 2003.

Stagg, J. C. A. *Mr. Madison's War: Politics, Diplomacy, and Warfare in the Early American Republic, 1783–1830*. Princeton, NJ, 1983.

Stampp, Kenneth M. *The Imperiled Union: Essays on the Background of the Civil War*. New York, 1980.

Steel, Ronald. *Walter Lippmann and the American Century*. New York, 1981.

Stourzh, Gerald. *Alexander Hamilton and the Idea of Republican Government*. Stanford, CA, 1970.

Stromberg, Roland N. *Collective Security and American Foreign Policy: From the League of Nations to NATO*. New York, 1963.

Sullivan, Mark. *Our Times: America at the Birth of the Twentieth Century.* Edited by Dan Rather. New York, 1996 [1926].

Tannenbaum, Frank. *The American Tradition in Foreign Policy.* Norman, OK, 1955.

Thompson, John A. *Woodrow Wilson.* New York, 2002.

Tucker, Robert W. *The Radical Left and American Foreign Policy.* Baltimore, 1971.

———. *Woodrow Wilson and the Great War: Reconsidering Wilson's Neutrality, 1914–1917.* Charlottesville, VA, 2007.

Tucker, Robert W., and David C. Hendrickson. *Empire of Liberty: The Statecraft of Thomas Jefferson.* New York, 1990.

Turner, Frederick Jackson. *The Significance of Sections in American History.* Edited by Max Farrand and Avery Craven. New York, 1932.

Van Deusen, Glyndon G. *William Henry Seward.* New York, 1967.

Walling, Karl-Friedrich. *Republican Empire: Alexander Hamilton on War and Free Government.* Lawrence, KS, 1999.

Weinberg, Albert K. *Manifest Destiny: A Study of Nationalist Expansionism in American History.* Baltimore, 1935.

Whitaker, Arthur P. *The United States and the Independence of Latin America, 1800–1930.* New York, 1964 [1941].

———. *The Western Hemisphere Idea: Its Rise and Decline.* Ithaca, NY, 1954.

Widenor, William C. *Henry Cabot Lodge and the Search for an American Foreign Policy.* Berkeley, CA, 1980.

Wight, Martin. *International Theory: The Three Traditions.* Edited by Gabriele Wight and Brian Porter. New York, 1992.

Wilkinson, Charles. *American Indians, Time, and the Law: Native Societies in a Modern Constitutional Democracy.* New Haven, CT, 1987.

Williams, William Appleman. *Empire as a Way of Life.* New York, 1982.

———. *The Tragedy of American Diplomacy.* New York, 1962.

Wolfers, Arnold, and Laurence W. Martin, *The Anglo-American Tradition in Foreign Affairs: Readings from Thomas More to Woodrow Wilson.* New Haven, CT, 1956.

Wooley, Wesley T. *Alternatives to Anarchy: American Supranationalism since World War II.* Bloomington, IN, 1988.

Zimmermann, Warren. *First Great Triumph: How Five Americans Made Their Country a World Power.* New York, 2002.

NOTES

Preface and Acknowledgements

1. For various axioms in the "Whig science of politics," see Gordon S. Wood, *The Creation of the American Republic, 1776–1787* (Chapel Hill, NC, 1969). For a rousing defense of the relevance of the pre-1945 experience, see Mead, *Special Providence*, 3–29.

2. This tradition—unionist, federalist, internationalist—is notable by its absence in the valuable review of the historiography of American diplomacy in Jerald A. Combs, *American Diplomatic History: Two Centuries of Changing Interpretations* (Berkeley, CA, 1983). The seminal piece in the new historiographical turn emphasizing union and federation is Peter S. Onuf, "A Declaration of Independence for Diplomatic Historians," *Diplomatic History* 22 (1998): 71–83. See also the introduction of Emily S. Rosenberg, "A Call to Revolution: A Roundtable on Early US Foreign Relations," ibid., 63–70.

3. Speech of James Wilson, in Farrand, *Records*, 1: 405.

4. Henry Kissinger, *Diplomacy* (New York, 1994), 20.

5. Deudney, *Bounding Power*. Michael Lind, *American Way*, develops a conceptual apparatus in which empire and anarchy figure as fundamental threats, just as they do in "the unionist paradigm" and "republican security theory."

6. Pocock, *Barbarism and Religion*, 2: 220.

7. Important works in the history of international thought are cited in Hendrickson, *Peace Pact*, 314n3. See also the lucid survey of John A. R. Marriott, *Commonwealth or Anarchy? A Survey of Projects of Peace* (London, 1939).

8. Kagan, *Dangerous Nation*; McDougall, *Promised Land*, 3–5; Mead, *Special Providence*; Lind, *Next American Nation*, and idem, *American Way*; Lieven, *America Right or Wrong*.

Chapter 1. The Problem and Its Modes

1. Alfred Zimmern, "How Can Europe Unite?" *Vital Speeches* 17 (1951): 677–80. A good short statement of this "constitutional partnership" may be found in Daniel Deudney and G. John Ikenberry, "The Logic of the West," *World Policy Journal* 10 (1993/94): 17–25. See also Ikenberry, *Liberal Order and Imperial Ambition: Essays on American Power and International Order* (New York, 2006); and *After Victory: Institutions, Strategic Restraint, and the Rebuilding of Order after Major Wars* (Princeton, NJ, 2001), esp. chapter 6. The "governance institutions" of the American-led order, Ikenberry observes, saw sustained investments "in alliances, partnerships, multilateral institutions, special relationships, great power concerts, cooperative security pacts, and democratic security communities" (Ikenberry, "Liberal Order Building," in *To Lead the World: American Strategy after the Bush Doctrine*, ed. Melvyn P. Leffler and Jeffrey W. Legro [New York, 2008], 87). Variations on this theme are also presented in Deudney, *Bounding Power*; Timothy Garton Ash, *Free World: America, Europe, and the Surprising Future of the West* (New York,

2004); Ruggie, *Winning the Peace*; David C. Hendrickson, "In Our Own Image: The Sources of American Conduct in World Affairs," *National Interest* 50 (Winter 1997–1998): 9–21; Michael Doyle, "An International Liberal Community," in *Rethinking America's Security*, ed. Graham Allison and Gregory F. Treverton (New York, 1992), 307–33; Eugene V. Rostow, *Toward Managed Peace* (New Haven, CT, 1993), 5; Ernest May, "The American Commitment to Germany, 1949–1955," *Diplomatic History* 13 (1989): 431–60; and Samuel P. Huntington, *The Clash of Civilizations and the Remaking of World Order* (New York, 1996), 53, where Huntington writes that "the emerging universal state of Western civilization is not an empire but rather a compound of federations, confederations, and international regimes and organizations."

2. The most important recent book investigating the significance of nationalism is Lieven, *America Right or Wrong*. Michael S. Sherry, *In the Shadow of War: The United States since the 1930s* (New Haven, CT, 1995), emphasizes domestic compulsions rather than external provocations in dictating U.S. conduct. For other studies in the nationalist vein, see below, chapter 3.

3. A good introduction to the vast literature on imperialism is Frank Ninkovich, "Imperialism," in Schulzinger, *Companion*, 79–102. Much of the literature charging imperialism upon the United States has, in recent years, been focused on the Iraq war that began in 2003 and the foreign policy of the George W. Bush administration. Most internationalists joined in the condemnation of Bush's "imperial" policies, but a number of scholars rejected the assumption that Bush's policies represented a dramatic departure from the record of past administrations. Of those writers, the most prominent has been Andrew J. Bacevich. In *American Empire*, Bacevich revived the "open door" interpretation of Charles Beard and William Appleman Williams; in *The New American Militarism: How Americans Are Seduced by War* (New York, 2005), Bacevich developed a cultural interpretation emphasizing the growth of a militarism oddly spawned by the memory of defeat in Vietnam; in *The Limits of Power: The End of American Exceptionalism* (New York, 2008), he stressed the sheer improvidence of an incoherent and corrupt worldview. Bacevich also edited a formidable reconsideration of U.S. national security policies, *The Long War: A New History of U.S. National Security Policy since World War II* (New York, 2007). In three successive books, Chalmers Johnson has also developed the imperial interpretation and has insisted, like Bacevich, that the proclivity long predates the first decade of the twenty-first century: *Blowback: The Costs and Consequences of American Empire* (New York, 2000); *The Sorrows of Empire: Militarism, Secrecy, and the End of the Republic* (New York, 2004); and *Nemesis: The Last Days of the American Republic* (New York, 2007). There are also important new interpretations in the imperial vein covering the post-1945 period in Gareth Porter, *Perils of Dominance: Imbalance of Power and the Road to Vietnam* (Berkeley, CA, 2005), and Christopher Layne, *The Peace of Illusions: American Grand Strategy from 1940 to the Present* (Ithaca, NY, 2006). The views of foreign policy historians are gathered in Lloyd C. Gardner and Marilyn B. Young, eds., *The New American Empire* (New York, 2005). The locus classicus of the imperial interpretation is William Appleman Williams, *Tragedy*, and idem, *Empire as a Way of Life*. For consideration of the "Wisconsin school"—also called "New Left," "radical," "revisionist," and "progressive"—see Tucker, *Radical Left*.

4. Cf. the lucid formulation, insufficiently grasped in the American science of

international politics, of Robert Jackson and Georg Sorensen, *Introduction to International Relations* (New York, 1999), 29. "People often expect states to uphold certain key values: security, freedom, order, justice, and welfare. IR theory concerns the ways in which states do or do not ensure those values." See also Jackson, *Global Covenant*, for a trenchant defense of this methodological perspective.

5. Meinig, *Shaping of America*, 2: xv. Empire, federation, and nation form vital organizing concepts in Meinig's magisterial series.

Chapter 2. American Internationalism

1. A. A. Berle Jr., assistant secretary of state, "No, Says Berle," *New York Times*, January 14, 1940.

2. Kennan, *American Diplomacy*, 95–96. On early twentieth-century American internationalism, see the studies cited in chapter 35. A good short introduction, though at odds with my approach in certain respects, is Warren F. Kuehl and Gary B. Ostrower, "Internationalism," *Encyclopedia of American Foreign Policy*, 2nd ed., ed. Alexander DeConde et al. (New York, 2002).

3. Carsten Holbraad, *Internationalism and Nationalism in European Political Thought* (New York, 2003), 1.

4. For various expressions of this pervasive theme, see, for example, Kuehl, *Seeking World Order*; McDougall, *Promised Land*; and Prestowitz, *Rogue Nation*. Hans Jonas, "Internationalism as a Current in the Peace Movement: A Symposium," in *Peace Movements in America*, ed. Charles Chatfield (New York, 1973), 174–75, argues that "aside from pacifist visionaries like William Ladd and Elihu Burritt, dabblers in international relations like Andrew Carnegie and Edward Ginn, and theorists like Josiah Royce and Thorstein Veblen whose primary concerns really lay elsewhere, there were virtually no prominent Americans prior to the First World War who can be meaningfully described as internationalists, and there was certainly no internationalist movement of any significance."

5. A felicitous expression of Ninkovich, *Modernity and Power*, 173.

6. Memorial Day Address, May 30, 1916, *Wilson Speeches*, 197–98.

7. Burke's idea of "conservative reform" always had great appeal to Wilson. On Wilsonianism as a "tremendously original intellectual achievement," see Ninkovich, *The Wilsonian Century*, 49–50. A Wilson without antecedents is also an assumption in Michael Mandelbaum, *The Ideas That Conquered the World* (New York, 2002). This view is not unusual. The towering figures of early twentieth-century diplomacy, Theodore Roosevelt and Woodrow Wilson, are invariably seen as anticipations of things to come later, and justly so. But there is value also in seeing them from the vantage point of the long nineteenth century. Wilson, Roosevelt, and Henry Cabot Lodge were keen students of American history and had spent years absorbing its debates and contestations. Wilson wrote, among other works, a very creditable five-volume American history for the general public. Alice Roosevelt Longworth, TR's mercurial daughter, recalled as an old woman that she could still "hear my father and Cabot Lodge talking about Jefferson as if he were an obnoxious neighbor of theirs." Kauffman, *America First!* 104. On Lodge's use of history, see Widenor, *Lodge*, 1–43, 171–220.

8. Madison, Eighth Annual Message, December 3, 1816; Webster, "The Revolution in Greece," January 19, 1824, *Webster Works* (1890), 3: 75. What Wight

felicitously termed "the constitutional tradition in diplomacy" is explored in Martin Wight, "Western Values in International Relations," in *Diplomatic Investigations: Essays in the Theories of International Politics*, ed. Martin Wight and Herbert Butterfield (Cambridge, MA, 1966), 90–91. For further investigations of what he called "the broad middle ground" of Western thought, see Wight, *International Theory*; Hedley Bull, *The Anarchical Society: A Study of Order in World Politics* (New York, 1977); and Jackson, *Global Covenant*. The classic exposition of American membership in this society was given by Chancellor Kent: "The law of nations, so far as it is founded on the principles of natural law, is equally binding in every age, and upon all mankind. But the Christian nations of Europe, and their descendants on this side of the Atlantic, . . . have established a law of nations peculiar to themselves. They form together a community of nations, united by religion, manners, morals, humanity, and science, and united also by the mutual advantages of commercial intercourse, by the habit of forming alliances and treaties with each other, of interchanging ambassadors, and of studying and recognizing the same writers and systems of public law." James Kent, *Commentaries on American Law* (New York, 1826), 1: 3–4. Attesting to this membership are the eight volumes of John Bassett Moore's *Digest of International Law*, first compiled in 1906, and Charles Cheney Hyde, *International Law . . . as Interpreted and Applied by the United States* (Boston, 1922). See also discussions in Lind, *American Way*; Hendrickson, *Peace Pact*; and Daniel Patrick Moynihan, *On the Law of Nations* (New York, 1990).

9. John Adams to James Warren, *Adams Papers*, 6: 348. See further Onuf and Onuf, *Federal Union*, 103–8.

10. The definitive review, though stopping at 1861, is Onuf and Onuf, *Nations, Markets, and War*. Douglas A. Irwin, *Against the Tide: An Intellectual History of Free Trade* (Princeton, NJ, 1996), fails to develop this very significant aspect of the free trade argument.

11. William Graham Sumner, *War, and Other Essays* (New Haven, CT, 1911), 317. The not-quite-made-up aspect of the American mind is also suggested in the quip of John Bassett Moore, characterizing "fair trade" or "reciprocity," that it was "a policy recommended by free-traders as an escape from protection, and by protectionists as an escape from free trade, but distrusted by both and supported by neither." *The Principles of American Diplomacy* (New York, 1918), 160.

12. On "security communities" and "international regimes," see G. John Ikenberry, *After Victory: Institutions, Strategic Restraint, and the Rebuilding of Order after Major Wars* (Princeton, NJ, 2001), and Helga Haftendorn, Robert O. Keohane, and Celeste A. Wallender, eds., *Imperfect Unions: Security Institutions over Time and Space* (New York, 1999).

13. Davis, *Federal Principle*, 38, 3, 215–16.

14. Robert C. Binkley, *Realism and Nationalism, 1852–1871* (New York, 1935), xix.

15. Samuel V. LaSelva, *The Moral Foundations of Canadian Federalism* (Montreal, 1996), 40, 46.

16. Hans J. Morgenthau, *In Defense of the National Interest* (New York, 1951), 4.

17. Horace Kallen, *The Structure of a Lasting Peace: An Inquiry into the Motives of War and Peace* (Boston, 1918), 136–37; Lewis S. Feuer, "Horace M. Kallen on War and Peace," *Modern Judaism* 4 (1984): 201; James Brown Scott, *The United States of America: A Study in International Organization* (New York, 1920); and

idem, *James Madison's Notes of Debates in the Federal Convention of 1787 and Their Relation to a More Perfect Society of Nations* (New York, 1918). This essential continuity is emphasized by Daniel Deudney, *Bounding Power*, 186–87, who argues that the liberal internationalist agenda advanced by Wilson was "Madisonianism in the context of global interdependence . . . the continuation of isolationist republicanism in interdependent circumstances." According to Deudney, it was above all the transformation in military technology and communication that occurred in the global industrial era—producing an intense level of "violence interdependence"—that forced the United States "to either transform the system or be transformed by it."

18. The cluster of values I am identifying with union, the federal principle, and internationalism is also registered in liberalism and republicanism. These relations, however, are complicated, and there is a sense in which the unionist tradition may be considered as both compatible and also as in some degree of tension with both liberalism and republicanism. The unionist tradition is liberal because it seeks an international environment in which power is tamed and individual liberty preserved and fostered. But it is in tension with liberalism insofar as the latter doctrine is understood as privileging individual rights to life, liberty, and property to the utter exclusion of communal values. In my reading of the liberal tradition, rights to separate national development and autonomy are given strong representation, though admittedly the strain stressing human rights over communal rights has become more dominant over the last twenty or thirty years. A similar dual relationship exists with the republican paradigm. The unionist tradition is republican because it recognizes the freedom and independence of the commonwealth as something which union must secure. But it is in tension with republicanism insofar as that is understood as proposing a reason of state in which the interests of the commonwealth trump all other values. Despite these differences of emphasis, liberalism and republicanism in their American variants have been tenacious in defense of free government—that is, of government resting on the consent of the people, featuring plural and countervailing sources of authority in politics, economy, and society. An outstanding survey of republics that have embodied the principle of countervailing power is Scott Gordon, *Controlling the State: Constitutionalism from Ancient Athens to Today* (Cambridge, MA, 1999).

Terminological questions are devilishly complicated and cannot be dispensed with in the study of political thought. But it is useful to observe that the important point is not the name but the thing. I suggest, therefore, that when we see in history the attempt to instantiate or make effective the norms of good faith, cooperation, reciprocity, and law among independent states or free peoples, with the objective of steering between anarchy and despotism, we ought to have no hesitation in seeing such ideas as part of a liberal and enlightened tradition, one that discloses fundamental values of the American republic.

Chapter 3. Imperialism and Nationalism

1. Ronald Steel, "Totem and Taboo," *Nation*, September 20, 2004; Anderson and Cayton, *Dominion of War*, xiii; and Williams, *Empire as a Way of Life*.

2. Lippmann, *U.S. War Aims*, 24.

3. Charles Beard and William Appleman Williams saw an "imperialism of antiimperialism" in American foreign policy, for which see Bacevich, *American Empire*,

11–31. The idea was revived by Niall Ferguson, *Colossus: The Price of America's Empire* (New York, 2004).

4. Jonathan Schell, "Tomgram: Jonathan Schell on the Empire That Fell as It Rose," August 19, 2004, www.tomdispatch.com; Ferguson, *Colossus*, 2; and John Lewis Gaddis, *Surprise, Security, and the American Experience* (Cambridge, MA), 2004, 22. To similar effect, see Melvyn Leffler, "Think Again: Bush Foreign Policy," *Foreign Policy*, September/October 2004. Whether these public disavowals reflected inner conviction is very doubtful, as is suggested by the famous confession of an unnamed senior administration official who declared: "We're an empire now." See Ron Suskind, "Faith, Certainty and the Presidency of George W. Bush," *New York Times Magazine*, October 17, 2004. I consider these contemporary issues in David C. Hendrickson, "A Dissenter's Guide to Foreign Policy," *World Policy Journal* 21 (2004): 102–13; and idem, "The Curious Case of American Hegemony: Imperial Aspirations and National Decline," ibid., 22 (2005): 1–22.

5. Lind, *Next American Nation*, 4, 6.

6. Kohn, *American Nationalism*, ix.

7. Meaning "master-race democracy." See Bender, *Nation among Nations*, 181, 331n; George Frederickson, *The Black Image in the White Mind: The Debate on Afro-American Character and Destiny, 1817–1914* (New York, 1971); and Lind, *Next American Nation*.

8. Horace Kallen, "Democracy versus the Melting Pot: A Study of American Nationality," *Nation*, February 25, 1915.

9. Mead, *Special Providence*, 218–63. For Roosevelt, see below, part 8.

10. Reinhold Niebuhr, *Moral Man and Immoral Society* (New York, 1960), 91. Lieven, *America Right or Wrong*, gives an analysis of American nationalism that is Niebuhrian in sensibility. This perspective is also advanced in Anatol Lieven and John Hulsman, *Ethical Realism* (New York, 2007).

11. See explications in Lieven, *America Right or Wrong*, and Prestowitz, *Rogue Nation*.

12. A judgment regarding the benign or malign nature of liberal capitalism is at stake in much of this historiography: what to liberal historians is an instance of mutually beneficial exchange or progressive economic development, to be classed as a form of internationalism, is seen by leftist historians as a site of exploitation, a source of disorder, and a form of imperialism. See below, chapter 33, note 6. The controversy here is not whether such liberal beliefs regarding the foundations of economic order entered strongly into the pattern of American diplomacy—that is generally stressed by both sides in the debate—but rather whether the institutions and practices these beliefs foster run more toward mutually beneficial exchange or one-sided exploitation.

13. Lieven, *America Right or Wrong*, x, 1–18, 36–40; eulogy of Henry Clay, July 6, 1852, *Lincoln Speeches*, 1: 264.

14. Novanglus VII, *Adams Papers* 2: 314, 320; General Orders, April 18, 1783, *Washington Writings*, 513. For the distinction between "being" and "having" an empire, see the thoughtful reflections of Charles S. Maier, *Among Empires: American Ascendancy and Its Predecessors* (Cambridge, MA, 2006). For European theories, see Pagden, *Lords of All the World*.

15. Lippmann, *U.S. War Aims*, 193–94.

16. Thomas I. Cook and Malcolm Moos, "The American Idea of International

Interest," *American Political Science Review* 47 (1953): 28–44, at 30. For the distinction between "hard" and "soft" versions of realism, essentially equivalent to the selfsame versions of nationalism, see Wight, *International Theory*, 30–37, 47. "Hard realism" has its most important representative in the German tradition of *Machtpolitik*. Germany's significance, as Lippmann wrote in 1917, was "to demonstrate *ad nauseam* the doctrine of competitive nationalism. Other nations had applied it here and there cautiously and timidly. No other nation in our time had ever applied it with absolute logic, with absolute preparation, and with absolute disregard of the consequences. Other nations had dallied with it, compromised about it, muddled along with it. But Germany followed through, and Germany taught the world just where the doctrine leads." Walter Lippmann, "The World Conflict in Its Relation to American Democracy," *Annals of the American Academy of Political and Social Science* 72 (July 1917): 1–10, at 7. John J. Mearsheimer, *The Tragedy of Great Power Politics* (New York, 2001), 11, seems to identify himself with this tradition of "hard realism," but Mearsheimer's stance is quite atypical of American realism as a whole. Most of the leading figures—George Kennan, Reinhold Niebuhr, Walter Lippmann—are indubitably "soft realists." Hans J. Morgenthau and Henry Kissinger are more difficult to classify. Morgenthau talked like a hard realist but acted like a soft one: he invariably opposed the use of U.S. military force and was a leading anti-interventionist critic of the Vietnam War. (Mearsheimer, who opposed the 2003 Iraq War, is like Morgenthau in this regard.) Kissinger, on the other hand, talked like a soft realist but acted like a hard one: he invariably supported the use of U.S. military force in the postwar era and at last report still, like Cleon, wants more. The two best introductions to the American realists are Jack Donnelly, *Realism and International Relations* (Cambridge, UK, 2000), and Michael J. Smith, *Realist Thought from Weber to Kissinger* (Baton Rouge, LA, 1986). On Morgenthau, see especially Richard Ned Lebow, *The Tragic Vision of Politics: Ethics, Interests and Orders* (Cambridge, UK, 2003).

17. Hans J. Morgenthau, *Politics among Nations* (New York, 1967), 322–23.

18. Polk, Fourth Annual Message, December 5, 1848; Webster to Everett, "The Case of the Brig Creole," January 29, 1842, *Webster Writings*, 14: 379.

19. This understanding is emphasized in Lind, *American Way*, 28. See also the luminous study of David Armitage, *The Declaration of Independence: A Global History* (Cambridge, MA, 2007). A classic statement was that of Lincoln and associates in 1852. The committee resolved, "1. That it is the right of any people, sufficiently numerous for national independence, to throw off, to revolutionize, their existing form of government, and to establish such other in its stead as they may choose. 2. That it is the duty of our government to neither foment, nor assist, such revolutions in other governments. 3. That, as we may not legally or warrantably interfere abroad, *to aid*, so no other government may interfere abroad, *to suppress* such revolutions; and that we should at once, announce to the world, our determination to insist upon this *mutuality* of nonintervention, as a sacred principle of international law." Subsequent resolutions condemned Russia's interference in Hungary, held that "to have resisted Russia . . . would be no violation of our own cherished principles of non-intervention," but on the contrary would have been meritorious, and urged tribute to the patriotic efforts under way in Ireland, Germany, and France "to establish free governments, based upon the principles of true religious and civil liberty." January 9, 1852, *Lincoln Works*, 2: 115–16. This standard is very similar to that set

forth by John Stuart Mill in his essay, "A Few Words on Nonintervention" (1859), in Mill, *Dissertations and Discussions* (London, 1867), 3: 153–78. It was also Woodrow Wilson's view, for which see below, part 9.

20. The contrary view is taken in Kagan, *Dangerous Nation*, in his brilliant but perverse reconstruction of the American diplomatic tradition. He argues, in effect, that "nationalistic universalism" was the keystone of American policy from the beginning.

21. The choice posed in this work among internationalism, imperialism, and nationalism invites comparison to the choice that Samuel P. Huntington poses among "cosmopolitanism, imperialism, and nationalism" in his *Who Are We?* Cosmopolitans, Huntington writes, would have America become the world; imperialists would have the world become America, and nationalists want America to remain America. Huntington's idea of a tripartite choice is in concurrence with my own, but we differ on the first term, with Huntington emphasizing a cosmopolitanism to which he is indefatigably opposed because it renounces nationalist values and identities, and my interpretation stressing union, federation, and internationalism as a coherent alternative tradition. Unfortunately, Huntington's presentation of the alternatives leaves no room for an internationalism that involves intimate cooperation yet does not seek to renounce national identity—which seeks, in other words, the classic federal relationship of a "coming together to stay apart." Perhaps most strikingly, it leaves no room for "the West," which is unaccountably absent in *Who Are We?* but which in Huntington's previous work tapped an important symbol of American identity.

While cosmopolitanism may reasonably be regarded as one strand of internationalism, it is, so far as political history is concerned, a very muted strand and by no means the characteristic one. At least that is true in the American experience. Insofar as cosmopolitan sympathies have entailed a rejection of national identities and interests, the conception has been rejected by American internationalists. Internationalists did not contend that the national interest would be sacrificed or abandoned by the pursuit of the measures they recommended, but instead proposed good faith, law, cooperation, and reciprocity as just and necessary means to the realization of such interests.

Chapter 4. The Rival Systems of Hamilton and Jefferson

1. Madison to Daniel Webster, May 27, 1830, *Madison Letters*, 4: 85; House of Representatives, September 3, 1789, *Madison Papers*, 12: 372; Henry Lee to James Madison, ibid., 13: 102–3, 137, in Banning, *Sacred Fire*.

2. William Gordon to John Adams, September 7, 1782, in Joseph L. Davis, *Sectionalism in American Politics, 1774–1787* (Madison, WI, 1977), 60–66; Josiah Quincy, 1804, in Carter, *Revolt against Destiny*, 74; Richard Henry Lee to George Mason, October 1, 1787, in *The Debate on the Constitution: Federalist and Antifederalist Speeches, Articles, and Letters during the Struggle over Ratification*, ed. Bernard Bailyn (New York, 1993), 1: 45.

3. Fisher Ames, "A Sketch of Character of Alexander Hamilton," July 1804, *Ames Works*, 514.

4. Jefferson to Washington, May 23, 1792, Peterson, *Writings*, 988; Washington to Hamilton, August 26, 1792, in *The Writings of George Washington*, ed. W. C. Ford (New York, 1891), 12: 177.

5. Memorandum from John Taylor, May 11, 1794, *Madison Papers*, 15: 328–30.

6. Jefferson to Washington, September 9, 1792, *Jefferson Works* (1895), 6: 109; The Stand No. VII, April 21, 1798, *Hamilton Papers*, 21: 442.

7. The historian Drew McCoy, *Elusive Republic*, calls these contrasting visions "expansion across space" and "development through time." The opposing systems are also lucidly set forth in Peterson, *Jefferson and the New Nation*, and Forrest McDonald, *Alexander Hamilton* (New York, 1979).

8. The General Assembly of the Commonwealth of Virginia, December 16, 1790, Ames, *State Documents*, 5–6.

9. Jefferson to Lafayette, June 16, 1792, *Jefferson Works*, 7: 109.

10. Jefferson to William Short, January 3, 1793, Peterson, *Writings*, 1004. The "leading mountebank" later gave amused recollection of this delicious portrait: "The horrors of the French revolution, then raging, aided [the Federalists] mainly, and using that as a raw head and bloody bones they were enabled by their stratagems of X.Y.Z. in which this historian was a leading mountebank, their tales of tub-plots, Ocean massacres, bloody buoys, and pulpit lyings, and slanderings, and maniacal ravings of their Gardiners, their Osgoods and Parishes, to spread alarm into all but the firmest breasts." "The Anas—Selections," ibid., 672. At the time, as later, Adams thought both parties far gone in maniacal ravings. When, after their reconciliation, Jefferson reminded Adams of the wild charges that had been brought against the Virginian, Adams answered that he supposed his correspondent to be "fast asleep in philosophical Tranquility" when Republican demonstrators were out in force, ten thousand strong, in Philadelphia in 1799, inducing "Terror" in the house of the president. "Both parties," Adams observed, "have excited artificial Terrors and if I were summoned as a Witness to say upon Oath, which Party had excited, Machiavillialy, the most terror, and which had really felt the most, I could not give a more sincere Answer, than in the vulgar Style 'Put Them in a bagg and shake them, and then see which comes out first.'" Adams to Jefferson, June 30, 1813, Cappon, *Adams-Jefferson*, 2: 346–48.

11. "Political Observations," April 20, 1795, *Madison Letters*, 4: 491; Madison to Jefferson, June 10, 1793, *The Writings of James Madison*, ed. Gaillard Hunt (New York, 1900–1910), 6: 127; Jefferson to Thomas Mann Randolph, August 11, 1795, in Malone, *Jefferson*, 3: 247; and Jefferson to Rutledge, November 30, 1795, *Jefferson Writings*, 9: 314.

12. The Defense No. 5, August 5, 1795, *Hamilton Papers*, 19: 90.

13. Pacificus No. 2, July 3, 1793, *Hamilton Papers*, 15: 59–62; Jefferson to Thomas Mann Randolph, June 24, 1793, *Jefferson Works*, 7: 410.

14. A Hamilton that verges on "hard realism" is presented in John Lamberton Harper, *American Machiavelli: Alexander Hamilton and the Origins of U.S. Foreign Policy* (Cambridge, UK, 2004), whereas a "softer" realist is more convincingly portrayed in Walling, *Republican Empire*. Walling notes that "the essential yet paradoxical truth is that Hamilton was much more like Machiavelli than commonly believed and was at the same time fundamentally opposed to a kind of politics that we usually call Machiavellian." That fundamental opposition is also apparent in Daniel Lang, "Alexander Hamilton and the Law of Nations," in Graebner, *Traditions, 1790–1865*, 1–27. For Hamilton as a "Christian statesman," see Trevor Colbourn, ed., *Fame and the Founding Fathers: Essays by Douglass Adair* (Indianapolis,

IN, 1998 [1974]), 200–226. For his international thought more broadly, see Stourzh, *Alexander Hamilton.* For Jefferson as a practical idealist, see discussion and further references in Tucker and Hendrickson, *Empire of Liberty,* 4.

15. Pacificus No. IV, July 10, 1793, *Hamilton Papers,* 15: 86; Jefferson to Madison, August 28, 1789, *Jefferson Writings,* 7: 449.

16. Montesquieu, *Spirit of the Laws,* 3, 7; Alexander Hamilton, The Defense No. 20, October 23 and 24, 1795, *Hamilton Papers,* 19: 341. See also Daniel G. Lang, *Foreign Policy in the Early Republic* (Baton Rouge, LA, 1985).

17. The Stand No. IV, April 12, 1798, 21: 413. Washington to McHenry (drafted by Hamilton), December 13, 1798, *Hamilton Papers,* 22: 345.

18. LC, May 8, 1798, 1632–33 (Gallatin).

19. Jefferson, "Thoughts on Lotteries," February 1826, *Jefferson Works* (1905), 12: 445.

20. Jefferson to Madison, October 1, 1792, Smith, *Republic of Letters,* 2: 740–41 (emphasis in original); Ellis, *American Creation,* 184–85.

21. Hamilton to Jonathan Dayton, 1799, *Hamilton Works,* 10: 335. On the tremors of the 1790s, see James Rogers Sharp, *American Politics in the Early Republic: The New Nation in Crisis* (New Haven, CT, 1993), and the magisterial study of Stanley Elkins and Eric McKitrick, *The Age of Federalism* (New York, 1993). Cf. Bender, *Nation among Nations,* 155, who discounts fears of separation before the mid–nineteenth century.

Chapter 5. The Causes of War

1. *Federalist* 7 (Hamilton); *Federalist* 41 (Madison).

2. Centinel XI, January 12, 1788, in Storing, *Anti-Federalist,* 2: 186.

3. Elliot, *Debates,* 3: 212, 209. See also the speeches of Melancton Smith and Thomas Tredwell in the New York Ratifying Convention, ibid., 2: 223–24, 396–97. On the pacific effects of commercial intercourse among the American states, see Agrippa VIII [James Winthrop] of Massachusetts, December 25, 1787, Storing, *Anti-Federalist,* 4: 84.

4. "Defense of the Funding System," July 1795, *Hamilton Papers,* 19: 56.

5. "A Sketch of the Character of Alexander Hamilton," July 1804, *Ames Works,* 1: 517.

6. Thomas Paine, *Rights of Man,* Part One, *Paine Writings,* 539, 473, 540. See also *Rights of Man, Part the Second,* ibid., 650–57, and, for Paine's earlier statement of the democratic peace theory in *Common Sense* (February 14, 1776), ibid., 32. See also David M. Fitzsimons, "Tom Paine's New World Order: Idealistic Internationalism in the Ideology of Early American Foreign Relations," *Diplomatic History* 19 (1995): 569–82. Jefferson's view of war, and especially the just war, is considered in Reginald C. Stuart, *The Half-way Pacifist: Thomas Jefferson's View of War* (Toronto, 1978).

7. James Madison, "Universal Peace," January 31, 1792, *Madison Papers,* 14: 206–9.

8. Jean-Jacques Rousseau, *Abstract and Judgement of Saint Pierre's Project for Perpetual Peace* (1756), in *Rousseau on International Relations,* ed. Stanley Hoffman and David P. Fidler (Oxford, 1991), 85, 88, 90–91. Doubtless it was the subversive character of the *Judgement,* with its far more critical account of European

monarchy, that delayed its publication. Though Hoffmann and Fidler, xxii–xxiv, properly criticize contemporary scholarship for misinterpreting Rousseau (based evidently on familiarity with the *Abstract* alone), Madison's case is more interesting because their views on the basic questions, independently discovered, are largely congruent.

9. John Quincy Adams to Thomas Boylston Adams, February 14, 1801, *JQA Writings*, 2: 499–502. This was a long-standing preoccupation of John Quincy Adams. For similar statements before and after, see JQA to Charles Adams, June 9, 1796, ibid., 1: 494; JQA to John Adams, August 31, 1811, and October 31, 1811, ibid., 4: 209, 266; JQA to Alexander Hill Everett, July 16, 1814, ibid., 5: 63.

10. Jefferson to Spencer Roane, September 6, 1819, *Jefferson Works*, 10: 140; Peterson, *Jefferson and the New Nation*, 655.

11. Kenneth N. Waltz, *Man, the State, and War* (New York, 1959).

12. Walling, *Republican Empire*, notes that Hamilton's passages in *The Federalist* denying the pacific implications of commerce do not capture the full complexity of his thought. On the Anti-Federalists, see Herbert Storing, with Murray Dry, *What the Anti-Federalists Were For* (Chicago, 1981).

13. "Universal Peace," *Madison Papers*, 14:208; Smith, *Wealth of Nations*, 863, 872, 878. "No national debt shall be contracted in connection with the external affairs of the state" formed the fourth of six "preliminary articles" in Kant's plan for perpetual peace. *Perpetual Peace: A Philosophical Sketch* (1795), *Kant's Political Writings*, ed. H. S. Reiss (Cambridge, UK, 1970), 95. See discussion in Michael Doyle, *Ways of War and Peace: Realism, Liberalism, and Socialism* (New York, 1997), 251–300.

14. *Federalist* 41. Lance Banning provides an authoritative exposition of Madison's views on this subject in *Sacred Fire*.

15. American Envoys to Talleyrand, January 17, 1798, *The Papers of John Marshall*, ed. Herbert A. Johnson et al. (Chapel Hill, NC, 1974–), 3: 330–31, 333–35. Marshall was the author of this exposition of the American position, which was signed also by Charles Cotesworth Pinckney and Elbridge Gerry.

16. The depiction by scholar Charles Tilly of state formation in early modern Europe—"war made the state, and the state made war"—was an insight shared by these early American thinkers. Tilly, "Reflections on the History of European State-Making," in *The Formation of National States in Western Europe*, ed. Charles Tilly (Princeton, NJ, 1975), 42. The danger of simultaneous "anarchy" and "hierarchy"— and the relationship of these perilous states to war and free institutions—is key to the contemporary international theory of Daniel Deudney, *Bounding Power*, as it was to the early American consensus. Once the problem is viewed from this perspective, the hard realist prescription of aggregating state power as a solution to the security problem appears in potential contradiction with itself and hazardous to the liberty of the citizen. See also below, chapter 16.

17. The democratic peace, put differently, depended mightily on the proper adjustment of what Jefferson called "the partition of cares." As he wrote in his autobiography: "It is not by the consolidation, or concentration of powers, but by their distribution, that good government is effected. Were not this great country already divided into States, that division must be made, that each might do for itself what concerns itself directly, and what it can so much better do than a distant authority. Every State is again divided into counties, each to take care of what lies within its

local bounds; each county again into townships or wards, to manage minuter details; and every ward into farms, to be governed each by its individual proprietor. Were we directed from Washington when to sow, and when to reap, we should soon want bread. It is by this partition of cares, descending in gradation from general to particular, that the mass of human affairs may be best managed, for the good and prosperity of all." *Jefferson Writings*, 1: 122. See also Jefferson, *Notes on the State of Virginia* (New York, 1999 [1785]), 64, Query VI, where Jefferson remarks that the affections of the Indians weaken "as with us, from circle to circle, as they recede from the center." Alexander Hamilton gave a similar analysis of the social affections while emphasizing the dangers of excessive decentralization in his speech before the New York Ratifying Convention, June 27, 1788, *Hamilton Works*, 2: 70. Other statements of this "partition of cares"—essentially identical in content to the "principle of subsidiarity" found in Catholic teachings and in modern European Union constitutional doctrine—may be found in John Adams to Abigail Adams, October 29, 1775, *Annals of America*, 2: 367; and Alexis de Tocqueville, *The European Revolution and Correspondence with Gobineau* (New York, 1959), 169–70.

18. Niles is quoted in Merrill D. Peterson, *The Jefferson Image in the American Mind* (New York, 1960), 17. On the tension between "withdrawal and return," see Peterson, *Jefferson and the New Nation*. On the estimation of commerce more generally, see McCoy, *Elusive Republic*; Lance Banning, "Political Economy and the Creation of the Federal Republic," in Konig, *Devising Liberty*, 11–49; Stourzh, *Alexander Hamilton*; Lerner, *Thinking Revolutionary*; Onuf and Onuf, *Federal Union*; Hendrickson, *Peace Pact*; Felix Gilbert, *To the Farewell Address: Ideas of Early American Foreign Policy* (Princeton, NJ, 1961); and James H. Hutson, *John Adams and the Diplomacy of the American Revolution* (Lexington, KY, 1980).

19. Jefferson to G. K. van Hogendorp, October 13, 1785, *Jefferson Papers*, 8: 633. See also Jefferson to Brissot de Warville, August 16, 1786, ibid., 10: 262.

20. Vernon G. Setser, *The Commercial Reciprocity Policy of the United States, 1774–1829* (New York, 1969 [1937]).

21. *Common Sense*, February 14, 1776, *Paine Writings*, 22; Jefferson to Madison, March 1793, *Jefferson Writings*, 9: 33–34.

22. Burton Spivak, *Jefferson's English Crisis* (Charlottesville, VA, 1979). See the contrasting assessments of the commercial weapon and the embargo in Stagg, *Mr. Madison's War*; Tucker and Hendrickson, *Empire of Liberty*; and Onuf and Onuf, *Federal Union*.

23. Adams, *History*, 4: 265–66. Adams drew the moral that the Jeffersonian "statesmanship which made peace a passion could lead to no better result than had been reached by the barbarous system which made war its duty." Ibid., 4: 289.

24. Jefferson to Benjamin Stoddert, February 18, 1809, *Jefferson Writings*, 9: 245; Madison, "An Examination of the British Doctrine, Which Subjects to Capture a Neutral Trade, Not Open in Time of Peace" (1806), *Madison Letters*, 2: 227–391. See also Onuf and Onuf, *Federal Union*, 197–211.

25. Jefferson to the Secretary of the American Society for Encouragement of Domestic Manufactures, June 6, 1817, quoted in Peterson, *Great Triumvirate*, 507–8n. See also Report on Manufactures, December 5, 1790, *Hamilton Works*, 4: 102, and Jefferson to Benjamin Austin, January 9, 1816, *Jefferson Writings*, 14: 387–93, where Jefferson affirms that "experience has taught me that manufactures are now as necessary to our independence as to our comfort."

Chapter 6. Louisiana!

1. Napoleon cited in H. L. Mencken, *A New Dictionary of Quotations on Historical Principles from Ancient and Modern Sources* (New York, 1989), 897. On the Louisiana crisis, see Arthur P. Whitaker, *The Mississippi Question, 1795–1803* (New York, 1934); Alexander DeConde, *This Affair of Louisiana* (New York, 1976); Tucker and Hendrickson, *Empire of Liberty*; Peter S. Onuf, "The Expanding Union," Konig, *Devising Liberty*, 50–80; and McCoy, *Elusive Republic*, 185–208.

2. Allen Bowie Magruder, *Political, Commercial and Moral Reflections on the Late Cession of Louisiana to the United States* (Lexington, KY, 1803), 7, 35–36; David Ramsay, *An Oration on the Cession of Louisiana to the United States . . .* (Charleston, SC, 1804), 4, 8–9, 11; *National Intelligencer*, July 8, 1803, cited in Malone, *Jefferson*, 4: 297. See further Onuf and Onuf, *Federal Union*, 149–53.

3. Jefferson to Breckinridge, August 12, 1803, Peterson, *Writings*, 1138; Jefferson to Wilson Cary Nicholas, September 7, 1803, ibid., 1140.

4. "Proposed Constitutional Amendment," *Annals of America*, 4: 173; Adams, *History*, 2: 79, 118–23.

5. Clinton, February 22, 1803, Benton, *Debates*, 2: 678.

6. October 20, 1803, William Plumer Jr., *Life of William Plumer* (Boston, 1857), 285; Tracy, November 2, 1803, Adams, *History*, 2: 108.

7. Henry Adams, *Documents Relating to New England Federalism, 1800–1815* (Boston, 1877), 52–53; Pickering to Rufus King, March 4, 1804, ibid., 351.

8. Pickering to George Cabot, January 29, 1804; Pickering to King, March 4, 1804; Pickering to Theodore Lyman, February 11, 1804, all in Henry Cabot Lodge, *Life and Letters of George Cabot* (Boston, 1877), 441–53. See also Charles Raymond Brown, *The Northern Confederacy According to the Plans of the "Essex Junto" 1796–1814* (Princeton, NJ, 1915), and Garry Wills, *Negro President: Jefferson and the Slave Power* (Boston, 2003).

9. Hamilton to Theodore Sedgwick, July 10, 1804, *Hamilton Works*, 10: 458. Rufus King reporting his and Hamilton's views to John Quincy Adams, April 8, 1804, Adams, *Documents Relating to New England Federalism*, 148.

10. Second Inaugural Address, March 4, 1805; Jefferson to Breckinridge, August 12, 1803, *Jefferson Writings*, 9: 409–10.

11. Peterson, *Jefferson and the New Nation*, 872.

12. *Washington Federalist*, December 22, 1808, in Malone, *Jefferson*, 5: 642. "Report and Resolutions of Rhode Island on the Embargo," March 4, 1809, Ames, *State Documents*, 42–44.

Chapter 7. Balances of Power

1. Randolph, March 1806, Benton, *Debates*, 3: 425; The Stand, No. IV, April 12, 1798, *Hamilton Papers*, 21: 413; "The Successes of Bonaparte," March 1806, *Ames Works*, 1: 494–95.

2. Jefferson to Monroe, January 8, 1804, *Jefferson Works* (1905), 10: 67; Jefferson to Benjamin Rush, October 4, 1803, *Jefferson Writings*, 10: 422.

3. Jefferson to Thomas Lomax, January 11, 1806, Malone, *Jefferson*, 5: 95. Jefferson's ideas of the balance of power are admirably surveyed in Lawrence Kaplan, *Jefferson and France* (New Haven, CT, 1967).

4. Jefferson to Thomas Leiper, January 1, 1814, and June 12, 1815, *Jefferson Writings*, 14: 44, 307; Jefferson to Langdon, March 5, 1810, ibid., 12: 374–75.

5. Felix Grundy, December 9, 1811, in Hofstadter, *Great Issues*, 228–29.

6. The citations in the two preceding paragraphs are drawn from Randolph's speeches of December 10 and 16, 1811, and January 9, 1812. Excerpts from the former may be found in Hofstadter, ibid., 229–31. For his speech of January 9, see LC, 707–16.

7. Lyman Law, Representative from Connecticut, January 1813, Benton, *Debates*, 4: 628. On the motives and causes of the War of 1812, see Stagg, *Mr. Madison's War*; Reginald Horsman, *The Causes of the War of 1812* (Philadelphia, 1962); Roger H. Brown, *The Republic in Peril: 1812* (New York, 1971); Paul A. Varg, *Foreign Policies of the Founding Fathers* (East Lansing, MI, 1963); Donald R. Hickey, *The War of 1812* (Champaign, IL, 1990); Adams, *History*; and Julius W. Pratt, *Expansionists of 1812* (New York, 1925).

8. Crowninshield, March 5, 1806, LC, 552–54; Randolph, March 5, 1806, LC, 557.

9. December 31, 1811, *Clay Works*, 5: 39; Calhoun, December 12, 1811, Benton, *Debates*, 4: 449; Randolph, December 10, 1811, ibid., 4: 439.

10. Jefferson to Lafayette, May 14, 1817, Peterson, *Writings*, 1407; "Extract from . . . the Judges of Massachusetts on the Militia . . . ," 1812, Ames, *State Documents*, 57–59; "Connecticut on the Militia Question," August 25, 1812, ibid., 61.

11. Liverpool to Sir James Craig, April 4, 1810, Bradford Perkins, *Prologue to War: 1805–1812* (Berkeley, CA, 1961), 14; Josiah Quincy, January 14, 1811, Benton, *Debates*, 4: 327; *Centinel*, January and February 1814, in Banner, *To the Hartford Convention*, 316–17.

12. "Mr. Randolph's Letter," December 15, 1814, *Niles Weekly Register*, December 24, 1814, 258.

13. Report of the Hartford Convention, Theodore Dwight, *History of the Hartford Convention* (Boston, 1833), 345–46, 357, 361.

14. Ibid., 370–71.

15. Ibid., 378, 355.

16. Benton, February 2, 1830, Benton, *Debates*, 10: 449. See also Thomas Jefferson to William Branch Giles, December 26, 1825, Peterson, *Writings*, 1511, and Stephens, *Constitutional View*, 513. The graceful work of Banner, *To the Hartford Convention*, emphasizes the moderate character of the convention. Henry Adams notes that the leaders of the convention, like Cabot, were moderate but insists that they were not particularly representative of New England opinion. "The tone of the press and the elections bore out the belief that a popular majority would have supported an abrupt and violent course" had the war continued. Adams, *History*, 8: 305. Emphasizing the perils to the union in the last year of the war are Stagg, *Mr. Madison's War*, and Lewis, *American Union*.

17. "Massachusetts Decides," Adams, *History*, 8: 3.

18. Jefferson to William Short, November 28, 1814, *Jefferson Writings*, 14: 218; Jefferson to John Adams, July 5, 1814, ibid., 14: 146–47.

19. Paul Johnson, *The Birth of the Modern: World Society, 1815–1830* (New York, 1991), 35–36.

20. Jefferson to Lafayette, February 14, 1815, *Jefferson Writings*, 14: 251–52. On the troop movements, see Stagg, *Mr. Madison's War*, 477–78.

21. John Adams to Thomas McKean, July 6, 1815, *Adams Works*, 10: 167–68; Jefferson to William H. Crawford, February 11, 1815, *Jefferson Writings*, 14: 244.

22. Albert Gallatin to Matthew Lyon, May 7, 1816, *Gallatin Writings*, 1: 700. Before getting carried away with too many "good feelings," the reader should consult the important corrective in Lewis, *American Union*, esp. 62–63. On the "new nationalism" after 1815, see also Adams, *History*. For the literature on early American nationalism, see Hendrickson, *Peace Pact*, 315n4, 316n11. Especially useful in considering the tenor of early American nationalism are John Murrin, "A Roof without Walls: The Dilemma of American National Identity," in *Beyond Confederation: Origins of the Constitution and American National Identity*, ed. Richard Beeman et al. (Chapel Hill, NC, 1987); Peter S. Onuf, "Federalism, Republicanism, and the Origins of American Sectionalism," in *All over the Map: Rethinking American Regions*, ed. Edward L. Ayers et al., (Baltimore, 1996); Liah Greenfeld, *Nationalism: Five Roads to Modernity* (Cambridge, MA, 1992), pt. 5; Nagel, *One Nation Indivisible*; and Kersh, *Dreams of a More Perfect Union*.

23. Jefferson to Gallatin, October 16, 1815, *Jefferson Writings*, 14: 356; Jefferson to Elbridge Gerry, June 21, 1798, ibid., 9: 406. For other expressions of the idea that war would threaten the union, see John Quincy Adams to John Adams, July 12, 1811, *JQA Writings*, 4: 147; Lewis, *American Union*, 49, 65, 69; and Henry Clay, March 13, 1818, *Clay Papers*, 2: 512–13.

Chapter 8. The Confederation of Europe

1. Gentz, in F. H. Hinsley, *Power and the Pursuit of Peace: Theory and Practice in the History of Relations between States* (Cambridge, UK, 1963), 197.

2. Friedrich von Gentz, *Fragments upon the Balance of Power in Europe* (London, 1806), xiii, 61.

3. Charles Louis de Montesquieu, *The Spirit of the Laws*, ed. Franz Neumann (New York, 1949 [1748]), bk. 9, chap. 1. For a review of the various usages of "federal" and "federative," see Martin Diamond, "What the Framers Meant by Federalism," in *A Nation of States*, ed. Robert A. Goldwin (Chicago, 1963), 24–41, and Raoul Berger, *Federalism: The Founders' Design* (Norman, OK, 1987).

4. Terry Nardin, *Law, Morality, and the Relations of States* (Princeton, NJ, 1983), 61–62; Brougham, "Balance of Power," *The Works of Henry Lord Brougham* (Edinburgh, 1872), 8:15. For "Europe as a republic," see further Deudney, *Bounding Power*, 136–60. Classic treatments of these federative ideas may be found in Walter Alison Phillips, *The Confederation of Europe: A Study of the European Alliance, 1813–1823, as an Experiment in the International Organization of Peace*, 2nd ed. (London, 1920), and Edward Vose Gulick, *Europe's Classical Balance of Power* (New York, 1955).

5. Friedrich von Gentz, *On the State of Europe before and after the French Revolution; Being an Answer to* L'Etat de la France à la Fin de l' An VIII (London, 1802), 22, 31, 34, 62–63. See discussion in Murray Forsyth, "The Old European States-System: Gentz versus Hauterive," *Historical Journal* 23 (1980): 521–38.

6. Gentz, *On the State of Europe*, 34, 60, 67.

7. Albert Sorel, *Europe and the French Revolution: The Political Traditions of the Old Regime*, ed. Alfred Cobban and J. W. Hunt (London, 1969), 35–36; Paul W. Schroeder, *The Transformation of European Politics, 1748–1848* (New York, 1994), 580.

8. Jefferson to Albert Gallatin, October 16, 1815, *Jefferson Writings*, 14: 358; Jefferson to Adams, January 11, 1816, Cappon, *Adams-Jefferson*, 2: 459.

9. Adams to Jefferson, February 2, 1816, Cappon, *Adams-Jefferson*, 2: 461–63.

10. "Memorandum on the Treaties of 1814 and 1815," Aix-La-Chapelle, October 1818, excerpted in Evan Luard, *Basic Texts in International Relations* (New York, 1992), 431. See above, chapter 5, for Madison and Rousseau.

11. The ill consequences of the 1815 settlement are stressed in Guglielmo Ferrero, *Problems of Peace from the Holy Alliance to the League of Nations* (New York, 1919). The most notable attempts to draw lessons from 1815 are Schroeder, *Transformation of European Politics*, and Henry A. Kissinger, *A World Restored: Metternich, Castlereagh and the Problems of Peace, 1812–1822* (Boston, 1957).

12. F. H. Hinsley, "The Development of the European States System since the Eighteenth Century," *Transactions of the Royal Historical Society*, 5th ser., 11 (1961): 73.

13. Paul W. Schroeder, "Did the Vienna Settlement Rest on a Balance of Power?" *American Historical Review* 97 (1992): 696. Both European legitimists and American republicans also execrated Bonaparte. "On this side of the water," wrote Alexander Hill Everett in 1830, "Napoleon is still the same tyrant, usurper, and enemy of liberty, that he always was." Such were the feelings of "the great mass" of Americans. "The Tone of British Criticism," *Prose Pieces and Correspondence*, ed. Elizabeth Evans (St. Paul, MN, 1975), 26. The fortunes of Bonaparte's reputation are traced in Pieter Geyl, *Napoleon: For and Against* (New Haven, CT, 1949).

14. George Armstrong Kelly, "Hegel's America," *Philosophy and Public Affairs* 2 (1972): 3–36; Leon Fraser, *English Opinion of the American Constitution and Government: 1783–1798* (New York, 1915).

15. Preamble to Treaty between Russia and Prussia, February 28, 1813, in Phillips, *Confederation of Europe*, 59; Henry Clay, "Speech on Recognition of the Independent Province of the River Plata," March 24–25, 1818, *Clay Papers*, 2: 532; and Adams to John Thornton Kirkland, November 30, 1815, *JQA Writings*, 5: 430–31. See Lewis, *American Union*, 73, for additional citations to the same effect.

16. JQA to John Adams, December 21, 1817, *JQA Writings*, 6:275–76; Adams to Deonis, March 12, 1818, *Clay Papers*, 2: 816n.

Chapter 9. New World and Old World

1. Jefferson to Claiborne, October 29, 1808, *Jefferson Writings*, 9: 213; Jefferson to Alexander Von Humbolt, December 6, 1813, ibid., 13: 21–22.

2. Clay, "Emancipation of the South American States," March 24, 1818, *Clay Works*, 5: 145, 244.

3. "Speech on South American Independence," May 10, 1820, *Clay Papers*, 2: 856–57; speech at Lexington, May 19, 1821, ibid., 3: 80.

4. David Trimble, March 28, 1822, Benton, *Debates*, 7: 298–99. See the discussion in Peterson, *Great Triumvirate*, 54, and Randolph Campbell, "The Spanish-American Aspect of Henry Clay's American System," *Americas* 24 (1967): 3–17.

5. Jared Sparks, *North American Review* 3 (1821): 433–35, in Whitaker, *The United States and the Independence of Latin America*, 336; September 19, 1820, *JQA Memoirs*, 5: 176; March 9, 1821, ibid., 5: 324–25.

6. Edward Everett, "Affairs of Greece," *North American Review* 18 (1822): 417.

7. Jefferson to Monsier A. Coray, October 31, 1823, *Jefferson Writings*, 15: 490.

8. The classic study is Edward Mead Earle, "American Interest in the Greek Cause," *American Historical Review* 33 (1927): 44–63. The contemporaneous rebellion of the Serbs against the Turks, notes Earle, failed to elicit in the United States much response at all. The Serbs, Earle suggests, "lacked a great name." Lafayette made a triumphal tour of the United States in 1824–1825 in which the cause of the Greeks figured prominently in his speeches. Americans of weight and stature in their communities who signed on enthusiastically, in addition to those mentioned in the text, included Nicholas Biddle, William Bayard, Charles King, Chancellor Kent, Mathew Carey, Noah Webster, and William Henry Harrison.

9. John Quincy Adams, *An Address Delivered . . . on the Occasion of Reading the Declaration of Independence* (Washington, DC, 1821), 29.

10. Review of Robert Walsh, *An Appeal from the Judgments of Great Britain . . .* , *Edinburgh Review* 66 (1820): 403–5. The context of Adams's 1821 address is well conveyed in Whitaker's great book, *The United States and the Independence of Latin America*, 344–69.

11. Jefferson to Monroe, October 24, 1823, Peterson, *Writings*, 1481–82.

12. August 22, 1823, Richard Rush, *Memoir of a Residence at the Court of London* (Philadelphia, 1845), 412–13.

13. Monroe to Madison, September 26, 1822, cited in Lewis, *American Union*, 172.

14. Ibid.; Jefferson to Monroe, October 24, 1823, Peterson, *Writings*, 1482–83.

15. November 16, 1819, *JQA Memoirs*, 4: 439; January 26–27, 1821, ibid., 5: 250–52.

16. James Monroe, Message to Congress, December 2, 1823; November 7, 1823, *JQA Memoirs*, 6: 177.

17. Lewis, *American Union*, 179. Most accounts, as Lewis notes, minimize Adams's apprehensions over the threat posed by the Holy Alliance. The best introduction to Adams's international thought is Norman Graebner, "John Quincy Adams and the Federalist Tradition," in Graebner, *Traditions, 1790–1865*, 97–127. Classic treatments are Samuel Flagg Bemis, *John Quincy Adams and the Foundations of American Foreign Policy* (New York, 1949), and Bradford Perkins, *Castlereagh and Adams: England and the United States, 1812–1823* (Berkeley, CA, 1964).

18. Madison to Jefferson, November 1, 1823, Smith, *Republic of Letters*, 3: 1879. Madison's letters to Monroe and Rush are cited in Ralph Ketcham, *James Madison* (Charlottesville, VA, 1990), 631. Madison had earlier expressed to Jefferson his fear that "the people of Spain as well as of Portugal need still further light and heat too from the American example before they will be a Match for the armies, the intrigues and the bribes of their Enemies, the treachery of their leaders, and what is most of all to be dreaded, their priests and their prejudices. Still their cause is so just, that whilst there is life in it, hope ought not to be abandoned." September 6, 1823, Smith, *Republic of Letters*, 3: 1877.

19. December 2, 1823, *JQA Memoirs*, 6: 224; November 22, 1823, ibid., 6: 197. After Adams's reply, Clay said that he did not have in mind a successful war, for that would indeed give rise to the "greatest danger," the creation of "military

influence and power." Clay did not want to go to war either; he appears to have been simply speculating that a defensive war for this object would have unifying effects at home.

20. Alexander Hill Everett, *America: or, A General Survey of the Political Situation of the Several Powers of the Western Continent, with Conjectures on Their Future Prospects* (Philadelphia, 1827), 36.

21. Ibid., 245, 45, 243–44.

22. Ibid., 329, 8–9.

23. Ibid., 10–11, 17–19.

24. Ibid., 245. It is notable that Everett's forecast preceded Tocqueville's far more famous prophecy at the end of book 1 of *Democracy in America*. Also in competition for the prize is Baron Friedrich von Grimm, Catherine's agent in France, who wrote to her in 1790 that "two empires will . . . divide between themselves all privileges of civilization and of intellectual, scientific, military, and industrial power: Russia in the east, and in the west America, so recently freed; and we other peoples in the present center of the world will be too degraded and humiliated to remember what we once were, except through a vague and stupid tradition." Cited in David Mayers, *The Ambassadors and America's Soviet Policy* (New York, 1995), 16.

25. Daniel Webster, "The Revolution in Greece," January 19, 1824, *Webster Works*, 3: 77.

26. Ibid., 67–68.

27. Ibid., 69–74.

28. Randolph, January 24, 1824, LC, 1182–90; *Webster Works* (1890), 3: 75.

29. *Webster Works* (1890), 3: 76–77.

30. Webster, April 14, 1826, Benton, *Debates*, 9: 164; Henry Wheaton, *Elements of International Law*, ed. Richard Henry Dana Jr. and George Grafton Wilson (London, 1936), 93n.

31. Everett, *America*, 234.

Chapter 10. To the Panama Congress

1. John Adams to James Lloyd, March 27, 1815, *Adams Works*, 10: 144–46. Adams was ridiculing the project of Francesco de Miranda to revolutionize South America, a scheme that had attracted the interest of both Alexander Hamilton and Rufus King in the crisis of 1798. Adams considered Miranda's project "visionary, though far less innocent than that of his countryman Gonzalez, of an excursion to the moon, in a car drawn by geese trained and disciplined for the purpose." There is a more favorable treatment of this famous scheme in Kagan, *Dangerous Nation*. Compare the more cautious analysis of Hamilton's role in Gilbert L. Lycan, *Alexander Hamilton and American Foreign Policy* (Norman, OK, 1970).

2. Antonio Muñoz Tébar, Secretary of State and Foreign Affairs, to Simón Bolívar, December 13, 1813, *Selected Writings of Bolívar*, ed. Vincente Lecuna and Harold A. Bierck Jr., 2 vols. (New York, 1951), 1: 56–57.

3. "Address Delivered at the Inauguration of the Second National Congress of Venezuela in Angostura," February 15, 1819, ibid., 1: 179–81; Bolívar to General Daniel F. O'Leary, September 13, 1829, ibid., 2: 738.

4. John J. Johnson, *Simon Bolívar and Spanish American Independence, 1783–1830* (New York, 1968), 75; Bolívar to [General Bernardo O'Higgins], Supreme

Director of Chile, January 8, 1822, *Selected Writings*, 1: 289; Bolívar to F[rancisco] de P[aula] Santander, Vice President of Colombia, January 6–7, 1825, ibid., 2: 461; *Mirada sobre América española* (Quito, 1829), in J. Fred Rippy, *Latin America: A Modern History* (Ann Arbor, MI, 1958), 242.

5. On the Panama Congress, see Whitaker, *The United States and the Independence of Latin America*; idem, *Western Hemisphere Idea*; Lewis, *American Union*; Andrew R. L. Cayton, "The Debate over the Panama Congress and the Origins of the Second American Party System," *Historian* 47 (1985): 219–38; and Mary W. M. Hargreaves, *The Presidency of John Quincy Adams* (Lawrence, KS, 1985).

6. *Clay Papers*, 5: 314; John Quincy Adams, The Panama Mission, March 15, 1826.

7. Charles Vaughan to Ward, February 13, 1826, in Lewis, *American Union*, 204.

8. See, however, [Benjamin Chew], *A Sketch of the Politics, Relations, and Statistics, of the Western World, and of Those Characteristics of European Policy Which Most Immediately Affect Its Interests: Intended to Demonstrate the Necessity of a Grand American Confederation and Alliance* (Philadelphia, 1827).

9. Hayne, Senator from South Carolina, March 14, 1826, Benton, *Debates*, 8: 421–29. For background, see Randolph Campbell, "Henry Clay and the Poinsett Pledge Controversy of 1826," *Americas* 28 (1972): 429–40.

10. Hayne, March 14, 1826, Benton, *Debates*, 8: 426.

11. Alexander Hill Everett, *America: or, A General Survey of the Political Situation of the Several Powers of the Western Continent, . . .* (Philadelphia, 1827), 234.

12. Hayne, Benton, *Debates*, 8: 421–29; George McDuffie, February 2, 1826, ibid., 8: 647; Thomas Hart Benton, March 14, 1826, ibid., 8: 461. The principle Benton applied to American diplomacy was equally applicable to his conception of federal union; here, too, he would urge distance and noninterference as peacemakers.

13. Webster, April 14, 1826, ibid., 8: 160–62.

14. Ibid. The best introduction to Webster's international thought is Kenneth E. Shewmaker, "Daniel Webster and American Conservatism," Graebner, *Traditions, 1790-1865*, 129–51.

Chapter 11. Into the Deep Freeze

1. Clay to Lafayette, August 10, 1827, *Clay Papers*, 6: 872–73.

2. Baylies in Richard B. Morris, *The Emerging Nations and the American Revolution* (New York, 1970), 145.

3. Storrs, May 15, 1830, LC, 6: 994–1016; Tocqueville, *Democracy in America*, 1: 169.

4. Webster to Johann Georg Hulsemann, December 21, 1850, *Webster Papers: Diplomatic*, 2: 53; Ashburton in Kenneth Bourne, *Britain and the Balance of Power in North America, 1815–1908* (Berkeley, CA, 1967), 70–71.

5. F. H. Hinsley, "The Development of the European States System since the Eighteenth Century," *Transactions of the Royal Historical Society*, 5th ser., 11 (1961): 75.

6. A similar comparison is made in Morison, *Oxford History*, 2: 332. On the "Philadelphian system," his name for the "American states-union, circa 1787–1861," see Deudney, *Bounding Power*, 161–89.

Chapter 12. Great and Fearfully Growing

1. Fisher Ames to Christopher Gore, October 3, 1803, *Ames Works*, 2: 1462.

2. *Niles' Register*, November 23, 1822, 171; [John O'Sullivan], Annexation, *Democratic Review* 17 (1845): 9.

3. For the "scale effect" and the general demonstration of the influence of geography and technology upon history, see Deudney, *Bounding Power*. See also various assessments in John Lauritz Larson, "'Bind the Republic Together': The National Union and the Struggle for a System of Internal Improvements," *Journal of American History* 74 (1987): 363–87; George Rogers Taylor, *The Transportation Revolution, 1815–1860* (New York, 1951); and Howe, *What Hath God Wrought*.

4. Charles Pinckney, Representative from South Carolina, February 14, 1820, LC, 1319–20; Monroe, May 7, 1822, *MP*, 2: 178.

5. Baylies, December 18, 1822, Benton, *Debates*, 7: 401–3; James Madison to Richard Rush, December 4, 1820, *Madison Letters*, 3: 195. On the background to Baylies's speech, see Meinig, *Shaping of America*, 2: 75. Madison's thinking is illuminated in McCoy, *Last of the Fathers*. See also Lewis, *American Union*, 21. This reasoning encouraged Republican leaders, especially Madison and Monroe, to reach across sectional boundaries in the search for a governing coalition. "They accepted," as Lewis describes their thinking, "what they expected would be a temporary division of the nation along party lines in order to prevent what they feared would be a permanent division of the union along sectional lines."

6. February 4, 1817, Benton, *Debates*, 5: 705–6. See also Calhoun's speech of April 4, 1816, where he remarked that disunion "comprehended almost the sum of our political dangers." Ibid., 5: 643.

7. Edmund Wilson, *Patriotic Gore: Studies in the Literature of the American Civil War* (New York, 1966), xi.

8. Fareed Zakaria, "The Myth of America's 'Free Security,'" *World Policy Journal* 14 (1997): 35–43, at 36; McDougall, *Promised Land*, 79.

9. Jefferson to Astor, May 24, 1812, *Jefferson Writings*, 13: 151; William M. Meigs, *The Life of Thomas Hart Benton* (Philadelphia, 1904), 416–17. See also Frederick Merk, *Manifest Destiny and Mission in American History* (New York, 1966). On sectionalism as a restraint upon expansion, see Scott A. Silverstone, *Divided Union: The Politics of War in the Early American Republic* (Ithaca, NY, 2004).

10. Horace Greeley, *The American Conflict* (New York, 1864), 354–55. To similar effect, see John Elliott Cairnes, *The Slave Power: Its Character, Career, and Probable Designs . . .* (New York, 1969 [1862]). Cf. John Quincy Adams, February 28, 1833, LC, 9: 59, where Adams speaks of territorial expansion and Indian removal as having served the "superabundantly, and excessively protected" interests of "the western and southern portions of this union." On the aggressiveness of the Slave Power, cf. Chauncey S. Boucher, "In Re That Aggressive Slavocracy," *Mississippi Valley Historical Review* 8 (1921): 13–79, with Richards, *Slave Power*. Studies of American expansion in which sectional factors are slight or invisible include Michael H. Hunt, *Ideology and U.S. Foreign Policy* (New Haven, CT, 1987), and Anders Stephanson, *Manifest Destiny: American Expansion and the Empire of Right* (New York, 1995). Important correctives may be found in Lewis, *American Union*; Robert E. May, *The Southern Dream of a Caribbean Empire, 1854–1861* (Athens,

GA, 1989); and idem, ed., *The Union, the Confederacy, and the Atlantic Rim* (West Lafayette, IN, 1995).

My general criticism also applies to Weinberg, *Manifest Destiny*. Weinberg's study, a real gem, treated laconically the fifteen different justifications for expansion that he found in American rhetoric from the eighteenth to the twentieth century. That these were a cover for manifest self-interest was his larger assumption: "Moral ideology was the partner of self-interest in the intimate alliance of which expansionism was the offspring." Weinburg's view is seconded by William Earl Weeks, "New Directions in the Study of Early American Foreign Relations," *Diplomatic History* 17 (1993): 73–96. Weeks argues, "It may be that the only truly realistic interpretations of American foreign policy are revisionist accounts that attribute every act, no matter how apparently altruistic, to a selfish nationalism" (82). This is reductionism that does not reduce far enough. It sees far too much unity of purpose amid the stipulated riot of selfishness. Nationalism is not the only vessel into which self-interest may be poured.

11. J. L. O'Sullivan to S. J. Tilden, May 6, 1861, Commager, *Civil War Archive*, 79; George Bancroft to Robert J .Walker, June 19, 1844, cited in Morrison, *Slavery and American West*, 31; Potter, *Impending Crisis*, 197–98.

12. Hamilton to Washington, September 15, 1790, *Hamilton Works*, 4: 336; Hamilton to Charles Cotesworth Pinckney, December 29, 1802, ibid., 10: 445–46; Jefferson, Second Inaugural Address, March 4, 1805.

Chapter 13. The Title Page

1. *McCulloch v. Maryland*, February Term, 1819, 17 U.S. 316, 404–5, 408, 421 (Wheat.).

2. March 31, 1820, *JQA Memoirs*, 5: 53; February 13 (Clay), ibid., 4: 525–26; Clay to Adam Beatty, January 22, 1820, *Clay Papers*, 2: 766; Monroe to Madison, February 19, 1820, cited in the outstanding treatment of Lewis, *American Union*, 134. On the Missouri crisis, see also Glover Moore, *The Missouri Crisis, 1819–1821* (Lexington, KY, 1953); George Dangerfield, *The Era of Good Feelings* (New York, 1952), 199–245; idem, *The Awakening of American Nationalism 1815–1828* (New York, 1965); Don E. Fehrenbacher, *The South and Three Sectional Crises* (Baton Rouge, LA, 1980), 9–23; Donald Robinson, *Slavery in the Structure of American Politics: 1765–1820* (New York, 1971), 402–21; Major L. Wilson, *Space, Time, and Freedom: The Quest for Nationality and the Irrepressible Conflict, 1815–1861* (Westport, CT, 1974), 49–72; and Howe, *What Hath God Wrought*.

3. Clay, February 5 and 6, 1850, *Clay Works* (1863), 3: 305.

4. Jefferson to John Adams, January 22, 1821, *Jefferson Writings*, 15: 309; John Elliott, Senator from Georgia, LC, January 17, 1820, 133–34. John Adams had noted in 1784 that "America will have external enemies to dread longer than seems to be here supposed. This may be no harm, for, when she has no enemy, she will be in danger of dividing." In Thorton Anderson, review of *John Adams and the Prophets of Progress*, by Zoltan Haraszti, *Journal of Politics* 14 (1952): 743.

5. Jefferson to Gallatin, December 26, 1820, Peterson, *Writings*, 1449.

6. Ibid; Jefferson to John Holmes, April 22, 1820, ibid., 1434–35; Jefferson to John Adams, January 22, 1821, *Jefferson Writings*, 15: 309; Jefferson to Gallatin,

ibid., 450; Lewis, *American Union*, 133. "Invective and irony" from *A Defense of the Legislature of Massachusetts; Or, The Rights of New England Vindicated* (Boston, 1804), 4. See also the provocative treatment of Jefferson's reaction to the Missouri crisis in Peter S. Onuf, "Thomas Jefferson, Missouri, and the 'Empire for Liberty,'" in *Thomas Jefferson and the Changing West*, ed. James P. Ronda (Albuquerque, NM, 1997), 111–53. Jefferson, writes Onuf, "knew the union he cherished was in jeopardy because he could not stop himself from imagining its destruction" (115).

7. Adams to Jefferson, February 3, 1821; Jefferson to Adams, December 10, 1819; Adams to Jefferson, December 21, 1819; Cappon, *Adams-Jefferson*, 2: 571, 548, 551.

8. January 10, 1820, *JQA Memoirs*, 4: 502.

9. February 24, 1820, *JQA Memoirs*, 4: 530–31; March 4 and 5, 1820, ibid., 5: 4–12.

10. Clay, December 30, 1819, LC, 841.

11. The tariff, Benton exclaimed, "sheds the whole of its benign influence upon the Northeast; it reserves all its baleful effects for the South and West!" March 1832, Benton, *Debates*, 11: 424.

12. Ray Allen Billington, with the collaboration of James Blaine Hedges, *Westward Expansion: A History of the American Frontier*, 3rd ed. (New York, 1967), 353; Webster, "Encouragement of Enlistments," January 14, 1814, *Webster Writings* (1903), 14: 32; Clay, November 16, 1825, *JQA Memoirs*, 7: 63.

Chapter 14. Constitutional Disorder

1. Extract of a letter from Jefferson to ⸻, *Jefferson Writings*, 15: 328–29. Madison's position is reviewed in Banning, *Sacred Fire*. Webster, "Veto of the Bank Bill," July 11, 1832, *Webster Papers: Speeches*, 1: 529; "The Judiciary," January 4 and 25, 1826, ibid., 1: 186–87.

2. "The Constitution Not a Compact," *Webster Papers: Speeches*, 1: 604; Benton, *Debates*, February 1832, 11: 385–86.

3. *A Disquisition on Government*, in Calhoun, *Union and Liberty*, 24, 28–29.

4. "The Constitution Not a Compact," *Webster Papers: Speeches*, 1: 604–5.

5. Ibid., 1: 607.

6. Various denunciations of nullification are exhibited in Ellis, *Union at Risk*; Jackson, Nullification Proclamation, December 10, 1832; John M. Clayton, Senator from Delaware, Benton, *Debates*, 12: 69. On Randolph, see Russell Kirk, *The Conservative Mind from Burke to Eliot* (Chicago, 1960), 197. In his memoirs Jefferson Davis contended that nullification was "a doctrine to which I have never assented." Jefferson Davis, *The Rise and Fall of the Confederate Government* (New York, 1881), 1: 230.

7. Jackson, Bank Veto Message, July 10, 1832. The debate over the union is subtly examined in Kenneth M. Stampp, "The Concept of Perpetual Union," *Imperiled Union*, 3–36. See also Alpheus Thomas Mason, "The Nature of Our Federal Union Reconsidered," *Political Science Quarterly* 65 (1950): 502–21; Herman Belz, "Theories of the Union," *Encyclopedia of the American Constitution*, ed. Leonard W. Levy et al. (New York, 1986), 1885–89; Arthur Bestor, "The American Civil War as a Constitutional Crisis," *American Historical Review* 69 (1964): 327–52; and

Walter H. Bennett, *American Theories of Federalism* (University, AL, 1964). The constitutional problem is set dramatically in political context by Forrest McDonald, *States' Rights and the Union: Imperium in Imperio, 1776–1876* (Lawrence, KS, 2000). For the nationalist case, see especially Story, *Commentaries*. For the compact school, Stephens, *Constitutional View*.

8. *McCulloch v. Maryland*, February Term, 1819, 17 U.S. 399 (Wheat.).

9. William Pinkney, February 15, 1820, Benton, *Debates*, 6: 437.

10. Richard C. Vitzthum, *The American Compromise: Theme and Method in the Histories of Bancroft, Parkman, and Adams* (Norman, OK, 1974), 7–8.

11. Webster's change of view is assessed in Maurice G. Baxter, *One and Inseparable: Daniel Webster and the Union* (Cambridge, MA, 1984), and Peterson, *Great Triumvirate*. Of "the doctrine of state rights," Morison comments that "almost every man in public life between 1798 and 1860 spurned it when his section was in the saddle, and embraced it when his constituents deemed themselves oppressed." *Oxford History*, 2: 78. Though typically rendered as "states' rights" today, the characteristic form of the expression before the Civil War was "State rights."

12. Henry Clay to Francis Brooke, January 17, 1833, *Clay Papers*, 8: 613; July 30, 1834, *JQA Memoirs*, 9: 162.

13. "The Union," May 1829, *The Works of William E. Channing* (Boston, 1875), 630; St. George Tucker: As the prevention of "intestine wars" and "frequent and violent contests with each other . . . was among the most cogent reasons to induce the adoption of the union, so ought it to be among the most powerful, to prevent a dissolution" (St. George Tucker, *View of the Constitution of the United States* [Indianapolis, IN, 1999 (1803)], 87); William Rawle, *A View of the Constitution* (Philadelphia, 1825), 298–300; Joseph Story: "Let the history of the Grecian and Italian republics warn us of our dangers. The national constitution is our last, and our only security" (Story, *Commentaries*, 3: 758–59). See also James Monroe, *The People, the Sovereigns*, ed. Samuel L. Gouverneur (Cumberland, VA, 1987 [1867]), 3–4. "Two dangers menace" the American system, Monroe affirmed: "disunion and consolidation. Either would be ruinous. It was by the Union that we achieved our independence and liberties, and by it alone can they be maintained."

14. Rufus Choate, "On the Preservation of the Union," November 26, 1850, *Choate Works*, 2: 314–15; [Alexander B. Johnson], "The Philosophy of the American Union," *Democratic Review* 28 (1851): 15.

15. Legaré to I. E. Holmes, April 8, 1833, and October 2, 1832, *The Writings of Hugh Swinton Legaré* (Charleston, SC, 1846): 1: 215, 208, 221, 207. A luminous study of "probably the most learned American of his day" is Michael O'Brien, *A Character of Hugh Legaré* (Knoxville, TN, 1985).

Chapter 15. Decentralizing Tendencies

1. *Federalist* 45 (Madison).

2. U.S. Constitution, Article 1, Section 8. Charles Pinckney, Representative from South Carolina, February 14, 1820, LC, 1328. On the "recessed" character of the Constitution's military clauses, see Deudney, *Bounding Power*. See also discussion in Inis L. Claude, *Power and International Relations* (New York, 1962).

3. Tocqueville, *Democracy in America*, 1: 403; "Speech on the Revenue Collection [Force] Bill," February 15–16, 1833, Calhoun, *Union and Liberty*, 431.

4. "There is an all but unanimous belief" in British opinion, wrote Richard Cobden to Charles Sumner after the Seven Days' Battle in June 1862, "that you *cannot* subject the South to the Union." July 11, 1862, J. A. Hobson, *Richard Cobden: The International Man* (New York, 1919), 365. The criterion of a "monopoly on the use of legitimate violence," among theorists of international relations, is widely held to constitute the dividing line between a state and a state system. Max Weber, Raymond Aron, Hans Morgenthau, and Kenneth Waltz, among others, place key importance on this criterion. If their view is sound, and if the American system departed from it in the respects noted in the text, it would follow that many of these selfsame theorists are mistaken in regarding the American experience as outside the domain of "international relations." Objection may be raised to "duopoly" because there were many state governments and only one general government, but the issue of coercion tended strongly to produce a bipolar pattern closely related to the anticipated strength of the sections. At the end of the day, you were either for or against the use of force as a means to maintain the union. This was, at the same time, the limiting condition from which the Constitution "averted its eyes." For this apt expression, see James Barbour, *Eulogium upon the Life and Character of James Madison* (Washington, DC, 1836).

5. Webster, May 25, 1832, Benton, *Debates*, 11: 464. To similar effect, see "Considerations on the Currency and Banking System of the United States," 1831, in Gallatin, *Selected Writings*, 392–93. The classic work dealing with monetary matters during the early period is Bray Hammond, *Banks and Politics in America from the Revolution to the Civil War* (Princeton, NJ, 1957); Hammond cites Kendall at 325. For a new guide through the monetary maze, see Stephen Mihm, *A Nation of Counterfeiters* (Cambridge, MA, 2007). Lawrence Ingrassia, "Will the Euro Be a Success? History Might Suggest 'No,'" *Wall Street Journal*, January 13, 1998, reports that James Haxby's *Standard Catalog of Obsolete United States Bank Notes, 1782–1866* carries photographs of about 72,000 notes.

6. Eckes, *Opening America's Market*, 10; Clay, "On the Protection of Home Industry," April 26, 1820, *Clay Works*, 6: 228.

7. Potter, *Impending Crisis*, for growing interdependence; Webster in Patrick J. Buchanan, *The Great Betrayal* (Boston, 1998); "Rough Draft of South Carolina Exposition and Protest," in Calhoun, *Union and Liberty*, 328–29.

8. "Report on Manufactures," April 17, 1810, Gallatin, *Selected Writings*, 262; James Buchanan, Senator from Pennsylvania, June 8, 1844, LC, 721 (Appendix). Gallatin's remarks are cited favorably in the protectionist work of H. C. Carey, *Principles of Political Economy* (Philadelphia, 1837), 33.

9. George Mifflin Dallas, Senator from Pennsylvania, February 23, 1832, Benton, *Debates*, 11: 404. Dallas was later vice president under Polk.

10. Clay, "The Compromise Tariff," February 25, 1833, *Clay Works*, 5: 558; "Rough Draft of . . . South Carolina Exposition," December 19, 1828, Calhoun, *Union and Liberty*, 320–21, 324, 328–29. This view was shared by British opinion. William Cobbett, the free trader, noted in 1833: "All these Southern and Western States are, commercially speaking, closely connected with Birmingham, Sheffield, Manchester, and Leeds; . . . they have no such connection with the Northern States, and there is no tie whatsoever to bind them together, except that which is of a mere political nature. . . . Here is a natural division of interests, and of interests so powerful, too, as not to be counteracted by any thing that man can do. The heavy duties

imposed by the Congress upon British manufactured goods [are] neither more nor less than so many millions a year taken from the Southern and Western States, and given to the Northern States." Cited in [Acton], "Political Causes of the American Revolution," *Rambler* 5 (1861): 37. Acton added that Cobbett "knew America better than any Englishman of that day."

11. Thomas Cooper, *Lectures on the Elements of Political Economy* (Columbia, SC, 1926), 119–20; "Free Trade," *Democratic Review* 9 (1841): 329–42, at 341–42. Here, and in the four paragraphs to follow, the discussion is indebted to Onuf and Onuf, *Nations, Markets, and War*, esp. 256–65.

12. Cooper, *Lectures on Political Economy*, 51, 25, 14–15, preface. Liberalism is associated with both the "commercial peace" and the ideal of peace through law. Interestingly, Cooper, though a commercial liberal, poured scorn on the utility—nay, the reality—of the law of nations. "All monarchs and monarchies are yet in a savage state," he declared. "They seem to have no bond of union but mutual protection in plunder. Theoretical writers like Grotius, Puffendorf, Barbeyrac, Heineccius, Vattel, Rutherforth, Burlemaqui and others, boast of a law of nature or nations existing. When was it enacted? By whom? Or by what power has it been sanctioned?" The law of nations, Cooper concluded, "exists no where but in the closest speculations of well meaning writers, as to what might be usefully acknowledged as binding with each other" (53–54). In Cooper's reckoning, his calculations were raised on the solid ground of interest, not the ephemeral world of legal writ and desiccated parchment. Cooper's embrace of free trade and his rejection of international law, as the preferred route to international peace, mimic the contemporary dispute between the "rational choice" and "constructivist" schools (focusing, respectively, on "interests" and "norms") in contemporary international relations theory. Our initial inclination was to put Cooper down as a rational choice theorist, but he did acknowledge that statesmen might, as they had in the past, act on a mistaken view of their interest. This acknowledgment was also made by one of Cooper's predecessors, Thomas Pownall, *Memorial to the Sovereigns of Europe, on the Present State of Affairs between the Old and New World*, 2nd ed. (London, 1780), 85, 103–4.

13. Alexander Hill Everett, *Memorial of the New York Convention*, March 26, 1832, *Executive Documents of House of Representatives* (Washington, DC, 1832), 5: 21; "On the Protection of Home Industry," April 26, 1820, *Clay Works*, 5: 228.

14. Joseph Seawell Jones to Daniel M. Barringer, December 11, 1832, in McCardell, *Idea of a Southern Nation*, 5; Calvin Colton, "Public Economy for the United States," *Western Journal* 1 (1848): 481; Clay, "On American Industry," March 30 and 31, 1824, *Clay Works*, 5: 281.

15. McDuffie, Inaugural Address, January 7, 1835, in Onuf and Onuf, *Nations, Markets, and War*, 270. For essential background, see Brian Schoen, "Calculating the Price of the Union: Republican Economic Nationalism and the Origins of Southern Sectionalism, 1790–1828," *Journal of the Early Republic* 23 (2003): 173–206.

16. William Seward, "The Destiny of America," September 14, 1853, *Seward Works*, 4: 123; "The Irrepressible Conflict," October 25, 1858, ibid., 4: 292.

17. LC, December 10, 1851, 51 (Stockton); Story, *Commentaries*, 3: 758. For a broad assessment of centripetal and centrifugal pressures in the decade before the Civil War, see Nevins, *Ordeal of the Union*, and Potter, *Impending Crisis*. Tocqueville's remains one of the best assessments of the centrifugal forces at work in the union; *Democracy in America*, 1: 397–433.

The relationship between nationalism and sectionalism is complex and resists any easy summary. As David Potter noted, "Northern support for a sectional tariff or for sectional internal improvements, adopted by sectional majorities in the national government, was no less sectional than Southern opposition to them." Nationalism, Potter speculated, "may be the terminal result of a full development of strong sectional forces, while sectionalism may be an emergent nationalism which has not yet matured." David M. Potter, "The Historian's Use of Nationalism and Vice Versa," *The South and Sectional Conflict* (Baton Rouge, 1968), 34–83, at 65 and 47. See also David M. Potter and Thomas G. Manning, *Nationalism and Sectionalism in America, 1775–1877* (New York, 1949). On the character of southern sectionalism, see McCardell, *Idea of Southern Nation;* Drew Gilpin Faust, *The Creation of Confederate Nationalism* (Baton Rouge, LA, 1980); William J. Cooper, *The South and the Politics of Slavery, 1828–1856* (Baton Rouge, LA, 1978); Jesse T. Carpenter, *The South as a Conscious Minority* (New York, 1930); William R. Taylor, *Cavalier and Yankee* (New York, 1961); and John Richard Alden, *The First South* (Baton Rouge, LA, 1961).

Chapter 16. The Hope of the World

1. "The Character of Washington," February 22, 1832, *Webster Works* (1851), 1: 230. See also the observations of Albert Gallatin in 1832, cited below in chapter 23, note 14.

2. Allan Bowie Magruder, *Political, Commercial and Moral Reflections, on the Late Cession of Louisiana, to the United States* (Lexington, KY, 1803), 73–74, discussed in Onuf and Onuf, *Federal Union,* 153; letter to the Legislature of Massachusetts, May 14, 1851, *Sumner Works,* 2: 439. Madison quoted in Ralph Ketcham, *James Madison* (Charlottesville, VA, 1990), 632. Ketcham records that this passage was found amid Madison's notes of the federal convention. The paper bore an 1817 watermark "indicating Madison made the notes during his retirement, while reflecting on issues raised in the 1787 debates" (725).

3. Kuehl, *Seeking World Order,* 18; William Ladd, *An Essay on a Congress of Nations for the Adjustment of International Disputes without Resort to Arms,* ed. James Brown Scott (New York, 1916 [1840]). Ladd was also the editor of *Prize Essays on a Congress of Nations for the Adjustment of International Disputes, and for the Promotion of Universal Peace without Resort to Arms* (Boston, 1840). The volume made a peculiar journal to publication, the story of which offers a cautionary tale to devotees of peace. In 1828, at the first meeting of the American Peace Society, $30 was offered for the best essay on a Congress of Nations. When initial returns proved disappointing, "two gentlemen" came forward in 1831 with an offer of $500—a very considerable sum in those days. Joseph Story, William Wirt, and John McLean, eminent legal figures, agreed to serve as jury members. Unable to reach agreement on which was the best essay, but finding merit in many, they recommended that the prize be divided among the five top entrants, whom they designated. Unfortunately, as Ladd recalled the sad tale, "This plan did not suit the gentlemen who offered the premium, and they did not consider themselves bound by it. They therefore rejected it, and immediately raised the premium to one thousand dollars for the best Essay only . . . and they appointed the Hon. John Q. Adams, Chancellor Kent and Thomas S. Grimké the committee of award. The much lamented Grimké died of the cholera,

in 1834, by which the cause of Peace suffered an irreparable loss. The Hon. Daniel Webster consented to take his place in the committee. . . . The second committee were no more fortunate than the first, and could not agree in awarding the prize to any one candidate; and it was found impossible to get either committee to revise their labors, being gentlemen of high standing in society, and their time precious; and the gentlemen who offered the prize declined having any thing further to do with the business." Perplexed by this turn of events, yet undaunted, the American Peace Society ensured publication of the five best essays, offered premiums to the successful writers, and widely distributed the book. In appealing for financial support, Ladd noted that "it requires much printing, lecturing and preaching, to bring the world to the same state of opinion and feeling on this subject which prevails in the State of Massachusetts" (iii–iv, xii).

4. Hugh S. Legaré (Committee on Foreign Affairs), "Report on the Foregoing Petition of the New York Peace Society," in Ladd, *Essay on a Congress of Nations*, 134–43. See further review of John Ware, address delivered before the Massachusetts Peace Society, December 25, 1824, in *North American Review* 20 (1825): 455–58. Legaré's emphasis that peace leads to democracy is the inverse of the contemporary fascination with whether democracy leads to peace. As Michael Lind cogently observes: "Liberal utopians are correct that trade and cooperation among states tend to be correlated with international peace. They are also correct that the combination of liberalism and democracy within states tends to be correlated with international peace. But they get cause and effect backward. Economic interdependence, international cooperation, liberalism, and democracy are not the causes of international peace; they are its results." *American Way*, 35–36. See also Mark E. Pietrzyk, *International Order and Individual Liberty: Effects of War and Peace on the Development of Governments* (Lanham, MD, 2002); Otto Hintze, "Military Organization and the Organization of the State" (1906), *The Historical Essays of Otto Hintze*, ed. Felix Gilbert (New York, 1975), 178–215; and above, chapter 5.

5. James Polk, Fourth Annual Message, December 5, 1848; John G. Gazley, *American Opinion of German Unification, 1848–1871* (New York, 1926).

6. "The Character of Washington," *Webster Works*, 1: 231.

Chapter 17. Reds and Whites

1. Montesquieu, *Spirit of the Laws*, 142 (bk. 10, chap. 4); Emmerich de Vattel, *The Law of Nations or the Principles of Natural Law applied to the Conduct and to the Affairs of Nations and of Sovereigns*, ed. Charles G. Fenwick (Washington, DC, 1916 [1758]), 85 (bk. 1, chap. 18); James Madison, "Population and Emigration," *Madison Papers*, 14: 117–22. For general background, see Onuf, *Jefferson's Empire*; Pagden, *Lords of All the World*; J.G.A. Pocock, *Barbarism and Religion*, vol. 4, *Barbarians, Savages and Empires* (Cambridge, UK, 2005); Edward Keene, *International Political Theory: A Historical Introduction* (Malden, MA, 2005); Keene, *Beyond the Anarchical Society: Grotius, Colonialism and Order in World Politics* (Cambridge, UK, 2002); *Diderot: Political Writings*, ed. John Hope Mason and Robert Wokler (Cambridge, UK, 1992); Sankar Muthu, *Enlightenment against Empire* (Princeton, NJ, 2003); and Jennifer Pitts, *A Turn to Empire: The Rise of Imperial Liberalism in Britain and France* (Princeton, NJ, 2005).

2. Carl Schurz, "Present Aspects of the Indian Problem," July 1881, *Schurz*

Papers, 4: 117; Knox to Washington, December 29, 1794, *ASP: Indian Affairs*, 1: 544. Knox's reports are shrewdly examined in Ralph Lerner, "Reds and Whites, Rights and Wrongs," *Thinking Revolutionary*.

3. Theda Perdue, "The Origins of Removal and the Fate of the Southeastern Indians," Paterson, *Major Problems*, 1: 217–43.

4. Meinig, *Shaping of America*, 1: 370.

5. Ibid., 415–16.

6. See also Meinig's stunning depiction of the eastern half of North America as a "ragged, bloody edge of empire" in 1750, in *Atlantic America*, 212, the first volume of his series. Ironically, what is otherwise so marked a feature of Meinig's great work—probing the understanding of contemporaries in relation to geographic position and cultural perspective—is almost completely cast aside in his treatment of white-Indian relations. On the limited ability of the federal government "to regulate violence at its periphery," see also Deudney, "Philadelphian System," 204. This distribution of power was relevant not only to "filibustering" expeditions on land but also to privateering and arms dealing at sea. Taking note of the bustling activities in American seaports directed toward the wars of independence in South America, Henry Clay remarked on "the spectacle of a people at war and a government at peace." Clay deprecated that spectacle, holding that "we ought to perform our neutral duties, while we are neutral, without regard to the undressed injuries inflicted upon us by old Spain on the one hand, or to the glorious object of the struggle of the South American patriots on the other." January 24, 1817, *Clay Papers*, 2: 291.

7. George Washington, Third Annual Message, October 25, 1791.

8. Jefferson to General Andrew Jackson, February 16, 1803, *Jefferson Writings*, 10: 357–58; Bernard W. Sheehan, *Seeds of Extinction: Jeffersonian Philanthropy and the American Indian* (Chapel Hill, NC, 1973); Onuf, *Jefferson's Empire*, 40–45.

9. Jefferson to William H. Harrison, February 27, 1803, *Jefferson Writings*, 10: 368–73. Debt slavery was an expedient that would unavoidably occur to a Virginian. For the long and sordid tale of Jefferson's relationship to debt, see Herbert E. Sloan, *Principle and Interest: Thomas Jefferson and the Problem of Debt* (New York, 1995).

10. On these events, see Gregory Evans Dowd, *A Spirited Resistance: The North American Indian Struggle for Unity, 1745–1815* (Baltimore, 1992); Richard White, *The Middle Ground: Indians, Empires, and Republics in the Great Lakes Region, 1650–1815* (New York, 1991); Alan Taylor, "Land and Liberty on the Post-Revolutionary Frontier," Konig, *Devising Liberty*, 81–104; Anderson and Cayton, *Dominion of War*; Alfred Leroy Burt, *The United States, Great Britain and British North America [to] 1812* (New Haven, CT, 1940); and Reginald Horsman, *Expansion and American Indian Policy, 1783–1812* (Norman, OK, 1992).

11. Clay, "On the Seminole War," January 1819, in *The Speeches of Henry Clay* (Philadelphia, 1827), 155, 144, 150–51; Benton, *Debates*, 6: 245. Cf. John Lewis Gaddis, *Surprise, Security, and the American Experience* (Cambridge, MA, 2004). See also Frank Lawrence Owsley Jr. and Gene A. Smith, *Filibusters and Expansionists: Jeffersonian Manifest Destiny, 1800–1821* (Tuscaloosa, AL, 1997).

12. Calhoun in John Niven, *John C. Calhoun and the Price of Union* (Baton Rouge, LA, 1988), 69; Adams to Erving, November 28, 1818, *JQA Writings*, 6: 475, 482, 486, 483.

13. Henry A. Wise, *Seven Decades of the Union* (Philadelphia, 1876), 151–52.

Wise approved of Jackson's view: "Jackson cared only for his justification; but Adams was horrified at its mode. Jackson made law, Adams quoted it." See also John William Ward, *Andrew Jackson: Symbol for an Age* (New York, 1962), 62–63.

14. Pinkney, February 15, 1820, LC, 402.

15. Samuel B. Payne, "The Iroquois League, the Articles of Confederation, and the Constitution," *William and Mary Quarterly*, 3rd ser., 53 (1996): 605–20, is a good introduction to this controversy.

16. *A Disquisition on Government*, in Calhoun, *Union and Liberty*, 54; Ellis, *American Creation*, 149; "The Song of Hiawatha" (1855), *Henry Wadsworth Longfellow: Poems and Other Writings*, ed. J. D. McClatchy (New York, 2000). An article by an international relations scholar that brilliantly sets Iroquois institutions in the context of theories of "security communities" and "the democratic peace" is Neta C. Crawford, "A Security Regime among Democracies: Cooperation among Iroquois Nations," *International Organization* 48 (Summer 1994): 345–85. On Indian unity and disunity, see the works of Dowd, White, and Taylor (esp. 94–96) in note 10 above. For Iroquois institutions, see Lawrence H. Gipson, *The British Empire before the American Revolution*, 15 vols. (New York, 1936–1970), 5: 64–112; Daniel K. Richter, *The Ordeal of the Long-House* (Chapel Hill, NC, 1992); and Francis Jennings, *The Ambiguous Iroquois Empire* (New York, 1984). On mutual recognition of disunity, see James Duane to George Clinton, March 13, 1778, *Letters of Delegates to Congress, 1774–1789*, ed. Paul H. Smith et al. (Washington, DC, 1976–1993), 9: 289: "An Onandagoe Chief," speaking for the tribes that had gone over to the British, "threw the Blame on the Headstrong warriors who no longer would listen to advice, [and] laid a proper Stress on the example of our own internal Divisions and Oppositions." For Canadian perceptions, see Sidney F. Wise and Robert Craig Brown, *Canada Views the United States: Nineteenth Century Political Attitudes* (Seattle, WA, 1967). On Spanish and Mexican perceptions, see the handsome study of David J. Weber, *The Spanish Frontier in North America* (New Haven, CT, 1992), and Cecil Robinson, ed., *The View from Chapultepec: Mexican Writers on the Mexican-American War* (Tucson, 1989).

Chapter 18. The Removal of the Cherokee

1. Quoted in Jeremiah Evarts, *Essays on the Present Crisis in the Condition of the American Indians* (Boston, 1829), 74.

2. *Worcester v. Georgia*, 6 Peters at 544. See the lucid discussion in Wilkinson, *American Indians*. See also James Tully, *Strange Multiplicity: Constitutionalism in an Age of Diversity* (New York, 1995), 116–24, and William R. Polk, *Neighbors and Strangers: The Fundamentals of Foreign Affairs* (Chicago, 1998). On the significance of "faith and honor," see the contrasting discussions in Francis Paul Prucha, *American Indian Treaties: The History of a Political Anomaly* (Berkeley, CA, 1995), 16–19, and Vine Deloria Jr., *Custer Died for Your Sins: An Indian Manifesto* (New York, 1969).

3. For discussion of a "suzerain-state system," see Martin Wight, *Systems of States* (Leicester, UK, 1977), and Adam Watson, *The Evolution of International Society* (London, 1992), 15.

4. "Resolutions of the [Georgia] Legislature Relative to the Cherokee Controversy," December 27, 1827, Ames, *State Documents*, 37–38.

5. James Barbour, "Preservation and Civilization of the Indians," February 3, 1826, *ASP: Indian Affairs*, 2: 646–49; and discussion in Lerner, "Reds and Whites, Rights and Wrongs," *Thinking Revolutionary*.

6. Storrs, May 15, 1830, LC, 6: 994–1016.

7. Ibid. Clay had suggested a similar consequence in 1819; Benton, *Debates*, 6: 246. For a different interpretation of those "gorgeous decorations," see Vivien Green Fryd, *Art and Empire: The Politics of Ethnicity in the United States Capitol, 1815–1860* (New Haven, CT, 1992).

8. LC, May 15, 1830, 6: 1014–15.

9. Wilson Lumpkin, Representative from Georgia, May 17, 1830, ibid., 6: 1016–26, at 1022. A critique very similar to Lumpkin's appears in [John Taylor], *A Definition of Parties* (Philadelphia, 1794), which is probed in Onuf, *Jefferson's Empire*, 40–45. Noting the Indian treaties made by the Federalists, Taylor argued, "'Instead of encroaching upon the barbarians,' the Federalists were encouraging 'the barbarians to encroach upon us'" (44).

10. *Van Buren Autobiography*, 2: 288; Thomas Foster, Representative from Georgia, May 17, 1830, LC, 6: 1031. On the war that Hayne "carried into the enemy's country," see Webster, "Second Speech on Foot's Resolution," *Webster Writings* (1851), 3: 308–9.

11. *Memoirs of the Life of William Wirt*, 2 vols., ed. John P. Kennedy (Philadelphia, 1850), 2: 250. Wirt used "the phrase of an eloquent historian" (Thomas Babington Macaulay, in his *History of England*). Tocqueville, *Democracy in America*, 1: 368–69, 365.

12. Albert J. Beveridge, *The Life of John Marshall*, 4 vols. (Boston, 1919), 4: 542–43.

13. *Worcester v. Georgia*, 6 Peters, 515–97, at 595.

14. Ibid., 570–71. Marshall to Story, September 22, 1832, cited in Beveridge, *Life of Marshall*, 4: 559. The legacy of *Worcester* is assessed in Wilkinson, *American Indians*.

Chapter 19. Annexation of Texas and War with Mexico

1. On Texas annexation and the decade after 1836, see David M. Pletcher, *The Diplomacy of Annexation: Texas, Oregon, and the Mexican War* (Columbia, MO, 1973); Frederick Merk, with Lois Bannister Merk, *Slavery and the Annexation of Texas* (New York, 1972); Thomas R. Hietala, *Manifest Design: Anxious Aggrandizement in Late Jacksonian America* (Ithaca, NY, 1985); Kinley J. Brauer, *Cotton versus Conscience: Massachusetts Whig Politics and Southwestern Expansion, 1843–1848* (Lexington, KY, 1967); Norman Graebner, ed., *Manifest Destiny* (Indianapolis, IN, 1968); Peterson, *Great Triumvirate*; and Howe, *What Hath God Wrought*.

2. For background, see Franklin A. Doty, "Florida, Iowa, and the National 'Balance of Power,' 1845," *Florida Historical Quarterly* 25 (1956): 30–59.

3. Remarks in Senate, December 27–28, 1837, *Calhoun Works*, 3: 141, 154.

4. [Thomas Hart Benton], *Thirty Years' View* (New York, 1893 [1856]), 2: 601.

5. Bartlett, *Record*, 191; Benton, *Thirty Years' View*, 614. Peterson, *Great Triumvirate*, calls Benton's charges "hallucinatory."

6. See Hermann von Holst, *John C. Calhoun* (New York, 1980 [1882]), 245–46, 253–55, for consideration of the glaring inconsistency. Had Texas formed as

many as five states, it was not likely that slavery would exist in all of them, but that the South would gain the political advantage from Texas annexation, though disputed by some advocates, was blindingly obvious to critics. On the constitutional background, see Everett S. Brown, *The Constitutional History of the United States, 1803–1812* (Berkley, CA, 1920), and W. Stull Holt, *Treaties Defeated by the Senate* (Baltimore, 1933). For Polk, see Benton, *Thirty Years' View*, 632–38.

7. Benton, *Debates*, December 23, 1845, 15: 302.

8. On Democratic support for the All-Mexico Movement, see Johannsen, *Stephen Douglas*, 216–17, and Merk and Merk, *Manifest Destiny*, 118–23, where the *Herald* is cited. Nicholas Trist to Virginia Trist, July 8, 1864, in Howe, *What Hath God Wrought*, 805. See the map showing the expansion of Polk's aims in ibid., 804.

9. See Potter, *Impending Crisis*, 1–15, for a riveting depiction of these hectic days. The Treaty of Guadaloupe Hidalgo with Mexico was ratified, by a vote of 38 to 14, on March 10, 1848.

Chapter 20. The Great Debate of 1848

1. Eulogy on John Quincy Adams, April 6, 1848, *Seward Works*, 3: 75–103, at 75–77; February 19, 1845, *JQA Memoirs*, 12: 171; William Lee Miller, *Arguing about Slavery: John Quincy Adams and the Great Battle in the United States Congress* (New York, 1995).

2. James McDowell, Representative from Virginia, Benton, *Thirty Years' View*, 708.

3. Speech in Lexington, KY, November 13, 1847, *Clay Papers*, 10: 362. See the depiction of Webster in Theodore Parker, *A Discourse Occasioned by the Death of Daniel Webster* (Boston, 1853), 104–5.

4. "Raleigh Letter," April 17, 1844, *Clay Papers*, 10: 44–45. Clay seemed to prevaricate on Texas annexation in his later Alabama letter. See discussion in Peterson, *Great Triumvirate*, and Knupfer, *Union as It Is*, 154.

5. "The Mexican War," March 1, 1848, *Webster Writings*, 5: 256–58.

6. Speech on Annexation of Texas, August 19, 1844, *Choate Works*, 2: 267–83.

7. Daniel Webster, "Letter on the Annexation of Texas," extracted in *The Portfolio* 3 (1844): 312; Garrett Davis, January 14, 1845, LC, Appendix, 341–42.

8. November 13, 1847, *Clay Papers*, 10: 362. On the spirit of wild adventure roused by the Mexican War, see Robert W. Johannsen, *To the Halls of the Montezumas: The Mexican War in the American Imagination* (New York, 1985).

9. Daniel Webster, "Public Dinner at Philadelphia," December 2, 1846, *Webster Writings*, 4: 31–32, cited in Howe, *What Hath God Wrought*, 763.

10. For Clay, the threat of Bonapartism was of long standing; see "Speech at Farewell Dinner," March 7, 1829, *Clay Papers*, 8: 4–5.

11. Horsman, *Race and Manifest Destiny*. The British correspondent was William H. Russell of the London *Times*, writing in 1861.

12. January 4, 1848, *Calhoun Works*, 4: 421.

13. Tyler, April 22, 1844, MP, 4: 310.

14. Guizot cited in Richard W. Van Alstyne, "The Monroe Doctrine," *Encyclopedia of American Foreign Policy*, ed. Alexander Deconde (New York, 1978),

588–89. Emphasizing preclusive or preventive motives are Norman A. Graebner, *Empire on the Pacific* (New York, 1955); Meinig, *Shaping of America*, 2: 203; and Lind, *American Way*, 64–70.

15. April 17, 1844, *Clay Papers*, 10: 45.

16. "Re-annexation of Texas," June 4, 1844, *Writings of Levi Woodbury*, 3 vols. (Boston, 1852), 1: 357. Woodbury attributed these sentiments to a speaker opposing Josiah Quincy in 1811. He also made reference to Edward D. Mansfield, *The Political Grammar of the United States* (Cincinnati, OH, 1836), 147, whose formulation differed somewhat from Woodbury's. One of the cardinal principles of the American system, according to Mansfield, was "that a colony settled upon an adjacent territory, and within the jurisdiction of the United States, whether it be composed of citizens of the Union or emigrants from foreign nations, Europeans, or Asiatics, shall, on enumerating a specific population, be admitted to equal rights, privileges, and powers with the original states. This principle is likewise unlimited in respect to the number, distance, or settlement of the colonies." The original states that had formed the government, Mansfield noted, would ultimately be left in a minority "in that government which they formed, and of which they were the sole possessors. They make the whole world partners with themselves, in an inheritance of liberty and power and wealth."

17. Robert Sampson, *John L. O'Sullivan and His Times* (Kent, OH, 2003), 201–4; Howe, *What Hath God Wrought*, 764; *State Register* and part of Breese quotation in Johannsen, *Stephen Douglas*, 216–17; Stockton, Speech at Philadelphia, December 30, 1847, in *Manifest Destiny*, ed. Norman A. Graebner (Indianapolis, IN, 1968), 213–14; Breese, Speech in Senate, February 14, 1848, ibid., 216–17.

18. "The Late Negotiations for Peace," *American Whig Review* 6 (November 1847): 446, 452. Bernard is cited in Anders Stephanson, *Manifest Destiny* (New York, 1995), 57, who notes this to be a "prediction of considerable historical insight."

19. *Clay Papers*, 10: 368–69.

20. January 4, 1848, *Calhoun Works*, 4: 410, 415.

21. Ibid., 411–12.

22. Ibid., 413; Henry Hillard, September 1852, "The Life and Character of Henry Clay," in *Monument to the Memory of Henry Clay* (Cincinnati, OH, 1857), 466.

23. "Objects of the Mexican War," March 17, 1848, *Webster Writings*, 5: 289, 292. On the significance of borough mongering, see Bernard Bailyn, *The Ideological Origins of the American Revolution* (Cambridge, MA, 1967), 47, 250. For the constitutional deformities resulting from vesting thinly peopled states with an impregnable bastion in the Senate, see the discussion in Lind, *Next American Nation*.

24. Adams, *Life of Albert Gallatin*, 672–73, 676; *Peace with Mexico* (1847), in *Gallatin Writings*, 3: 582. See discussion in Horsman, *Race and Manifest Destiny*, 271. "The clarity of the eighteenth century," as Horsman comments, "revealed the tawdriness of much of mid-nineteenth-century nationalistic thought."

Chapter 21. Intervention for Nonintervention: The Kossuth Tour

1. John Berrien, Senator from Georgia (Whig), December 9, 1851, LC, 43. Kossuth emphasized that an affirmative response to his pleas of support would be

a means of preventing war; "Hereditary Policy of America," December 11, 1851, *Select Speeches of Kossuth*, ed. Francis W. Newman (New York, 1854), 65–66. The standard works are Donald S. Spencer, *Louis Kossuth and Young America: A Study of Sectionalism and Foreign Policy, 1848–1852* (Columbia, MO, 1977); and Merle E. Curti, "Young America," *American Historical Review* 32 (1926): 34–55.

2. *Webster Papers: Diplomatic*, 2: 90n; Rufus Choate, "A Discourse Commemorative of Daniel Webster," July 27, 1853, *Choate Works*, 1: 520; Spencer, *Kossuth and Young America*.

3. Last Speech of Mr. Clay, January 9, 1852, *Clay Works*, 3: 222–24.

4. Toasts were drunk to this prospect at an 1854 dinner in London held by George N. Sanders, the American consul, whose guests included seven revolutionaries—Mazzini, Garibaldi, and Orsini of Italy, Louis Kossuth of Hungary, Arnold Rage of Germany, Ledru-Rollin of France, and Alexander Herzen of Russia. The American minister in attendance, James Buchanan, sat next to Mrs. Sanders at dinner and "asked her if she was not afraid the combustible materials about her would explode and blow us all up." Potter, *Impending Crisis*, 178. Two other remarkable documents in this vein from the 1850s are *Proceedings of the Congress of the People's League of the Old and New World* (Philadelphia, 1852) and Theodore Poesche and Charles Goepp, *The New Rome; or the United States of the World* (New York, 1853). See discussion in Kohn, *American Nationalism*, 175–76. In the opinion of Poesche, an immigrant from Germany, and Goepp, a Pennsylvania farmer of German origin, "every people, upon throwing off the yoke of its tyrants, ought to demand admission into the league of states already free, that is, into the American Union; so that these states may become the nucleus of the political organization of the human family, and the starting point of the World's Republic."

Robert Walker, the former secretary of the Treasury, also vouchsafed a vision, confessedly millennial, of "a confederacy of the whole world . . . foretold in Holy Writ and prophecy" that would be based upon the principles of the American Constitution. Though acknowledging that such a state of things could "only exist after the lapse of centuries, and after a great change in the condition of the world," Walker saw an intermediate step toward this "grand result" in the "fusion" of Britain and America, though this too he acknowledged to be a remote prospect. Rejecting the proposal of an English correspondent that Americans reunite with Britain by receiving representation in the British Parliament, Walker declared this to be impossible. "If this union between the two countries ever takes place, it must be by all becoming States of our Union, with equal rights and privileges, by reciprocal re-annexation and re-union, but under the provisions of our Constitution." The Hon. R. J. Walker to Arthur Davies, January 12, 1852, in Walker and Davies, *An Outline of the Empire of the West* (London, 1852), 21–23. See discussion in Horsman, *Race and Manifest Destiny*, 293–97.

5. Cass, January 20, 1852, in Curti, "Young America," 36; Johannsen, *Stephen Douglas*, 330–31.

6. Robert Stockton, December 10, 1851, LC, 51.

7. William Seward, Senator from New York, December 9, 1851, LC, 41–42.

8. Charles Sumner, Senator from Massachusetts, December 10, 1851, LC, 51; Lewis Cass, Senator from Michigan, December 11, 1851, ibid., 68.

9. Jacob Miller, Senator from New Jersey (Whig), December 9, 1851, LC, 45; Cass, ibid., 68.

10. William Seward, Senator from New York (Whig), December 9, 1851, ibid., 42; Jeremiah Clemens, Senator from Alabama (Democrat), December 10, ibid., 53.

11. Tyler to James S. Whitney, February 3, 1852, *Proceedings of the Massachusetts Historical Society* 47 (1914): 472–75.

12. Joseph Underwood, Senator from Kentucky (Whig), December 3, 1851, LC, 26.

13. Webster to George Ticknor, January 16, 1851, *Webster Papers: Diplomatic*, 2: 64.

14. "Mr. Cass's Resolution," January 7, 1850, *Clay Works* (1863), 3: 107. See Spencer, *Kossuth and Young America*, for Kossuth's travails in navigating the sectional conflict.

15. Stephen Douglas, December 11, 1851, LC, 70; "Two Letters on the Extension of Slavery . . . ," May 3, 1850, Horace Mann, *Slavery: Letters and Speeches* (Boston, 1851), 312–13; John Parker Hale, January 7, 1850, in Arthur M. Schlesinger Jr., "Human Rights and the American Tradition," *Cycles*, 90–92.

16. "The Slave Oligarchy and Its Usurpations," November 2, 1855, Charles Sumner, *Recent Speeches and Addresses* (Boston 1856), 556.

Chapter 22. Invitation to a Beheading

1. Henry Clay, February 5 and 6, 1850, LC, 116; John Calhoun, March 4, 1850, Calhoun, *Union and Liberty*, 591. On the 1850s, see especially Potter, *Impending Crisis*; McPherson, *Battle Cry of Freedom*; Nevins, *Ordeal of the Union*; and Morrison, *Slavery and American West*.

2. Polk, Fourth Annual Message, December 5, 1848; Henry Foote in Morrison, *Slavery and American West*, 103.

3. Clay, January 29, 1850, LC, 244–47; March 7, 1850, *Webster Works* (1881), 5: 352.

4. Potter, *Impending Crisis*, 121–44.

5. Ibid.; Don Fehrenbacher, *The South and Three Sectional Crises* (Baton Rouge, LA, 1980), 33.

6. Appeal, January 19, 1854, Hofstadter, *Great Issues*, 355; Douglas, 1850, in Potter, *Impending Crisis*, 171; "Connecticut Opposes the Kansas-Nebraska Bill," May 1854, Ames, *State Documents*, 282–83. See the contrasting treatments in Harry Jaffa, *Crisis of the House Divided: An Interpretation of the Issues in the Lincoln-Douglas Debates* (Chicago, 1982), and Johannsen, *Stephen Douglas*.

7. See Robert E. May, "A 'Southern Strategy' for the 1850s: Northern Democrats, the Tropics, and the Expansion of the National Domain," *Louisiana Studies* 14 (Winter 1975): 333–59, at 335.

8. William Marcy in Robert E. May, *The Southern Dream of a Caribbean Empire: 1854–1861* (Athens, GA, 1989), 60; Nevins, *Ordeal of the Union*, 2: 363.

9. "The Ostend Report," October 18, 1854, *Buchanan Works*, 9: 260–66. See also Potter, *Impending Crisis*, 177–98, and Nevins, *Ordeal of the Union*, 2: 347–79.

10. Kenneth Stampp, *America in 1857* (New York, 1990), 92–93; Catron at 96.

11. Rufus Choate, "American Nationality," July 5, 1858, *Choate Works*, 2: 429.

Chapter 23. Causes of the War, Causes of the Peace

1. On the war's causes, see the works cited in chapter 22, note 1. Good collections with diverse viewpoints may be found in Edwin C. Rozwenc, ed., *The Causes of the American Civil War* (Boston, 1961); Kenneth Stampp, ed., *The Causes of the Civil War* (New York, 1991); Gabor S. Boritt, ed., *Why the Civil War Came* (New York, 1996); Hans L. Trefousse, *The Causes of the Civil War: Institutional Failure or Human Blunder?* (New York, 1971); and Thomas J. Pressly, *Americans Interpret Their Civil War* (Princeton, NJ, 1954). "Needless war" is from George Fort Milton, *Eve of Conflict: Stephen A. Douglas and the Needless War* (New York, 1934). The seminal piece in the post–World War II revaluation was Arthur M. Schlesinger Jr., "The Causes of the Civil War: A Note on Historical Sentimentalism," *Partisan Review* 16 (October 1949): 969–81.

2. Meinig, *Shaping of America*, 2: 457.

3. Madison to C. J. Ingersoll, January 8, 1830, in McCoy, *Last of the Fathers*, 248.

4. Ames to Christopher Gore, October 3, 1803, *Ames Works*, 2: 1463. See also Robert V. Bruce, "The Shadow of a Coming War," Boritt, *Lincoln, the War President*, 3–28.

5. March 4, 1850, Calhoun, *Union and Liberty*, 575; Davis, in McCardell, *Idea of a Southern Nation*, 231. Cf. Frank Owsley, "The Irrepressible Conflict," from *I'll Take My Stand: The South and the Agrarian Tradition*, by Twelve Southerners (Baton Rouge, LA, 1977 [1930]), 73. On the significance of unequal growth in international relations, see Robert Gilpin, *War and Change in World Politics* (Cambridge and New York, 1981).

6. Davis in Nevins, *Ordeal of the Union*, 1: 341; cf. 1: 282; *Clay Papers*, 10: 729.

7. Maldwyn Allen Jones, *American Immigration* (Chicago, 1960), 172, notes that during the Civil War "many southerners were firmly convinced that the overwhelming majority of Federal soldiers were of foreign origin, and it was to this fact that in later years they often attributed the defeat of the Confederacy." Jones believes it "probable," however, that "the number of foreign-born soldiers in the union did not much exceed half a million, which was only about one-fifth of the total number of enlistments." The *New Orleans Daily Crescent* observed, June 15, 1860, that "enough foreigners to constitute a constituency for four or five additional representatives" had come to the United States in 1860. The *Crescent* denied that slavery was the reason they settled in the North. It cited two other reasons: "a general law of emigration" that inclined people to "settle down where the climate is the nearest approach to that which they left behind," and the ability of immigrants to "buy rich and productive Government lands for a mere trifle." This policy of "giving away the public lands, millions of acres at a time," was one of the factors that "tend to aggrandize the Northern section of the Union." "Sumner's Statistics," *Southern Editorials on Secession*, ed. Dwight Lowell Dumond (Gloucester, MA, 1964 [1931]), 126–27. For an earlier appreciation of the effects of migration in shifting the sectional balance of power, see the speech of Charles Pinckney, February 14, 1820, LC, 1316–17. On the effect of immigration on the sectional balance of power, see also Fischer, *Albion's Seed*, 854; James M. McPherson, *Ordeal by Fire* (New York, 1982), 23–25; idem, *Battle Cry of Freedom*, 40; Lind, *Next American Nation*, 48–54; and Higham,

Strangers in the Land. See Potter, *Impending Crisis*, for consideration of the implications of a war fought in 1850.

8. C. Vann Woodward, "Equality: America's Deferred Commitment" (1958), in *The American Scholar Reader*, ed. Hiram Haydn and Betsy Saunders (New York, 1960), 472.

9. Avery O. Craven, *Civil War in the Making, 1815–1860* (Baton Rouge, LA, 1959), 108.

10. March 4, 1850, *Calhoun Works*, 4: 556–57.

11. On the southern critique of northern capitalism, see Richard Hofstadter, "John C. Calhoun: The Marx of the Master Class," *The American Political Tradition* (New York, 1948), 68–92; Eric McKitrick, ed., *Slavery Defended: The Views of the Old South* (Englewood Cliffs, NJ, 1963); George Fitzhugh, *Cannibals All! Or Slaves without Masters*, ed. C. Vann Woodward (Cambridge, MA, 1988 [1857]). Woodward notes, xxv, that Fitzhugh "exploited and quoted extensively from many of the sources that Karl Marx used ten years later in the first volume of *Capital* to marshal evidence of the inhumanity of British industrial capitalism." The southern sensibility is beautifully rendered in Eugene D. Genovese, *The Southern Tradition: The Achievement and Limitations of an American Conservatism* (Cambridge, MA, 1994).

12. October 16, 1854, *Lincoln Works*, 2: 255.

13. See the discussion in Geoffrey Blainey, *The Causes of War* (New York, 1988 [1973]), 3. "For every thousand pages published on the causes of wars," Blainey notes, "there is less than one page directly on the causes of peace." Logically, as Blainey observed, the causes of war and peace "should dovetail into one another. A weak explanation of why Europe was at peace will lead to a weak explanation of why Europe was at war. A valid diagnosis of war will be reflected in a valid diagnosis of peace."

14. Albert Gallatin, "Memorial of the Committee of the Free Trade Convention," January 23, 1832, in *State Papers and Speeches on the Tariff*, ed. F. W. Taussig (Cambridge, MA, 1895), 213; "Speech on the Annexation of Texas," April 24, 1844, in Adams, *Life of Albert Gallatin*, 673.

15. *Federalist* 7 (Hamilton); Clay in Peterson, *Great Triumvirate*, 119; "The Tariff," April 1–2, 1824, *Webster Papers: Speeches*, 1: 116. Cf. Calhoun, February 28, 1842, in the Senate: "Instead of a nation, we are in reality an assemblance of nations, or peoples." *Calhoun Works*, 4: 81.

16. "Letter to a Public Meeting," November 19, 1850, *Buchanan Works*, 8: 391–92. For numerous expressions of the bonds of union created by mutual dependence in the early years of the Republic, see Cathy D. Matson and Peter S. Onuf, *A Union of Interests: Political and Economic Thought in Revolutionary America* (Lawrence, KS, 1990).

17. Alexander Stephens, November 14, 1860, *Secession Debated: Georgia's Showdown in 1860*, ed. William W. Freehling and Craig M. Simpson (New York, 1992), 64–67.

18. Amendments to the Constitution, June 8, 1789, *Madison Papers*, 12: 198, 209; Banning, *Sacred Fire*, 286–87; Clay, February 12, 1833, *Clay Works* (1897), 5: 546; Lincoln, October 16, 1854, *Lincoln Works*, 2: 253.

19. Adams, January 1832, in Peterson, *Great Triumvirate*, 202; Shields, April 5, 1850, in Knupfer, *Union as It Is*, 158; Johannsen, *Stephen Douglas*, 819. Knupfer

provides an excellent depiction of what I have termed the normative order of federal union. On compromise see also Thomas Brown, *Politics and Statesmanship: Essays on the American Whig Party* (New York, 1985).

20. Robert G. Gunderson, *Old Gentlemen's Convention: The Washington Peace Conference of 1861* (Madison, WI, 1961). On the anticipations of a coming war (written during the "great debate" of 1939–1941, when the same puzzle was a dominating factor), see the first book of David M. Potter, *Lincoln and the Secession Crisis* (New Haven, CT, 1942).

21. *Van Buren Autobiography*, 2: 416.

Chapter 24. D.I.V.O.R.C.E.

1. "To the Massachusetts Convention," April 5, 1851, *Seward Works* (1887), 3: 447.

2. Chatham and Prior in Bedford Brown, Senator from North Carolina (Democrat), February 1833, colloquy with William Wilkins, Senator from Pennsylvania (Democrat), Benton, *Debates*, 12: 53.

3. January 9, 1838, *Clay Papers*, 9: 125.

4. Phillips, January 20, 1861, in Nagel, *One Nation Indivisible*, 257; Adams to William Vans Murray, April 7, 1801, *JQA Writings*, 2: 526.

5. John Quincy Adams, *The Jubilee of the Constitution . . . Being the Fiftieth Anniversary of the Inauguration of George Washington . . .*, April 30, 1839 (Washington, DC, 1839), 69. Nagel cites these and other examples of marital metaphors in his pathbreaking study of the union, *One Nation Indivisible*. (It broke a path for me.) For other instances, see Alfred Iverson, Senator from Georgia (Democrat), December 5, 1860, and Edward Dickinson Baker, Senator from Oregon (Republican), March 2, 1861, LC, 12, 1384.

6. Seward, "The True Greatness of Our Country," 1844 and 1848, *Seward Works* (1853), 3: 22 (Baker gives the date as 1848 but writes that in substance the same lecture was given twice by Seward in 1844); Jefferson to Richard Rush, October 20, 1820, *Jefferson Writings*, 15: 284. See also Onuf, *Jefferson's Empire*, 114–16.

7. James Madison to Mark L. Hill, April 1820, *Madison Letters*, 3: 175; Lincoln, First Inaugural Address, March 4, 1861.

8. Webster, March 7, 1850, Benton, *Debates*, 16: 430; the *Times* in Robert V. Bruce, "The Shadow of a Coming War," Boritt, *Lincoln, the War President*, 23.

9. See John C. Calhoun, February 26, 1833, *Calhoun Works*, 2: 304–5; Stephens, *Constitutional View*, 542–43. Reviewing Pickering's proposals for peaceable secession during the oppressive reign of the Jeffersonians (for which see above, chapter 6), Jefferson Davis noted that "Mr. Pickering seems to have had a correct and intelligent perception of the altogether pacific character of the secession which he proposed, and of the mutual advantages likely to accrue to both sections from a peaceable separation." Jefferson Davis, *The Rise and Fall of the Confederate Government* (New York, 1881), 1: 72–73.

10. See discussions in Bruce Russert, *Grasping the Democratic Peace* (Princeton, NJ, 1994); John M. Owen, *Liberal Peace, Liberal War: American Politics and International Security* (Ithaca, NY, 1997), 124–38; Christopher Layne, "Kant or Cant: The Myth of the Democratic Peace," *International Security* 19 (1994): 5–49, and

Debating the Democratic Peace: An International Security Reader, ed. Michael E. Brown et al. (Cambridge, MA, 1996). Cf. Seward (1848): "Democracies are prone to war, and war consumes them." *Seward Works* (1853), 3: 88. On English opinion, see Martin Crawford, *The Anglo-American Crisis of the Mid-Nineteenth Century: The Times* and *America, 1850–1862* (Athens, GA, 1987).

11. "Second Speech on Foot's Resolution," January 26, 1830, *Webster Works* (1858), 3: 342. Cf. Clay, February 12, 1833, *Clay Works*, 5: 550.

12. *Federalist* 9 (Hamilton); Andrew Jackson, Farewell Address, March 4, 1837; Lincoln, First Inaugural Address, March 4, 1861. To similar effect, see Jefferson to John Taylor, June 4, 1798, *Jefferson Writings*, 17: 208.

13. *Federalist* 13 (Hamilton); Madison to Andrew Stevenson, February 10, 1833, *Madison Letters*, 4: 272–73.

14. Douglas, March 13 and 14, 1850, LC, Appendix, 365.

15. June 25, 1851, George Ticknor Curtis, *Life of Daniel Webster* (New York, 1889), 2: 519; Potter, *Impending Crisis*, 132.

16. "A Discourse Commemorative of Daniel Webster," July 27, 1853, *Choate Works*, 1: 555.

17. July 10, 1858, *Lincoln Works*, 2: 492; July 17, 1858, ibid., 514; Stephens, November 14, 1860, *The Rebellion Record* (New York, 1861), 227, 220.

18. Bensel, *Yankee Leviathan*, 12, 62.

19. October 16, 1854, *Lincoln Speeches*, 1: 308.

20. December 29, 1832, Letter in London *Patriot*, in Oliver Johnson, *William Lloyd Garrison and His Times* (Boston, 1881), 132; John Elliott Cairnes, *The Slave Power* (New York, 1969 [1863]), 26. On Lincoln's political navigation, see Robert W. Johannsen, *Lincoln, the South, and Slavery* (Baton Rouge, LA, 1991).

21. Clement Eaton, *Freedom of Thought in the Old South* (Durham, NC, 1940), 300–375; Jefferson to St. George Tucker, August 28, 1797, *Jefferson Writings*, 9: 417–19. See the discussion in James Rogers Sharp, *American Politics in the Early Republic* (New Haven, CT, 1993), 241; and Onuf, *Jefferson's Empire*.

22. Edward Gibbon, *The History of the Decline and Fall of The Roman Empire* (1776), ed. J. B. Bury (London, 1897), 1: 68; Montesquieu, *Spirit of the Laws* (Nugent), bk. 5, chap. 19.

Chapter 25. The Tragedy of Civil War

1. Calhoun, March 4, 1850, Benton, *Debates*, 16: 409; Webster, March 7, 1850, ibid., 16: 430.

2. Mary Chestnut, *Diary from Dixie*, 182, 245, in J. G. Randall and David Donald, *The Civil War and Reconstruction* (Lexington, MA, 1969), 517–18.

3. March 4, 1861, "First Inaugural Address—First Edition and Revisions," *Lincoln Works*, 4: 260.

4. James P. Holcombe, *Address . . . at Washington and Lee*, January 19, 1871, *Personal Reminiscences, Anecdotes, and Letters of Gen. Robert E. Lee*, ed. J. William Jones (New York, 1875), 494–95.

5. S. A. Goodwin, 1889, *The Davis Memorial Volume*, ed. J. William Jones (New Orleans, 1890), 654. Vernon Parrington, *Main Currents of American Thought*, 3 vols. (New York, 1927), 2: 93, expressed the tragic theme in a yet different vein: "That the principle of local-self government should have been committed to the

cause of slavery, that it was loaded with an incubus certain to alienate the liberalism of the North, may be accounted one of the tragedies of American history. It was disastrous to American democracy, for it removed the last brake on the movement of consolidation, submerging the democratic individualism of the South in an unwieldy mass will, and surrendering the country to the principle of capitalistic exploitation." It follows from Parrington's formulation that the avowed best friends of state rights and local autonomy were in fact its worst enemies.

6. Fourth Annual Message, December 3, 1860, *MP*, 7: 3161–62, 3166–67.

7. Seward, *New York Evening Post*, December 6, 1860, in Kenneth M. Stampp, *And the War Came: The North and the Secession Crisis, 1860–61* (Chicago, 1950), 56.

8. "The State of the Union," *Seward Works*, 4: 658–62.

9. Lee's eulogist noted, "The great Italian poet has placed those who, during the civil wars of Florence, sought escape from the dangers and responsibilities of citizenship by avoiding the discharge of its highest duty, in the vestibule of his Inferno, as men who, having never truly lived, were disdained alike by Justice and by Mercy, and unworthy of even a passing glance from mortal eye. This doom of scornful oblivion, pronounced in undying verse, has been confirmed by the accordant sentiment of all succeeding ages." Holcombe, *Address*, 495.

10. Rufus Choate, "On the Preservation of the Union," in Faneuil Hall, November 26, 1850, *Choate Works*, 2: 326.

Chapter 26. The New Nation

1. Frederick Douglass, "Reconstruction," December 1866, *Atlantic Monthly*; Twain in McPherson, *Abraham Lincoln*, 24.

2. See the discussion in Raymond Aron, *Peace and War* (New York, 1966), and Robert Gilpin, "The Theory of Hegemonic War," *The Origin and Prevention of Major Wars*, ed. Robert I. Rotberg and Theodore K. Rabb (New York, 1989).

3. W. L. Morton, "British North America and a Continent in Dissolution, 1861–1871," *History* 47 (1962): 139–56. On the transformative effect of the Civil War, see especially McPherson, *Abraham Lincoln*, and idem, *Battle Cry of Freedom*. Other entries in the rich literature on the war's effects include Bensel, *Yankee Leviathan*; Forsyth, *Unions of States*; Meinig, *Shaping of America*, vol. 2; Bender, *Nation among Nations*; Lind, *Next American Nation*; Peterson, *Lincoln*; Porter, *War and the Rise of the State*; Bernard Schwartz, *From Confederation to Nation: The American Constitution, 1835–1877* (Baltimore, 1973); Harold M. Hyman, *A More Perfect Union: The Impact of the Civil War and Reconstruction on the Constitution* (Boston, 1975); Roy F. Nichols, "Federalism versus Democracy: The Significance of the Civil War in the History of United States Federalism," in Nichols et al., *Federalism as a Democratic Process* (New Brunswick, NJ, 1942); Carl N. Degler, "One among Many: The United States and National Unification," and Kenneth M. Stampp, "One Alone? The United States and National Self-Determination," both in Borritt, *Lincoln, the War President*, 89–144.

4. Nicholas Murray Butler, *Building the American Nation* (New York, 1923), 265–66, discussed in Forsyth, *Unions of States*, 70–71.

5. Charles Sumner, *Are We a Nation?* November 19, 1867 (New York, 1867), 35.

6. These famous passages are, respectively, from William Tecumseh Sherman

and Philip Sheridan, both cited in James M. McPherson, "From Limited to Total War, 1861–1865," *Drawn with the Sword: Reflections on the American Civil War* (New York, 1996), 83–84.

7. See comments of George Ticknor, quoted in McPherson, *Abraham Lincoln*, vii; Bender, *Nation among Nations*, 170; Kohn, *American Nationalism*, 124; Huntington, *Who Are We?* 108. For a deeper sense of southern identity, see Fischer, *Albion's Seed*, and Meinig, *Shaping of America*, 2: 513. On the relationship of nationalism to regionalism, see Michael O'Brien, *Henry Adams & the Southern Question* (Athens, GA, 2005), esp. 73–74.

8. Keller, *Affairs of State*; James Blaine (1866), *Twenty Years of Congress: From Lincoln to Garfield* (Norwich, CT, 1886), 2: 160; McPherson, *Abraham Lincoln*, viii; Bensel, *Yankee Leviathan*, 2. See also Leonard P. Curry, *Blueprint for Modern America: Nonmilitary Legislation of the First Civil War Congress* (Nashville, TN, 1968).

9. *Ex parte Milligan* 4 Wall. 120 (1866); Lind, *American Way*, 18–19; Randall, *Constitutional Problems*; Henry S. Foote, *War of the Rebellion; or, Scylla and Charybdis . . .* (New York, 1866), 49. See also Marshall L. DeRosa, *The Confederate Constitution of 1861: An Inquiry into American Constitutionalism* (Columbia, MO, 1991). The unprecedented scale of power created by the war is evoked in Henry Adams, *The Education of Henry Adams* (Boston, 1918), 169. The costs are tallied in Mark E. Neely Jr., *The Fate of Liberty: Abraham Lincoln and Civil Liberties* (New York, 1991).

10. Porter, *War and the Rise of the State*, 258–68; Eric Helleiner, *The Making of National Money: Territorial Currencies in Historical Perspective* (Ithaca, NY, 2003).

11. Eckes, *Opening America's Market*, 46, 28, 47; David A. Lake, *Power, Protection, and Free Trade* (Ithaca, NY, 1988), 7.

12. Speech of Fisher Ames, Massachusetts Ratifying Convention, Elliot, *Debates*, 2: 158–59. Cf. Oliver Wendell Holmes, "Brother Jonathan's Lament for Sister Caroline," March 25, 1861, Commager, *Civil War Archive*, 44. "Much nationality" from Fredrika Bremer, *The Homes of the New World* (New York, 1853), 2: 129, who marveled that the Senate's mode of representation brought forth "much that is picturesque in the living, peculiar life of each state." The American states, "each so separate and so peculiar in situation, scenery, climate, products, population, stand forth in Congress as individuals, and take part in the treatment of public questions, which are interesting to the whole human race, according to characteristics which are peculiar to themselves and common to all."

Chapter 27. A New Birth of Freedom?

1. Nicholas Murray Butler, *Building the American Nation* (New York, 1923), 266.

2. See Eric Foner, *Reconstruction: America's Unfinished Revolution, 1863–1877* (New York, 1988), 425.

3. Lincoln to Horace Greeley, August 22, 1862, *Lincoln Speeches*, 2: 358; interview with George Thompson, an English antislavery orator, *Recollected Words of Abraham Lincoln*, ed. Don Fehrenbacher and Virginia Fehrenbacher (Stanford, CA, 1996), 83–84; Second Inaugural Address, March 4, 1865.

4. Frederick Douglass, *Oration Delivered on the Occasion of the Unveiling of the Freedman's Monument in Memory of Abraham Lincoln* (Washington, DC, April 14, 1876), 16–17.

5. Ibid., 14–15; Douglass, address, April 16, 1888, in David W. Blight, "'For Something beyond the Battlefield': Frederick Douglass and the Struggle for the Memory of the Civil War," *Journal of American History* 75 (1989): 1156–78, at 1170; idem, *Race and Reunion: The Civil War in American Memory* (Cambridge, MA, 2001).

6. Charles Sumner, *Are We a Nation?* (New York, 1867), 34.

7. See the analysis in Lind, *What Lincoln Believed*, 221–24.

8. Seward to Adams, August 26, 1867, *Executive Documents of . . . House of Representatives* (Washington, DC, 1867–1868), 1: 130; Van Deusen, *Seward*, 428–30; Keller, *Affairs of State*, 92.

9. Foote added, staking his claim to political science, that "the experience of nations is uniform on this subject; and even had no such fatal example of the ruin of freedom heretofore occurred, it would really seem that a mere statement of this proposition, as a yet *unproven theorem*, ought to be sufficient to enforce the important truth referred to upon the most opaque intellect." Henry S. Foote, *War of the Rebellion; or, Scylla and Charybdis . . .* (New York, 1866), 434.

10. Keller, *Affairs of State*, cites many instances of this theme.

11. Godkin in Bender, *Nation among Nations*, 181; Frederick Douglass, "Reconstruction," *Atlantic Monthly*, December 1866.

12. Nina Silber, *The Romance of Reunion: Northerners and the South, 1865–1900* (Chapel Hill, NC, 1993); "The New North," *Century* 33 (March 1887): 807; Henry W. Grady, "The New South," address before the New England Society in New York, December 22, 1886, *New England Magazine* 8 (March 1890): 85–90; R.E. Colston, formerly Brigadier-General, C.S.A., "Union Sentiment among Confederate Veterans," *Century* 34 (June, 1887): 309; Watterson in Peterson, *Lincoln*, 49. The salience of nationalism in this era, including the growth of flag worship, is given a crisp summary in Huntington, *Who Are We?* 119–28.

13. Kagan, *Dangerous Nation*, 285.

Chapter 28. "Free Security" and "Imperial Understretch"

1. Grover Cleveland, First Inaugural Address, March 4, 1885; Van Buren, June 9, 1829, Moore, *Digest*, 6: 14.

2. On free security, see C. Vann Woodward, "The Age of Reinterpretation," *American Historical Review* 66 (1960): 1–19.

3. Donald G. Creighton, *The Road to Confederation: The Emergence of Canada, 1863–1867* (Boston, 1965); C. P. Stacey, "Britain's Withdrawal from North America, 1864–1871," *Canadian Historical Review* 36 (1955); and W. L. Morton, "British North America and a Continent in Dissolution, 1861–1871," *History* 47 (1962): 139–56; John H. Thompson and Stephen J. Randall, *Canada and the United States: Ambivalent Allies* (Athens, GA, 2002); Reginald C. Stuart, *United States Expansionism and British North America, 1775–1871* (Chapel Hill, NC, 1988); Blaine in Richard van Alstyne, *The Rising American Empire* (New York, 1960), 163–64.

4. Welles in Paolino, *Foundations of the American Empire*, 14; Banks (1866) and Johnson in Keller, *Affairs of State*, 86, 91; Fareed Zakaria, *From Wealth to Power: The Unusual Origins of America's World Role* (Princeton, NJ, 1998), 44–89.

5. *Ulysses S. Grant: Memoirs and Selected Letters*, ed. Mary Drake McFeely and William S. McFeely (New York, 1990), 42. This continued to be the verdict of New England historians long after the war. See Tannenbaum, *American Tradition*, 83–86.

6. "If Mr. Buchanan be elected, he will follow the bloody policy of this administration, whose sins and glories—Greytown, Ostend, Kansas, and all—decorate and oppress him." Henry Winter Davis, "A Plea for the Country against the Sections," August 7, 1856, *Speeches . . . by Henry Winter Davis, of Maryland* (New York, 1867), 60; Davis, "The Empire of Mexico," April 4, 1864, ibid., 395–96. Davis resolved "that it does not accord with the policy of the United States to acknowledge any monarchical government erected on the ruins of any republican government under the auspices of any European power." The resolution passed the House of Representatives unanimously.

7. Orestes A. Brownson, *The American Republic: Its Constitution, Tendencies and Destiny* (1866), *Brownson Works*, 18: 221; Charles Sumner, *Prophetic Voices Concerning America* (Boston, 1874), 175.

8. "The Confederacy Lures the British with Cotton, 1861," Paterson, *Major Problems*, 1: 309.

9. "Naboth's Vineyard," speech in Senate, December 21, 1870, *Sumner Works*, 14: 120–21. A notable reflection of the climate of opinion on the constitutional means of annexation is Hermann von Holst, *John C. Calhoun* (Boston, 1882), noted above in chapter 19.

10. "The Destiny of America," September 14, 1853, *Seward Works* (1854), 1: 330. The standard work is Donald F. Warner, *The Idea of Continental Union: Agitation for the Annexation of Canada to the United States, 1849–1893* (Lexington, KY, 1960).

11. *Harper's Weekly* (1870) and Sumner in Keller, *Affairs of State*, 94–95, 97; Grant's motives in Eric T. L. Love, *Race over Empire: Racism and U.S. Imperialism, 1865–1900* (Chapel Hill, NC, 2004). For Sumner's wide-ranging objections to annexation, which charged Grant with having violated both international and constitutional law, see speech in Senate, March 17, 1871, *Sumner Works*, 14: 168–70. For debate among historians, see Donald M. Dozer, "Anti-expansionism during the Johnson Administration," *Pacific Historical Review* 12 (1943): 256–57; LaFeber, *The New Empire*; Robert L. Beisner, *From the Old Diplomacy to the New, 1865–1900* (New York, 1975); Marilyn Young, "American Expansion, 1870–1900," in *Towards a New Past: Dissenting Essays in American History*, ed. Barton E. Bernstein (New York, 1968); and Ernest May, *American Imperialism: A Speculative Essay* (Chicago, 1991 [1967]).

12. Fish, April 10, 1872, Moore, *Digest*, 6: 359–60; Blaine to minister to Russia, February 18, 1891, ibid., 353–56; Fish to Sickles, April 30, 1873, in Keller, *Affairs of State*, 89. For background, see Mayers, *Dissenting Voices*, 138–58.

13. James J. Sheehan, *German History, 1770–1866* (New York, 1989), 6; Acton, "Political Causes of the American Revolution," *Rambler* 5 (1861): 19. For a depiction of Europe's federative crisis in the 1860s, see Robert C. Binkley, *Realism and Nationalism, 1852–1871* (New York, 1935). Despite the historic legitimacy of federative forms and the widespread interest in "the federative reconstruction of Europe," the "grand monument began to crumble" in the 1850s and came crashing down in

the 1860s, out of which "emerged in the next decade the new national states of Italy and Germany, and the international system of the armed peace" (157–63). See also Hermann Wellenreuther, ed., *German and American Constitutional Thought* (New York, 1990).

Chapter 29. A World of Its Own

1. This was Justice Oliver Wendell Holmes's characterization of the purport of Supreme Court decisions in his dissenting opinion in *Lochner v. New York*. The process by which this occurred is investigated in Bruce Ackerman, *We the People*, vol. 2, *Transformations* (Cambridge, MA, 2000), and Alexander Bickel, *The Least Dangerous Branch* (Indianapolis, IN, 1962).

2. Benton, *Debates*, 11: 404; Henry C. Carey, *The Way to Outdo England without Fighting Her* (Philadelphia, 1865). The key ideas of the "national school"— Carey, Daniel Raymond, Friedrich List, and Henry Clay—are evoked in Michael Lind, *Hamilton's Republic: Readings in the American Democratic Nationalist Tradition* (New York, 1997), 232–53; idem, *What Lincoln Believed*; and Onuf and Onuf, *Nations, Markets, and War*.

3. Fulbright (1948) in Kauffman, *America First!* 149.

4. Hay in Eckes, *Opening America's Market*, 60. For commercial and industrial anxieties, see LaFeber, *New Empire*.

5. Smith, *Wealth of Nations*, 591; Carl Schurz, "Parker vs. Roosevelt: An Open Letter to the Independent Voter," September 1904, *Schurz Papers*, 6: 362. See also the statements against and for the tariff by David Starr Jordan (August 1908) and William Howard Taft (September 17, 1909) in *Annals of America*, 13: 147–49, 176–80. These essays do not take up the question of the implication of protection or free trade for international peace. In the United States, at least, the question appears to have died out in this era, perhaps because something like absolute security had seemingly been achieved.

6. Eisenhower in David Fromkin, *In the Time of the Americans* (New York, 1995), 55.

7. J. Hector St. John De Crèvecoeur, *Letters from an American Farmer* (New York, 1997 [1783]); Horace Kallen, "Democracy versus the Melting Pot: A Study of American Nationality," *Nation*, February 25, 1915. On the successive antagonisms arising out of the English civil wars, see Kevin Philips, *The Cousins' Wars: Religion, Politics, and the Triumph of Anglo-America* (New York, 2000). Among the towering works dealing with America's "peopling," see especially Meinig, *Shaping of America*; Fischer, *Albion's Seed*, and Stephan Thernstrom, ed., *The Harvard Encyclopedia of American Ethnic Groups* (Cambridge, MA, 1980).

8. "Trans-national America," *Atlantic Monthly* (July 1916), in Randolph Bourne, *War and the Intellectuals, Collected Essays, 1915–1919*, ed. Carl Resek (New York, 1964), 107–23; Kallen, "Democracy vs. Melting Pot." The professor cited by Kallen was Barrett Wendell, his former English teacher at Harvard; Priscilla Wald, *Constituting Americans: Cultural Anxiety and Narrative Form* (Durham, NC, 1995), 244.

9. Insightful explorations of changing American identity during this period may be found in Kohn, *American Nationalism*; Huntington, *Who Are We?*; Lind, *Next*

American Nation; Bender, *Nation among Nations*; Higham, *Strangers in the Land*; John J. Miller, *The Unmaking of Americans* (New York, 1998); and Thernstrom, *Harvard Encyclopedia*.

10. Ernest May, "National Security in American History," in *Rethinking America's Security*, ed. Graham Allison and Gregory T. Treverton (New York, 1992), 97–99. On the changed treatment of Indians after 1865, see Wilkinson, *American Indians*, 14. Congress in Bender, *Nation among Nations*, 162.

11. "The Significance of the Frontier in American History," July 12, 1893, Frederick Jackson Turner, *The Frontier in American History* (New York, 1962).

Chapter 30. The Unionist Paradigm Revisited

1. John Fiske, *American Political Ideas Viewed from the Standpoint of Universal History* (New York, 1885), 99–100, 135–36. Part of the work appeared as "Manifest Destiny" in *Harper's*.

2. Ibid., 144–52.

3. Cf. Tocqueville, *Democracy in America*, 1: 400: "Single nations have therefore a natural tendency to centralization, and confederations to dismemberment."

4. Richard Hofstadter, *Social Darwinism in American Thought* (Boston, 1955), 177. Ulysses S. Grant, in his second inaugural address, professed his faith "that our great Maker is preparing the world, in his own good time, to become one nation, speaking one language, and when armies and navies will no longer be required."

5. Bryce, *American Commonwealth*, 1: 310.

6. Fiske, *American Political Ideas*, 107.

7. Martti Koskenniemi, *The Gentle Civilizer of Nations: The Rise and Fall of International Law, 1870–1960* (Cambridge, UK, 2001), 155–66; Henry Cabot Lodge, "Our Blundering Foreign Policy," *Forum* 19 (March 1895): 12–15.

Chapter 31. The New Nationalism and the Spanish War

1. Edward Henry Strobel, *Mr. Blaine and His Foreign Policy* (Boston, 1884), 27, 68–69; Edward P. Crapol, *James G. Blaine: Architect of Empire* (Wilmington, DE, 2000); David Healy, *James G. Blaine and Latin America* (Columbia, MO, 2001).

2. Benjamin Harrison, First Annual Message, December 3, 1889.

3. Whitaker, *Western Hemisphere Idea*, 74–85. Though the project for a customs union failed of adoption, the conference did recommend the establishment of "an International American Monetary Union" which would issue "international coin or coins . . . which shall be uniform in weight and fineness, and which may be used in all the countries represented in this Conference." James Brown Scott, ed., *The International Conferences of American States, 1889–1928* (New York, 1931), 32–33.

4. Ninkovich, *U.S. and Imperialism*, 13–15. See above, chapter 10.

5. Alfred Thayer Mahan, *The Influence of Sea Power upon History, 1660–1783* (Boston, 1890). For the outlook of these "neo-Hamiltonians," who dubiously claimed the legacy of Alexander Hamilton, see Zimmermann, *First Great Triumph*; Widenor, *Lodge*; Samuel P. Huntington, *The Soldier and the State* (Cambridge, MA, 1957); John A. S. Grenville and George Berkeley Young, *Politics, Strategy, and*

American Diplomacy, 1873–1917 (New Haven, CT, 1966); Judis, *Folly of Empire*; and Ninkovich, *U.S. and Imperialism.*

6. Smith, *Commonwealth or Empire*, 21. Moltke quoted in Trueblood, *Federation of the World*, 4. The South's attraction to these attitudes as a means of redemption, reintegration, and leadership within the national community is explored in John Pettegrew, "'The Soldier's Faith': Turn-of-the-Century Memory of the Civil War and the Emergence of Modern American Nationalism," *Journal of Contemporary History* 31 (1996): 49–73.

7. H. L. Mencken, "Roosevelt: An Autopsy," *Prejudices: A Selection*, ed. James T. Farrell (New York, 1958), 53–54.

8. Charles W. Eliot, "Five American Contributions to Civilization," *Atlantic Monthly* 78 (1896): 433–47. For a clarifying discussion of how various forms of militarism and pacifism related to social Darwinism, see Deudney, *Bounding Power*, 202–4.

9. McKinley, War Message to Congress, April 11, 1898; First Annual Message, December 1897. In his first inaugural address, McKinley had affirmed the traditional American policy: "Our diplomacy should seek nothing more and accept nothing less than is due us. We want no wars of conquest; we must avoid the temptation of territorial aggression. War should never be entered upon until every agency of peace has failed; peace is preferable to war in almost every contingency. Arbitration is the true method of settlement of international as well as local or individual differences."

10. Elbert J. Benton, *International Law and Diplomacy of the Spanish-American War* (Baltimore, 1908), 108, 95. Two good introductions to the historiography on the war are Thomas G. Patterson, "United States Intervention in Cuba, 1898: Interpretations of the Spanish-American-Cuban-Filipino War," *History Teacher* 29 (1996): 341–61; and Richard E. Welch Jr., "William McKinley: Reluctant Warrior, Cautious Imperialist," in Graebner, *Traditions, 1865–1945*, 29–52.

11. Wood to Roosevelt, in LaFeber, *American Search*, 152; Herbert Croly, *The Promise of American Life* (New York, 1912), 302–3; Archibald Cary Coolidge, *The United States as a World Power* (New York, 1908), 129–30; William Howard Taft, *The United States and Peace* (New York, 1914), 27–28. See further Ninkovich, *U.S. and Imperialism*; Judis, *Folly of Empire*, 48–49; and Jules Robert Benjamin, *The United States and Cuba* (Pittsburgh, 1977), for the delegitimation of Cuban governments created by their dependency on the United States.

Chapter 32. Imperialism and the Conquest of the Philippines

1. Ninkovich, *U.S. and Imperialism*, 30–34. For an account stressing McKinley's foreknowledge, see Walter Karp, *The Politics of War* (New York, 2003), 100. Though most historians today insist on a strict separation between the Philippine acquisition and the Spanish war, Sumner, a shrewd observer, commented in early 1899 that "it was morally certain that we should come out of any war with Spain with conquered territory on our hands, and the people who wanted the war, or who consented to it, hoped that we would do so." Sumner, *Conquest of U.S.*, 5.

2. Sumner, *Conquest of U.S.*, 9. The pamphlet was based on a speech given at Yale University on January 16, 1899.

3. Beveridge, "March of the Flag," September 16, 1898; Speech in Senate,

January 9, 1900, in Graebner, *Ideas and Diplomacy,* 372–73; Ernest Lee Tuveson, *Redeemer Nation: The Idea of America's Millennial Role* (Chicago, 1968), vii; Frank M. Russell, review of Rippy, *America and the Strife of Europe, Annals of the American Academy of Political and Social Science* 202 (1939): 252–53.

4. Weinburg, *Manifest Destiny,* 321.

5. Lodge, March 7, 1900, in Dorothea R. Muller, "Josiah Strong and American Nationalism: A Reevaluation," *Journal of American History* 53 (1966): 487–503, at 500–501. The author makes the case for Strong as an internationalist who took exception to Lodge's selfish nationalism in 1900.

6. Beveridge and Roosevelt cited in Judis, *Folly of Empire,* 44.

7. Mahan in Ninkovich, *U.S. and Imperialism,* 37; Beveridge, "March of the Flag"; Theodore Roosevelt, *The Winning of the West,* 6 vols. (New York, 1903), 1: vii; Lodge in Judis, *Folly of Empire,* 44; Adler, *Isolationist Impulse,* 26.

8. Roosevelt to Wolcott, September 15, 1900, in Judis, *Folly of Empire,* 60n.

9. Fisher Ames to Timothy Dwight, October 31, 1803, *Ames Works,* 1: 329.

10. "Expansion and Peace," *Independent,* December 21, 1899, *Roosevelt Works,* 15: 282–92.

11. See discussion in Stanley Karnow, *In Our Own Image: America's Empire in the Philippines* (New York, 1989), and H. W. Brands, *Bound to Empire: The United States and the Philippines* (New York, 1992).

12. Smith, *Commonwealth or Empire,* 74. Predictions of the invigorating effect on American manhood suffered from news reports regarding atrocities and widespread prostitution. On the backlash in American opinion, see Ninkovich, *U.S. and Imperialism,* 53–54; Zimmermann, *First Great Triumph*; Richard E. Welch Jr., *Response to Imperialism: The United States and the Philippine War, 1899–1902* (Chapel Hill, NC, 1965); and Kristin Hoganson, *Fighting for American Manhood: How Gender Politics Provoked the Spanish-American and Philippine-American Wars* (New Haven, CT, 1998). For a careful review of the evidence regarding war deaths, see John M. Gates, "War-Related Deaths in the Philippines, 1898–1902," *Pacific Historical Review* 53 (August 1984): 367–78. A good compendium of contrasting historiographical opinions is Thomas G. Paterson, ed., *American Imperialism and Anti-imperialism* (New York, 1973).

13. Sumner, *Conquest of U.S.,* 3; Hoar in Ninkovich, *U.S. and Imperialism,* 45.

14. Roosevelt in Kohn, *American Nationalism,* 193; Smith, *Commonwealth or Empire,* 34.

15. Beisner, *Twelve against Empire,* 228, 219. Benjamin Trueblood, the peace advocate, noted in November 1898 "that the older statesmen of the nation are almost without exception opposed to the colonial imperialistic policy now so much talked of." Quoted in Patterson, *Toward a Warless World,* 285n82. See also E. Berkeley Tompkins, *Anti-imperialism in the United States: The Great Debate, 1890–1920* (Philadelphia, 1970), the excellent short treatments in Mayers, *Dissenting Voices,* 190–218, and idem, *Wars and Peace,* 23–37. There is a good collection of primary sources in William Jennings Bryan et al., eds., *Republic or Empire? The Philippine Question* (Chicago, 1899).

16. Sumner, *Conquest of U.S.,* 12; Smith, *Commonwealth or Empire,* 55; George Hoar, April 17, 1899, quoted in Beisner, *Twelve against Empire,* 160–61.

17. Smith, *Commonwealth or Empire,* 36; Sumner, *Conquest of U.S.,* 26.

18. Sumner, *Conquest of U.S.,* 21–22.

19. Ninkovich, *U.S. and Imperialism*, 2, 40–41.

20. Hon. John Barrett, Late United States Minister to Siam, "The Problem of the Philippines," *North American Review* 167 (September 1898): 259–67; Frank A. Vanderlip, Assistant Secretary of the Treasury, "Facts about the Philippines, with a Discussion of Pending Problems," *Century* 56 (August 1898): 555–63.

21. David Healy, *US Expansionism: The Imperialist Urge in the 1890s* (Madison, WI, 1970), 5. See also, among other excellent works by Healy, *Drive to Hegemony: The United States in the Caribbean, 1898–1917* (Madison, WI, 1988).

22. Osgood, *Ideals and Self-Interest*, 87. As Walter McDougall cogently observes, the United States "prides itself equally on its idealism and pragmatism, *and likes to believe they are identical.*" The tension in American history "is not one between idealism and realism at all, but between competing conceptions of what is both moral and realistic." McDougall, *Promised Land*, 9.

23. See the animadversions on the court's opinion in Lind, *American Way*, 87. Also Sanford Levinson, "Why the Canon Should Be Expanded to Include the Insular Cases and the Saga of American Expansionism," *Constitutional Commentary* 17 (2000): 241.

Chapter 33. Informal Empire and the Protection of Nationals

1. *Boston Evening Transcript*, April 15, 1899, in Beisner, *Twelve against Empire*, 43.

2. Cf. contrasting assessments in Osgood, *Ideals and Self-Interest*, 85, and Lewis Gould, *The Presidency of Theodore Roosevelt* (Lawrence, KS, 1991), 253.

3. The locus classicus of this perspective within the American government was a 1928 State Department memorandum, J. Rueben Clark to Henry Stimson, December 17, 1928, in Bartlett, *Record*, 546–49.

4. This is an important theme in Ninkovich, *U.S. and Imperialism*.

5. Ibid.; Carl Schurz, "Parker vs. Roosevelt: An Open Letter to the Independent Voter," September 1904, *Schurz Papers*, 6: 390–92.

6. Butler in Max Boot, "Neither New nor Nefarious: The Liberal Empire Strikes Back," *Current History* 102 (November 2003): 363; Paul W. Drake, "From Good Men to Good Neighbors: 1912–1932," in *Exporting Democracy: The United States and Latin America, Themes and Issues*, ed. Abraham Lowenthal (Baltimore, 1991), 7. On the role of public opinion, Mark Peceny, *Democracy at the Point of Bayonets* (University Park, PA, 1999), is suggestive but limited in his treatment of this period. For various assessments of the record, see Ninkovich, *The U.S. and Imperialism*, and Julius Pratt, *America's Colonial Experiment* (New York, 1950). The argument that the United States exported more anarchy than order in its colonial interventions is advanced in Amy Kaplan, *Anarchy of Empire in the Making of U.S. Culture* (Cambridge, MA), 2002, and LaFeber, *American Search*, in ironic contrast with Robert H. Wiebe, *The Search for Order, 1877–1920* (New York, 1967).

7. Patrick Devlin, *Too Proud to Fight: Woodrow Wilson's Neutrality* (New York, 1975), 120.

8. The missionary was Samuel Guy Inman, April 1911, in Robert David Johnson, "Transformation of Pan Americanism," *On Cultural Ground: Essays in International History* (Chicago, 1994), 173.

9. LC, Senate, December 13, 1909, 108. See also Borah's subsequent review of

the 1909 intervention, of which he was extremely critical, in ibid., January 13, 1927, 1555–61; and Kinzer, *Overthrow*, 62–70.

10. Theodore Roosevelt, Annual Message, December 6, 1904.

11. Roosevelt to Bishop, February 23, 1904, Joseph Bucklin Bishop, *Theodore Roosevelt and His Time* (New York, 1920), 1: 430–31; September 1904, *Schurz Papers*, 6: 395–96.

12. Elihu Root, "The Monroe Doctrine," December 22, 1904, *Miscellaneous Addresses*, ed. Robert Bacon and James Brown Scott (Cambridge, MA, 1917), 272, 271; Root, "The Real Monroe Doctrine," April 22, 1914, *Addresses on International Subjects*, ed. Robert Bacon and James Brown Scott (Cambridge, MA, 1916), 114–15.

13. Adler, *Isolationist Impulse*, 26. See further Tyler Dennett, *Americans in East Asia* (New York, 1922), and A. Whitney Griswold, *The Far Eastern Policy of the United States* (New Haven, CT, 1938).

14. "John Quincy Adams: The Opium War and the Sanctity of Commercial Reciprocity," *Proceedings of the Massachusetts Historical Society* 42 (1909/1910): 303–25; Ninkovich, *U.S. and Imperialism*, 158.

15. "Hon. Anson Burlingame's Mission," *New York Times*, February 6, 1868; Frederick W. Williams, *Anson Burlingame and the First Chinese Mission to Foreign Powers* (New York, 1912).

16. *Spectator* (London), 1898, quoted in LaFeber, *American Search*, 177.

17. William R. Manning, "China and the Powers since the Boxer Movement," *American Journal of International Law* 4 (1910): 856; Max Boot, *The Savage Wars of Peace: Small Wars and the Rise of American Power* (New York, 2002), 96.

18. Smith, *Commonwealth or Empire*, 42.

19. Hay to Adee, September 14, 1900, in LaFeber, *American Search*, 175.

20. Henry Clews, *The Wall Street Point of View* (New York, 1900), 248–52.

Chapter 34. Seward and the New Imperialism

1. Cf. Samuel Flagg Bemis, *A Diplomatic History of the United States* (New York, 1936), with Weinberg, *Manifest Destiny* (1935).

2. Richard W. Van Alstyne, *The Rising American Empire* (New York, 1960), 176; Paolino, *Foundations of the American Empire*, 212; Julius W. Pratt, "The 'Large Policy' of 1898," *Mississippi Valley Historical Review* 19 (1932): 223; LaFeber, *New Empire*, vii. To similar effect, Bender, *Nation among Nations*, 214, and Williams, *Tragedy*. "In the unfolding drama of the new empire," as LaFeber observes, Seward "appears as the prince of players. Grant, Hamilton Fish, William M. Evarts, James G. Blaine, Frederick T. Frelinghuysen, and Thomas F. Bayard assume secondary roles" (24). I agree with Keller, *Affairs of State*, 92n, that Paolino's interpretation mistakenly identifies Seward's commercial expansionism with end-of-the-century territorial imperialism, but Paolino does scrupulously provide in his fine reconstruction the materials for a different interpretation. The best short treatment of Seward's thought is Norman B. Ferris, "William H. Seward and the Faith of a Nation," Graebner, *Traditions, 1790-1865*, 153–77. See also the valuable study of Van Deusen, *Seward*. Essential in considering continuity versus discontinuity are Robert L. Beisner, *From the Old Diplomacy to the New, 1865-1900* (Arlington Heights, IL, 1986), and Charles

S. Campbell, *The Transformation of American Foreign Relations, 1865–1900* (New York, 1976). Beisner's work has a valuable bibliographical guide to the era.

3. Charles Vevier, "American Continentalism: An Idea of Expansion," *American Historical Review* 65 (1960): 323–35; Keller, *Affairs of State.*

4. "The Darien Canal," February 23, 1869, *Seward Works*, 5: 589–92; Paolino, *Foundations of the American Empire*, 142.

5. "The Destiny of America," September 14, 1853, *Seward Works*, 4: 122; "Nebraska and Kansas, Second Speech," May 25, 1854, ibid., 4: 476.

6. February 10, 1853, LC, Appendix, 147. See also Seward to Bigelow, September 6, 1865, *Seward Works*, 5: 423.

7. "Speech at a Whig Mass Meeting," October 29, 1844, *Seward Works*, 1: 267. "To the Chatauque Convention," March 31, 1846, ibid. (1853), 3: 409; preliminary draft of speech, February 1866, in Paolino, *Foundations of the American Empire*, 11–12.

8. "Ireland and Irishmen," March 15, 1844, *Seward Works*, 3: 498–99; Paolino, *Foundations of the American Empire*, 27.

9. George Seward to Hamilton Fish, April 27, 1870, Keller, *Affairs of State*, 95–96.

10. "The Destiny of America," September 14, 1853, *Seward Works*, 4: 128; Letter, March 15, 1844, *The Life of William Seward*, ed. George E. Baker (New York, 1855), 230.

11. Beisner, *Twelve against Empire*, 160, 162.

Chapter 35. Before the Deluge

1. September 5, 1901, John W. Tyler, *The Life of William McKinley* (Philadelphia, 1901), 148; speech in San Francisco, May 13, 1903, *A Compilation of the Messages and Speeches of Theodore Roosevelt*, ed. Alfred H. Lewis (Washington, DC, 1906), 1: 387.

2. John Hay, February 27, 1902, *Memorial Address on the Life and Character of William McKinley* (Washington, DC, 1903), 50–51.

3. Sullivan, *Our Times*, 54; Osgood, *Ideals and Self-Interest*, 84–85.

4. Beard, *A Foreign Policy for America*, 91–92. For a striking depiction of the growth of transnational ties, see Daniel T. Rodgers, *Atlantic Crossings: Social Politics in a Progressive Age* (Cambridge, MA, 1998). Rodgers's dissatisfaction with "histories lopped off at precisely those junctures where the nation-state's permeability might be brought into view" was a sentiment shared by internationalists; they, too, warned that "the boundaries of the nation-state" should not "become an analytical cage" (2). The transnational movement of ideas was an element that helped produce what Akira Iriye calls "cultural internationalism," whose proponents held that a peaceful world might "best be fostered through cross-national cultural communication, understanding, and cooperation." Akira Iriye, *Cultural Internationalism and World Order* (Baltimore, 1997), 27. On the growth of international organizations, both intergovernmental and nongovernmental, before 1914, see idem, *Global Community: The Role of International Organizations in the Making of the Contemporary World* (Berkeley, CA, 2002), 9–23. The growth of cultural and economic influence is imaginatively explored in Emily S. Rosenberg, *Financial Missionaries to the World:*

The Politics and Culture of Dollar Diplomacy, 1900–1930 (Durham, NC, 2003); idem, *Spreading the American Dream: American Economic and Cultural Expansion, 1890–1945* (New York, 1982); and Robert W. Rydell and Rob Kroes, *Buffalo Bill in Bologna: The Americanization of the World, 1869–1922* (Chicago, 2005).

5. Benjamin Trueblood, 1895, in Homer L. Boyle, *History of Peace* (Grand Rapids, MI, 1902), 151; Hamilton Holt, "The Way to Disarm: A Practical Proposal," *Independent*, September 28, 1914, in John Whiteclay Chambers II, *The Eagle and the Dove: The American Peace Movement and United States Foreign Policy, 1900–1922* (Syracuse, NY, 1991), 45. On Holt, see Kuehl, *Hamilton Holt*. Here, and in *Seeking World Order*, Kuehl tells the story of the figures—"probably less than a dozen"—who considered the subject of international organization fully from 1900 to 1914.

6. William I. Hull, *The New Peace Movement* (Boston, 1912), 147–50.

7. Edwin D. Mead, in Edward Everett Hale and David J. Brewster, *Mohonk Addresses* (Boston, 1910), xx; Theodore Roosevelt, "International Peace," Address before the Nobel Prize Committee Delivered at Christiania, Norway, May 5, 1910, *Outlook*, May 10, 1910, 20.

8. William Howard Taft, *Peace: Patriotic and Religious Addresses* (New York, 1912), 67; Philander C. Knox, June 1910, quoted in Holt, "A League of Peace," in Chambers, *The Eagle and the Dove*, 19. The rethinking of America's role in the international system prompted in some the search for a usable past. In one of his first books, Walter Lippmann drew attention to the extension of European rivalry into "archaic and unorganized portions of the globe" and believed that struggle explained the European war. Americans, he noted, should have "every reason to understand the dangers of unorganized territory, to realize clearly why it is a 'problem.' Our Civil War was preceded by thirty or forty years of diplomatic struggle for a balance of power in the West. . . . We were virtually two nations, each trying to upset the balance of power in its own favor. And when the South saw that it was beaten, that is to say 'encircled,' when its place in the Western sun was denied, the South seceded and fought. Until the problem of organizing the West had been settled, peace and federal union were impossible." The world's problem in 1915, Lippmann believed, was "the same problem tremendously magnified and complicated." Walter Lippmann, *The Stakes of Diplomacy* (New York, 1915), 114, 109–10. Frederick Jackson Turner, in his essays on sectionalism in the 1920s, gave an account of American expansion very similar to Lippmann's. Turner described rival societies "marching side by side into the unoccupied lands of the West, each attempting to dominate the back country, the hinterland, working out agreements from time to time, something like the diplomatic treaties of European nations, defining spheres of influence, and awarding mandates [trusteeships], such as in the Missouri compromise, the Compromise of 1850, and the Kansas-Nebraska Act." Turner, *Significance of Sections*, 27. The themes of this essay are partly anticipated in a memorandum sent by Turner to Wilson, just before the president left for the Paris Peace Conference, that sought to think through the analogy between America's old federal problem and the task Wilson confronted at Paris; November [30?], 1918, *Wilson Papers*, 53: 264–70.

9. Walter E. Weyl, *American World Policies* (New York, 1917), 8.

10. For various expressions of this rosy outlook, see David Starr Jordan, *War and Wastage* (New York, 1913), and Adler, *Isolationist Impulse*, 28. One congressman, relates Adler, noted in 1910 that "the likelihood of a war involving the United

States was 'as chimerical, and unlikely as a descent on our coasts of an army from the moon.'"

11. Norman Angell, *The Fruits of Victory: A Sequel to "The Great Illusion"* (New York, 1921), 255–56. This book contains an extended discussion in part 2 of the misunderstandings that grew up over his book *The Great Illusion: A Study of the Relation of Military Power in Nations to Their Economic and Social Advantage* (New York, 1910). For the conventional criticism of Angell, see M. S. Anderson, *The Rise of Modern Diplomacy, 1450–1919* (London, 1993), 273–79. There are more positive and convincing portraits in J.D.B. Miller, *Norman Angell and the Futility of War: Peace and the Public Mind* (New York, 1986), and John Mueller, *Retreat from Doomsday: The Obsolescence of Major War* (New York, 1989).

12. Trueblood, *Federation of the World*, 16, 46, 26, 52. See also Daniel Pick, *War Machine: The Rationalization of Slaughter in the Modern Age* (New Haven, CT, 1993), 189.

13. Widenor, *Lodge*, 138–39, 151; Taft to Knox, September 9, 1911, in Lars Schoultz, *Beneath the United States: A History of U.S. Policy toward Latin America* (Cambridge, MA, 1998), 134; Knock, *To End All Wars*, 49; Root in Stromberg, *Collective Security*, 6. An absorbing study of the legalists is Francis Anthony Boyle, *Foundations of World Order: The Legalist Approach to International Relations, 1898–1922* (Durham, NC, 1999). See also Frederic L. Kirgis, "The Formative Years of the American Society of International Law," *American Journal of International Law* 90 (1996): 559–89.

14. See Henry Adams to John Hay, May 3, 1905, and to Elizabeth Cameron, August 27, 1905, cited and discussed in Cushing Strout, *The American Image of the Old World* (New York, 1963), 155; Adams to Charles Gaskell, June 8, 1917, quoted in Ernest Samuels, *Henry Adams: The Major Phase* (Cambridge, MA, 1964), 575. A view similar to Adams's was maintained by Lewis Einstein in essays published in January 1913 and November 1914 in London's *National Review*, in Lewis Einstein, *A Prophecy of the War (1913–1914)*, foreword by Theodore Roosevelt (New York, 1918); William T. Stead, *The Americanization of the World, or The Trend of the Twentieth Century* (New York, 1972 [1902]). The alternative for Britain's "imperial federalists" of a union with the white settler colonies faced daunting logistical and geographic obstacles. See Daniel Deudney, "Greater Britain or Greater Synthesis? Seeley, Mackinder and Wells on Britain in the Global Industrial Era," *Review of International Studies* 27 (2001): 187–208.

15. Richard Olney, *Atlantic Monthly*, May 1898, in John R. Dos Passos, *The Anglo-Saxon Century and the Unification of the English-Speaking People* (New York, 1903), 226. Skeptical about any imminent reunion, and cautious about rushing it, were Alfred T. Mahan and Charles Beresford, "Possibilities of an Anglo-American Reunion," *North American Review* 159 (1894): 555.

16. Among the fine studies of prewar internationalism, scholars differ in their characterization of the various schools of thought. Sondra R. Herman, *Eleven against War: Studies in American Internationalist Thought, 1898–1921* (Stanford, CA, 1969), emphasizes a distinction between "polity internationalists" and "community internationalists." The former were those, like Elihu Root or William Howard Taft, who were conservative in economics but worshiped the law and believed in the advance of international comity through arbitration and the codification of international law; the latter were those, like Jane Addams, Thorstein Veblen, and Josiah

Royce, who emphasized the existence of transnational communities (of women and labor, for instance) and were emphatic in their rejection of militarism and imperialism. Herman's categorization basically corresponds to the distinction drawn in Knock, *To End All Wars*, between conservative and progressive internationalism, the latter of which comprised various shades of socialists, feminists, peace workers, and labor organizations. Kuehl, *Seeking World Order*, and Patterson, *Toward a Warless World*, identify four schools—pacifists, generalists, legalists, and federalists—though Patterson stresses the "ambiguous motives, divided loyalties, flawed perceptions, misguided tactics and strategy, and ideological heterogeneity of peace spokesmen" (viii). On the creation of new "publics," see the analysis of John Dewey in Deudney, *Bounding Power*, 208–10.

Chapter 36. "Great Utterance" and Madisonian Moment

1. Walter Weyl, *American World Policies* (New York, 1917), 32.

2. George Peabody Gooch, "Politics and Morality," *Studies in Diplomacy and Statecraft* (London, 1946), 335.

3. Roland N. Stromberg, "Uncertainties and Obscurities about the League of Nations," *Journal of the History of Ideas* 33 (1972): 139–54, at 143–44.

4. Theodore Roosevelt, "The World War: Its Tragedies and Its Lessons," *Outlook*, September 23, 1914, 178; idem, "International Peace," *Outlook*, May 10, 1910, 21; Lodge in Bartlett, *League to Enforce Peace*, 51.

5. Hamilton Holt, "A Declaration of Interdependence," *Independent*, June 5, 1916; Holt to Wilson, May 29, 1916, in Kuehl, *Hamilton Holt*, 137; Wilson, address at League to Enforce Peace, May 27, 1916, *Wilson Speeches*, 189–95.

6. Unsigned editorial, "Mr. Wilson's Great Utterance," *New Republic*, June 3, 1916; Walter Lippmann, *Force and Ideas: The Early* Writings, ed. Arthur M. Schlesinger Jr. (New Brunswick, NJ, 2000), 40.

7. Tucker, *Wilson*, 145–73.

8. *Roosevelt Works*, 20: 304; 21: 357, 447; Editorial Notes, *New Republic*, February 3, 1917, 2.

9. Henry Cabot Lodge to John T. Morse Jr., August 18, 1919, in Ruggie, *Winning the Peace*, 14.

10. Beveridge to Roosevelt, July 14, 1918, in Osgood, *Ideals and Self-Interest*, 281.

11. Albert Sorel, quoted in E. H. Carr, *The Twenty Years Crisis, 1919–1939: An Introduction to the Study of International Relations*, 2nd ed. (London, 1946), 12. For Wilson's "higher realism," see Arthur S. Link, *The Higher Realism of Woodrow Wilson* (Nashville, TN, 1971).

12. Wells in Edward Mead Earle, "H. G. Wells, British Patriot in Search of a World State," *World Politics* 2 (January 1950): 181–208.

13. Bryce, *American Commonwealth*, 1: 356; and above, chapter 30. See also assessment in Meinig, *Shaping of America*, 1: 385–95.

Chapter 37. Safe for Democracy

1. Tucker, *Wilson*, 188–214.

2. John L. Heaton, ed., *Cobb of "The World"* (New York, 1971), 267–70; Nordholt, *Wilson*, 224–25.

3. War Address, April 2, 1917.

4. Ibid.

5. "Sound Nationalism and Sound Internationalism," *Roosevelt Works*, 21: 351.

6. Jefferson to Robert R. Livingston, September 9, 1801, *Jefferson Writings*, 9: 280. On Wilson's relation to the nineteenth-century law of neutrality, see Tucker, *Wilson*, 53–71. See also Charles Francis Adams, *The Struggle for Neutrality in America*, December 13, 1870 (New York, 1871). The "great victory" that had been won in that struggle, Adams argued, was "the right of the United States to remain at peace, no matter what parties may choose the fearful work of mutual destruction." The nation would "'Sway the rest' not by its power, but by its example; not by dictation, but by adhering, in the day of its strength, to the same pure and honorable policy which it proclaimed and defended when relatively weak" (45–46). Madison had affirmed the same principle in 1806: "The progress of the law of nations, under the influence of science and humanity, is mitigating the evils of war, and diminishing the motives to it, by favoring the rights of those remaining at peace, rather than of those who enter into war." Examination of the British Doctrine," *Madison Letters*, 2: 232.

7. Milwaukee, January 31, 1916, in Harley Notter, *The Origins of the Foreign Policy of Woodrow Wilson* (Baltimore, 1937), 481; speech of October 26, 1916. See also Wilson's "Prolegomenon to a Peace Note," ca. November 25, 1916, *Wilson Papers*, 40: 67–70nn.

8. Robert Lansing, "The President's Attitude toward Great Britain and Its Dangers," September 1916, *Confidential Memoranda*, LC, 1: 40. Wilson's change of heart is also registered in his speech on the S.S. *George Washington* on July 4, 1919: "America did not at first see the full meaning of the war. It looked like a natural raking out of the pent-up jealousies and rivalries of the complicated politics of Europe." Cited in Kennan, *American Diplomacy*, 63.

9. James Bryce et al., *The War of Democracy: The Allies Statement* (Garden City, NY, 1917), xxii. Walter Hines Page, the Anglophile ambassador to Britain, shared Bryce's sentiments and was deeply embarrassed by Wilson's policy of neutrality for this reason.

10. Link, *Wilson*; remarks to foreign correspondents, April 8, 1918, *Wilson Papers*, 47: 288; and discussion in Thompson, *Wilson*, 169. In the technical language of international law, Wilson was fighting for "external self-determination" rather than "internal self-determination," the right of the peoples to be free from foreign interference so that they might determine for themselves the methods and forms by which they might be ruled. For this distinction, see Michla Pomerance, "The United States and Self-Determination: Perspectives on the Wilsonian Conception," *American Journal of International Law* 70 (1976): 1–27. On the insufficiency of democracy as a factor for peace, with heavy emphasis on the early American example, see George H. Blakeslee, "Will Democracy Make the World Safe?" October 7, 1917, Phelps, *League of Nations*, 243–49.

11. Brenda Gayle Plumer, "Haiti," in *Encyclopedia of U.S. Foreign Relations*, ed. Bruce W. Jentleson and Thomas G. Paterson (New York, 1997), 2: 275; idem, *Haiti and the United States* (Athens, GA, 1992), 86–100; "Sound Nationalism and Sound Internationalism," August 4, 1918, Theodore Roosevelt, *Roosevelt in the Kansas City Star* (1921), 192. On press censorship, see the contemporaneous account of

Herbert J. Seligmann, "The Conquest of Haiti," July 10, 1920, in *The Nation: 1865–1990*, ed. Katrina Vanden Heuvel (New York, 1990), 36–40.

12. "Our Purposes in Mexico," November 24, 1913, *Wilson Papers*, 28: 585–86.

13. Bryan to Carothers and Silliman (from Wilson draft), July 23 and 31, 1914, *Wilson Papers*, 30: 297–98, 322; Wilson to Garrison, August 8, 1914, *Wilson Papers*, 30: 362. The discrepancy is highlighted in Robert W. Tucker, "Woodrow Wilson's 'New Diplomacy,'" *World Policy Journal* 21 (2004): 92–107.

14. March 11, 1913, *Wilson Papers*, 27: 172–73.

15. White House talk with Democratic National Committee, December 8, 1915, cited in Tucker, "Woodrow Wilson's 'New Diplomacy,'" 98; Walter Lippmann, "The Case for Wilson," *New Republic*, October 14, 1916. In his Jackson Day Address, January 8, 1915, Wilson declared it a "fundamental principle that every people has a right to determine its own form of government." Though sympathizing with the 80 percent of Mexicans who had never had a voice in their own governance, Wilson insisted that it was none of his business "how long they take in determining it" and pledged "so far as my influence goes while I am President nobody shall interfere with them." *Wilson Papers*, 32: 38–39. The fine study of Judis, *Folly of Empire*, exhibits a Wilson who learns from his mistakes. Tucker, "New Diplomacy," is more skeptical on this point.

16. Wilson in Betty Miller Unterberger, "Russian Revolution," in *Woodrow Wilson and a Revolutionary World*, ed. Arthur S. Link (Chapel Hill, NC, 1982), 73.

Chapter 38. The Liberal Peace Program Goes to Paris

1. This composite is drawn from Wilson's speeches of January 22, 1917, and January 8, 1918, and a memorandum he prepared in the spring of 1917, "Bases of Peace," printed in Link, *Wilson*, 76–77. Walter Lippmann, "America's Relation to the World Conflict," *Annals of the American Academy of Political and Social Science* 72 (July 1917): 1–10. On the liberal peace program, see Knock, *To End All Wars*; Link, *Wilson*; Notter, *Origins*; and Laurence Martin, *Peace without Victory: Woodrow Wilson and the British Liberals* (New Haven, CT, 1958).

2. Niall Ferguson, *The War of the World* (New York, 2006), 166.

3. Frank Vanderlip, *What Next in Europe?* (New York, 1922), 74.

4. *Nation*, January 5, 1921, 4, in Stromberg, *Collective Security*.

5. Emile Joseph Dillon, *The Inside Story of the Peace Conference* (New York, 1920), 509–10, 513.

6. Sullivan, *Our Times*, 581.

7. Lippmann, "The Political Scene," *New Republic*, March 22, 1919, 3.

8. Roosevelt in Thompson, *Wilson*, 176; Norman Angell, *The Fruits of Victory* (New York, 1921), 114.

9. Grayson diary, December 8, 1918, *Wilson Papers*, 53: 335–37; Wilson to House, October 28, 1918, ibid., 51: 473; Thompson, *Wilson*, 176–77. Cf. Kennan, *American Diplomacy*, 67n.

10. On the various misunderstandings arising out of the armistice, see David Fromkin, *In The Time of the Americans* (New York, 1995). On the British blockade of Germany, see Mayers, *Wars and Peace*, and Michael Walzer, *Just and Unjust Wars* (New York, 1977).

11. R.A.C. Parker, *Europe, 1919–1945* (New York, 1970). Wilson's attitude toward the Germans is explored in depth in Klaus Schwabe, *Woodrow Wilson, Revolutionary Germany, and Peacemaking, 1918–1919* (Chapel Hill, NC, 1985), and N. Gordon Levin Jr., *Woodrow Wilson and World Politics* (New York, 1968). The peace conference has a large historiography. Recent comprehensive studies include Margaret Macmillan, *Paris 1919* (New York, 2003); Arthur Walworth, *Wilson and His Peacemakers: American Diplomacy at the Paris Peace Conference, 1919* (New York, 1986); and Zara Steiner, *The Lights That Failed: European International History, 1919–1933* (Oxford, 2005).

12. Carter Glass to Wilson, *Wilson Papers*, December 19, 1918, 53: 441.

13. From revised draft given by Wilson to French government, March 28, 1919, in Lind, *American* Way, 99. The vicious cycle is portrayed in Melvyn P. Leffler, *The Elusive Quest: America's Pursuit of European Stability and French Security, 1919–1933* (Chapel Hill, NC, 1979). The dilemma between a particular and a universal guarantee is brilliantly explored in Stromberg, *Collective Security*. On the French security treaty, see William Keylor, "The Rise and Demise of the Franco-American Guarantee Pact, 1919–1921," in *The Legacy of the Great War: Peacemaking, 1919* (Boston, 1998), 96–105, and Lloyd E. Ambrosius, "Wilson, the Republicans, and French Security after World War I," *Journal of American History* 59 (1972): 341–52.

14. Paul Birdsall, *Versailles Twenty Years After* (London, 1941), 16.

15. Lippmann to Norman Hapgood, July 28, 1919, *Public Philosopher: Selected Letters of Walter Lippmann*, ed. John Morton Blum (New York, 1985), 123; Steel, *Walter Lippmann*, 160.

16. Lippmann, March 22, 1919, *New Republic*, 2; John Maynard Keynes, *The Economic Consequences of the Peace* (New York, 1920), 226.

17. Keynes, *Economic Consequences*, 51–54.

18. "A Memorandum by Robert Lansing," August 20, 1919, *Wilson Papers*, 62: 428–49; Thompson, *Woodrow Wilson*, 234.

19. Thomas, July 29, 1919, in Nordholt, *Wilson*, 371; Robert Lansing, *The Peace Negotiations: A Personal Narrative* (Boston, 1921), 96–98.

20. Thompson, *Wilson*, 172–73, points out that Lansing (the subsequent critic of self-determination) had observed to Wilson that, "from the standpoint of winning the war," there was now a strong case for encouraging the nationalities' hopes for independence. Wilson told a British official that "he disliked most intensely" the idea of "setting the Austrian people against their own government by plots and intrigues. We were not good at that work, and generally made a mess of it, but he saw no other way. He intended to support the Czechs, Poles, and Jugo-Slavs." Lansing to Wilson, May 10, 1918, and Sir William Wiseman to Sir Eric Drummond, May 30, 1918, *Wilson Papers*, 47: 589–91; 48: 205–6.

21. The views that "the state system won't be transcended until it has been completed" and that stateless peoples must first achieve states before they can turn to international cooperation were Wilsonian convictions that are given a stout defense in Michael Walzer, "The Reform of the International System," in *Studies of War and Peace*, ed. Øyvind Østerud (Oslo, 1986), 227–40.

22. Harold Nicolson, *Peacemaking 1919* (London, 1944), 33. On the larger association between nationalism and liberalism in the nineteenth century, and how it broke down in the first half of the twentieth century, see Isaiah Berlin, "Political

Ideas in the Twentieth Century" (1949), *Four Essays on Liberty* (New York, 1969), 3–40.

Chapter 39. The Great Debate of 1919

1. Wilson, address to Senate, July 10, 1919, *Wilson Papers*, 61: 436. See Woodrow Wilson, *Constitutional Government in the United States* (New York, 1917 [1907]), 77–78; cf. 139–40 for a more conciliatory view of the Senate's prerogatives. Its political merit apart, Wilson's estimate of presidential power was not an especially convincing lesson to draw from the record of executive-Senate interaction, for many treaties negotiated by the executive in the nineteenth century had failed to cross the high hurdle of a two-thirds vote in the Senate. See W. Stull Holt, *Treaties Defeated by the Senate* (Baltimore, 1933). For the great debate, see especially Lloyd Ambrosius, "Woodrow Wilson and the Quest for Orderly Progress," in Graebner, *Traditions, 1865–1945*, 73–100; idem, *Woodrow Wilson and the American Diplomatic Tradition: The Treaty Fight in Perspective* (New York, 1987); John Milton Cooper, *Breaking the Heart of the World* (New York, 2001); Ralph Stone, *The Irreconcilables: The Fight against the League of Nations* (Lexington, KY, 1970); D. F. Fleming, *The United States and the League of Nations, 1918–1920* (New York, 1932); Stromberg, *Collective Security*, 22–45; Widenor, *Lodge*, 266–353; Mayers, *Dissenting Voices*, 242–53; Johnson, *Peace Progressives*, 70–104; and Thompson, *Wilson*. Ambrosius has a fine bibliographical survey for the whole Wilson period in Schulzinger, *Companion*, 148–67.

2. Succinct expositions of the covenant may be found in J. L. Brierly, *The Law of Nations: An Introduction to the International Law of Peace*, 6th ed. (New York, 1963), 105–20, 397–412; and Inis L. Claude Jr., *Swords into Plowshares: The Problems and Progress of International Organization* (New York, 1984). Its confederal features are examined in Paul Rivlin, "The League of Nations as Confederacy," *International Relations* 4 (1976): 1121–38.

3. H. G. Wells, "A League of Free Nations," November 23, 1918, *Saturday Evening Post*, in Phelps, *League of Nations*, 101–8.

4. Root to Will Hays, March 29, 1919, and Root to Lodge, June 21, 1919, in *Men and Policies*, ed. Robert Bacon and James Brown Scott (Freeport, NY, 1968 [1924]), 254, 269–70.

5. These sources are cited and discussed in Knock, *To End All Wars*, 252–54.

6. Adler, *Isolationist Impulse*, 90–111.

7. Borah in Kohn, *American Nationalism*, 213; Lippmann to Hapgood, July 28, 1919, Blum, *Public Philosopher*, 123; Knock, *To End All Wars*, 257.

8. Borah in Charles W. Toth, "Isolationism and the Emergence of Borah: An Appeal to American Tradition," *Western Political Quarterly* 14 (1961): 555–68, which contains a discussion of Borah's nationalism, internationalism, and anti-imperialism. On that theme, see also Johnson, *Peace Progressives*.

9. "The League of Nations," *Roosevelt Works*, 21: 304.

10. "Lodge Addresses Senate," *New York Times*, December 22, 1918; Widenor, *Lodge*, 296–97.

11. For the reservations, see Henry Cabot Lodge, *The Senate and the League of Nations* (New York, 1925), and the meticulous investigation in Cooper, *Breaking the Heart*.

12. Root to Hay, *Men and Policies*, 265–66.

13. Elihu Root to Henry Cabot Lodge, "Revised Draft of the Proposed Covenant," June 21, 1919, ibid., 274.

14. Wilson to John St. Loe Strachey, April 5, 1918, *Wilson Papers*, 47: 258. See the critical discussion of this vital point in Stromberg, *Collective Security*, passim, and the more sympathetic treatment in Ninkovich, *Modernity and Power*, 53.

15. See analysis and sources in Knock, *To End All Wars*, 261.

16. Quoted in Borchard and Lage, *Neutrality*, 236–37. See also the discussion in Bartlett, *League to Enforce Peace*, 53; and Harley Notter, *The Origins of the Foreign Policy of Woodrow Wilson* (Baltimore, 1937).

17. "Notes of Conversations with Wilson by William Emmanuel Rappard," November 20, 1918, *Wilson Papers*, 63: 627.

18. On Wilson's ideas for the hemisphere, see Mark T. Gilderhus, *Pan American Visions: Woodrow Wilson in the Western Hemisphere, 1913–1921* (Tucson, AZ, 1986); and Knock, *To End All Wars*.

19. *Federalist* 22 and 15. The "epidemical rage in Europe" for "triple and quadruple" alliances in the first half of the eighteenth century had benefits, Hamilton noted, that were "fondly hoped for" but "never realized." The fact that these alliances were no sooner formed than broken showed "how little dependence is to be placed on treaties which have no other sanction than the obligations of good faith, and which oppose general considerations of peace and justice to the impulse of any immediate interest or passion." The problem of "cooperation under anarchy" was thoroughly scrutinized by the Founders and was central to the unionist paradigm. Benjamin Franklin gave it famous expression in his comments on the inherent frailties of "the requisition system," which left each "assembly waiting to see what another will do, being afraid of doing more than its share, or desirous of doing less; or refusing to do anything, because its country is not at present so much exposed as others, or because another will reap more immediate advantage." "Reasons and Motives [for Albany Plan of Union]," July 1754, *Franklin Writings*, 3: 203. The inadequacies of this system, as Madison insisted, resulted "naturally from the number and independent authority of the States." A system of voluntary contributions could "never succeed" because "some States will be more just than others, some less just: Some will be more patriotic; others less patriotic; some will be more, some less immediately concerned in the evil to be guarded against or in the good to be obtained. The States therefore not feeling equal motives will not furnish equal aids: Those who furnish most will complain of those who furnish least." "Vices of the Political System of the United States," April 1787, *Madison Papers*, 9: 348; Madison to George Thompson, January 29, 1789, ibid., 11: 433–34.

20. Lippmann, *U.S. War Aims*, 178.

21. Ibid., 171–72.

22. Forsyth, *Unions of States*, 197–98.

23. James Reed, Senator from Missouri, "Reed Denounces League Plan," December 29, 1918, in Phelps, *League of Nations*, 192. To similar effect, "Poindexter Opens Senate Attack on League of Nations," *New York Times*, February 20, 1919. "'Make believe,'" wrote the speculator Dickson G. Watts, "is a game society plays as well as children." The debate over the league is a classic instance. Neither side could admit to the league's weaknesses. Critics had an interest in exaggerating its power; so did Wilson. So it got exaggerated in the debate.

24. Gilbert Hitchcock, February 4, 1919, and James Hamilton Lewis, Senator from Illinois, in Stone, *Irreconcilables*, 49–50.

25. Wilson to Hitchcock, March 8, 1920, *Wilson Papers*, 65: 70–71.

26. Cooper, *Breaking the Heart*, follows Arthur Link in emphasizing that Wilson's rigidity was borne of his illness. For keen studies of Wilson's mental makeup, see John Morton Blum, *Woodrow Wilson and the Politics of Morality* (Boston, 1956); Alexander L. George and Juliette L. George, *Woodrow Wilson and Colonel House* (New York, 1964); Nordholt, *Wilson*; and Tucker, *Wilson*, 17–52.

27. TR to Albert Jeremiah Beveridge, October 31, 1918, *The Letters of Theodore Roosevelt*, ed. Elting E. Morison et al. (Cambridge, MA, 1954), 8: 1385; Beveridge, TR, and Lodge in Judis, *Folly of Empire*, 113; "Aladdin's lamp" in Adler, *Isolationist Impulse*, as excerpted in Ralph A. Stone, ed., *Wilson and the League of Nations* (New York, 1967), 42.

28. H. G. Wells, in collaboration with Viscount Grey, Lionel Curtis, William Archer, H. Wickham Steed, A. E. Zimmern, J. A. Spender, Viscount Bryce, and Gilbert Murray, *The Idea of a League of Nations* (Boston, 1919), 6. To similar effect, see Wilson's "Prolegomenon to a Peace Note," ca. November 25, 1916, *Wilson Papers*, 40: 67–70. The small number of liberal republics that endured over time in modern Europe, notes Lind, *American Way*, 81, "usually enjoyed low security costs because they had natural geographic defenses." The enlargement and intensification of war, he argues, had by 1915 rendered this traditional reliance "obsolescent." To similar effect, see Deudney, *Bounding Power*. Deudney calls this an increase in the level of "violence interdependence."

29. "The Great Debate," *New Republic*, March 8, 1919, 164–65. For other expositions of this theme (by Horace Kallen and James Brown Scott), see above, chapter 2, note 17, and Samuel J. Graham, "League of Nations to Avert International Anarchy," *New York Times*, January 12, 1919, in Phelps, *League of Nations*, 257–66. See also *New Republic*, March 1, 1919, for discussion of Herbert Croly, *The Promise of American Life* (New York, 1909), 312, where Croly argued that "peace will prevail in international relations, just as order prevails within a nation, because of the righteous use of superior force—because the power which makes for pacific organization is stronger than the power which makes for warlike organization." If American power were thrown into the balance, it might be sufficient "to tip the scales in favor of a comparatively peaceful settlement of international complications."

30. Root and Beard in Knock, *To End All Wars*, 237; Lippmann to Newton D. Baker, January 17, 1920, in Steel, *Lippmann*, 167. See also David M. Kennedy, *Over Here: The First World War and American Society* (New York, 1980), and Robert Nisbet, *The Present Age: Progress and Anarchy in Modern America* (New York, 1988). Randolph Bourne, the promising writer who foresaw this devil's bargain, became a hero to many after the war. Bourne died of the flu at the age of thirty-two in late 1918. See Lillian Schissel, ed., *The World of Randolph Bourne* (New York, 1965), 147–203. On fears for domestic institutions and civil liberties before American entry, see John A. Thompson, *Reformers and War: American Progressive Publicists and the First World War* (New York, 1987), and John Milton Cooper, *The Vanity of Power: American Isolationism and the First World War, 1914–1917* (Westport, CT, 1969).

31. Link, *Wilson*, 104–28. Widenor, *Lodge*, presents the most convincing case

for Lodge as an "internationalist." See also discussion in Stromberg, *Collective Security*, 33–39.

32. Interview with Rathenau, Frank Vanderlip, *What Next in Europe?* (New York, 1922), 98.

33. Lippmann argued this point in mid-1916 in "What Program Shall the United States Stand for in International Relations?" *Annals of the American Academy of Political and Social Science* 66 (July 1916): 66: "It seems to me that in an Anglo-American alliance, Great Britain and France would find so much safety that they could risk a conciliatory policy towards Germany after the war. I for one should be inclined to say that the United States must insist on that as one of the terms of our bargain."

34. Imperial War Cabinet Minutes, December 31, 1918 (summarizing viewpoint of Lloyd George), cited in George W. Egerton, "Britain and the 'Great Betrayal': Anglo-American Relations and the Struggle for United States Ratification of the Treaty of Versailles, 1919–1920," *Historical Journal* 4 (1978): 885–911, at 885–86. French thinking is succinctly set forth in A. W. DePorte, *Europe between the Superpowers* (New Haven, CT, 1979).

35. Henry W. Taft, in William H. Taft et al., *The Covenantor: An American Exposition of the Covenant of the League of Nations* (New York, 1919), 49–50.

36. On Wilson's "supreme infanticide," see Thomas A. Bailey, *Woodrow Wilson and the Great Betrayal* (New York, 1945), 271–87.

37. "Borah Declares That Harding Speech Is 'Great'; Says It Shows the Nominee Bars 'This League,'" *New York Times*, October 8, 1920.

38. Knock, *To End All Wars*, 229.

39. "League Men Explain Support of Harding," *New York Times*, October 15, 1920; "Harding Rejects the League Outright," ibid., Oct 8, 1920; Kuehl, *Keeping the Covenant*, 9–17.

40. Thompson, *Wilson*, 242–43.

41. H. L. Mencken, "The Last Round," October 4, 1920, *A Carnival of Buncombe: Writings on Politics* (Chicago, 1984), 26–27. Wilson's final years are movingly described in Gene Smith, *When the Cheering Stopped: The Last Years of Woodrow Wilson* (New York, 1964). The psychological "turning in" is well conveyed in Adler, *Isolationist Impulse*, 90–111, and Stromberg, *Collective Security*, 40–45.

Chapter 40. Nationalism, Internationalism, and Imperialism in the 1920s

1. Edwin L. James, "Enlightened Nationalism," *New York Times*, August 20, 1930. On the fortunes of various American internationalists in the interwar period, see Kuehl, *Keeping the Covenant*.

2. A comment of Sir William H. Beveridge, director of the London School of Economics, in a radio address, "World Slump Cure Viewed as Political," *New York Times*, January 11, 1932.

3. Ninkovich, *U.S. and Imperialism*.

4. Melvyn P. Leffler, "Open Door Expansionism, World Order, and Domestic Constraints," in Paterson, *Major Problems* (1989), 2: 126–47.

5. Thomas J. McCormick, *America's Half-Century* (Baltimore, 1989), 24–28.

6. A notorious expression of H. G. Wells, quoted in James, "Enlightened Nationalism." When, asked James, "do we make Mr. Wells apologize" for saying that?

7. "La Follette Fears Imperialism Here," *New York Times*, October 31, 1924. The contours of the debate are examined in Johnson, *Peace Progressives*, 105–50.

8. John Dewey, "Imperialism Is Easy," *New Republic*, March 23, 1927.

9. "Mexico Involved as Borah Assails Nicaraguan Policy," *New York Times*, January 8, 1927; "Coolidge Openly Accuses Mexico," ibid., January 11, 1927; "Moscow Directly Accused," ibid., January 13, 1927.

10. "Sees US Entangled in Central America," *New York Times*, January 12, 1927; "Paris Press Is Harsh," ibid., December 30, 1926. Further intervention in Mexico was also the anticipation of Dewey in "Imperialism Is Easy."

11. Walter Lippmann, "Empire: The Days of Our Nonage Are Over," in *Men of Destiny* (New York, 1927), 215–22.

12. For Hoover's attitude, see Williams, *Tragedy*, and Ninkovich, *Modernity and Power*.

13. Coolidge, Message to Congress, December 7, 1926, *Foreign Relations of the United States* (Washington, DC, 1941), 1: xxvi.

14. Lewis Einstein, "Our Still Dubious Foreign Policy," September 1931, *The North American Review*, in Graebner, *Ideas and Diplomacy*, 542.

Chapter 41. The Great Depression and Economic Nationalism

1. William C. White, "Nationalism Darkens World Outlook," *New York Times*, January 1, 1933.

2. "Debt Criticism Here Arouses British Ire," *New York Times*, December 21, 1931.

3. "Roosevelt's First Year: 12 Epochal Months," *New York Times*, March 4, 1934. On the triumph of nationalism over internationalism more generally, see Frank H. Simonds, "The Collapse of the Peace Movement," *Annals of the American Academy of Political and Social Science* 174 (July 1934): 116–20.

4. Hoover in Ninkovich, *Modernity and Power*, 347n31.

5. Hubert Clinton Herring, "Charles A. Beard: Free Lance among the Historians," *Harper's*, May 1939, 649–50.

6. Ibid., 650; Charles and Mary Beard, *America at Midpassage* (New York, 1939), 455; Charles Beard, *The Idea of the National Interest* (New York, 1934); idem, *The Open Door at Home* (New York, 1935). See further Osgood, *Ideals and Self-Interest*, 372–76; Bacevich, *American Empire*, 11–23; Brands, *What America Owes*, 109–43.

7. Clarence Berdahl, Kenneth Colegrove, Walter Rice Sharp, and Quincy Wright, "Cooperation of States Held Necessary to World Peace," *New York Times*, November 12, 1939; Edward Mead Earle, "The New Mercantilism," *Political Science Quarterly* 40 (1925): 595. On tariff barriers as "potential breeders of war," see also James D. Mooney and Alan C. Reiley, *Onward Industry!* (New York, 1931). Mooney was vice president of General Motors, and Reiley an advertising manager at Remington Typewriter Company. "Discern War Peril in Tariff Barriers," *New York Times*, June 22, 1931.

Chapter 42. Isolation and Neutrality

1. Chautauqua address, August 14, 1936, in Ninkovich, *Wilsonian Century*, 121.

2. Osgood, *Ideals and Self-Interest*, 364.

3. Paul Scheffer, "The United States and War Debts: The Political Aspect," *International Affairs* (Royal Institute), 11 (1932): 441–59, at 451; Charles A. Beard, "In Time of Peace Prepare for War," *New Republic*, March 18, 1936; C. Hartley Grattan, "No More Excursions! The Defense of Democracy Begins at Home," *Harper's*, April 1939, 457.

4. E. H. Carr, *The Twenty Years' Crisis* (New York, 1946). Borchard (1936) cited in Jonas, *Isolationism in America*, 110. Carr's work is one of the seminal realist tracts in the emerging discipline of international relations. But the first edition of the book in 1939 supported the Chamberlain policy of appeasement rather than the Churchill policy of resistance. Much of Carr's ire was directed against Norman Angell, who supported resistance to Hitler. (See Norman Angell, *America's Dilemma: Alone or Allied?* [New York, 1940].) There were, in fact, self-understood "realists" and "idealists" on both sides of the debate over intervention.

5. See Selig Adler, "The War-Guilt Question and American Disillusionment, 1918–1928," *Journal of Modern History* 23 (1951): 1–28; Warren Cohen, *The American Revisionists: The Lessons of Intervention in World War I* (Chicago, 1967); the riposte to the revisionists in D. F. Fleming, "Our Entry into the World War in 1917: The Revised Version," *Journal of Politics* 2 (1940): 75–86; Jonas, *Isolationism*, 150–216; and Tucker, *Wilson*, 56–58.

6. Borchard, *Neutrality*, 56; Jonas, *Isolationism*, 136–68.

7. Borchard and Lage, *Neutrality*, 237; Kuehl, *Keeping the Covenant*, 180.

8. George Gallup, "What We, the People, Think about Europe," *New York Times*, April 30, 1939.

9. The nonrecognition policy was not consistently applied. Wilson's State Department recognized the government brought to power in Peru in 1914 in a military coup. Just as Hoover was beginning to abandon nonrecognition in the Western Hemisphere, his administration adopted the policy, under the leadership of Secretary of State Stimson, against Japan's creation of a puppet state in Manchuria in 1931.

10. Sumner Welles, February 16, 1942, *The World of the Four Freedoms* (New York, 1943), 45; idem, *A Time for Decision* (New York, 1944), 198–99.

11. Welles, February 16 and May 30, 1942, *Four Freedoms*, 45, 91–92.

Chapter 43. The Final Reckoning

1. Hanson W. Baldwin, "Impregnable America," *American Mercury* 47 (July 1939): 267; Jonas, *Isolationism*, 121–35, at 127. See Philip Guedall, "Hitler and Napoleon," *New York Times*, April 9, 1939, on the brittleness of German power and "a grave shortage of almost everything an army needs to fight with." See also Stromberg, *Collective Security*, 127–29, and Justus D. Doenecke, *Storm on the Horizon: The Challenge to American Intervention, 1939–1941* (Lanham, MD, 2000), 119–38. The large historiography is reviewed in Doenecke, "The United States and the European War, 1939–1941: A Historiographical Review," and Michael A.

Barnhart, "The Origins of the Second World War in Asia and the Pacific: Synthesis Impossible?" in Hogan, *Path to Power*, 224–95.

2. Gallup, *New York Times*, April 30, 1939; Lodge in Osgood, *Ideals and Self-Interest*, 407. The 1940 poll is cited in Stromberg, *Collective Security*, 129.

3. Newspaperman in Osgood, *Ideals and Self-Interest*, 408; Arthur Schlesinger Jr., "Back to the Womb?" *Foreign Affairs*, July/August 1995. Cf. John Hay's depiction of the winter of 1860–1861 in *Memorial Address on the Life and Character of William McKinley* (Washington, DC, 1903), 13–16.

4. Address at Charlottesville, June 10, 1940, Franklin D. Roosevelt, *My Friends* (Whitefish, MT, 2005), 64.

5. "Radio Address: Shall the United States Enter the European War?" May 17, 1941, *The Papers of Robert A. Taft*, ed. Clarence E. Wunderlin Jr. et al. (Kent, OH, 2001), 2: 245–46.

6. Borah to J. B. Eldridge, July 24, 1939, in Stromberg, *Collective Security*, 152n; Oswald Garrison Villard, "Valedictory," *Nation*, June 29, 1940, 782; "Radio Address: Shall the United States Enter the European War?" May 17, 1941, *Taft Papers*, 2: 246.

7. "Beard Hits Intervening," *New York Times*, September 9, 1940. For other rejections of the isolationist label, see statement of Ludlow, excerpted in Charles Beard, *American Foreign Policy in the Making, 1932–1940* (New Haven, CT, 1946), 242.

8. This was said, in later years, of Charles Beard by Lewis Mumford in a letter to the *Saturday Review of Literature*, cited in Ronald Radosh, *Prophets on the Right: Profiles of Conservative Critics of American Globalism* (New York, 1975), 39. The writer Bill Kauffman calls isolationists like Borah and Wheeler "retro-progressives"—"desultorily organized defenders of an America that was too big for body bags and too small to fit into a gross national product." Kauffman, *America First!* See also the fine portraits of these figures in idem, *Ain't My America*; Wayne S. Cole, *Roosevelt and the Isolationists: 1932–1945* (Lincoln, NE, 1983), 37–38; and Johnson, *Peace Progressives*.

9. "White Says Motive Is Shunning of War," *New York Times*, December 24, 1940; editorial, "Mr. White Did His Job," ibid., January 4, 1941.

10. Osgood, *Ideals and Self-Interest*, is the classic statement of the realist or nationalist viewpoint. For the revisionists, see Williams, *Tragedy*, and discussion in chapter 3. For internationalist interpretations, see sources in chapter 1, note 1.

11. Steel, *Lippmann*, 378–92, and Edward Mead Earle, *Against This Torrent* (Princeton, NJ, 1941). Osgood, *Ideals and Self-Interest*, was particularly insistent on the dominance of realistic considerations tied to national security. It is true that many interventionists were perfectly willing, for purposes of the argument, to put all "morality" aside in demonstrating the threat to American security; they saw the merit of Livingston Hartley's argument, cited in Osgood, that "it seems wisest to consider our defensive problem not in the light of principles upon which Americans may divide, but in the light of national interests toward which Americans should be unanimous." But this gambit did not really reflect their true position, which was heavily imbued with moral and ideological features.

Were the interventionists persuasive in making the appeal to physical security? The question is not easy to determine, but there are reasons for questioning the threat to America's *physical* security in 1941. As Charles Lindbergh pointed out, the very factors that made an American amphibious assault on continental Europe treacherous made a German assault on the Americas doubly so. Lindbergh, Radio Address in New York, April 23, 1941, in Graebner, *Ideas and Diplomacy*, 604–8. It was impossible to believe that the Royal Navy would pass into the hands of the Germans; the more likely result, if defeat should stare England in the face, was its removal to Canada. The argument that physical security was endangered was also weakened once Hitler invaded Russia in the summer of 1941. See Bruce Russett, *No Clear and Present Danger: A Skeptical View of the United States Entry into World War II* (New York, 1972), and discussion and sources in Christopher Layne, *The Peace of Illusions: American Grand Strategy from 1940 to the Present* (Ithaca, NY, 2006), 184–86.

12. Ellsworth Barnard, "War and the Verities," *Harper's*, January 1940, 113–28, at 127; Lippmann, October 30, 1941, in Steel, *Walter Lippmann*, 390–91. The sentiment was reciprocated: "National socialism," said Hitler, "aims at the extirpation of internationalism of every sort, including the interconnection of capital, of news, of fraternal lodges, and so forth." "Nazis Aim to Exclude 'Internationalism,' Even of News," *New York Times*, June 25, 1933.

13. Earle, *Against This Torrent*, 51–52. On the "disillusion with disillusion," see Osgood, *Ideals and Self-Interest*, 383.

14. Gerald W. Johnson, "The Ghost of Woodrow Wilson," *Harper's*, June 1941, 7, 9.

15. Barnard, "War and the Verities," 122.

16. Acheson quoted in Bruce Cumings, "Is America an Imperial Power?" *Current History* 102 (November 2003): 355–60, at 356.

17. A. A. Berle Jr., "No, Says Berle," *New York Times*, January 14, 1940.

18. Felix Belair, "Roosevelt Warns Americas to Meet Force with Force," *New York Times*, April 16, 1940. See Bryce Wood, *The Making of the Good Neighbor Policy* (New York, 1961); Warren F. Kimball, *The Juggler: Franklin Roosevelt as Wartime Statesman* (Princeton, NJ, 1991), 107–25; and Robert Dallek, *Franklin D. Roosevelt and American Foreign Policy, 1932–1945* (New York, 1995). For FDR's winning touch with Latin America, see especially Frederick B. Pike, *FDR's Good Neighbor Policy* (Austin, TX, 1995).

19. Rippy in Charles A. Beard, "Giddy Minds and Foreign Quarrels," *Harper's*, September 1939, 341; Belair, "Roosevelt Warns," *New York Times*, April 16, 1940. The administration identified five essential principles of the hemispheric order: "1. Respect for the integrity and importance of other States. 2. Self restraint and acceptance of the equal rights of neighbors. 3. Non-intervention in the domestic affairs of neighboring States. 4. Settlement of disputes by friendly negotiation in accordance with justice and equity, rather than by force. 5. Provision for access to materials and opportunities necessary to a rising standard of living for all American peoples." Very similar principles were stated by the State Department in its last note to Japan (November 26, 1941) preceding the outbreak of war: "(1) The principle of inviolability of territorial integrity and sovereignty of each and all nations. (2) The principle of noninterference in the internal affairs of other countries. (3) The principle of equality, including equality of commercial opportunity and treatment. (4) The principle of reliance upon international cooperation and conciliation for the prevention and pacific settlement of controversies and for improvement of international conditions by peaceful methods and processes." Cited in Robert W. Tucker, *Nation or Empire? The Debate over American Foreign Policy* (Baltimore, 1968), 54n.

20. Address to Congress, January 6, 1941; Douglas Brinkley and David R. Facey-Crowther, eds., *The Atlantic Charter* (New York, 1994).

21. Beard, *A Foreign Policy for America*, 33, 21, 34–35, 29.

22. Seward, December 9, 1851, LC, 41–42.

23. Jefferson to Thomas Leiper, June 12, 1815, *Jefferson Writings*, 14: 307–8; Jefferson to Thomas Lomax, January 11, 1806, in Malone, *Jefferson*, 5: 95.

24. Jefferson to Langdon, March 5, 1810, *Jefferson Writings*, 12: 374–75.

25. The "garrison state" was a concept associated with political scientist Harold Lasswell, who began developing in the late 1930s the terrifying specter of a world divided into states that were "dictatorial, governmentalized, centralized, integrated." See Harold Lasswell, "The Garrison State versus the Civilian State," *China Quarterly* 2 (1937): 643–49, and idem, "The Universal Peril: Perpetual Crisis and the Garrison-Prison State," in *Perspectives on a Troubled Decade*, ed. Lyman Bryson et al. (New York, 1950).

Lasswell's position was essentially a restatement, in altered technological conditions, of the old specter central to the unionist paradigm that found despotism and "continual compulsion upon the people" to be an inexorable consequence of anarchy. The whole problem of foreign policy was—and is—reducible to whether liberty was most imperiled through too little or too much power in the state. Two books that give extensive consideration to this fundamental problem (though with the focus on the post–World War II era) are Aaron L. Friedberg, *In the Shadow of the Garrison State* (Princeton, NJ, 2000), and Michael J. Hogan, *A Cross of Iron: Harry S. Truman and the Origins of the National Security State, 1945–1954* (Cambridge, UK, 1998). The best statement of the problem, showing its ubiquity in "republican security theory," is Deudney, *Bounding Power*. It also forms an important theme in Lind, *American Way*. The specific content of the "garrison state" idea, though in essence a simple renaming of an old perception, was powerfully shaped in the late 1930s by the emergence of totalitarianism as a recognizably new political type. Its characteristics are described in Abbott Gleason, "A New Kind of State," *Totalitarianism: The Inner History of the Cold War* (New York, 1995), 31–50.

26. House Diary, *Wilson Papers*, 30: 462.

27. "President on the Russian Treaties," April 6, 1918, *New York Times Current History: The European War* (New York, 1918), 15: 277. See A.J.P. Taylor, *The Struggle for Mastery in Europe* (New York, 1954), xx, for explication of the idea of an automatic balance. Writing of the era from 1848 to 1918, Taylor held that the "Balance of Power . . . seemed to be the political equivalent of the laws of economics, both self-operating. If every man followed his own interest, all would be prosperous; and if every state followed its own interest, all would be peaceful and secure." Striking as this formulation is, it entails a false analogy to Adam Smith's thinking, for Smith understood that the pursuit of individual advantage in a market society was not possible without a state enforcing rules of justice. Taylor's formulation also obscures an important point about the balance. To treat it as a mechanism is to ignore its status as a standard of conduct. The balance of power, in Calhoun's expression, "made the constitution" of international society, insofar as it had a constitution, because it provided the limiting power of interposition or veto that could, in a pinch, check irresponsible power. The deficiencies of the balance lay not in the ideal of equilibrium or in its rejection of universal empire but in its susceptibility to war and in the ease with which states might pursue their selfish interests in its name, but not in

its spirit—applying "the terms, sound policy, system of equilibrium, maintenance or restoration of the balance of power ... to what, in fact, was only an abuse of power, or the exercise of arbitrary will" (see above, chapter 8, note 5). Wilson's ideas of the balance are explored in Ninkovich, *Modernity and Power*; Edward H. Buehrig, *Woodrow Wilson and the Balance of Power* (Bloomington, IN, 1955), and Osgood, *Ideals and Self-Interest*.

28. Johnson, "Ghost of Woodrow Wilson," 9.

29. Walter Lippmann, *Some Notes on War and Peace* (New York, 1940), 46–47.

30. Ross Hoffman, *The Great Republic: A Historical View of the International Community and the Organization of Peace* (New York, 1942), xiii; Divine, *Second Chance*, 29–46, 57–58.

31. Clarence Streit, *Union Now: A Proposal for a Federal Union of the Democracies of the North Atlantic* (New York, 1939). This was followed by idem, *Union Now with Britain* (New York, 1941). The gist of Streit's idea is set forth in Clarence K. Streit, "Democracy versus Absolutism: A World-Wide Survey," *New York Times*, November 25, 1934. See further Divine, *Second Chance*; Wooley, *Alternatives to Anarchy*, 89–99; James Huntley, *Pax Democratica* (New York, 1998); and Joseph P. Baratta, *The Politics of World Federation* (Westport, CT, 2004).

32. Ross Hoffman, review of *World Order in Historical Perspective* (1942), by Hans Kohn, *Journal of Modern History* 15 (1943): 155–56.

33. Russell H. Bastert, "The Two American Diplomacies," *Yale Review* 49 (1960): 523; Walter Lippmann, *U.S. Foreign Policy: Shield of the Republic* (Boston, 1943), 132; idem, *U.S. War Aims* (Boston, 1944), 78. A universalistic approach, as Kennan wrote after the war, looked toward rules and procedures that would be applicable to all countries; it sought a "top-down" solution to the international anarchy by championing certain universal principles—for example, the "indivisibility of peace" for purposes of collective security, or "nondiscrimination" for purposes of forming a liberal international economic order. The particularized approach, to which Kennan and Lippmann were committed, took things from the other end. It was "bottom-up," not "top-down," and it looked toward the formation of a community among the "older, mellower, and more advanced nations of the world—nations for which the concept of order, as opposed to power, has value and meaning." Kennan noted in 1948 that the government was "conducting a dual policy, which combines elements of both of these approaches"—a duality, he observed, "to which we are now deeply committed." George Kennan to Robert Lovett, February 24, 1948, PPS/23, *The State Department Policy Planning Staff Papers, 1947–1949*, ed. Anna Kasten Nelson (New York, 1983), 2: 124–26.

John Gerard Ruggie, *Winning the Peace*, 34, improperly excludes "the particularists" from the domain of internationalism and multilateralism. The liberal realists, like Kennan, Lippmann, and Niebuhr, accepted the "ultimate ideal of a world at peace under the reign of law." Lippmann, *U.S. War Aims*, 187. They objected not to internationalism but to the doctrine that "there are no legitimate entities between national states on the one hand and the universal society on the other, between the atom and the cosmos." Idem, *Isolation and Alliances: An American Speaks to the British* (Boston, 1952), 41. In a 1949 essay, Niebuhr acknowledged that "the forces which are operating to integrate the world community are limited" but refused to conclude "that all striving for a higher and wider integration of the world community is in vain. That task must and will engage the conscience of mankind for ages to come." But he also warned that "the edifice of government which we build will be sound and useful if its height is proportionate to the strength of the materials from which it is constructed." Reinhold Niebuhr, "The Illusion of World Government," *Foreign Affairs* 27 (1949): 379–88, at 388.

34. Evgeny Krieger, *From Moscow to the Prussian Frontier* (1945), cited in Martin Wight, "Why Is There No International Theory?" in *Diplomatic Investigations*, ed. Martin Wight and Herbert Butterfield (Cambridge, MA, 1966), 28–29.

35. See Mayers, *Wars and Peace*, 81–82, for somber reflections in this vein.

36. "The ideal perfection of civil society" from Hugh S. Legaré, report on petition of the New York Peace Society, in *Prize Essays on a Congress of Nations for the Adjustment of International Disputes, and For the Promotion of Universal Peace Without Resort to Arms*, ed. William Ladd (Boston, 1840), 667.

INDEX

Index